CAMBRIDGE UNIVERSITY LIBRARY
A HISTORY

CAMBRIDGE UNIVERSITY LIBRARY

A HISTORY

THE EIGHTEENTH AND NINETEENTH CENTURIES

DAVID McKITTERICK

FELLOW OF DARWIN COLLEGE AND
UNDER-LIBRARIAN, UNIVERSITY LIBRARY

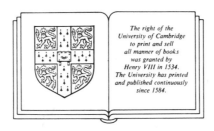

The right of the
University of Cambridge
to print and sell
all manner of books
was granted by
Henry VIII in 1534.
The University has printed
and published continuously
since 1584.

CAMBRIDGE UNIVERSITY PRESS

CAMBRIDGE

LONDON   NEW YORK   NEW ROCHELLE

MELBOURNE   SYDNEY

Published by the Press Syndicate of the University of Cambridge
The Pitt Building, Trumpington Street, Cambridge CB2 1RP
32 East 57th Street, New York, NY 10022, USA
10 Stamford Road, Oakleigh, Melbourne 3166, Australia

© Cambridge University Press 1986

First published 1986

Printed in Great Britain at
the University Press, Cambridge

British Library Cataloguing in Publication Data
McKitterick, David
Cambridge University Library : a history : the
eighteenth and nineteenth centuries.
1. Cambridge University Library – History
I. Title
0.27.7426'59   Z921.C18

Library of Congress Cataloguing in Publication Data
McKitterick, David.
Cambridge University Library.
Includes index.
1. Cambridge University Library – History.
2. Libraries, University and college – England –
Cambridge (Cambridgeshire) – History. I. Title.
Z792.C18M33   1986   027.7426'59   85–17471

ISBN 0 521 30655 8

CONTENTS

v

ILLUSTRATIONS

Illustrations are reproduced by courtesy of the following: the Master and Fellows, Clare College, Cambridge (fig. 2); the Master and Fellows, St John's College, Cambridge (fig. 7); the Syndics of the Fitzwilliam Museum, Cambridge (figs. 5, 10 and 15); Bernard Quaritch Ltd (fig. 26); Edward Sandars, Esq. (fig. 27 d). All others are by courtesy of the Syndics, Cambridge University Library.

PREFACE

I have sought in this book, which follows John Oates' account of the University Library down to 1710, to do three things. First, to explain the background to the present collections in the Library as they have developed over nearly two hundred years; second, to examine the steps taken to organize the Library as it increased and had more demands made of it; and third, to establish the context in which these developments took place, in the University, in the country, and in the world at large.

While to most the current bookstock of the Library is of over-riding concern, the manner in which the University spent its funds (sometimes extremely limited), and the extent to which endowments were able to support them, have an obvious relevance to the strengths and weaknesses of the Library today. Under the Licensing Acts of the late seventeenth century, and continuously since the Copyright Act of 1710, the Library has been entitled to a copy of every book published in this country. The implications of this for a university library, and the limitations of the legislation, are not as widely appreciated as might have been hoped following the work of Barrington Partridge and Oates, while the workings of the Acts of 1814, 1836 and 1842, and the degree of success attained by the joint agency established by a number of the copyright libraries in 1863 are still matters for exploration. Because of its crucial importance, I have deliberately paid especial attention to the history of copyright deposit as it has affected the University Library; much of this will have considerable bearings on the other copyright libraries, but the extent of shared experiences in this respect, and the differences between the various libraries, remain to be investigated more thoroughly. Copyright deposit lies at the core of national library provision in Britain, and this book examines the question as it has affected the historical growth of one Library in more detail and over a longer period than has been published for any other library.

Apart from copyright deposit and miscellaneous purchases and donations, each collection to arrive has had implications for the long-term development of the Library (and frequently therefore for the University) – if not always quite so obviously as in the case of John Moore's library, given by George I in 1715, or the consignments received from the Indian sub-continent in the second half of the nineteenth century. For each (and particularly for Moore's, the most important the Library has ever received) I have described something of its formation and the rationale of its contents.

My second principal concern is with library organization, most obviously with the means by which the Library's contents were made available to readers, whether in catalogues or in the arrangement of books on the shelves. The minutiae of a library's organization do not always make the most stimulat-ing reading on a cursory inspection, but they directly influence the Library's effectiveness, and also reflect the changing attitudes to the Library both as an institution and as a collection of books. The curious will also find some information on the history of the library profession, its training, expectations, and conditions of work: the Library Association was founded only in 1877, at the end of my period, and not one of the staff mentioned in the following pages had any formal training of the kind widely expected today.

Third, and most particularly, I have sought to provide a context for all this activity. I have approached this from four directions. The first is familiar in histories of libraries: the means by which books and manuscripts were acquired, by gift, in the trade, whether new or second-hand, from retail booksellers or at auction, from local, metropolitan or foreign sources. In this Cambridge is fortunate, since besides the ordinary accessions and donations registers there also survive for much of the eighteenth and nineteenth centuries the individual invoices from suppliers, one of the largest such accumulations of their kind in the country. The second is the University Library's relations with members of the University at all levels, with the colleges, and with other institutions in the University. Until the end of the eighteenth century it was usual to ignore such questions. But in the nineteenth century new attention to undergraduate teaching and examination, the rise of the scientific departments with their own particular needs, greatly increased general expenditure and the concomitant hopes of saving money, and external interest expressed in such documents as the report of the Graham Commission of 1852–3, drew the University's libraries closer together (albeit in different combinations) when the provision of modern books was under consideration. On the other hand, the development of popular interest in older printed books, going beyond earlier attention to incunabula and English books of the early sixteenth century, stimulated attention to the collections in college libraries and, coupled with talk in national bibliographical circles of major projects in retrospective bibliography, led to a call for a union catalogue of the college libraries' older books. Thirdly, the Library's relations with scholars outside Cambridge became more and more complex. They were international long before the opening of this volume, but the requirements of classical, theological, historical, literary, antiquarian and art historical scholarship brought the collections of the Library, like those of many another public or semi-public institution, more and more before the eyes of an expanding and increasingly critical reading public; the development of facsimile techniques and the cheap mass reproduction of photographs made their own contribution to this expansion of the Library's audience. Of all the Librarians whose terms of office are contained in this volume, only Bradshaw's incoming correspondence survives in anything like its complete form: it is an indication of the degree to which the Library was acting as a reference library at levels, in subjects, and for people that a century earlier would not have been expected. In this respect the penny post and the growth of the railways had an effect on the Library no less important than changes in secondary and tertiary education, or the development (faster elsewhere than in Cambridge) of religious tolerance.

There remains the question of the Library's relationship to other libraries outside Cambridge, in a period when library co-operation became a necessity. I have already alluded to copyright deposit, which remained the most obvious feature in this respect. Despite the fact that Conyers Middleton, Thomas Kerrich and Edward Daniel Clarke all travelled considerably in Europe, they showed little inclination to introduce changes at Cambridge as a result of their observations elsewhere. So far as I can discover, the subsequently much quoted example of the University Library at Göttingen became a topic for discussion only well after it had shown what could be achieved in an academic library with imaginative management and the funds to match. In the cataloguing of the collections as a whole, Cambridge and Oxford moved together to the extent that Cambridge relied for access to much of its stock until the early nineteenth century on the printed author catalogue of the Bodleian Library published in 1738. Despite the examples of William Reading's printed catalogue of Sion College Library (1724) and that of Leiden University Library (1716) the University Library remained without a subject catalogue: both John Taylor's efforts in the 1730s, and thoughts of a catalogue modelled on Brunet in the first years of the nineteenth century, came to nothing. Calls were frequently made for a printed catalogue of the entire library, or for one of the Royal Library alone, but none was ever produced. Yet on the other hand, when the Library introduced a guardbook catalogue using printed slips in 1861 it did so before the British Museum, which looked to Cambridge for guidance. It was against this background, just as much as the gradually unfolding ones of university reform, ever more diverse demands of scholarship, and a changing book trade, that the Library's influence and place in the world gradually developed.

My debt to the work of four men will be obvious in the notes to the following pages. Henry Bradshaw was the first to attempt a serious history of the Library; Henry Richards Luard was responsible for the printed list of many of its records; John Willis Clark wrote a still unequalled history of its buildings; and Charles Edward Sayle compiled the *Annals* which have until now been the principal source for its chronology. Without these men, my path would have been much more tangled.

This book owes it origins, however, to John Oates, who hoped to write about the period himself until it became clear that the better course was to concentrate on the period down to 1710. The numerous references to his work are no more than a token of what this book owes to his knowledge, kindness and encouragement. He has read much of it in typescript, to the benefit of author, book and reader alike. Parts have also been read by Hugh Amory, Paul Needham and Frank Stubbings, and their various suggestions for improvements have been of the greatest help.

While research and writing have had inevitably to be fitted into spare time, usually first thing in the mornings, in the evenings, or at week-ends, my colleagues during the day in the Library and University Archives have been aware for some years of my importunities, and they have been generous in their patience, interest and support. Outside the Library, in Cambridge I am indebted to the staffs of the libraries at Corpus Christi College, King's College, St John's College and Trinity College. Elsewhere in the United Kingdom it is a pleasure to thank the staffs of the Bodleian Library (especially on this occasion Alan Bell, Paul Morgan, Julian Roberts and Timothy Rogers), the British Library (especially Robin Alston, Jean

Archibald, Nicolas Barker, Mirjam Foot, Philip Harris, Lotte Hellinga, Mervyn Janetta, Dennis Rhodes, Ian Willison and Christopher Wright), the County Record Office at Bury St Edmunds, Eastbourne Public Library, Edinburgh University Library, Glasgow University Library, the John Rylands University Library of Manchester, Lambeth Palace Library and the National Library of Scotland. Abroad, I have been similarly helped at the Bibliothèque Nationale, the Grolier Club, the Houghton Library at Harvard (especially by Hugh Amory), the Clements Library at the University of Michigan, the Pierpont Morgan Library (especially by Paul Needham), the Watkinson Library at Trinity College, Hartford, Connecticut (especially by Jeffrey Kaimowitz) and the Baillie/Howe Library at the University of Vermont (especially by John Buechler). Outside all these institutions, whose staffs number so many friends, I record here also the particular and varied contributions of Terry Belanger, Tom Birrell, John Feather, Arthur Freeman, Edith Hazen, Frans Korsten, Robin Myers, Graham Pollard, Nicholas Poole-Wilson, Paul Quarrie, Robert Rosenthal and Katherine Swift. The troublesome labours of proofreading have been cheered by the informed help of Alan Bell, Brian Jenkins, Elisabeth Leedham-Green and Paul Needham, who are of course innocent of any blemishes that remain.

None, however, has contributed as much as my wife Rosamond, who has nurtured this book at every turn, and by her knowledge and understanding improved it from beginning to end. For this, I can only be thankful, and trust that others will be likewise.

Cambridge, August 1984

ABBREVIATIONS

All books are published in London unless otherwise stated.

Baker–Mayor	Thomas Baker *History of the College of St. John the Evangelist, Cambridge* ed. J. E. B. Mayor 2 vols. (Cambridge 1869)
Bernard *Catalogi*	[Edward Bernard] *Catalogi librorum manuscriptorum Angliae et Hiberniae in unum collecti* (Oxford 1697)
Bradshaw *Correspondence*	*Henry Bradshaw's correspondence on incunabula with J. W. Holtrop and M. F. A. G. Campbell* ed. Wytze and Lotte Hellinga 2 vols. (Amsterdam 1966 [1968] − 78)
Browne *Catalogue*	E. G. Browne *A catalogue of the Persian manuscripts in the library of the University of Cambridge* (Cambridge 1896)
Cambridge under Queen Anne	*Cambridge under Queen Anne, illustrated by memoir of Ambrose Bonwicke and diaries of Francis Burman and Zacharias Conrad von Uffenbach* ed. J. E. B. Mayor (Cambridge Antiquarian Soc. 1911)
Christian *Vindication*	Edward Christian *A vindication of the right of the universities of Great Britain to a copy of every new publication* (Cambridge 1807)
Clark *Endowments*	*Endowments of the University of Cambridge* ed. J. W. Clark (Cambridge 1904)
Cooper *Annals*	C. H. Cooper *Annals of Cambridge* 5 vols. (Cambridge 1842–1908)
Craster	Sir Edmund Craster *History of the Bodleian Library 1845–1945* (Oxford 1952)
DNB	*Dictionary of national biography*
Duff	E. Gordon Duff *Fifteenth century English books; a bibliography of books and documents*

	printed in England and of books for the English market printed abroad (Bibliographical Soc. 1917)
Dyer *Privileges*	George Dyer *The privileges of the University of Cambridge* 2 vols. (1824)
Esdaile *British Museum Library*	Arundell Esdaile *The British Museum Library* (1946)
Foxon	D. F. Foxon *English verse 1701–1750; a catalogue of separately printed poems with notes on contemporary collected editions* 2 vols. (Cambridge 1975)
Goodison *Cambridge portraits*	J. W. Goodison *Catalogue of Cambridge portraits* 1. *The University collection* (Cambridge 1955)
Gunning *Reminiscences*	Henry Gunning *Reminiscences of the University, town and county of Cambridge* 2 vols. (Cambridge 1854)
GW	*Gesamtkatalog der Wiegendrucke* Bd 1 etc. (Leipzig 1925 etc.)
Hartshorne *Book rarities*	C. H. Hartshorne *The book rarities in the University of Cambridge* (1829)
Hearne *Remarks and collections*	Thomas Hearne *Remarks and collections* ed. C. E. Doble etc. 11 vols. (Oxford Historical Soc. 1885–1921)
Historical Monuments Commission *Cambridge*	Royal Commission on Historical Monuments *An inventory of the historical monuments in the City of Cambridge* 2 vols. + maps (1959)
Historical register	*The historical register of the University of Cambridge...to the year 1910* ed. J. R. Tanner (Cambridge 1917)
HMC	Royal Commission on Historical Manuscripts
Ker *Medieval libraries*	*Medieval libraries of Great Britain; a list of surviving books* ed. N. R. Ker 2nd ed. (Royal Historical Society 1964)
Luard	[H. R. Luard] *A chronological list of the Graces, documents, and other papers in the University Registry which concern the University Library* (Cambridge 1870)
Luard *Adversaria*	*A catalogue of adversaria and printed books*

	containing MS. notes, preserved in the Library of the University of Cambridge ed. H. R. Luard (Cambridge 1864)
McKenzie *Cambridge University Press*	D. F. McKenzie *The Cambridge University Press 1696–1712; a bibliographical study* 2 vols. (Cambridge 1966)
Macray *Annals*	W. D. Macray *Annals of the Bodleian Library, Oxford, with a notice of the earlier library of the University* 2nd ed. (Oxford 1890)
Monk *Bentley*	J. H. Monk *The life of Richard Bentley, D.D.* 2nd ed. 2 vols. (1833)
Munby *Phillipps studies*	A. N. L. Munby *Phillipps studies* 5 vols. (Cambridge 1951–60)
Nichols *Illustrations*	J. and J. B. Nichols *Illustrations of the literary history of the eighteenth century* 8 vols. (1817–58)
Nichols *Literary anecdotes*	J. Nichols *Literary anecdotes of the eighteenth century* 9 vols. (1812–16)
Oates *Catalogue*	J. C. T. Oates *A catalogue of the fifteenth-century printed books in the University Library, Cambridge* (Cambridge 1954)
Oates 'Copyright Act'	J. C. T. Oates 'Cambridge and the Copyright Act of Queen Anne (1710 –1814)' in Larry S. Champion (ed.) *Quick springs of sense* (Athens, Ga. 1974) pp. 61–73
Oates *History*	J. C. T. Oates *Cambridge University Library; a history. From the beginnings to the Copyright Act of Queen Anne* (Cambridge 1986)
Oates 'Reform of the Copyright Act'	J. C. T. Oates 'Cambridge University and the reform of the Copyright Act, 1805–1813' *The Library* 5th ser. 27 (1972) pp. 275–92
Partridge *Legal deposit*	R. C. Barrington Partridge *The history of the legal deposit of books throughout the British Empire* (1938)
Philip	I. Philip *The Bodleian Library in the seventeenth and eighteenth centuries* (Oxford 1983)
Prothero *Bradshaw*	G. W. Prothero *A memoir of Henry Bradshaw* (1888)
Reporter	*Cambridge University Reporter*

Sayle *Annals*	C. E. Sayle *Annals of Cambridge University Library 1278–1900* (Cambridge 1916)
Schiller-Szinessy	S. M. Schiller-Szinessy *Catalogue of the Hebrew manuscripts preserved in the University Library, Cambridge* 1 (Cambridge 1876)
STC	A. W. Pollard and G. R. Redgrave *A short-title catalogue of books printed in England, Scotland, & Ireland and of English books printed abroad 1475–1640* (Bibliographical Soc. 1926) 2nd ed., revised and enlarged by W. A. Jackson, F. S. Ferguson and Katharine F. Pantzer. Vol. 2 (Bibliographical Soc. 1976)
Venn *Al. Cant.*	J. and J. A. Venn *Alumni Cantabrigienses; a biographical list of all known students, graduates and holders of office in the University of Cambridge to 1900* 10 vols. (Cambridge 1922–54)
Willis & Clark	Robert Willis and John Willis Clark *The architectural history of the University of Cambridge and of the colleges of Cambridge and Eton* 4 vols. (Cambridge 1886)
Winstanley *Early Victorian Cambridge*	D. A. Winstanley *Early Victorian Cambridge* (Cambridge 1940)
Winstanley *Eighteenth century*	D. A. Winstanley *The University of Cambridge in the eighteenth century* (Cambridge 1922)
Winstanley *Later Victorian Cambridge*	D. A. Winstanley *Later Victorian Cambridge* (Cambridge 1947)
Winstanley *Unreformed Cambridge*	D. A. Winstanley *Unreformed Cambridge* (Cambridge 1935)
Wright *Catalogue*	W. Wright *A catalogue of the Syriac manuscripts preserved in the library of the University of Cambridge* 2 vols. (Cambridge 1903)

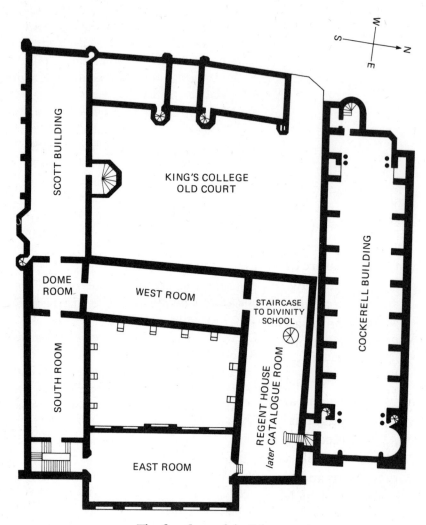

The first floor of the Library.

1

INTRODUCTION: NATIONAL EXPECTATIONS

WHEN IN 1869 Henry Bradshaw, the new University Librarian, contributed a series of articles on the history of the Library to the *Cambridge University Gazette*,[1] he chose to interrupt his account not at 1710 but at 1715: with the arrival of George I's gift of one of the finest private libraries in the country rather than with the Copyright Act of Queen Anne. The *Gazette* was a journal of liberal, even advanced, opinions, but it is a measure of how preoccupations have developed since that it should now seem more appropriate to start with the earlier year – a date which places more emphasis on the gradual accumulation of a research library with both university and national obligations, than on the arrival of a single collection, however grand or fundamental to the surviving corpus of early books and manuscripts. Bradshaw did not even mention the 1710 Act, and alluded to its successors in the Statute Book only in passing. His brief history – almost the first of its kind[2] – was prompted by Macray's *Annals of the Bodleian Library*, published in 1868, which laid especial emphasis on the arrival of collections and major treasures. But while on the one hand he recognized in Macray's work proof that at Oxford 'the Library has been, as indeed it should be, the centre of the literary activity of the University' and on the other opposed to it the equally obvious belief current in Cambridge that 'books are wanted for working purposes', he seemed disinclined to pursue the implications of his remarks. To Bradshaw, indeed,

---

[1] Reprinted as *The University Library* (Cambridge 1881) and in his *Collected papers* (Cambridge 1889) pp. 181–205.
[2] It was preceded only by C. H. Hartshorne's inaccurate and incomplete account in *The book rarities in the University of Cambridge* (1829).

it seemed that for many the subject of the history of the Library was scarcely respectable: 'Any regard for the Library, except as a place from which we can carry off the books we want to use, is looked upon by our highest authorities as a matter of merely antiquarian curiosity.'[3]

The following pages will, it is to be hoped, satisfy some of that 'merely antiquarian curiosity'. They do not spurn the anecdotal, or even sometimes the trivial, and they have been written in the belief that a degree of antiquarian connoisseurship is not only occasionally appropriate to interpret episodes in the Library's history, but that it also helps to explain something of the Library's museum role at the end of the twentieth century. Beyond these parochial minutiae, however, lie considerations of a more complex kind, that force attention past the traditional narrative and local concerns of library history. I have attempted in this book also to pay attention to the place of the Library not only within the University, but also in the country at large and in the international scholarly community: to its fortunes and importance as a copyright deposit library, as well as its growth as one of the major national research collections. Within Cambridge itself, there is still no satisfactory account of eighteenth- and nineteenth-century reading habits, among either senior or junior members; and while some modern studies exist of the curricula during the period,[4] these have taken little or no notice of either the college or the university libraries, or of the local book trade. Whereas the sixteenth and seventeenth centuries have attracted several significant investigations into these central questions of university history,[5] even the nineteenth-

---

[3] *The University Library* p. 5.

[4] Most recently M. M. Garland *Cambridge before Darwin: the ideal of a liberal education 1800–1860* (Cambridge 1980). Christopher Wordsworth's *Social life at the English universities in the eighteenth century* (Cambridge 1874) and *Scholae academicae; some account of the studies at the English universities in the eighteenth century* (Cambridge 1877) remain alone of their kind after over a century.

[5] Cf. (among many) Sears Jayne *Library catalogues of the English renaissance* (Berkeley 1956, rev. ed. Godalming 1983); Mark H. Curtis 'Library catalogues and Tudor Oxford and Cambridge' *Studies in the Renaissance* 5 (1958) pp. 111–20; Mark H. Curtis *Oxford and*

century reform period remains uncharted. In 1869 Bradshaw apologized for the lack of any Cambridge volume to balance Macray's *Annals* by complaining of a lack of records: 'a handful of stray papers, a few mutilated old catalogues, the account books (very incomplete) for the last fifteen years, and one or two very meagre entry books (also imperfect) stretching back to about 1780 – these are all that the University Library contains of the history of the last two hundred years'. Even after the publication in 1870 of H. R. Luard's list of papers relating to the Library housed in the University Registry, Bradshaw still spoke of the 'melancholy scantiness' of the records.[6] In fact, these records are very far from scanty, but this book can do no more than suggest how their use might be developed.

While a comprehensive study of overall library provision and its impact on scholarship, teaching and leisure in eighteenth- and nineteenth-century Cambridge must await another occasion, a definition of the University Library's evolving position within the University is an essential prerequisite; it must indeed also be a central factor in any account of the development of the collections. Throughout the period covered in this volume, which ends with the death of Henry Bradshaw, the Library was geographically at the centre of the University. Its topographical position changed only in 1934 when, after over five hundred years, a new purpose-built library was opened on the other side of the River Cam in what in the nineteenth century were still open fields. This topographical pre-eminence within the University was confirmed

Cambridge in transition 1558–1642 (Oxford 1959); William T. Costello *The scholastic curriculum at early seventeenth-century Cambridge* (Cambridge, Mass. 1958); Lisa Jardine 'The place of dialectic teaching in sixteenth-century Cambridge' *Studies in the Renaissance* 21 (1974) pp. 31–62; David McKitterick 'Two sixteenth-century catalogues of St John's College library' *Trans. Cambridge Bibliographical Soc.* 7 (1978) pp. 135–55; Philip Gaskell *Trinity College library; the first 150 years* (Cambridge 1980). For an isolated example from a slightly later period see Bruce Dickins 'Henry Gostling's library; a young don's books in 1674' *Trans. Cambridge Bibliographical Soc.* 3 (1961) pp. 216–24. These remarks were written before the publication of a valuable paper by J. C. Mays 'Coleridge's borrowings from Jesus College library, 1791–94' *Trans. Cambridge Bibliographical Soc.* 8 (1985). 6 Bradshaw *The University Library* pp. 4, 5.

1　The Old Schools viewed from the east. Engraving by David Loggan, 1688. In 1710 the Library occupied the first floors of the east and south ranges. Size of original 349 × 410 mm.

by the Library's proximity to the other organs of university administration and influence – the Schools themselves (fig. 1), the Senate House and the University Church. Until the mid-nineteenth century these were the most obvious manifestations of the University's, as distinct from the colleges', existence. Neither the Botanic Garden (between the modern Downing Street and the Corn Exchange), conveyed to the University in 1762, nor the building in Queens' Lane assigned to the Professors of Anatomy and Chemistry in 1716, nor the University Press next to it, was of obvious importance to passers-by, while the University accounts repeat the emphasis on the Library, Schools (containing most of what lecture

4

rooms there were) and Senate House. But while the Library had a public and obvious function as the showpiece which epitomized the University as a whole, and was accordingly included in the itineraries of important visitors as well as in the pocket guide books that began to make their appearance in the mid-eighteenth century, its position was also defined by the nature of the University itself. The authority of the colleges, expressed in university organization in the controlling power of the professors and Heads of Houses, was challenged successfully only in the nineteenth century. While the University Library enjoyed a pre-eminent position in some respects, in others it was subordinate in the unreformed University to the requirements of the colleges and their ability to attract benefactions.

It has been remarked before now that the college libraries gained more from major donations than the University Library for most of the eighteenth and nineteenth centuries. Even setting aside the unique attention that Trinity College attracted with the erection of the Wren Library, including the gifts of Sir Henry Puckering in 1691 (among them the autograph drafts of *Lycidas* and *Comus*), the Gale manuscripts in 1738, and Edward Capell's Shakespeare collection in 1779,[7] the colleges often proved a stronger magnet for benefactors than the University Library. Besides the bequest of Thomas Baker in 1740, St John's received important collections from Domenico Antonio Ferrari in 1744, John Newcome in 1765 (including a number of incunables from the Harleian Library),[8] and Thomas Gisborne in 1804. Thomas Sherlock's

[7] M. R. James *The western manuscripts in the library of Trinity College, Cambridge* 3 (Cambridge 1902) pp. v–xiii; *Catalogue of Mr Capell's Shakespeariana, presented by him to Trinity College Cambridge* (privately pr. 1779), ed. W. W. Greg (Cambridge 1903).

[8] M. Cowie *A descriptive catalogue of the manuscripts and scarce books in the library of St John's College, Cambridge* (Cambridge 1843) pp. 115–34; Valdo Vinay 'Domenico Antonio Ferrari, bibliofilo Napoletano in Inghilterra nella prima metà del XVIII secolo' *Studi di letteratura, storia e filosofia in onore di Bruno Revel* (Firenze 1965) pp. 597–615; Howard Nixon 'Harleian bindings' *Studies in the book trade in honour of Graham Pollard* ed. R. W. Hunt, I. G. Philip and R. J. Roberts (Oxford 1975) pp. 153–94; R. F. Scott (ed.) *Admissions to the College of St John the Evangelist* 3 (Cambridge 1903) pp. 544–55; Baker–Mayor p. 1034.

bequest to St Catharine's in 1761 set the college library on its feet, and formed the basis of a printed catalogue – the first of a Cambridge college library – in 1771.[9] F. S. Parris, Master of Sidney Sussex College, chose to leave his books to his college rather than to the University Library where he had been *Protobibliothecarius*. In 1777 David Hughes left to Queens' a library of over two thousand volumes including several hundred tracts, some of the greatest rarity. Isaac Milner left his library to Queens' in 1820.[10] And in 1813 John Bowtell bequeathed his fundamental collections on the history of the town and University to Downing College, founded thirteen years previously.[11] The dispositions of the collections belonging to librarians other than Parris only serve to emphasize further the limited extent to which the University Library was expected to act as a repository for common knowledge. That of John Taylor, the most active of the librarians in the mid-eighteenth century, had been gathered not least from among the cast-offs of the University Library itself, and so served more usefully as a bequest to his old school at Shrewsbury.[12] But the auction of the books of his successor at several removes, Richard Farmer, was a major loss to Cambridge of which the Library appears to have taken no active notice.[13] Even in 1872, when the books and other possessions of Thomas Kerrich, Farmer's successor, were bequeathed by his son to the University, their desirability was – still – the object of shameful and public debate.[14]

The Kerrich collection, of paintings and other works of art as well as books and manuscripts, was left to the Fitzwilliam

[9] *Catalogus librorum in bibliotheca Aulae Divae Catharinae Cantabrigiae* (Cambridge 1771).

[10] T. H. Horne *A catalogue of the library of Queens' College, Cambridge* 2 vols. (Cambridge 1827).

[11] Historical Manuscripts Commission *Third Report* (1872) pp. 320–7; A. B. Gray 'John Bowtell of Cambridge' *Proc. Cambridge Antiquarian Soc.* 11 (1907) pp. 346–84.

[12] See below, p. 190.

[13] E. S. Shuckburgh *Laurence Chaderton, D.D.; Richard Farmer* (Cambridge 1884); Sir Sydney Roberts *Richard Farmer (1735–1797)* (1961); L. J. Lloyd 'Dr Richard Farmer, 1735–97' *The Book Collector* 26 (1977) pp. 524–36. The books were auctioned by King in London in May–June 1798. See also below, pp. 296–301.

[14] Prothero *Bradshaw* pp. 180–3 and below, pp. 747–8.

Museum. From its opening in 1848, thirty-two years after Viscount Fitzwilliam's bequest, the Museum not only offered an alternative to the University Library as a repository for newly acquired rare books and modern works on the fine arts, but also relieved the Library of its long-standing duties as curator of coins, sculpture, and, to some extent, pictures. Less publicly, but no less importantly, the Museum was part of a university, rather than college, based administration. In that sense it was an extension of the principles already implied in the expansion of laboratory space for the sciences. When in the 1820s the University contemplated rebuilding the old Schools, it did so not only because there was no longer sufficient space for the Library. Pressure for drastic reconstruction of existing university facilities for teaching came not least from those responsible for the natural sciences, while in 1828 William Whewell prepared a long statement on the needs for university teaching, in botany, mineralogy, anatomy, chemistry, medicine, modern history, Greek, natural philosophy and mathematics. Only if space for all these was made available, he believed, would the University emerge from its state of near atrophy, and respond to the needs of the new century.

Without some provision for lecture-rooms and for Collections, in addition to what Cambridge now possesses, she will have the mortification to see herself left behind in the cultivation of such studies as are above-mentioned; at a time when her Professors are as zealous as they have ever been, and are not charged with incapacity; when her Students are daily growing in activity and intelligence; and when her scientific possessions are such as to offer no mean foundation for future times to raise into complete collections.[15]

These and similar university developments all redefined the context of the Library itself, which could no longer exist in unquestioned supremacy. Its position was redefined more directly in 1825, with the introduction of a 'library tax' of 1s. 6d. a quarter on all members of the University apart from sizars, the poorest of the undergraduates.[16] The innovation at

---

[15] Willis & Clark 3 p. 100.   [16] Grace Book *N* p. 107.

last provided the Library with a regular income for purchases from a source other than private benefactions, but it removed some of its old independence and was the source of dispute in the 1860s when further efforts were made to reorganize the Library's financial relations with the University.

In other words, as the need for specialist teaching space and other institutions increased, the prerogative of the colleges was threatened and was finally balanced against a more centralized and powerful university organization. The most conspicuous manifestations of the nineteenth-century reforms in administration were the disappearance of the Caput, a small, influential and thoroughly unrepresentative body,[17] in 1856, and its replacement by a new Council of the Senate, to be supplemented in 1878 by the decision also to create a General Board of Studies.[18] Curriculum and examination reform similarly broke up the entrenched autonomy of the colleges; and while the Royal Commissioners of 1852 refrained from prolonged direct attack on some aspects of college administration, their recommendations for university boards for each discipline, for dividing responsibility for undergraduate teaching between college and University (the latter being responsible for more advanced work), and for colleges to contribute from tuition fees towards the expenses of the University, all attacked a loose, separatist structure in favour of a central authority.

Undergraduates were an unusual sight in the Library until the late nineteenth century. Barred from using it in 1471–2 after a series of thefts convinced the Regent Masters that it would be more convenient if they were not generally admitted, few of them seem to have shown very much resentment at their exclusion or to have sought special permission for admittance over nearly three centuries. The

---

[17] Winstanley *Early Victorian Cambridge* pp. 238–9.
[18] *Cambridge University Reporter* 13 December 1878. Winstanley *Later Victorian Cambridge* p. 304.

attitude of the senior members meanwhile was conditioned partly by well publicized thefts and partly by the knowledge that the curriculum could not be said to require use of a large library. George Pryme, Professor of Political Economy from 1828 to 1863, recalled the curriculum of early nineteenth-century Cambridge at its worst:

It would scarcely be believed how very little knowledge was required for a *mere* degree when I first knew Cambridge. Two books of Euclid's *Geometry*, Simple and Quadratic Equations, and the early parts of Paley's *Moral Philosophy*, were deemed amply sufficient. Yet in the year 1800 three students failed to pass even this test.[19]

The uneven advance in the eighteenth century of written examinations organized by colleges, and the establishment of the Senate House examination from about 1750, marked, at the least, aspirations towards better supervision of the under-graduate curriculum, but in themselves they had little effect on the demands made of the University Library.[20] With some exceptions, teaching was in the hands of the colleges, and increasingly, as the tripos system was developed, of private coaches. It was therefore only natural, given a course of instruction dependent principally on colleges and privately arranged tuition,[21] and a curriculum that did not compel candidates to read or study over a very wide range of topics, that even when undergraduate needs for books were acknowl-edged they were met not at university but at college level. Trinity College, well in the van, established a separate collection of books for undergraduate use in 1700, more to fill

---

[19] George Pryme *Autobiographic recollections* (Cambridge 1870) p. 92; see also Winstanley *Unreformed Cambridge* pp. 41–57, and *Early Victorian Cambridge* pp. 151–2.

[20] Winstanley doubted whether any of the Knightbridge Professors of Moral Philosophy lectured at all between the chair's being established in 1683 and the nineteenth century, whether Edward Waring, Lucasian Professor of Mathematics from 1760 to 1798 ever lectured, and whether any of the three Regius Professors of Physic between 1700 and 1817 either lectured or advanced their subject in any other way. They were by no means the only notorious offenders (Winstanley *Unreformed Cambridge* pp. 127, 131–2, 138).

[21] For one polemic on the relation of college to university teaching in the mid-nineteenth century see J. W. Donaldson *Classical scholarship and classical learning* (Cambridge 1856).

9

the embarrassing spaces in the newly built Wren Library than out of ideological conviction.[22] Most other colleges were content to wait until the nineteenth century or later, when text books on more subjects, and more varied and numerous than ever before, forced the more imaginative colleges to expand their libraries drastically. In the case of St John's, curriculum reading and various benefactions entailed the expansion of the library into converted sets of rooms below the old seventeenth-century library; Pembroke built a new library entirely. At the opposite extreme, however, Trinity Hall possessed a separate undergraduate reading room only at the end of the century,[23] and Clare College possessed no special undergraduate library even in 1930.[24] In the University at large, when the modern departmental collections began to emerge, they owed their existence at first not so much to the University as to the impetus of private individuals: of John Martyn in botany, of John Symonds, William Smyth and Oscar Browning in history, of George Pryme and Alfred Marshall in economics.

Curriculum and teaching reform in the nineteenth century brought inevitable demands for better provision. The first formal call for undergraduates to be allowed to use the University Library more liberally appears to have been made in 1831. At first it was sought to confine them to a separate reading room, where they could be supervised and their specialist needs be met the more easily. But this proved to be impracticable. Not only were there insufficient staff to fetch and carry books, or to supervise a general reading room, but changes in the nature of teaching made virtually unlimited access seem almost a necessity. Max Müller's comment on Charles Kingsley's lectures as Professor of Modern History in

---

[22] Philip Gaskell and Robert Robson *The library of Trinity College, Cambridge: a short history* (Cambridge 1971) pp. 24–5. Christopher Wordsworth, who came up to Trinity in October 1793, used the college library not only for his needs as a student but also as a place in which to 'lounge' (C. Wordsworth *Social life at the English universities in the eighteenth century* (Cambridge 1874) pp. 587–94).

[23] Charles Crawley *Trinity Hall; the history of a Cambridge college 1350–1975* (Cambridge 1976) p. 130.

[24] Mansfield D. Forbes (ed.) *Clare College 1326–1926* 2 vols. (Cambridge 1928–30) 2 p. 353.

the 1860s was applied to libraries in general, not just to the University Library, and was, perhaps, exaggerated as to the generality of students: 'They stirred up the interest of young men, and made them ask for books which Undergraduates had never asked for before at the University libraries.'[25] Whatever its truth, the interest of his remark is that he saw any need to make it at all. Among much else, the changes in mid-nineteenth-century Cambridge brought a reform and extension of the curriculum, the appointment of new university teaching staff and, equally importantly, changes in teaching methods themselves. The Historical Tripos was not founded until 1873, but under Seeley and Oscar Browning developed an emphasis on independent and wide-ranging enquiry that had been nowhere evident in the eighteenth or early nineteenth centuries; even so, it did not escape criticism for providing insufficient opportunity for candidates to use primary sources.[26] To his contemporaries, Oscar Browning's emphasis (shared with Seeley) on the political aspects of history, in the belief that they were of most everyday modern importance, seemed arguable (and his undisputed seriousness of purpose was made the more comic by his risible political career);[27] but his opinions were founded on the same liberal utilitarianism that had prompted the establishment of the Natural Sciences Tripos, and that provided arguments in favour of introducing triposes in the Indian and Semitic languages.[28] The slow and painful reform of the Classical Tripos in the 1860s and 1870s, freeing it from its old link with mathematics (which had persisted since 1822) and requiring less purely philological skill from candidates,[29] implied a

---

[25] Preface to Charles Kingsley *The Roman and the Teuton* (1875) pp. xi–xii.

[26] G. W. Prothero 'The historical tripos' *Cambridge Review* 5 (1884–5) pp. 163–6; Deborah Wormell *Sir John Seeley and the uses of history* (Cambridge 1980) pp. 110–15.

[27] Oscar Browning *Memories of sixty years at Eton, Cambridge and elsewhere* (1910) pp. 234–5.

[28] Winstanley *Later Victorian Cambridge* pp. 208–9. See also Roy Porter 'The natural sciences tripos and the "Cambridge School of Geology", 1850–1914' *History of Universities* 2 (1982) pp. 193–216.

[29] Winstanley *Later Victorian Cambridge* pp. 209–27.

similar distaste for the straitjacket of earlier doctrines. These and changes in other disciplines recognized that the University was for most of its members no longer (as it had become in the eighteenth century) either simply the path to an ecclesiastical career or an agreeable means of filling in the last years before adulthood.

To these educational and academic reforms, statistics added their own comment, and one that could be less easily ignored. The alarming success of the copyright deposit legislation, once the University had accepted its responsibility, meant that the shelves were filled faster than ever before, while the increase in undergraduate admissions to the University threatened both college and university provision. At the beginning of the eighteenth century annual matriculations stood at about two hundred. This figure declined as the century wore on, dropping to little over a hundred in 1760–70, but there was a steep rise in the early years of the nineteenth century, to an average of well over four hundred between 1820 and 1860. After 1860 it climbed spectacularly, reaching 993 in 1885. In 1748 there were 1500 names on college boards in all, including both undergraduates and members of the Senate. By 1824 this had risen to 4489, and in 1884 it was 11,958, of whom somewhat over three thousand were resident.[30]

These developments had a crucial effect on the Library's position in the University. What had been clear to the more alert members of the University forty years before became desperately obvious to all in the 1870s despite the addition of a new building: that there was sufficient space neither for books nor, increasingly, for readers. After years of discussion on the means of dealing with undergraduate needs, and the often querulous fears on the subject expressed by the Library staff, much of the problem was removed by the establishment of specialist subject libraries designed in most cases specifically to answer the needs of the Tripos or to provide services that the

---

[30] J. A. Venn *Oxford and Cambridge matriculations 1544–1906* (Cambridge 1908), frontispiece; *Cambridge University calendar* 1885 p. 675.

University Library because of its size could not encompass. The change in library provision in the latter part of the nineteenth century was dramatic, but no more so than the changes in the University that led the way. The beginnings of modern departmental organization were reflected in the memorandum addressed to the Library Syndicate in November 1864 by the Regius Professor of Physic and nine others in medicine and chemistry appealing for more liberality in borrowing books essential for their work:[31] but the answer lay not so much in special provision within the Library as in further provision outside it.

New specialist libraries[32] were begun for Divinity in 1879, with the opening of the new Divinity School in St John's Street, for Music in 1880, for Zoology in 1883, when the University received the books of Francis Maitland Balfour, Professor of Animal Morphology, and for Moral Sciences in about 1885, through the initiative of Alfred Marshall and Henry Sidgwick. The library of the Mineralogical Museum was enhanced in 1880 by the bequest of W. H. Miller, while in 1881 the University reached agreement with the Cambridge Philosophical Society to provide accommodation and staff for the Society's library in return for access to the collections.[33] In 1884 Oscar Browning launched an appeal to bring up to date the historical library established in 1807 under the terms of the will of John Symonds, Regius Professor of Modern History, and to make it of use to ordinary undergraduate needs.[34] Older

[31] The memorandum was signed by Henry J. H. Bond (Regius Professor of Physic), William Clark (Professor of Anatomy), G. E. Paget (Linacre Lecturer), W. W. Fisher (Downing Professor of Medicine), W. H. Drosier (Clark's deputy), G. M. Humphrey (Lecturer in Anatomy), G. D. Liveing (Professor of Chemistry), P. W. Latham (lecturer and on the staff of Addenbrooke's Hospital), Adam Sedgwick (Woodwardian Professor) and Charles Lestourgeon (lecturer on surgery and pathology at Addenbrooke's).

[32] The history of departmental libraries is gathered most conveniently in *Cambridge University Reporter* 28 March 1969 pp. 1236–311.

[33] One aspect of the Philosophical Library's position in the University is described in Norma C. Neudoerffer 'The function of a nineteenth-century catalogue belonging to the Cambridge Philosophical Library' *Trans. Cambridge Bibliographical Soc.* 4 (1967) pp. 293–301. See also below, pp. 746–7.

[34] For Browning and the History Library see CUL Cambridge Papers FA 4528.

specialist libraries already existed for geology (in the Woodwardian Museum, from 1842 until the first years of the twentieth century housed on the ground floor of the Cockerell Building of the University Library), botany (founded on the botanical library presented by John Martyn in 1765), anatomy, and astronomy (dating back to the 1820s and to be transformed by John Couch Adams' bequest of part of his valuable library of early astronomical books in 1892). By then there were also specialist libraries in physics (1887), chemistry (1888), and engineering (1891). A separate law library was finally established after many years' anxiety in 1898, and one for modern languages in about 1900. Not all of these were intended for undergraduates. The interest of George Pryme's bequest of his early economics books and pamphlets was primarily historical even when he made it, quite apart from the fact that there was no Tripos in the subject. Oscar Browning's appeal was, indeed, unique in that it was launched specifically for undergraduates.

This extra library provision was intended to meet the needs of all the various strata of the University, both at undergraduate and at teaching or research levels, but it also expressed emphatically a new spirit that would have found few sympathizers in the previous century. The organization of the University had changed, but so had its expectations of itself. The same was true also of the University Library – not only in its attitude to undergraduates but also in its assessment of itself as a research collection. When the books of John Moore, Bishop of Ely, were presented by the King in 1715, they approximately trebled the size of the Library, to perhaps 45,000 volumes. No other collection to compare with it arrived until the gift of Lord Acton's library of about 60,000 volumes in 1902, but more seriously the University Library neither bought books and manuscripts nor sought gifts with much enthusiasm or organization for a century and more after the arrival of George I's gift. Moore's books took decades to catalogue and house, but the consequences and obligations of such a collection were not acknowledged in library policy until the 1860s. Indigestion gave way to torpor. In the late eighteenth century one attempt was made to assert the place of the Library as a centre of research, with a major series of purchases at the sale of Anthony Askew's manuscripts in 1785; the impetus, however, came not from the Library itself but from the University's short-lived hopes for a new programme of scholarly publication by the University Press, and the experiment was not repeated.[35] The degree to which the University flouted its statutes, ignored its responsibilities and sought to lead a comfortable existence unhindered by outside opinion has been examined elsewhere,[36] and needs no extended repetition. Yet by the 1870s the position of the Library as a national research institution had a direct influence on the manner in which provision in the University was made for undergraduates and for departmental or research needs.

In other words, just as the Library could no longer develop unhampered by very much interference from the rest of the University, and became subject to a complex structure of financial, educational and scholarly demands, so also in the context of the nation it was no longer possible to pursue a path that took no notice of outside opinion or needs.

The 1710 Copyright Act confirmed privileges for the University which had existed intermittently under the successive Licensing Acts from 1662 to 1695,[37] and since after a very few years it proved in this respect little more of an inducement to the trade than had been the case with its predecessors, the Library was only a little better off than previously. Copyright deposit was further restricted by the Library's own attitude to books which it might, technically, have claimed: a lack of interest, lack of will, and a natural lack of sympathy for much that was published. Even setting aside the Library's inability to cope with its own internal administration in the early eighteenth century under the weight of George I's gift, attitudes to copyright deposit remained almost

---

[35] See below, pp. 326–35.   [36] Winstanley *Unreformed Cambridge*.
[37] J. C. T. Oates 'The deposit of books at Cambridge under the Licensing Acts, 1662–79, 1685–95' *Trans. Cambridge Bibliographical Soc.* 2 (1957) pp. 290–304; *idem* 'Cambridge and the Copyright Act of Queen Anne (1710–1814)' *Quick springs of sense* ed. Larry S. Champion (Athens, Ga. 1974) pp. 61–73.

immovably conservative: it seemed that the privilege existed solely to support the University, and by implication therefore involved no further national obligations. The transformation of an inward-looking university library to a national institution that contrived simultaneously to answer the needs of an expanded and altered university was not accomplished smoothly or quickly. The process required changes in attitudes as much as growth in the stock of books, but it had been accomplished, if not perfected, by the date of Bradshaw's death in 1886.

George I's gift of John Moore's library, the finest private collection in the country, did much to silence criticism of the Hanoverian succession, and in that respect was politically astute: the results of Townshend's manoeuvrings to acquire the collection for Cambridge were quickly recognized in contemporary verse.[38] But the political nature of the gift was given extra emphasis in a further, and unremarked, respect, on which no contemporary comment appears to have survived: that the King, having bought the books, then gave them away. It was not only that such an act would have been unimaginable in France, where under Louis XIV the Royal Library advanced its collection by purchase and gifts in return for favours on an unprecedented scale:[39] had Moore's books been in France it is unlikely that they would have escaped the attentions of Le Tellier and those responsible for improving the royal collections. But the comparison with France is nonetheless suggestive. Following the removal of responsibility for the royal library from the superintendent of buildings to a librarian answerable directly to the King, the French royal collections were made available to any scholar who wished to study them.[40] By contrast, the English Royal Library had fallen into disrepair, and for all his efforts Richard Bentley, as King's Librarian, had been unable to restore it. It was open to

---

[38] See below, pp. 150–1, n. 152

[39] L. Delisle *Le cabinet des Manuscrits de la Bibliothèque Impériale* (4 vols. Paris 1868–81) I pp. 261–356.   [40] *Ibid.*, I p. 299.

interested scholars, but not until the foundation of the British Museum in 1753 did the country have a public library after the model of the French example, and even then it was meagre by comparison.[41] In 1697 Bentley had pointed out that both de Thou's and Marquard Gude's libraries were available to the Royal Library for purchase; either would have provided the conclusive intellectual and national authority for which he strove,[42] and which the French Royal Library so obviously possessed. The saving of Moore's collection for Cambridge therefore accomplished two aims at once. It was a *douceur* to university loyalty; and in preserving it in the public library of one of the two English universities there was an unstated belief in the ability of the University not merely to maintain it but also to recognize in it the basis of the authority and responsibilities of a national library. In other words, the University Library was advanced to a station in the hierarchy of the country's libraries above even the Royal Library. Richard Bentley's opinion on the Crown's buying just such a library as he had hoped for, and then giving it away to his own university where he was not a popular figure, is not recorded: although he became a member of the syndicate appointed to organize the library's reception in Cambridge, salt was later to be rubbed in the wound with the election of Conyers

---

[41] It was reckoned by Arundell Esdaile (*The British Museum Library* (1946) p. 180) that in 1757 the old Royal Library contained about nine thousand printed books. On Louis XIV's death in 1715 the French Royal Library contained over sixty thousand volumes (Le Prince *Essai historique sur la Bibliothèque du Roi* (Paris 1856) p. 74). See also I. R. Willison's suggestive 'The foundation of the British national library, 1600–1800' *Öffentliche und private Bibliotheken im 17. und 18. Jahrhundert; Raritätkammern, Forschungsinstrumente oder Bildungstätten?* ed. P. Raabe (Wolfenbüttel 1977) pp. 33–61.

[42] Richard Bentley *A proposal for building a royal library, and establishing it by Act of Parliament*. Reprinted in A. T. Bartholomew *Richard Bentley, D.D.; a bibliography* (Cambridge 1908) pp. 93–6. De Thou's library passed mostly into the Menars library (sale at The Hague, 1720) and then into the Soubise library (sale at Paris, 1789). For Marquard Gude's library, sold at Hamburg in 1706, see L. Nielsen *Danske privatbiblioteker gennem tiderne* 1 (Copenhagen 1946) pp. 212–16. Samuel Johnson alluded to the loss to the country of Vossius' library (sold in 1690 to the University of Leiden) even in 1742 (*Gentleman's Magazine* 1742 p. 639: his account of the Harleian Library was also printed in Thomas Osborne's *Proposals for printing the two first volumes of the Bibliotheca Harleiana* (1742) and in the subsequent *Catalogus Bibliothecae Harleianae* (1743)).

Middleton, the figurehead of opposition to him, as librarian of the new collection. In this respect party interest threatened the Library's interest. Bentley was one of the very few people in Cambridge who could have appreciated the implications of George I's gift – implications that the University at first failed miserably to exploit.[43]

If the University, or the Library, gave very much thought in the eighteenth century to matters of policy beyond everyday administration, little evidence of it has survived. In contrast with the wealth of some colleges, the University itself was poor. Its funds would not allow extensive purchases to add to the commanding presence of Moore's books coupled with the old library of before 1715. Legal provisions for copyright deposit were weak, and from 1751 the authorities found it more convenient to sell off such publications as they deemed useless among the parcels arriving from Stationers' Hall. In 1735, in correspondence with Lord Hervey, Middleton was scathing of a new publication brought to his attention, *The Persian letters continued* (purporting to be by George Lyttelton), which he clearly thought unnecessary for the Library to keep. 'The Persian Letters have not yet reached us, productions of that sort find no great market here, where ye little money that we have, is reserv'd for what is more necessary. I have order'd them however to be sent for, & shall not fail to give them a reading as soon as they come to hand.'[44] Interesting though his remarks are for the glimpse they provide of the relationship of the Library with, in this case, probably the Stationers' Company, his equation of current market demand with responsible librarianship is far more illuminating: the Univer-

---

[43] Bentley's attempts to influence thinking at Cambridge are also reflected in his acquaintance Daniel Maichel's *Introductio ad historiam literariam de praecipuis bibliothecis Parisiensibus, locupletata annotationibus, atque methodo*, published by Crownfield at Cambridge in 1721 and sold in London by James Knapton, Robert Knaplock and Paul Vaillant: the book was reprinted at Leipzig later in the same year.

[44] Middleton to Hervey 27 March 1735. Bury St Edmunds Record Office, Hervey papers 941/47/8.

sity Library seemed perilously close to applying the criteria of the circulating library, supplying a superior equivalent of the local bookseller 'Maps' Nicholson's 'most choice collection of Lounging Books that the genius of Indolence could desire'.[45]

It was therefore the more irksome that when, following legal proceedings in 1812 and new copyright legislation in 1814, novels and other light literature came in ever increasing quantities, and the Library was forced to abandon its policy of disposing of unwelcome material, market forces again came to the fore. On the one hand a reform movement pressed for better financial support for the Library, and steps were taken to repair the faults of the previous century, while on the other the ideals of scholarly universality and national record were welcomed for reasons which were, no doubt, predicted by those unsympathetic with the new spirit. 'The flourishing state of our Public Library, has lately become a subject of pride and constant interest to every resident and to many non-resident, Members of the Senate', rejoiced George Peacock in 1831. 'Every exertion is made to supply its deficiencies, not for purposes of ostentation, but of use, and it promises to become, if its progress be not arrested, in a very few years, the best consulting library in the kingdom.'[46] Peacock's model was Göttingen, 'the best consulting library in Europe' and certainly better than the British Museum which, for all its riches, had acquired books only irregularly and interruptedly. The ideal of a universal research library, embodied in Münchhausen's work at Göttingen University Library and expressed by Christian Gottlob Heyne in 1810 as 'a comprehensive collection of the most important writings of all times and all nations in all

45 *Gradus ad Cantabrigiam* (Cambridge 1803) p. 59. On Nicholson (whose portrait now hangs in the Entrance Hall of the Library; see below, p. 311) see Gunning *Reminiscences* I pp. 198–200; *Gentleman's Magazine* 1796, pt 2 pp. 708, 781; and Wordsworth *Social life at the English universities* pp. 378–85.
46 [George Peacock] *Observations on the plans for a new library* (Cambridge 1831) p. 59.

branches of learning',[47] had taken nearly a century to reach Cambridge; but it dogged the Library and Librarians (not always to their unalloyed delight) and finally won acceptance. The implied supremacy of the new spirit was asserted by Cockerell's Greek Revival designs for a completely new library, of which only one range was ever completed (see figs. 18–20): the University's decision to erect a new library in this, rather than any other, style, neatly echoed Smirke's appeal to neo-classical authority in the new King's Library of the British Museum completed a few years earlier.[48] The University Library's failure to affirm its position in the century following the arrival of Moore's collection began, belatedly, to be made good, both in increased accessions and in retrospective improvement, and in the Library's attitude to the scholarly community outside Cambridge. After much talk, the printed catalogue of Moore's books which would have established the supremacy of the Cambridge library in company with the Bodleian, and encouraged further attention,[49] had been finally abandoned, the victim of insufficient money and energy to endorse the authority of his collection by printed testimony. By the early nineteenth century Moore's books were becoming of less over-riding importance, but the publication of catalogues of manuscripts – first of the Burckhardt oriental manuscripts in 1853 and then of all the western manuscripts in 1856–67 – at last established the Library's national ascendancy in these fields. In addition, the vogue for loan exhibitions –

[47] Translated and quoted in B. Fabian 'An eighteenth-century research collection; English books at Göttingen University Library' *The Library* 6th ser. 1 (1979) pp. 209–24 at p. 212. See also *idem* 'Göttingen als Forschungsbibliothek im achtzehnten Jahrhundert. Plädoyer für eine neue Bibliotheksgeschichte' *Öffentliche und private Bibliotheken im 17. und 18. Jahrhundert; Raritätkammern, Forschungsinstrumente oder Bildungstätten?* ed. P. Raabe (Wolfenbüttel 1977) pp. 209–39. On Göttingen more generally see Charles E. McClelland *State, society, and university in Germany 1700–1914* (Cambridge 1980) and the references cited there.

[48] J. Mordaunt Crook *The British Museum: a case study in architectural politics* (Harmondsworth 1973) pp. 129–30.

[49] The desirability of a printed catalogue had of course been felt before 1715 as well, for example by Joseph Wasse in 1706 (Thomas Hearne *Remarks and collections* 1 ed. C. E. Doble (Oxford 1885) p. 200).

prompted by the British Institution and redoubled in the wake of 1851 – provided further opportunities for the Library's place to be asserted and evaluated in a national context, whether in loans of portraits to the new South Kensington Museum in 1866–8[50] or in contributing to the array of books printed by Caxton in the Caxton quatercentenary exhibition ten years later.[51] The coalescence of organized knowledge in Victorian Britain, exemplified in the increase of national learned societies, the development of the major metropolitan museums and galleries, and the rapid multiplication of learned journals and nationalist co-operative enterprises such as the *Dictionary of national biography* or James Murray's English dictionary, was expressed within the library world with the foundation of the Library Association in 1877; but the interdependence and mutual interests of the copyright libraries were stated in the foundation of a Copyright Agency in 1863 and in the increasing consultation, co-operation and comparison with the British Museum.

Within the Library this transition, at both University and national level, was reflected in innumerable ways, but nowhere more vividly than at the shelves of recent novels, acquired as copyright deposit copies and no longer discarded. In this case, however, the change was prompted more by opportunities offered than by idealism. The purposes of a copyright deposit library, its obligation to collect and preserve the printed output of the national literature regardless of the contemporary whims or educational needs of the University, were grasped generally only in the second half of the nineteenth century. If in the eighteenth century novels only entered the collections occasionally and even sometimes (as, seemingly, in the case of *Gulliver's travels*) by mistake, and there seemed no great need for them in the first years of the

---

[50] *Catalogue of the first (–third) special exhibition of national portraits ... on loan to the South Kensington Museum* (1866–8). The associated photographs and papers relating to the loan stand at S405·8.b.8.5.

[51] George Bullen *Caxton celebration, 1877; catalogue of a loan collection connected with the art of printing* (1877).

nineteenth century, by the 1840s opinion had changed remarkably. Like most other towns, Cambridge was not without its circulating libraries, but the University Library was found to offer an incomparably richer selection for recreational reading. The Novel Room became an object of previously unwonted interest; and since ladies were officially barred from borrowing books in a university open only to men, the convenient fiction was born that resident senior members taking books away from there did so on behalf of their lady friends.

As the worn bindings of many of the Library's mid-nineteenth-century novels testify, this was no casual affair. In 1865 J. E. B. Mayor noted that for years the principal work of the Library had been to compete with the circulating libraries, to the waste of assistants' time and of money spent on rebinding.[52] The system of quarter days, when all books were to be returned to the Library, meant that four times each year virtually all the books in the Library were in their places on the shelves. In the absence of any machinery for reserving books for would-be readers, these occasions were critical. Joseph Romilly, the University Registrary, was only one among several couriers who ministered to the needs of their friends who were otherwise unable to borrow. He borrowed books so that his sister could know what to feed young blackbirds on, as well as indulge her taste for sermons.[53] But this was a light chore compared with the demands from his friends at Madingley Hall, Lady Cotton (widow of Admiral Sir Charles Cotton), and her two children, the agreeable Miss Philadelphia Letitia Cotton and Sir St Vincent Cotton, a once colourful figure who squandered the family inheritance and who became wretched, toothless, prematurely aged and finally

[52] Mayor to Edward Atkinson 24 January 1865.
[53] MS. Add. 6826, 15 July 1850; MS. Add. 6829, 16 October 1852. Borrowing registers survive only for the period 1846–7, but record Romilly taking out not only Le Neve, Alison, Masters on Corpus Christi College, Debrett, a life of Bishop Fisher, and Caius *De antiquitate Cantabrigiensis academiae*, but also novels by Mrs Bremer, Fanny Burney, Disraeli, Mrs Gore, Samuel Lover and Captain Marryat.

paralysed. The family were voracious readers, and came to rely on the University Library to while away the winters: as Romilly could borrow virtually as many books as he wished, he found himself sending off parcels of anything from half a dozen to eighteen volumes. The autumn of 1853 was particularly active. Miss Cotton sent in a list of twenty works in the middle of October, and then wrote again on 1 November explaining that as her brother was confined to his room he wanted more. A few were returned three days later, but as Romilly was finding it difficult to make suitable selections for Madingley himself, he wrote to ask for a further list of books which Sir St Vincent would like. Romilly's patience was running thin, however, and the arrival of a 'very long' list of books in Miss Cotton's execrable handwriting put him in no good temper for her arrival a little later:

I dont think I was very civil in subst^{ce} tho I was rather doucereux in manner. I told her that one of her excellencies was not the clearness of her writ & that therefore I had copied out her list for the library keepers: – she said that Sir St Vincent was a rapid devourer of books now he was ill, for he was a bad sleeper & read at night: – I said I was certainly surprised at hav^g 8 vols returned on Sat. w$\overline{c}$h had been received on Wed^y, & that I wondered Sir St Vincent didn't subscribe to a circul^g Library.[54]

Nonetheless, in the end Romilly's good temper – and quite extraordinary patience – prevailed. Christmas Eve, the first day of the new Library quarter, found him on the steps of the Library in the midst of a gathering that was clearly a regular occasion:

I followed Lucy's advice & planted myself at the Library-door 5' before 10: there were congregated about 20 persons waiting for the opening of the door: among these were Shaw, Rusby, Shilleto, E. Walker, Skinner, old Pearce &c &c: I had a good deal of fun in talk^g to them & saying how it reminded me of my early opera-going days. – I placed myself quite close to the door, & Rusby told me that I must run upstairs as hard as I could, for that every body would try to pass me: – I made up my mind that nobody should do that: – so away we went helter-skelter I keeping ahead: I rushed into compartm^t Y & seized on 'Lewis Arundel' & then turned to catch

[54] MS. Add. 6831, 7 November 1853.

'Heir of Redclyffe', but it was snapt up & so was 'My Novel': – I rather
hope that Rusby carried off 'Heir of R.' as he said he was come to get a
novel beginn^g with R for a Lady. – Skinner (every action & every word of
whom is always unpleas^g to me) was humbug enough to say 'whenever I
find another person wants the same book as myself I give it up to him'!! If
so what possessed him to come to get the 1st chance?[55]

Romilly was able to appreciate the comedy of the scramble,
but not everyone found it easy to regard with equanimity the
phenomenon of the law of the land's being exploited in such a
way. The anonymous editor of William Everett's *On the Cam*,
a series of lectures delivered in Boston in 1864, felt it necessary
to correct Everett's remark that the copyright privilege
'which, if the library strictly availed itself of it, would soon
become like the gift of an elephant, is chiefly exercised in
procuring all the new novels, at the instance of the professors'
wives and other ladies connected with the University'. With
some local knowledge, the English editor noted starchly that
'works of more intrinsic value and lasting interest are applied
for with greater regularity and sooner after publication than
the novels, which are often not supplied until the demand for
them at the lending libraries has well nigh passed away'.[56] It
was, and is, a useful corrective. Nonetheless, in the 1860s the
Library was scandalized to discover that its copyright copies of
other books were being used as textbooks in local schools, and
J. E. B. Mayor (who came nearer to achieving an overdue
metamorphosis for the Library than any other single individual) was outraged as well as concerned at the threat such acts
seemed to pose to copyright deposit. 'By a flagrant abuse of the
privilege granted by the Copyright Act – an abuse of which the
booksellers are well aware,' he fumed to the Master of Clare
College, Edward Atkinson, 'it has become customary for
schoolmasters to supply their scholars with class-books –
dictionaries, grammars, reading-books, and exercises, from

[55] MS. Add. 6832, 24 December 1853.
[56] William Everett *On the Cam* (1866) p. 36.

the University Library; nay, infants are taught to spell from books supplied to us by Act of Parliament.'[57] In 1866 he was further angered to be told by one of his assistants that a female reader introduced by an M.A. had been borrowing books that had nothing to do with scholarly endeavour. A letter from her was brief, but revealed a situation that had clearly become absurd: 'Mrs. So and So's compliments. She returns the novel, and will be glad of another; also of a book for the child.'[58]

Borrowing of novels could scarcely be stopped, but such irregularities as these could be, and were, brought under control. Mayor's warning of the same year, though applied more to the weight of deposit copies coming into the Library in 1867, was an apt reminder of the narrow path the Library walked between a university and a national library of record, where parliamentary legislation could only provide guidelines. 'It should be remembered that we are not bound to welcome every spelling book or seedsman's catalogue: the act requires us to claim, and we may waive our claim, as the Berlin librarian Dr Pertz does.'[59] It was an argument that had been used, for different books, in the eighteenth century, and it was one that was contained within successive copyright legislation into the present century, but it was not easy to elaborate in practice. It enshrined a definition of a copyright deposit library that was worked out painfully and spasmodically over two centuries. The route by which it was achieved, and the consequences for the Library and University alike, form a recurrent theme in the following chapters. In 1836, Panizzi found it easy to distinguish between a university library and a national collection when he gave evidence to the Select Committee on the British Museum, and brushed aside any claim that Göttingen University Library had any relevance to the Museum. 'It is a library for the education of the persons

---

[57] Mayor to Edward Atkinson 24 January 1865.
[58] [J. E. B. Mayor] *Statement made to the Syndics of the Library, 7 March 1866* (Cambridge 1866) p. 3n.   [59] *Ibid.*, p. 11.

attending the university, and not a national collection, like that of the British Museum. It is not a library for research, as ours ought to be, but a library for education.'[60] For Cambridge the distinction could provide no such escape. The Library had to contrive to be both.

[60] *Reports from Committees* 1836 10, para. 4794. See also I. R. Willison 'The political and cultural context of Panizzi's reform of the British Museum Department of Printed Books as a national research library' *Bibliotheken im gesellschaftlichen und kulturellen Wandel des 19. Jahrhunderts* ed. G. Liebers and P. Vodosek (Hamburg 1982) pp. 53–73.

2

THE COPYRIGHT ACT OF 1710

THE SO-CALLED 'Copyright Act of Queen Anne', more properly entitled 'An act for the encouragement of learning, by vesting the copies of printed books in the authors or purchasers of such copies, during the times therein mentioned', received the Royal Assent on 4 April 1710.[1] Its legal ancestors were the Printing Act of 1662 and its successors, referred to generally as the Licensing Acts and which, while enjoining the deposit of copies of books in the privileged

[1] *Journals of the House of Lords* 19 p. 144. The privileges as a library of copyright deposit conferred on the Library (together with the Royal Library and the Bodleian) under the Licensing Act of 1662 and its successors had ended with the final expiry of the series on 3 May 1695. Between then and April 1710 there was no legislation to support any attempt to add to the Library by means of legal deposit. There is no evidence that the University, faced with such a predicament, appealed to the booksellers to support scholarship any further. Both event and consequences went unremarked in the University's records, but the same was not true of the other libraries deprived in like manner. Richard Bentley, as Royal Librarian, still pursued copyright deposit copies even in 1698, though with predictably little success, while at Oxford in 1695 Thomas Hyde sought to repair the situation by reverting to Sir Thomas Bodley's original agreement with the Stationers' Company of 1611. Hyde had almost equally little success: a few books were indeed delivered to Oxford, but only through the goodwill or ignorance of the booksellers. No books were deposited formally at Stationers' Hall for the whole of the period. (Monk *Bentley* 1 p. 99; Macray *Annals* pp. 40–1; Partridge *Legal deposit* p. 32 notes 4 and 5; Philip *Bodleian Library* pp. 68–9 and 76–8). The only evidence that Cambridge took any steps to continue the provisions for deposit under the Licensing Acts is in an undated memorandum 'Particulars to be considerd, & offerd, in order to be confirmd by an Act of Parliament': the last item of all on what is apparently an agenda for a meeting in Cambridge was 'To make that Clause of the Statute about printing perpetuall, for giving one Book of every printed Copy to ye publick Library of either University for Ever' (Baker transcripts, MS. Mm.2.23 p. 309). The same meeting was to consider the confirmation of the University's charters: the necessary Bill relating to this subject was introduced in Parliament in December 1689, but it was rejected in February 1691/2 (Cooper *Annals* 4 pp. 11, 17–18). I have found no further information at Cambridge on the part that the University may have taken in the unsuccessful Copyright Bill (which was to contain provisions for deposit) of 1706/7 (*ibid.* p. 79). For an account of the political background of the 1710 Act see John Feather 'The book trade in politics; the making of the Copyright Act of 1710' *Publishing History* 8 (1980) pp. 19–44, and Harry Ransom *The first copyright statute* (Austin 1956) (with the text of the Act).

libraries (then the Royal Library, and those of the two English universities), were designed not least for the purposes of censorship. The new Act of 1710 continued and extended the regulations for deposit, but instead of censorship was designed primarily to protect owners of copyrights against infringement by rival publishers or booksellers – for a term of twenty-one years in the case of books published before 10 April and for fourteen years in the case of those published subsequently. In order to achieve this, it was commanded that all titles, both of new books and of reprints, were to be entered in the Register Book at Stationers' Hall before publication, the Clerk of the Company providing a certificate of entry when requested, and also being required to make the Register available for inspection by any bookseller, printer or other interested person at all reasonable times. 'Whereas', the Act archly remarked, 'many persons may through ignorance offend against this Act unless some provision be made whereby the property in every such book, as is intended by this Act to be secured to the proprietor or proprietors thereof, may be ascertained, as likewise the consent of such proprietor or proprietors for the printing or reprinting of such book or books may from time to time be known'. The Stationers' Register was re-established as at once a record of ownership and (theoretically) a reference instrument for any bookseller who wished to consult it; it was therefore also the proprietors' most important witness to their properties.

By another clause in the same Act the number of copies of each book to be deposited was tripled from the old figure used in the Licensing Acts, from three to nine. After some unsuccessful lobbying on the part of the Cottonian Library and St Paul's Cathedral, and the addition at the last minute in committee stage and the House of Lords of five Scottish libraries, the list of deposit libraries comprised the Royal Library, the Bodleian, Cambridge University Library, Sion College (taking the place of St Paul's), the Faculty of

Advocates in Edinburgh, and the four Scottish universities.[2]

Many of the difficulties in administering the 1710 Act (so far as the University Library and other deposit libraries were concerned)[3] arose from the failure of these two separate but related parts, concerning copyright entry and deposit, to succeed in the way that had been intended. The first few days after the passing of the Act into law saw a predictable flush of enthusiasm for entry in the Register: on 12 April Tonson entered forty-seven copies, and on the next day Richard Sare entered thirty-five. But many of these early entries were 'old' copies, already published, and even though a substantial number of books was entered in the rest of the year the total at the end fell far short of the output of the press as a whole. Subsequent years saw further decline. The Act imposed no penalty for not entering a work in the Register, and the only incentive to comply with it lay in the bookseller's or publisher's fear of piracy. Even by September 1710 Henry Dodwell was complaining to Thomas Hearne in Oxford that the new Act was proving insufficient protection for booksellers' copyrights.[4] Rather than rely on the inadequate protection of the Act, some proprietors (particularly of costly enterprises) found it preferable to seek protection in the time-honoured device of the royal patent: among many, Bernard Lintot protected his property in this way when publishing Pope's *Iliad* in 1715, and Henry van der Esch did the same in 1734 for the new edition by Thomas Birch and others of Bayle's *Dictionary*. This procedure in itself did not of course require the deposit of

[2] Partridge *Legal deposit* pp. 33–4. Since 1925 the privileges accorded to the library of the Faculty of Advocates have been exercised by the National Library of Scotland, which was founded in that year.

[3] Copyright deposit at Cambridge has been surveyed in Oates 'Copyright Act'. For some of the other libraries see John P. Chalmers 'Bodleian copyright survivors, 1710 –1726' (Oxford B.Litt. thesis 1974); Philip pp. 76–9; P. Ardagh 'St Andrews University Library and the copyright acts' *Edinburgh Bibliographical Soc. Transactions* 3 (1956) pp. 183–209; A. Nairn 'A 1731 copyright list from Glasgow University archives' *The Bibliotheck* 2 [1959] pp. 30–2; S. M. Simpson 'An early copyright list in Edinburgh University Library' *The Bibliotheck* 4 (1965) pp. 202–4; E. H. Pearce *Sion College and Library* (Cambridge 1913) pp. 282–5.   [4] Hearne *Remarks and collections* 3 p. 45.

copies in the privileged libraries. On the other hand some sought to save a little money by spuriously claiming that their publications were correctly entered:[5] the practice was to become widespread in the nineteenth century, and no real effort was ever made to prevent it. The risk of not entering a book proved in most cases to be not worth the trouble or expense of doing so, and although (especially in the first decade of the working of the Act) the list of books entered at Stationers' Hall contained many works of scholarship, it degenerated with alarming rapidity to include an ever greater proportion of sermons, minor pamphleteering and titles of little obvious interest to a university library whose clientele was restricted for most purposes to the senior members of the University.

If the arrangements for entry were thus so ineffectual, those for deposit proved to be equally imperfect. The Act, to be sure, specified a stiff penalty for non-deposit of nine copies: offending booksellers or printers, besides forfeiting the value of the copies not delivered, were also to be fined five pounds for each undelivered copy, the fine to be recovered, with costs, by the Crown and by the governing authorities of the other copyright libraries. The Warehouse-Keeper at Stationers' Hall, who was to receive the books and who was to deliver them up to the several libraries within ten days of their demanding them, faced a similar penalty for non-compliance. There were thus two further holes through which copies might escape. In 1710, for example, Tonson had entered but did not deliver copies of his edition of Congreve, and in 1718 a large London conger did not produce at Stationers' Hall the requisite nine copies of Dugdale's *Monasticon*. Both books had been entered correctly in the Register, but plans for the *Monasticon* had changed since Richard Smith had entered, as a precaution, an ambitious four-volume edition on his own in 1716; likewise, John Urry's edition of Chaucer was entered in

---

[5] For example the broadside *The D– of M– turn'd conjuror* (J. Cramphorn, 1712: Foxon D2) and William Forbes' *The rattle-snake, or, a bastinado for a Whig* (Richard Gunning, 1712/13: Foxon F 192).

August 1714, but it was not published until 1721, after his death, and Lintot did not bother to deliver copies. In no case was any action taken by the Library. William Reading, Librarian of Sion College, echoed the feelings of the other libraries when in 1724 he complained,

They [the booksellers] enter such *English* Sermons, Histories, Poems and Pamphlets, as they are apprehensive will quickly be reprinted by others in cheaper Paper and Character: but commonly neglect to enter large and learned Works, which are not easily reprinted, or not vendible in lesser Forms. However, even such Books are sometimes entered: and I believe the Books we have received from *Stationers* Hall, by Virtue of this Act, have been worth about five Pounds *per Annum*, one year with another.[6]

In Cambridge, weaknesses in the Library staff at the beginning of the century, and the lack of incentive consequent on the poor prospects of obtaining what might have been most needed, each contributed to a situation exacerbated by the increasing poverty of the list of books in the Stationers' Register; the three together led to an accessions policy (*de facto*: none was ever set down) for English books that for much of the eighteenth century was less than adequate even by the unambitious standards that obtained for most of the time.

Next to no documentation survives of the dealings between the University and the Stationers' Company. It was the Warehouse-Keeper's responsibility to send copies of everything delivered within ten days of demand being made by the libraries, but on the other hand it was quickly found to be convenient in Cambridge to receive parcels at half-yearly or even yearly intervals.[7] (The annual accounts submitted to the Vice-Chancellor by Jonathan Pindar, the Library assistant, show carriage costs of amounts varying from half a crown to

---

[6] W. Reading *The history of the ancient and present state of Sion-College* (1724), annexed to his *Bibliothecae cleri Londinensis in Collegio Sionensi catalogus* (1724), p. 38.

[7] In 1719 two parcels were sent up at the same time from Stationers' Hall. In January 1721/2 the Library received, besides a parcel containing two sets of engraved plates, another made up of two packets in one, the whole consisting of the fruits of the previous ten months: but thirty-four titles in all (Accessions Register 16 January 1721/2). A further parcel, of four books, arrived on 21 April 1722. These are the sole official records of accessions for this period.

three shillings for a single parcel.) From about 1723 it became usual for parcels to be sent twice a year, at Lady Day and Michaelmas, but this quickening of the rate heralded no increase in the number of books received: in 1724 and 1726 the carriage of the two parcels together cost each year only two shillings. From early on it was the practice of the Library to pay the Warehouse-Keeper at Stationers' Hall an annual sum for his pains: the earliest record for this is dated 13 September 1714, when Joseph Collyer acknowledged receipt of £1.1s.6d., the odd eighteen pence being presumably for carriage of a parcel of books. In addition, Robert Knaplock received ten shillings on 15 September 1714 'for so much layd out by me at several times to porters, and for packing books sent from Stationers Hall to the publick library',[8] but it is not known for how long Knaplock, one of the principal booksellers in St Paul's Churchyard, acted as forwarding agent in this manner. Later on it became the custom for Collyer (or Collier), and from 1725 his successor Thomas Simpson, to be paid quarterly, though the deliveries continued half-yearly; subsequently this smooth arrangement (attributable to the meticulously neat Samuel Hadderton, *Bibliothecarius* from 1721 to 1732) was allowed to deteriorate, and payments fell years behind.[9]

The sole surviving letter to pass between the Stationers' Company (in the person of Thomas Simpson) and the Library (in the person of Hadderton) dates from February 1725/6. Simpson refers in it to a list of thirteen books, all that had been entered in the Stationers' Register between 30 December 1725 and 16 February 1725/6. 'S^r: I received yours dated the 11th Instant, & according to your desire have sent y^o the above … being all wch are entered & come to my hands since my letter to you: at Lady Day God willing I shall take care to send all that comes to my hands to you …'.[10] It assumes that Hadderton was anxious to pursue the University's rights: and certainly his librarianship saw the only recorded attempt in these years to

---

[8] Vouchers.   [9] See below, p. 274.   [10] Luard 181.

enforce the Act. In 1722 Nicholas Fazakerley was paid a guinea 'for his opinion ab^t our right to copies', and a further five shillings was paid to Serjeant Reynolds' clerk, but the absence of further legal payments suggests that the matter was taken no further in the courts.[11] The episode does suggest, however, that there was some unease in the University at the failure of the 1710 Act to secure all that was wanted. It was shared by Oxford, who on 15 October 1726 inserted a notice in the *London Gazette* announcing that the London booksellers William and John Innys (publishers of the monthly *Memoirs of literature*) had been appointed to collect copies of books due under the Act but not yet delivered to Stationers' Hall, and to receive Oxford's books in the future: the opportunity was also taken to warn defaulters that action would be taken against them.[12] The Bodleian had selected more books than Cambridge, but its attempt was not viewed with much optimism by Simpson, writing from Stationers' Hall:

As for your Advertism^t in the Gazett 'tis my opinion 't will be of little Service to you: for some People do not think themselves Oblidg'd to Register their Coppy: but if they do they know by the Act they are to deliver Nine Books but they say & think it is in their Option whether they will Register or not.[13]

And a month later, in response to pressure from Oxford, he was forced to refuse to do more than the Act insisted on:

I shall be always both ready & willing to serve you in any thing that lyes in my Power, but as for makeing a demand in Your Name for One Coppy of all Books Printed, for your University, is what I cannot Possibly do: by reason my business will not permitt me: As for the Books that are brought to me to be Regestered & in my Custody shall be sent to you once a month as you desire or as often as you please.[14]

---

[11] Vouchers. The payment was made (and recovered from the Vice-Chancellor) by Conyers Middleton, even though as *Protobibliothecarius* (see below, p. 169) he was responsible primarily for the Royal Library. Fazakerley was University Counsel from 1738 to 1757: see also *DNB*.

[12] Macray *Annals* p. 205; Partridge *Legal deposit* pp. 301–2. On 12 November a further advertisement substituted the name of John Brooks for that of Innys.

[13] Simpson to Joseph Bowles (Bodley's Librarian) 27 October 1726 (Bodleian Library Records, Copyright Correspondence 1726–1912 fo. 1).

[14] Simpson to Bowles 24 November 1726 (*ibid*. fo. 3). Philip *Bodleian Library* p. 79.

The problem of how much Stationers' Hall could be expected, or be persuaded, to do persisted for as long as the universities remained tied to it; the question was solved, with much pain and embarrassment, only in the latter half of the nineteenth century. It seemed that without the Stationers' co-operation the privileged libraries could accomplish little; while as the operation and deficiencies of the 1710 Act became more familiar to the booksellers, who were members of the same company, there was less and less cause to promote the libraries' interests that were the booksellers' loss. In the face of ill-conceived legislation the libraries had a legal claim that meant only as much as the booksellers would allow. Such a situation was not conducive to concern in the University; and unconcern was nurtured to breed laziness and no serious consideration of the consequences for a library that was, technically at least, a national one.

It will be easily appreciated, in view of the minute charges for transport of the books from London, that the University Library in these years did not receive unmanageable quantities of deposit copies. Like the other copyright libraries it continued to buy books published in England that ought to have come by law. But, in theory at least, between 1710 and 1725 the Library might have drawn on 1257 titles that were marked as received in the requisite number of copies at Stationers' Hall:[15] the total number of entries in the Register for the same period was 2154, a figure that however included a large number of reprints and 'old copies' as well as some oddities and (since entry was supposed to be before publication) even one or two complete miscarriages. The first years of the Act witnessed registration on a scale that can, when compared with later performances, only be called enthusiastic. Less than nine months in 1710 brought 734 titles, many of them old copies: the figure was further swelled by the pamphlets provoked by the Sacheverell affair. In 1711 the figure dropped

---

[15] Figures in this paragraph are based principally on those in John P. Chalmers' thesis (see note 3 above).

to 269, and in 1712 rose again to 323.[16] Subsequent years saw a dramatic decline, from 113 in 1713 to 45 in 1718 and a tiny cluster of thirty titles in 1724. The Library did not take all that was available even in this last year, and the bill for carriage at Michaelmas was sixpence.

Not everything that was entered was deposited at Stationers' Hall, and not everything that was deposited there found a permanent home in the copyright libraries. In modern literature, Cambridge retained, for example, Anne Finch, Countess of Winchelsea's *Miscellany poems* (1713), Alan Ramsay's *Poems* (1721), Parnell's *Poems on several occasions* (1722) and Edward Bysshe's *British Parnassus* (1714). Plays, generally speaking, were avoided, then and for many years to come, even though they formed a staple part of the diet of the entries in the Register. So the Library ignored Cibber's *Caesar in Egypt* (1725) and his comedy *The non-juror* (1718). It was not interested in Addison's *Cato* (1713) or *The drummer* (1722), but accepted the quarto *Works* in four volumes in 1721. It spurned John Bingley's poem *The fair Quakers* (1713), even though it had taken Edward Ward's *Aminadab, or the Quaker's vision* in 1710: scarcely surprisingly, it did take William Sewel's *History of the Quakers* when that appeared in 1722. Shaftesbury's *Characteristicks* (1711) was allowed to go, but Philippe de Commines' *Memoirs* (1712) came, as did Defoe's *General history of the pyrates* (1724) as well as both parts of *Robinson Crusoe*: perhaps this last, like *Gulliver's travels* in 1726, was mistaken for a serious account of overseas travel and exploration. Books of music, whether Henry Carey's *Cantatas for a*

16 No definitive figures are yet available as to what ought – had everything proceeded in accordance with the 1710 Act – to have been passed on to the libraries, i.e. new titles and revisions of earlier works. Some idea of the inadequacy of the Stationers' Register coverage may be gained from figures in W. T. and C. S. Morgan *A bibliography of British history, 1700–1715* 2 (Bloomington, Ind., 1937). In a survey which, while admittedly including a few earlier books reprinted, omitted many songs and ballads and did not attempt to be comprehensive in Scotland, Ireland or Wales, the Morgans nevertheless listed 770 books for 1710, 670 for 1711, 758 for 1712, 681 for 1713, 755 for 1714, 651 for 1715 and 495 for 1716: the figures do not of course take account of all subjects.

voice with accompanyment (1724) or Jeremiah Clarke's *Choice lessons for the harpsichord or spinett* (1710) were ignored generally – one of the few classes of books (single plays being another) where any blanket policy seems to have been successfully exercised. There was certainly no attempt in medicine to collect everything, though a higher proportion of titles was found acceptable in this subject than in many others. Richard Carr's *Medicinal epistles on several occasions* (1714), Boerhaave's *Method of studying physick* (1719) and William Cheseldon's *Anatomy of the humane body* (1722) were all judged suitable, but neither of two works by George Cheyne, his *Essay on the gout* (1721) and *Essay of health and long life* (1724). Sometimes a connection with the University helped. In 1724 Richard Bradley became first Professor of Botany and, undeterred by an almost complete ignorance of Latin or Greek, managed to publish *A survey of the ancient husbandry and gardening* the following year. The Library acquired a copyright deposit copy of this, though it had shown no interest in his two earlier and more practical books the *Gentleman and gardeners kalendar* (1718) and *New improvements of planting and gardening* (1717-18: perhaps the period and subject matter helped the choice for the Library, but the 1725 book did contain a plan for a garden in Cambridge itself, and therefore had some extra local interest).

There was no formal collaboration between Cambridge and the other copyright libraries. In the first sixteen years' operation of the Act a total of 727 deposit copies have been identified in the Bodleian Library, just over half the number possible. The equivalent figure for Cambridge is certainly lower.[17] But while the two institutions frequently retained copies of the same book, Cambridge also kept many that did not apparently find favour at the other university. These included both standard works and minor ephemera. George Crawford's *Peerage of Scotland* (Edinburgh 1716) and William

---

[17] Again, I have relied here on Chalmers' thesis (see note 3 above).

Strahan's translation of Domat's *Civil law in its natural order* (1722), W. Gibson's *Farrier's new guide* (1720) and Edward Laurence's *Young surveyor's guide* (1716) were accepted along with a *Select century of Cordery's colloquies* compiled by John Clarke, a schoolmaster at Hull, and published in 1718, as well as chapbooks such as *The lives and characters of the Dutchess of Marlborough's four daughters* (1710) and *The amazing wonder: or a full and true relation of the dismal condition of one John Sexton, A Blew-Coat boy in Christ Hospital* published in the same year: the Library quickly learned, unfortunately, to dismiss this last class of literature from its considerations. Part of the difficulty seems to have been (to judge by the results) that the titles were not always a reliable guide to the contents: *Robinson Crusoe*, otherwise *The life and strange surprizing adventures of Robinson Crusoe, of York, mariner* (1719) has already been mentioned, but there was also some room for uncertainty in the title of *An account of the damnable prizes in Old Nick's lottery* (1712) – a pamphlet about a Bill on duelling that had failed to pass through Parliament; the Bodleian apparently acquired neither.

According to the Act, the nine deposited copies were to be on the 'best paper', but this proved to be as impossible to insist on as the rest of this peculiarly unsatisfactory piece of legislation. Benjamin Motte abided by the letter of the law in depositing large paper copies of Bradley's *Survey of the ancient husbandry* in 1725 and of *Gulliver's travels* the next year; and so too the deposit copy of Burnet's *History of his own time* (vol. 1, 1724) is on large paper, as is Jeremy Collier's *Several discourses upon practical subjects*, printed by William Bowyer for the author in 1725.[18] But others were not. The Library acquired a true large paper copy of Geoffrey Keating's *General history of Ireland* (1723) only in 1870, through Henry Bradshaw, though it had had a deposit copy since shortly after the book's first publication. Deposit copies of Nicholas Rowe's translation of Lucan's *Pharsalia*, published by subscription by Tonson in

---

[18] The Bowyer ledgers record that fifty copies were printed on special paper.

1718, were only on ordinary paper, and it was remarked in the Accessions Register that Addison's *Works* (1721) were on small paper. Throughout the century, books published by subscription gave endless difficulties that the Library never solved satisfactorily. There was always a slight risk of both a deposit copy and a subscription copy turning up, but Cambridge avoided the risk by subscribing to scarcely anything in the first half of the century. It finally bought the enlarged edition of Strype's *History of the Reformation* with John Newcome's benefaction of 1758: none of the copyright libraries subscribed, though in Cambridge alone the list of subscribers included Thomas Baker, Samuel Knight, and the libraries at St John's, Queens' and Trinity.

Only one serious attempt was made in the first half of the century to remedy the deficiencies of the 1710 Act. The initiative came not from the libraries, but from the booksellers and authors, who saw their publications printed abroad and imported for sale more cheaply (thanks particularly to the heavy tax on paper) than it was possible to manufacture and sell them in England. The 1710 Act provided no defence whatever against imports of books in Latin, Greek or other foreign languages, and Samuel Buckley, publisher and editor of the seven-volume edition of de Thou's *Historiae* (1733) sought to protect his position by a private Act of Parliament (7 George II pr. *c.* 34). The Act stipulated that he was to deliver a copy to each of the libraries, and in Cambridge William Bonner charged for its binding on 23 February 1736/7. Among those who contributed to the edition was Thomas Carte, who was subsequently moved to seek more protection for authors as well. In March 1734/5, in response to a petition from proprietors of copyrights and others in the book trade complaining of piracies (and particularly foreign piracies), the House of Commons appointed a committee to consider the threat thus posed to the trade. But although in February 1736/7 the Warehouse-Keeper of the Stationers' Company was ordered to lay before the House an account of the books demanded of him by the several libraries, and the Clerk of the Company had to report on the number of books entered in the Register, the deposit clause of the Act does not seem to have been a principal issue – at least on this occasion. The subsequent Bill[19] (which incidentally added five of London's law libraries as places of deposit) received its first reading in March 1736/7, and while an attempt was made in it to protect the interests of authors in particular, and to reduce the damage wrought by foreign piracies, no penalty for non-delivery of copies to Stationers' Hall was specified beyond the consequent loss of protection by the Act. It is therefore doubtful whether the libraries would have received any benefit. The University accounts record the payment of a guinea to 'Mr Townshends servant' (Thomas Townshend then being one of the University's two Members of Parliament, and a member of the Commons committee) in the financial year 1736–7, when he brought a copy of the Bill to Cambridge: as the Bill was also designed to improve the regulations covering the drawback on paper duties imposed in 1712 and 1714, it affected the University's interests doubly.[20] Eventually, however, the question came to relate more to piracies than deposit, and after the first Bill had been killed the Act that finally received the Royal Assent in June 1739 (12 George II c. 36) was concerned primarily with importations, and not at all with the libraries.

In the absence of any accessions register for virtually the whole of the first half-century after the passing of the 1710 Act, the identification of deposit copies depends largely on evidence of a sometimes tenuous, and even negative kind. The sole extensive records of the approximate order in which books

---

[19] One version of the Bill is printed, from a copy in the St Bride Printing Library, in Partridge *Legal deposit*, pp. 304–6. The other libraries were those of the Inner Temple, Middle Temple, Gray's Inn, Lincoln's Inn, and the Advocates in Doctors' Commons, Warwick Lane.

[20] *Journals of the House of Commons* 22 p. 400 (3 March 1734/5: petition and committee): pp. 411–12 (12 March 1734/5: report); p. 761 (24 February 1736/7: officers of the Stationers' Company); p. 764 (28 February 1736/7: they attend the House); 3 March 1736/7: first reading). For a collection of papers on the affair cf. Bodleian Library MS. Carte 207. Partridge *Legal deposit* p. 40 gives further references.

came into the Library are the contemporary shelf-lists, and bills submitted by a variety of local binders, notably Francis Hopkins, Henry Crow, Charles Wright, John Richardson and William Bonner:[21] since books were usually sent from Stationers' Hall in quires, most copyright books had to pass through their hands.[22] The earliest of these bills to have survived is one from Francis Hopkins dated 15 March 1713/14, listing twenty-seven volumes bound for a total of twenty-six shillings. With one exception, the books dated from between 1710 and 1713,[23] and included sermons by Fleetwood, Tilly, Bull and several lesser figures, Burnet's *Discourse of the pastoral care*, Hotman's *Franco-Gallia* and Bulstrode's letters, Aesop and Justinus, a book on the peerage and Ecton on tithes, Swift's *Conduct of the allies* and *Some remarks on the Barrier Treaty*, Townshend's *Barrier Treaty vindicated, Telemachus* in English verse, and Edward Ward's life of Don Quixote in Hudibrastick verse, the *History of the October Club*, Thomas Ellwood's *Davideis*, and volumes of verses that can no longer be identified. But while all these books were bound up, sometimes into pamphlet volumes, in 1713/14, no evidence survives of when exactly they arrived or what prompted such an assortment.

Apart from these sources, for a period from about 1721[24] to 1731 Samuel Hadderton made a practice of writing on the versos of the title-pages of some books, both English and

---

[21] Many of the books listed in these bills were identified some years ago by J. C. T. Oates, who arranged for them to be placed in groups in class Rel. f., for their more convenient study.

[22] One of the very few exceptions was Thomas Blennerhaysett's sermon *Legal obedience* (1716), which arrived in a binding commemorating the simultaneous victories over the Jacobites at Preston and at Sherriffmuir on 13 November 1715. The deposit copy in the National Library of Scotland is in a binding of the same design. Despite the fact that Cheselden's *Anatomy of the humane body* 2nd ed. (1722) has printed on its title-page 'Price Bound in Calf 5s.' it is in a Cambridge binding, comparable with that on Parnell's *Poems on several occasions* (1722): no doubt there are other similar examples.

[23] Apart from Francis Bugg's *Quakerism withering* (1694).

[24] The earliest I have found is Charles King's *The British merchant; or, commerce preserv'd* (3 vols. 1721) marked 'Ex dono Autoris. 1721' and annotated by Hadderton 'Sic Compactus & Ornatus Sumptibus Authoris.'

foreign, the date (and even occasionally the means) of arrival; in this way he documented the gift from the new Russian Academy of Sciences of its *Sermones* in June 1727, for example.[25] He did not, however, follow this useful practice when dealing with deposit copies. In June 1722, Henry Jones, Fellow of King's College, presented two bound volumes of his *Philosophical transactions abridg'd*, a month after the arrival of André Tacquet's Euclid from the Cambridge press 'sic compactus & ornatus sumptibus Corn. Crownfield Typographi Academ.'. Archibald Hutchison's *Three treatises* arrived in a special binding as a gift in January 1723/4, and John Lewis' edition of Wyclif's *New Testament* (1731) in September 1731, 'sic compactus & ornatus sumptibus Editoris'. None of these, nor William Reading's catalogue of Sion College Library (1724, received on 3 August that year), Zachary Grey's *Defence of our antient and modern historians* (2nd ed. 1725, received 19 September) nor William Whiston's *Praelectiones physico-mathematicae* (Benjamin Motte 1726, received 25 August 1727), had been entered in the Stationers' Register. Nor had a small volume prepared by John Martyn chiefly for undergraduates attending his lectures at Cambridge: his *Methodus plantarum circa Cantabrigiam nascentium*, drawing heavily on the work of John Ray sixty years earlier, arrived on 21 April 1727 and may well have been a present to the Library.[26] However, not all books can be so readily explained even if they do bear Hadderton's notes. Richard Fiddes' *Life of Cardinal Wolsey* (1724) was dedicated to the Universities of Oxford and Cambridge and published by subscription. The Bodleian Library appears in the list of subscribers for a large paper copy, but Cambridge does not. The book was entered in the Stationers' Register on 12 February 1723/4, and a large paper copy was received, according to Hadderton's note on the title leaf, on 6 July 1724. It was bound by Francis Hopkins by 9

---

25 *Sermones in primo solenni Academiae Scientiarum Imperialis conventu die XXVII. Decembris anni MDCCXXV* (Petropoli [1726]), now 7690.b.2.

26 He followed this up in June 1729 with his *First lecture of a course of botany* (1729).

July. Despite the fact that this copy, on large paper as required by the Act, was available from Stationers' Hall, there must be some doubt as to whether it is a deposit copy: Hadderton was not wont to write in such books.

Although the pace of arrival of copyright books steadied after the first enthusiasm of 1710–11, the Library staff began to find increasing difficulty in dealing with them and with some of the other purchases or gifts, in premises that were overwhelmed by the presence of the library of John Moore, given in 1715 and not set properly in order until the 1750s.[27] Most of the Library's everyday organization fell on the Library and Schools Keeper Jonathan Pindar, and he and his successor hit upon the simple procedure of storing some of these books temporarily in the turret (clearly visible in Loggan's engraving) above the stairs leading up to the Library room on Rotherham's old east front; there they remained until the building was demolished in 1754. Most of the books tucked away in this neglected corner, uncatalogued and barely remembered, were modern English books, not all of them acquired under the Copyright Act.[28] In later years, with a much greater copyright intake, the Library was to develop and refine a system for separating the useful from the apparently trivial, but no such discrimination was exercised in the second, third and fourth decades of the eighteenth century. There was, to be sure, much in this attic that did not fall within the contemporary curriculum, such as *Moll Flanders, Robinson Crusoe, Gulliver's travels,* Mrs Manley's novels, and *The London spy,* or poetry by Parnell, Pope, William Broome, James Thomson, Mary Barber, Mary Monk (*Marinda,* 1716) and the anonymous *Mother Gin, a tragi-comical eclogue: being a*

[27] See below, Ch. 5.
[28] The only surviving list is in Bodleian Library, MS. Gough Camb. 62, fos. 122–39, listing about 433 titles, of which the latest I have noted is of 1748. The list does not seem to be complete, as it does not, for example, include William Hodson's *Divine cosmographer* (Cambridge 1640) seen in the turret by William Cole (J. P. Malcolm (ed.) *Letters between the Rev. James Granger and many of the most eminent literary men of his times* (1805) p. 335).

paraphrastical imitation of the Daphnis of Virgil (1737). Several volumes of the street literature acquired in the first few months of the Act's working found their way there too, with an assortment of music including songs by John Blow, sonatas by William Corbett, Adam Craig's Scotch tunes and Johann Ernst Galliard's *Six sonatas for the bassoon or violoncello*. Among the medical books were works by Alexander Monro, John Quincy and Boerhaave, which jostled with Jethro Tull's *Horse-hoeing husbandry* (1733) and Batty Langley's *Practical geometry* (1726), Woodward on fossils, William Gibson's *Farrier's guide* (1720), books of travel and local history, on law, shorthand, the Sacheverell affair and heraldry.

It is possible to see why these had been set aside for the present. But apart from these and similar books that did not seem to fall within the most strictly defined limits of an eighteenth-century academic library there were many whose banishment to the turret now seems a mystery, including Burnet's *History of his own time* (1724–34), the collected works of Addison (1721) and Francis Bacon (1740), William Reading's catalogue of Sion College Library (1724), Joseph Butler's *Analogy of religion* (1736), Nicholas Saunderson's *Elements of algebra* (1740) besides dozens of sermons and classical texts. Among the older or foreign ones were Francis Junius' Latin Bible of 1592–3, Lambert Bos' edition of the Septuagint (1709, bought in February 1713/14), Isaac Verburg's edition of Cicero (Amsterdam 1724) and Peder Terpager's *Rituale ecclesiarum Daniae et Norvegiae* (Copenhagen 1706, given by Crownfield in March 1721/2), all of more obvious use than some of the minor copyright literature. Among these books were a very few, such as Elizabeth Elstob's *English-Saxon homily* (1709, bought by the Library in 1712/13 for fifteen shillings) and various works by William Whiston that were also represented by copies downstairs among John Moore's books, but the overwhelming majority were not. And since these books were uncatalogued they were for all practical purposes unobtainable.

Apart from some books that were mislaid, or, perhaps, disposed of deliberately, all these books, as well as the whole of the rest of the Library's printed books apart from Moore's collection, were eventually entered in an interleaved copy, purchased in 1752, of the printed Bodleian catalogue of 1738.[29] The work of compiling most of the catalogue fell to Thomas Goodall, whose handwriting is thereby a guide to the date of arrival of many of the books acquired for the Library in the eighteenth century. He did not always find his task easy. The Bodleian Library's holdings, while very similar to those of Cambridge, were not comprehensive for English books published since 1710 and deposited at Stationers' Hall, while Oxford also lacked many of the earlier books, both English and foreign, that had been received at Cambridge in the series of libraries acquired in the seventeenth century. The headings chosen for anonymous books, or for alternative forms of names of authors, caused Goodall further difficulties. It is not obvious, from Goodall's interpretation of the catalogue, that the Library had by 1752 already acquired the two volumes of *Robinson Crusoe*: on spotting the Bodleian entry for Defoe's *Serious reflections during the life . . . of Robinson Crusoe* (1720), he adapted it to catalogue the original story, merely altering the date from 1720 to 1719 and so incidentally creating a more misleading error than the several examples of the same book's appearing twice over in the catalogue, once as printed in the Bodleian's holdings and once as added in manuscript on a quite different page by Goodall. But despite these drawbacks, these four volumes of the interleaved Bodleian catalogue remained, with the separate catalogue of the Royal Library described below on pp. 190–5, the catalogue of the Library's printed books until the end of the century.

As Zacharias Conrad von Uffenbach, a sceptical, sometimes over-critical, and consequently sometimes gullible, connois-

[29] Now Adv. bb. 64.1–4.

seur from Frankfurt, [30] discovered when he visited Cambridge in the summer of 1710 in the course of a tour through England, the Library was at that time cared for by two men: Jonathan Pindar (who was also one of the three University Printers – at a stipend of £5 per annum – and who supplemented his salary at the Library by looking after the rest of the schools as well), and a Librarian who enjoyed a well-deserved reputation for his learning.[31] John Laughton, Fellow of Trinity, had been University Librarian since 1686, and before that had served for a brief spell as Librarian to his own college, where he had been responsible for reporting the manuscripts to the editors of the Oxford *Catalogi* of 1698. Apart from many kindnesses to others, his principal scholarly achievement was the quarto edition of Virgil printed at the University Press and published by Tonson in 1701, which he edited anonymously. He was among the first Curators of the Press to be appointed in January 1697/8, though he took less part in its business than his title of *Academiae Architypographus* might seem to imply.[32] As University Librarian he had seen through two major reforms, in the visual revolution entailed in the reversal of all the books in the Library so that their spines now pointed outwards rather than inwards, and in the complete recataloguing of the collection by Samuel Knight in 1708–9; but otherwise his term of office could be counted only a mixed success. Despite his work on the Trinity manuscripts, for those in the University Library the Oxford editors had to be content with Thomas James' old list of 1600, while in his failure to ensure

[30] On von Uffenbach see, besides the references in *Cambridge under Queen Anne*, G. A. E. Bogeng 'Über Zacharias Conrad von Uffenbachs Erfahrungen und Erlebnisse bei der Benutzung deutscher, englischer, holländischer öffentlicher Büchersammlungen in den Jahren 1709–1711' in A. Hortzschansky (ed.) *Beiträge zum Bibliotheks– und Buchwesen; Paul Schwenke zum 20 März 1913 gewidmet* (Berlin 1913) pp. 30–46.

[31] *Cambridge under Queen Anne* p. 140. Francis Burman was much impressed by his erudition when Laughton showed him round in 1702 (*ibid.* pp. 116–17). For a brief biography see Robert Sinker *Biographical notes on the librarians of Trinity College* (Cambridge Antiquarian Soc. 1897) pp. 19–25, and see also Oates *History* p. 462.

[32] McKenzie *Cambridge University Press* I pp. 96–7.

that the Library kept abreast of modern books he had done the University a serious disservice.[33] He died on 4 September 1712, leaving a private library that was sold at auction the following month, and a valuable collection of coins, while his papers were acquired by a young Fellow of Jesus named George Paul.[34]

The Librarian was paid £35 a year, besides various fees due from the Proctors that could usually be expected to total between six and seven pounds: the stipend may be compared on the one hand with the dividend paid in 1711/12 of £12 to each junior fellow of St John's and £16 to each of the senior fellows, and on the other hand with the annual stipend of £20 paid to the University Organist, £40 to the Sir Thomas Adams Professor of Arabic, and with the Regius Professorship of Divinity, said in 1717 to be worth £300 a year.[35] Paul was anxious for Laughton's post, and despite only a brief acquaintance prevailed on Humfrey Wanley to write to John Covel, Master of Christ's, in his support.[36] He was however one of six candidates, and was ousted in the first stage of the election, the choice lying finally between Thomas Macro, Fellow of Gonville and Caius, and Philip Brooke, who had entered St John's College as a pensioner from Manchester in 1695 aged sixteen and had been a Fellow since 1701. Brooke, with overwhelming support from Trinity, Queens', Jesus and King's, was elected on 3 October without a vote being necessary.[37] To him fell the task of dealing with the arrival of the library of John Moore, Bishop of Ely, a collection far in excess of anything the Library had ever faced previously or that the Copyright Act was to provide for years to come.

---

[33] Cf. Oates *History* p. 466.
[34] Hearne *Remarks and collections* 3 pp. 458, 477; Paul to Strype 21 August 1713 (MS. Add. 7 no. 85).   [35] Monk *Bentley* 2 p. 23.
[36] Wanley to Covel 30 September 1712 (British Library MS. Add. 22911 fo. 146^r).
[37] Grace Book Θ p. 603. For further details see Edward Rud's *Diary* ed. H. R. Luard (Cambridge Antiquarian Soc. 1860) p. 8.

3

JOHN MOORE AND HIS CIRCLE

AS YET, THE PRESENT Bishop of *Ely's* Library is universally and most justly reputed the best furnish'd of any (within the Queen's Dominions) that this age has seen in the Hands of any private Clergyman; the Reverend and Learned Proprietor, having from his Youth, been peculiarly diligent in collecting the fairest Editions of the *Greek* and *Latin* Classicks, Fathers, Councils, Ecclesiastical and Civil Historians, Law-writers, Confessions of Faith and Formularies of Worship, in all Languages, Ancient and Modern, Books of Physick, Surgery, Mathematicks, *&c.* in one Word, the choicest *Supellex Libraria* that could be met with (by Himself, or his Friends) in public Auctions, or the Shops of private Stationers, at home or abroad.[1]

Thus wrote William Nicolson, Bishop of Carlisle, a few months before the death of John Moore (fig. 2) in 1714. He was, like many of his contemporaries, acquainted with this 'supellex libraria' as a visitor; but he had examined it to an extent matched only by a few. Its size was well known, at least in approximate terms, and of its importance there was no doubt in the minds of all that saw it. It was a lodestone for scholars and casual visitors alike: not only for Englishmen visiting London such as Ralph Thoresby, who became a friend of Moore and paid repeated visits,[2] but also for an enthusiastic throng of foreigners. Francis Burman, visiting London in 1702, called on Moore one morning in November in the company of Richard Bentley, the day after he had met Newton for the first time and a few hours before viewing Bedlam and watching a firework display in honour of the King. Moore, he recorded, 'received me in the most friendly way, shaking hands and offering chocolate. He showed me his *London* library, and begged me to visit him daily, during the

---

[1] W. Nicolson *The English historical library* 2nd ed. (London 1714) p. xii.
[2] *The diary of Ralph Thoresby*, ed. J. Hunter (London 1830) 1 pp. 334–5, 342, 2 pp. 116, 212.

2   John Moore (1646–1714), Bishop of Ely. From a painting by Sir Godfrey Kneller, 1705. Size of original 124.5 × 100.3 cm.

remainder of my stay in England.'[3] Zacharias Conrad von Uffenbach was less fortunate. He too had marked Moore's house out for a visit during his tour of English libraries in 1710, but missed it because he called at the wrong address.[4]

[3] *Cambridge under Queen Anne* pp. 323–34.   [4] *Ibid.*, p. 372.

As the largest private collection of Moore's generation, and in the absence of comparable public collections, quite apart from the rarities it contained – whether manuscripts, adversaria, or printed books (many, in varying degrees, made known to the world with the publication of descriptions in Bernard's *Catalogi* in 1697-8) – it was in practice much more than a private affair. Hardly surprisingly, it was strongest in theology and ecclesiastical matters, classics (not least for the series of annotated volumes from the Casaubons' library, which were described in the *Catalogi*), and history; but these strengths were lent distinction by other parts of the 'supellex libraria'. In 1811 Dibdin coined the description of Moore as 'the father of black-letter collectors in this country'.[5] He could invent no higher accolade for the man whose remarkable collection of early printed books he saw on the shelves at Cambridge. The phrase has survived better than many of Dibdin's inventions: there was much truth in it, even if it was not absolutely accurate. In the late seventeenth century Moore's collection of early printed books was comparable only with that of Richard Smith (sold at auction, in a catalogue that did little justice to it, in 1682), and it was challenged by others only in the latter years of his life. The Mainz *Catholicon* of '1460' caught the notice of Humfrey Wanley as supposedly the first book ever to have been printed (Moore was curiously unaware of continental scholarship on this point);[6] but the Caxtons (over forty in all, including a unique volume of quarto pamphlets acquired from John Bagford in the 1690s),

[5] T. F. Dibdin *Bibliomania* (1811) p. 421.

[6] On 8 March 1697, in answer to an enquiry from Humfrey Wanley in connection with Bernard's *Catalogi*, Moore wrote, 'Having a little enquired into ye original of printing I did observe, that it was a controversy who were the Authors & Inventors of it at the time it first appeared, & lawsuits were commenced about it. the first discoverers meaning to apply their skill more to their own peculiar advantage, than to the service of the Public. So that we are not, I take it, to hope for a satisfactory account of that now, wch had so much uncertainty in it from the beginning. I do find that from about the year 1450 they were labouring to bring the art of Printing to perfection, & did print some little matters on one side, as you intimate, of the paper only; but cannot discover any ground to believe any book was compleatly printed before ye Catholicon. what I find next is the Bible, wch was printed 2 years after it' (British Library MS. Harley 3780 (169)).

Wynkyn de Wordes (Bernard's *Catalogi* devoted almost a column to two volumes of his tracts), Pynsons, Aldines and early sixteenth-century books all commanded the respect, wonder and admiration of everyone who heard of them. Dibdin's phrase, however, ignored Moore's manuscripts, numbering something over seventeen hundred and including not only the most celebrated such as the eighth-century Bede, the ninth-century Book of Cerne, the tenth-century Book of Deer, and the thirteenth-century illustrated life of Edward the Confessor,[7] but also those whose interest has been recognized only more recently, such as the Findern anthology of medieval English literature. It also under-estimated Moore's general library, and ignored completely Moore's position at the centre of the Cambridge Newtonians, intimately associated with such figures as Whiston, Samuel Clarke, Richard Laughton, Charles Morgan and Richard Bentley.[8] Moore had other purposes to his collecting besides early printed books, and some emerged in the circle of acquaintances that gathered round his library, the largest late seventeenth-century private collection in England to have survived more or less intact.

After Moore's death, and after some abortive attempts to dispose of it elsewhere, the collection was bought *en bloc* by George I, and given to the University of Cambridge. To the

[7] Cf., among much more, on the Moore Bede (MS. Kk.5.16) *The Moore Bede, Cambridge University Library MS Kk.5.16* with preface by P. Hunter Blair and contribution by Sir Roger Mynors (Early English Manuscripts in Facsimile 9, Copenhagen 1959) and below, pp. 135–7; on the Book of Cerne (MS. Ll.1.10) A. B. Kuypers *The Book of Cerne* (Cambridge 1902) and J. J. G. Alexander *Insular manuscripts, 6th to the 9th century* (Survey of Manuscripts illuminated in the British Isles 1978) pp. 84–5, with further references; on the Book of Deer (MS. Ii.6.32) *The Book of Deer* ed. John Stuart (Spalding Club 1869), Alexander *op. cit.* pp. 86–7, again with further references, and below, pp. 50, 129; and on the Life of Edward the Confessor (MS. Ee.3.59) *La estoire de Seint Aedward le Rei ... reproduced in facsimile from the unique manuscript (Cambridge University Library Ee.3.59)* introd. M. R. James (Roxburghe Club 1920), and below, p. 131.

[8] The most influential book on this group is by Margaret C. Jacob *The Newtonians and the English revolution, 1689–1720* (Hassocks 1976), though some of her tenets as to the political ideology of the Cambridge Newtonians are now being disputed. See also John Gascoigne '"The Holy Alliance"; the rise and diffusion of Newtonian natural philosophy and latitudinarian theology within Cambridge from the Restoration to the accession of George II' (Cambridge Ph.D. thesis 1981) and *idem* 'Politics, patronage and Newtonianism: the Cambridge example' *Historical Journal* 27 (1984) pp. 1–24.

troubles it brought, the excitement it caused, and the manner in which it was administered, I shall pass in Chapter 5. Its arrival transformed the University Library, and with the provisions of the Copyright Act of 1710 marks the beginning of a national library of a kind that the University had not known hitherto.

The biographical particulars of Moore's life have been sketched on various occasions before,[9] and if there is little of significance to be added to them, they can be supplemented in detail at many points. His first modern biographer, Cecil Moore, followed Polwhele in tracing his antecedents back to the early twelfth century, with some omissions, and to the Moores of Collumpton in Devon. His father, Thomas, was the second son of John Moore, a man of radical views and rector of Knaptoft,[10] a tiny and contracting village north-east of Lutterworth in Leicestershire. The new John, eldest son of Thomas and Elizabeth his wife, was born at Sutton-juxta-Broughton, a hamlet a few miles to the west of Knaptoft, in 1646. He was educated at Market Harborough, where his father had settled as an ironmonger, and on 28 June 1662 was admitted at Clare Hall, Cambridge. In 1665/6 he took his B.A., and in 1669 his M.A., while in September 1667 he was elected Fellow of his college. His consequent ordination was, according to Robert Martin of Stamford, far from pleasing to his father, who was of a 'rigid persuasion'; and 'tho' he gave his son ye university Educacōn, yet he never intended him for ye

---

9 Cf. Cecil Moore *The father of black-letter collectors* (London 1885, reprinted from *The Bibliographer*); idem 'Bishop Moore, the father of black-letter collectors' *Book-lore* 1 (1885) pp. 75–82; and W. P. Courtney in *DNB*. See also W. Harrod *The history of Market-Harborough* (Market Harborough 1808) p. 40, and J. Nichols *The history and antiquities of the County of Leicester* 2 part 2 (London 1798) pp. 502–3. For surviving portraits of him see John Ingamells *The English episcopal portrait 1559–1835* (Paul Mellon Centre 1981) pp. 299–30. Robert White's engraving is datable to 1694, when Moore paid him £5 (Cambridge University Library MS. Dd.14.26(2)). Kneller's portrait (now in Clare College, Cambridge) is dated 1705, but on 2 December 1699 Moore's private accounts record payment of £21.10s.0d. to Kneller for 'drawing your Lordship's picture'. The painting in the entrance hall of Cambridge University Library was copied from Kneller's portrait by Isaac Whood in 1736.

10 Author of *The crying sin of England* (1653) and *A scripture-word against inclosure* (1656).

Episcopate order, & when he saw he would comply wth Church principles, he angrily (I am told) made him account for & Refund w^t. he cost at Cambridge & ye Bp. [John Moore] pd him'.[11] But while relations with his father suffered a setback, his position in the world was considerably advanced with his attachment in 1670 to the circle of Heneage Finch, later first Earl of Nottingham, who in May of that year became Solicitor-General. Finch became Lord Keeper in 1673 and Lord Chancellor in December 1675. Under his wing Moore's fortune was made. In 1676 he received the royal rectory of Blaby in his native Leicestershire, only a few miles from his birthplace, and he held the living until 1686. In 1679 he was also installed as a prebendary of Ely Cathedral, a month after marrying Rose Butler of Barnwell Priory, Cambridge. He received his D.D. from the University two years later, and in 1687 was presented to the London rectory of St Augustine, Old Change, where he remained for less than two years before being presented to the royal living (and another new Wren church) of St Andrew's, Holborn, in succession to Edward Stillingfleet, recently consecrated Bishop of Worcester.[12] He seems to have first moved into London in June 1686, when he rented a house in Sutton Street, a narrow street running off the east of Soho (or King) Square between the houses of the Earl of Carlisle and Viscount Fauconberg and now known as Sutton Row: at the time it was only recently developed from the Soho fields. It was a fashionable as well as a convenient place to live, and an area much favoured by the Whig gentry.[13]

He added to his incumbency the post of minister at the new neighbouring church of St Anne's, Soho, and he became a royal chaplain. These years were also marked by the death of his wife in 1689; she had borne him three sons and three

[11] Cambridge University Library MS. Add. 2, no. 148, letter to John Strype. On his death in 1686 Moore's father left an estate valued at £1518.17s.7d. (Moore *The father of black-letter collectors* p. 5). His will was proved on 23 June 1686 (PRO Prob 11/383).

[12] The churches were both bombed in the Second World War, and St Andrew's has since been restored. For their earlier appearance see Royal Commission on Historical Monuments. *London 4 The City* (London 1929) pp. 107–9, 120–3, and plates.

[13] CUL MS. Dd.3.67, 7 June 1686; *Survey of London 33 The parish of St. Anne Soho* (London 1966) chapters 2–4.

daughters, and was buried in St Giles in the Fields. His second marriage a little later, however, established him even more firmly in what had become a prominent social position. Dorothy, his second wife, came from County Durham, and had outlived her first two husbands Michael Blackett (of the wealthy Newcastle coal dynasty) and Sir Richard Browne, grandson of the Lord Mayor of London.[14] She was to bear him three more sons.

Moore was an obvious candidate for the episcopal bench, and his chance came quickly. On 5 July 1691, following the deprivation of the non-juring William Lloyd, he was consecrated Bishop of Norwich. He remained in the see until 31 July 1707,[15] living partly at Norwich and partly in Charles Street, St James's Square. His translation to the much richer see of Ely, where he succeeded Simon Patrick, brought him to Ely House in Holborn, the ancient (and decrepit) palace of the Bishops of Ely: the house was considerably more spacious than that in Charles Street, sprawling the length of the modern Ely Place, though only St Etheldreda's church now remains of it.[16] While Bishop of Norwich, Moore kept his books partly in the capital and partly in the country, where by 1707 they occupied several rooms,[17] but on his translation he seems to have been able to amalgamate the various portions of his collection in Ely House, in rooms round the old cloister.[18]

[14] G.E.C. *Complete baronetage* (Exeter 1900–6) 3 p. 92.

[15] For some account of the events following the deaths of the Bishops of Winchester, Chester and Ely within seven months in 1706–7, and the background to Moore's translation to succeed Simon Patrick, see E. Carpenter *Thomas Tenison, Archbishop of Canterbury, his life and times* (London 1948) pp. 179–83.

[16] The extent of the palace can be most easily appreciated in Rocque's map of London (1745). See also, among much else, E. Williams *Early Holborn and the legal quarter of London* (London 1927) 1 pp. 336–431, with illustrations, and Sir Gilbert Scott 'Remarks on Ely Palace, Holborn, accompanying some original drawings of the same made in 1772' *Trans. London and Middlesex Archaeological Soc.* 5 (1881) pp. 494–503, with clear plans of the palace.

[17] Thomas Tanner to Arthur Charlett 25 June 1707. Bodleian Library MS. Ballard 4 fo. 84.

[18] In 1712 Thoresby visited Moore in the company of Ludolph Kuster, editor of the Cambridge Suidas, and noted, 'We were both surprised with the Bishop's yet growing library, eight chambers (as I remember) that almost surround the quadrangle' (*Diary* ed. J. Hunter (London 1830) 2 p. 116).

It is no purpose of this book to offer an account of Moore's everyday ecclesiastical or indeed political affairs;[19] but if the accusations brought by his contemporaries and by subsequent generations against him, that he pilfered what was not his, and formed at least part of his library by taking books away from their rightful owners, are to be appreciated, then something of his reputation in ordinary diocesan matters needs to be understood, and his position as Bishop remembered.

Unfortunately little is recorded of his reputation in his diocese after his translation, but in Norwich it was a mixed one. Many were impressed by his humanity and compassion, whether as Bishop or as one ready to provide a prescription to cure disease: medicine was one of his hobbies, and his collections on the subject were extensive.[20] Samuel Crisp, one of his parish clergy and at odds with his parishioners in 1694–5, wrote appreciatively of him to Strype,

You seem very *sollicitous* that I should give you an *acct* of our *new* Bp. who has made the *largest Steps* of any amongst us: and *since* we had the *cursed occasion* to part with our *old one*, to whom I *stand greatly oblig'd* by *many personal favours*, I think we are *mighty happy* to have so *good a man* to *succeed* him, *who*, for ought I have heard, *gives a general satisfaction*.[21]

But others, including Humphrey Prideaux, Archdeacon of Sudbury and later Dean of Norwich, were less enthusiastic:

He is a close designeing man that will reguard little but what tends to his own or relations interests, and I would by noe means advise any friend of mine to list himselfe under him. Whatever yᵉ Church may be advantaged by others of yᵉ new promotion, I expect it will be very little by him. He is indeed my old friend and acquaintance; however, it grieves me to se this diocese sacrificed to his secular interest, he beeing one that will by noe means answere its needs, and I thinke there is noe diocesse in England needs a good Bishop more than this. You see the London ministers gett all yᵉ preferments . . .[22]

---

[19] For the background see principally Carpenter *Thomas Tenison*; Norman Sykes *William Wake* (Cambridge 1957); and G. V. Bennett 'King William III and the episcopate' in G. V. Bennett and J. D. Walsh (ed.) *Essays in modern English church history in memory of Norman Sykes* (London 1966) pp. 104–31.

[20] See below, pp. 90–4. [21] British Library MS. Add. 5853 p. 398 (copy).

[22] *Letters of Humphrey Prideaux to John Ellis* ed. E. M. Thompson Camden Soc. 1875) p. 148. Moore was elected Bishop on 21 May, and the letter is dated 7 June 1691, shortly before he was consecrated.

Prideaux regarded Moore, not unjustifiably, as an opportunist, acting 'as wise and cunning a part as possibly a man can doe'.[23] While Prideaux enjoyed a reputation for quite unusual saintliness, his letters on the subject of Moore are tinged with malice and, not impossibly, jealousy: he too was a member of the Nottingham circle. Prideaux continued his intermittent rancorous gossip even after Moore had left Norwich for Ely:

That man hath lately made one D[r] Canon a Prebendary of his church, on contract to marry his daughter; and it is hard to say w[ch] is the greatest fool of the two in this matter. Canon is about 50 years and a very infirme man, beeing exceedingly troubled with y[e] falleing of y[e] gut, w[ch] usually takes him up all the morneing to get it up; and she is a young sanguine girle of about 24. That he should at all marry in such a case and such an one as will be sure to loath him, or that y[e] other should marry such a daughter to such a man, is a folly on both sides w[ch] is not to be accounted for, and must end ill on both sides.[24]

Robert Cannon, collated to his stall in February 1709, nevertheless lived for several years after Prideaux' gloomy predictions, and died as dean of Lincoln in 1722.

The circumstances of Moore's death on 31 July 1714, six weeks after the opening of his hearing of the case between the Fellows of Trinity College and their Master Richard Bentley, are well known. The fatal chill he caught in the great hall at Ely House saved Bentley from removal from office, and he died only one day before the Queen herself.[25] His body was taken to Ely, to be buried in the cathedral, and in the south ambulatory a monument was set up to his memory: the lengthy epitaph[26] on it has been ascribed to Samuel Clarke. The monument was, appropriately, near to the cathedral library which Moore had fostered in his years as prebendary from 1679.

The inscription speaks of his power as a preacher, his loyalty, his benevolence and his political acumen. It also singles out the

23 Prideaux to Ellis 11 December 1693 (*ed. cit.* p. 162).
24 Prideaux to Ellis 11 June 1709 (*ed. cit.* p. 201).
25 J. H. Monk *The life of Richard Bentley, D.D.* 2nd ed. (London 1833) 1 p. 364.
26 Transcribed in James Bentham *The history and antiquities of the conventual & cathedral church of Ely* 2nd ed. (Norwich 1812) p. 207. Bentham's plan of the cathedral in 1770 (pl. 40) shows Moore's monument in a slightly different position from its present one.

facts not only that his library now rests in Cambridge, but also that in his lifetime Moore readily provided access to it for those in need of it, 'ut a multis fere annis nihil editum fuerit de meliore Notâ, cui non ex instructissimâ ejus Bibliothecâ materiae aliquid accesserit'.

Long before his translation to Ely, Moore possessed a library of national importance, and as a consequence faced demands on it to which he was by no means averse on most occasions. Its significance as a collection was to be recognized in the decision by George I (encouraged by Lord Townshend) to buy it *en bloc* and present it to Cambridge; but this transaction (in one respect at least) simply put on a formal footing what had been long known informally to a wide circle in London, much of the provinces, and even overseas. Most of those who have left accounts of the collection have done so either as sightseers – recording impressions that were inevitably somewhat general – or as scholars who had benefited from one or other particular part. The most notable exception was John Bagford who, in the course of his account of the London libraries prepared for Robert Harley, alone took a view that was at once panoramic and heightened with local detail whose choice bore the mark of his personal enthusiasms. He had supplied Moore with books for several years, and won his respect to such an extent that in due course Moore was to help him to a place as pensioner in the Charterhouse. Bagford was indeed unique, not only one of Moore's library. His account of the collection at Charles Street, sharing with him a curiosity about the history of printing that formed one of the principal purposes and justifications of Moore's library. His account of the collection at Charles Street written perhaps some time between May 1703 and July 1707, was by one who had helped in its formation, as well as one who had explored the shelves and who sympathized with some of its most important components:

The R^t Reverend ye B^p of Norwich, hath a Large & moste incomparable Library. There are vast quantitie, both of printed Books & MSS in all

Faculties. There are great variety of MSS: admirable both for Antiquity & fair Writing. A Capgrave ye finest in England, there is but one more & y^t is in Bennet College Library in Cambridge; wth many others of great Value to long to inserte. He hath ye old Printed books at ye first beginning of printing. That at Mentz 1460 & other printed at Rome & several other Cities in Italy, Germany, France & Holland before 1500. Those printed in England by ye first Printers at Oxford 1469; St Albans, Westminst^r by Caxton, Winken de Worde, Pynson &c ye greatest collection of any in England. Other books printed on Vellum & curiously illuminated so as to pass for MSS. a fine Pliny & Livy in 2 Vol^s both printed on Vellum and many such like: Abundance of Exemplars of Books printed by ye famous Printers, The Aldi, Junti, Gryphius, Vascosanus, Stephens, Elzevirs &c. It were heartily to be wisht his Lo^pps Catalogue were printed, for I believe it would be ye best y^t ever appeared, I mean here in England.[27]

Bagford's enthusiasm for the Capgrave (MS. Gg.4.12) is understandable;[28] but he might also have pointed out that the Corpus copy of the text (MS. 167) is of about forty years later.

On printed books Bagford was on firmer ground. Moore possessed the '1460' *Catholicon* by March 1697/8. The Pliny was Jenson's Italian edition of 1476: it was indeed one of the prizes of the library, decorated with a lavishness that attracted the eye of Waagen in 1835, and it is unfortunate that the arms of the original owner have been erased. Waagen gave a detailed account of the first, heavily ornate, page in particular, as 'a convincing proof to what a degree, even after the invention of printing, it remained customary to ornament books with miniatures, so that the serious occupation of learning might not be without the beautiful and cheerful ornament of art', and was inclined to believe that the work was Milanese. Most recently the decoration has been attributed to Venice, and associated with the same workshop as that responsible for a Jenson Pliny of 1472 now in the British

---

27 British Library MS. Harley 5900, f. 49; see also Moore *The father of black-letter collectors* pp. 29–30. The notes in Harley 5900 were written after Pepys' death in 1703. Bagford's contributions to Moore's library are discussed below, pp. 111–15.
28 Tanner noted that it 'videtur esse autographum' (*Bibliotheca Britannico-Hibernica* art. Capgrave). See also Edmund Colledge 'The Capgrave "autographs"' *Trans. Cambridge Bibliographical Soc.* 6 (1974) pp. 137–48.

Library.[29] The book had been in England for some time before Moore bought it in April 1701 for £2.10s.0d. And finally of those that Bagford singled out for special mention, the two-volume edition of Livy on vellum is that printed by Schoeffer in Mainz in 1518, described immodestly by a later Cambridge admirer C. H. Hartshorne in 1829 as 'amongst the finest vellum books in the world'.[30]

As bishop, Moore was relieved of much of the necessity of dealing in person with payments to booksellers, and on many occasions the task, with sundry other mundane ones, fell to his chaplains. To this post he appointed a succession of scholars whose duties were clearly as much bibliothecarial as spiritual. Richard Laughton,[31] who graduated from Moore's own college in 1684/5, was chaplain to him by 1693, and though he published little he commanded the respect of many both in England and overseas; he also came to enjoy the friendship of Newton and Bentley. But in 1694 he was appointed a college tutor, and in his place Moore installed William Whiston, who had come up to Clare in 1686 and had been elected a Fellow of his college five years later. Whiston remained attached to Moore until 1698, when his patron presented him to the living of Lowestoft. The controversies surrounding Whiston's subsequent career, his Arianism, his dismissal from the University and his eventual career as a nonconformist need not concern us here; but as Lucasian Professor of Mathematics (in succession to Newton) he dedicated one book to his former patron, *A short view of the chronology of the Old Testament, and of the harmony of*

---

[29] G. F. Waagen *Treasures of art in Great Britain* (London 1854) 3 p. 452. Lilian Armstrong *Renaissance miniature painters & classical imagery; the Master of the Putti and his Venetian workshop* (London 1981) no. 41. J. J. G. Alexander has attributed it to Venetian or Paduan artists, and has compared it with a small group of manuscripts, including a Eusebius (MS. Harley 4965), prepared for the Aragon kings of Naples ('Notes on some Veneto-Paduan illuminated books of the Renaissance' *Arte Veneta* 23 (1969)).

[30] Hartshorne *Book rarities* p. 41, echoing Dibdin's remark 'among the finest vellum books in the world!!!' (MS. notebook in the possession of the Earl of Plymouth). In 1878 Samuel Sandars *(An annotated list of books printed on vellum to be found in the University and college libraries at Cambridge)* knew of one other copy on vellum, at Vienna.

[31] Details of his life are set out in the *DNB*.

the four Evangelists, published at Cambridge in 1702, a year before he gave up his living.[32] His successors as chaplains included three outstanding men, Samuel Clarke, Thomas Tanner and Charles Morgan, later Master of Clare College. Clarke and Tanner in particular both made extensive use of Moore's library and bore much of the responsibility for its organization.

Samuel Clarke, a native of Norwich and already a Fellow of Gonville and Caius College, was introduced to Moore by Whiston in 1697,[33] and on the latter's removal to Lowestoft the following year became chaplain at the age of twenty-three. On him fell the task of compiling a catalogue of Moore's printed books,[34] a project continued by various others with diminishing enthusiasm after about 1700. Clarke remained in his post as chaplain for nearly twelve years, accepting the rectory of Drayton in Norfolk (conveniently close to Norwich) in 1699, in 1707 that of St Benet's, Paul's Wharf, and in 1709 the royal living of St James, Piccadilly. He became a chaplain to Queen Anne on the recommendation of Moore who, in Hoadly's words, 'was in every day confirmed in the high Opinion of his Superior Talents, and Excellent Qualifications', and 'very justly thought that there was No place so deserving of such a person, and so fit for Such Abilities to exert Themselves in, for the Good of Mankind, as the *Metropolis* of the Kingdom'.[35] Whether or not Clarke himself appreciated Moore's high opinion of his talents may be doubted, for Humphrey Prideaux alleged that he was not unwilling to leave

---

[32] On Whiston see *Memoirs of the life and writings of Mr. William Whiston ... written by himself* (London 1749).

[33] W. Whiston *Historical memoirs of the life of Dr. Samuel Clarke* (London 1730) pp. 5–8.

[34] There exist now two series of catalogues of Moore's printed books, the first made while he was still collecting and the second compiled in the mid-eighteenth century by members of the staff of Cambridge University Library. Neither is completely reliable as a guide to what Moore actually owned, and by the time that the second was compiled many of his books had been mislaid or sold. The first (divided between Cambridge (MS. Oo.7.49) and the Bodleian (MSS. Add. D.81 and Add. D.81*)) contains comparatively few accessions after *c.* 1700.

[35] Samuel Clarke *Works* ed. B. Hoadly (London 1738) preface, p. iii.

Moore's service. 'His greatest preferment, in being made Rector of your parish,' Prideaux wrote to John Ellis on 11 July 1709, 'is in that hereby he is emancipated from the Bishop of Ely, whose service and ways he was heartily weary of.'[36] Prideaux was not, however, an unprejudiced observer, and he may possibly have exaggerated Clarke's feelings. A prolific author and a close friend of Newton, Clarke was an obvious choice as Boyle Lecturer in 1704–5, and the published version of his discourses, *A demonstration of the being and attributes of God*, is among a number of books by him in black or red gilt turkey leather bindings which he presumably presented to Moore. In 1697 he dedicated his first book, an annotated edition of Rohault's *Physica*, to Moore (it reached a third edition, supplemented with essays contributed by Charles Morgan, in 1710), and added later both his *Three practical essays, on baptism, confirmation, &c.* (1699) and his *Paraphrase on the Gospels of St Mark and St Luke* (1702).[37] His monumental folio edition of Caesar published by Tonson in 1712, acclaimed by Addison,[38] though it owed more to Bentley and Robert Cannon (who made available material from Isaac Vossius) owed something as well to Moore, in particular to the French fifteenth-century manuscript in his possession which had been also used by the Cambridge scholar John Davies in 1706. (The manuscript, MS. Nn.3.5, is of no great textual significance.) In design and appearance, Clarke's edition, dedicated appropriately to the Duke of Marlborough, was Tonson's masterpiece, a book which easily rivalled French book design at its grandest and echoed in its typographical arrangement some of the Imprimerie Royale's most illustrious products.

Despite Prideaux' adverse report in 1709, and despite the

---

[36] Prideaux *Letters* ed. Thompson p. 201.
[37] Apart from the gifts mentioned here, I know of only one book from Clarke's library which passed into the hands of Moore, and so to Cambridge, J. Buxtorf *Florilegium hebraicum* (Basel 1648), bought by Clarke for 3s.6d. Charles Morgan's contributions to the 1710 edition of Clarke's Rohault were later printed in an English translation by John Clarke as *Six philosophical dissertations* (Cambridge 1770).
[38] Cf. *The Spectator* no. 367.

taint of heresy in his book *The scripture-doctrine of the Trinity* (1712), Clarke appears to have remained on terms of trust and friendship with Moore; in 1714 he was to become his executor. For a time he shared his duties with another man, of quite different talents. Thomas Tanner, born in 1674 and appointed chaplain of All Souls College two days after his twenty-first birthday, had already published his *Notitia monastica*[39] when he was introduced to Moore. In 1698 he became his chaplain, a post he retained until March 1701, when he was collated to the Chancellorship of the diocese of Norwich: his official diocesan business allowed him ample time to collaborate with Moore as consultant on his manuscripts. In 1701 he married his patron's daughter Rose, and if Hearne's venomous pen is to be trusted the union brought little happiness. Hearne's description of her was not flattering: 'She was remarkable for drinking of Brandy. She was a short squabb dame, & uncapable of having Children, or else *Tom* not able to do it. After he had married her he was forc'd to lay aside Books, She not caring he should follow them, & ingage himself in Law Suits, relating to the Chancellor-ship of *Norwich* which the Bp. gave him, which made the poor man wish for a return to *Oxon* again.'[40] Rose died in 1707, and Tanner was subsequently twice remarried, but his disappearance from Oxford convinced Hearne that he was pursuing no scholarly work. He accused him privately of being distracted by Rose and her father's library at the expense of the continuation of Wood's *Athenae*, and considered Tanner dilatory in his work on a revision of Leland's notes.

While it is true that Tanner published virtually nothing while chaplain to Moore, his surviving papers and his annotations on many of Moore's manuscripts and printed books show him preparing much of the groundwork for the *Bibliotheca Britannico-Hibernica* published posthumously in

---

[39] Of the ten copies printed on large paper of this his first book, one was in Moore's library, but there is no direct evidence to suggest that it was a gift.

[40] Thomas Hearne *Remarks and collections* 2 p. 9. On Tanner's achievement as an antiquarian cf. M. J. Sommerlad 'The historical and antiquarian interests of Thomas Tanner' (Oxford D.Phil. thesis 1962).

1748. This displays most obviously his familiarity with Moore's library, and particularly with the medieval manuscripts. And yet, if Tanner can with some justice be charged with lassitude over its publication, no such accusation can be preferred against him as custodian, for a relatively short period, of Moore's library. He bought books for it from the London booksellers, wrote about it when Moore was away in the country, and catalogued many of the manuscripts acquired in the months immediately following the publication of Bernard's *Catalogi*. As Moore's temporary librarian in the summer of 1698 it was to him that Arthur Charlett wrote on 26 June enquiring as to the bishop's possible interest in the books of William Levinz, President of St John's College, Oxford, which were to be sold by Edward Millington at Oxford three days later;[41] and it was to him too, that Wanley reported on the small group of books including Erasmus, Scioppius, Carolus Stephanus, Claudian, Heinsius and Apicius bought at the same auction for a total outlay of £1.8s.9d.[42]

Among Tanner's first tasks at Charles Street were duties attending the publication of the Oxford *Catalogi*, which was finally issued to the public in November 1698. That August he organized the manuscripts into the order in which they appeared in the printed catalogue,[43] before returning to his other work at Oxford. But the project was not finished. Moore's enthusiasm pursued him there too, and he had barely arrived when Moore sent news of further manuscripts,[44] which were to arrive just too late for inclusion in the printed catalogue. The new attractions were the volumes relating to Bury St Edmunds, formerly in the possession of the Bacon family and of John Cradock of Rickinghall, Suffolk, now MSS. Ee.3.60, Ff.2.29, Ff.2.33, Ff.4.35, Gg.4.4 and Mm.4.19, containing charters, registers and various other documents

---

[41] Bodleian Library MS. Tanner 22 (16).

[42] *Ibid.* (98). Wanley acted as agent at the sale for both Moore and William Wake, and considered the prices high. (Wanley to Tanner 6 July 1698, Bodleian Library MS. Tanner 22 (34)). [43] Tanner to Moore [August 1698] (Tanner 22 (105)).

[44] Moore to Tanner 26 August 1698 (Tanner 22 (89)).

relating to the abbey.[45] Tanner later incorporated them into his continuation of the printed catalogue of the manuscripts, but he meanwhile wrote to congratulate Moore not simply on their acquisition:

I can't but congratulate your Lp upon the happy deliverance of your house and Library from Fire. Mr Charles, who in his return from Worcester call'd here on me last week, gave me the first account of that accident: and as nobody would have been (next to your Lordship) more sensible of its loss than I, whose use and value I [*illegible*], so for your Lps sake and ye Publick I am very glad and thankfull to providence for its preservation. I am mightily pleased to hear of ye 6. vol. belonging to S. Edm. Bury, that are likely to get in your Lps hands; I shall be glad to see them one time or other, but shall not have time to peruse them this winter.[46]

Tanner was not however so distracted that he did not have time to seek out one or two books for Moore at Oxford, including a copy of Virgil published at Venice in 1510 (no longer among Moore's library) and an edition of Valerius Maximus; he also discovered a copy of 'Vincentius Bellovacensis Speculū compleat in a huge fol. *Venet.* 1484. fol wh^{ch} I can have for very little more than ye price of wast paper, if your Ldp has it not already'. Moore's reply to this offer has not survived, but the book may be identical with Hermann Liechtenstein's printing of the *Speculum doctrinale* (1494), rebacked since Moore's time but still incorrectly labelled 1484 on the spine.[47]

Tanner's surviving correspondence with Moore extends principally over the brief period from August 1698 to June 1699, and is tantalizingly incomplete. It covers the auctions of the books of William Levinz, as has been mentioned, but there

---

45 R. M. Thomson *The archives of the Abbey of Bury St Edmunds* (Woodbridge 1980) nos. 1280, 1284, 1296, 1285, 1299 and 1277. See also M. R. James *On the Abbey of S. Edmund at Bury* (Cambridge Antiquarian Soc. 1895) p. 97 *et passim*. Tanner also borrowed one subsequently, and in 1741 it was among four volumes restored to Cambridge by the Bodleian Library: cf. John Batteley *Antiquitates S. Edmundi Burgi ad annum MCCLXXII* (Oxford 1745) and Macray *Annals* p. 210. Cambridge University Library acquired the Bury St Edmunds Cellarer's register, forming the sequel to MS. Gg.4.4, at the sale of Sir Henry Bunbury's books at Sotheby's on 15 February 1904 (now MS. Add. 4220).

46 Tanner to Moore (draft) [autumn 1698] (Bodleian Library MS. Tanner 22 (92)).

47 Inc. 1893.

is only one brief reference to that of the much more important library of Francis Bernard, M.D., sold in October 1698. These few letters need not be accounted necessarily typical, but they are almost the sole witnesses to the excitement which a promising sale could engender in Moore, and are thus of unique interest.

Tanner was the natural choice as agent for Moore at the sales of the books of William Anderton and John Oxlad, two members of the book trade, at Oxford in March 1699. Moore's complicated instructions were not always definite as to how far he wished to bid, but for the second sale (seemingly the first to be organized by Benjamin Shirley), entailing books from one of the established bookselling families of Oxford, he provided Tanner with a list of twenty-two desiderata, all but two or three of them priced. They were a mixed bag, including the Paris Chrysostom of 1621–4, Andreas *Bibliotheca Belgica* (1642), Léry *Historia navigationis in Brasiliam* (1586), the 1668 (1670) edition of *Ignoramus*, Beveridge's Syriac grammar (1658), a collected Petrarch published in Basel, and Sir Richard Hawkins' *Observations* on his voyage of 1593, published in 1622. He enjoyed some success, but the Chrysostom turned out to be imperfect and had to be returned, Moore being 'loth at this time of day to buy books wth any defect' – a requirement that was several times remarked on by his contemporaries. This was, however, a rather less complicated matter than the next sale for which he required Tanner's services.

The owner of the *Bibliotheca Graeco-Latina*, sold by John Bullord from 23 May 1699, is no longer known: it is not impossible that it was simply a miscellaneous sale designed to dispose of stock, like two others organized by Bullord in the same year. Moore, on his way to Norwich and then at Norwich itself, read the catalogue several times over, and sent his first instructions on bids off to Tanner on 16 May, writing from Bury St Edmunds. Extensive though his bids were, he failed to secure most of the books he hoped for. This much is clear from his letter to Tanner of 2 June, when he mourned 'so few books fall to my share that I could be content wth the Herbal ... and wth the Malabar. hortus'. But he did acquire Baluze's *Capitularia regum Francorum*, which he asked to have packed and sent up to Norwich. Thanks to gaps in the correspondence and repairs and rebindings to the books since, it is now impossible to establish how much further he was successful, and the matter is further complicated by Moore's need to make up sets. His letter of 2 June suggested that he badly wanted van Rheede's illustrated *Hortus Indicus Malabaricus*, described in the catalogue as being in twelve volumes although the twelfth and last was not published until 1704. Moore's set almost certainly came from elsewhere, as it bears the signature of Walter Charleton, dated 1682, in the first volume, and Charleton did not die until 1707. Likewise it seems that the copy of Graevius' *Thesaurus* now among Moore's books was not acquired at the sale, and that the lot (of eight rather than the full twelve volumes), for which Moore was prepared to pay the curious sum of £8.5s.6d., was one of the many lost. His copy, bound uniformly in red turkey leather, came most probably from David Mortier, whose engraved label is on the first blank leaf. But his bid for Phavorinus *Lexicon Graecum* (1538), which he wished to acquire for the grammar school at Bury St Edmunds, was apparently successful, for in 1700 he presented a copy of the same edition to the school, together with Stuckius *Antiquitatum convivialium libri III* (1597) and Henninius' edition of Juvenal (1685) – gifts followed up in 1702 by Vossius *Commentariorum rhetoricorum libri VI* (1643).[48]

Moore's and Tanner's interests, potentially so close, do not appear to have clashed at these sales. The relationship cannot always have been so easy. Tanner's antiquarian tastes were forming before ever he met Moore, and the similarity of their collections, for all the difference in size, is in one respect

---

[48] Cambridge University Library MS. Add. 7930, the school's library catalogue and donors' register. The headmaster from 1663 to 1707 was the classicist Edward Leedes, who gave Moore a copy of his *Methodus Graecam linguam docendi* (Cambridge 1699).

immediately and inescapably obvious.[49] Both were enthusiastic collectors of English books printed in the century following Caxton's establishment of his press at Westminster; and although Dibdin awarded the laurel to Moore as the greater and earlier of the two, Tanner's own collections were very far from negligible by the time of his death. It is impossible to establish to what exact degree his tastes anticipated or echoed those of his patron, but there remain among Moore's books a number bearing Tanner's signature. They include Nowell's *Catechisme* (1570), an imperfect copy of the primer of ?1538 bound up with the Epistles and Gospels, on yellow paper, John Bale's *Declaration of Edmonde Bonners articles* (1561), and the 1629 edition of John Boys' *Workes*, as well as the much later edition by Edmund Gibson of William Drummond's *Polemo-Middinia* (1691). To these was also added, more surprisingly since Moore possessed two other copies as well, Caxton's edition of Cicero on old age (1481), though admittedly none of the three is quite complete.

The traffic was, however, not all in one direction, and in one case Tanner's behaviour seems to have been a little less than open. In 1862 Henry Bradshaw believed that he had identified Moore's copy of the St Albans *Rhetorica nova* of 1480 in a sale of Bodleian duplicates, chiefly from the Tanner collection, when it fetched over one-sixth of the total for the entire sale. He bought it from Boone after the sale for £100 plus a duplicate copy of the *Royal book* as an exchange, acquiring by this transaction not Moore's copy, as he supposed, but William Laud's, which for some reason had been sold in place of the Moore–Tanner copy. The copy that remained at Oxford had been taken from Moore's library on 15 May 1714 by Tanner himself, and had never been returned after its owner's death a few weeks later.[50] It was presumably borrowed honestly, though the person recording the loan felt aggrieved or

---

[49] Cf. Philip p. 81.

[50] On Bradshaw's negotiations see below, p. 593, Oates *Catalogue* p. 26 and *idem* 'The sale of a duplicate' *Bodleian Library Record* 3 (1950–1) pp. 175–6. The record of Tanner's loan, and its subsequent defacement (Bodleian Library MS. Add. D.81 f.466ᵛ), was unknown to Mr Oates.

uncertain enough to add 'as is supposed': an amateurish attempt made later to excise Tanner's name from the entry does nothing to dispel doubts as to his conduct.

The means by which Moore collected his library have been questioned on many occasions, from the eighteenth century onwards, and Richard Gough's opinion, repeated by Dibdin, is familiar: 'The bishop collected it by plundering the libraries of the clergy in his diocese; some he paid with sermons or more modern books; others only with *quid illiterati cum libris?*'[51] The antiquary William Cole noted in similar vein several years earlier, 'It was well known the Bp. if he could obtain his Books, scrupled not much *how* he *came by them*. I have *often heard* it *so affirmed.*'[52] His own dioceses of Norwich and Ely were not the only areas to suffer, according to Francis Drake, writing from York years after Moore's death. In February 1730/1 he remarked to the Earl of Oxford,

I shall from time to time advertise your Lordship with what curiosities I meet with. I am in pursuit of a MS. Bede of great antiquity, but whether I shall come up to it or no is uncertain. People in this country are not such great strangers to things of this nature as I could wish them; the late Bishop of Ely plundered these parts excessively when he was down in person amongst us, and Dr Man—g, Prebendary of Durham, another Church-man, makes no scruple to beg, borrow or st—l all he can lay his hands on.[53]

And from Northamptonshire there was further complaint:

Mr. *Tew* the late incumbent found walled up in the chancel a Greek MS. of three of the gospels, St. *Mark's* being wanting, conjectured to be about six hundred years old. It was communicated by him to Dr. *Cumberland* then bishop of the diocese, of whom it was borrowed by Dr. *Moore* bishop of *Ely*, who when pressed to return it said, he had mislaid or could not find it. From this circumstance it hath been suspected that the MS. was much older than it was thought to be, and is perhaps preserved with the books he gave to the University of *Cambridge*.[54]

[51] T. F. Dibdin *Bibliomania* (London 1811) p. 420n. See also Richard Gough *British topography* (London 1780) I p. 224.   [52] British Library MS. Add. 5853 p.483.

[53] HMC Portland 6 p. 35. 'Man—g' was presumably Thomas Mangey, editor of Philo-Judaeus and prebendary of Durham from 1721 to 1755.

[54] John Bridges *History and antiquities of Northamptonshire* ed. P. Whalley (Oxford 1791) 2 p. 45. See also Nichols *Literary anecdotes* 9 (London 1815) p. 612. George Tew (d. 1702) was rector of Loddington, near Kettering.

Two hundred years later it is difficult to distinguish rumour from the truth, but it is relevant to recall the rapacious collecting of men such as Charles-Maurice Le Tellier, Archbishop of Rheims, who were roughly contemporary with Moore.[55] He may have been casual in his attitude to others' property, but it is by no means clear how far he exploited his position of privilege, while the notion of preservation by getting a book into sympathetic hands is not always to be dismissed cavalierly as misappropriation.

In 1770 the University Library returned to the authorities at Norwich two manuscripts relating to the diocese which had been in Moore's possession since the late 1690s,[56] but these were by no means the only items concerning the see that found their way into his collection. A *Liber valorum* of *c.* 1570 (MS. Dd.4.19), a seventeenth-century *valor ecclesiasticus* (MS. Ff.5.13) and an early sixteenth-century note of the taxation imposed on parishes in the archdeaconries of Suffolk and Sudbury (MS. Dd.10.34) might all, in a different period, be regarded as belonging more properly to the diocesan archives than to an individual bishop, but such a distinction was less than obvious in more than one English diocese in the seventeenth century. The circumstances in which Moore acquired several bundles of computus rolls relating to the bishopric of Richard Nykke during the reign of Henry VIII are ambiguous. They were given to him by one Thurston in October 1697, and several explanations are of course possible: they may have been an unsolicited gift, Moore may himself have suggested them as an appropriate present, Thurston may have been seeking Moore's patronage, or, perhaps most plausibly, the Bishop's library may have seemed to Thurston, puzzled as to where to place them, the most seemly repository.

[55] L. Delisle *Le cabinet des manuscrits* (Paris 1868–81) I pp. 302–7.
[56] Formerly Cambridge University Library MSS. Ee.3.57 (no. 859 in Tanner's manuscript continuation of the list of Moore's manuscripts in Bernard's *Catalogi* (MS. Oo.7.50²)) and Gg.4.1 (University Grace Book *K* p. 498). The Norwich muniments were badly cared for at the end of the seventeenth century: cf. Barbara Dodwell (ed.) *The Charters of Norwich Cathedral Priory* I (Pipe Roll Soc. 1974) pp. xxiii–xxiv.

Speculation is unrewarding and unproductive. That many of Moore's books came from private libraries in the diocese of Norwich is clear,[57] but unlike many bought at London or Oxford auctions (for example) few can be assigned to dated transactions. His private accounts, kept almost entirely in London, record only a handful of purchases in Norwich, and do not mention even so large an acquisition (totalling at least four hundred items) as the Knyvett collection in about 1693.[58]

Not everyone could afford, or wished, to be a critic. Books were dedicated to him not only by scholars whom he helped or encouraged, and by medical figures recognizing his interest in their profession, but also by the parish clergy. In 1695 Charles Rowbotham, rector of Fakenham and of Reepham and Kerdiston, dedicated to him his *Disquisitio in hypothesin Baxterianam de foedere gratiae*, and in 1710 Nicholas Clagett, appointed archdeacon of Sudbury by Moore in 1693, dedicated to him his confutation of Whiston's *Accomplishment of scripture prophecies* entitled *Truth defended, and boldness in error rebuk'd*. Nor did everything reach the formality of print. Robert Warren's translation of Erasmus, *A practical discourse concerning the magnitude of God's mercy*, may perhaps date from as late as 1702, but the dedication copy was a rough affair, more a revised draft than a finished article for presentation.[59] On the other hand, a much more elaborate manuscript came not from one of Moore's diocesan clergy but from Thomas Davies, vicar of Syston in Leicestershire, who preached before Moore in Norwich Cathedral in August 1699. His sermon, *Agur's wish*, was written out subsequently in careful pen facsimile,[60]

---

[57] One volume of printed tracts, mostly sermons printed between *c.* 1690 and 1704, has an inscription to the effect that it is from the Plume Library at Maldon in Essex.

[58] Cf. D. McKitterick *The library of Sir Thomas Knyvett of Ashwellthorpe c. 1539–1618* (Cambridge 1978).

[59] Cambridge University Library MS. Gg.5.23. Warren was a member of Christ's College, ordained at Rochester in January 1701/2, and appointed to Sir John Morden's college at Blackheath; in 1704 he became rector of Charlton. Moore's copy of his translation *The tablet of Cebes the Theban philosopher* (Cambridge: John Pindar 1699) is bound in black turkey leather, and was presumably a gift.

[60] Cambridge University Library MS. Ff.4.20.

but despite his care in presentation and his choice of text he does not appear to have received further encouragement in the church. Others, too, came from outside the diocese. In July 1707 Peter Allix, then Treasurer of Salisbury Cathedral, dedicated to Moore his *Two treatises* in answer to Whiston, explaining simply that he had intended to dedicate the book to his predecessor at Ely, Simon Patrick, but that Patrick being dead he addressed it to Moore 'By Right of Succession'. The case of Humphrey Ditton, friend of Whiston and formerly a nonconformist preacher but then through Newton's influence appointed mathematics master at Christ's Hospital, was less impersonal: in 1712 Ditton dedicated his *Discourse concerning the Resurrection* to Moore in acknowledgement of his patronage, and two years later he followed this by adding to Moore's library what is almost certainly a presentation copy (to judge from the binding: Sir Isaac Newton's copy is identical) of his *New law of fluids* (1714).

When in 1730 William Whiston recalled his first meeting with his successor as chaplain, Samuel Clarke, he recalled also something of Moore, a characteristic which does much to explain his unusual appetite for books of all kinds: 'He was ever ambitious of being, and of being esteemed a Patron of Learning, and learned Men.'[61] His chaplains were very far from the only beneficiaries. From abroad, Johann Albert Fabricius acknowledged Moore's pre-eminence when he selected him as the only Englishman to receive the dedication of one of the fourteen volumes of his *Bibliotheca Graeca*: by 1707, he emphasized, Moore's reputation had spread even to Germany.[62] The notes of loans made by Moore, or on his behalf, to others, recorded partly in one of the volumes of his library catalogue but also scattered in other places with little

[61] William Whiston *Historical memoirs of the life of Dr. Samuel Clarke* (London 1730) p. 7; quoted in *Cambridge under Queen Anne* p. 283.
[62] J. A. Fabricius *Bibliotheca Graeca* 2 (Hamburg 1707). For Moore's possible connection with the London edition (1703) of Fabricius' *Bibliotheca Latina*, see H. S. Reimar *De vita et scriptis Joannis Albertis Fabricii* (Hamburg 1737) p. 111.

organization, are quite clearly only fragmentary, but they offer invaluable evidence of the uses to which his library was put.

At one stage during the proceedings against him at Ely House in 1714, Richard Bentley is reported to have fainted. It is not to be presumed that he did so through a failure of *sang-froid* in the face of his enemies, the Fellows of Trinity College. He was standing trial before Moore as Visitor of the College; but Moore was also Bishop of the diocese where he was archdeacon, and, most eloquently of all, the two men were friends in scholarship and bibliophily. For years Bentley had contrived to keep his friendship with Moore separate from the arguments in Trinity. His vitriolic letter to Moore published in 1710 to defend himself from the barbs of the Trinity Fellowship certainly did not imply that relations on any other topic needed to be anything other than cordial. In 1711 he dedicated his Horace to Robert Harley, whose protection he needed at that stage above all. On this occasion, Moore's library had little to offer save by way of printed editions, but nonetheless one of the most ornate bindings among his books is a copy of Bentley's edition, published by Cambridge University Press and bound in red turkey leather by Richard Balley. The earliest records of Bentley at work among Moore's books date from August 1698, when he borrowed the Jesuit Juan de Mariana's *De rege et regis institutione* (Mainz 1605), Casaubon's edition of Persius (1615) and works by Scaliger, Snellius, Budé and Graevius on the Roman coinage. Two years later he had manuscripts of Homer and Hephaestion, a volume of Castelvetro and an assortment of editions of Horace.[63] On another occasion he borrowed eight editions of Virgil,[64] and in 1712 he collated the eleventh-century manuscript of Nonius

---

[63] Bodleian Library MS. Add. D.81.
[64] MS. Dd.12.40 fo. 108ᵛ. Bentley's annotated copy of Hephaestion's Ἐγχειρίδιον (Paris 1553) is in Trinity College, Cambridge, and his collation of the manuscript (now part of MS. Dd.11.70) was published by Gaisford in 1810.

Marcellus (MS. Mm.5.22).[65] There still remain among Moore's books Bentley's own heavily annotated copies of Robert Stephanus' editions of Juvenal, Persius and Horace (1544), bound up in a single volume. The exact date when Bentley turned his attention to Terence with a view to editing the text is not known, and his edition did not appear until many years later, in 1726, eventually completed in less than eighteen months and spurred into publication by Francis Hare's inadequate edition of 1724. But most of the work had been done several years previously. Though his preface mentions merely that he had used Cambridge libraries, whose collections included for example the rough late manuscript which had been in the University Library since the sixteenth century,[66] Bentley had in fact found particular aid in Moore's collection long before. He followed in the steps of John Leng, Fellow of St Catharine's and editor of the Tonson–Cambridge edition of 1701, who had used Moore's library for Isaac Casaubon's copiously annotated copy of the diminutive Lyon edition of 1576 and for Le Fèvre's of Heinsius' edition of 1635. Bentley's borrowings for the purpose also included the Aldine edition of 1541, Boecler's of 1657, the Gryphius edition of 1554, the scarce edition published in 1488 by Jean Dupré of Lyon, and, somewhat less usefully, a French manuscript of the thirteenth century with commentaries added two centuries later.[67] It is to these that Bentley most probably referred in a letter to James Lisle of Staple Inn on 10 August 1714, just after Moore's death, requesting him to collect the Trinity College statutes and other documents, and mentioning that he had 'about a dozen Books of the Bishop's', which he would return as soon as desired:[68] in the end they were not returned to the library until January 1722/3.

[65] Note in B. Aretius *Commentarii in Epistolam ad Galatos* (1583) and B. Ochino *Espositione sopra la Epistole à i Galati* (1546); note in Bentley's copy of Mercer's edition of Nonius Marcellus (Paris 1614: British Library 684.c.14).   [66] MS. Ff.4.39.
[67] Bodleian Library MS. Add. D 81 fo. 466ʳ. The Terence is now MS. Ff.6.4, probably acquired by Moore through Alexander Cunningham in 1701.
[68] Richard Bentley *Correspondence* (London 1842) 1 p. 484.

Bentley never completed one further project for which he drew much of his reading from Moore's library. Nothing has appeared in print of his Suetonius, save for a list of readings which he appended to a letter addressed to John Walker, a Trinity Fellow, who was in Paris in September 1719 collating manuscripts for Bentley's proposed edition of the New Testament. He asked Walker to examine two of the earliest Suetonius manuscripts known to him, but he also revealed that he still had not begun his text.[69] As with Terence, he had been at work on Suetonius sporadically for several years. In July 1713 Peter Needham had borrowed, presumably for Bentley's use, one of Moore's manuscripts for this purpose, and on 2 January following he borrowed 'for yᵉ use of Dʳ Bentley' three further versions of the text, a further manuscript, the Sweynheym and Pannartz edition of 1472 (Moore did not possess the *editio princeps*) and the Milan edition of 1480 – the last bound up with Justinus *Epitome*.

If the opportunities afforded to classical scholars were perhaps most fruitful in the case of Bentley, Moore was equally willing to help others as well. Ludolph Kuster, professor of Greek at Berlin and editor of the great Cambridge Suidas (1705), marked his appreciation of Moore's scholarly benevolence by dedicating to him his edition of Iamblichus *De vita Pythagorica* published at Amsterdam in 1707.[70] Peter Needham was far more typical. Admitted to St John's College, Cambridge in 1693 from Norfolk he was elected to a Fellowship in 1698, and in May 1706 was ordained priest by Moore in Norwich; in the same year he was presented to the rectory of Ovington, a small village to the west of Norwich, which he held for five years before taking livings at the Cambridgeshire villages of Madingley and Conington. An accomplished scholar, he dedicated his first major published work to Moore, an edition of the Γεωπονικά printed at Cambridge University

<hr />

[69] *Ibid.*, 2 pp. 552–8.
[70] He also presented to Moore his *Diatribe anti-Gronoviana* (Amsterdam 1712), now Dd*.3.8¹(D).

Press in 1704 and undertaken with Moore's active support. Needham had begun serious work on the text probably some time in 1700, and on 6 December that year Moore wrote to Hans Sloane requesting the loan of material to help his young protégé. 'I have a request to make relating to a book, wch your study, that has almost all physic books, hardly can want. tis the Translation of the last 8 books of the Geoponica by Andreas a Lacuna. if it be in your possession & you will please to lend me it, after the use thereof I will carefully return it wth hearty thanks.'[71] Moore did not elucidate further, but Sloane guessed the purpose, and at the end of January Moore addressed to him one of the few letters of a scholarly nature to have survived from his pen:

What you suppose is tru, I am encouraging a young man to publish again the Geoponica: I have obtain'd in order to it a Collation of good MSS in Sr John Cottons hands; I have out of my own study furnisht him wth a Collation of anoth^r MSS by Isaac Casaubon, & wth a fragment of a MSS wch is valuable so far as it goes; & also wth Junus Cornarius's translation, wch has great faults, I believe chiefly, thro' want of a good Greek copy. for in his translation of Plato he seems to have outdone both Ficinus & Serranus: neither is he less happy in translating Hippocrates & Epiphanius. what you mention at Venice would be most welcome, & I would willingly bear the charge of transcribing or collating as there should be occasion. it may be sufficient to collate a printed book wth ye MSS, and perhaps the best way to have ye differences exactly between the print & MSS unless we had a Transcriber well skill'd in Greek. Didymus & other Authors, if any there be, are to be copy'd, & I shall thankfully perform any bargain on this occasion you shall make, either to copy him, or ye whole Geoponica as shall be best liked. if there be anything in Lacuna's Apology concerning the version of our Author then the use of it would be very acceptable. I beg when you are pleased to write to Venice that enquiry there may be made after Lacunas version, & that it may be bought, or if in a Library compared with Cornarius. you may ask our good friend Mr Bernard, or any other that have good books whether they have Lacuna.[72]

Casaubon's 'collation', an annotated copy of Brassicanus' edition published at Basel in 1539, is not now among Moore's

---

[71] British Library MS. Sloane 4038 fo. 101.
[72] *Ibid.*, fo. 126. Hearne had a low opinion of Needham: see *Remarks and collections* I p. 78.

books.[73] Moore had possessed Cornarius' translation (Basel 1540) for several years, having acquired it with the Knyvett books in the early 1690s, but it is not known how long he had owned the manuscript fragment.[74] As for the book which Sloane mentioned as being at Venice, and which so aroused Moore's curiosity, this may perhaps have been Marciana 294, a copy of the fourteenth or fifteenth century, or Marciana 524, of the fourteenth: in the event Needham restricted his study of late manuscripts to those nearer home, and paid more attention to the early ones in the French Royal Library.

Much of Needham's work on Hierocles' commentary on Pythagoras, published in 1709 and also printed at Cambridge, was made possible by Moore, who lent him the *editio princeps* printed at Padua in 1474, and once again Moore received a copy in a presentation binding:[75] on this occasion the book was dedicated to William Cowper, the Lord Chancellor, but in 1712 Needham dedicated a further book to Moore, his edition of Theophrastus published, like his former works, at Cambridge.[76] Other work was never completed. It was, for example, left to Anthony Askew to further Needham's labours on Aeschylus. In January 1712/13 Needham borrowed Stanley's own copiously annotated copy of his edition of 1663, and with it he took Casaubon's annotated copy of the Stephanus edition of 1557 and an anonymously annotated copy of the Aldine edition of 1518, as well as the ninth-century manuscript of Palladius (MS. Kk.5.13) acquired ten years previously. Askew subsequently obtained some of Needham's

---

73 The loan is recorded in the Oxford almanack for 1699 (Adv.e.38.15).

74 MS. Dd.3.86 no. 11, dated s.xv in the printed catalogue of manuscripts. It is no. 87 in Bernard's *Catalogi*, among a group of manuscripts from the Knyvett library – a circumstance that suggests but does not prove that Moore acquired it at about the same time.

75 This book was awaited for some time by the learned world: cf. McKenzie *Cambridge University Press* 1 pp. 317–18, quoting Hearne and the *Journal des Sçavans*.

76 This is notable for the inclusion of James Duport's *Praelectiones*, wrongly attributed to Thomas Stanley (editor of Aeschylus) in Bernard's *Catalogi*. Duport's manuscript, annotated by Needham, is now MS. Ff.4.33; the notes on it added in the printing house are discussed in McKenzie *Cambridge University Press* 1 p. 346.

notes, but in turn his projected edition of Aeschylus reached no further than a preliminary specimen: Needham's contributions were finally published only in the nineteenth century, in Samuel Butler's edition of 1809–26.

Further evidence of the extent to which Bentley's embarrassing behaviour was not allowed to affect relations in scholarly matters between Moore and his supporters emerges in Moore's treatment of John Davies, one of Bentley's principal champions. Davies was elected Fellow of Queens' College in 1701, and in 1709 his edition of the *Tusculanae disputationes* was published by the Cambridge bookseller Edmund Jeffery. He received considerable editorial assistance from Bentley, but from Moore he obtained a copy of the Stephanus edition, invaluable for its annotations listing variant readings in manuscripts outside Cambridge: unlike Needham, who ranged to Oxford (with the help of Hearne) and far beyond in his search for sources, Davies was apparently content to conduct his research almost wholly in Cambridge, principally in the University Library and in Peterhouse. Moore responded to the compliment of the dedication by presenting Davies to the living of Fen Ditton in 1711: he was collated to a prebendal stall in Ely Cathedral the same year. The edition of the *Tusculanae disputationes* proved to be the first of a long series of Cicero texts edited by Davies, but it was the only one to appear in Moore's lifetime: when in 1723 a second, revised, edition was called for, he added a note of his patron's death, and quoted from the Emperor Julian's third oration (expressing Julian's gratitude to the Empress Eusebia for her care and friendship during his stay in Milan, where he was surrounded by intrigue) in what was clearly intended to be a parallel with Cambridge politics of the early eighteenth century.

Bentley, Needham and Davies, all classical scholars, were among the most frequent users of the library, but there were many others. Joshua Barnes, Regius Professor of Greek at Cambridge, borrowed Melanchthon's copy of the *Iliad* (Venice 1504) in preparation for his edition of Homer published in 1701, though he used it very little. Moore also helped him more generally, in 1699 for example lending him his valued copy of the Stephanus *Poetae Graeci principes heroici carminis* (1566) bearing Isaac Casaubon's annotations, of which Barnes transcribed sections into his own copy.[77] Another Cambridge figure to benefit was Simon Ockley, appointed Professor of Arabic in his early thirties, who borrowed 'An Arabick MS containing some account of ye life of Mahomet' in March 1711/12. Among those from Oxford were J. E. Grabe, allowed to take away two Septuagints and the first volume of the Antwerp polyglot in April 1703,[78] and John Mill, who included a collation of Moore's eleventh-century Greek *Evangelistarium* (MS. Dd.8.49) in his edition of the New Testament in 1707. By no means all were from the universities. In July 1713 'One Mr Ward a Dissenter' borrowed a volume containing works by Rapicius, Robortellus and Victorius, and both the episcopal bench and the London clergy made use of the collection. William Wake borrowed an assortment of books in 1697;[79] John Williams, Bishop of Chichester, took away Vialart's *Geographia sacra* (Paris 1641) in May 1701;[80] Francis Hare, later Bishop of Chichester but then a prebendary of St Paul's, borrowed Foy-Vaillant's *Historia Ptolemaeorum Aegypti regum ad finem numismatum accommodata* (Amsterdam 1701) as well as von Pufendorf's *De rebus gestis Friderici Wilhelmi Magni* (Berlin 1695); and 12 February 1712/13 saw John Turner, vicar of Greenwich and later chaplain to George I, borrowing Morinus *Commentarius historicus de disciplina in administratione sacramenti poenitentiae tredecim primis seculis in ecclesia occidentali* (Paris 1651). One non-clerical borrower whose loans were noted in the library catalogue was 'M^r. Spanheim', otherwise Freiherr Ezechiel von Spanheim, numismatist, classical scholar and Ambassador of Frederick the Great, who was in London briefly in May–July 1701 and

---

[77] Both Moore's and Barnes' copies are now in Cambridge University Library. On 19 April 1699 Barnes wrote to Richard Laughton at Clare College, pleading to be allowed to retain the 'Heroick Poets' a little longer (MS. Dd.3.64 fos. 66–7).

[78] Adv.e.38.16, flyleaf. His transcript of the Codex Alexandrinus was published in 1707–9.   [79] MS. Ff.5.19 fo. 87^v.   [80] MS. Dd.12.40 fo. 110^v.

returned there the following December to remain until his death on 25 November 1710. Moore, who himself also borrowed from Spanheim, lent him copies of Horace and Strabo in March 1703/4,[81] and the first notes of all on loans in the catalogue are to him, of Gronovius' edition of Aulus Gellius, Rittershusius' of Oppian, and Gronovius' *Supplementa lacunarum in Aenea Tactico Dione Cassio et Arriano de expeditione Alexandri* (Leiden 1675). Those to Spanheim were followed by a series of entries, similarly undated, beginning with 'Livies to Mr Hern', presumably the occasion when Hearne borrowed Lipsius' unfinished edition of 1579 in February 1706[82], and continuing with records of loans to Edward Chandler, John Woodward, and others.

These last were of odd volumes only; but Jacob Tonson obtained rather more. Tonson's proposals for publishing, in a series of quarto volumes to be printed at the newly reformed Cambridge University Press, the works of Horace, Virgil, Terence, Catullus, Tibullus and Propertius, appeared in 1698: the Horace was the first to appear, in 1699, followed in 1701 by Virgil and Terence. In 1702 Arthur Annesley's edition of Catullus, Tibullus and Propertius was issued. It thus seems likely that Moore's loans to Tonson of these last authors, for the use of Annesley, were perhaps as early as 1699 or before: work on the edition began at the University Press in 1700.[83] The loans included a folio edition of Propertius published in

---

81 British Library MS. Add. 22911 fo. 38ʳ. See also V. Loewe *Ein Diplomat und Gelehrter, Ezechiel Spanheim (1629–1710)* (Berlin 1924) pp. 146–56. Moore's large paper copy of Spanheim's edition of Callimachus (Utrecht 1697), in a special binding, was perhaps a gift. He also possessed a large paper copy of Spanheim's *Dissertationes de praestantia et usu numismatum antiquorum* (London 1706), in which Spanheim paid him a fulsome tribute.

82 Hearne *Remarks and collections* I pp. 183–4.

83 On this project see McKenzie *Cambridge University Press* I pp. 15 etc. The Syndics gave Tonson leave to proceed on 23 August 1698 (McKenzie 2 p. 1). On 24 January 1697/8 (the month in which the Press was formally established) Moore paid Bentley £15 'towards the subscription of the Typography of yᵉ University of Cambridge' (Moore's private accounts, Cambridge University Library Church Commissioners papers 95579); this does not appear in the Vice-Chancellor's accounts (see McKenzie 2 pp. 30–3), and it does not seem to have formed part of the original funding of the Press (McKenzie 1 p. 13 and 2 p. 30), to which Moore had already contributed £25.

1478 and an edition of Tibullus of 1488 'in Vellum': neither edition is known to modern bibliographers, and some error seems probable. The entries are not crossed through as they usually are for books returned to Moore, so the books may never have come back. At the same time, Annesley borrowed Michel de Marolles' edition of Tibullus and Propertius; and on two subsequent occasions Tonson took away, some presumably for Annesley's use, Sebastian Gryphius' edition of Catullus (1548), Statius' Catullus of 1566, and Antonius Gryphius' edition of 1578, as well as Muretus' Tibullus and Propertius of 1562. His borrowings also included the 1494 Venice edition of Caesar's *Commentaries* and Hyginus *De castris Romanis* (Amsterdam 1660). Only two of them, the 1548 Catullus and the Hyginus, can now be found in the library.

Not all the loans were of a classical or ecclesiastical nature. While John Laughton, Fellow of Trinity College and University Librarian, borrowed Valeriano's *Castigationes Virgilianae lectionis* (Rome 1521), he also removed on another occasion an account of the revolution in Sweden.[84] Laughton's was a less unexpected name than that of George Hickes, whose politics (but not his interests) were the antithesis of Moore's. Hickes' remarkable personality, his outstanding scholarship, and the magnetic quality of his subject matter, drew many Whigs to his aid, particularly White Kennett.[85] Moore, well entrenched in his ecclesiastical position and even owing it as Bishop of Norwich to the eviction of his non-juring predecessor, was a less likely patron still. Nevertheless, he made available to Hickes in April 1700,[86] when he was at work on his Thesaurus, a group of Swedish works, among them a series of sagas including the 1664 printing of *Gautreks saga*, the 1666 *Herrauds och Bosa saga* and the 1672 *Hervarer saga*. With these Hickes also borrowed a volume of early Swedish legal texts, edited by Johann Hadorph, bound up with Olaus Verelius *Manuductio ad*

[84] MS. Ff.5.19 fo. 87ᵛ.
[85] Cf. David C. Douglas *English scholars* (London 1939) ch.4.
[86] MS. Dd.12.40 fo. 109ᵛ.

runographiam scandicam antiquam (1675) and his *Index linguae veteris Scytho-Scandiae* (1691), a further volume of Scandinavian law, Loccenius *Lexicon iuris Sueo-Gothici* (3rd ed. Holmiae 1674) and, to round off the collection on a slightly different topic, 'An old English and Latin vocabulary'.

Hickes left an unusually full and signed receipt for his books,[87] and restored them in due course. But there were occasional and inevitable losses as a result of Moore's generous policy in lending his books. Another was lost after it had been returned, for the manuscript of Florus borrowed by John Hudson (then still at University College, and not yet Bodley's Librarian) in November 1699 and duly sent back,[88] cannot now be found at Cambridge. Moore took considerable risks with his books, and did so willingly, but had to face the consequent losses. He was also in the unenviable position of being known to possess books and being expected to lend them to anyone who asked. So the exiled Alexander Cunningham, writing to his nephew from The Hague on 22 February 1709, spoke of his needs:

I must lykewise borrow from The B^P of Ely Antonius Augustinus de propriis nominibus. his Lo: had it from me and since his Lo: is very ready to lend books to those who are upon any publick work I am confident his Lo: will not refuse me the use of it since his Lo: had it from me. his Lo: knows me too well to have the least suspicion that I should have any design not to restore it to his Lo: and I have no other design in borrowing it than because it is absolutely necessary for the foresaid worke I design shortly to publish, but of this I shall shortly write to his Lo: in the mean time read the whole letter to my L of Ely and give his Lo: my most humble duty ...[89]

Cunningham sought to reassure himself; but relations with Hudson were less even-footed. Unlike Cunningham, who had rendered Moore considerable service, Hudson in 1705 had no

---

[87] J. E. Grabe, at work on his edition of the Septuagint (Oxford 1707–20), also left a signed receipt, in a volume of almanacs for 1703: 'Borrowed then out of My Lords of Norwich Library Aldus & the Roman Edition of the Septuagint, as also the first Volum of the Antwerp Bibel, with this Assurance, that I shall restore them without any damnage at demand.' (Adv.e.38.16). Grabe acknowledged his considerable debt to Moore in the Prolegomenon to vol. 1 (Cap.3).

[88] MS. Dd.12.40 fo. 54^v.   [89] MS. Dd.3.64 (56).

such command. In 1701 he had retained a copy of Rufus Festus for some considerable time.[90] Thomas Hearne, his sympathies for once with Hudson, was quick to note the strain between Bodley's Librarian (presiding, ironically, over a library that did not lend) and Moore, whose private library had apparently come to be regarded in some quarters as all but public property:

D[r]. Hudson shew'd me a Letter to-day w[ch] he rec[d] from the B[p]. of Norwich in Answer to one sent lately to him, complaining of his L[d]ship's Backwardness in Lending certain Books, (to y[e] great detriment of the Publick): his L[d]ship declar'd himself sorry y[t] the D[r]. should take it amiss, & promis'd to lend him for y[e] future any Book he should have occasion for out of his study.[91]

Within a few weeks Hearne, too, was to borrow from Moore's library.[92]

No such difficulties seem to have intruded themselves into Moore's relations with two much more amiable men, Burnet and Strype. When Burnet began his work on the history of the Reformation, Moore had not formed his collection, and for Burnet the task was made no easier by his being refused access even to the Cotton library for a time. But the third part of the *History of the Reformation* appeared in 1715, and in it Burnet paid more than the demands of courtesy in his acknowledgements: 'No Curiosity pleased me more than that Noble Record of the Legate's Proceedings in the Matter of King *Henry*'s Divorce; of which I had the free Use, as of every Thing else that was in the Library of my Learned, and Dear Brother, the late Bishop of *Ely*; in whose Death the Church, and all his Friends, and none more than my self, have had an Invaluable Loss.'[93] The loss was indeed great, for by the time these words were

---

90 MS. Dd.12.40 fo. 54[v]. Among other books borrowed by Hudson was Isaac Casaubon's annotated copy of St Cyril of Jerusalem's catechetical lectures (Paris 1609) (note in Adv.e.34.15).

91 Hearne *Remarks and collections* 1 p. 64 (3 November 1705). On Hearne's later relations with Hudson see Macray *Annals* pp. 191–3.

92 Hearne *Remarks and collections* 1 pp. 183–4.

93 Burnet *The history of the Reformation* 3 (London 1715) p. vii. He returned to the subject on p. 46 in discussing the question more minutely.

published Moore's books had been moved away from London to Cambridge. In fact, however, there is less evidence of Burnet's using Moore's library than his remarks might lead one to suppose. Thomas Baker, with access to the books after their arrival at Cambridge, was able to supplement Burnet at a number of points,[94] and Moore's books make comparatively few appearances in the final volume of the *History of the Reformation*. John Strype seems to have been far better acquainted with the library as a scholar, and he too was able to supplement Burnet on one point, sending him a note of Moore's manuscript copy of Edmund Bonner's injunctions to his clergy in 1542 which provided a list of twenty-six further titles to the thirteen listed by Burnet as having been proscribed.[95]

Strype was among the most regular consultants of Moore's books. Three years older than Moore, he entered Jesus College, Cambridge, at the same time that the latter went up to Clare, though he moved to Catharine Hall a year later. The two had many interests in common, and in the preface to his life of Thomas Cranmer (1694) Strype expressed indirectly one of the purposes for which Moore's library has proved to be most valuable since. Writing wistfully of the dearth of ecclesiastical historians during the sixteenth and early seventeenth centuries, and the accompanying lack of contemporary evidence (as it seemed to him), he attributed these phenomena to the 'slothfulness of that age', relieved only by the industry of John Foxe. Strype himself owned Foxe's surviving papers, but failed to grasp the most obvious point, that the writing of religious history, inescapably partisan in the seventeenth century, was fraught with more dangers than the simply scholarly, and that the Reformation had until very recently been historically and politically too close for anything other than propaganda or apologetic to have found a wide and sympathetic audience. Strype noted a change 'of late years, when by length of time, and destruction of many Original MSS. by the Civil Wars,

---

[94] Baker's annotated copy is now Adv.a.52.2.
[95] Burnet *The history of the Reformation* 3 appendix p. 418, and MS. Nn.3.1.

divers remarkable Transactions were buried and lost', and 'some few Learned Men employed themselves in Collecting and Publishing what Memorials of Religion and the Church they could retrieve; as namely, Dr. *Fuller*, Dr. *Heylin*, and especially Dr. *Burnet*, now the Right Reverend Bishop of *Sarum*; to whom the *English* Church must be ever beholden for his great and happy Pains contributed hereunto'. He built his work on these, and continued, 'But yet there be good Gleanings after these Writers; and many things of remark there are, relating to the Church in those Three busie Reigns of *Henry*, *Edward*, and *Mary*, whereof these Historians are either wholly silent, or speak imperfectly, or erroneously: Some whereof in my Searches I have met with; which I have disposed in these Memorials.'[96]

Strype's biographer in the *Dictionary of National Biography* was scathing of his accuracy both as an historian and as a transcriber of the documents which form such long appendices to his works. In many cases these documents were drawn from Moore's library. Of the collections mentioned in the prefatory acknowledgements to his life of John Aylmer (1701), for example, this was the only private library to merit recognition by name, together with the State Paper Office, the Lambeth Palace Library, the records of the diocese of London, and the College of Heralds. 'The Right Reverend the Lord Bishop of Norwich,' he wrote, 'the Possessor of a great and curious Collection of MSS. and other antient printed Pieces, (little inferior to MSS. in regard of their Scarceness) hath also been very considerably assistant to me as well in this present Work, as in others, by that free Leave, nay and Invitation he hath given me to peruse, and make Transcriptions out of any of them.'[97] He turned to the library again for his *Annals of the Reformation* (1709) and his life of Edmund Grindal (1710), for

---

[96] J. Strype *Memorials of the Most Reverend Father in God, Thomas Cranmer* (London 1694) p. iii. For Strype see also W. D. J. Cargill Thompson 'John Strype as a source for the study of sixteenth-century English church history' in Derek Baker (ed.) *The materials, sources and methods of ecclesiastical history* (Studies in Church History 11, 1975) pp. 237-47.

[97] J. Strype *Historical collections of the life and acts of John Aylmer, Bishop of London* (London 1701) a2^r.

the latter working also from the libraries of Cotton, Robert Harley and Sir William Petyt and transcribing from Moore's collection material relating to the Dutch Church in London. A year later his life of Matthew Parker (1711) included long passages from a manuscript relating to Parker's gifts to Cambridge (MS. Gg.4.8) and from the pregnant correspondence of John Parkhurst, Bishop of Norwich from 1560 to 1575.[98] Moore took a particular interest in the life of Parker, and even agreed to support it publicly. John Wyat, the publisher of the book, sent Strype an account of his reception when he applied for the Bishop's recommendation during his efforts to gain the express goodwill of the episcopacy:

When your servt was here for the manuscript I was gone to my Lord of Ely's where I had been once before this morning & twice on monday but could not be admitted. But now I was. My Lord s^d: he wondred he had not seen me before. I told him how many times I had been to wait upon him. He said nobody had told him. He was very kind in shewing me the original paper he had drawn up to Recomend your Book, wch he afterwards got his Chaplain to Transcribe Fair, & when he had so done my Lord signed it. I send you a Coppy of it at ye Bottom. I think it is as ample a Recomendation as we could have desired ...

'whereas the Learned mr Strype has with much Faithfulness & skill written the Life of Arch Bishop Cranmer, & other Treatises containing many original papers relating to ye Ecclesiastical & Civil Affairs of this Realm, wherein the Rights & supremacy of ye Crown are maintained, the objections of papists confuted, & the piety, Justice & wisdom of ye first Reformers defended: And whereas he is now writeing the Life of ABp Parker in which he will Further Justify the Reformation of ye Church of England, & give Light in a number of particulars to ye History of it, wch will be of true Advantage to ye protestant Cause & Interest.

We do therefore earnestly Recomend his usefull & Judicious Labours to ye Learned as being truly worthy of their Favour & Encouragement.'[99]

In return for so many and great favours, Strype did what was in his power to thank Moore. In the winter of 1696/7 he offered three small notebooks containing John Lightfoot's manuscript diary relating principally to the Westminster

---

[98] MS. Ee.2.34. Cf. *The letter book of John Parkhurst, Bishop of Norwich ... 1571–5* ed. R. A. Houlbrooke (Norfolk Record Soc. 1975).   [99] MS. Add. 5 (181).

Assembly.[100] In 1700 he offered another, unidentified, printed book, but it was imperfect, and Wyat, acting as intermediary, was forced to write back to Strype, 'I perceive he is not willing to give any Great Rate for it, for he says he does not love Imperfect bookes.'[101] But Moore did welcome (according to Wyat) the dedication to him of Strype's edition of Lightfoot's *Remains*, published in 1700. In April that year Wyat showed him the proposed dedication, 'which he Read twice over, & objected nothing at all against it, & said you were very kind'. Appropriately, it paid especial attention to what Moore uniquely could offer:

I was willing also this way to express my Sense of Your Lordship's obliging Favours towards me, which You have been pleased to shew, not only upon Account of our antient Acquaintance, and equal Standing in the University, but chiefly in respect of those Studies I have of late addicted my self to; which You (a known Patron and Furtherer of all good Learning) have been always ready to assist and promote. You have, *my Lord*, afforded me the free Use of Your singular Library, stored with so many and so choice Manuscripts, together with such Antique, and to the present Generation scarce heard of, Books and Treatises, when Printing was but, as it were, in its Infancy. And besides, You have got me the sight of other valuable Manuscripts. Whereby I must gratefully acknowledge the considerable Improvements I have made in my Searches into the Historical Affairs of this Church, when it first began to reform Abuses, and to vindicate it self from *Rome*, and as it happily proceeded under our two first Protestant Princes ...[102]

Moore could only approve the sentiments, and there is some evidence that his collecting, taking full account of the history of anti-Catholic sentiment, was in part motivated by the same feelings. But although Strype, with his wide interests and ambitious projects, was in a better position than most to appreciate the scope of Moore's library, even he could not comment intelligently on all of it. Like everyone else faced

100 MSS. Dd.14.21–3. For Moore's letters on the subject cf. MSS. Add. 2 (192) and Add. 5 (205). Moore had hoped to acquire them in time to include them in Bernard's *Catalogi*, but negotiations became protracted and they arrived too late.
101 MS. Add. 2 (244).
102 Dedication to Lightfoot's *Genuine remains* (1700).

with a collection beyond everyday comprehension, he inevitably concentrated on details, and on what he knew; Bagford, naturally, did the same, and made the mistake (a curiously modern one) of failing to see the essential continuity between the manuscripts and early printed books on the one hand, and the modern portion of the collection on the other.

Both men were, in truth, faced with a library that for all Moore's personal interests was more akin to a national collection, where more appropriate terms of reference might have been couched in general principles, than to one of a private individual. But, as was to be proved after Moore's death in 1714, this was a perspective shared by only the most far-sighted in the early eighteenth century, and of which Cambridge was to show a practical understanding only very gradually.

4

THE MAKING OF THE ROYAL
LIBRARY

DESPITE THE DEMANDS of the scholarly world,[1] Moore's library was originally, and always remained to a great extent, a personal collection, begun at Cambridge and reflecting in the end innumerable interests. It was also one that contained, accidentally or deliberately, the tools of the late seventeenth-century ecclesiastical establishment, fully representative of theological debate of all periods: under this head can be included much history, geography, and law, as well as philosophy and the more obvious works of theological polemic. If it was, occasionally, less up to date than (for example) that of Evelyn in its coverage of modern books of general interest,[2] that was of little importance in the context of Moore's overall purposes. His curiosity about the history of printing led him to collect the earliest products of the press, and with conspicuous success in the case of English books. But many of his printed books of the fifteenth and early sixteenth centuries were amassed equally or more for their theological and historical interest as for their value as *curiosa*. Years later, Dibdin[3] remarked the comparative dearth of classical *editiones principes* in the University Library − an observation the less surprising in coming from the librarian of one whose passion they (fashionably) were. Much of the reason for this dearth was that Moore had taken no especial pains to collect them, and the University Library had come to rely on his collection of early

---

[1] See above, Ch. 3.

[2] On Evelyn's library cf. Sir Geoffrey Keynes *John Evelyn; a study in bibliophily with a bibliography of his writings* 2nd ed. (Oxford 1968). Evelyn's library was finally dispersed by Christie's in 1977−8.

[3] Notebook relating to a visit to Cambridge, now in the possession of the Duke of Plymouth.

printed books without considering very seriously where it might be improved.

Aside from his friendship with and patronage of the scholarly and ecclesiastical world, there is but little evidence of Moore's keenest interests beyond his library. Though a friend of scholars, and retaining his connections with Cambridge throughout his adult life, as well as with Oxford for a shorter period,[4] he wrote nothing himself beyond the calls of duty. His first published sermon,[5] preached before his namesake the Lord Mayor of London on 28 May 1682, appeared in print while he was yet chaplain to Heneage Finch, Earl of Nottingham, and twenty months later he preached before a similar congregation in the Guildhall on a subject of particularly topical interest, 'Of patience and submission to authority'. But it was as a preacher before the Queen that he gained renown, and two sermons in August 1690 were followed in March 1691/2 by a Lenten one 'Of religious melancholy' – a discourse that went into three editions that year and which Henry Hills thought it worth while to issue as late as 1708. He preached before the Queen again on Palm Sunday 1694, before the King in April 1696, in Westminster Abbey in January 1697/8, and on Anne's accession preached twice at court in February and March 1705/6. So much is recorded in his printed sermons.[6] When necessary his pastoral concerns could be tinged with other, political, reflections. The troubled months following the Rye House Plot, and the questions that accompanied them, are fully reflected in his sermon 'Of patience and submission to

[4] Moore was incorporated M.A. at Oxford on 15 July 1673. For Moore's later connections with Clare College see especially J. R. Wardale (ed.) *Clare College letters and documents* (Cambridge 1903) and W.J. Harrison *Life in Clare Hall, Cambridge, 1658–1713* (Cambridge 1958). His gifts to the College library included (in 1683) theological works by Jonas Schlichting, Johann Crell and Faustus Socinus, in 1684 the collected works of John Lightfoot published that year, and in 1705 the collected Erasmus (Basel 1540) and two editions of La Bigne's *Bibliotheca veterum patrum*.

[5] Many of his sermons, published separately in his lifetime, were gathered together by Samuel Clarke and published in collected form in 1715. In 1724 this volume was reissued with a new title-page and further sermons drawn from Moore's surviving papers.

[6] Besides his printed sermons, others survive in manuscript: cf. MSS. Dd.14.9, Dd.14.13 and Dd.14.15.

authority'. The Jesuits' decree against the Oath of Allegiance, passed in Ghent in 1681, was an obvious target for attack; but he also turned to history (and in particular to Pope Gregory VII) in a veritable orgy of historical allusion drawn from his own library. The most notable of his authorities included Sigebert of Gembloux, Otto of Freising, Trithemius, Onuphrius Panvinius, Pithou's Frankish Annals, Hotman's *Francogallia*, Paulus Aemylius' life of Childeric, Bellarmine, Cardinal Benno, Reinerius Reineccius, Labbé's Councils, Cuspinian, and Gilles' *Croniques et annales de France* – the last no longer among his books. Whatever Moore's bibliophilic interests, his collection was also a weapon of some power.

A few years later, on somewhat surer ground, he was still acidic on the subject of foreign Catholics. His sermon preached before William III, shortly after the attempt on the King's life planned at Richmond Park had been foiled in the spring of 1696, was similarly coloured by the contents of his library: on this occasion his authorities included Camden and two volumes of *numismata*, du Molinet's *Historia summorum pontificum per eorum numismata* (Paris 1679) and the Jesuit Claude François Menestrier's *Histoire du roy Louis le Grand par les médailles* (Paris 1689) – the last a work which drew Moore's particular opprobrium for Louis XIV 'who has suffered so many things to be said of him, not only full of rank Flattery, but which savour much of Blasphemy'.[7] In a more domestic key, he could draw on his collection when preaching to the House of Lords in 1697 on the anniversary of the execution of Charles I, quoting from Ussher's letters, Samuel Bochart, Milton's Εἰκονοκλάστης and his *Character of the Long Parliament*, as well as a small pamphlet containing *The humble advice and earnest desires of certain well-affected ministers, lecturers of Banbury and Brackley* (1649) and his manuscript of Thomas

---

7 *A sermon preached before the King at St. James's, April 16. 1696. Being a day of public thanksgiving* (1696) p. 12. The original 1689 edition of Menestrier's work is no longer among Moore's books, but there is a copy of the scurrilous Amsterdam piracy of 1691 including five extra plates denigrating Louis XIV: Moore's copy is bound up with N. Chevalier's *Histoire de Guillaume III . . . par médailles* (1692).

Fairfax's *Memorials written by himself*,[8] a work not published until it appeared in a much edited form in 1699, though several copies seem to have been in circulation before then. On a happier occasion he could turn to his books for the history of missionary endeavour when preaching to the Society for the Propagation of the Gospel in February 1712/13.

By no means all his sermons were forced to bear such a weight of printed evidence, and they were well enough regarded to be translated into Dutch by the same W. van Schie who supplied him with books for several years, and so be published at Delft in 1700.[9] Their publication abroad was one further reminder of Moore's close connections with the Low Countries, most obvious to the world in his relations with William III. When a collection of the King's private prayers, composed by Tillotson, appeared in 1704, it was Moore who provided the introduction to them: Moore's copy, printed on vellum, is at Cambridge with the manuscript of the prayers.[10] The little book proved an instant success, and two thousand copies were sold within a fortnight[11] – a circumstance which no doubt encouraged the appearance of a Dutch edition at The Hague, published by Joh. Kitto, while a French edition, translated by a Huguenot minister David Mazel, was published by Mortier and John Barnes (the latter the publisher of the English original) in 1704.

Moore's sermons were drawn particularly from the historical and theological portions of his library. But amidst a large general collection one subject stands out with particular prominence. His interest in medicine, in all its branches, can be traced from his days as an undergraduate in Cambridge. It was rare for him to put his signature in any of his books, and there are fewer than a dozen such examples to be found in his

---

[8] MS. Dd.14.25.   [9] *Zielroerende predicatien* (Delft 1700). See also below, pp.119–20.
[10] *A form of prayers used by His late Majesty, King William III. When he received the Holy Sacrament*, Sel.6.82 and MSS. Dd.14.11 and Dd.11.55. For Moore's account of the final illness of the King, contained in a letter to John Sharp on 7 March 1701/2, see A. Tindal Hart *The life and times of John Sharp, Archbishop of York* (1949) p. 210 n.2.
[11] Note to the Dutch edition *Koning Williams ziel-zugtingen* (The Hague, n.d.).

collection today. Among them are a pocket Lambinus edition of Cicero's *Epistolae ad familiares* (1585), acquired in his youth and, less expectedly, William Harvey's *Exercitationes de generatione animalium* (Amsterdam 1651) for which he paid 3s.8d. at Cambridge in 1663. By the time of his death there were few major – or indeed minor – medical books of the sixteenth and seventeenth centuries that were not in his library, though the fifteenth century was more meagrely treated. He gained a reputation for his willingness to dispense simple medicines, and was thus open to the importunities of those unable to reach or afford more qualified advice, and many of his books contain supplementary prescriptions added in his own hand.[12] His interest in the subject stretched from Galen to his own time, encompassing not only major standard works but also a host of less enduring products of more recent enthusiasms such as Lodowick Rowzee's *Queens wells, that is a treatise of the nature and vertues of Tunbridge water* (1671) or Robert Pierce's *Bath memories: or, observations in three and forty years practice, at the Bath* (Bristol 1697). When William Cowper's *Anatomy of humane bodies*, easily the largest and most striking medical book to appear in England in Moore's lifetime, was published in 1698, he had it specially bound in turkey leather by Christopher Hussey.[13]

Scarcely surprisingly, Moore's medical curiosity attracted the attention of authors as well as of patients. His namesake, practising as an apothecary in Abchurch Lane in the City, dedicated his *Arcana Mooreana; or, a succinct and lucid discourse of the origine ... and cure of the cholick* to him in 1713. The

[12] Cf. MSS. Dd.3.64 (53), a letter from Thomas Moore in Yarmouth to Moore, 19 December 1690, requesting medicine to treat jaundice for his sister-in-law, and Dd.3.64 (65), a letter from Elizabeth Newett to Moore as Bishop of Ely, asking for medicine. Moore's penchant was sufficiently well known to be celebrated in verse in 1709 in *The chimney-sweeper in disgrace, or a dialogue between the Lord Bishop of — and T.N. chimney-sweeper in St. Margaret's parish* (Foxon C 150; cf. Hearne *Remarks and collections* 2 p. 110 (25 May 1708)).

[13] Private accounts (Cambridge University Library Church Commissioners Papers CC 95579–80) 6 July 1698; the binding of this and another unidentified book cost him 13s.6d., which suggests that he provided the leather. The volume now stands at Tab.b.135. Moore called on Hussey's services regularly in 1697–8.

apothecary was not held in universal esteem by other members of the medical world; being under an 'indispensible necessity ... to vindicate [my] reputation in the *knowledge* and *practice* of physick, against the malicious calumnies and detractions of my *enemies*,' he explained, 'I hope I shall not be charg'd either with *vanity* or *rashness* in publishing these brief *essays*; which are design'd for no other end, but that by reading this little *manual*, those that are strangers to my person, may be convinc'd ... that I am legally qualified for the exercise of the *art* I profess, maugre the inveterate *malice* of all opposers'.[14] Conrad Sprengell, formerly of Leipzig and practising in London, dedicated his *Aphorisms of Hippocrates, to which are added, aphorisms upon the small-pox, measles, and other distempers, not so well known to former more temperate ages* (1708) to Moore as well. Like the apothecary Moore, Sprengell was not a member of the established medical circles in London, though he was later to be admitted to the College of Physicians, and he managed in his dedication to draw a neat, if hackneyed, parallel between Moore's dual concerns for the soul and the body: 'To render the Operations of the Mind Regular, which is the Province of a Divine, it is necessary to preserve the Body in its due Tone and Order, as being the Instrument of its operations.'[15]

Moore was not of course unique in his interests in medical books. Francis Bernard was a competitor both for them and for Caxtons until his death in 1698; and Sloane was an equally strong contender from the early 1680s;[16] these circumstances may partly explain the absence of many fifteenth-century editions from his library: his copy of Ketham's *Fasciculus medicinae* in the Venice edition of 1500 came from the Knyvett family, and never passed through the hands of the metropolitan trade. Nonetheless, in his medical manuscripts he outshone

---

[14] *Arcana Mooreana* (1713), Epistle dedicatory. The dedication did not protect him from Pope, whose verses 'To the ingenious Mr. Moore, author of the celebrated worm-powder' appeared in 1716: cf. Foxon P 978 etc.
[15] *The aphorisms of Hippocrates* (1708), Dedication.
[16] Cf. J. L. Wood in *Factotum* 2 (June 1978) and Jeremiah S. Finch 'Sir Hans Sloane's printed books' *The Library* 4th ser. 22 (1942) pp. 67–72.

Bernard with ease, while his printed books were in several cases remarkable for their provenance. Among those from seventeenth-century libraries may be instanced in this respect Sir George Ent's own copy of the first edition (1651) of Harvey's *De generatione animalium*, acquired presumably on or shortly after Ent's death in 1689: Ent had been responsible for persuading Harvey to publish this his third and final major work, and his manuscript notes as well as a congratulatory poem by Harvey's family doctor Baldwin Hamey are spread across the flyleaves. From Sir Théodore de Mayerne's library Moore acquired a valuable group of manuscripts and some printed books. On his death in 1655 Mayerne had left his library to the College of Physicians, where most of it was consequently destroyed in the Great Fire in 1666 that burned Harvey's books. But a number of his manuscripts and more important books seem never to have been received by the College, and now survive in various libraries. Several went to Sloane,[17] and among those which passed to Moore were a substantial group of manuscript notebooks kept by Mayerne including case-books and pharmacopoeiae,[18] his annotated copy of the *Pharmacopoeia Londinensis* (1618) for which he had been partially responsible, and his copy of Vesalius *De humani corporis fabrica* (Basel 1543): it was in some ways the core of Mayerne's working library, while Moore's own particular interest in James I's physician received acknowledgement in the dedication to him of Joseph Browne's edition of Mayerne's works published in 1700.[19]

Walter Charleton's library also yielded a useful group of books, which, though less spectacular than those belonging to Mayerne, nevertheless included a copy of the *Pharmacopoeia*

---

[17] Cf. Edward J. Scott *Index to the Sloane manuscripts in the British Museum* (1904) pp. 349–50.

[18] MSS. Dd.4.21, Dd.4.33 (marked 'No. 23' on the cover), Dd.5.24 (no. 36), Dd.5.25 (no. 20), Dd.5.26, Dd.10.65 and Dd.11.85 (no. 49). Several of Mayerne's books were sold with Sir John Colladon's library (2 February 1713), but none of those belonging to Moore appears in the catalogue.

[19] The other dedicatees were William III, John Radcliffe and William Gibbons. For Joseph Browne see *DNB*.

Collegii Regalis Londini (1677) with additional biographical notes and prescriptions written out by Charleton himself. The spoils on this occasion also included a number of books of less immediate medical interest: Zenocarus *De vita Caroli Quinti* (Antwerp 1596), Prideaux *Marmora Oxoniensia* (1676, acquired by Charleton in 1677) and Sir John Marsham *Chronicus canon, aegyptiacus, ebraicus, graecus* (1672, a gift from the author). In this connection, too, may be mentioned two works by Charleton (rather than from his library) in Moore's collection bearing adversaria, his *Physiologia Epicuro-Gassendo-Charletoniana* (1654) annotated by William Brouncker, and his *Onomasticon Zoicon* (1668) with notes by an anonymous hand. I have been unable to discover by what means Moore acquired these, nor can much light be shed on the manner in which a group of Charles Bernard's books came into his hands. Bernard's books were sold at auction in March 1711; and as it was a sale that came towards the end of Moore's life, when his collection of medical books was already well formed, the books bearing Bernard's signature are of some interest. They include four medical books, Eustachius *Opuscula anatomica* (Venice 1564), van Horne Μικροτεχνη (Leiden 1668), Hornung *Cista medica* (Nuremburg 1626) and Thomas Bartholin *De luce animalium* (Leiden 1647), besides two books of a quite different nature, Gilles Ménage's *Discours* on Terence's *Heautontimorumenos* (Utrecht 1690) and du Fresnoy's *L'art de peinture* (Paris 1673). The Eustachius had been bought at the auction by a recently established bookseller, Benjamin Cowse of St Paul's Churchyard, for £1.7s.0d., and there is no reason to suppose that he was acting on commission from Moore, who must be presumed to have gathered Bernard's copies of these books from the booksellers piecemeal.

Moore's interests were wide,[20] and when his library arrived

---

[20] He was involved in the rebuilding of St Paul's Cathedral (HMC Portland 10 pp. 101, 114), and his collection contains most of the major sixteenth- and seventeenth-century architectural authorities.

at Cambridge in 1715 it was a startlingly different collection compared with what was already in the University Library. In the first years after their arrival Thomas Baker, the most knowledgeable person about the Library at the time, naturally – in view of his own interests – seized on the early books; and for many years the logistics of cataloguing Moore's library tended to obscure the exact nature of the additions outside this most obvious of fields. But of major late seventeenth-century works alone the list of those now in the University Library for the first time was prodigious. So Newton's *Principia* (1687) and *Opticks* (1704), Burnet's *Theory of the earth* (1684–90), Halley's *Miscellanea curiosa* (1705–7), and both the quarto and folio *Opera* of John Wallis (1665–7 and 1693–9) arrived where none had been before. Boyle's *Sceptical chymist* also made its first entry, in the second edition of 1680. In the other natural sciences, the Library had not hitherto possessed Hooke's *Micrographia* (1655), Lister's *Historia conchyliorum* (1685–92), Lhuyd's *Lithophylacii Britannici ichnographia* (1699), Ray's *Synopsis animalium* (1693), or Willoughby's *Ichthyographia* (1685) and *De historia piscium* (1686). Moore's medical library has already been remarked on, and the additions to the Cambridge collection were legion, including even such standard works as Willis's *Cerebri anatome* (1664) and *Pharmaceutice rationalis* (1674), Lower's *De corde* (1669) and Harvey's *Anatomical exercises* (1653). Nor could it be said that the sciences generally were less strong than the humanities, where the Library might – perhaps – have been expected to be more representative. Here too examples must suffice. They ranged from Henry More's *Antidote against swearing* (1653) and Glanvill's *Vanity of dogmatizing* (1661) to Locke's *Essay concerning humane understanding* (1690) and his first and second *Letters* concerning toleration (Moore's copy of the first was the second edition, of 1690), Petty's *Political arithmetick* (1690) and *Political anatomy of Ireland* (1691), and Potter's *Archaeologiae Graecae* (Oxford 1697). The gaps in editions of classical authors that were now filled included even Hudson's Thucydides (1696) and Josephus (1702), Bentley's editions of Horace (Cambridge 1711) and Callimachus (1697), and Joshua Barnes' of Homer (Cambridge 1711). Rather different, Ogilby's *Iliad* (1660) and *Odyssey* (1669) had not hitherto belonged to the Library, nor Dryden's more recent Virgil published in 1697. And, also for the first time, early editions of Milton now graced the University Library shelves, among them the 1669 *Paradise lost*, the first edition of *Paradise regain'd* and *Samson Agonistes* (1671), three editions of the History of Britain (1670, 1671 and 1677) and the two crucial collections of his poetry published in 1645 and 1673. The University Library acquired in Moore's collection its first collected Shakespeare (the fourth folio of 1685) – the earliest it was to possess for nearly two hundred years, until Samuel Sandars left a complete set of all four folios on his death in 1894. There was a modest collection of contemporary drama; the Dennis–Collier pamphlet war was well represented; but in contemporary or near contemporary poets Moore's library offered an abundance that the University Library had never attempted. Dryden was present in several editions of his *Religio laici* and in his *Fables* (1700) and *Comedies* (1701), but here also were half a dozen editions of Waller and the verses of lesser luminaries such as Alexander Radcliffe, Lady Mary Chudleigh, Charles Cotton, and Joshua Poole of Clare College, whose *English Parnassus: or a help to English poesie, containing a collection of all the rhyming monosyllables* had appeared posthumously in 1677. For the University Library, the collection broke completely new ground in also bringing an assortment of newspapers for the first time and one or two modern writing books including John Ayres' *Tutor to penmanship* (1698, bought for £1.1s.6d. on 27 April 1700) and Shelley's *Penman's magazine* (1705).

Nor did Moore's interests stop at books. Like a growing number of collectors he possessed a series of engravings, of portraits, views, dress, street cries, and reproductions of paintings and sculpture, besides separate engravings, most of which have been dispersed.[21] Unlike books, engravings were not cheap. 'A large picture of St. Peter's Church' cost £2.5s.od. on 5 January 1705, the London bookseller Luke Stokoe received £7.5s.od. for a large folio collection of sixty-two 'cutts' in February 1707, 'Two large books of Cutts' bought from Cooper in January 1704 cost £7.10s.6d., a smaller collection of illustrations to the Bible from the same source the following month cost £1.15s.od., and an unidentified picture of Erasmus cost thirty shillings in February 1700.[22]

The University Library had received no significant collection of modern foreign literature since the bequest of Henry Lucas in 1664, and had done little to buy any. Moore's library introduced for the first time Bossuet's *Discours sur l'histoire universelle* (Paris 1681) and Spinoza's *Tractatus theologico politico* ('Hamburg' 1670), and began to make good the omissions. But despite this wealth there were inevitable lacunae, that were to become most noticeable in English literature. The fourth folio and the 1655 *King Lear* were Moore's sum collection of Shakespearean drama, and he did not attempt to collect other late Elizabethan or Jacobean literature to anything like the same extent as he did for the earlier part of the sixteenth century; on the whole he remained content with collected editions. The books perhaps lacked that appeal of age that led him to amass the finest collection extant for many years of literary texts published by Caxton, Wynkyn de Worde and Pynson, while the books of the first half of the sixteenth century, the period of the Reformation, were of peculiar and even topical interest in their own right.

---

21 The best were transferred to the Fitzwilliam Museum in 1876 (see below, pp. 747–8), but two volumes remain (LE.40.30 and F165.bb.2.2) containing views of Rome, reproductions of paintings including Raphael's *School of Athens* and his *Battle of the Milvian Bridge* – both by the fertile G. G. de Rossi. Moore's collection of de Rossi's publications included also his engravings of Raphael's *Imagines Veteris ac Novi Testamenti* (Rome 1674) and a copy of *Veteres arcus Augustorum triumphis insignes* (Rome 1690) perhaps bound specially for Moore. Copies of G. G. de Rossi's catalogue of 1699 and of that of his heir Domenico de Rossi (1709) are among Moore's books. Most of the engravings in LE.40.30 are by de Rossi, but the volume also includes several by Orlandi and Silvestre as well as a series of architectural engravings of Blenheim Palace.

22 Details from Moore's private accounts (see note 13 above).

Moore's collection of incunabula has been fully described and catalogued elsewhere.[23] But notable as it is, and renowned as it was in his own lifetime, it is now smaller than it was once. In the eighteenth century John Taylor drew up a list of the University Library's fifteenth-century printed books, of which he identified 382, among them 240 from Moore's collection. Thanks to fresh knowledge of undated and anonymously printed books, and to prolonged searches on the shelves by Henry Bradshaw and his successors, some 469 items are now attributed to Moore's collection in the current catalogue of incunabula. But while no acceptable catalogue of his incunabula (or of his other early printed books) was made until the 1720s,[24] in the 1690s their importance was considered to be sufficient for them to be included in Bernard's *Catalogi* – a work whose concern was more with manuscripts than with printed books. Not always accurate, and occasionally frustratingly incomplete in its details, the list printed in the *Catalogi* is nevertheless the fullest reliable record available of the point to which Moore's collecting had taken him by the mid-nineties,[25] and it is of further interest in having been compiled just before the influence of Harley and Wanley came to dominate the trade in early books, whether manuscript or printed. The list is not an entirely satisfactory tool for detailed analysis, but if its mistranscriptions and other inadequacies are set aside, and only an approximation of the collection attempted, then it appears that by the summer of 1697 Moore possessed something over one-quarter of the final total of incunabula he was eventually to accumulate: this is likely to be a serious underestimate, as it ignores all books not identified as having been printed in the fifteenth century and does not treat

---

[23] By J. C. T. Oates in his *Catalogue*.   [24] See below, p. 184.

[25] The only catalogue of Moore's printed books as a whole (and that incomplete) was begun in the mid-nineties, and is divided into three parts roughly according to format, Bodleian Library MSS. Add. D.81 and D.81* (respectively octavos etc. and folios) and Cambridge University Library MS. Oo.7.49 (quartos). Unfortunately they were continued only intermittently after the first few years, and although books were still being added in 1713 coverage in Moore's latter years is poor. For the catalogue of his books compiled at Cambridge see below, pp. 193–5.

single volumes containing several texts in a consistent manner. But on this basis it appears that his collection of Caxtons (not, on the whole, difficult to identify) was still less than half-way to its final total. On the other hand he already possessed virtually all the Aldus imprints he was to obtain: in the following seventeen years he added only about seven more fifteenth-century editions. Again, the Aldines were easy to pick out, and the statistical distortions in the rest of the collection can only be surmised.

Of those early English books that were already in Moore's possession in 1697, and attracted the attention of the cata-loguer, the Caxtons comprised the Bruges *Game and play of chess* (but none of Moore's eventual three copies of the *Recuyell of the histories of Troy*), the *Dicts or sayings of the philosophers*, the double volume containing the *Description of Britain* and the *Chronicles of England*, Cicero on old age, and one of his two copies of Higden's *Polychronicon*, as well as a volume described laconically in the *Catalogi* as 'English Poems, by Chaucer, &c.', almost certainly to be identified with the celebrated collection of quartos, several unique, that has continued to attract fascinated scholars ever since. The similar, if less obviously spectacular, collections of pamphlets printed by Wynkyn de Worde were described in detail, unlike the Caxton volume, and to these products of the later English press described in the *Catalogi* may also be added Wynkyn de Worde's *Polychronicon* and his *Jerome*, three products of Pynson's press, and the St Albans *Rhetorica nova* now in the Bodleian Library. Moore already possessed the copy of the Oxford Rufinus ('1468') that had once belonged to James Goldwell, his ancestor in the see of Norwich, as well as Alexander ab Alexandria's *Expositio super libros Aristotelis De anima*, but not yet (apparently) the Oxford editions of John Lathbury, Terence, Richard Rolle or William Lyndewode. And to continue the litany of English books before passing abroad, his early sixteenth-century books numbered, among many, Richard Whitford's *Werke for housholders*, now unique, and such rarities as Walter Burley's

Tractatus perbrevis de materia et forma printed by John Scolar in
1518, and Edmund Becke's translation of Erasmus' *Two
dyaloges* printed by John Mychell in Canterbury in about 1550.
The achievement of such a collection seems clear enough, but
thanks to misprints and misunderstandings the list appears also
to include several books that may be more properly described
as ghosts: the Oxford Lyndewode *Provinciale* [1483], just
mentioned, almost certainly lurks behind an alleged (and
otherwise unknown) edition of ten years later.

To turn from English incunables to continental is to face a
wealth to which selection can do scant justice; for although
Moore was (apparently) to strengthen and improve his
collection to a degree not equalled by any preceding generation of English book collectors, by 1697 he had laid the
foundations and many of the most important books in this
category were already in his possession. Of major *editiones
principes* he possessed Aristotle and Aristophanes, as well as the
Florence Homer of 1488. Among the Aldines, already alluded
to, were the *Thesaurus* of 1496 and Politian of 1498 and, in
the post-incunabular period, Pollux *Vocabularium* (1502),
Philoponus on Aristotle (1504), Philostratus *De vita Apollonii
Tyanei*, Stephanus *De urbibus* (1502), Erasmus *Adagia* (1508) and
Bessarion (1503), as well as (probably – the evidence is not
quite conclusive) the 1513 Plato. Of five books printed by the
first printers at Rome listed as his in the modern catalogue of
incunables, he possessed, according to the *Catalogi* list, only
Cyprian (1471). So far he had met with more success in
collecting the earliest Venetian printing, notably the De Spira
De civitate Dei and a volume of the 1470 Livy,[26] and from
Jenson's press (singled out like Aldus for particular notice in the
list) the 1470 Cicero *Rhetorica* and Laurentius Valla of 1471.
The 1471 Valdarfer Cicero *Orationes* was also in Moore's
possession by 1697, as was a rare work from the press of
Balthazar Azoguidus, the first printer at Bologna, Andrea da

---

[26] Later to be much celebrated and shown to visitors at Cambridge: see Oates *Catalogue*
p. 287.

Barberino's *Vita del magnifico cavaliero Guerino* (1475). Of various minor errors in the list of Venetian incunabula one proved somewhat more misleading than others. No. 82 described a *Decameron* published at Venice in 1470, whose true identity was not established until many years later. It misled the eighteenth century, and Dibdin profferred a correction on a visit to Cambridge, when he wrote a note in the volume: 'I can most confidently pronounce it to be an extremely defective and barbarously cut copy of the edition printed by Petrus Adam de Michaelibus at Mantua in 1472' – an assertion repeated by Hartshorne in 1829.[27] The confidence of both men turned out to be misplaced, and the misleading information on the added manuscript title-page has now been set aside in Mr Oates' catalogue: the book is in fact Balthazar Azoguidus' edition printed in Bologna in 1476,[28] and not the earliest, otherwise unknown, edition of the *Decameron* at all.

Of the French incunables which Moore had acquired by 1697, one of the most arresting was a volume containing two works of Franciscus de Platea, printed by the first Paris printers, and Albrecht von Eyb's *Margarita poetica*, the product of Gering alone. So far as can be gathered from Bernard's list, Moore did not yet possess the celebrated Bible of 1476/7 with its date altered to read 1463 – a falsehood which misled Maittaire and which set the Harleys on a hopeless chase.[29] Nor did he yet own the *Speculum humanae vitae* of 1472, still the earliest book in the University Library to have been printed in France. But two notable *liturgica* were already among his books, the *Missale Xanctonense* printed by Higman in Paris in 1491 and the much less bulky Sarum *Horae* printed by Pigouchet in 1498, both on vellum. And finally, to remove from France and to return as it were to the beginning, the earliest printed book listed in the 1697 catalogue was the Mainz *Catholicon* dated 1460, to which the compiler of the list (perhaps Wanley himself at this point) gave exceptionally detailed treatment. Moore also had one of

---

[27] Hartshorne *Book rarities* p. 46.   [28] Oates *Catalogue* no. 2474.   [29] *Ibid.*, p. 19.

his eventual two copies of the Nuremberg Chronicle (1493), Koberger's Latin Bible in four volumes (1497, since reduced by loss to two) and a volume of unusual curiosity on the Ottomans comprising Georgius de Hungaria *De moribus Turcorum* (Urach, n.d.), Mahomet II *Epistolae magni Turci* (Cologne, n.d.), the *Historia septem sapientum Romae* (Gouda, n.d.) and Ludovicus Brunus *Carmina in adventu et coniugio Maximiliani* (Louvain 1477).

This part of Moore's library therefore, impressive as it was by the summer of 1698 as the last sheets of Bernard's *Catalogi* were being printed, was only a fraction of what he was to accumulate by 1714. While there are almost certainly lacunae in the printed list, and various mistakes either in the cataloguing or its printing may mislead the unwary, he was, on the basis of this evidence, still to amass the greater part of his collection. Thus he appears to have acquired after 1697 Adolf Rusch's edition of Dionysius on Valerius Maximus in a 'Maioli' binding, Cicero *De officiis* in the editions of 1465 and 1466, Breydenbach's *Itinerarium* (1486), a group of five further books published by Vindelinus de Spira, Boccaccio *Genealogiae* (Venice 1494/5) in a binding by the late sixteenth-century University Printer Thomas Thomas,[30] a Greek *Psalter* (Venice 1486) formerly in the possession of the Jesuits in Paris, the first edition of Trithemius (1494), and the volume containing two scarce devotional works in French (both printed at Lyon): Pierre Desrey's Life of Christ printed by Balsarin in 1498/9 and Maurice de Sully's *Expositions des Évangiles* attributed to Martin Havard.

On the other hand a number have been lost. Of the 240 books listed by Taylor in the eighteenth century, six were

---

[30] This may well have been missed by the cataloguer, being bound after a copy of Hyginus' *Fabularum liber* (Basel 1535). The volume once belonged to Thomas Bradocke, Fellow of Christ's from 1579 to 1587, Headmaster of Reading School and translator of Jewell into Latin; but although his initials are on the top cover it is not clear that he was responsible for the binding (on which cf. Shrewsbury School A.VI.1 : J. B. Oldham *Shrewsbury School bindings; a catalogue* (Oxford 1943) p. 20), and John Morris 'Thomas Thomas, Printer to the University of Cambridge 1583–8. Part 2' *Trans. Cambridge Bibliographical Soc.* 4 (1968) pp. 339–62, at p. 351.

recognized as having been lost by 4 February 1736, and in his work on the incunabula Mr Oates was able to identify fourteen now missing from the Royal Library including Taylor's six.[31] Some may have been sold, but there is no evidence for this.[32] The list is headed by the *editio princeps* of Cicero *De officiis* printed by Fust and Schoeffer in 1465 on vellum; it includes also the *editio princeps* of Sallust (V. de Spira, Venice 1470) and two important books from the Low Countries, Boccaccio *De claris mulieribus* (Louvain 1487) and a *Directorium Sarisburiense* (Gerard Leeu, Antwerp 1488) of which Duff records but half a dozen copies. To these can be added several, not listed in the modern catalogue of incunabula, which appear in the catalogues of Moore's library begun by Samuel Clarke in the 1690s and which, however incomplete, offer further particulars of the collection. The details in these catalogues are not always accurate, and over a dozen editions unknown to modern bibliographers must be set aside as either actual or possible errors. But after these have been omitted the list includes a group of classical editions, notably Poliziano's translation of Herodian (Rome 1493), a Juvenal (Venice 1494), a Terence (Venice 1494) and Pliny's *Historia naturalis* (Venice 1496); other Italian books include Beroaldus *De felicitate* (Bologna 1499) and *Declamatio philosophi* (Bologna 1497), Angelus de Clavasio *Summa angelica* (Venice 1492), Jacobus Brutus *Corona aurea* (Venice 1496/7), Gaietanus *Expositio in libros Aristotelis de caelo*

---

[31] Oates *Catalogue* pp. 50–1.

[32] Some have been sold since the eighteenth century, including a copy of Caxton's *Royal Book*, disposed of in 1862, and a second copy of *The doctrinal of sapyence* formerly bound up with a *Royal Book*, *The book of good manners* and *The dicts or sayings of the philosophers*, exchanged with Ellis in 1870 and sold at the Huth sale on 13 June 1912 for £310 to Quaritch, (See below, p. 664, and S. de Ricci *A census of Caxtons* (Bibliographical Soc. 1909) p. 51.) One further (Oates 3837, the *Recuyell of the histories of Troy*) has since been exchanged (in 1960) as a duplicate with H. P. Kraus in return for the Ripon Cathedral copy of Caxton's *Vocabulary* (now Inc. 4084.5), one of four copies known; some leaves of Inc. 3837 were transferred to the copy retained (Inc. 3838) before the transaction was completed. See J. C. T. Oates and L. C. Harmer *Vocabulary in French and English; a facsimile of Caxton's edition c. 1480* (Cambridge 1964), *Fifty-five books printed before 1525 representing the work of England's first printers; an exhibition from the collection of Paul Mellon* (Grolier Club 1968) pp. 3–4, and H. P. Kraus *A rare book saga* (New York 1978) pp. 246–8.

et mundo (Venice 1484), Laurentius Valla *Elegantiae linguae latinae* (Venice 1496), a *Legenda aurea* (Venice 1500), a second copy of the Jenson Bible of 1476 and one of Jenson's edition of 1479. The German disappearances are much less numerous (Moore never possessed as many German incunables as he did Italian), and comprise principally Koberger's edition of Guillermus Parisiensis (1496) and the 1496 Grüninger edition of the *Legenda aurea*. Of the Low Countries books, several entries cannot be substantiated, but they include a volume containing Isidore's *Synonyma* (Antwerp 1488), Petrus de Alliaco *Libellus sacramentalis* (Louvain 1487) and an unidentified edition of Gerson *De regulis mandatorum*. Finally, among books printed for the English trade there were several rarities, including Mirk's *Liber festivalis* in the Rouen edition of 1495. The St Albans *Rhetorica nova* (1480), borrowed by Thomas Tanner, was never returned.[33] The list is hardly an encouraging one, and although the University sold off duplicates from the Royal Library in the 1740s, no incunabula were sold on these occasions, and the losses point to theft.

By the time he died, Moore had acquired books from most of the major collections sold in England since the auction of Lazarus Seaman's library in 1676.[34] Volumes from the Bysshe, Richard Smith, Anglesey, Cecil, Lauderdale, Britton, Bernard and Spanheim sales can all still be identified on the shelves, amid many more whose provenance has been forgotten. Others – a majority – came from collections that had never been auctioned. But the evidence of how or when Moore bought his books, and of the order in which he assembled his collection, is disappointingly sparse. Very little of his correspondence still exists, and even less relating to his books; his diaries, scribbled in the blank leaves of almanacs, are meagre and incomplete; the booksellers' and auctioneers' catalogues in

[33] See p. 66 above.
[34] He gave one book from Seaman's library (Cl. Paradin's *Quadrins historiques de la Bible* (J. de Tournes, Lyon 1558)) to his son Daniel. The volume came to the University Library among Sir Geoffrey Keynes' books in 1982.

his collection bear few annotations; and even in those few surviving auction catalogues that bear names of buyers as well as notes of prices realized, his name occurs only infrequently. Apart from a series of general domestic accounts kept between 1691 and 1710, maintained naturally with no especial care in matters relating to the library, the principal sources of information among his surviving books and papers are therefore the books themselves.

Moore's opportunities for, and consequent successes in, gathering local treasures were much less than those enjoyed by some of his contemporaries on the continent, who could exploit the hopes and fears of religious houses. As a diocese, Norwich proved comparatively profitable; but in the diocese of Ely the situation was different, and the poverty of most of the area covered by the diocese, coupled with the proximity of Cambridge, help to explain the lack of books culled locally there compared with the conspicuous numbers amassed in the richer and more populous counties of Norfolk and Suffolk. The largest local collection to pass into his hands from the diocese of Norwich was the library of the Knyvett family of Ashwellthorpe, a few miles south of Wymondham.[35] The collection, founded in the early years of the sixteenth century but built mainly by Sir Thomas Knyvett (c. 1539–1618) had been added to by his grandson, and on the extinction of the direct male line of descent it was dispersed. Almost all the seventy manuscripts (including an important group of Middle English manuscripts) that had once belonged to Knyvett came into Moore's hands, together with printed books on subjects ranging from astronomy to cookery, zoology, architecture and the law, and including a particularly fine collection of sixteenth-century illustrated books, a carefully selected group of medical books, and a number of books in Spanish and

---

[35] Cf. D. McKitterick *The library of Sir Thomas Knyvett of Ashwellthorpe (c. 1539–1618)* (Cambridge 1978). Moore acquired the Knyvett books presumably in or some time after 1693. On 12 April 1695 he paid twenty-seven shillings for carriage of books from Norwich to London, but there is nothing to connect this with the Knyvett books: he kept books in both places. See also below, p. 128.

Italian; as usual it had been formed with no particular eye to modern English literature.

But if this was the largest cache to come from a Norfolk private library, there were also many smaller additions. Emanating from the library of his predecessor James Goldwell (Bishop of Norwich from 1472 to 1499) came two fifteenth-century printed books, Rufinus *Expositio Symboli S. Hieronymi* (1478, the first book printed at Oxford, in which it seems possible that Goldwell was intimately involved as patron)[36] and an exceedingly rare edition of Ovid *Metamorphoses* printed by Bocard in Paris in 1496. Trechsel's edition of Augustine *Opus quaestionum* (Lyon 1497) had been in Norwich certainly in 1617, and the itinerant Jean de Vingle's edition of Cicero *Epistolae ad familiares* (Lyon 1496) came from the Feckenham family. From the library of George Gardiner, dean of Norwich from 1573 to 1589, came Amerbach's folio Bible in seven volumes with Hugo de S. Caro's commentary. And to these early printed books may be added as an additional example Moore's copy of Payne Fisher *Tombes, monuments, and sepulchral inscriptions, lately visible in St. Paul's Cathedral,* printed for the author in 1684 and given by him to Sir Robert Baldock, Recorder of Yarmouth: Baldock died in 1691, and Moore presumably acquired it shortly after, either in London or in Norfolk. Many such books with local provenances had of course already travelled up to town before Moore ever saw them. An edition of Bertrandus *De jurisdictione ecclesiastica contra Petrum de Cugneriis* (1496) issued and still bound up as usual with the *Vita et processus sancti Thomae Cantuariensis,* printed by Philippi in Paris, had been in Wigginhall St Mary, away to the west of the county, in the sixteenth century, but had passed into the hands of the antiquary and Royalist pamphleteer Fabian Philipps (d. 1690). Among manuscripts, Coke's autograph notes on legal cases in 1608–10 had been in London at least since 1658, when they had been in the

---

[36] A. C. de la Mare and Lotte Hellinga 'The first book printed in Oxford: the *Expositio symboli* of Rufinus' *Trans. Cambridge Bibliographical Soc.* 7 (1978) pp. 184–244.

possession of Henry Twyford;[37] but it seems unlikely that the
Elizabethan Bishop of Norwich John Parkhurst's correspondence with the continental reformers, Matthew Parker and
others, had ever left Norwich.[38] A crudely illuminated and
now battered fifteenth-century Sarum *Horae* had once been in
the hands of the Colman family and of William Barber of New
Buckenham, and a second *Horae* came from another Norfolk
source, bearing the names of Tilney and Derham.

As for institutional rather than private provenances, by the
end of the seventeenth century there were comparatively few
manuscripts of monastic origin for sale compared with a
century previously. Many of those from Norwich Cathedral
priory, for example, had already found their way into
Cambridge University Library and Corpus Christi College
thanks to Andrew Perne and Matthew Parker.[39] Moore
managed to accumulate a small group of five of them
nevertheless, though only two of these bear ownership
inscriptions. The five comprised a thirteenth-century pseudo-
Dionysius etc., a fourteenth-century collection of astronomical notes, a thirteenth-century Avicenna among the Knyvett
manuscripts (given to Sir Thomas Knyvett by a Norwich
bookseller in 1567), a fifteenth-century pseudo-Augustine,
and a gift from Peter Le Neve, a thirteenth-century miscellany
by John Beleth, Alanus de Insulis etc. which had belonged
formerly to Bassingbourne Gawdy of West Harling.[40] In 1698
there came into his hands – not from any local source but via
the London trade – a group of records relating to Bury St
Edmunds. Moore already possessed a fifteenth-century *Horae*
associated with the church there,[41] but though he never owned

37 See J. H. Baker 'Coke's notebooks and the sources of his reports' *Cambridge Law Journal* 30 (1972) pp. 59–86.
38 MS. Ee.2.34. See *The letter book of John Parkhurst, Bishop of Norwich . . . 1571–5* ed. R. A. Houlbrooke (Norfolk Record Soc. 1975).
39 N. R. Ker 'Medieval manuscripts from Norwich Cathedral Priory' *Trans. Cambridge Bibliographical Soc.* 1 (1949) pp. 1–28. Oates *History* pp. 137–8.
40 MSS. respectively Ee.1.4, Gg.6.3, Mm.3.16, Ff.6.44 and Ff.5.28.
41 MS. Ee.1.14 (Ker *Medieval libraries* p. 219).

any books from the abbey library he now acquired half a dozen manuscripts relating to its possessions.[42]

Norwich had long been the second city in England, the centre of one of the most populous and prosperous areas of the country, accessible from Cambridge and the west as well as from the sea and from the south of East Anglia.[43] The diocese had in the fourteenth century supported a very considerable trade in manuscripts, quite apart from importing specially commissioned ones from the London shops.[44] But by the end of the seventeenth century the region was not only challenged in its economic supremacy: it had also been well gleaned, particularly of its early manuscripts, and to a lesser extent of its early printed books. The assiduous collecting of men such as Sir Thomas Knyvett and Sir Lionel Tollemache, followed by Peter Le Neve and Henry Spelman, meant an inevitable depletion of available books. Moore was one of the last for many years to be able to discover and obtain manuscripts from local collections in worthwhile quantities. But he was almost first in his search for printed books.

The dearth, real or imaginary, seemed sometimes to extend even to Norwich itself. Where London could boast (for all their limitations) the Cotton, Sion College, Tenison and Royal Libraries, Norwich possessed a library with a proud history going back to 1608 but one naturally modest by comparison, and not intended for specialist scholarly demands. A printed *Catalogue of the books in the library of the city of Norwich* appeared in 1706, listing just over 920 volumes, and it remained a reference library until 1716. Both Moore and Tanner were among its benefactors, and the list of subscribers included both William Whiston and Samuel Clarke, besides Tanner.[45] In the

---

[42] MSS. Ee.3.60, Ff.2.29, Ff.2.33, Ff.4.35, Gg.4.4 and Mm.4.19. Cf. R. M. Thomson *The archives of the Abbey of Bury St Edmunds* (Woodbridge, Suffolk, 1980).

[43] Cf. Penelope Corfield 'A provincial capital in the late seventeenth century' in Peter Clark and Paul Slack (ed.) *Crisis and order in English towns 1500–1700* (1972) pp. 263–310, and John T. Evans *Seventeenth-century Norwich; politics, religion and government, 1620–1690* (Oxford 1979).

[44] See especially P. Lasko and N. J. Morgan (ed.) *Medieval art in East Anglia 1300–1520* (Norwich 1973).

[45] G. A. Stephen *Three centuries of a city library* (Norwich 1917) especially pl. 2 and p. 54.

Close, things were little better. The cathedral library, recently refurbished, was adequate only for everyday needs, and those clergy who could afford to do so amassed their own private collections – there as everywhere else. Robert Pepper, Chancellor of the diocese since 1673, possessed a library which made up in an impressive coverage of legal textbooks what it lacked in general reading.[46] His successor, Tanner, appointed three months after his death in December 1700, was far more catholic in his tastes (and eventually owner of a much greater library), but he found himself in difficulties away from London and Oxford. So long as Moore's books were available all was well; but with Moore's translation to Ely in 1707 there went also Moore's books. The only other library Tanner had found to be of use was that of Charles Trimnell (1663–1723), archdeacon of Norfolk since 1698, whose abilities, aided by a royal chaplaincy (obtained no doubt with Moore's help) led him to St James, Piccadilly, in October 1706. Faced with such a dearth in the midst of his work on his *Bibliotheca*, Tanner's asperity in a letter to Arthur Charlett at Oxford towards those who seemed to cross him is understandable:

One g^t. discouragem^t to me here is that we have nothing in this town that deserves the name of a Public Library, and the Supellex literaria in private hands diminishes dayly; that varlet H. Wanly came down into this Country and privily carried off the best Library in the Diocese for the use of Secretary Harley I mean Sr Simonds Dewes's. D^r. Trimnell last year carried hence as many books (tho' not so good) as you have and now the B^p. is packing up 2. or 3. Rooms he had here.[47]

Trimnell in fact succeeded Moore to the bishopric, having remained in London for only a few months, and so his books were again available until his translation to Winchester in 1721. But had Moore acquired Sir Simonds D'Ewes' manuscripts from Stow Hall in Suffolk he would have added a collection of some six hundred items which would have rivalled in itself all those he already possessed in 1706. Instead, Humfrey Wanley's social address at the right moment, and energy in the chase,

---

[46] Moore's eldest son John married Pepper's daughter. (Moore *The father of black-letter collectors* p. 11).

[47] Bodleian Library MS. Ballard 4 f. 84, Tanner to Charlett 25 June 1707.

supported with Harley's money, carried off the prize. There is no direct evidence that Moore ever seriously contemplated buying the collection; but Wanley himself, in reporting to Harley on 20 November 1703 (at the outset of what turned out to be protracted negotiations), explained that 'many have their Eies upon this Collection, but none as yet have ask'd the Price of them'. He was an astute librarian. The manuscripts, offered for sale by the grandson of the founder of the collection, added to the Harleian Library an assemblage of outstanding antiquarian interest, noticeably strong (in a collection that offered much variety) in numismatics and containing a number of important Anglo-Saxon manuscripts: one which would, in other words, have ideally complemented Moore's collection, but for which he had no Wanley.[48] Harley bought it for £450, Wanley having beaten D'Ewes down from £500, and if indeed Moore ever had any opportunity to purchase it he may well have found this to be too much. By comparison with Harley, his means were modest.

Such of his personal accounts as survive span only a few years, but by far the largest single payment for books which they record is for seventy guineas in August 1701. To this transaction we shall return. It fell in the same month as one other considerable purchase, at a time of exceptional expenditure by Moore on his library even if the sums do seem paltry by comparison with those spent by Harley or Sunderland, or, a few years later, the Earl of Pembroke. This second transaction concerned the library of William Savile, second Marquess of Halifax, whose books were kept partly in London and partly at Rufford in Nottinghamshire. Halifax had died in 1700, leaving his second wife to whom he had been married for but five years. His library, formed chiefly by his father and containing an unusually fine collection of French books, composed of

[48] See Andrew G. Watson *The library of Sir Simonds D'Ewes* (1966) *passim* and, for its purchase by Harley, pp. 56–61. For further details see also the introduction (pp. xviii–xix) to *The diary of Humfrey Wanley* ed. C. E. and Ruth C. Wright (Bibliographical Soc. 1966).

history, geography, memoirs, classical authors and affairs of state, as well as good sections of Italian books, came thus onto the market, there being no heir to the title. Moore was in a singularly fortunate position to engage with the family, Lady Halifax being Lady Mary Finch, grand-daughter of his patron the Earl of Nottingham. It was a happy opportunity and one which he seized, purchasing books through his agent Mr Meadows to the value of £36. On the whole the books he thus obtained were modern ones, including a presentation copy from the author of Nathaniel Johnson's *The king's visitorial power asserted* (1688) and a two volume edition of Grotius *De iure belli ac pacis* (The Hague 1680), but he also acquired two catalogues in manuscript of the first marquess' library.[49]

While the ties of patronage and local influence could accomplish much, Moore inherited few, if any books from his family, and for most of his acquisitions depended on the ordinary trade. His library was not alone in being familiar to John Bagford,[50] whose knowledge and engaging (if somewhat undisciplined) manner won widespread respect. As other collectors realized no less easily than Moore, Bagford's familiarity with the history of early printing was unmatched in Britain; but it was Moore who, for a time, made the best use of it.

Of the manuscripts and printed books supplied by Bagford, most dated from the sixteenth century and before. The incunabula so added to the collection included an edition of

---

[49] The Halifax printed books are, in the main, characterized by a number written in the top right hand corner of the first flyleaf, as on those mentioned here and on, for example, Wicquefort's *L'ambassadeur et ses fonctions* (The Hague 1681). The library catalogues are MSS. Dd.2.14 ('A catalogue of the books in the lower library, London, 1692') and Dd.9.51 ('A catalogue of the books in the library of Rufford belonging to My Lord Marquiss of Halifax for the year 1693').

[50] On Bagford see principally A. F. Johnson 'John Bagford, antiquary, 1650–1716' in his *Selected essays on books and printing* ed. P. H. Muir (Amsterdam 1970) pp. 378–80, and Melvin H. Wolf *Catalogue and indexes to the title-pages of English printed books preserved in the British Library's Bagford collection* (1974).

Eusebius *Evangelica preparatio* (Venice 1497; Inc. 1924) bound up with Iamblichus Chalcidensis *De mysteriis* (Venice 1497; Inc. 2178), supplied with a dozen other 'tractes printed by Aldas' for seven shillings in July 1703 in a group of books that was headed by a manuscript and Ulrich Gering's edition of Albrecht von Eyb's *Margarita poetica* (Paris 1478; Inc. 2880) at the price of 4s.6d.[51] Bagford's scanty accounts in MS. Harley 5998 span 1703 to 1708, and while they clearly do not record all his transactions with Moore, they do provide a picture of the general character of most of the books handled in his business. The great majority of the entries are for incunabula, early English printed books, and manuscripts, and of the most miscellaneous character. On 11 December 1705, for example, Bagford supplied Moore with four items, ranging from a collection of Greek manuscripts (not identified) for £2.3s.od. to a small book of prescriptions, Dr Trigg's *Secrets, arcana's & panacea's* (1665) for sixpence.[52] From the same source in 1703 there had arrived a much more considerable order, including Albertus Magnus *Compendium theologicae veritatis* (Venice 1476; Inc. 1687), a copy that had been in England since the fifteenth century, for two shillings, and a 16° Psalter printed by Gerard Leeu (Antwerp 1490; Inc. 3928) for a shilling. One of John Rastell's attacks on Jewell cost fourpence, and for sixpence Bagford sold to Moore an unspecified edition of the scarce *Lyttle treatyse called the image of idlenesse* by Walter Wedlocke, allegedly translated by Oliver Oldwanton from the 'Troyane or Cornyshe tounge': the copy does not survive at Cambridge. Bagford's notes, poorly spelt, sometimes atrociously written, and frequently lamentably parsimonious in detail, permit identification of fewer books still in Moore's collection than might be wished.[53] Manuscripts in particular

---

[51] British Library MS. Harley 5998 fo. 1ʳ. [52] *Ibid.*, fo. 35ʳ.

[53] Bagford's notes can also be seen in some of Moore's books, including for example Pynson's *Promptorius puerorum* (1499: Inc. 4199), 'Arnold's chronicle' (Antwerp 1503?) (STC 782), and MS. Ee.2.15, a much mutilated collection of medieval English poetry containing a slip of paper in his hand. A leaf from MS. Mm.4.25 (a glossed s.xii Psalter) survives in the University of Missouri collection of fragments assembled by Bagford, sold at Sotheby's on 12 December 1967, Lot 51. (I am grateful to Dr M. Gatch for drawing this to my attention.)

are difficult to identify, but it seems that an imperfect copy of the Sarum Antiphoner printed at Paris by Hopyl in 1520 was also supplied on this occasion, for a shilling: containing little more than the Psalter and lacking two months of the calendar, the copy now classed as Sel.2.25 was supplemented apparently in the sixteenth century by the insertion of an illuminated fifteenth-century manuscript Sarum calendar for the whole year. The book conforms with, and is probably to be identified with, Bagford's 'psalter vere ould partley prented & MS'.[54] It came from Shropshire, and in common with most other early printed books bought by Moore was far from expensive.

In amassing a collection of early English printing, a task in which he was significantly aided by Bagford, Moore was collecting for several years in an area both unfamiliar and unfashionable. Prices for historical texts and notable editions of the classics were higher than most, reflecting the fields that were most popular. Few collectors at the end of the seventeenth century recognized the value not merely of chronicles, but of the mass of minor literature of the past as well. Besides these, Caxtons, known (on the whole) and already the centre of a cult of connoisseurship, were a little more expensive. Demand, moreover, was growing. Bagford's account submitted to Moore on 20 March 1704/5 includes, besides half a dozen manuscripts, 'a volom of Caxtones tractes 4°', priced at four shillings,[55] but increasingly Moore was in competition with Sloane and with Harley. It was from Bagford that Sloane apparently secured for five shillings in January 1703/4 the first edition of the *Canterbury tales*,[56] a book that Moore never seems to have possessed. And although Bagford's scanty

---

[54] British Library MS. Harley 5998 fo. 8ʳ.

[55] It is not clear to what exactly this refers. In 1697 or 1698 Moore already possessed among his printed books the volume of 'English Poems, by Chaucer, &c.' (Inc. 4070 etc.; Bernard *Catalogi* 2 p. 382 no. 158; British Library MS. Add. 6262 fo.39ʳ), and in 1713 Hearne noted that it too had come into Moore's possession from Bagford (Hearne *Remarks and collections* 4 p. 261). Most probably, Bagford's reference is to the volume opening with Lydgate's *Horse, sheep and goose* (Inc. 4069) and including *The play of the wether* etc. (now Sel.5.51–63)); but four shillings seems a small price for a volume that Bagford is unlikely to have failed to recognize, however imperfectly, for its rarity and interest.   [56] Not identified in de Ricci *A census of Caxtons*. Harley 5998 fo. 9ʳ.

accounts include in all some eighty-four titles supplied to Moore between July 1703 and March 1704/5, there is some indication that the next few years saw Moore supplanted by the other two. The demands of Sloane and Harley outweighed those of the older customer, an impression confirmed in Moore's private accounts. Moore's payments fell off sharply after 1701 and 1702, dwindling (at least according to the written accounts) to nil in 1705 and followed by only three payments in 1706 and 1707. Meanwhile in November 1706 Bagford sold to Harley a copy of Cicero's *Epistolae ad Atticum* (Venice 1470)[57] for the unusually high price of £1.1s.6d., and in the following March a Josephus (Venice 1499) for five shillings and Ovid's *Fasti* (1501) for 2s.6d. In September 1708 Jacob Bellaert's Dutch edition of Bartholomeus Anglicus *De proprietatibus rerum* (Haarlem 1485) went the same way for 7s.6d.[58] So far as can be ascertained, Moore possessed none of these books, yet all fell well within his means and his province as a collector. The conclusion that Bagford was increasingly turning his attention to newer collectors, anxious to amass libraries and offering ample opportunities to reliable booksellers, seems inescapable. He died only in 1716, having supplied Harley also with manuscripts and other 'out-of-course' books for many years.[59]

Bagford's name recurs more frequently in Moore's private accounts than that of any other bookseller, as supplier not only of books and manuscripts but also of maps and engravings, as agent at auctions, and even, once, as amanuensis.[60] Moore rarely recorded the source of his purchase in a book, but I am aware of two that can be identified by notes (not by Moore) inside them as having been acquired from Bagford. Giovanni Cinelli's *Le bellezze della città di Firenze* (Florence 1677) and Gasparo Alveri's *Roma in ogni stato* (2 vols., Rome 1664) both

[57] Harley 5998 fo. 53ᵛ. This is perhaps the copy now in St John's College, Cambridge, given by John Newcome in 1765.   [58] Harley 5998 fos. 56ʳ, 75ʳ.

[59] *Diary of Humfrey Wanley* I p. 182 etc. On Moore's nomination, Bagford was made a pensioner of the Charterhouse.

[60] 'Paid Mr Bagford for transcribing the manuscript 1–10–0' (22 December 1696). I have not identified the manuscript in question.

came apparently from the same library, for 1s.10d. and 8s.2d. respectively. A further volume also probably from Bagford, but from another library, contained three works by C. G. Bachet published at Bourg en Bresse in 1626, for which Moore paid £1.1s.6d. on 15 May 1701.

Moore's private accounts offer a tantalizing, and deceptive, picture of his more regular dealings with the book trade, recording payments for books not only to booksellers but also to his chaplains, friends, domestic servants and other agents. Their incomplete and irregular nature has already been remarked on, and while they do not, for example, usually distinguish between the three booksellers named Bateman in Plomer's *Dictionary*, they do sometimes mention 'young Mr Bateman' or 'Mr Bateman senior'. The sums paid to one or other of the men (and seemingly mostly to Christopher Bateman) were considerable. In 1691 Christopher received at least £40, and in March–June 1697 the Batemans between them received over £60.[61] Christopher Bateman was both bookseller and auctioneer, and some of the larger payments must almost certainly have been to meet the cost of books bought at auction; but he also had two shops full, according to von Uffenbach, of Latin books. Von Uffenbach visited him during his stay in London in 1710 and, warm with the discovery of the 1681 edition of Mabillon's *De re diplomatica* for only two guineas, wrote of him in his journal as 'the most eminent man in London – nay, in the whole of England – who deals in old bound volumes and also in Latin books. In other places one finds hardly any Latin books and what one does see is like a store of rough volumes. But Bateman has two great shops full, and in such quantities that they lie in heaps on the ground.'[62]

---

61 In September 1690 Moore and Bateman were already well enough acquainted for Bateman to give him a copy of the octavo Greek New Testament printed at Cambridge in 1632 that after being given by the printer to William Sancroft passed in turn to Walter Adams (Fellow of Emmanuel from 1645), John Worthington (also a Fellow of the College) and the Duke of Lauderdale, whose library was sold at auction. The volume is now Syn.5.63.14.

62 Zacharias Conrad von Uffenbach *London in 1710* ed. and transl. W. H. Quarrell and M. Mare (1934) p. 18.

Many of Moore's French printed books came, according to his accounts, from David Mortier, a Frenchman whose shop at Erasmus' Head in the western part of the Strand was also the agency by which Moore bought books from Holland to the value of £10 in November 1701. Mortier's bills, too, were frequently considerable and sometimes recorded settlements following auctions: in April 1707 Moore paid £10.12s.od. apparently (the evidence is not quite conclusive) following the sale of an unidentified clergyman's library conducted by Mortier on 19 March. Quantities of books came from Mortier's countryman Paul Vaillant; one payment is recorded to H. Riboteau, also in the Strand, in 1699; and on various occasions a French woman in Pall Mall supplied books in the same language; she is unnamed, but in 1702 a Mme Sauvage was paid three pounds, and this may have been her.

In Norwich, between 1692 and 1707, Moore bought from members of the Oliver family, though it cannot be said that his dealings with them were either extensive or prolonged. He bought mostly Bibles from them, but he also used Thomas Goddard, to whom seven payments are recorded in the years 1698 to 1704, and Samuel Selfe, from whom he bought two books in 1706 and 1707.[63] Books also came regularly from Oxford, but for many years (according to the accounts) few seem to have been bought in Cambridge. In 1699 and again in 1706 he was buying in Ipswich, and on the second occasion he travelled on to Bury St Edmunds and King's Lynn, buying more books in both places. Further books came from Great Yarmouth, the home of his brother. As well as these domestic travels in East Anglia, the accounts also record two longer journeys in the course of which he was able to add a little to his collection. The longer of the two took place in 1700 and entailed an excursion to Newcastle, the home of his second wife's relations, lasting from August to October, with pauses to allow book buying at Sheffield (15 August), Newcastle (10

[63] On these see David Stoker 'The Norwich book trades before 1800' *Trans. Cambridge Bibliographical Soc.* 8 (1981) pp. 79–125.

September), York (21 September), Doncaster (26 September) and Market Harborough, his home town, from at least 30 September until 3 October. In April–May 1703 he journeyed to Reading, Marlborough (where the only recorded bookseller then was John Buckridge) and Bath, where he bought from the Hammonds: the accounts for this journey include payments for 'removing of books' and for two men to help with them, a circumstance that suggests that many more books were involved than casual purchases.

While Moore encouraged, and even apparently expected, his chaplains to forage for him, he seems also to have explored bookshops and bookstalls for himself. There are several records of payments to the man who kept 'the little stand at White Hall', usually of a few shillings, and elsewhere in London the addresses of booksellers stretch from Westminster Hall to St Paul's Churchyard. But for most of his career he seems to have attended auctions only on the rarest of occasions, and to have preferred instead either to deal through an agent or to wait until after a sale and then apply to the booksellers.

Sometimes he managed to make a selection before a major public sale. The library of Henry Coventry, Secretary of State, was not auctioned until 1687, after his death, but Moore bought a handful from the owner in 1680.[64] Thomas Britton's books went under the hammer in November 1694, eight months after Moore had paid twelve pounds in a private transaction. His private accounts are incomplete, but they do not suggest that he ever bought very extensively even on those occasions when either he or his representative attended a sale. At the auction of Anthony Horneck's library in April 1697 he spent only £3.13s.2d.; the library of Robert Woodward, dean of Salisbury, sold by Edward Millington in November 1702, elicited only £2.3s.8d.; that of William Hodges, rector of St Swithin's, London, a mere thirteen shillings in March 1702/3; that of Robert Hooke in April 1703 but 19s.6d.; and that of

---

64 Entry in Rider's *British Merlin*, 1680 (Adv.e.38.8).

Sackville Crow the following December £3.0s.10d.
Varenne's sale of foreign imports in March 1704 was exceptional in costing Moore a total of ten pounds.[65] In the
surviving catalogues of auctions that record names of buyers,
his appears scarcely at all. In this respect he was quite unlike Sir
Hans Sloane, who attended regularly and bid frequently. But
one of the few occasions when Moore did make a personal
appearance (and long before he was consecrated Bishop of
Norwich) was at the Anglesey sale in October 1686. The first
Earl of Anglesey had followed a political career of conspicuous
success until his dismissal in 1682, and had founded his
collection when he was still an undergraduate at Magdalen
College, Oxford. It contained very little really early material,
but it had gained renown both for its size and also, more
importantly, for containing the library of Henry Oldenburg,
Secretary of the Royal Society.[66] Its sale inevitably attracted
unusual interest from collectors and scholars, and among the
most determined buyers was John Evelyn. Others who
attended included Sloane, Hickes, the naturalist Leonard
Plukenet, Lord Falkland, Isaac Vossius, Dr Bernard, and Sir
Henry Herbert, as well as the London trade, notably Walter
Kettilby and Bagford – the last of whom bought very little,
however. Among most of these, Moore's successes were
modest. He was still not rector of a London parish, and he does
not appear to have attended more than one or two sessions.
Nevertheless, he acquired by these means a run of Jean de
Launay's works, Fortunius Licetus *Hieroglyphica* (1653),
Kirchmann *De funeribus Romanorum* (1661), Quenstedt
Sepultura veterum (1648) and John Pits' account of English
historical writers (1619). Some, but not all, can still be
identified at Cambridge as the Anglesey copies, while in

---

[65] Details from his private accounts: see above, n. 13.
[66] Cf. the notes of Bagford and William Oldys on London libraries (*Notes and Queries* 2nd
ser. 11 (1861) pp. 442–3. The unique marked copy of the sale catalogue of the Anglesey
books is in Lambeth Palace Library.

addition he bought subsequently a number of books which also originated from the library: Hieronymus Henninges' collection of plates *Genealogia aliquot familiarum in Saxonia* (1590), for example, belonged to the translator Philip Ayres, whose books were not sold until 1713, a few months before Moore's death.[67]

The purchase of books from foreign countries presented peculiar problems. England, in alliance with the States General, was at war with France almost continuously from 1689 until the Treaty of Utrecht in 1713, a condition broken only by an uneasy truce between the Treaty of Ryswick in 1697 and the outbreak of the War of the Spanish Succession in 1702. Trade in books, as in other commodities, from France was difficult, and was not infrequently conducted through Dutch and Huguenot intermediaries; the close commercial, religious and family ties between the Dutch and English trades made it comparatively easy to obtain books through the Dutch and other north European ports. Moore exploited every available channel, with considerable success, and included scholars and clergy among his agents besides the regular booksellers. In August 1694 he bought from W. van Schie in Delft a group of books including Goltz *Opera* (5 vols., Antwerp 1644–5), Théophile Bonet *Polyalthes* (3 vols., Geneva 1692) and eighteen volumes of the *Miscellanea curiosa*. The total came to 152 guilders, to which was added the cost of packing, 1g.18st. for a cask, and a 'Paspoort, en connoissement' calculated at 5g.7st. Moore and van Schie were familiar with each other, and in the same post by which he sent the bill the bookseller added a friendly postscript that he was in hopes of receiving another consignment of books from Paris. He added too a further list of new books, including the Imprimerie Royale edition of various Greek mathematicians (1693), a run of the *Acta eruditorum* from 1681 to 1693 in fourteen volumes,

---

[67] A volume of thirty-four political tracts of 1642–3 from the Anglesey library, annotated with prices and dates of purchase, is now Syn.7.64.118; it fetched half a crown at the sale.

the catalogue of the Le Tellier library, and Junius *De pictura veterum libri III* (Rotterdam 1694).[68] Moore returned to him again, and his accounts record payments to van Schie for £9.13s.8d. on 9 January 1698/9 and similar sums subsequently until January 1702/3. Apart from van Schie, Moore also dealt with other Dutch booksellers whose names are recognizable only through a veil of Anglicized spelling in his private accounts: Pieter van der Aa of Leiden, 'Mrs Vanderbush' (or rather, van den Bosch), and Johann Heinrich Wetstein of Amsterdam. Much of his buying was done through a third party. On at least three occasions it involved the ministers of the Dutch church in London, and in February 1705/6 Sir Andrew Fountaine was paid £2.11s.0d. for books he had imported from Holland and France. Sometimes the Norwich booksellers and other merchants were employed.[69] Of the London booksellers, Samuel Smith was in regular contact with Holland,[70] and bought extensively at auctions there, while both Mortier and Vaillant were able to supply Dutch titles as well. Indeed, according to rumour Vaillant was the means by which Moore acquired one of his two copies of the folio *Médailles* (1702) of Louis XIV. Writing to Sir William Trumbull in October 1709, John Bridges explained that the book was only given away as a present, on the instructions of Louis XIV, but that Vaillant had obtained a copy in Holland and was asking twenty guineas for it.[71] The price may have been outrageous, but even if he had not succeeded in selling it to Moore, as Bridges speculated, the suggestion that such a thing was possible is a striking comment on Moore's status as a book collector.

Few of Moore's books can now be identified as having been bought at auction in the Low Countries on his instructions, but

---

[68] Bodleian Library, Tanner correspondence.
[69] On 12 February 1700/1 a Mr Thurston's account for £20 'for books from Holland' was settled, and on 12 July 1705 Samuel Selfe, the Norwich bookseller, received £10.11s.6d. for the same.
[70] N. Hodgson and C. Blagden *The notebook of Thomas Bennet and Henry Clements (1686–1719)* (Oxford Bibliographical Soc. 1956) p. 21.   [71] HMC Downshire 2 p. 881.

two small groups call for attention. Lipsius' edition of Tacitus (Antwerp 1574), an account of the Council of Trent (Venice 1600), Possel *Calligraphia oratoria linguae graecae* (Frankfurt 1615) and a collection of French pamphlets on naval matters published at Rouen between 1612 and 1620 all bear notes that they were bought at The Hague on 21–2 September 1697, and two others, a Horace (Amsterdam 1664) and Alessandro Citolini *La tipocosmia* (Venice 1561) were bought at Leiden on 9–10 October. But the greater part of Moore's Dutch purchases remains anonymous, since the presence or otherwise of a Dutch signature in a book is obviously no guide as to where or when Moore acquired it.[72]

Booksellers did not by any means have a monopoly in this international trade. To the classical scholar Alexander Cunningham Moore owed some of his most important manuscripts, while from a man of much less exalted status he received help over books which, if they failed to cause such a widespread scholarly stir on their arrival, nevertheless contributed materially to the ultimate importance of his library. Little seems to be known of the activities in the book trade of Irenaeus Crusius, a Huguenot whose denization in London was recorded on 10 July 1696, when he was described simply as 'clerk'.[73] Records of payments to him date only in the period 1702 to 1705, and may suggest a date for the acquisition of one of Hans Lufft's German Bibles, published at Wittenberg in

---

[72] At least seven volumes can be traced to the library of the classical scholar Willem van der Goes, sold in April 1687, including the Aldine Sedulius and Juvencus (1502), Giovio's *Illustrium virorum vitae* (Florence 1551) and Fulvio Orsini's *Imagines et elogia virorum illustrium* (Rome 1570). Although in the end Moore came to own several volumes from the library of Nicolaas Heinsius, including Gruterus' own copy of his edition of Seneca (1604: Adv.e.32.4), Scaliger's copy of Herodotus (1570: Adv.a.19.2), and the works of St Basil (1551: Adv.a.19.8) there is no evidence that he was represented at the auction in 1683. (On the Heinsius volumes see M. H. Hoeflich 'Two Heinsius-related volumes in the University Library, Cambridge' *Trans. Cambridge Bibliographical Soc.* 6 (1975) pp. 262–5).

[73] William A. Shaw (ed.) *Letters of denization and acts of naturalization for aliens in England and Ireland 1603–1700* (Publications of the Huguenot Society 18, Lymington 1911) p. 242. His son entered St John's College in 1719 (R. F. Scott (ed.) *Admissions to the College of St John the Evangelist* 3 (Cambridge 1903) p. 19).

1540, a copy not quite complete but of some interest as having belonged to one Matthew Pauly in London in 1618. Crusius alluded to his overseas trade in a postscript to a letter addressed to Moore on the subject of the book, but most of his sole surviving letter to Moore was taken up with the Bible itself:

When this great German Bible was brought to me; I remembered that My Lord was pleased to say, he would haue such a one if it was for a reasonable price therefore I haue ordered the Bearer of this to shew you the same. It is one of the very first Bibles that Dr Luther printed, as may appear by the fifth Chapter of the first Epistel of St John where Testimonium S.S. Trinitatis is omitted and was put in the very next or second Edition. In short it is reckoned a great Curiosity, and would yield a double price in Germany, whereas the owner is willing to sell it for halfe a Guinea. I should haue giuen me self the honour to wait on you, sir, but being tormented with the Gout, beyond all Expression, I can but subscribe my self . . .[74]

As for his buying of current English books, Moore's advance was irregular. As I have hinted, there is no evidence that he made a consistent attempt to stay abreast of fresh publications, particularly in topics other than ecclesiastical, even though his library came eventually to be comprehensive in several subjects. Subscription lists, which came to enjoy considerable popularity, and to be used regularly for the first time during his career, are one guide to this in the absence of properly detailed accounts or other records, but they need to be treated with some caution. Sometimes he lagged behind the closing date, and was thus omitted from the list of subscribers, as was the case with John Harris' *Lexicon technicum* (1704), which he bought only in December 1706. At other times he could be more prompt: in June of the year of publication he paid Richard Smith £2.17s.0d. for George Bull's *Opera omnia* (1703), in time to be included in the list of subscribers. Yet speed was not always rewarded with inclusion. Royaumont's *History of the Old and New Testament*, of which the third edition appeared in

---

[74] Letter inserted in Syn.3.54.5. On I John V.7 see *The Cambridge history of the Bible* 3 (Cambridge 1963) pp. 10 etc.

1705, was 'printed for the undertaker R. Blome, Her Majesty's Cosmographical Printer and sold by S. Sprint and Jo. Nicholson', and carried a note at the head of the list of 'subscribers to the first impression' explaining that it was 'an alphabetical account of the names of the subscribers to this work, who returned their names to be inserted amongst the Benefactors to each impression; a considerable number being omitted, as not returning their names to the undertakers, but subscribing to the booksellers'. The lack of Moore's name (or of that of any collector) in a list by no means implied a lack of interest or failure to pay on time: it was frequently simply the accident of the trade, depending solely on who took in the payment. Equally, by no means all books published by subscription carried lists of subscribers: of many examples that might be quoted, Matthew Poole's *Annotations upon the Holy Bible* (1700) is but one, Moore's accounts recording 'subscriptions of Poole's two volumes $\frac{1}{2}$ down 1–5–0' on 12 January 1699/1700.

If, with these provisos, any pattern is to be observed, it is an untidy one. Books with which Moore had been closely associated, as owner of source material, tend (scarcely surprisingly) to include his name among the subscribers, such as Strype's *Annals* (1709) and his lives of Edmund Grindal (1710) and Matthew Parker (1711). The same was true of books of a theological or ecclesiastical nature, where he was usually only one of many on the episcopal bench: this category includes John Gregory's New Testament in Greek (Oxford 1703), Grabe's Septuagint (Oxford 1707), Edmund Gibson's *Codex iuris ecclesiastici anglicani* (1713), Jeremy Collier's *Ecclesiastical history of Great Britain* (1708–14: Moore's name appears only in the second volume), and Walker's *Attempt towards recovering an account of the numbers and suffering of the clergy* (1714). For many books of scholarship, such as John Hudson's edition of Dionysius Halicarnassus (Oxford 1704), it would have been difficult not to subscribe. Among the few books on completely lay subjects in which Moore's name figured were Charles Leigh's *Natural history of Lancashire, Cheshire and the Peak* (Oxford 1700 – a book since stigmatized as a 'dreadful muddle')[75] and Elizabeth Elstob's *English–Saxon homily*, printed by Bowyer in 1709, but neither of these can be described as being very far removed from his everyday circle. As is to be expected, he subscribed to *The lucubrations of Isaac Bickerstaff Esq* (1710), and moving rather further afield, he did the same for John Browne's *Myographia nova: or, a graphical description of all the muscles in the humane body* (1698) – a work of limited originality but of inevitable appeal to his fascination with medical topics. Of the various large compendia that appeared round the turn of the century, reflections in their way of a new distribution of affluence, Harris' *Lexicon* has already been mentioned. Others similarly appear to have failed to engage Moore's attention when subscriptions were being gathered: his accounts record payments on 3 June 1701, exceptionally, of 'the second payment of subscription for the Geographical Dictionary 1–2–6'. Thus Harris' *Compleat collection of voyages and travels* (2 vols. 1705), *A compleat history of England* (2 vols. 1706) and Samuel Stebbings' *Genealogical history of the kings and queens of England* (1707) all appeared without his name. So too did John James' translation of Perrault's *Treatise of the five orders of columns in architecture* (1708), whose subscribers were almost entirely practical craftsmen rather than scholars. Yet all these books found their way into his library.

With two books he was associated in a far less casual manner. In 1705 Bowyer printed a small edition, consisting of 120 copies only, of Martin Lister's edition of Apicius, the latest of a series of books by Lister that had almost all been published in extremely limited quantities, from his earliest appearance in York to the made up copies of the privately circulated

[75] Harry Carter *A history of the Oxford University Press* 1 (Oxford 1975) p. 323. On the question of subscriptions more generally, see P. J. Wallis 'Book subscription lists' *The Library* 5th ser. 29 (1974) pp. 255–86.

illustrations of shells issued in the 1690s. For reasons no longer known, the cost was defrayed by a group of scientists and bibliophiles, including the Earl of Sunderland, Lord Sommers, Robert Harley, Newton, Flamsteed, Sloane, Wren, the Archbishop of Canterbury, and Moore.

Lister also gave Moore a copy of his *Exercitatio anatomica altera: de buccinis fluviatilibus & marinis* (1695), and the other book with which Moore was associated in this close way was also one of natural history. There is no record of the circumstances in which he first met Leonard Plukenet, whose reputation has been obscured by his two greater contemporaries John Ray and Sir Hans Sloane, neither of whom regarded his work on dried plants with wholehearted admiration. (Ray nevertheless drew extensively from Plukenet's work for his own *Historia plantarum*, and his criticisms were tempered by friendship for a man anxious for his position.) Appointed her Regius Professor by Queen Mary in 1689 and placed in charge of the gardens of Hampton Court, Plukenet also established a small herbarium at Westminster, and had plenty of opportunities to make Moore's acquaintance. Like Lister, he published most of his work at his own expense, the first of his lavishly illustrated books, *Phytographia*, appearing in 1691–6. This was followed by *Almagestum botanicum* in 1696, *Almagesti botanici mantissa* in 1700, and *Amaltheum botanicum* in 1705. Moore possessed all of them, uniformly bound in red goatskin splendour, and on 23 May 1705 he disbursed ten pounds to Plukenet himself: *Amaltheum botanicum* was supported by a consortium of eleven subscribers (who each contributed five guineas) headed by Thomas Tenison and including, besides Moore, Henry Compton, the Bishop of London, Sunderland, Sommers, the Earl of Portland, Lord Paget and Lord Wharton – a group of men united in their politics and on the whole in their love of books. Plukenet died a year later, in 1706, and his collections are now in the British Museum of Natural History, having (according to one authority) been acquired by Moore and by him sold to Sloane, who added them to his own rather more considerable accumulations.[76]

Moore was never rich, even after his translation to Ely,[77] and so far as can now be established the summer of 1697 was the only period in which he displayed something of the same acquisitive showmanship that characterized so much of the formation of the Harleian Library. The occasion was the purchase not of printed books but of manuscripts, and the cause may perhaps have lain partly in the fact that Bernard's *Catalogi*, in which Moore's library was to figure prominently, was in the last stages of production. By mid-1697 Moore possessed about 850 manuscripts (the counting following the method of the *Catalogi*, and therefore including one or two printed books) out of a total reported later by Thomas Baker as 1790 – that is, about 47% of the eventual whole.[78] The preparation and production of Bernard's *Catalogi*, supervised in its later stages by Arthur Charlett, had been started before 1692. In 1694 Bernard issued an appeal for private collectors to send him lists of their manuscripts, and among the last to be included was that of Moore. The book was long going through the press, and the final five sheets were not printed off until 1698.[79]

The name of the person responsible for compiling the list of Moore's manuscripts in the *Catalogi* is not certain. Thomas Tanner, one of the few people capable of such a task, did not join Moore's household until after the compilation of the first part of the list, containing the first 674 items. But on 12 May

76 On Plukenet see C. E. Raven *John Ray* (Cambridge 1942) pp. 231–2 etc., and on Moore's part in the preservation of his specimens H. Trimen and W. T. Dyer *Flora of Middlesex* (1869) p. 376 and B. Henrey *British botanical and horticultural literature before 1800* (Oxford 1975) I p. 142.

77 For an analysis of Moore's clerical income and expenses between 1692 and 1707 see D. R. Hirschberg 'Episcopal incomes and expenses' in Rosemary O'Day and Felicity Heal (ed.) *Princes and paupers in the English church 1500–1800* (Leicester 1981) pp. 211–30, table 12. 78 Sayle *Annals* p. 92; Hartshorne *Book rarities* p. 23.

79 Carter *A history of the Oxford University Press* I p. 246; Percy Simpson *Proof-reading in the sixteenth, seventeenth and eighteenth centuries* (Oxford 1935) pp. 210–11.

1697 a Mr Davis was paid £1.8s.0d. for 'the writing the catalogue of manuscripts'. Moore's household accounts are not any more specific than this, but they refer almost certainly to Thomas Davies, who was in correspondence with Wanley on Moore's behalf the following October,[80] sending a further list of manuscripts at Norwich, and who was again in touch with Wanley concerning a visit by the latter to Moore's London house in Charles Street in April 1698:[81] he was still acting for Moore in 1709.[82]

It is unlikely that so small an amount as twenty-eight shillings was for more than either a catalogue of a small part of the collection or for transcription from some existing list. In any case, most of the cataloguing of the major part of the manuscripts had already been done by October 1696, seven months previously, probably by either Wanley or Davies. Bagford was then entrusted with the making of a transcript, while the Oxford editors began to grow anxious and gave to Edmund Gibson the task of supervising the preparation of a copy for the press of the description of Moore's ever growing library. On 27 October Gibson wrote to Moore in some disquiet,

I am to beg your Lordship's pardon, for not taking soe much care of your Catalogue, as to see it fairly transcrib'd. But I was hurry'd out o'Town on a sudden, and am got home again but very lately, after a long and tedious journey. I have not yet seen M^r. Bagford; but doe hope that he took care to get the transcript finisht, and to have it sent to your Lordship. Our University are very uneasie for want of it; to that degree, that Dr Charlett sent me a Letter as far as Carlisle, with orders to take an opportunity of writing to your Lordship about it. I suppose, you may think fitt not to part with it, till you have review'd some of ye Manuscripts and are satisfy'd that the titles are right.[83]

A month later the crucial papers at last arrived, and he felt able to write in a more cheerful vein – taking care to allay Moore's

---

[80] British Library MS. Harley 3778 (168).
[81] British Library MS. Harley 3778 (166).
[82] Davies to Hearne 21 June 1709 (Bodleian Library MS. Rawlinson 4.111).
[83] Bodleian Library MS. Tanner 24 fo. 218.

fears and anxieties as much as possible: the subject was clearly a delicate one:

Yesterday I recieved the Catalogues; and will care to send the fair Copy to Oxford by the first safe hand. If your Lordship thinks of being in London before Christmass, I will desire that the several sheets may be sent up, to have your own correction and approbation before they goe to the Press. But if you continue at Norwich, I will take care (however) that the sheets shall goe through two or three hands, that are both accurate and judicious.[84]

It is a reflection of the pace at which Moore was at this time adding to his manuscripts that an *Appendix librorum quorundam omissorum*, listing both manuscripts and printed books, needed to be added, and a yet further *Modicum catalogi manuscriptorum, penes ... D. D. Joannem More* completed both the cataloguing of his manuscripts and the whole national survey apart from yet more addenda and emendanda, adding three manuscripts and revising the entries as far as no. 664, the tenth-century Pictish Gospel Book with Gaelic notes known as the Book of Deer.[85] It also seems probable that some of the manuscripts in the two principal lists of addenda had been in Moore's possession for some time, and at first had either escaped notice or were not recorded because of uncertainties over their true nature. The volume of 'poems and translations by Sir Tho. Knyvett' (no. 693)[86] may well have fallen into this category, the bulk of the Knyvett manuscripts having been recorded several pages earlier. But overall it appears that the later lists are very largely of recent purchases or gifts. The first, and largest, list of Moore's manuscripts published in the *Catalogi* represented a virtually complete account of acquisitions up to May 1697, apart from one or two strays. No. 603, a fifteenth-century manuscript of Jacobus de Theramo *Consolatio peccatorum* (MS. Ff.2.16) was given to Moore by Jean

---

[84] *Ibid.*, fo. 162.
[85] MS. Ii.6.32. See, most recently, Kathleen Hughes *Celtic Britain in the early middle ages; studies in Scottish and Welsh sources* (Woodbridge, Suffolk, 1980) pp. 22–37, and above p. 50.   [86] MS. Dd.9.23.

Dubourdieu, a minister at the French Savoy chapel,[87] on 7 April that year, while amongst the last to be entered was a group of manuscripts by Thomas Stanley for which Moore paid ten pounds to his descendants on 22 May: they included a copy of Stanley's edition of Aeschylus (1663) interleaved in eight volumes and containing a wealth of further matter.[88] The Book of Deer, entered three items before the Stanley manuscripts, may also have been acquired that spring.[89]

The first of the lists of additions, *Appendix librorum quorundam omissorum*, contained both manuscripts and printed books, and included twenty-one manuscripts (numbered 51 to 71) of which one, no. 62 (Lightfoot's *Journal*) was acquired in June 1697.[90] It was only a small group, but the last main accumulation to be reported was much more extensive and contained nos. 675–827, the numbering omitting the previous appendix. This contained several notabilia, among them a fifteenth-century volume of English poetry and prose (MS. Ff.2.38), a fourteenth-century martyrology (the only surviving book known to have belonged to the Dominicans at Guildford (MS. Ll.2.9)),[91] a volume dated 1556 once part of the official papers of the Kingdom of Sicily (MS. Ff.2.25), as well as quantities of estate documents and a copy of Thomas Legge's Latin tragedy *Richard III* acted at St John's College, Cambridge, in 1579 (MS. Mm.4.40): there was also a late transcript of two other Cambridge Latin plays, William Alabaster's *Roxana* and Guarini's *Il pastor fido* in a translation acted at King's College (MS. Ff.2.9). The dates of acquisition of the items in this section are not all clear, but two of them, the group of Norwich computus rolls (MSS. Dd.3.61–2) were

[87] W. and S. Minet (ed.) *Régistres des églises de la Savoie de Spring Gardens et des Grecs 1684–1900* (Huguenot Society 1922).

[88] On these see M. Flower 'Thomas Stanley (1625–1678): a bibliography of his writings in prose and verse (1647–1743)' *Trans. Cambridge Bibliographical Soc.* 1 (1950) pp. 139–72.

[89] Moore did not possess it in March 1695, when it was in the hands of Thomas Gale and shown to Evelyn: see *The diary of John Evelyn* ed. E. S. de Beer (Oxford 1955) 5 p. 206.

[90] See above, pp. 84–5.   [91] Ker *Medieval libraries* p. 94.

given to Moore on 26 October 1697. If, as seems likely[92] Thomas Davies was responsible for reporting Moore's recent additions to Wanley for the *Catalogi*, it would seem that when he reported 'some things he has at Norwich' on 14 October he provided details of nos. 675–804, these being arranged in order of size, from the largest to the smallest and concluding with the computus rolls, and that the remainder of this section (nos. 805–27) consisted of still later additions, ending with a fifteenth-century manuscript of Peter of Blois. Finally, the last addenda of all added only three further manuscripts, numbered I to III, and with that the printed record of Moore's manuscripts came to an end.

Moore was to live for another sixteen years after the completion of Bernard's *Catalogi*, and by 1697 he had been in London for only about twelve years. Yet by that date he had not only laid the foundations of his collection of manuscripts: he had also acquired almost all the most important items in it, and with a very few exceptions was not to add substantially to it after about 1702. Wanley's work for Lord Harley ensured that there could not be so many opportunities again of such a kind for years to come. The list of Moore's manuscripts in the *Catalogi* began with a group of Latin Bibles including, first of all, an early fourteenth-century copy with illustrations in the style of the artist of the Queen Mary Psalter;[93] but one of the earliest in date was one of the last to be added to the list before the 'Appendix' of books omitted from the main list, the tenth-century Book of Deer (MS. Ii.6.32). Oldest of all was the Book of Cerne (MS. Ll.1.10), an anthology of Passion narratives from the Gospels with hymns and prayers, written in the early ninth century either in or in a place influenced by Mercia.[94] He

[92] British Library MS. Harley 3778 (168).
[93] MS. Dd.1.14. See Margaret Rickert *Painting in Britain; the middles ages* 2nd ed. (Harmondsworth 1965) p. 128.
[94] Rickert *Painting in Britain* p. 25; D. N. Dumville 'Liturgical drama and panegyric responsory from the eighth century? A re-examination of the origin and contents of the ninth-century section of the Book of Cerne' *Journal of Theological Studies* 22 (1972) pp. 374–406. See also p. 50 n. 7.

had a twelfth-century Pontifical from Winchester (MS. Ee.2.3) and another perhaps from Ely (MS. Ll.2.10). The thirteenth-century life of Edward the Confessor in French verse (MS. Ee.3.59), whose lavish illuminations have been attributed to an assistant of Matthew Paris,[95] was the finest illuminated manuscript he was ever to obtain, though it seems to have attracted little interest among his contemporaries. As we have seen, Bagford singled out the copy of Capgrave's *Chronicle of England* (MS. Gg.4.12) as being especially worthy of notice,[96] and it has been suggested that this may have been the copy intended for presentation to Edward IV.[97] Among humanist manuscripts, Moore might have pointed on the one hand to John Gunthorpe's copy of a Latin translation of Homer (MS. Mm.3.4) and on the other to a small Horace since discovered to have been written by Bartolomeo di San Vito (MS Dd.15.13).[98] Among the Knyvett books, in about 1693, he had acquired a tenth-century copy of Smaragdus on the Rule of St Benedict, probably written at Glastonbury (MS. Ee.2.4),[99] an extremely fine early thirteenth-century illustrated Bible (MS. Ee.2.23),[100] the unique manuscript of the Arthurian *Roman d'Yder* (MS. Ee.4.26),[101] a Sarum Antiphoner of the late fourteenth or early fifteenth century (MS. Mm.2.9),[102] and the so-called Findern manuscript of

---

[95] Rickert p. 109; facsimile ed. M. R. James *La estoire de Seint Aedward le Rei* (Roxburghe Club 1920). For further references see J. J. G. Alexander and C. M. Kauffmann *English illuminated manuscripts 700–1500* (Bibliothèque Royale Albert Iᵉʳ, Brussels 1973) no. 48.

[96] See above, p. 57.

[97] Peter J. Lucas 'John Capgrave O. S. A. (1393–1464), scribe and publisher' *Trans. Cambridge Bibliographical Soc.* 5 (1969) pp. 1–35; the manuscript is no. 5 in Lucas' list.

[98] Cecil H. Clough 'The library of Bernardo and of Pietro Bembo' *Book Collector* 33 (1984) pp. 305–31, at p. 309 and pl. 5.

[99] T. A. M. Bishop 'An early example of insular-caroline' *Trans. Cambridge Bibliographical Soc.* 4 (1968) pp. 396–400, with references to the parts of the manuscript separated from the main bulk.

[100] N. J. Morgan *Early gothic manuscripts* [1] *1190–1250* (1982) no. 65.

[101] Ed. H. Gelzer *Die altfranzösische Yderroman* (Gesellschaft für Romanische Literatur Bd 31, Dresden 1913), and Alison Adams *The romance of Yder* (Arthurian Studies 8, Woodbridge, Suffolk, 1983).

[102] Ed. W. H. Frere *Antiphonale Sarisburiense; a reproduction in facsimile of a manuscript of the thirteenth century* (Plainsong and Mediaeval Music Society) 1901–15.

English literary texts, compiled in the fifteenth and sixteenth centuries.[103]

As for the foreign manuscripts, Montfaucon[104] found scarcely anything of interest among the Greek manuscripts listed in the *Catalogi*: in this field, more than in any other, Moore was to make notable gains after 1697, but he already possessed the early eleventh-century *Evangelistarium* (MS. Dd.8.49), of which Mill was to make use in his edition of the Greek New Testament, and a copy of the Gospels written in 1297 bound up with a late fourteenth-century copy of the Apocalypse and collection of prayers written probably at Constantinople (MS. Dd.9.69).[105] Beyond the Bosphorus, it may be doubted how much Moore knew of Turkish, Syriac, Persian or Japanese, yet examples of all these are recorded in the *Catalogi*, besides Hebrew, concentrated in a group between nos. 612 and 657. Bernard's list included four said to be in Chinese, two of them printed books, but only one can now be confidently identified, a copy of the Japanese *Azuma kagami* or history of Japan between 1180 and 1266 first compiled in about 1300 and printed in about 1615 (MS. Ll.1.3).

Overall, the collection was by and large one of books written in England. Difficult communications with the continent, constantly distracted by war, prohibited any very ambitious programme of acquisition such as the Harleys, Thomas Coke of Norfolk, Sir Andrew Fountaine and the Earl of Sunderland were to be able to pursue with regard to Italian manuscripts a little later.[106] Of the few fourteenth- and fifteenth-century Italian manuscripts in his collection added to the meagre collection obtained by 1697, the two volumes of Bonaventura's commentary on the *Sententia* from the library of

---

[103] Ed. in facsimile by Richard Beadle and A. E. B. Owen (1977). Cf. also Kate Harris 'The origins and make-up of Cambridge University Library MS. Ff.1.6' *Trans. Cambridge Bibliographical Soc.* 8 (1983) pp. 299–333.

[104] *Palaeographia Graeca* (Paris 1708) p. xxviii.

[105] A. Turyn *Dated Greek manuscripts of the thirteenth and fourteenth centuries in the libraries of Great Britain* (Dumbarton Oaks Studies 17, 1980) pp. 63–6.

[106] Cf. C. E. Wright 'Manuscripts of Italian provenance in the Harleian collection in the British Museum' in Cecil H. Clough (ed.) *Cultural aspects of the Italian Renaissance; essays in honour of Paul Oskar Kristeller* (Manchester 1976) pp. 462–84.

Giovanni of Aragon (MSS. Gg.3.22–3)[107] and a Dante (MS. Mm.2.3)[108] came via French libraries, and his manuscript of Virgil (MS. Ee.5.5)[109] came via Holland, while a copy of Pliny's *Natural history* was mentioned by Tanner in his continuation of Bernard's list only two entries before the Moore Bede which also came from a foreign source.[110] Even after the Treaty of Ryswick, the French establishment allowed few opportunities for serious acquisitions from France, and Moore was to enjoy only one brief, but spectacular, triumph in 1701.

There remains a further portion of a catalogue of his manuscripts made in his lifetime, continuing the list in the *Catalogi* and beginning with no. 831. This was the work of Thomas Tanner, and the list is now MS. Oo.7.50². It furnishes a conspectus, with some gaps, up to no. 1025, and, again, it was an amalgam of new acquisitions mingled with books previously missed. Nos. 831–913 were apparently entered at about the same time, being arranged by sizes from folio downwards, but they are further distinguished, in a way that had not been followed hitherto, according to whether they are on paper or vellum. Among them were several that had belonged to Moore for some years, such as the catalogue of Sir Thomas Knyvett's library made in the early years of the century, and two were entered for a second time before the duplication was discovered: no. 868, a compilation of instructions for the Master of Wards and Liveries (MS. Ff.4.22), had already been catalogued as no. 460, and no. 860 (MSS. Hh.3.12 and Mm.4.30) as no. 457. But duplicate entries and earlier possessions apart, the section covered over a year of accessions, for the group of Bury St Edmunds manuscripts (nos. 839–44)

---

[107] Perhaps two of the manuscripts sold by Frederic III of Naples, probably after 1501, and acquired by Cardinal Georges d'Amboise, Archbishop of Rouen. (Delisle *Le cabinet des manuscrits* I pp. 234–5).

[108] From the library of Julien Brodeau (d. 1653), dispersed in 1698 or 1699 (Delisle *Le cabinet des manuscrits* I pp. 300–1).

[109] Sold at the sale of Paulus van Uchelen's books in Amsterdam in 1702, for the equivalent of £9.8s.0d., and so acquired by Moore after that date.

[110] See below, pp. 135–7.

came in August 1698, so missing the *Catalogi* itself by only a few weeks, and item 845, a thirteenth-century miscellany from Norwich Cathedral priory containing theological pieces by John Beleth and others (MS. Ff.5.28) was given to Moore by Peter Le Neve in April 1699.[111] The section also includes Davies' sermon preached at Norwich on 13 August 1699 (no. 866). Nos. 914–17 may well also belong to this group, but this is not certain since 914–15 are described in a slightly different manner from the preceding. If, as seems reasonable, it is assumed that Tanner entered the manuscripts in groups, thus being able to follow a very broad arrangement by size, he next began with no. 918, a series of bulky volumes containing an index to law reports. Once again he proceeded through the sizes, this time mixing paper and vellum together, and so reached no. 970, having entered on the way one printed book, Adolphus Occo's *Impp. Romanorum numismata* (Antwerp 1579) interleaved with manuscript notes on the collection of Jacobus Golius and Abraham Ortelius. There then followed one odd volume, a thirteenth-century manuscript from Durham Cathedral containing the Bible and various minor texts,[112] before the next, and final, group.

[111] Not 1639, as the printed catalogue of manuscripts in the Library ludicrously has it.
[112] The manuscript (Kk.5.10) had formerly belonged to the Yorkshire antiquary Walter Stonehouse, whose copy of Nicholas Fuller's *Miscellaneorum theologicorum libri tres* (Oxford 1616) was also in Moore's library. The manuscript was the second from Durham Cathedral to come into Moore's possession. He had possessed a fourteenth-century collection of sermons for several years (MS. Mm.3.14), and besides these eventually owned some six incunabula, including the editiones principes of Tibullus etc. (Venice 1472) and Seneca (Ferrara *c.* 1484), and Guillaume Le Signerre of Milan's folio collected Cicero of 1498–9: the last had once belonged to Thomas Linacre, and came to Moore via the Durham librarian John Milner in whose possession it was still in May 1703. (Cf. Oates *Catalogue* nos. 1613, 1697, 1953, 2225, 2237, and 2323. There is some doubt as to whether these belonged to Durham before or after the dissolution in 1539: see A. J. Piper 'The libraries of the monks of Durham' in M. B. Parkes and Andrew G. Watson (ed.) *Medieval scribes, manuscripts & libraries; essays presented to N. R. Ker* (1978) pp. 213–49.) Despite these numbers, there is no direct evidence that Moore managed on a larger scale to imitate Pepys (who contrived to extract from the Durham authorities a fragment of an eighth-century Gospel Book (MS. A.ii.17) or Harley, who was given a fifteenth-century Suidas in 1715 (Harley 3100; exchanged for D'Achéry's *Spicilegium* in 1715: Wright (ed.) *Diary of Humfrey Wanley* I pp. 13 and 227).

The list closed with fifty-three items, beginning with the largest and breaking off before the smallest had been reached. The group contained the core of Moore's collection of Greek manuscripts, and appears to have come, for the most part, from the continent; it has attracted particular attention[113] because it contains Moore's most widely trumpeted manuscript, one of the two earliest copies extant of Bede's *Historia ecclesiastica*, written perhaps in about 734–7 at Wearmouth or Jarrow and so falling conceivably within Bede's own lifetime (MS. Kk.5.16).[114] The manuscript found its way to Charlemagne's court, and subsequently to Le Mans where it remained until the seventeenth century. The date of Moore's acquisition of so major a manuscript, and its re-entry into England, has exercised various scholars, who have arrived at a consensus of 1697–1702,[115] but there is some evidence to suggest that Moore bought it in August 1701. Wanley referred to it in 1705, and recalled that it had come after the Treaty of Ryswick in 1697: 'In Gallia conservatus fuit Codex satis diligenter, usque ad conclusionem Foederis initis inter Gulielmum Magnae Britanniae Regem & Ludovicum Regem Christianissimum apud Ryswickum, cum vir quidam doctissimus eum cum multis aliis Codd. rarissimis tam Graecis quam Latinis, &c. publica Auctione emerit, & nuperrime eos omnes admodum

---

[113] See for example P. Hunter Blair in *The Moore Bede* (Early English manuscripts in facsimile 9 (Copenhagen 1959)) pp. 25–6; P. E. Easterling 'Two Greek manuscripts of Spanish provenance in Bishop Moore's collection' *Trans. Cambridge Bibliographical Soc.* 3 (1961) pp. 257–62; and R. H. Rodgers 'The Moore Palladius' *ibid.* 5 (1971) pp. 203–16. All stress the homogeneity of MSS. 972–1025, but in fact there are several intruders, as the next paragraphs explain.

[114] On this see, besides the facsimile mentioned in n. 113, the review by David H. Wright in *Anglia* 32 (1964) pp. 110–17; P. McGurk 'Citation marks in early Latin manuscripts' *Scriptorium* 15 (1961) pp. 3–13; O. Arngardt 'On the dating of early Bede manuscripts' *Studia Neophilologica* 45 (1973) pp. 47–52; and M. B. Parkes *The scriptorium of Wearmouth–Jarrow* (Jarrow lecture 1982). It is now thought that the manuscript may have been copied from an exemplar datable to 737. For its place in Charlemagne's library cf. B. Bischoff 'Die Hofbibliothek Karls des Grossen' in W. Braunfels (ed.) *Karl der Grosse; Lebenswerk und Nachleben* (Düsseldorf 1965) II *Das Geistige Leben* ed. B. Bischoff pp. 42–62. The current edition is by B. Colgrave and R. A. B. Mynors, *Bede's Ecclesiastical history of the English people* (Oxford 1969).

[115] Besides the authorities just cited, see N. R. Ker *Catalogue of manuscripts containing Anglo-Saxon* (Oxford 1957) pp. 38–9.

Reverendo Domino Possessori vendiderit.'[116] William Nicolson saw it on 19 January 1701/2, when he dined with Moore in London (and noted incidentally that his library was 'in five rooms, besides Closets');[117] and in 1703 Wanley noted in a letter to John Smith the Saxonist, rector of Gateshead and prebendary of Durham, that 'the book remained in France till after the Peace of Ryswick, when one Mr Cuningham a Scotch Gentleman (who is about a new Edition of the Justinian Code, &c.) brought it with many other valuable MSS. Greek, Latin, &c. at a public auction, & having brought them all over, sold them to my Lord of Norwich'.[118] Unfortunately Wanley gave no further details of this 'Mr Cuningham', but of the two men named Alexander Cunningham then at large on the continent it was probably the classicist whose library, strong in law books, was sold at Leiden in 1730. Friend of numerous Scottish scholars, and editor in 1721 of Horace, he certainly knew Moore and enjoyed close contacts with the Low Countries: he also acted as agent to Sunderland at The Hague. His namesake the historian was also known to Moore, and in August 1701 was in Paris ostensibly on a trade mission but in fact under instructions to discover the state of the French army: if the books were sold in Paris he was thus in a better position to bid for them. It is not known where the auction alluded to by Wanley took place, but in view of the ardour of French collectors in the capital, who would not have allowed such treasures to go, it seems unlikely that it was in Paris. The evidence all points to the first, rather than the second, of the two men.[119] Wanley implied that whoever it was did not have a commission from Moore; but on 21 August 1701 Moore paid

---

[116] H. Wanley *Antiquae literaturae septentrionalis liber alter* (Oxford 1705) p. 288.

[117] 'Bishop Nicolson's diaries' *Trans. Cumberland & Westmorland Antiquarian and Archaeological Soc.* NS I (1901) p. 39.

[118] Bodleian Library MS. Eng. Hist. c. 6 fo. 40, 28 August 1703.

[119] Easterling 'Two Greek manuscripts' p. 257. Besides her references see A. Cunningham *The history of Great Britain from the revolution in 1688, to the accession of George the First* (1787) I pp. xiii and 238, and, for two letters from Cunningham to William Carstares dated from Paris 22 and 26 August 1701, *State-papers and letters addressed to William Carstares* (Edinburgh 1774) pp. 709–10.

'Mr Cunningham' seventy guineas for books, a sum far larger than any other recorded in his accounts relating to his library.[120] It almost certainly included the payment for the Moore Bede.

The manuscript has received almost constant attention since its first arrival. Wanley considered it to have been written at Wearmouth in 737, and by August 1703 he was in correspondence with John Smith, who was anxious to know whether he had any thought of editing it for publication. Smith had mooted a new edition of the *Historia ecclesiastica* for some time previously, and radically altered his plans after 1703: his edition was finally printed by the Cambridge University Press in 1722 under the care of his son, Smith himself having died at Cambridge in 1715. It was the first fresh edition to have appeared since Abraham Whelock's in 1644, and was the first to be based on the Moore manuscript of the Latin text. It remained the standard edition until Plummer's in 1896. Smith had done his work thoroughly, consulting three of the principal early manuscripts, and in the preface was set out the history not only of the Moore manuscript (repeating Wanley's account for Hickes) but also of the text itself, both written and printed. The work was magisterial, but, as Laistner was able to remark of Plummer's work nearly two centuries later, it was regrettably insular. The Leningrad Bede, roughly contemporary with the Moore manuscript, remained apparently unremarked in western Europe until 1880,[121] while other eighth- and ninth-century manuscripts of the text remained unstudied until even more recently.[122]

The Bede was only one among many, and the remainder were by no means uniform. Of the final group of fifty-three, twenty-eight were Greek and the rest a mixture of continental and English origin. In date the Greek manuscripts ranged from

---

[120] Private accounts (see n. 13 above). On 24 June he had also paid Cunningham £10, and he paid another £10.2s.6d. on 15 July.   [121] *Neues Archiv* 5 (1880) p. 260.

[122] M. L. W. Laistner and H. H. King *A hand-list of Bede manuscripts* (Ithaca 1943) pp. 93–4. See also D. Douglas *English scholars* (1939) pp. 73–6.

the eleventh to the seventeenth century, the earliest being a copy of the Acts and Epistles (MS. Kk.6.4) noted with some accuracy by Tanner as being written 'ante annos 600.' and a copy of Aristotle's Nichomachean Ethics written in Sicily in 1279 (MS. Ii.5.44). Most,[123] however, were of the sixteenth century. Two came from Spain, a copy of Demetrius Chomatenus and Constantine Harmenopulos written partly by Nicolas de la Torre (MS. Ff.4.3), and another volume written entirely by de la Torre at Salamanca in 1564 containing the *Synopsis Basilicorum* (MS. Kk.5.11). These appear to have arrived in France in the early seventeenth century. Among the sixteenth-century manuscripts prepared in France itself were a volume of Onosander and Aelian written by Angelos Vergekios in 1569 (MS. Kk.5.31) and a Procopius, with other texts, partly in the hand of Constantine Palaeocappa (MS. Ff.4.2). One, a collection of mathematical works by Aristoxenes and others (MS. Kk.5.26), had once belonged to François I, who had acquired it from Jérome Fondule in 1529: unfortunately it now lacks the binding that it bore in the library at Fontainebleau.[124] Two came from the library of Jacques Mentel (d. 1671), whose medical career has been eclipsed by his fraudulent attempts to prove that his namesake Mentelin invented printing at Strasbourg: Mentel's Greek manuscripts were less controversial, of Erotianus' Lexicon to Hippocrates, Oribasius and Alexander Aphrodisias (MS. Kk.5.7), and a collection of medical works (MS. Mm.1.17). A collection of the letters of Philostratus and others, in the hand of George Hermonymos (MS. Kk.6.23), had once belonged to Guillaume Budé. Many of these manuscripts bear the signature of Jean-Baptiste Hautin (*c.* 1580–1640), the numismatist;[125] his name appears, for example, on the eleventh-century Acts and Epistles and on the Onosander and Aelian, both mentioned

---

[123] For details of several of these manuscripts I am grateful to Mrs. P. E. Easterling.

[124] See H. Omont *Catalogues des manuscrits grecs de Fontainebleau sous François 1er et Henri II* (Paris 1889) p. 371: it is no. 44 in the catalogue of 1550.

[125] On Hautin see, besides Delisle *Le cabinet des manuscrits*, the remarks in Louis Jacob *Traicté des plus belles bibliothèques* (Paris 1644) pp. 514–15.

above, on a Euripides (MS. Mm.1.11), a small Aristides formerly in the possession of Janus Lascaris (MS. Nn.4.42), and further sixteenth-century copies. Besides these Greek texts, Hautin had also inscribed his name on a collection of Wandalbert's works of the late tenth or early eleventh century (MS. Dd.12.54), a volume of Cicero and Boethius of the twelfth or thirteenth century (MS. Ii.6.6), a thirteenth-century group of texts including Julius Firmicus and Macrobius (MS. Kk.6.25), and a fifteenth-century copy of Valerius Maximus (MS. Gg.6.2). Several of these volumes contain notes of contents in the same hand that appears providing similar details in the Moore Bede and a late twelfth-century collection containing Henry of Huntingdon and Bede, for example. Like the Bede, the Henry of Huntingdon (MS. Gg.2.21)[126] had once belonged to Le Mans Cathedral, and they were among several manuscripts from French religious houses that had come into the market only in the seventeenth century. So Moore also gained in 1701 a thirteenth-century Priscian from S. Sulpice, Bourges (MS. Gg.2.32),[127] an eleventh-century manuscript (perhaps also from Bourges) of Nonius Marcellus (MS. Mm.5.22)[128] marked simply 'De Sancto Sulpicio', a fifteenth-century Cicero from Langres (MS. Mm.5.18) and, more important than any of these later manuscripts, a copy of Palladius' *Opus agriculturae* (MS. Kk.5.13) written at St Denis in the second quarter of the ninth century,[129] the earliest complete text of the first thirteen books of this author and still at St Denis in the fourteenth century. Besides these the group included a catalogue of the manuscripts of the comtes de Brienne,[130] a magnificent Sephardi Hebrew Bible (MS. Mm.5.27) of the twelfth century, two copies of Dante, and a

---

[126] This bears the initials 'J. H. 3 ian. 1619' in the capital C on fo. 3ʳ (I am grateful to Miss Sarah Foot for drawing this to my attention).

[127] Cf. Delisle *Le cabinet des manuscrits* 2 pp. 411 and 508.

[128] This manuscript was subsequently collated, in 1712, by Richard Bentley against the 1614 edition: his marked copy is in the British Library, 684.c.14.

[129] R. H. Rodgers 'The Moore Palladius' *Trans. Cambridge Bibliographical Soc.* 5 (1971) pp. 203–16. [130] MS. Mm.2.11; Delisle *Le Cabinet des manuscrits* 1 pp. 214–17.

miscellaneous group of seventeenth-century papers that clearly came from English sources. With (so far as I know) only one exception, all the books from this source and bearing a brief contents list on the flyleaf in the hand that appears, for example, on the manuscript of Henry of Huntingdon, were manuscripts. The exception is a volume (now U.3.53) containing the 1595 catalogue of the Greek manuscripts at Vienna and a copy of Lamprias *De scriptis Plutarchi* (1597). Precisely which of all these had belonged to Hautin, which had been bought by Cunningham, and which had come into Moore's library by other routes remains obscure. Hautin's collection had been broken up as early as April–May 1674, when Baluze purchased several hundred books and manuscripts for Colbert's library.[131] Baluze would have been unlikely to have missed such treasures as the Moore Bede and the Palladius, and it must therefore be assumed that either he was not shown them or that they never belonged to Hautin at all: the distinctive lists of contents in the front of each of the volumes in this group may, in this case, have been made by or for a later collector.

Tanner's descriptions of Moore's manuscripts were considerably more detailed than had been the case for the first items to be entered in Bernard's list (which had, it will be remembered, required some supplementation). He omitted descriptions of books in Arabic, simply assigning such manuscripts numbers in his sequence, but otherwise he compiled his list with commendable comprehensiveness. Monastic provenances were recorded where there was a clear inscription, as for example no. 911 (MS. Ii.6.5), a miscellaneous volume containing the *Viaticum Constantini* etc. from Bury St Edmunds, and no. 881 (MS. Hh.6.11), a thirteenth-century manuscript of Hugh of St Victor etc. from Ramsey Abbey. Particularly beautiful manuscripts were noted, he mentioned the gilt edges

---

131 Bibliothèque Nationale MS. Baluze 100 fo. 60ʳ etc., with a list of books bought. In addition Baluze himself bought a dozen Greek manuscripts, which passed into the royal library in 1719: see H. Omont *Inventaire sommaire des manuscrits grecs de la Bibliothèque Nationale* 4 (Paris 1898) p. xviii. See also, for a list of Hautin's Latin manuscripts in Baluze's collection, Delisle *Le Cabinet des manuscrits* 1 p. 365.

of the Hebrew Bible (no. 1006), and those of notable age were classed as either 'vetustus' (no. 936, an assortment of the eleventh and early twelfth centuries opening with Boethius *De arithmetica*, perhaps once at Glastonbury), 'antiquum' for slightly more modern books, or, in the case of the Bede, 'pervetustus'; falling midway, the early ninth-century Palladius was classed as 'exemplar vetustissimum'. With one exception (already alluded to), he made no attempt to date the Greek or Hebrew manuscripts (Montfaucon's *Palaeographia Graeca* did not appear until 1708),[132] and his solitary attempt was in connection with no. 1014 (MS. Kk.6.4), 'Acta Apostolorum, Epistolae Canonicae et Pauli Graece (ante annos 600 script.)', a volume written in the eleventh century.

Tanner's manuscript continuation of the lists published in Bernard's *Catalogi* ends with no. 1025. It thus breaks off in the middle of the group of Greek manuscripts and others imported from France, omitting the smaller-sized ones. A further eight can be identified as belonging to the group, seven of them in Greek and four bearing Hautin's name. These have been considered with the rest of the group above, but with the end of Tanner's list, evidence of the contents of Moore's collection of manuscripts becomes sparse. Most of the loose papers had not been described at all, and their incorporation into the rest of the collection once it was in the University Library swelled the overall numbers very substantially: in 1829 C. H. Hartshorne repeated the number first quoted by Samuel Knight, dean of Ely, to Thomas Baker, and claimed that Moore had owned 1790 manuscripts, but it is not clear how they were counted. In 1736 the University Library authorities commissioned a bookplate to be pasted into all Moore's books, but it was not used with complete accuracy or discrimination. Therefore, although the numbering was continued in the eighteenth century up to no. 1060, and many of Moore's

---

[132] On early attempts to date Greek manuscripts see P. E. Easterling 'Before palaeography; notes on early descriptions and datings of Greek manuscripts' *Studia Codicologica* 1977 pp. 179–87.

manuscripts are to be found in this further, and final, supplement — including James Duport's commentary on Theophrastus reprinted by Needham in his edition published at Cambridge in 1712, and Robert Warren's translation of Erasmus dedicated to Moore as Bishop of Norwich – the group is by no means obvious. The catalogue of Richard Holdsworth's library, for example, had been written for the Library by William Crow of Caius in 1663–4, and was entered among these additional miscellanea as no. 1034. It stands as a warning against too hasty conclusions; but there is a strong likelihood that the Clare College copy of John Scott's late sixteenth-century account of the University (MS. Gg.5.21; no. 1059) came from Moore's collection, if only because of Moore's connection with the college. Another manuscript (*olim* Gg.4.1; no. 1057) was restored (with MS. Ee.3.57) to Norwich in 1770,[133] and two more, both Greek (MSS. Ff.6.32 and Gg.1.2; nos. 1043 and 1047) bear the same handwriting as the 'Hautin' group discussed above. Amidst so many uncertainties, however, one thing seems clear: that once Tanner stopped his work in the first months of the eighteenth century, no further list of Moore's manuscripts was compiled until long after they had arrived in Cambridge.

Moore died on 31 July 1714, the day before Queen Anne, with whom he had been so closely associated. He had acquired fewer manuscripts in his last years, and most of his early printed books had been in his possession by 1705-10. The first years of the new century brought a new generation of book collectors who, if they were not quite the first great collectors of printed books, as de Ricci has described them,[134] undoubtedly wielded longer purses than Moore. The Duke of Devonshire, the Duke of Roxburghe, the Earl of Sunderland, and Robert Harley, Earl of Oxford, were all battling for what Moore had once been

---

[133] Grace Book *K* p. 498.
[134] S. de Ricci *English collectors of books and manuscripts (1530–1930)* (Cambridge 1930) p. 33.

able to command virtually alone, and their activities, coupled with the already large size of his library, inevitably affected his collecting in his later years.

The disposition of his library thus posed problems and difficulties quite different from those of a previous generation. It was large, even vast by contemporary standards, and it contained many things of value for which there was a ready market. The possibilities consequent on purchasing such a collection were not lost at least on Harley, who within days of Moore's death was seriously considering buying the manuscript collection outright. By 30 August Wanley (already familiar with much of the collection) was able to report in some detail on the position:

1. Whereas my Lord Bishop formerly did cause his MSS. to be numbered successively as they were brought in; that good order was discontinued divers years before his decease; so that those necessary marks are wanting in many of them.

2. Many books which have been so marked do now want the said numbers; either by being newly bound, or by being mangled through negligence or petulancy.

3. Many others which still have their marks cannot easily be found in the printed catalogue, because they were either erroneously marked at first; or else the print is faulty; or both.

4. Divers MSS. of value mentioned in the said printed Catalogue could not be produced to me, being either lent out, mislaid, or lost. Such are, Two Copies of Suetonius, said to belong to Dr. Bentley. A fine Register of the See of Hereford, said to be lent to the present Lord Bishop of Hereford.[135] Ovidius de Nuce, an exceeding old copy, lent or mislaid. Tullie's Tusculan Questions, mentioned in the said printed Catalogue. No.32. Original Epistles of our ancient learned Protestant Divines. No.125. Statutes of Norwich Cathedral temp. R. Hen. VIII. No.203. Charters of Westminster Church. No.223. Old Chartulary of Ely. No.236. Books of Queen Elizabeth's Jewels. No.254, 255. Pars Γεωπονικων[136] cum aliis Graecis, man. vet. No.87. Index Librorum Graecorum Bibliothecae Palatinae per Dav. Hamaxungum. No.671.[137]

---

[135] In 1714 the Bishop of Hereford was Philip Bisse; Wanley presumably refers to MS. Dd.10.18, a fourteenth-century cartulary. [136] The original reads Γεω πορικωμ. [137] MS. Dd.12.70. Cf. P. E. Easterling 'Another copy of Sylburg's catalogue of the Palatini Graeci' *Byzant. Zeitschrift* 56 (1963) pp. 261–4.

The Original Foundation Charter of the Cathedral Church of Norwich. No.160. Bedae Histor. Eccles. formerly belonging to the Monastery of Plympton;[138] and many others too tedious here to enumerate.

5. Through the negligence or petulancy above-mentioned, or else mere stupidity, books which were out of their bindings have been quite disjoined, so that their several parts cannot be found and put together: which is the fault of the Leiger book of Ossulverstone and others. In like sort the modern letters were thrown on the ground and trodden under foot; nay, very lately part of them were burned on purpose, and others industriously mangled with the penknife.

6. This management needed not to have been introduced into that place, where my Lord Bishop bought all manuscripts that offered, good, bad, or indifferent, without making any delectus. This custom hath in process of time raised the vast number of old books of small or no value, which I found there, such as vulgar Latin Bibles, Psalters, Primers, and other Books of Superstitious Devotion, Old Scholemen, Postils, Sermons, and such trash; heaps of common place Books and Notes of Divinity, Law, Physic, Chirurgery, Heraldry, Philosopher's Stone, &c. Rubbish Reports and such trumpery stuff that make one sick to look at them, being really fitter for any other room in the house rather than the library.

7. Another thing hath been omitted that might have advanced the price of the Collection; I mean, the putting down some note of the curiosity and usefulness of such a book or books. My Lord of Ely was certainly apprised of such matters; as that this was the work of such a person; or the handwriting of such another; or fit to be consulted on such an occasion; but this knowledge being now dead with him, the price of those books is lowered thereby.

8. Some manuscripts have been found placed among the printed books of the classical kind: as to this sort of MSS. here I find the Latin Classicks to be almost all of them recent copies. As to the Greek manuscripts (taking them in the whole), there are but two very ancient books among them, both which are imperfect; the rest being, for the far greater part (like the Latin classics), later copies and paper transcripts.

9. As to the parcel of Oriental Manuscripts lately belonging to Dr. Sike, of Cambridge,[139] most of them suffer by being unknown. Moreover, the parcel seems to have been garbled before my Lord of Ely bought it, and

---

[138] British Library MS. Add.14250, a twelfth-century manuscript acquired at the sale of the library of Jeremiah Milles, dean of Exeter, on 15 April 1843.

[139] I.e. Henry Sykes or Sike, Regius Professor of Hebrew 1705-12, who came from Bremen and hanged himself at Trinity College in May 1712. He had owned MS. Dd.9.49, a treatise on Mohammedan law and ritual.

wanting the proper titles, the languages being not cultivated, it can now be but of little worth.[140]

Despite all the imperfections and gaps in the collection, its attractions easily outweighed its disadvantages, and Wanley seems to have been confident of his prey. On 4 September, in reply to a letter from him on the subject, the Saxonist John Smith replied, 'I am rejoyced to hear y[t.] y[e.] B[P.] of Elys Library is in so fair a way of coming to y[e] Harleyan Collection. Tw[d.] be a Thous[d.] pittys y[e.] Booksellers sh[d.] have it to squander away again, Indeed no Body sh[d.] have it but my Lord who has so Noble a Treasure of his own to bring it to.'[141] But Moore's sole executor, his erstwhile chaplain Samuel Clarke, quickly brought less cheerful news, and replied to Wanley on the same day that 'The Persons concerned in the Division of my late Lord of Ely's Estate cannot think of offering the Books at less than eight thousand pounds. It will be your care to let me know my Lord Harley's Intention, as soon as conveniently you can; the Persons concerned, being minded to agree with any One that shall make the first reasonable Offer.'[142] Harley thought this too high a price for the printed books and the manuscripts (and Wanley's main interest was in the manuscripts), and almost two months later was finally forced to conclude that he would have to risk their going elsewhere: 'I do not think to give so much money for it as they ask: I think the best way is to let Bateman bye it or let it come to an auction and get the valuable books, and those that I have a mind for, without the trouble of all the rubish and Duplicates: this is my opinion but I would have you ask my Father what his Thoughts are.'[143]

Whether or not Christopher Bateman, the leading second-hand bookseller in London and from whom Moore had bought many of his books, was ever a serious contender for the

[140] *European Magazine* June 1801 pp. 407–8.
[141] British Library MS. Harley 3781 fo. 108[r].
[142] British Library MS. Harley 3778 fo. 75. See also Hartshorne *Book rarities* p. 20.
[143] Letter of 16 November, quoted Wright (ed.) *Diary of Humfrey Wanley* I p. xxvi.

library, is unclear. The price was a high one for a bookseller to find unless he was to be allowed to sell gradually on commission, and the only real choice lay between outright sale of the printed books and manuscripts either together or in two separate parts (as had happened to Stillingfleet's library in 1707, the manuscripts going to Harley and the books to Narcissus Marsh), and auction. Wanley may have feared that the booksellers and auctioneers were potentially well placed: Moore had been now dead for several months, and there was still no sale; but he was proved wrong.

Nor was he alone in his interest, for although by November Harley had been forced to his reluctant conclusion despite Wanley's hopes, Wanley himself had also been sounding out other possible contenders. One such was Dr John Radcliffe, physician to the late Queen, and known to be in the throes of composing his will that summer. Tanner had hoped for some months that Radcliffe would leave a substantial sum of money to the Bodleian for purchases of books (his intention of providing for the building of a library in Oxford had been known since 1712), and the previous December Tanner had hoped even for five hundred or a thousand pounds a year. Moore's death in July put Radcliffe's possible benefactions in another light, however, and prompted him to write the following month, 'I believe there is nothing as yet determined about the manner of the sale of late L^d. of Elys library – wch would be a noble present for Dr Radcliff or some other generous benefactor to make to Oxford.' In the event Radcliffe divided the bulk of his estate between University College and what became the Radcliffe Trustees, with £40,000 left specifically for 'building a library in Oxford' (the present Radcliffe Camera) and only a hundred pounds a year for buying books. He died on 1 November, and his will was proved on 8 December. The interval allowed ample room for speculation as to his final wishes, and the possibility that there might be further money for Bodleian purchases was an attractive one.[144] So, with Oxford's buying power in theory so much increased, Wanley enquired of Bodley's Librarian John Hudson as to his intentions. Hudson was frank:

We know little more of Dr Radcliffe's great Benefaction y^n what is in ye news-papers: We intend to buy ye B^p of Ely's books, if we can have y^m upon reasonable terms. I am sure we shall not want half of y^m: & I am afraid, y^t if we were ye purchasers, ye oth^r half would sell for a 1000^l. I perswade myself y^t what we should leave, would be of greater value y^n w^t we take: & yet for all this I'll venture a wager, yt ye remaind^r does not sell for above what I have mention'd. Unless y^e King buys y^e Study, I know not who will bid agst us. For since y^e madness of private persons is not so great, as to throw away vast sums of money for no real use or advantage to y^{m}selves or oth^{rs} This $Bιβλιομανία$ yt has prevail'd so much (to ye great prejudice of Learning) will by degrees cool & grow out of fashion: I perswade myself yt after two or three persons drop, books will goe at easier rates y^n ever.[145]

Hudson's hopes were, however, dashed; and while Oxford received one of the most remarkable endowments in its history, eventually permitting the building of an architectural masterpiece, Moore's books went to Cambridge.

It is not known to whose inspiration Cambridge owes the acquisition of the library. But there were political, economic and scholarly points that could all be made in its favour, and Cambridge owed most to the acumen and sympathy of Charles, 2nd Viscount Townshend. He had been educated at King's College, where he had matriculated as a Fellow Commoner in 1691. As Lord Lieutenant of Norfolk he had been well acquainted with Moore, the Bishop of Norwich, and on 17 September 1714 he became Secretary of State in the new Hanoverian government. It was he who was persuaded, and persuaded the new King George I, to purchase the library outright. In pressing the claims of Cambridge (Moore's own university) he might – had he wished: there is no direct

144 Details on Radcliffe are from Francis Atterbury *Epistolary correspondence* (1784) 3 p. 307, quoted in *Bibliotheca Radcliviana 1749–1949* (Bodleian Library exhibition catalogue 1949) p. 10, and S. G. Gillam *The building accounts of the Radcliffe Camera* (Oxford Historical Society 1958) p. vii.
145 Hudson to Wanley 13 November 1714 (British Library MS. Harley 3779 fo. 320).

evidence – have pointed to Radcliffe's plans for Oxford, or to the ostentatious display of loyalty by the University to the new house in its address to the King on 24 September 1714; or he might simply have pointed to the need for a better collection of books at Cambridge. The gift was motivated at once by political acumen and by an element of sheer generosity, and in subsequent years the University naturally fastened on the latter. Politically, the University was as uncertain of the new dynasty as elsewhere,[146] but Hearne for one, writing in Oxford, did not miss any favours shown to one university over the other. On 28 September he noted of the previous Friday's events, when the two universities presented their loyal addresses, 'As for the Cambridge Address, wch is rather more base and flattering than Oxford, it was immediately presented, together with their Verses, & they were much better receiv'd than the Gentlemen of Oxford.' He could scarcely be enthusiastic about the Hanoverian monarch, but Oxford's reception had been somewhat more cool by comparison – despite their address which Hearne described as 'flattering, cringing, & unbecoming loyal Men'.[147]

It became known only the following May that the King intended to purchase Moore's library,[148] and give it to Cambridge; but the formal announcement was delayed until well over a year after Moore's death. On 20 September 1715

---

[146] Cf. W. Matthews (ed.) *The diary of Dudley Ryder, 1715–1716* (1939) p. 189: 'Dined at brother's. There was Cousin John Ryder come from Cambridge. He says the great majority there are against the King, though they all, except five or six, take the oaths to him. They are also much inclined towards popery and are introducing its several practices and doctrines by degrees ...' This was after the 1715 rebellion. The Vice-Chancellor himself, Thomas Sherlock, did not make his own views public until after the battle of Preston. On the political opinions of the two universities see also Christopher Wordsworth *Social life at the English universities in the eighteenth century* (Cambridge 1874) pp. 40–7, and, for continuing Jacobitism at Oxford, Eveline Cruickshanks' remarks in Romney Sedgwick *The House of Commons 1715–1754* (1970) pp. 306–7.

[147] Hearne *Remarks and collections* 4 p. 410. According to Hearne, the subsequent coronation celebrations at Oxford were no more than tepid.

[148] Thomas Baker to John Strype 7 May 1715: 'Just now I am told, the King intends to make a gift of the late Bp: of Ely's Library, to the University of Cambridge' (MS. Add. 10 fo. 92).

Townshend was able, at last, to write formally to Thomas Sherlock, Vice-Chancellor and Master of St Catharine's,

Reverend Sir

I have received His Majesty's commands to acquaint you that for the incouragement of Learning, and as a mark of His Royall Favour he gives to the University of Cambridge the Library of the late Bishop of Ely. It is with great satisfaction I send you this notice, which I desire you will communicate to the Heads of Houses and Senate.[149]

His letter was read out to the full Senate on the 22nd, and two days later the same body approved a formal letter of thanks to him as a corollary to that already addressed to the King. 'Had not your Lordship remembered the place of your Education with a kindness almost peculiar to your self, we had wanted that great Encouragement of Learning, which now by your Lordships powerfull interposition on our behalfe we enjoy from the King's Bounty.'[150] To this Townshend was properly self-depreciatory: the gift came from the King, not from him. According to his account he had done no more than suggest an 'agreable' mode in which the King might signify his favour to the University. Political acuteness or no, the gift was a truly royal one in every sense:

I am much obliged to you for the Honour of your Letter and for the kind acknowledgments which you are pleased to bestow on my endeavours for your service; but I should be guilty of Ingratitude to His Ma^{ty}. and of Injustice to you did I suffer that to be ascribed to my Interposition which was so entirely owing to His Majesty's generous inclination to encourage His Faithfull University of Cambridge. The only part I can assume to myself is that of having suggested to His Ma^{ty's}. wishes such a method of conveying his Royal Favour as I hoped might prove most agreable to you; nor was it possible that much sollicitation should be necessary to induce Him to furnish you with those Materials of Learning which He was Secure would become so many Weapons in your hands to guard and maintain the Faith of the Church, the Rights of the Crown and the Libertys of the British Constitution.

I hope you will continue me the justice to believe that I shall gladly embrace every opportunity of testifying the unfeigned affection and

---

[149] Luard 153 (1).
[150] Luard 153 (2). The copy sent to Townshend is now MS. Add. 6211 (1).

CAMBRIDGE UNIVERSITY LIBRARY

gratitude I shall ever retain for that University within which I had the Happiness to receive my Education.[151]

Sherlock presented the second address from the University to the King in the space of just over a year on 29 September accompanied by a deputation from Cambridge and introduced by Townshend. He alluded indirectly to the time spent at King's both by Townshend and by Robert Walpole (who had entered the same college as a scholar four years later), and to earlier royal benefactions; he was also quick to remark, on the King's qualities as patron and encourager of learning, that 'such Royal qualities must necessarily produce the proper returns of Duty & affection: Your University will endeavour as she is bound to do by the strongest tyes of Interest and Gratitude, to promote the happiness of your Government' And as for the gift itself, he was able to announce at the same time that it was to be known by the title it has retained ever since, to the mystification of generations of readers and the perplexity of those who remember other 'royal libraries' in the British Museum:

The noble collection of Books & Manuscripts gathered in many years by the great industry & accurate Judgment of the late Bishop of Ely, tho' in itself exceedingly valuable, is upon no account so welcome to your University, as that it is a Testimony of your Royal favour: the Memory of which will be constantly preserved by this ample benefaction, worthy to bear the title of the Donor, & to be for ever styled THE ROYAL LIBRARY.[152]

---

[151] MS. Add. 6211 (2). See also Grace Book Θ, insertion between pp. 652 and 653.

[152] Cooper *Annals* 4 pp. 140–1; see also Grace Book Θ pp. 641–5 and the *London Gazette* October 1715. Cooper also prints, with some variations, the verses attributed variously to Joseph Trapp and Thomas Warton (both Professors of Poetry at Oxford) occasioned by a sortie to Oxford in pursuit of some Jacobite army officers. The lines are usually quoted as

> The King observing with judicious eyes
> The state of both his universities,
> To Oxford sent a troop of horse; and why?
> That learned body wanted loyalty.
> To Cambridge books he sent, as well discerning
> How much that loyal body wanted learning.

This later provoked a retort from Sir William Browne (donor of the Browne medal for classical composition):

The warrant for payment of the price of the collection, £6450 'for the Library of ye Printed Books and Manuscripts of the said Bishop, which were left at Ely House in Holbourn at the time of his Decease, or were Lent out by him before his Death' was issued on 24 October, and Samuel Clarke received payment in full from the Civil List on 9 November, one of the last items to go through in the financial year.[153]

The gift of so celebrated and valuable a library was rightly acclaimed by the University as a whole. By his outstanding act of generosity the King had done much more than provide Cambridge with a collection of early books and manuscripts. He had also endowed it with a collection of national importance, in many respects more important than the Royal Library itself; and this in turn entailed obligations and expectations that the University realized only gradually.[154] But apart from the manuscripts, which had so entranced Wanley, and the early printed books and other rarities, recognized or unknown, the collection also included quantities of modern books that had been regarded with dismay by some who would have acquired the library. The University was to tackle the question of duplicates only in the 1740s, and it proved a relatively minor worry. Much more importantly, the acquisition of Moore's books also did much to repair the neglect, mismanagement and laziness of the University over the previous thirty or more years, and in addition provided what the meagre funds of the Library and the inadequate provisions for deposit under the Licensing Acts had failed to

The King to Oxford sent a troop of horse,
For Tories own no argument but force;
With equal skill to Cambridge books he sent,
For Whigs admit no force but argument.
(See Wordsworth *Social life at the English universities* p. 5.)

[153] The Treasury order (MS. Add. 4357) was presented to the Library by J. C. Fox in 1905, after it had been saved in 1840 from a fishmonger in Hungerford market who had bought it with other Exchequer records at £8 a ton.

[154] 'I do not so much rejoice as might be expected, at it', wrote William Wake to William King, Archbishop of Dublin, in July 1715. 'They will neither make use of them, nor be obliged by the gift of them.' (Quoted in Norman Sykes *William Wake, Archbishop of Canterbury, 1657–1737* (Cambridge 1957) 2 p. 132.)

provide. Moore's library, a research library long before it arrived in Cambridge, easily outnumbered the books already in the University Library as regards both early and more recent works, and thrust it into international prominence.

The University Library had received no major gift of books since Richard Holdsworth's and Henry Lucas' bequests in 1663–4, and the rather smaller collection of John Hacket in 1670. It still relied almost solely for purchases on the income from the estates bought with Tobias Rustat's gift of 1666–7; and although the University had been empowered for much of the time since 1662 to receive one copy of every book printed in Great Britain, under the Licensing Acts and the more recent Copyright Act of Queen Anne, the number of books entering the Library had not been great. In 1710 von Uffenbach, clearly unimpressed, had been moved to remark as we shall see, that the Library was kept 'in two mean rooms of moderate size', and that the printed books were 'very ill arranged, in utter confusion'.[155] These two rooms contained between them in 1709 a total of 16,297 volumes, of which 658 were manuscripts. Of these, 12,623 printed books were in the 'Great Room' (i.e. the South Room), and 3016 printed books with the manuscripts in the 'Lesser Room', Rotherham's old library, later to be rebuilt as the East Room.[156] To these were now added Moore's library, estimated as containing 28,965 volumes of printed books and 1790 of manuscripts.[157] The Library was thus all but trebled in simple numerical terms, while the existing collections were transformed at every point.

---

[155] *Cambridge under Queen Anne* p. 140.
[156] Luard 207. See also Oates *History* p. 481, and pp. 154–5 below.
[157] The figures quoted by Hartshorne in 1829, p. 23, based on a note by Thomas Baker who had been provided with them by Samuel Knight (1675–1746), the biographer of Erasmus.

5

THE CHALLENGE OF THE ROYAL LIBRARY

THE UNIVERSITY, having thus enacted its public business, turned at once to the practical details of transferring its latest asset to Cambridge. The associated problems admitted of no easy answer. Existing space in the Library was hopelessly – and obviously – inadequate, while the number of books suddenly needing to be sorted, classified and catalogued was overwhelming, and both the University and the Library faced a crisis. The ways in which they responded to this challenge, the means employed to cope with the books, the erratic search for staff competent to look after them, the losses, sales and eventual success in imposing order on the collection after thirty-odd years, form the subject of the next pages.

So far from reducing members of the University to silence, the magnitude of the task began to attract a variety of proposals of more or less imagination. Of the most grandiose of all new building schemes at first put forward, no formal record remains, and it progressed (for the moment) no further than gossip. On 16 October Thomas Baker wrote to Strype,

As to a new Library, I have nothing certain to inform. The Law Schools have been spoke of, but as there is hardly roome enough, so they that think of that, seem neither to consult the honor of the Donor, or of the University. The great design, wch. is likewise spoke of, is a new Building to front ye present Schools, on either side the Regent Walks, with an Arch in the middle. For this money is wanting, & yet if it were begun, I should hope, such a public work would hardly stick for want of encouragement. In the meanwhile that wing of the Library is spoke of for the MSS:, in part of wch the present MSS are lodg'd already, & the printed Books to be remov'd.[1]

---

[1] MS. Add. 10 fo. 96.

The authorities moved in their own way, however, and a syndicate to organize the operation was appointed on 9 November. Richard Bentley, to the fore here as so often, and already familiar with Moore's library, was joined by William Grigg, Master of Moore's own college, Thomas Crosse (Proctor a year later and subsequently Master of St Catharine's), Benjamin Langwith and Henry Bull of Queens', and Theophilus Shelton of Magdalene. Philip Brooke, the Library Keeper since 1712 and Fellow of St John's, was not among these men, who were appointed to arrange both for the removal of the books and for their proper safety until bookcases could be built.[2] Work began at Ely House within a few days. The main contractor for the London packing was the bookseller Christopher Bateman who, as has been seen, had himself once entertained hopes of selling the collection. He was assisted by a joiner to build suitable boxes, a porter, and four assistants who between them packed the books into bags and cases. Their work was supervised by Francis Say, secretary to Moore and his successors until he was appointed librarian to Queen Caroline in 1737; and by 14 December thirty-one cases and 212 bags had been despatched to Cambridge. The work was finished by Christmas, and the University paid the last of the attendant bills on 9 February.[3]

The task had been completed with admirable speed and efficiency, but no such claims can be made for the subsequent events. The most pressing difficulty lay in the Library building itself. There had been no need for any expansion into other parts of the Schools building since 1649, and the total accommodation for the Library thus remained the east and south rooms on the first floor. In 1710 Zacharias Conrad von Uffenbach had visited Cambridge and set down, in characteristically pained tones, his views of the Library as it was then:

In the morning we went into the *collegium publicum*, commonly called *the school*, in which are the *auditoria publica* and the library. It is an old, mean building. We saw below too a small room in which the academic council

[2] Grace Book Θ pp. 654–5.
[3] For details, see Vouchers for 1715–16 (University Archives).

meets: there is nothing however remarkable in it, except the representation of the senate, copied from an ancient picture, as the inscription upon it states, amongst other matters. Above is the library in two mean rooms of moderate size. In the first, on the left hand side, are the printed books, but very ill arranged, in utter confusion. The catalogue is only alphabetical, and lately compiled on the basis of the Bodleian catalogue. It is also local, indicating where the books are to be sought. In the second room, which is half empty, there were some more printed books, and then the MSS., of which however we could see nothing well, because the librarian, Dr. *Laughton* (or as they pronounce it, *Laffton*) was absent; which vexed me not a little.[4]

With both rooms thus on the first floor, the entire ground floor as well as the west and north rooms upstairs were left to the other needs of the University. The building programme which gradually emerged over the next forty or so years, involving the abandoning of the old Regent House, on the first floor at the north end, to the needs of the Library, and the erection of a new Senate House, was the direct result of the need for space for Moore's books. No-one foresaw in 1716, however, to what measures the University would be driven. It lacked enough money to embark at once on an ambitious scheme such as that described by Baker in October 1715, and as a result proceeded in a series of compromises. Where a modern librarian, faced with such a Herculean need as an immediate two hundred per cent increase in his shelf space, might compute its practical implications in a few minutes, one of the most remarkable features of developments after 1716 was that no-one seems to have calculated the shelving required for Moore's library. Baker, powerless as *socius ejectus* in St John's, was one of the few to foresee the difficulties. 'We seem', he wrote to Strype, 'to have come to a resolution, to fit up the Law Schools for the Bp: of Ely's Books, but as the execution will be slow, so I am sure, there will want rooms for a great part of them.'[5] The authorities proceeded piecemeal, their attention being first engaged by the western range of the Schools. After their arrival from London, the books seem to have been stored here first, but on the ground floor, while the room above, the

4 *Cambridge under Queen Anne* p. 140.   5 MS. Add. 10 fo. 99 [June 1716].

school of law, was an obvious repository of a more permanent nature. It was on the same level as the rest of the Library, but in order for it to be made more accessible some further measures were needed. As Loggan's view of 1688 clearly shows (see fig. 1), this range had no direct connection with the south range. The corner between the west end of the south range and the south end of the west was owned by King's College and occupied by a single-storey porters' lodge for their old court. Negotiations were successfully concluded with the College with little delay, and the University leased the space over this lodge in which was constructed a link room between the south and west ranges. The new room (fig. 3), fitted out with wall cases from floor to ceiling, was dominated by carved wooden columns 'after the composed order', as the carver, John Woodward, phrased it in his bill of 3 October 1720.[6] From the first, this new room, decidedly modern in taste, had been designed to house the manuscripts, and it became the focal point of views depicting the interior of the Library. Meanwhile the West Room, newly accessible through the south end, had been drastically modernized, with new sets of windows, and had been fitted out with bookcases made by John Austin,[7] who had made the bookcases for Archbishop Sancroft's library at Emmanuel in 1705–7 and who with Cornelius Austin and Grinling Gibbons had been responsible for much of the woodwork in the Wren Library at Trinity.[8] The alterations to the West Room were completed in the middle of 1718, but the expense to the University of so much building work between 1715 and 1720 was so formidable that, according to Baker, purchases of books had to be seriously curtailed.[9]

[6] Vouchers 3 October 1720. See also Willis & Clark 3 p. 33.
[7] Willis & Clark 3 p. 33. These cases are now in the north and south galleries of the first floor in the University Library.
[8] For the Austins' surviving work in the colleges see *An inventory of the historical monuments in the City of Cambridge* (1959) p. cxxi *et passim*.
[9] On 8 March 1717/18 he wrote to Strype, 'Your book in Royal Paper would be very fit for the University, if they had moneys to spare, but they are at such expence in fitting up Libraries (one part whereof is almost finisht, tho' it will not hold much above half the Books) that they have nothing left to purchase Books: so that unless you be inclin'd to be a Benefactor, I doubt, we shall want a usefull Book.' MS. Add. 10, fo. 117.

3   The Dome Room in the early nineteenth century, showing the Lewis cabinet (see pp. 236, 240–1). Size of original 108 × 173 mm.

Baker, an inexhaustible correspondent, recounted the latest events to White Kennett, with whom he was in touch on antiquarian matters:

We are now partly come to a Resolution of taking in yᵉ Regent House or whole Square to make room for his Majesties Books. A new Regent House or place of Assembly is spoke off, and I am told our new vicechan: is now at London, solliciting that affair having had encouragemᵗ. from our Chancellor & others. The necessity of this might have been foreseen at first, for by yᵉ best Computation I can make the Law Schools (now almost fitted up) will not receive much more than half yᵉ Books: & if I am not out in my Computation we can hardly have yᵉ Use of yᵉ Books, these two Years yet at soonest, I shall be glad to be mistaken.[10]

He was right. The books were still not all housed. Even the expedient of building a large bookcase down the centre of the whole length of the new West Room still left more lying round in heaps.[11]

[10]   British Library MS. Lansdowne 988 fo. 266ᵛ: Baker to Kennett 14 December [1717?].
[11]   Conyers Middleton *Bibliothecae Cantabrigiensis ordinandae methodus* (Cambridge 1723).

Further building to the east of the schools, over the land occupied by the houses in Regent Walk, had been talked of in 1715, as we have seen, and this was at last put on a formal footing in March 1718/19 with the appointment of another syndicate to purchase the north side of Regent Walk. With a whiff in the air of further financial help from London, all seemed set for one of the most ambitious plans ever to be put forward for the University. The new syndicate, faced with properties belonging to Caius and with the house of the Regius Professor of Physic, found it necessary to appeal to the House of Lords to bring in a Bill enabling the University to acquire the land for development. The Act became law on 11 June 1720, and the buildings were gradually acquired over the next four years.[12] So far the proposed schemes had, officially at least, included no more than a new Senate House, to replace the old Regent House that members of the University had felt to be so inadequate since at least 1673 (the Sheldonian Theatre at Oxford was built in 1664–9).[13] Unofficially there was also talk of extending the east front of the Library. But the scheme now put forward, inspired by James Burrough, Fellow of Caius, was of much greater daring. In 1720 Burrough was no more than thirty years old, and he was to live to become in turn Esquire Bedell and Master of his college; but he left his mark most effectively on the University in thirty years as an architect and 'improver' to half a dozen colleges, where he showed himself to be a designer of some skill. His proposal for the new Senate House was however his first essay (or at least, the first to command recognition) in this art, and was one of refreshing originality. In brief, Burrough proposed to build a new east front to the Library in front of Rotherham's, and to add two arms to the east, the northern to be a new Senate House and the southern to contain what became designated as the Consistory and Register Office.[14] Details emerged only gradually, and

---

[12] See Grace Book *I* pp. 22–3, and Willis & Clark 3 pp. 43–4 (quoting the University's petition to the King) and 48. The University had acquired some of this land in 1674: see Willis & Clark 3 pp. 40–1.   [13] Willis & Clark 3 p. 40.

[14] For Burrough's career see J. W. Clark in *DNB* and J. Venn *Biographical history of Gonville and Caius College* 3 (Cambridge 1901) pp. 126–9.

were indeed unclear to the University at large until the publication of an engraving of the proposed design in 1722. Even Baker could raise only uncertain hopes when he wrote to Kennett on 25 April 1721:

We are very busy in pulling down houses to make way for a new building, whether Library, or Theatre, or Regent House I do not well know; I should be glad to see a new building rise. They cut down their trees at Kings College, & cleared the ground for a magnificent design, and yet all is like to be blasted by their misfortunes in yᵉ south Sea. I wish the times were more propitious for building.[15]

He was to be proved rightly pessimistic about the completion of the scheme, but not for the reasons he feared. The bursting of the South Sea Bubble in the autumn of 1720 had put an end to much financial speculation and King's hopes for Hawksmoor's plans for the College,[16] but it did not seriously affect the University.

But whereas the idea for the new three-sided court facing Great St Mary's seems to have been originally Burrough's, the execution of it was placed in the hands of James Gibbs, a man already familiar to some circles at Cambridge as the protégé of Lord Harley at Wimpole and friend of Matthew Prior, who in 1719 had been the instrument of the Master of St John's in an unsuccessful attempt to persuade Harley to provide money for a new college chapel.[17] Had Harley come forward with the capital, the chapel was to have been designed by Gibbs, but the scheme came to nothing. Two years later, however, the new University Library, offices, and Senate House seemed to offer a more certain future. Gibbs had produced tentative plans by

[15] British Library MS. Lansdowne 988 fo. 228ᵛ.
[16] Willis & Clark 1 pp. 556–60, though the authors did not realize the College's misfortunes. On Hawksmoor in Cambridge see also S. Lang, 'Cambridge and Oxford transformed: Hawksmoor as town planner' *Architectural Review* (April 1948) pp. 157–60; D. Roberts *The town of Cambridge as it ought to be reformed* (privately printed, Cambridge 1955); and Kerry Downes *Hawksmoor* (2nd ed. 1979) pp. 110–21.
[17] See Bryan Little *The life and work of James Gibbs, 1682–1754* (1955) pp. 53–4. A letter from Baker to Hearne (13 December 1719), describing a reception in honour of the Harleys in the college library, at which Prior spoke some verses 'with some Intimation of a charitable design' is quoted in Hearne's *Remarks and collections* 7 (Oxford 1906) p. 80. See also Matthew Prior, *Literary works* ed. H. Bunker Wright and Monroe K. Spears (2nd ed. Oxford 1971) 1 pp. 521–2 and 2 pp. 978–9.

December 1721, and on the 11th Edward Lany, Master of Pembroke and a member of the building syndicate, wrote to Lord Harley acknowledging their receipt.

I am very much obliged to your care to send Mr. Gibbs's design for our building. I design to offer it to the Syndics as soon as they meet. I have not skill enough myself to judge of it, but I doubt we have already a design very near the same from Mr. Burroughs, only his is upon rustic pillars, not unlike those that support Lincoln's Inn Chapel.[18]

With the schemes of Burrough and Gibbs thus before them, on 8 March 1721/2 the building syndicate agreed 'That Mr James Gibbs do take with him to London Mr Burrough's Plan of the Intended publick Buildings and make what improvements he shall think necessary upon it, and that the said Mr Gibbs be imploy'd and retained to supervise and conduct the said work, and be paid for his assistance and directions therein by the Vice-chancellor for the time being'.[19] The plan (fig. 4) as modified by Gibbs did away with the rustic pillars Burrough had proposed, but was still to go through several further changes in the next months. While the three-sided court, open to the east, was never in dispute, many of the details of each of its member blocks were. Gibbs first proposed a scheme where not only was most of the stonework rusticated (rather than smoothly finished, as in the present Senate House), but the south side of the Senate House, and the echoing north side of the Consistory and Register Office, were to have been decorated merely with a line of flat Corinthian pilasters, unrelieved by any central pediment. The east front of the projected Royal Library, connecting the two sides, had at its centre a pediment supported by four rounded half-pillars exactly matching those proposed for the east ends of the two wings. Copies of the design, engraved by Heinrich Hulsbergh, were struck off in the summer of 1722.[20] Over the next few

---

[18] HMC Portland 5 p. 630.   [19] Willis & Clark 3 p. 44.

[20] Vouchers 2 and 23 July 1722. A view of the proposed buildings is in University Archives, P.xxix.2, and is reproduced in A. E. Shipley *Cambridge cameos* (1924) opposite p. 92, and in J. Summerson *Architecture in Britain 1530–1830* (Harmondsworth 1963) pl. 127B. Another version engraved by Hulsbergh, which would have placed the

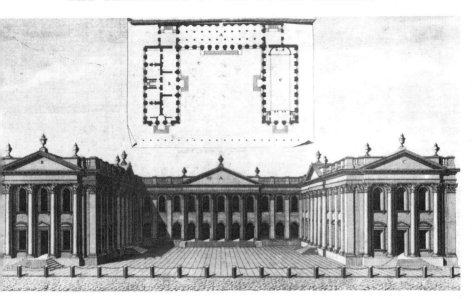

4 James Gibbs' abandoned plans for the public buildings at Cam-
bridge, showing (centre) the Royal Library, (left) the 'Consistory &
Register Office' and (right) the Senate House. From an engraving by
Edward Kirkall. Size of original 263 × 400 mm.

years, however, as work on the Senate House gradually went
forward, Gibbs modified his design. The rustic stonework
disappeared; the windows on the ground floor of the Senate
House and its pair were given alternating triangular and
curved pediments; and the north and south sides of the court
were relieved by the three central bays of each being brought
forward slightly, provided with round fluted half-pillars to
support pediments. More dramatically, by 1728 the court was
planned to be wider, and where Gibbs had envisaged a wall to
the Library of five bays and two half bays, this was later
extended to eleven bays, the pediment at the centre being

staircases in the two wings, is in the Map Room, Views x.2 (22), and yet another,
engraved by E. Kirkall, stands at Views x.2 (21); a smaller copy of the scheme was
engraved by J. Clark in 1724 (copy in Map Room, Views x.5 (48)). These complicated
modifications are surveyed in Terry Friedman *James Gibbs* (New Haven 1984) pp. 225–
32, with reproductions of Gibbs' drawings of 1721 (general view from the east) and
1724 (ground plan showing staircases and a completely rebuilt east room), both of
which are now in the Ashmolean Museum.

enlarged to five bays in proportion. By then, too, he had abandoned his scheme to keep the level of the central court roughly at that of the present Senate House. In none of its forms did the project pay any attention to existing floor levels in Rotherham's old east front, but this scarcely mattered as the building was to have been quite separate, the Royal Library being housed in a room running the length of the range facing the University Church and reached by staircases leading from an open cloister beneath. The Senate House was sufficiently far advanced in 1728 for Gibbs to be able to record it in his *Book of architecture* as 'built', though in fact it was not ready for public use until 1730.[21]

As far as the Library was concerned, this was the end for the moment of a design which, had it been executed, would have dominated Cambridge. The proposed Royal Library was never built, and indeed rose no higher than a trench 160 feet long across the east front of the Schools, dug in 1726 and partially filled in just before a royal visit in April 1728. It foundered on university politics, opposed in the end by Caius because it would have obstructed their light or, as Thomas Gooch, the college's Master, put it in a letter to the Vice-Chancellor in May 1727, 'so effectively shut out all view of that noble fabrick Kings-Chapell, that I wonder how the University or that College can bear it'.[22] When the subject of a new east front to the Library was raised again in the 1750s, somewhat different results were to emerge.[23]

The opening of the new Senate House at last freed the Regent House for library purposes, and on 5 August 1730 the University gave its formal permission for the expansion.[24] The work of alteration was placed under the care of a local builder, James Essex, who had already worked with Gibbs on the new

---

[21] Willis & Clark 3 p. 54.
[22] Willis & Clark 3 pp. 49–53. The rival 'attached' and 'detached' schemes, which had no effect on the University Library, are discussed *ibid.* pp. 48–54.
[23] See below, pp. 255–9.   [24] Grace Book *I* p. 277.

Senate House and whose son of the same name was to be connected with the University almost until his death in 1784. The reconstruction proceeded in two stages over the next three years, Essex having completed enough by August 1731 to justify submitting a bill for £200 'towards Floring & classing yᵉ Old Regent House'.[25]

In its fittings, the room thus added to the Library was somewhat different from the rooms on the other three sides of the court, and marked a new departure. Whereas when the West Room had been fitted up, in the years just after the arrival of the Royal Library, and additional windows were inserted to correspond with the new bookcases placed at right angles to the wall between each, no such alterations were made to the fenestration of the old Regent House. Instead Essex made use of all the available wall space, so that the bookcases at right angles to the walls were continued round the walls as far as the window jambs. The plan was not revolutionary, for wall cases had been built in the Wren Library in the 1690s and at St Catharine's twenty or so years later. It meant, however, in the University Library, that the distance between each case was more than doubled; and the effect of so much space must have been startling to those accustomed to the cramped shadows of the rest of the Library.[26] In the details of the design of his bookcases Essex was commensurably ambitious. Austin's work in the West Room had been restrained, the case-ends simply panelled and relieved only by a minute cartouche at the top: the little flamboyance in his work had been restricted to the carvings on the gates, decorated with foliage and the royal

---

[25] Vouchers, 1731.
[26] Willis & Clark 3 pp. 468–70 and 4 Library fig. 9. Bookcases were not added under the windows until much later. By the time the Library was moved out in 1934 the refurbished Regent House was so cluttered as to require considerable imagination to envisage its appearance in the 1730s. As in the rest of the first floor, extra cases had been introduced between the old ones; the walls were shelved up to the ceiling, rolls of paper were heaped on the tops of the cases, and down the centre of the room ran the racks, over six feet high, housing the General Catalogue.

5 The West Room and Dome Room, 1809. From a watercolour by
Thomas Rowlandson. Size of original 189 × 275 mm.

arms, dividing off four studies at the four corners of the room
(fig. 5). Essex however created cases of rather more complexity, each end with a scrolled pediment decorated with a scallop
shell, a large royal cypher or coat of arms under a crown, and
with a centre panel that opened out to reveal a shelf-list of the
books in that case.[27] There was nothing else in the Library to
compare with them, although there had been convenient shelf-
lists similarly placed, on a rather smaller scale, in St John's
College library since the 1620s.

With the alterations to the Regent House well under way,
the University also agreed in June 1732 to tidy up the north-
west corner of the Schools by removing a staircase at the north

[27] Most of the cases are now in the Morison Room and the Photocopying Room of the
Library.

end of the West Room, and to widen the building at that point so that the room would extend in uniform breadth right up to the door through to the newly acquired north range. Eleven months later it agreed to the equally sensible measure of breaking a door through to link Rotherham's east room and the east end of the Regent House, and so at last the Library was in full possession of four interconnecting sides of the schools. The university accounts record payments in 1734 of £61.3s.od. 'to 4 Scholars for assisting in Setting up the King's books and in making the Catalogue', and £13.9s.3d. 'To Labourers in the Library for Removing and Cleaning books', by which time it must be supposed that the Royal Library books were housed – even if they were not yet formally catalogued.[28]

Quite apart from the questions surrounding where and in what style to house the Royal Library, the putting into order and cataloguing of about 30,000 volumes presented problems so vast that neither the Library authorities nor the University at large managed to face them properly for about twenty years. The books could not be tackled until space was available for their shelving, but even if all possible allowance is made for the kind of delays beloved by administrators out of their depth, there were still some in the University who found the position thoroughly unsatisfactory. In September 1717, with the King about to visit Newmarket, Baker remarked to Strype that 'not one Book is yet put up, nor one class towards receiving them',[29] and although some manuscripts were available within a few years of their arrival he still felt sufficiently ill-served to write to Strype in January 1720 that 'The late Bp: of Ely's MSS: are not yet opened'.[30] Seven years later, when James West of Balliol College, Oxford, was shown round the Library by Baker, the books were still in heaps.[31] And writing

[28] Willis & Clark 3 pp. 75–6.
[29] Baker to Strype 28 September 1717: MS. Add. 10 fo. 107.
[30] Baker to Strype 13 January 1719/20: MS. Add. 10 fo. 119.
[31] *Reliquiae Hearnianae* 2 p. 661. See also Hearne *Remarks and collections* 9 p. 301.

to another correspondent Baker was forced to be even more circumstantial in his apologies:

I am sorry, I can give you no better account of the Bp: of Ely's Library; the printed books are set out, but all of them in such confusion, & many of them at such a height, that there is no coming at them without a long ladder (of how many *gressus* I cannot say) so that they are of little use. The MSS: are not yet opened, nor any possibility of coming at them, to those that most want or desire them, & it not being agreed where to place them, they are like to continue useless, longer than I am willing to say.[32]

All this was scarcely surprising, for it was only decided to take the Regent House into the Library in 1730;[33] and although the university accounts record a payment of five guineas to a Mr Say for work on the catalogues of the Royal Library in 1718–19, the publication of Conyers Middleton's *Bibliothecae Cantabrigiensis ordinandae methodus* in 1723 indicates how little had by then been done. Not until the 1730s, with the conversion of the Regent House and West Room completed and the appointment of a Librarian determined to put an end to the delays, was any real progress made, while the cataloguing processes for the printed books could not be said to have been completed until 1753 and the manuscripts not until 1761.[34]

In 1715 the entire staff of the Library still consisted of two men. Philip Brooke, Fellow of St John's, had been Librarian since 3 October 1712, when he had succeeded John Laughton, and he was assisted by Jonathan Pindar, the latest in a dynasty whose services stretched back to the 1650s. Brooke's qualifications for his post are no longer obvious, for although he presided over the arrival of the largest gift that the Library had ever received, he left little permanent mark on his place of office. Instead, his term in the post was cut abruptly short, and the manner of his exit seems to have been easily the most remarkable episode of his career. In 1717, as a non-juror, he lost

---

[32] Bodleian Library MS. Willis 39, fo. 49: the letter bears no year, but the rest of the volume is *c.* 1729.   [33] Willis & Clark 3 pp. 74–5.
[34] The dates of the last bills for these tasks in the vouchers.

his college fellowship.[35] But more serious trouble developed in the summer of the following year. On 5 July 1718 the Vice-Chancellor summoned Brooke and admonished him for not having taken the oaths of allegiance. Exactly what circumstances had enabled Brooke to avoid this difficulty for over a year after being ejected from his fellowship for this very reason are not recorded, but he parried the Vice-Chancellor's attack by alleging, perfectly truthfully, that he had already taken the oaths when he was appointed Librarian in 1712 – under Queen Anne. Refusal to comply on this new occasion, however, threatened his post, and his difficulties were aggravated by Thomas Gooch's admonitions. In the words of the papers relating to his case, 'He likewise reprimanded Mr Brooke for not attending better to the Business of his Place, & made him promise greater Care & Caution for the future. He also told him, that upon any future Neglect, He or any succeeding Vice-Chanc^r would declare his Place void.' Nor was this all. Brooke wished to dispense with the services of Pindar, and to introduce another assistant; and he had so far overstepped his mark in withholding Pindar's salary, which it was his duty to meet, that the Vice-Chancellor took personal responsibility for seeing that Pindar received the money in the future. The last were, perhaps, no more than misdemeanours, though they were scarcely excusable. But the question of the oaths of allegiance allowed no such forbearance, and Brooke was accordingly prosecuted in the Vice-Chancellor's court the following December. He resigned on 10 December 1718, to the disappointment of those who wished Gooch to vaunt the University's loyalty in pressing the prosecution further. Brooke did not die until 1759, but unlike his fellow non-juror Baker he played no further part in Cambridge life.[36]

He was immediately succeeded as Librarian by his opponent

---

[35] On Brooke, see Venn *Al. Cant.* and Baker–Mayor pp. 301, 1008.
[36] See Luard 161, and, for the Vice-Chancellor's court under Gooch, etc., University Archives V. C. Ct.I.15; J. H. Monk *The life of Richard Bentley* (1833) 2 p. 45, and Cooper *Annals* 4 p. 160.

in the election of 1712, Thomas Macro, Fellow of Gonville and Caius. The elder brother of the antiquary and collector of manuscripts Cox Macro, Thomas had been born at Bury St Edmunds, and entered Caius in 1700 aged eighteen. He had held the living of Babraham since 1716, and during his career as Fellow of his college held a variety of college offices. As University Librarian his reign was brief, for he remained in the post only until 1721, in a period dominated by negotiations over extra space for the Royal Library. The remaining twenty-three years of his life were spent mostly away from Cambridge, and he died as minister of St Nicholas, Great Yarmouth, in 1744.

Macro was the last Librarian to enjoy sole charge of the Library until the nineteenth century. On his resignation in 1721 not only was he followed in this post by Samuel Hadderton of Trinity, who had already begun to classify the Royal Library books in March 1719/20;[37] but a second post of *Protobibliothecarius* was created in the same month. It was an obvious enough reform to increase the Library staff following the accession of so unwieldy a collection as the Royal Library; but the manner of its execution, and the direction chosen, reflected less an understanding of the Library's real needs for assistants capable of organizing the books under the guidance of an active head, than the provincial Grub Street disputes surrounding Bentley's governance at Cambridge. The *Protobibliothecarius*, charged with the organization and care of the Royal Library, proved a mixed success, and not until a small army – by the Library's standards – was engaged and paid piecework several years later was Moore's library brought under control. The election of the first to hold the post was surrounded by the bitterness of party faction, and it was later recalled that John Symonds, Fellow of St John's, 'with five or six more of that house, formed the whole number that had

---

[37] On Macro, see J. Venn *Biographical history of Gonville and Caius College* 1 (Cambridge 1897) p. 506. For Hadderton's early work see Baker to Hearne, 27 February [1719/20], summarized in Hearne *Remarks and collections* 7 p. 102.

sense, honesty, and courage enough to vote against the creating a useless place on such an occasion; but so high did party run, and so low had it descended, that the very mob in the street hooted them all their way home'.[38]

Hadderton, as Macro's successor, and Conyers Middleton, the first to hold the new creation, were both sworn in on 15 December, and from that day until 1828 the Library was ruled by a junta of two men. From the first the *Protobibliothecarius* was the senior of the two, as the title implies, and the list of those who filled the post at various times was to include four who were at the same time also Heads of Houses: F. S. Parris of Sidney, Edmund Law of Peterhouse, John Barnardiston of Corpus, and Richard Farmer of Emmanuel. In 1787–8 Richard Farmer was at the same time both *Protobibliothecarius* and Vice-Chancellor, a plurality in which his contemporaries seem to have seen nothing very extraordinary. The post was thus of considerably greater importance than the old Librarianship; and by creating one that could be interpreted by its holder as requiring little or no attention to the everyday routines of running a library, the University found itself in time in possession of the services of a series of most distinguished scholars. None of those in the post took his title to entail anything like full-time application to the books placed in his charge, but the work of Middleton and Farmer on the history of printing and literature, and of Thomas Kerrich on the history of illustration and painting, did at least show some awareness of those studies increasingly expected of a scholar-librarian.

The relationship between *Protobibliothecarius* and *Bibliothecarius* evolved and changed in the century of their joint existence. But if it was never of the kind described a year before their merger by the university wit who alleged that the former's job was 'to lay books on the shelf', and the latter's 'to

---

[38] Quoted in J. Nichols *Literary anecdotes of the eighteenth century* (1812) 5 p. 410. Hadderton's rival in the election of *Bibliothecarius* on 15 December was George Birkett, Fellow of Peterhouse (Grace Book *I* p. 54).

brush the dust of them',[39] it was fathered by politics more than by scholarship. In 1717 Richard Bentley, as Regius Professor of Divinity, had claimed a fee of four guineas over and above what was customary from the incepting Doctors of Divinity at the visit of George I to the University. Among them was Conyers Middleton, Fellow of Trinity until his marriage in 1710, and one of the thirty fellows of his college who in February 1709/10 had petitioned the Bishop of Ely, as Visitor of the College, against their Master. Marriage, though it deprived him of his fellowship, did not distract him from the plight of Trinity. So, already undisposed in 1717 to forgo opportunity to cross Bentley, he refused to comply with Bentley's demands until he had written assurance that the money would be repaid if it was ever later proved to have been elicited improperly. There followed some of the more ludicrous episodes of Bentley's prolonged altercation with members of his college and of the University.[40] On Middleton's suing him in the Vice-Chancellor's court for the return of the four guineas, he refused to settle the matter out of court and the Vice-Chancellor thereupon issued a decree for his arrest. He still refused to comply, and was suspended from all his degrees – a proceeding which, in the words of his biographer J. H. Monk, 'struck with amazement the audience in the Consistory'. There is no need to repeat the details of the ensuing pamphlet war here, for they have been retold amply by Monk. Middleton emerged from it as the hero of the anti-Bentley faction, and proved to be more than a match at invective. He further earned the admiration of his party by enduring a wearisome and inconclusive attendance at the Court of King's Bench in Westminster at the suit of Bentley, who alleged that he had libelled the government in his tract *A*

---

[39] J. M. F. Wright *Alma mater, or seven years at the University of Cambridge* (1827) 2 p. 172.
[40] The best account is in J. H. Monk *The life of Richard Bentley* 2 vols. (1833), especially chapters 13–14. See also A. T. Bartholomew *Richard Bentley, D.D.: a bibliography of his works and of all the literature called forth by his acts or his writings* (Cambridge 1908) pp. 66–70.

true account of the present state of Trinity College. Middleton was convicted, but his offence was recognized for the academic bickering it was. Yet though no sentence was ever passed, the financial loss to him was a heavy one. Not only did he have to maintain himself in London for several months, but he had also to pay both his own legal expenses and much of those of Bentley too. The matter was brought to a temporary end on 24 November 1721 by Bentley's accepting Middleton's proffered apology.

There the affair could, however, scarcely be allowed to rest. The ingenious mode chosen by Middleton's friends to make some restitution for his expenses, and at the same time to goad Bentley further, was to create the new post of *Protobibliothecarius*, at a salary of £50 per annum, and to move Middleton's election to it. They lost little time, for the office was established and Middleton elected three weeks after the settling of the case in King's Bench. Entrusted specifically with the Royal Library,[41] Middleton came with few manifest accomplishments for his post. His reputation was as a controversialist, and a controversialist he remained, whether over Bentley, Richard Mead and medicine in classical Rome, or Daniel Waterland and the Deist controversy. Even his life of Cicero,[42] ridiculed by Fielding in *Shamela*[43] but still reprinted into the nineteenth century and published also in both Basel and Madrid, became the target of criticism culminating in its being convicted as a plagiary in 1787 by Samuel Parr.[44] Leslie Stephen did not mince his words in the *Dictionary of national biography*: 'Middleton was probably one of the few divines who can be fairly accused of conscious insincerity.' Yet he was

---

[41] Grace Book *I* p. 53.

[42] The portrait now hanging in the Library, presented by Mrs Heberden in 1802, shows Middleton holding a book labelled 'M.T. Ciceronis Opera', but according to J. W. Goodison (*Catalogue of Cambridge portraits* I (Cambridge 1955) p. 41) was painted somewhat before 1741; for a reproduction see *ibid.*, pl. 10.

[43] See also W. L. Cross *The history of Henry Fielding* (New Haven 1918) I pp. 306–10.

[44] In his *Praefatio ad Bellendenum de statu libri tres*; but see also M. L. Clarke 'Conyers Middleton's alleged plagiarism' *Notes and Queries* N.S. 30 (1983) pp. 44–6.

still admired by Horace Walpole, who owned the portrait of him by J G. Eckhardt painted in 1746.[45] Walpole also bought Middleton's eclectic collection of antiquities in 1743, and thought enough of him to write a memoir and to draw up a comprehensive list of his writings.[46] William Cole likewise composed a sympathetic biography, rather more personal in its contents, but (like the rest of his memoranda on Cambridge) written for posterity – even to the extent of including a note of his appearance: 'I never saw him in my life, except on a journey, but dressed in his gown and cassock and square cap, if in the University: and was one of the cleanest and neatest men in his person that could be met with.'[47]

But though neither Walpole nor Cole took much notice of his career as librarian, Middleton in fact at first paid more attention to the general needs of the Library and to its contents than any librarian since Abraham Whelock. In the day to day affairs Whelock had spent more time than Middleton, but Middleton's two published sallies into the field, one on the organization of the Library and one on Caxton, were marked by originality, common sense and scholarship, all qualities which had not been very obvious for some years. They related, principally, to the Royal Library. He recognized the urgent need to dispose of duplicates as early as 1722, on 14 July that year visiting Humfrey Wanley and leaving with him a (now lost) catalogue of Moore's early printed books. The two men agreed that Harley should select duplicates listed there in

---

[45] Now in the National Portrait Gallery. The earliest portrait, on G. B. Pozzo's medallion, was made on Middleton's visit to Rome in 1724 (see below).

[46] *Horace Walpole's correspondence with Sir David Dalrymple [etc.]* ed. W. S. Lewis et al. (1952) pp. 14–19 and 291–304.

[47] *Ibid.*, pp. 305–15. Another observer described him in a little more detail: 'As to his person, he was of a proper middle stature, and a thin habit; his eye very lively, but small; he was a little out-mouthed; of a manly complexion; and, to use the Painters phrase, there was a very expressive motion in every feature, though his whole deportment was composed to gravity' (*Biographia Britannica* (1760) p. 3100). He was a close friend of Thomas Gray, to whom Middleton's house was 'the only easy Place one could find to converse in at Cambridge' (Thomas Gray *Correspondence* ed. Paget Toynbee and Leonard Whibley, with corrections by H. W. Starr (Oxford 1971) 1 p. 328).

exchange for books from his own shelves;[48] but no more came of the proposal, and although in the end many of the Royal Library duplicates were sold off at auction in 1742 few inroads were made into the earliest books until the nineteenth century. As an official of the University Middleton was in a more taxing position when negotiating over his own, as distinct from the University's, books. The Library, for instance, possessed no copy of Lyndewode's *Constitutiones provinciales*, printed by Wynkyn de Worde in 1496 (and did not do so until Samuel Sandars presented one in 1892), but in July 1723 Middleton was offering his own copy to Wanley, with a cartulary of the Cluniac priory of Monks Horton in Kent (the property, perhaps, of a friend), in exchange for 'some old duplicate Printed Book'.[49] He could scarcely have sold either the Lyndewode or the cartulary to the Library of which he had charge at a time when its annual purchase fund was both tiny and devoted entirely to modern works.

As a theorist he proved in the long run to have greater success. His quarto pamphlet *Bibliothecae Cantabrigiensis ordinandae methodus*, published privately in 1723, anticipated many of the questions posed by the Royal Library, and some of the solutions which in the end were arrived at only after prolonged delays. He recommended the taking over of the Regent House and the building of a separate room for manuscripts and particularly valuable printed books, he sought reforms in a borrowing system which allowed Bentley to have the Codex Bezae out of the Library for five or more years, he emphasized the need for standard reference works such as dictionaries and bibliographies to be reserved for reference only, and he set out a classification scheme for the Royal Library. There, however, Middleton's exertions as a custodian in the narrowest sense came to an end. In August 1723 he

---

[48] Wanley *Diary* 1 p. 153.
[49] *Ibid.* 2 p. 248. The cartulary belonged to 'a friend' on 9 October 1725, when Middleton again besought Wanley to acquire it.

successfully applied for leave of absence from the University until the following summer to travel abroad 'for ye Recovery of his health, & for ye viewing of foreign libraries'.[50] With so many pressing questions about the library of which he had only recently been placed in charge, the decision to travel abroad may seem a little premature. But, as his sympathetic biographer in the *Biographia Britannica* explained:

The truth is, the Librarian's place [i.e. the place of *Protobibliothecarius*] had been established long enough before there was any necessity for it: the foundation of the new Senate-house was scarcely laid, nor so much as the plan settled for altering the old one; consequently, with regard to the duty of his office, the Librarian was entirely at leisure, from the present state of the library, where the King's books, it was easy to see, must unavoidably remain in the same useless confusion they then lay, for a much longer time than would be spent upon his travels. This, in reality, furnished a sufficient excuse for his absence, but it was such an one, as it became himself, at least, to be very shy of mentioning. However, the ill state of his health supplied another, which was both unanswerable and indispensible. He had now a good while felt the bad effects of that juvenile temerity which has been already taken notice of; he was actually grown extremely thin, and seemed to be in a dangerous marasmus from a continual spitting. In order, therefore, at once to satisfy the most scrupulous of his friends, and silence the most clamorous among his foes, he laid his case before Dr Mead, who fully gave his opinion in writing, that it was necessary for his health that he should remove into a warmer climate. By this means, though not without a good deal of difficulty, he obtained a special grace for the purpose, and shortly after set out upon his much desired journey with Lord Coleraine. They went together to Paris, where his Lordship, who was known to most of the literati abroad, introduced his fellow-traveller to the celebrated Mr Montfaucon. Not many days after they parted from Paris, his Lordship stepping aside to see some curiosities that lay at a good distance from the direct road to Rome, left our author to pursue his own rout, which was to take the shortest way to that city. He arrived there early in the year of 1724, and passed about twelve months in it entirely to his satisfaction. On his first coming he met with an accident, which made him resolve to support his residence here in such a degree of dignity as should be some credit to his station at Cambridge.

[50] Grace Book *I* p. 83. Leslie Stephen, in the *DNB*, was unequivocal about his health: 'He was athletic in his youth, but injured his health by an injudicious diet, intended to suppress a tendency to corpulence.'

He made use of this character to get himself introduced to his Brother-Librarian at the *Vatican*, who received him with great politeness; but upon his mentioning Cambridge, said he did not know before, that there was any university in England of that name, and at the same time took notice, that he was no stranger to that of Oxford, for which he expressed a great esteem. This touched the honour of our new Librarian, who took some pains to convince his brother not only of the real existence, but of the real dignity of his university of Cambridge. At last, the Keeper of the Vatican acknowledged, that, upon recollection, he did indeed remember to have heard of a celebrated school in England of that name, which was a kind of nursery where youth were educated and prepared for their admission at Oxford: and Dr Middleton left him at present, in that sentiment. But this unexpected indignity put him upon his mettle, and he agreed to give 400*l. per ann.* for a *hôtel* with all accommodations fit for the reception of those of the first rank in Rome.[51]

Middleton also went to the further expense of having his portrait engraved by Giovanni Battista Pozzo (fig. 6), and cast as a medallion, with library furnishings appropriate to his professional prominence on the reverse.[52]

By February 1724/5 he was back in England,[53] his fortune much depleted, and again visiting Wanley, this time with much more attractive temptations. He had already sent a box of manuscripts and printed books to Harley at Wimpole, but this was not all. 'He saith,' noted Wanley, 'that he ha's another parcel of MSS. (besides those that he hath already offer'd to sell my Lord) now coming for England; among which, some are in Greek, as also some choice pieces of Antiquity. Farther that a Bookseller at Pisa hath a good parcel of MSS. Also, that Monsignor Passionei at Rome, hath several very choice Manuscripts; among which, is a Tetravangelion in old Greek Capitals.'[54] Harley bought forty-seven manuscripts from

---

[51] *Biographia Britannica* (1760) pp. 3095–6 and note.
[52] E. Hawkins *Medallic illustrations of the history of Great Britain and Ireland to the death of George II* (British Museum 1885) 2 p. 460, no. 71. Copies exist both in bronze and gilt. An ivory carving of the same medallion is in the Victoria and Albert Museum (Ivory A16.1941), and the design was later issued by Wedgwood: see R. Reilly and George Savage *Wedgwood; the portrait medallions* (1973) p. 241.
[53] Not late in 1725, as in *Biographia Britannica*.   [54] Wanley *Diary* 2 p. 334.

6 Conyers Middleton (1683–1750), *Protobibliothecarius*. From a medallion by Giovanni Battista Pozzo, 1724. Diameter of original 85 mm.

Middleton, in Latin, Greek, Spanish, Italian, and one in Persian
'pro more Persico inluminatus'.[55] Most of them dated from
the fifteenth or sixteenth century, and had been written in
Italy. They presented a mixed bag of classical, liturgical and
monastic texts. Among them were an illuminated copy of
Bonaventura's Legend of St Francis executed in Florence in
1504 for a member of the Malatesta family, a copy of Cicero *De
officiis* written in Rome in 1498 by Bartolomeo di San Vito of

---

[55] *Ibid.*, 2 pp. 335–6 and 341–4. See also C. E. Wright *Fontes Harleiani* (1972) p. 239.

Padua, a collection of Spanish historical papers relating to the 1570s and, most notably, a Greek Gospel book dating from the twelfth century.[56] Harley was already taking full advantage of the great exodus of Italian books, and Middleton had grasped his opportunities no more successfully than many others.[57] Once again, however, and this time with the need to recoup some of the expenses of his continental tour, Middleton felt it useless – if indeed it occurred to him – to offer his treasures to the University Library, which had neither the money nor the inclination to add to the riches brought by the gift of George I.

In 1727 he felt unable to take up an offer to the University of Greek manuscripts from Mount Athos. The monastery of Pantokrátor made various efforts to raise money in the 1720s and 1730s, through embassies to western Europe, and it applied for this purpose to both Oxford and Cambridge, as well as elsewhere. But while Oxford found the resources to produce fifty pounds for half a dozen manuscripts,[58] the monastery's approach to Cambridge proved less fruitful. On 31 May 1727 Bartholomew Cassano, 'a Greek priest', wrote to Middleton, sending a catalogue and explaining that some manuscripts had

[56] For details of them see, besides Wanley's *Diary* and the catalogue of the Harleian manuscripts, Andrew G. Watson *Catalogue of dated and datable manuscripts, c. 700–1600, in the Department of Manuscripts, the British Library* 2 vols. (1979) and, for the Gospels (now Harley 5785) K. Aland *Kurzgefasste Liste der Griechischen Handschriften des Neuen Testaments* I (Berlin 1963) p. 212: Wanley described the manuscript as 'venustissimum; 800 fere abhinc annis exaratum' (*Diary* 2 p. 336). Harley's career as a collector is discussed in C. E. Wright, 'Edward Harley, 2nd Earl of Oxford, 1689-1741' *The Book Collector* 11 (1962) pp. 158–74, and (with a section devoted to Middleton) in *idem* 'Manuscripts of Italian provenance in the Harleian collection in the British Museum' in Cecil H. Clough (ed.) *Cultural aspects of the Italian Renaissance; essays in honour of Paul Oskar Kristeller* (Manchester 1976) pp. 462–84.

[57] In February 1724/5, for example, Wanley also received a long list of Italian manuscripts from John Gibson who acquired them from agents in Florence. Joseph Smith, later British Consul at Venice, had also begun collecting in Italy by the 1720s, and was trading in manuscripts with the Earl of Sunderland in December that year. See Wanley *Diary* 2 pp. 336–41, 461, etc. For a more general account, see Lesley Lewis *Connoisseurs and secret agents in eighteenth century Rome* (1961).

[58] Macray *Annals* p. 205; F. Madan *Summary catalogue of western manuscripts in the Bodleian Library at Oxford* 5 (Oxford 1905) p. 331; R. M. Dawkins *The monks of Athos* (1936) pp. 324–36; F. Stubbings 'Anthony Askew's *Liber amicorum*' *Trans. Cambridge Bibliographical Soc.* 6 (1976) pp. 306–21, esp. p. 316.

already been delivered to Lambeth and to Oxford.[59] The catalogue no longer survives, and Middleton bought none. Various Mount Athos manuscripts came to the Library with Anthony Askew's books in 1785,[60] and Richard Bentley took advantage of opportunities for acquiring Greek manuscripts in England,[61] but between them Middleton and the University were content to allow this offer to slip away.

The university authorities, quite apart from Middleton, were in no position to sympathize with suggestions as to how the stock of the Library's manuscripts might be improved. Even the Rawlinson sales passed by without raising very much interest, though Thomas Baker did what he could to ensure that catalogues were put into the right hands.[62] 'The Dr. [Middleton] has a public Purse and, I hope, may be a good Customer', he wrote in April 1729[63] on the occasion of the thirteenth auction, but nothing seems to have come of his hopes. In 1733 he was again in correspondence with Richard Rawlinson, this time over a collection of papers now unidentifiable (Thomas Rawlinson's manuscripts were auctioned by Ballard finally in March 1733/4) but extensive enough to warrant the involvement of the Vice-Chancellor Charles Morgan, Master of Clare. Morgan proved unreceptive, and after Middleton had heard his verdict Baker had the task as intermediary of writing to Rawlinson that 'Dr Middleton has at last receiv'd the Vicechan^s. Answere, wch tho' in soft words is plainly a negative: So the Papers must be dispos'd of according to your Orders & Direction. We are a strange Body, you are wiser at Oxford.'[64] Neither Baker nor Rawlinson was yet defeated, however, and notwithstanding

[59] British Library MS. Add. 32457, fo. 60. Three manuscripts are in the Wake collection at Christ Church, Oxford.   [60] See below, pp. 330–3.

[61] M. R. James *The western manuscripts in the library of Trinity College, Cambridge* I (Cambridge 1900) pp. xx, xxii, etc.

[62] B. J. Enright 'The later auction sales of Thomas Rawlinson's library, 1727–34' *The Library* 5th ser. 11 (1956) pp. 23–40 and 103–13, at p. 35 n. 3.

[63] Bodleian Library MS. Rawl. letters 30 fo. 126, 13 April 1729, quoted *ibid.*, p. 39.

[64] Rawl. letters 30, no. 100.

this rebuff took advantage of the annual change of Vice-Chancellor to approach Roger Long, Master of Pembroke. In May the following year Baker agreed to ask Middleton to re-open the subject, but not even this second attempt carried. Whatever his personal opinions, Long was forced to be swayed by other counsels from other Heads, and in July Baker had to write again,

I deliver'd your last Sheet to Dr Middleton, w^{ch}: came in good time, for he has since shown it &c: to the vice-chancellor, for his perusall, & approbation to have enlodg'd in the University Library in the manner you desire. What Answere may be expected, he does not yet know, but he seems somewhat discourag'd by the Answere he receiv'd from the late vicechan:, after conference with two or three more of the Heads.

The project proved impossible, and Baker let slip to his fellow non-juror some of his annoyance in remarking sarcastically that 'we are very Loyall, & are now putting up the late King George's Picture, in one of the wings of the Library, wch now from his Gift, bears the Title of the Royall Library'.[65] Whatever the collection, whether Rawlinson papers, or Greek manuscripts from Middleton or Mount Athos, the University was in no mood to receive them. It was completely absorbed in the Royal Library.

Nonetheless, while Middleton perhaps despaired of the Library in parting with his manuscripts, his investigations on his return into Moore's early English printed books, one of the most celebrated parts of the collection, reaped most satisfying results. His account of the earliest printing in England, following on from the work of Maittaire, proved to be one of the cornerstones of subsequent research. Middleton's *Dissertation concerning the origin of printing in England* was published by William Thurlbourn in Cambridge in 1735, the title page

---

[65] *Ibid.*, no. 107. There is no such portrait of George I now in the University's collection, and Baker presumably refers here to the preliminaries of the discussion that led to Lord Townshend's gift of Rysbrack's statue, which arrived in 1739 and now stands in the Squire Law Library.

graced by an engraving of the proposed new university buildings.[66] As a piece of research in the modern sense it has many faults,[67] but it laid to rest two erroneous beliefs about the subject that had bedevilled accounts since the mid-seventeenth century – one the creation (so Middleton was inclined to believe) of the 'bold and vain' Richard Atkyns in his book *The original and growth of printing* (1664). He dealt easily with Atkyns' account of the 'Lambeth record', and the inventions surrounding the fictitious Frederick Corsellis, and objected to the statement that Gutenberg had invented the art at Haarlem, pointing out that political conditions in the late 1450s would have made Corsellis' supposed journeys to England impossible in the manner described, that Caxton kept uncharacteristically silent about it, and that Caxton himself had learned to print not in England but in Cologne: the final nail to seal down the coffin was that prolonged research had failed to unearth so valuable a document from where it was alleged to be. He dealt equally summarily with the Oxford Rufinus of '1468'. Not all the evidence that he adduced was at all new, but he pointed out that mis-dated books were by no means uncommon. Part of the difficulty of the '1468' book, moreover, was that there was apparently a lacuna of eleven years subsequently for which there was no reasonable explanation. Though he also had the benefit of notes made by John Lewis of Margate,[68] much of

[66] Middleton's *Dissertation* was also published in Paris by D. C. Couturier in 1775, with a fulsome preface by the translator D. G. Imbert.

[67] His discussion of the history of signatures in early books came under attack only a generation later, by John Nichols and William Bowyer, for example. These two were reluctant to cede the argument about Corsellis without a struggle, and suggested (*The origin of printing* (1774) p. 43) that Leland's statement that Caxton was the first printer in England was 'not inconsistent with Corsellis's having printed earlier at Oxford with separate Types cut in Wood, which was the only method he had learnt at Harleim [*sic*]'; their remark drew acid comment from Richard Farmer, 'Had Mr Bowyer seen the famous *Oxford* book, dated 1468, He would have immediately found it was not printed in *wooden* types; & consequently that his argument against *Caxton* falls to the ground' (MS. note in his copy of the *Origin*, CUL 7850.d.12).

[68] Middleton *Dissertation* p. 10n. Lewis' biography of Caxton was published in 1737. For an account of the history of Lewis' papers see F. C. Bigmore and C. W. H. Wyman *A bibliography of printing* (1880–6) 1 pp. 436–7.

Middleton's pamphlet (which also had a good deal to say generally on the beginnings of printing in Oxford) was based on copies of books actually in the University Library. Thus he was able, with some reservations as to whether such methods could be conclusive, to begin to compare the types used in different books. But here he relied heavily on previous authorities, not least Lewis, and this aspect of his work was less impressive. In describing the work of the printers in the City of London, for example, he could assemble Lettou's edition of Thomas Wallensis' *Expositiones super Psalterium* and three copies of the Lettou–Machlinia edition of Littleton's *Tenores*: a copy of Machlinia's edition of John Wotton's *Speculum christiani* said by Middleton to have been in the Library is no longer there.[69] All three books have clearly signed colophons, and it is not without significance that Middleton did not note Machlinia's unsigned Terence, or a Lettou–Machlinia volume of statutes and yearbooks, both of which had arrived with the Royal Library. Typographical analysis could scarcely be described as being even in its infancy (though Ames was to begin to investigate Caxton's types in 1749),[70] and Middleton relied heavily on the statements of colophons alone. When he turned to the St Albans Printer, Moore's collection had already suffered one loss: unknown to Middleton (though he knew Moore had once possessed it) Thomas Tanner had never returned Laurentius de Saona's *Rhetorica nova. The book of hawking, hunting and blasing of arms* was however there; but Middleton missed the unique *Elegantiolae* of Augustinus Datus, a book with a clear colophon but whose presence in the Library was concealed by its being bound up with a collection of foreign pamphlets. He had missed one treasure, but the last pages of his brief treatise (the whole took a mere twenty-nine pages) were occupied with a chronological catalogue of the output of Caxton's press, the first specially printed catalogue of

---

[69] *Dissertation* p. 12. The present Library copy was rejected as a duplicate by the British Museum in 1831.   [70] In his *Typographical antiquities* (1749).

any part of the Library's incunabula. The list did not attempt to distinguish between Caxton's career at Bruges and at Westminster, and contained two stray books that should properly have been omitted as the work of Wynkyn de Worde, but it presented an immense advance on previous knowledge. Understandably, he was misled by the wrong date on Gower's *Confessio amantis*, dated 1493 instead of 1483, yet this was trivial beside the results of the research that had been made possible thanks to the enlightened pertinacity of John Moore thirty or more years previously: all but one of the Caxtons listed by Middleton had belonged to him.[71]

As custodian of the most extensive gathering of Caxtons in an English public collection, Middleton's choice of subject seemed in every way fitting. He was, however, prompted by more than scholarly curiosity. Ever anxious to improve his position (in December 1733 he had cast his eyes on the Professorship of Modern History),[72] he undertook his work on Caxton in characteristic spirit. 'Your Lordship', he wrote to Lord Hervey, 'will think me sadly employed in turning over such rubbish, but it is just ye reverse in ye learned of what it is in ye active world: ye more obscure & trifling our pursuits are, ye greater fame of learning is acquired by attempting them; & a few more performances of ye kind may raise me to a rank of glory wth the great Hearne of Oxford.'[73] He was never to rival Hearne in his knowledge of English antiquities, but on this occasion at least he was right where his Oxford peer was wrong. Unable to give Middleton due credit for the contents of his 'twelvepenny Pamphlett in English', as he snootily described it, Hearne stuck blindly to local prejudice:

His whole performance is poor & mean, and tho' he endeavours to rob Oxford of an honour, that no one pretended to take from her, yet Middleton *detrahere ausus Haerentem capiti multi cum laude coronam*, hath

---

[71] The *Directorium* listed by Middleton on p. 28 is now in the British Library, where its old Royal Library class-mark can still be made out: it was missing from Cambridge in 1778. See Oates *Catalogue* p. 50.
[72] Middleton to Hervey 26 December 1733. Bury St Edmunds Record Office, Hervey papers 941/47/8. [73] Middleton to Hervey 24 October 1734 *ibid.*

plainly shewed that he envys us this glory, which no one need wonder at, that considers a much bolder stroke of his lately, which made a great noise, & very deservedly blasted his reputation, which was his book (for he is known to be the author, tho' his name be not to it) to prove that Moses was not an inspired writer. 'Tis certain, that Middleton is an ingenious man, but he soars at all; and considerable, very uncommon, must be the Genius that succeeds.[74]

Middleton had picked the plums from the Royal Library, at least as regards the printed books, but his scholarly labours on Caxton and his successors did very little to advance the cataloguing of the library as a whole. He had no taste for the drudgery of cataloguing, and (English incunables apart) not even any sense of the probability of fresh discoveries that is an inseparable part of arranging and listing a collection for the first time.

My time has been wholly employed for these six weeks past [he wrote to Hervey in August 1734] in a close attendance on yᵉ Publick Library, where we are now drawing up a Catalogue of yᵉ books, & ranging them in order. books were never disagreeable to me before, but this drudgery of dealing wᵗʰ yᵉ outsides onely has almost surfeited me . . . this is a task, that I must submit to for many months, or rather years to come, unless I will part wᵗʰ yᵉ onely prefermᵗ I have in yᵉ world; with a salary of 50 pᵈˢ pʳ ann.[75]

Despite the impression given by Baker, some printed books at least had been available for use comparatively shortly after 1715. By a Grace of 22 August 1719, for example, a Mr Hayley (presumably John Hayley, Fellow of King's and Junior Proctor) was allowed to borrow Moore's copy of Pomponius Mela printed at Milan in 1471;[76] and on 11 June the following year Mr Drake (probably Samuel Drake, Fellow of St John's) was permitted two copies of Matthew Parker's *De antiquitate Britannicae ecclesiae Cantuariensis* (1572).[77] No real beginning seems to have been made, however, until the incunabula were separated off and listed by Middleton with the help of an

[74] Hearne *Remarks and collections* 11 p. 432 (3 March 1734/5).
[75] Middleton to Hervey 18 August 1734. Bury St Edmunds Record Office, Hervey papers 941/47/8.
[76] Grace Book *I* p. 11; Luard 167.   [77] Grace Book *I* p. 24; Luard 170.

unnamed assistant.[78] This was in roughly chronological order, beginning with the Mainz *Catholicon* dated 1460, and as it listed the Library's incunables as a whole, from both the old and the Royal libraries, there seems to be some evidence that this was only incidentally a part of cataloguing the latter. Either this list or a copy of it was made available by Middleton in 1722 to Michael Maittaire,[79] who included notes of fifty-seven Cambridge incunables in the second edition of the first volume of his *Annales* (1733). By March 1719/20 a start had also been made on some of the more urgent binding work in the Royal Library,[80] but although various attempts were made to begin work on a full catalogue of Moore's books, the surviving evidence tells a story of incomprehension and muddle.

The man whose organizing genius and enthusiasm for dogged hard work put an end to this sorry state of affairs was John Taylor, who succeeded Samuel Hadderton as *Bibliothecarius* on 18 March 1732. By this time it had become clear that if anything was to be done about the Royal Library it would have to be by someone other than the man technically in charge, Middleton, who, as Hearne noted in December 1731, had 'no authority as chief Librarian ... over M[r]. Hadderton ...; their authority is equal, only the D[r]. has the preference of Order and Honor. But there is no Statute to determine their Privileges. The D[r]. ... will not contend for power, whilst M[r]. Hadderton does most of the business, and the D[r]. will have less leisure, now that he is to be their Woodward Professor.' But a few weeks later Hadderton was

---

[78] MS. Add. 2671. For fuller details of the cataloguing of the incunables see the introduction to Oates *Catalogue*, pp. 17–23. A further catalogue of the early printed books, not mentioned by Oates, is in Bodleian Library MS. Gough Camb. 62 (SC 17817) fos. 88 *et seq.*, and lists both the Royal and the older collections. This quotes the numbers on the books alluded to by Oates (pp. 17–18), the highest being 17487 on a volume printed by Wynkyn de Worde. It includes nos. 9–14 of those books described by Oates (pp. 50–1) as missing in 1736, and nos. 18 and 22 from the separate notebook labelled 'Libri antiquiores'.

[79] Maittaire's letter of acknowledgement, dated 29 October 1722, is now British Library MS. Add. 32457, fos. 9–10.

[80] A bill survives among the Vouchers from Charles Wright, receipted 19 March 1719/20.

dead, mourned by Hearne and no doubt by his informant Baker as a 'true Drudg', and his place taken by Taylor, 'an ingenious Man, but not so well fitted for drudgery as his predecessor'.[81]

Middleton had come into his office on a wave of sympathy; but by the beginning of the 1730s knew himself to be unpopular with many. While Baker fed gossip to Hearne that in itself was not necessarily malicious, his position was made further insecure by increasingly unconventional theology. He clashed in print with Daniel Waterland, Master of Magdalene College, in 1731, in a pamphlet published anonymously but whose authorship quickly became generally known; and though in the face of an attack by Zachary Pearce he was contrite in writing to Lord Harley (''tis my intention to push matters no further, but to silence all clamour by slipping as quietly as I can out of ye squabble'), the University was indignant. Others, more jealous, found the excuse they had sought, provoked the further by Middleton's appointment in July 1731 as the first Woodwardian Professor of Geology. It was for these reasons, rather than for his incompetence as *Protobibliothecarius*, that a plot was hatched to abolish his post in the Library and to apply the stipend to the Common Chest. In February 1731/2, before any copy of Pearce's pamphlet had reached Cambridge, but when its general contents were already known, Robert Lambert, Master of St John's, and James Bate, Fellow of the college, headed the attack at a meeting of the Caput whose agreement was necessary to promote the appropriate Grace. While Lambert (no friend of Middleton since a particularly complicated election to the college's Mastership in 1727) argued that Middleton should not be allowed to hold two university posts, the Senate debated the theological aspects of the matter informally outside. Nothing came of these proceedings, but the matter was not formally silenced until 24 March, six weeks later, with

---

[81] Hearne *Remarks and collections* 11 p. 10; *ibid.*, pp. 46–7.

the defeat of a Grace that described Middleton's post in the Library as *inutile* and *onerosum*. Middleton was at last able to report to Harley

The Grace to abolish my Office was offered to ye Caput yesterday morning & stopt there by Dr Gooch & Dr Dickins. I have not yet heard what resentment there is in ye Body on this occasion, or in what form they design their next attack, I am apt to think, y^t they will hardly drop it as yet, & y^t ye New Librarian is engaged in ye scheme, thro' ye vanity of getting rid of a superior in Office, for I have not so much as seen him, since my coming hither.

He had found friends in Thomas Gooch (Master of Gonville and Caius) and Francis Dickins (Regius Professor of Civil Law, and Fellow of Trinity Hall), discovered an unexpected enemy in Bate ('a Creature & first minister of ye Master who is ye raiser & fomenter of all this spleen to me'), and had had confirmed his low opinion of Samuel Drake, another candidate for the St John's mastership in 1727. Had the college succeeded in its attack, Taylor would have been sole librarian. But it had not, and perhaps wisely Middleton left the new man as much as possible to himself.[82]

John Taylor, or Demosthenes Taylor (fig. 7) as he came to be called after his editorial *magnum opus*, was born in 1704, the son of a barber in Shrewsbury. He entered St John's College from Shrewsbury School on 7 June 1721 and took his B.A. in 1724. Elected a Fellow of his college in 1726, he became a Law Fellow in 1732 and so contrived to remain a layman until his ordination in 1751, when his academic career virtually ended.[83] He was elected *Bibliothecarius* in succession to Hadderton on 18 March 1731/2, the runner-up being G. H. Rooke, Fellow (and later Master) of Christ's,[84] and remained in that office until 1734 when he became Registry. His election came in the aftermath of extensive thefts of books by Philip Nichols, described below, and with the Library at a

---

[82] Middleton to Harley 29 January, 8 February, 21 March 1731/2 and 25 March 1732. Portland papers (British Library MS. Loan 29/167). The St John's election is discussed in Baker–Mayor 2 pp. 1015–17.

[83] *Admissions to the College of St John the Evangelist*, ed. R. F. Scott 3 (Cambridge 1903) pp. 27, 339–41.   [84] Grace Book *I* p. 315.

7   John ('Demosthenes') Taylor (1704–1766), *Bibliothecarius*. From a
drawing by an unknown artist. Size of original 138 × 90 mm.

critical stage in its extensions. He also faced the task,
notwithstanding Middleton, of cataloguing the Royal Library. To all this and more he gave unsparing attention. By
nature a scholar, with interests quite removed from the
ordinary husbandry of books, he had already published in 1732
proposals for an edition of Lysias, which appeared in 1739. It
was followed in 1743 by an account, *Marmor Sandvicense*, of a

marble dating from the fourth century B.C.,[85] and by volumes two and three of his edition of Demosthenes in 1748 and 1757: the first was never published. Such were his major scholarly accomplishments, but he achieved considerable renown, not to say notoriety, as the author of *Elements of the civil law* (1755),[86] was one of the contributors to the revised edition of Stephanus' *Thesaurus* published in 1734–5, found time to write about Roman inscriptions discovered in Cumberland and on Hadrian's Wall as well as about an earthquake at Portsmouth in March 1749/50, and put forward proposals for a scholarly review modelled on the *Mémoires de l'Académie Royale des Inscriptions et Belles Lettres*.[87] He was elected to the Society of Antiquaries in 1759, and quickly became Vice-President and Director.[88] On his ordination in 1751 (a scrambled affair to allow him to take advantage of a vacancy in the St John's living of Lawford in Essex) he resigned as University Registrary and embarked on another career as archdeacon of Buckingham from 1753 and canon residentiary of St Paul's from July 1757: this last position provided him with a house in Amen Corner, where he remained until his death in 1766. He is buried in St Paul's Cathedral.

The one occasion recorded by Boswell when Taylor and Samuel Johnson met was not a social success. 'Demosthenes Taylor, as he was called ... was ... the merest statue of a man that I have ever seen. I once dined in company with him, and all he said during the whole time was no more than *Richard*. How a man should say only Richard, it is not easy to imagine. But it was thus: Dr. Douglas was talking of Dr. Zachary Grey, and ascribing to him something that was written by Dr. Richard

---

[85] The marble was given to Trinity College by the Countess of Bute in 1766. See P. Gaskell and R. Robson *The library of Trinity College Cambridge: a short history* (Cambridge 1971) p. 28. Taylor's own annotated copy of his book is in the Bodleian Library.

[86] For details of its reception see J. Nichols' account in Roger Long and John Taylor *Two music speeches at Cambridge* (1819) pp. xviii–xxii.

[87] His proposals, dated 1742, are reprinted *ibid.* pp. 58–64.

[88] Contrary to the *DNB*, he was not an FRS.

Grey. So, to correct him, Taylor said, (imitating his affected sententious emphasis and nod,) "Richard".'[89] Among his friends, however, Taylor's shyness left him. A good raconteur, he also possessed the rare knack of being able to turn instantly from one pastime to another.

If you called on him in College after dinner, you were sure to find him sitting at an old oval walnut-tree table entirely covered with books, in which, as the common expression runs, he seemed to be buried; you began to make apologies for disturbing a person so well employed; but he immediately told you to advance, taking care to disturb, as little as you could, the books on the floor; and called out, 'John, John, bring pipes and glasses;' and then fell to procuring a small space for the bottle just to stand on, but which could hardly ever be done without shoving off an equal quantity of the furniture at the other end; and he instantly appeared as cheerful, good-humoured, and *degagé*, as if he had not been at all engaged or interrupted. Suppose now you had staid as long as you would, and been entertained by him most agreeably, you took your leave, and got half-way down the stairs; but, recollecting somewhat that you had more to say to him, you go in again: the bottle and glasses were gone, the books had expanded themselves so as to re-occupy the whole table, and he was just as much buried in them as when you first broke in on him. I never knew this convenient faculty to an equal degree in any other scholar.[90]

[89] Boswell's *Life* 25 April 1778.
[90] George Ashby, President of St John's, quoted in *Two music speeches* (1819) p. xxxi. Ashby's account, communicated to John Nichols, continued a little later: 'His voice to me, who know nothing of music, appeared remarkably pleasing and harmonious, whether he talked or read English, Latin, or Greek prose, owing to his speaking through his lips much advanced, which always produces softness: this practice, or habit, I believe, he learnt from a speaking-master, to whom he applied to correct some natural defect; for which purpose he always kept near him an ordinary small swing-glass, the use of which was unknown to his friends; but in preaching, which he was fond of, one might perceive a shrillness or sharpness that was not agreeable; perhaps he could not speak so loud as was required, and at the same time keep his lips advanced and near together, as he had learned to do in common conversation. He understood perfectly, as a gentleman and scholar, all that belongs to making a book handsome, as the choice of paper, types, and the disposition of text, version, and notes.
He excelled in many small accomplishments. He was fond of carving, which he did with much elegance; an agreeable practice, but which, notwithstanding what Lord Chesterfield says, some persons who have frequented good tables all their life-time cannot do, though they can blow their nose passing well. He always appeared handsomely in full dress as a Clergyman, was grand in his looks, yet affable, flowing, and polite. Latterly he grew too plump, with an appearance of doughy paleness, which occasioned uneasiness to those who loved him, whose number, I think, must be considerable' (*ibid.* p. xxxiii). The same volume also contains various poems by Taylor (pp. 38–54). All these details were repeated from Nichols' *Literary anecdotes of the eighteenth century* 4 (1812).

His own library was celebrated, and he paid more attention to that than to the furniture of his rooms in college. After his move to London, and so away from the University Library, he spent even more on it, while on his death he bequeathed the printed books to his old school and the manuscripts and annotated volumes to Anthony Askew.[91] His disposition of the former met with less than universal approval,[92] and the latter were the cause of much later bitterness. Askew was criticized for his custody of Taylor's notes,[93] while the University's ungainly attempt to acquire his papers and books from Askew's library at the auction in 1785 will be described later.

Despite Hearne's doubts, Taylor proved an ideal choice as *Bibliothecarius*. He held the post technically for only two years, before taking up his appointment as Registrary, but he remained *de facto* in charge of cataloguing Moore's books even after he had relinquished the post to Thomas Parne in 1734.[94] His hand is everywhere to be seen in the organization of the books that had been so neglected. It was he who classified the books, wrote many of the draft class catalogues, corrected mistakes in the cataloguing, compiled cataloguing rules, listed the early printed books more fully and accurately than Middleton had, and even toyed with making a subject catalogue. His neat writing belies the speed at which he must have worked, although he used shorthand on occasion for brief memoranda intended only for his personal use. In February

---

[91] *Cambridge Chronicle* 12 April 1766. Cf. J. B. Oldham 'Shrewsbury School Library: its history and contents' *Trans. Shropshire Archaeological Soc.* 51 (1941–3) pp. 53–81; *idem*, *Shrewsbury School Library bindings* (Oxford 1943); *idem*, *A history of Shrewsbury School* (Oxford 1952) pp. 260, 263–4.

[92] Ashby considered that Taylor ought merely to have left standard sets of classical authors, dictionaries, etc. to Shrewsbury. 'Not so with the many curious articles that he had picked up singly at a great expence from foreign parts as he could hear of them. These are not likely to be of much service in the Country; but might probably have been looked into in the University, which also would have been a place for distant Literati to have inquired for them, where access would be remarkably easy and agreeable' (*Two music speeches* p. xxxviii).   [93] *Ibid.*, p. xxx.

[94] Cf., for example, his request to the Vice-Chancellor for payment to be made to H. Mickelson 'for work done in the King's Library' (Vouchers, 24 December 1741).

1735/6 – after he had officially resigned from the Library – he checked the fifteenth-century books, using the list prepared under Middleton's supervision, and between then and December 1740 began work on a proper catalogue of the incunables in the Royal Library, a project he abandoned after entering only forty-two items.[95] His attack on the rest of the printed books was on the other hand sustained, and permanent in its effect. His methods of classification were, by his own admission, inspired at least partly by the need for speed.

He used to say, that, throwing the books into heaps for general divisions, he saw one whose title-page mentioned somewhat of *height*, and another of salt. The first he cast among those of Mensuration, the other to those of Chemistry or Cookery; that he was startled, when he came to examine them, to find the first was 'Longinus de Sublimitate,' and the other 'A Theological Discourse on the Salt of the World, that good Christians ought to be seasoned with.'[96]

Despite such mishaps, he was the first to impose a new classification scheme on the Library for half a century, and his execution of the task had many merits. It was not achieved without some difficulty, and some parts of the Library which were too hastily catalogued had to be reclassified, including, for example, many of the liturgies. As it finally emerged, the scheme differed somewhat from that proposed by Middleton in 1723, and the classes stood as follows – repeating Taylor's own terminology for subjects as far as possible:

A	Bibles
B	Commentaries; Biblical history; concordances
C	Commentaries; Jewish writings; early Christianity; comparative theology
D	Greek and Latin Fathers
E	Latin Fathers
F	Polemical theology; dogma; sermons
G	Liturgy
H	Canon law; civil law
I/J	Civil law

[95] MS. Oo.7.58. This also includes Taylor's list of adversaria in the Royal Library.
[96] Roger Long and John Taylor *Two music speeches at Cambridge* (1819): preface by J. Nichols, p. ix, quoting George Ashby.

K	Medicine; anatomy; surgery
L	Ancient philosophy; materia medica
M	Ancient philosophy; mathematics; astronomy; architecture; warfare; other sciences
N	Philosophy; chronology; geography
O	Travel; general history; politics
P	Ecclesiastical history
Q	Ancient history
R	History of the British Isles
S	History of France and Italy
T	History of the rest of the world
U/V	Dictionaries; bibliographies; library catalogues
W	Orators; ancient and modern imaginative literature; letters
X	Latin plays and poems
Y	Greek plays and poems; modern plays and poems in all languages
Z	Archaeology; antiquities; numismatics; inscriptions
Aa★,Bb★	Dictionaries; pamphlet volumes of a miscellaneous nature[97]

By August 1734 matters were sufficiently far advanced for the University Press to print thirty-nine quires of sheets of numbers and figures to be pasted onto the spines of the books.[98]

At various times attempts had been made to set records straight as a preliminary to cataloguing the library by recalling all books which had been borrowed. There was, therefore, nothing out of the ordinary in yet another recall in the autumn of 1737. This occasion was more urgent than usual, however, for when the Library Syndics agreed to it on 28 September, they also agreed that Taylor should be 'desired to prepare an Abstract of the State of the Royal Library by Friday morning next', i.e. in forty-eight hours. By then he had presumably done so, for on the Friday they were able to tackle the question in detail. Taylor was requested to reduce the class of Bibles (class A)

---

[97] These categories, which obviously do not mention all subjects, are based wherever possible on the titles pasted to the outsides of the draft class catalogues, and therefore do not necessarily and invariably correspond with the books as arranged on the shelves.

[98] Vouchers, 1733–4.

into order, to draw up a shelf-list, and to report back to the Syndics in order that they could 'judge of the method in disposing them'.[99] Having thus been given his head, Taylor set to work with some speed, and in mid-November the Syndics were able to give permission for two further classes of theological books to be dealt with similarly. They also wisely agreed that 'no persons whatsoever' should be allowed to enter the Royal Library until Taylor had it in order, save with the Vice-Chancellor's express permission.[100] This determined attack promised an end to a situation that had become a disgrace to the University, and thus far everything had gone extraordinarily smoothly. But the whole procedure relied on one man, and he was seriously overworked. In a letter to Richard Rawlinson written probably in 1738, and dated 10 March, Thomas Baker sounded a preliminary alarm:

The Catalogue of Bp: Moors Books may probably be printed, wch is now taking by Mr Taylor, & will, I believe, be exact enough to be published. The first Class (viz: Bibles) I have seen, exceeding well taken, & the rest, I doubt not, will be like it. But I wish, he may have health (w^ch: he has wanted of late) to enable him to proceed. He is too much fatigu'd with business, both in the university & college, where he is Steward, to be applyd to for more, wherein I dare not give you too much encouragement, & his Book, you know, is yet upon his hands, besides other business.[101]

Equally seriously, in July that year the Syndics were constrained to report that the new catalogue of the Bibles had been stolen.[102] Taylor was entrusted with appealing to the University at large for its return, but he clearly required some help if the work of cataloguing the Library was ever to be completed.

In the end there were three series of class catalogues or shelf-lists, the first two having been so revised and annotated as to be unusable as documents of permanent record. The class catalogues were prerequisites for an alphabetical catalogue,

[99] University Archives Minutes of Syndicates 1737–1834 p. 7.
[100] Minutes of Syndicates 14 November 1737. Final approval to finish the catalogue was given on 26 May 1738. [101] Bodleian Library MS. Rawl. Letters 30 (127).
[102] Minutes of Syndicates. Min. Vl. 1 (1). 17 July 1738.

193

and rather than re-examine all the books for this next stage, an attempt was made to compile an author catalogue merely by rearranging the shelf-lists by authors' or editors' names. Taylor himself wrote many of the drafts, but he was assisted by a motley of undergraduates, young postgraduates, and local talent. Between 1738 and 1748 over two dozen names appear in the accounts as receiving various sums of money for cataloguing books. Chief among them was Henry Mickelson, who had entered St John's College as a sizar in June 1736 and who from 1743 until his early death in 1752 was a Fellow of Clare. He was employed from 1740 to 1745, and in 1741 alone earned far more than the £35 allowed to Thomas Parne as *Bibliothecarius*. The scheme adopted for cataloguing the library proved untidy and wasteful, and in the end it proved necessary to rewrite the alphabetical catalogue of authors as well: this too was successful at only the third attempt, both the earlier ones proving to be too compactly arranged to accommodate all the entries necessary. Finally, in October 1747, the third version of the alphabetical catalogue was begun by Robert Pitcher, school master at Fen Ditton. Into four vast volumes bound in reversed calf and supplied by the best of the local binders, Edwin Moor, Pitcher and a group of skilled calligraphers transcribed the labours of the previous decade. Even this was not enough, however, and their artistry was quickly disguised by the discovery of yet more omissions. The hand of Pindar's successor Thomas Goodall (unnervingly similar to that of F. S. Parris, Middleton's successor as *Protobibliothecarius*)[103] is to be seen at every turn in the library catalogues of the mid-century, as well as on the title pages of the greater part of the Royal Library. He had supervised work on the catalogues in 1746, wrote many of the class marks in the books, and now spent a considerable quantity of ink in adding entries to virtually every page of the new alphabetical catalogue. More unrecorded

---

[103] Plate 2 in Oates *Catalogue* is in Goodall's hand, not Parris'. The two may be conveniently compared in the Vouchers for the early 1750s. Goodall's name is to be found first on a binding bill dated 17 July 1725.

books continued to be spotted for some time afterwards. In addition to these four main volumes there was another, now lost, describing volumes of plates kept in a class by themselves signified simply by the letter A and a running number. Again, Goodall seems to have been responsible for this class, in which he placed Moore's many volumes of engravings indifferently with such later acquisitions as the catalogue of the Earl of Pembroke's numismatic collection, given in 1749, and the spectacular coloured copy, bound by Richard Balley, of J. Commelin's *Horti medici Amstelodamensis rariorum plantarum descriptio et icones* (Amsterdam 1697–1701). All four alphabetical catalogues are, it is needless to say, no longer in use, but the class catalogues of the Royal Library written in 1748 by W. Pitkin, Edmund Carter (author of a history of Cambridgeshire), Henry Gee, John Harris, John Hallam, John Foster, Charles Newling (recently graduated from St John's and subsequently Head Master of Shrewsbury School) and Richard Spenser of Trinity College (later a Fellow of Pembroke)[104] remain the same in use to this day.

Taylor had also listed[105] a subject catalogue as a desideratum, but this proved to be too ambitious, and although various incomplete drafts were made, the only substantial part to be completed was Taylor's own *Bibliotheca Biblica*, compiled probably by 1748.[106]

Few enterprises could have tried the patience of the University more, but there were also those who were unwilling to wait, for whom the presence of so large and ill-sorted a collection was overpoweringly tempting. Unsecured and unmarked, Moore's books had been pilfered almost from the moment they arrived in Cambridge, but it needed a thief to be apprehended before the authorities recognized the obvious

---

[104] Cf. Vouchers for 1748–9. A brief notice of Carter, 'a poor disabled writing-master', is given in *DNB*.   [105] In the same notebook as his notes on cataloguing rules etc.
[106] MS. Oo.7.60. It was bound by Edwin Moor on 21 July 1748: his receipted bill dated 2 November 1748 is among the Vouchers.

truth that a disorganized library is an open invitation to a thief. As we have seen, little had been achieved in the way of cataloguing the Royal Library by 1731; and access to it still relied on a catalogue (now lost) created in Moore's own lifetime which appears to have identified at least some of the books by single numbers either on their spines or written inside the front board or on a flyleaf.[107] Moreover, as Conyers Middleton had pointed out in 1723,[108] there was virtually no limit to the period for which a book might be borrowed. It also emerged from the investigation following a series of thefts by Philip Nichols, a Fellow of Trinity Hall, that no proper check was made of what was even legitimately borrowed. If further invitation was needed, none of the Royal Library books bore any mark of the University's ownership (as distinct from the old catalogue numbers) until bookplates were engraved for them by John Pine in 1736.[109]

Nichols did not confine his attention to the University Library,[110] and suspicions of him were first raised at St John's, who quickly found that the bookseller William Thurlbourn had also been robbed. They established that various books sold at auction in London on 13 November 1730 had been sent in by Nichols, and that one of them had belonged to the college. Only after their investigations were thus well advanced was Samuel Hadderton called in, as University Librarian, with the librarian of Trinity (Sandys Hutchinson) and various fellows of Nichols' own college. Nichols' room was found to contain books from St John's, Trinity, Trinity Hall and the University Library. He was expelled from his fellowship in July 1731, and

---

[107] Cf. Oates *Catalogue* pp. 17–18. It was these numbers by which Daniel Waterland referred to Moore's early printed Bibles when in correspondence with John Lewis in 1729 (D. Waterland *Works* (Oxford 1823–8) 10 pp. 316, 341).

[108] *Bibliothecae Cantabrigiensis ordinandae methodus* p. 13.

[109] On 8 July 1737 the University paid Pine's bill of £37.17s.6d. for engraving and printing 28,200 bookplates in four sizes (Luard 196); see also Audit Book 1660–1740 p. 635. Some of Pine's plates were later re-engraved by Joshua Baldrey, and copies printed off in 1785 (Vouchers).

[110] See Owen Chadwick 'The case of Philip Nichols, 1731' *Trans. Cambridge Bibliographical Soc.* I (1953) pp. 422–31.

deprived of his degrees on 6 August. He appears to have stolen books principally for money. Hints were dropped of a mistress, and little more proof is needed of his financial plight than the extraordinary revelation that he had mortgaged his fellowship for £100 in August 1730 to another Nichols living in Staffordshire. As a thief, in the mind of Thomas Baker at least, he aroused pity, but the case was closed without all his thefts being recovered. He confessed to taking fifteen items from the Library, including five from the Royal Library, in October 1731; but Hadderton's list of the books sold at auction in November 1730 that he believed to have come from the Library differed slightly from the culprit's confession. Most of them came from easily accessible parts of the building, either the old library or the unreserved Royal Library, but one came from 'a table in the Inner part of the said Library, from whence however a person by thrusting his arm thro' a Latticed partition might draw it out'.[111]

Hadderton died on 20 March 1731/2[112] just after the scandal and three days after the election of his successor. One of Taylor's first actions, after arranging for his office to be provided with fresh furniture,[113] was to issue an order in the name of the Vice-Chancellor and dated 3 June:

Whereas upon inquiry into the State of the Publick Library, it has been found, that a great number of Books borrowed thence many years ago have not to this time been returned into it; from which neglect the loss of many of the said Books may be apprehended, if timely care be not taken to prevent it; These are to require, that all Persons who have borrowed any books out of the Publick Library do return the same within Ten Days from the date hereof; and that from the date hereof no Books be delivered

---

[111] Hadderton's deposition, dated 4 August 1731, and Nichols' confession are in the Library archives (Luard 187). Only one of the books admitted to have been stolen was recovered: Cellarius' *Notitia orbis antiqui* (Cambridge 1703) was back in Hadderton's hands by 23 September 1731. A large paper copy of Dugdale's *A perfect copy of all summons to the nobility to the great councils and parliaments of this realm* (1685), bound in Turkey leather and taken from the Royal Library, was sold to the Earl of Oxford, but he was advised by his bookseller to keep it (HMC Portland 6 p. 39).

[112] *Gentleman's Magazine* 1732 p. 678.

[113] On 23 May the University paid £1.8s.0d. for four leather chairs for his room (Vouchers).

out of the Library, till all the Books have been Surveyed by the Catalogue, and the Library has been put into order.[114]

It was the first such census to have been carried out for many years, and the losses that were discovered were appalling. By 1736 it was established that, so far from only a few having been lost, several thousand had gone. Nichols and a further culprit who was now apprehended, Henry Justice,[115] were not the only thieves, but they were the only two to be identified and punished. The case of Justice brought considerable expense to the University in following up clues, pursuing missing books, and attending court in London when he came to trial,[116] but the cost was easily justified by the magnitude of his thefts. He had entered Trinity College in 1716, the son of an attorney in York. In the same year he was admitted to the Middle Temple, and in 1727 was called to the bar. In 1735 he returned to Cambridge, and took up residence in Trinity while at the same time keeping his chambers in Elm Court in the Middle Temple. When, in the following January, his London rooms were searched, a quantity of books was found belonging to the University and to his college. He was unable to explain their presence satisfactorily, and so came to stand trial at the Old Bailey in May, where in the end he avoided further harassment by pleading guilty to thefts from the University Library, and was sued only for stealing from Trinity. He was sentenced to transportation to the American colonies for seven years. Ninety-six books were recovered from him, yet even this

---

[114] Luard 189. Nevertheless, when Matthew Lyne, Fellow of Emmanuel, wanted to borrow a manuscript Virgil and six early printed books, the customary Grace was passed as usual (Grace Book *I* p. 319, 1 July 1732).

[115] Cooper *Annals* 4 p. 223, and notes by George Chawner in MS. Add. 6107 p. 16. Cf. Philip Gaskell 'Henry Justice, a Cambridge book thief' *Trans. Cambridge Bibliographical Soc.* 1 (1952) pp. 348–57.

[116] Taylor's bills alone amounted to £65.5s.2d. Sandys Hutchinson, Librarian of Trinity, was reimbursed for £29.8s.0d., and the solicitor's bill was £44.0s.0d., quite apart from a host of smaller ones. On the day that Justice should have been tried for stealing from the University Library the Cambridge party celebrated the occasion by dining at Truby's coffee house in St Paul's Churchyard for a total of £3.8s.1d.; a 'consultation' shortly afterwards at the Ship Tavern cost £1.2s.0d. (Audit Book 1660–1740, accounts for 1735–6).

belied the scale of his operations with his accomplice and brother-in-law Jonas Thompson, once Mayor of York. The matter of Thompson was more serious, but the University began legal proceedings against him only in June.[117] Some time in the latter half of 1736 a draft petition was drawn up on behalf of the University, stating that 'several thousands of very valuable books', part of the Royal Library, were missing, and that it had been discovered that a 'very great quantity' of these, valued at upwards of £2000, had come into the hands of Thompson.[118] They had been shipped to Thompson via London and Bridlington, and the numbers had been such as to require four wagons to remove them from the port.[119] The matter was however even at this point less than likely to be resolved satisfactorily, for although the University sought an injunction to restrain Thompson and his associates from selling or otherwise disposing of the books, and pleaded for a subpoena to be served on him ordering his appearance before the Lord Chancellor, the University realized that at least part of its case was lost. He could not be charged with stealing any exact list of books, for no such list either existed or could be compiled, while he also threatened either to secrete the books in the country or to send them overseas. So far as Thompson was concerned, the matter had to be dropped.

Unlike the wretched Nichols, Justice was a bibliomaniac. He ended his life in Holland,[120] and when his books came to be auctioned at The Hague by Nicolas van Daalen in October and November 1763 the sale lasted sixteen days. By then the library was of very considerable value, particularly strong in classical authors, ancient and modern history and ancillary subjects. He also possessed a fine collection of prints. It was alleged at his

---

[117] The legal bills for the case are in the Vouchers for 1735-7.
[118] The draft petition prepared by the university counsel John Willes and William Noel (later Justice of the Common Pleas) is in the Library archives (Luard 195²).
[119] According to a note by Taylor dated 18 February 1735/6, Luard 195¹.
[120] 'Lately died at the Hague, one Mr. Justice, who was some years ago transported for stealing books belonging to the Public Library of this university' (*Cambridge Chronicle* 22 October 1763).

trial, according to the report in *The present state of Great Britain*, that he had also traded in books, and had already made several trips overseas for that purpose;[121] but this was only to further his ends as a collector. He had a much better eye for worthwhile books than Nichols, and among those stolen from Trinity there were, for example, the Complutensian Polyglot Bible (valued at his trial at 'about twenty guineas'), an Aldine New Testament valued at three or four guineas, Plutarch's *Vies des hommes illustres* (two guineas), Palladio's *Quattro libri dell'architettura* (£1 or more), and the first Duke of Newcastle's *Methode nouvelle et invention extraordinaire de dresser les chevaux*, valued at £10 or more.[122]

There was however one similarity with the Nichols case. In both detection followed suspicions by college authorities and, in the Justice affair, after thefts had been reported at the library of the Middle Temple.[123] In neither had the University Library raised the alarm. In such an atmosphere of incapacity and ineffectiveness it is more surprising that more books were not lost than that more thieves were not caught.

As will have emerged in the last few pages, Taylor continued to take a key part in running the Library even after he had resigned from formal responsibility. He was one of the few people competent to do so. But when on 5 December 1734 Lancelot Newton, Fellow of St John's and University Registrary since 1726, died in middle age, he left a post vacant which commanded an income of £80 or £90 per annum, well over twice that of the *Bibliothecarius*. Taylor grasped at the opportunity, and his election as Newton's successor[124] meant that the librarianship was again open. It also gave an opportunity for the factions of the University to practise their electoral skills, prompted once again by the controversies that

---

121 *The present state of Great Britain* 51 (1736) p. 567.
122 Cf. the report on the case in *The proceedings at the sessions of the peace* No. 4 pt 2 (1736) pp. 110–25 *passim*.
123 *Ibid.*, p. 116.   124 On 17 December. Grace Book *I* p. 371.

surrounded Middleton's scholarly and religious opinions. As Middleton explained to Lord Hervey,

We have had an election this week of a Register of ye University in ye room of an honest man lately dead, Dr Newton of St Johns, who was a true Whig: ye place is now given to as true a Tory, Mr Tailor of ye same Coll. who was ye other Librarian wth myself. ye onely Whig of three Candidates could not get pricked by ye defection of Waterland, who sent peremtory orders to his deputy to serve Tailor, for ye sake of vacating ye Librarian's place, & ye hopes of securing it to an Orthodox man, who had written for him agst me, one Chapman of King's: we are canvassing again for ye second Office, wch will be disposed of on Tuesday next, when Waterland's scheme seems ye most likely to succeed.[125]

John Chapman, Fellow of King's since 1727, had clashed with Middleton in a tract published three years previously, *Remarks on a letter to Dr Waterland, in relation to the natural account of languages.* But despite the powerful backing of Daniel Waterland, Middleton was unduly pessimistic. On 30 December two men were nominated to succeed Taylor in accordance with custom, Chapman and Thomas Parne, but it was Parne who was chosen the following day.[126] Whether Chapman (who later became archdeacon of Sudbury, and died in 1784 as rector of Mersham in Kent) would have made a more efficient librarian than Parne can scarcely be surmised. Middleton, however, was jubilant. The University had elected 'a worthy man, & hearty friend for my assistant', he wrote to Hervey.[127] More fortunately for the Library, its proximity to the Registrary's office gave every encouragement to Taylor to see through the work he had begun. From his room (which appears to have housed some of the early and more valuable books in the Royal Library for a time)[128] he continued as an active overseer of the ordering of the Library. He had need to be. Parne was undistinguished as a librarian and played scarcely any part in the everyday life of the collections of which he found himself in charge. The son of Richard Parne of Oxford,

---

[125] Middleton to Hervey 19 December 1734. Bury St Edmunds Record Office Hervey papers 941/47/8.   [126] Grace Book *I* p. 371.
[127] Middleton to Hervey 2 January 1734/5. Hervey papers 941/47/8.
[128] Oates *Catalogue* p. 21.

he had been educated at Bedford School, and entered Trinity as a sizar on 8 January 1714. He gained a scholarship in 1717, took his B.A. the following year, and in 1720 was elected to a fellowship. In 1722 he became a tutor (an appointment entirely unaffected by his appointment as Senior Dean in 1742 or as University *Bibliothecarius* in 1734), took his degree of B.D. in 1729 and of D.D. in 1739. To the misfortune of posterity, his history of his college, for which he published proposals in 1731,[129] never appeared.

His talents, however, were spoiled. A place seeker of more than average importunity even by the standards of the day, he had early marked himself, as a junior Fellow of Trinity, by joining John Colbatch in a hapless attempt to prosecute Bentley in 1728.[130] Bentley's biographer J. H. Monk described him as possessed of 'an intrepid spirit, but accompanied with a violent temper'.[131] He was, moreover, as a college tutor, in no position to withstand the letter of the statutes, which made tutors responsible for their pupils' bills. As an enemy of Bentley he was an easy target, and he became so embarrassed with debts incurred through no fault of his own that, as Monk recorded of the end of his life, 'the agitation of such circumstances operating on a mind which seems always to have been in a high degree of excitement, produced unequivocal symptoms of insanity; whereupon he was exiled from the College with an allowance for his support.'[132]

In the outside world, he could in 1722 already describe himself as chaplain to Anthony, Lord Lucas, the eldest son of the Duke of Kent, but this was merely a beginning to his long search for patronage. In 1730 he had been nominated as Public Orator, but was defeated in the election by Philip Williams, Fellow of St John's, thanks to the divided opinions of Trinity.[133] A

---

[129] 'It will be *grande volumen* and yet he gives expectation of a 2nd Part' (Hearne *Remarks and collections* 11 p. 10). For some of his notes cf. Bodleian Library MS. Gough Camb. 16 (SC17766).　　[130] Monk *The life of Richard Bentley* 2 p. 267.

[131] Monk *The life of Richard Bentley* 2 p. 267.

[132] *Ibid.*, p. 420.　　[133] *Ibid.*, pp. 296–7.

temporary truce with Bentley, by which Bentley agreed not to block his preferment and Parne agreed not to be party to any attempt to displace the Master, made the way open for the advancement (and extra salary) that Parne so much desired, but the truce lasted no more than two or three years.[134] His failure to become University Orator was compensated by his successful bid for the librarianship, yet at the same time that he became *Bibliothecarius* he was also considering his chances of succeeding Richard Bradley as Professor of Botany[135] – despite the fact that so far as the world was aware he possessed little or no relevant knowledge. By the early 1740s he had joined the throng who pinned their hopes on the Duke of Newcastle. In July 1742, equipped with a D.D., he sought the Regius Professorship of Divinity in succession to Bentley,[136] but lost it to John Whalley, Master of Peterhouse and the candidate favoured by Newcastle.[137] In April 1743, having received a hint of a royal chaplaincy after his failure to gain the professorship, he wrote to Newcastle again, pleading that he was beginning to appear ludicrous in the eyes of his friends to whom he had boasted of his imminent appointment.[138] He was rewarded the following year, and could describe himself on the title-page to his sermon on the anniversary of the King's accession on 11 June 1744 as both Chaplain in Ordinary to His Majesty and rector of Walkington in Yorkshire.[139] Still not content, his hopes again rose early in 1746, and he approached Newcastle once more:

Being naturally of Too Great a spirit, & Buoyed up with Promising Hopes by several Persons of Eminence I lived many years (imprudently enough) at too much Expence. And what more deeply Embarassed me, had some Grievous Losses from some of my Pupils in yᵉ University. But about seven

---

[134] Ibid., pp. 354–5, 382–3.
[135] Winstanley *Unreformed Cambridge* pp. 162–3.
[136] British Library MS. Add. 32699 fos. 325–6.
[137] British Library MS. Add. 32699 fos. 619–20.
[138] British Library MS. Add. 32700 fo. 102.
[139] Although he issued proposals for a collection of his sermons in two volumes in 1744, no such collection ever appeared. A copy of the proposals is in CUL.

years ago, I Grew wiser, retrenched my Expences; & was in a Fair way of making my self, in a Few years intirely Easy. And had I obtained ye Divinity Professor^p. which seemed, as it were, to offer itself, I had not only been so, but amply Provided for, for Life.

On y^r. Graces introducing me to Court, & Giving me large views, w^{ch}, from ye Assurances you was pleased to give, I thought I might depend on; my Expences again increased, & my Affairs here went Backwards. on ye Failure at Canterbury last year,[140] my Credit is impaired, my mind shooked, my Health not a little indangered. Good y^r Grace, let not ye world, wch is but too apt to take any Handle to slander ye Great, have room to impute any of ye misfortunes wch. may Happen to me, to any but myself!

Y^r Grace, on my missing ye former, undertook to Engage to me ye next Prebend by Promise from his Majesty, & to write me ye success. Many months are since gone. Y^r doing it is so necessary for ye supporting both my spirits & my fortune, that they seem very many & long.[141]

Again his hopes were dashed, however. A further stall fell vacant later in the year, and on 25 October he was enquiring whether the Archbishop of Canterbury would introduce him to the King (in whose gift the stall lay), proposing to have his recent thanksgiving sermon at Cambridge printed so that he could use the occasion to present it.[142] The appeal was as unsuccessful as previous ones, and Parne's final attempt to win favour from Newcastle came two years afterwards. On 14 December 1748 Newcastle was elected Chancellor of the University, an event close enough to the death of John Whalley for Parne to be able to send his congratulations by the letter in which he sought once again the Regius Professorship of Divinity and with it a stipend of about £300 a year.[143] He had ceased to be tutor in his college in 1745, and Senior Dean in 1747, and his last years, beset by illness, ended on 11 July 1751. His contribution to the Library had been negligible, in stark contrast to Taylor's crucial, and unofficial, role.

Even before the books came to Cambridge, it was realized

---

[140] i.e. his failure to obtain David Wilkins' prebend.
[141] British Library MS. Add. 32707 fos. 1–2.
[142] British Library MS. Add. 32709 fos. 132–3.
[143] British Library MS. Add. 32717 fo. 450. For Newcastle's part in the election see Winstanley *Eighteenth century* pp. 182–9.

that Moore's library contained many duplicates. The catalogue of the collection made in his own lifetime, incomplete though it was, revealed something of the problem, which arose not least because he had kept libraries in both Norwich and London. So there were, in the late 1690s, copies of Hyde's catalogue of the Bodleian Library in both places, two copies each of Wood's *Athenae Oxonienses* and Wharton's *Anglia sacra*, and three or four copies of the 1567 Vitruvius.[144] In November 1737 the Library Syndics began to tackle the problem exposed by Taylor in the course of his cataloguing, and resolved 'that the Vice Chancellor do from time to time buy such books as shall be necessary as near as may be to the amount of yᵉ Duplicates' – a decision that is not straight-forward to interpret.[145]

The duplicates from the Royal Library were, in the main, disposed of through William Thurlbourn from about 1740 onwards. This was done principally in two auction sales held in March and December 1742[146] but, as will be seen, the Library was already acquiring books from him in exchange for duplicates several years earlier. No suggestion seems to have been made in 1715 that books in Moore's collection which duplicated items already in the University Library should be disposed of, and the auction sales consisted (apart from an 'appendix' of other books) almost entirely of duplicates from within the Royal Library itself, regardless of the old university collection. The catalogues, in the absence of any full inventory dating from Moore's own lifetime, make plain the limited extent of his control over his collection. If – and there is no direct evidence to the contrary – Thurlbourn's catalogues were

144 Bodleian Library MS. Add. D.80*.
145 University Archives Minutes of Syndicates 1737–1834 p. 8 (14 November 1737).
146 Sanctioned by the Library Syndicate on 17 February 1741/2 (Minutes of Syndicates 1737–1834 p. 81). On 16 May 1741 the Syndics had agreed that five hundred copies of a catalogue of Royal Library duplicates should be printed, but it is not clear that this referred to Thurlbourn's auction catalogue. A fragment of the manuscript of the catalogue prepared for the auction survives, and suggests that it was compiled under Taylor's supervision as much as Thurlbourn's.

not salted from elsewhere to any great extent, the duplication was of a nature that suggested more of careless extravagance than of deliberate policy. So there came on the market books as varied as the collected edition of Erasmus (1540), Charles Estienne's *De dissectione partium corporis humani* (Paris 1545), Ray's *Historia plantarum* (1686), Cowper's *Anatomy* (Oxford 1698), Moses Pitt's *Atlas* (Oxford 1680 etc.), architectural books by Vitruvius and Serlio, Baluze's *Capitularia* (1677) and Bartolocci's *Bibliotheca magna Rabbinica* (Rome 1675–94), quite apart from quantities of books in the classics. Even after one copy had been set aside for the Library, there still remained two copies to be sold of such books as the 1602 Chaucer, the 1666 Hooker, Cooper's Latin dictionary (1584), Burton's *Description of Leicestershire* (1622), John Parkinson's *Theatrum botanicum* (1640) and Plot's *Natural history of Staffordshire* (Oxford 1686).

There were, however, no incunables and few books published before 1520; it seems likely that the authorities decided to keep back from auction almost all books published before the mid-sixteenth century. This principle applied with particular strictness to early English books: among only about half a dozen published before 1550 to be included were the first edition of Tyndale's *Obedience of a christen man* (1528) and the 1525 edition of Lyndewode's *Constitutiones*. But despite these reservations, the two series of sales, spread over eighteen days, comprised over 2400 lots. The first sale was almost a family affair, virtually all those attending being members of the University; and though the auctioneer's marked up copy of the catalogue survives only for this one,[147] there is no reason to suppose that the second was dissimilar. Among those who bought most heavily were James Husband, Fellow of Caius, Roger Long, the Master of Pembroke, and Henry Plumptre, a member of Queens', but the first sale was dominated (if the number of lots bought is the criterion) by John Taylor,

---

[147] Cam.d.742.2. Luard 203.

formerly *Bibliothecarius* and now Registrary, and by George Townshend, Fellow-Commoner of St John's and later to achieve fame for his political caricatures and as a controversial Lord Lieutenant of Ireland. Of all those present, Taylor was of course most familiar with the books, and many came into his possession without the need for an auction. Financially the sale was only a mixed success, and after Thurlbourn's commission of fifteen per cent had been paid the University was left with a credit balance on the first sale of only £172.12s.11d.[148] The highest price paid was for Cowper's *Anatomy*, which reached £5.7s.0d., but this and the price of £4.5s.0d. paid for Walton's polyglot Bible easily outstripped all other lots. The 1540 Erasmus in seven volumes fetched eighteen shillings, but the collected works of St Basil (1551), Baluze's *Capitularia* (1677), Estienne's *De dissectione* (1545), Descartes' *Principia philosophiae* (Amsterdam 1644) and *Epistolae* (Amsterdam 1668), Grynaeus' *Novus orbis* (Basel 1537), Boyle's *Sceptical chymist* (1680) as well as two copies of John Fisher's *De veritate corporis et sanguinis Christi in Eucharistia* (Cologne 1527), all failed to find buyers. As usual, recent works of scholarship were sold without difficulty, but it could scarcely be claimed that competition was brisk even for these.

The University received a mere £90.11s.6d. from the second sale.[149] Onto the end of this was tagged a so-called 'Appendix' of which the origin is not clear: it included, besides books of the same kind as had graced the preceding days' sales, many published between 1715 and 1741 that can have formed no part of the Royal Library. But despite the fact that these also were sold in the public schools, it is difficult to adduce convincing evidence that they were in any sense the University's property, superfluous to the Library's needs either as gifts or as books received under the copyright legislation. Thurlbourn, who conducted regular auctions, avoided using

---

[148] Vouchers 9 November 1742.
[149] University Audit Book 1741–86, account for year ending November 1744. No record survives of individual purchases or of prices realized.

his shop at 1 Trinity Street (the present site of Bowes and Bowes) when selling large collections, and instead preferred a room at the Wrestlers or the Falcon Inn. It may, therefore, have been perhaps a mixture of his ordinary stock and unwanted Library books. On the one hand, for example, the Library might have been expected to retain Nicholas Trivet's *Annales sex regum Angliae* (Oxford 1719), the revised fourth edition of Whiston's *New theory of the earth* (1725) or Samuel von Pufendorf's *De officio hominis et civis iuxta legem naturalem* (second edition 1737), edited by Thomas Johnson, Fellow of Magdalene, who had died in 1737. On the other hand, however, such books as Mary Master's *Poems on several occasions* (1733), Elizabeth Rowe's *Miscellaneous works* (1738–9) and a French translation of *Don Quixote* were not characteristic of the kind of book that the Library sought to preserve in the mid-eighteenth century.

In addition to these revenues, the University also received the sum of £12.6s.6d. from Dr William George, Provost of King's and Vice-Chancellor in 1743–4.[150] As Headmaster of Eton until 1743, he had not participated in the first auction at least, but he did not buy direct from the University, and instead seems to have bought from among the items set aside as unsold by Thurlbourn in the sales of a year or so previously. William Cole also bought various books subsequently, at prices established by Thurlbourn. They were not the only ones to do so.[151] Thurlbourn closed his own part of the account as far as the University auditors were concerned in 1744–5, by reporting two sales totalling £13.15s.6d., receiving on them a

---

[150] University Audit Book 1741–86, account for year ending November 1744.

[151] Cf. Tasso *Gierusalemme liberata* (Mantua 1584: F158.c.2.2) with a note by Cole 'Jan: 26 1744/5, sent this Duplicate fr yᵉ. Royal Library to be valued by Mʳ. Thurlbourne yᵉ. Bookseller according to an Order of yᵉ. University'; Ludovico Petrucci *Apologia* (1619: Syn. 7.61.85) bears a similar note, as does the Christie-Miller copy (dated 4 March) of Edmund Gardiner's *Triall of tobacco* (1610) (Sotheby's 31 March 1925, lot 308). See also W. M. Palmer *William Cole of Milton* (Cambridge 1935) pp. 72–3. In July 1984 the Library bought the copy of the *editio princeps* of Longus *Daphnis and Chloe* (Florence 1598) mistakenly discarded as a duplicate presumably at about this time and sold to Mansfield Price, Fellow of St John's and a few years younger than Taylor.

commission of £4.1s.0d.[152] The matter was finally ended in 1748, with the purchase by Thomas Merrill, the other principal Cambridge bookseller, of the 'refuse' of the duplicates for £6.[153] The entire exercise had been a most necessary one, but it had not reaped enormous benefits. It was, moreover, a restrained one. Duplication with books already in the Library had been generally ignored, and any more radical proposals were firmly set aside on 10 December 1744, when a Grace proposing that duplicates from the old library should be sold was defeated.[154]

The process of trading duplicates for new books was of considerably more importance for the Library. In this way it was able to acquire, without charge to the University, a number of scholarly works of crucial importance which it had either ignored or been unable to afford in the years between the arrival of the Royal Library and the early 1740s. No full list of these exists, but in a notebook kept by Taylor in which he also entered rules for cataloguing the Library, a list of Boyle Lectures, and a chronological arrangement of the names of the church fathers, with other miscellanea, is a catalogue of ninety titles of 'Books sent in by M[r]. Thurlbourn in exchange for Duplicates, by order of the Syndics'. It is undated, but clearly records transactions completed shortly before the sales, containing, for example, only the first two volumes (out of four) of Muratori's *Novus thesaurus veterum inscriptionum* (Milan 1739–42) dated 1739–40. It also includes one item that can be shown to have come not from Thurlbourn but from Israel Lyons, a Polish Jew who had settled in Cambridge as a silversmith a few years earlier and who also earned a living as teacher of Hebrew: the university accounts record payment to him on 28 May 1740 of £6.5s.6d. for the recent edition of the Hebrew Bible published at Amsterdam in 1724–8. Among

---

[152] Vouchers 25 January 1745.
[153] University Audit Book 1741–86, account for year ending November 1748.
[154] British Library MS. Add. 5852 p. 111 (Diary of Henry Hubbard, transcribed by William Cole).

English books which might have been pursued under the Copyright Act of 1710 and which were now bought were David Wilkins' edition of Selden (1726), the collected works of Samuel Clarke (1738), Bayle's *Dictionary* in ten volumes, including Sale's contributions on oriental history (1734–41), and eleven volumes of the *Philosophical Transactions* of the Royal Society. A special attempt was made to obtain the most important antiquarian works, including Edmund Chishull's *Antiquitates Asiaticae* (1728), Stukeley's *Stonehenge* (1740), Maittaire's edition of the *Marmora Oxoniensia* (1732–3) among English publications, and Antonio Gori's *Inscriptiones antiquae* (Florence 1726), Christian Liebe's *Gotha numaria* (Amsterdam 1730) and the catalogue of the *Musei Theupoli antiqua numismata* (Venice 1736) among the foreign. There were new editions of John Chrysostom (by Montfaucon, thirteen volumes, 1718–38), St Basil (by Garnier, 1721–30) and Clement of Alexandria (by John Potter, Oxford 1715); of Thucydides (Dukerus, 1731), Josephus (Havercamp and John Hudson, 1726), Suetonius (Burmann, 1736), Herodotus (Gronovius, 1715–16), Lucretius (Havercamp, 1725), Terence (Francis Hare, London 1724), Manilius (Bentley, London 1739), a group of medical works by Friedrich Hoffmann mostly published in 1733–8, the first volume of the new catalogue of the French Royal Library, Montfaucon's catalogue of the Coislin collection of Greek manuscripts now in the Bibliothèque Nationale (1715) and his *Bibliotheca bibliothecarum manuscriptorum nova* (1739), Foppens' *Bibliotheca Belgica* (1739), Maittaire's *Annales typographici* (1722–33, the first volume in the revised edition), and Prosper Marchand's *Histoire de l'origine et des premiers progrès de l'imprimerie* (1740). And only in this manner, seemingly, was it possible to obtain one of the chief monuments of Cambridge eighteenth-century scholarship, the new edition of Stephanus' *Thesaurus* (1734–5) edited by Edmund Law, Thomas Johnson, Sandys Hutchinson and Taylor himself. The list – and these examples are by no means the whole even of the cream – was a reminder, if any was needed, of how far the Library had fallen behind in obtaining books essential to a university.

It also becomes clear from this list, which is certainly not and was never intended to be complete, that the practice of using Pine's bookplates for books other than those that had once belonged to Moore was not wanton. The bookplates read, with perfect accuracy, that the books they grace came as 'munificentia regia' (fig. 8), either as a direct gift or as a result of exchanging duplicates with Thurlbourn. The same principle appears to have been applied at least until 1751, for the bookplate is in Arringhi's *Roma subterranea* of that year, while the last volume of the *Philosophical Transactions* to bear it is that for 1756. All these fresh additions were placed with the rest of the Royal Library, and were catalogued with it rather than with the rest of the University Library's collections.

Although most of the theology was extracted in the nineteenth century to fill the shelves of the new Cockerell Building, and many of the early English books, the finest of the bindings, the oriental books, and various other categories were removed for protection against theft (the books were on open shelves until 1954)[155] or because generations of Librarians believed they could classify the books better, the Royal Library remains still the largest intact single collection in the Library as a whole, with the exception only of Lord Acton's books given in 1902.

Unlike the printed books, Moore's manuscripts presented relatively minor problems of organization. There were fewer of them; they were easily distinguishable apart from curiosities such as orientalia and volumes containing both printed and manuscript portions; and, most importantly, there already existed a catalogue of many of them, in Bernard's *Catalogi* of 1697 and in the handlist continued by Thomas Tanner.[156] It was only natural that they attracted the eye of the authorities first and so were the first to be shelved, in the Dome Room

---

[155] *Cambridge University Reporter* 1954–5 pp. 1659–60.
[156] MS. Oo.7.50². See above, pp. 133–41.

8   John Pine's engraved bookplate for the Royal Library, 1737. Size of
original 235 × 183 mm.

fitted up in 1719–20. But whereas it was an easy matter to
decide to keep Moore's printed books separate from the old
library, his manuscripts were eventually mingled with the
earlier collections in the manner in which they still remain.
This was not done until 1756, however, and between 1715 and
then there was considerable scope for misunderstanding.

The manuscripts in the old library were in 1732 still arranged as a separate collection.[157] In that year they were checked, and a list was made of those thought to be missing. Of twenty-four not found in their places, all but eight can now be found in the Library. The remarkable list of books so much misplaced that even a further check did not discover them is a sharp reminder that by no means only the Royal Library was not cared for punctiliously. Some manuscripts seemed to be missing simply because they had for one reason or another acquired duplicate numbers in the lists based on Thomas James' catalogue of 1600. Aelfric's eleventh-century Anglo-Saxon grammar and glossary,[158] for example, given by Matthew Parker in 1574, had been removed from the Library and on its recovery by Abraham Whelock had been given another number. Another volume given by Parker, containing texts by William of Malmesbury, Geoffrey of Monmouth and others, caused difficulties because it was not realized that it was no longer bound in two volumes.[159] In other words, they were no more lost than was the volume containing Aelfric's translation of Genesis and a collection of saints' lives in Anglo-Saxon,[160] which had acquired two numbers for no explicable reason at all. Six years later, in 1738, another check of all the old classes of manuscripts brought further difficulties and losses to light. Four volumes, among the thirteen or so (the record is not very exact) manuscripts listed as missing for the first time, are still absent from the Library today. But this time the roll-call also included the Codex Bezae, and this, the most valuable of the Library's possessions, was still not in its place in May 1748 when (owing to some repairs being done to the roof) the manuscripts were removed from their usual place and the opportunity taken of inspecting them as part of a general check of the whole library. The inspection is the last recorded in MS.

---

[157] The supplementary catalogue of manuscripts, continuing the numbering in Thomas James' *Ecloga* (1600) and repeated by Bernard, is now MS. Oo.7.59. The list used for checking missing items in 1732, including separate lists of lost books for that year, 1738 and 1748, is now MS. Add. 4451.   [158] MS. Hh.1.10.
[159] MS. Ff.1.25, nos. 244–5 in the old list.   [160] MS. Ii.1.3.

Add. 4451, and no record of any repetition survives until 1760.[161]

No account of any separate inspection of the Royal Library manuscripts exists before this latter year, but they had nonetheless been sorted out in the early 1750s, being finally taken in hand thirty-seven years after Moore's books had arrived at Cambridge, with a Grace passed on 6 July 1752 which remarked that the Dome Room was now properly ready for them and instructed that catalogues should be prepared at whatever expense seemed necessary.[162] As a result, all the Library's manuscripts were gathered together regardless of provenance. Moore's printed books reached class Bb; class Cc had been used for books from a variety of sources including the collection of John Colbatch, Vice-Master of Trinity, in 1748, and the next available class was thus Dd. By proceeding from stack to stack the manuscript classes at first reached to Mm.[163]

Generally speaking, manuscripts now in classes Dd to Mm (including Thomas Baker's volumes bequeathed in 1740) were thus in the Library by the mid-1750s. There are of course exceptions, both of exclusion and inclusion. The notes by Adam Wall (d. 1798) on university history, given to the Library by Dr Charles Sutton, vicar of Aldborough, Norfolk, in 1836, are now MSS. Mm.5.40–52, for example, whereas Moore's manuscript of Julius Caesar, used by Samuel Clarke and John Davies in the early eighteenth century, is now MS. Nn.3.5. The adventures of the Codex Bezae, for one reason or another absent from the shelves for so much of the early part of the century,[164] brought it finally to rest in a new place at

---

[161] Cf. the 'Catalogue of MSS. missing in 1760', a folio notebook in the Library archives.

[162] Grace Book *K* p. 188.

[163] There was also a small, and temporary, class A, consisting of a single sequence of numbers A1 etc.: the manuscript of Jean Robertet's letters and poems (now MS. Nn.3.2) was thus A145, for example. This catalogue too was the work of Goodall, but it had no long-term importance and was soon abandoned.

[164] Bentley was finally obliged to return it after keeping it in the Master's Lodge at Trinity for several years. In 1716 it was transcribed by J. J. Wetstein, then aged twenty-three. In 1732 or 1733 John Dickinson, an undergraduate of St John's, transcribed it for John

Nn.2.41. Other manuscripts found their way into class Nn because of the desire to distinguish rigidly between manuscripts and printed books regardless of any consideration of their history. As a result of this somewhat different professional failing, the Greek manuscript of Porphyrius' *Isagoge*, that had been bound up with two further Greek texts of Simplicius and Ammonius printed at Venice in 1499–1500 at least since they had been presented to the Library by Cuthbert Tunstall in 1528–9, was abstracted from its binding and classified as MS. Nn.1.24. A manuscript copy of *Aesop at Tunbridge, or a few select fables in verse* (the poem was also published in 1698), now MS. Nn.3.9, was similarly treated, for it almost certainly comes from one of Moore's pamphlet volumes. Besides this, Moore's adversaria were put into this further class Nn until they were removed into a new class Adv. in the 1930s.

Goodall copied out a list of the rearranged manuscripts into three volumes of a new class catalogue in 1754–6.[165] In doing so he drew heavily on already existing lists, principally in Bernard's *Catalogi*, where the accounts of the Library's old collections of manuscripts simply repeated those by Thomas James of 1600. His work shows little originality so far as the contents of the books, either in the old or the Royal Library, were concerned. Thus, for example, he repeated the description of part of Dd.1.17, a fourteenth-century English miscellany, by writing down 'Factura Mawnfylli Militis' where Sir John Mandeville was meant, and left out the name of Clement of Llanthony as author of a Latin harmony of the Gospels a little later in the volume, even though it was clearly written there. Both descriptions came from the old list of contents at

Jackson, of Leicester. In 1752 John Taylor presumably was able to refer to it when he wrote to Ducarel about its relationship to the Codex Claromontanus in the Royal Library at Paris; and in 1766 Thomas Craster, also of St John's, transcribed it for Kennicott, who sent the transcript to J. S. Semler. (F. H. Scrivener (ed.) *Bezae codex Cantabrigiensis* (Cambridge 1864) pp. xi–xii; John Nichols *Literary anecdotes* 1 (1812) p. 548).

165 MSS. Oo.7.53–5. The dates of Goodall's cataloguing tasks are again based on the vouchers; I have found no evidence for Bradshaw's belief that Stephen Whisson actually did the work (see Sayle *Annals* p. 100).

the front of the volume, which the catalogue of Moore's manuscripts provided in Bernard merely duplicated. As few of Moore's oriental manuscripts had been exactly described by Bernard, it was not surprising that Goodall found difficulty in coping with them. Dd.9.55, a book of some complication as it is an epitome of Muslim matrimonial law, with Malay glosses and some Javanese religious formulae, went down as 'A Book written on an odd sort of paper (perhaps a coarse Chinese) & stitch'd up in Common Blew Paper'.[166] He was less uncertain about Dd.9.49: 'This is thought to be the Book concerning the Rites of the Mahometan Religion written by a Moor in African Letters but Spanish Language', and was perfectly correct in describing it as such. Dd.9.50, a Koran, was entered as 'Liber, ut videtur, Arabica-Turcicus. in Engl. Binding': here he missed the book's title, but he was right as to the Turkish and Arabic interlineation while failing to note the Persian translation of part of the volume. The Arabic manuscripts which so defeated Goodall were more correctly described a few years later. In October 1772 the Dutch orientalist Hendrik Schultens visited the Bodleian Library in the course of a tour to England.[167] The following March he came to Cambridge, and on being shown the catalogue of manuscripts at once noticed a mistake in the manner in which one of those in Arabic had been treated. Further investigation revealed that fifty (according to one account: it was certainly several dozen) had been mis-catalogued, and he thereupon set the descriptions right. But, to the loss of the Library, which possessed no proper catalogue of its Arabic manuscripts until 1900, Schultens was unable to agree to Edmund Law's attempts to persuade him to provide a full catalogue of the collection.[168]

Over the years various scholars amended Goodall's list,

[166] E. G. Browne *A hand-list of the Muḥammadan manuscripts* (Cambridge 1900) no. 1018. See also Ph. S. van Ronkel, 'Account of six Malay manuscripts of the Cambridge University Library' *Bijdragen tot de Taal-, Land- en Volkenkunde van Nederlansch-Indie* 6ᵉ Volgr. 2 pp. 10–22.

[167] W. D. Macray *Annals of the Bodleian Library* 2nd ed. (Oxford 1890) p. 460.

[168] B. Glasius *Godgeleerd Nederland* ('s Hertogenbosch 1856) 3 p. 323.

inserting items he had omitted, providing titles to the oriental books, adding authors' names, and correcting spelling;[169] but within its limits and given the restricted circumstances in which he worked, his catalogues were as competent as could reasonably have been expected. Inasmuch as they also usually distinguished between Royal and other manuscripts, provided formats of a rough kind, and gave the Bernard numbers whenever possible, they also showed some imagination in trying to foresee readers' needs. His shelf-lists were made still more useful in 1761 by the addition of indexes to each of the three volumes which remained the fundamental catalogue of the Library's manuscripts until the work of James Nasmith in the 1790s.[170]

When in 1760 the Library again faced an inspection of the manuscript classes, their new arrangement should have made the task of spotting missing books somewhat easier. But Aelfric's grammar (today MS. Hh.1.10) and the text of Geoffrey of Monmouth (now MS. Ff.1.25), both reported lost in 1732, could still not be found. The number of 'permanently' lost volumes, in the sense that they are still missing today, had risen to fourteen, but the Codex Bezae had reappeared, to be assigned a new number presumably after the acquisition of Anthony Askew's manuscripts in 1785 which precede it on its shelf. The list of books missing in 1760 from both the old and the Royal Library was prepared by Stephen Whisson. Of the ninety-four Royal manuscripts he was unable to find, he remarked nine as having been missing when Humfrey Wanley carried out a similar check in 1714 on behalf of Lord Harley after Moore's death.[171] Wanley's survey was not complete, however, and the manuscripts marked in Whisson's list as

169 On 21 February 1760, for example, a Grace was passed authorizing payment of £30 per annum for three years to Benjamin Kennicott for collating Hebrew manuscripts (Grace Book K p. 326). The payment was renewed several times subsequently.

170 As well as the catalogue of the manuscripts in classes Dd to Mm (now MSS. Oo.7.53–5), Goodall also prepared a concordance of the manuscripts as numbered in Bernard etc. with the new Library class-marks. This, together with another copy written out by F. S. Parris and Stephen Whisson in 1753, is now MS. Oo.7.56.

171 See above, pp. 143–5.

unseen by Wanley end less than a quarter of the way through the inventory of 1760. There were, therefore (given the incomplete nature of the lists in Bernard's *Catalogi* and Tanner's continuation), no means of telling which manuscripts had been lost in the intervening forty-five years. As in the case of the old library manuscripts, some marked as missing were merely mislaid or eluded identification with existing descriptions. A translation of Sallust into English (Bernard 688), for example, was only lost in the Library, and is now MS. Nn.3.6; either Bernard no. 19 or his no. 456, both of which were marked as missing, is probably Nn.4.9, a Sarum *Horae*; and Bernard no. 208, 'A Catalogue of books abolished in the latter end of the reign of King Henry VIII', with injunctions given by Edmund Bonner, Bishop of London, is now part of Nn.3.1.[172] All, escaping Goodall's cataloguing, were finally placed in class Nn, while no. 952, a fragmentary record of the house of Augustinian canons at Cumbwell in Kent and said similarly to be lost, was subsequently bound up with various other oddments in Dd.3.88, one of a series of such composite volumes. Some manuscripts had already been catalogued, but were not found in Bernard, such as Sir Thomas Knyvett's Donatus (Bernard no. 62; MS. Dd.8.50) – a slip rather less readily explicable than Whisson's difficulties in recognizing 'Liber precum. Arabicè' as Dd.15.8 or 'Liber Chinensis' as Ll.1.3: the last in fact is three chapters of the Japanese imperial court chronicle of the thirteenth-century *Azuma Kagami*, in the edition (composed with moveable types) of *c.* 1615, which had been in England since at least 1626/7.[173] A few of those missing had more claim to remain in Norwich or Ely than in Moore's

---

[172] Once again, the cause of the confusion over Bernard no. 208 arose from a manuscript bound up with (in this case) two printed books, Erasmus' *Farrago nova epistolarum* (Basel 1519, now Tb.53.4) and Cicero's *Epistolae ad familiares* (Venice 1494, now Inc. 1982). The manuscript was excised when Nasmith recatalogued the manuscripts in the 1790s (Note in AB class catalogue).

[173] See Kawase Kazuma *Kokatsujiban no kenkyū* (Tokyo 1937) pp. 220–1. It may well have been one of the fifty-four Japanese books bought by Richard Cocks on 10 November 1616 during his stay in Japan: see E. M. Thompson (ed.) *Diary of Richard Cocks* (Hakluyt Society 1883) 1 p. 205.

private library, and the titles of others are too common to allow confident identification with manuscripts either at Cambridge or elsewhere, but the fate of one or two can be traced after they left the shelves of either Moore or the University Library. A volume listed by Tanner in his continuation of Bernard's list of Moore's manuscripts as no. 838 in the collection, 'Registrum Abbatiae de Langley in Com. Norfolc.' is probably now Bodleian Library MS. Bodley 242. In Tanner's posthumous *Notitia monastica* (1744) it was recorded as being at Cambridge,[174] but Tanner had, as we have seen, done his research on Moore's collection years before, and this was probably no more than an unchecked assumption on the part of the editor, John Tanner. In fact it seems to have remained in Tanner's own hands, one of several instances in which he was responsible for the disappearance of manuscripts from his patron's library; only in the mid-eighteenth century, almost sixty years later, were the results of some of his activities recognized, though it was not until the next century that his name was ever pinned publicly to manuscripts absent from Cambridge in 1760. Bernard's no. 435, for example, had not been missed by Wanley in 1714. It was a copy of Sir Thomas Browne's *Repertorium*, a tract on the monuments in Norwich cathedral, and may well have been used as the basis for the first publication of the work in 1712 even though two holograph copies are extant:[175] the manuscript is now MS. Tanner 445 in the Bodleian, part of Tanner's bequest of 1736. By the same means the Bodleian acquired the manuscript listed by Bernard under no. 537 as 'Formae instrumentorum in curiis ecclesiasticis. (Liber Joannis Cowell.)', a compilation mostly relating to Cambridge and the diocese of Ely dating from the end of the sixteenth century and now MS. Tanner 410. A third, less obvious, was a manuscript

---

[174] p. 353.

[175] Sir Thomas Browne *Works* ed. Sir Geoffrey Keynes (new ed. 1964) 3 p. xii. Moore is not mentioned in the editorial matter of the 1712 edition, though one plate, of the fifteenth-century bishop and bibliophile James Goldwell, is dedicated to him and was presumably paid for by him.

of rather greater importance. In 1705 Hickes included in his *Thesaurus* a poem on the so-called 'Land of Cokaygne', and acknowledged the help given by Tanner, then at All Souls, who had provided him with the manuscript. The means through which it passed from Hickes to the Harleian Library are not known (though it is worth remarking that Wanley and Hickes were close friends); but there was little to aid the Cambridge librarians in 1760 when they marked as missing Bernard's no. 784. The printed catalogue of the Harleian collections, largely written by Wanley, had appeared only the previous year, but had listed the book clearly enough to arouse the suspicions of anyone collating the descriptions given by Wanley and in Bernard: the clue was not however found. In addition the author of another piece in the same volume, Michael Kildare, had figured in Tanner's *Bibliotheca Britannico-Hibernica* in 1748 as the writer of a ballad in Moore's MS. 784. But the connection of MS. Harley 913, a fourteenth-century collection forming the most extensive source of early Anglo-Irish poetry extant, with the missing Cambridge volume, was not made until T. Crofton Croker, in 1839 in his *Popular songs of Ireland*, reprinted a ballad from the volume on the entrenchment of New Ross in 1265; Frederic Madden had drawn attention to the ballad in *Archaeologia* ten years before, without mentioning the connection, though he recalled it quickly enough when, on a visit to the University Library in 1846, he was shown the list of missing manuscripts.[176]

On the whole, therefore, Moore's manuscripts appear to have been reasonably cared for after their arrival at Cambridge. Despite the understandable fussings of one or two critics, there is no evidence of wholesale pillaging; and it seems

[176] Frederic Madden 'Ancient Norman French poem on the erection of the walls of New Ross, in Ireland, A. D. 1265' *Archaeologia* 22 (1829) pp. 307–22. The whole manuscript is discussed fully by W. Heuser in his *Die Kildare Gedichte: die ältesten mittelenglischen Denkmäler in Anglo-Irischer Überlieferung* (Bonner Beiträge zur Anglistik 14, Bonn 1904) and, in a wider context, by St J. D. Seymour in his *Anglo-Irish literature 1200–1582* (Cambridge 1929). See also *Sir Frederic Madden at Cambridge*, ed. T. D. Rogers (Cambridge 1980) p. 40. Neither the connection with Moore, nor the name of an earlier owner, George Wyse, is recorded in C. E. Wright *Fontes Harleiani* (1972).

more than likely that most of the losses first discovered in 1760 had occurred by 1715. Wanley himself had remarked that many of the items listed in Bernard could not be found then, and with that the authorities at Cambridge had to be content. The printed books proved to be another matter altogether, and to them we must now return.

The thefts by men such as Henry Justice, who had apparently stolen quantities of books from the Royal Library before they had even been catalogued, were unquantifiable, but even among those of which the Library did have some record the thefts proved to be on an alarming scale. It was such that on 12 April 1748 F. S. Parris, Vice-Chancellor and Master of Sidney Sussex College, issued a printed circular recalling all books to the Library so that a proper figure could be arrived at.

Whereas upon inquiry into the state of the Publick Library, it appears that near 800 Volumes are wanting there, and many of them have been so for several years:

These are therefore to require, that all Persons who have borrowed any Books out of either part of the same, do return them within 20 days from the date hereof. And that no Books be delivered out of either Library till they have all been survey'd by their Catalogues, and the whole Library has been put into order.[177]

The figure of eight hundred related solely to the old library, that is of classes A to T and the then classes I to XIX. Further investigation, however, based on counts of the numbers of books listed in the class catalogues and of the number of those on the shelves, revealed that in June, well after the expiry of Parris' mandate, 902 volumes were missing – solely, again, from the old library.[178] Anxious to maintain some momentum, Parris, the two official inspectors, Taylor as Registrary and Thomas Parne as Librarian, issued a further notice on 16 July, threatening fines of five pounds for each volume kept out beyond 15 August. They also took the unusual, and desperate, step of publishing the names of the culprits whom they could identify, with the class-marks and titles of a total of forty-four

<hr />

[177] Luard 209.   [178] Luard 210.

volumes from all parts of the Library that they were known to have borrowed. Their broadside,[179] an oddly frank document, revealed that Parne himself had seven volumes and Conyers Middleton five. Among the lesser fry, or those who had less reason to set an example, was Christopher Smart, whose six volumes included the works of Scarron, Donne's Letters, Thomas More's *Lucubrationes*, Abel Boyer's *Choice letters*, the Amsterdam edition of Menander (1709), and Vanbrugh's *Short vindication of The relapse*: all were restored to the Library.[180]

The year 1748 was crucial in the history of the Library. It marked, in the vigorous steps taken to recover or identify missing books, the virtual end of half a century of sloppy administration, and it saw the completion of the cataloguing of most of Moore's printed books. A fresh set of Orders for the Publick Library was passed by Grace on 11 June, as part of the campaign for the return of missing books and also to establish what its compilers no doubt hoped was a turning point. In an attempt to control borrowing it also introduced a system of quarter days on which all books were to be returned, that survived until 1982:

Orders for the Publick Library.

1. That no Person be allowed the use of the Library but members of the University Senate, and Batchelors of Law and Physick.

2. That no one take or borrow any Book out of the Library without first delivering a Note for the same to one of the Library-keepers or his Deputy in his own hand-writing, expressing his Name and College, and the Year and Day of the Month on which such Book is taken or borrowed, with the Classical Mark of the Book, on pain of forfeiting Five Pounds or double the value of such Book, at the discretion and in the judgment of the Vicechancellor.

3. That the Library-keepers or their Deputies preserve carefully all such Notes, till the Books so taken out be returned again to the Library; duly

---

[179] Luard 212.
[180] At least two were returned in September 1797 by Samuel Pegge Esq. of Scotland Yard: S*.2.12(B) (Xenophon, Basel 1569, given by Hacket), and Hhh.676 (a tract volume).

entering the same in a Book to be kept for that purpose, together with the day of the said return, and any damage done to any Book, on pain of Five Shillings for every omission, to be paid by them or any of them.

4. That every one who shall borrow or take any Book out of the Library, return it thither again on or before the next of the four following Days, viz. *Michaelmas-day*, St. *Thomas*, *Lady-day*, and *Midsummer-day*, or oftener if the Syndics see occasion and require it, under penalty of Two Shillings for every Folio or Quarto, and One Shilling for every Book of less size: The penalty to be repeated every Month till the Book be returned, or another of the same edition and equal value placed in its room.

5. That every Year, on the Friday next after the Commencement, or oftener if they see occasion, the Syndics shall meet in the Senate-House or elsewhere, at the appointment of the Vicechancellor, to give Orders and appoint Inspectors for a general survey of the Library the Monday following. These Inspectors with the Librarians shall make a full and true Catalogue of all Books wanting or much damaged, expressing in whose custody such Books are, or by whom damaged; and deliver the same signed by them to the Vicechancellor.

6. That all Books in this Catalogue be returned to the Library perfect and undamaged, or others of the same edition and equal value placed in their room there within Thirty days after notice given, on pain of forfeiting Five Pounds for every Volume not so returned, or the full value of the same, at the discretion and in the judgment of the Vicechancellor, to be paid by him who stands charged with it; or, in case no one stands charged with it, by the Library-keepers, or their Deputies, or any of them; unless it shall appear to the Vicechancellor that such loss or damage has not happened through any neglect or default of the said Library-keepers or Deputies.

7. That if after the said Thirty days, on inquiry and report to be made by the said Inspectors, or otherwise, it appears to the Vicechancellor that any Books be still wanting in the Library, or much damaged, he shall order others without delay to be procured at the expence of the Publick Chest, and put in their places.

8. That all the penalties abovementioned shall be levied as other penalties are by the Queen's Statutes, Chap. 50. and 90, one third to the Bedles who collect them, the rest to the Publick Chest.

9. That the Vicechancellor, Heads of Colleges, all Doctors in every Faculty, the Orator, and all publick Professors, together with the Proctors, Taxors and Scrutators be Syndics for the publick Library. And that the major part of these, or of so many of them as shall be met, on due notice to them all, provided such major part be not less than Five, of whom the Vicechancellor to be always one, shall have power to order such things as

shall be necessary for the better regulating and securing the same.

Lastly, that these Orders shall extend to both Libraries, and continue in force for three Years.

Lect. et Concess. 11 *Junii* 1748.[181]

Under the circumstances it is scarcely even curious that the rules (which were adopted in perpetuity three years later)[182] placed so much emphasis on what may be termed the protective aspects of a library.

The report in July 1754, when the whole of the printed books was again inspected, that only two books had gone astray in six years, must have given some satisfaction.[183] And of the two, a duodecimo *Book of Common Prayer* of 1713 and John Banister's *New ayres and dialogues for voice and viols* (1678), the second was subsequently returned. No-one, even then, can have been foolish enough to suppose that by flexing their administrative muscles the authorities could stamp out serious theft once and for all. Further major thefts occurred in 1777, when the Library fell victim to the ambitions of the nineteen-year-old son of the music historian Dr Burney within a few months of his coming to Caius.[184] But although books inevitably continued to disappear in a depressing manner, the task of discovering exactly what was missing was possible only after everything had been catalogued. The differences between the thefts which occurred between 1715 and 1750 or thereabouts and those which occurred later are that the later were measurable where the earlier were not, and that the earlier were almost openly encouraged by the state of chaos which it has never been the Library's misfortune to repeat.

[181] Luard 211. See also Grace Book *K* p. 74 and *Statuta Academiae Cantabrigiensis* (Cambridge 1785) pp. 424–5. [182] Grace Book *K* p. 159. [183] Luard 219².

[184] Cf. Ralph S. Walker 'Charles Burney's theft of books at Cambridge' *Trans. Cambridge Bibliographical Soc.* 3 (1962) pp. 313–26. The young Charles Burney left Cambridge abruptly and finished his education at King's College, Aberdeen. His library, remarkable for its editions of classical authors and unique in its collection of seventeenth- and eighteenth-century English newspapers, was bought by the British Museum in 1818. Sayle (*Annals* p. 101) is mistaken in stating that further large-scale thefts took place in 1757: he confused Burney's date of birth with the date of his thefts. See J. Venn *Biographical history of Gonville and Caius College* 2 (Cambridge 1898) p.99.

6

BENEFACTORS, CURIOSITIES AND STRANGERS

BETWEEN 1715, the date of the arrival of the Royal Library, and 1740, the date of Thomas Baker's death, Charles Sayle records in his *Annals* but two major donations. These two came, moreover, within two years of each other: a gift of printed books from John Worthington on 16 October 1725 and another, of oriental manuscripts and curiosities from George Lewis, archdeacon of Meath, in the spring of 1727. Benefactions were not, in fact, quite as sparse as Sayle suggests, and in the case of the first at least he seriously under-estimated the extent.

John Worthington, son of the more celebrated Cambridge Platonist (1618–71) of the same name who had as Master successfully steered Jesus College through the interregnum and who had so cheerfully welcomed the return of the ejected Master Richard Sterne in 1660 that he had organized a concert to celebrate the event, spent most of his later life in London.[1] Born in 1663 at Fen Ditton, where his father was vicar and lived for a short while after departing from Jesus College, Worthington was educated at St Albans school and at Eton. He entered Jesus as a pensioner in February 1680/1, and in the same year was awarded one of the seventeen scholarships recently founded by Tobias Rustat. He took his B.A. in 1684, and in 1688 was elected Perne Fellow of Peterhouse, a position he enjoyed for only three years, for in 1691 he lost his fellowship as a non-juror and thereafter lived away from Cambridge. In

[1] Cf. *The diary and correspondence of Dr. John Worthington* ed. J. Crossley and R. C. Christie (Chetham Society 13, 36 and 114 1847–86) and R. C. Christie *A bibliography of the works written and edited by Dr. John Worthington* (Chetham Society N.S. 13 1888). A. Gray's and F. Brittain's sympathetic picture of him (*A history of Jesus College Cambridge* (1960), pp. 84–7) is based on these works.

1660 his father had acquired an estate of about 220 acres of farm and heath land at Moulton, three miles beyond Newmarket,[2] and he now relied on this for his support: in 1730 it provided him with forty or fifty pounds a year.[3] Like Baker, Worthington used his enforced retirement to pursue his antiquarian interests. He corresponded with Strype in preparation for the new edition of Stow's *Survey of London* published in 1720, was a close friend of Baker himself, and in 1727 came to know Thomas Hearne after submitting to him some notes on Little Gidding: the two remained in correspondence until Hearne's death in 1735. Worthington died, like his father before him, at Hackney, and he was buried on 22 January 1737/8.[4]

The single entry in the University's Grace Book under the date 16 October 1725[5] records only one of Worthington's benefactions, since in October 1730 Hearne noted also that he was 'at this present' giving a further collection. Two years later he was still pursuing the good of the Library, and on 5 July 1732 wrote to Hearne, most probably with reference to his father's *Select discourses* published in 1725:

I have not met with that good Encouragement in disposing of the Books you hoped for; but by way of gift, I have had the Pleasure of seeing most of them disperse abroad in the World, maugre all the opposition of Booksellers. Some of those I presented to the University of Cambridge, to be sold for the Benefit of the Publick Library, are not as yet converted into money; when they are (as I shall let Dʳ. Middleton know the next time I see or write to him) it is my design that some of your books, either already or hereafter printed, may be bought therewith for the said Library.[6]

[2] *Diary and correspondence* 1 pp. 205–6.

[3] Hearne *Remarks and collections* 10 p. 339.

[4] For the younger Worthington's will, see Christie *Bibliography* pp. 80–3. He left his remaining books on law and husbandry to his nephew Nathaniel Turner, his 'lockt chest and cubard of books' to his godson John Worthington Turner, and the remainder of his books and manuscripts to the first son or grandson of one of his nephews to graduate at Oxford or Cambridge. In 1810 they were in the possession of John Turner of Putney (*ibid.* p. 74).

[5] Grace Book *I* p. 144. Two parcels of Worthington's books reached the Library in 1725: see Hadderton's account for 1725–6 in the Vouchers.

[6] Hearne *Remarks and collections* 11 p. 76. The presentation copy of *Select discourses* is now Pp*.2.294(D), and Worthington himself presented Hearne's edition of Thomas Otterbourne and John Whethamstede (Oxford 1732).

Worthington had devoted much labour and time to preserving the memory of his father's works, and in issuing them either for the first time or in revised editions based on the family's papers. *The doctrines of the Resurrection and the reward to come* and *Charitas evangelica* were first published in 1690 and 1691, a collection of *Miscellanies,* including Worthington's absorbing correspondence with Samuel Hartlib, in 1704, a revised edition of *A form of sound words, or a scripture catechism* in 1723, and, finally, the *Select discourses* mentioned above. He never published any of his own antiquarian investigations, but a quantity of his notes came to the Library among Baker's transcripts in 1740, and in 1859 the arrival of the Baumgartner papers, including many collected by Samuel Knight in the mid-eighteenth century, brought various notes by Worthington on the history of Cambridgeshire.

No list survives of Worthington's gifts,[7] and the books are now scattered among the older classes. His gift in 1725 consisted of about a hundred printed books and an unspecified number of manuscripts,[8] but he gave many more later. In order to mark their arrival a special bookplate was printed, once more enunciating the son's devotion to his father's memory. As usual, and unlike the Hacket and Royal Library bookplates, it was solely typographical, the inscription set within a border of arabesques: but it was not entirely practical, since Worthington's gift included large numbers of duodecimos into which the bookplates could be fitted only by making the text read vertically. Nor do there seem to have been enough. In the end Worthington gave several hundred

---

[7] Besides his presents to Cambridge, he also presented thirty volumes to Sion College: see W. Reading *The history of the ancient and present state of Sion-College* p. 48 (appended to his *Bibliothecae cleri Londinensis in Collegio Sionensi catalogus* (1724)).

[8] Like his printed books, Worthington's manuscripts were never listed separately. They included Dd.4.9 (a commonplace book once belonging to John Smith, Fellow of Queens', whose *Select discourses* the elder Worthington saw through the press in 1660); Nn.4.12, a fifteenth-century collection of theological and religious texts bearing a note that it had once belonged to Andrew Marvell, given to Worthington by Meshach Smith, prebendary of Wells (d. 1707); and probably Mm.3.22–4, three volumes of notes on the Old Testament drawn from Hebrew sources. These three last volumes bear Royal Library bookplates, but there is no record that Moore ever owned them, and Thomas Baker noted inside the front that they had been Worthington's.

volumes, but by no means all received the bookplate and many of them – perhaps a majority – can now be identified only by the initials J.W. written in his hand inside the front boards of almost all his books: as a consequence, of course, any volume that has since been rebound has risked losing this identification as well, and it is now impossible to reconstruct the whole of the collection.

Many of the books were of an age to have come from the library of his father, who had bequeathed his manuscripts and some of his printed books to his son in 1671.[9] Henry More's *Divine dialogues* (1668) has every appearance of having been a presentation copy, but it is by no means certain that any of the earlier part of the elder Worthington's library survived the Great Fire, when his house was destroyed. The copy of Nathaniel Ingelo's *Perfection, authority, and credibility of the holy scriptures*, a Commencement sermon preached in Cambridge in 1658 and dedicated to the elder Worthington together with the Heads and fellows of colleges, shows no sign of being a presentation copy. Ingelo, a Fellow of Queens' in 1644–6 and of Eton from 1650 until 1683, shared Worthington's musical interests and was a close family friend, baptizing his daughter Mary in 1658:[10] among the younger Worthington's gifts was also Ingelo's *Discourse concerning repentance* (1677), but I have discovered no marks of ownership here or elsewhere which explicitly denote that his father owned any that came to Cambridge.

As for the collection as a whole, it was as varied in its subject matter as Worthington's interests were wide. It contained few early printed books, the earliest so far to have been unearthed being Johann Reuchlin's *De accentibus et orthographia linguae Hebraicae* (1518). Most were of the seventeenth century, and the collection included besides Brice Bauderon's *Pharmacopoea* (1639) a useful group of pocket-sized medical works: Johann Hartmann, Jan van Heurn, J. C. Claudin, Johann Stocker, J. B.

[9] Worthington *Diary* 2 part 2 p. 169.   [10] Worthington *Diary* 1 pp. 36, 112, 119 etc.

van Helmont, and James Primrose, Gerard Blasius and Thomas Wharton on anatomy, Leonhart Fuchs' herbal in the octavo edition of 1551, and George Tonstall's *New-year's gift for Doctor Witty* – the last a contribution to the debate as to the efficacy of the waters at Scarborough. Thomas Willis' *Propositiones tentationum* (1615) came from the Pembroke library, having been presented to the third Earl by the author. The classical texts, similar in number, were likewise more suited for the pocket than for the library. They were mostly duodecimo Leiden or Amsterdam editions, and at least one, the Oxford Sallust of 1678, had been acquired by Worthington before he even came up to Cambridge. Besides these and books on philosophy (including Janson's edition of Descartes published in 1656), linguistics, theology (particularly modern controversy but also including the 1670 edition of Julian of Norwich) and law, there was an assortment of less serious reading. Among this could be counted Mignault's edition of Alciati's *Emblemata* (Antwerp 1581), the 1672 edition of the younger Evelyn's translation of Rapin *Of gardens*, Gerbier D'Ouvilly's *Brief discourse concerning the three chief principles of magnificent building* (1662), travel and history books on Italy and Portugal, a book on witches, John Hart's ingenious *Orthographie* (1569), suggesting a new system of phonetic spelling by means of a greatly enlarged alphabet, Pierre Muret's account of the ancient and modern funeral rites in Paul Lorrain's translation of 1683, and Sir Walter Raleigh's *Remains* (1681).

The 1640 edition of William Fulke's perennial book on meteors *A most pleasant prospect into the garden of natural contemplation*, Robert Gentilis' translation of *Le chemin abregé, or a compendious method for the attaining of sciences in a short time* (1654) and Boyle's *Chymista scepticus* (1662) represented other sides of Worthington's interests. His curiosity in heraldic matters was recorded in Edward Waterhouse's *Discourse and defence of arms and armory* (1660), annotated by Waterhouse himself, Sir John Doddridge's enlarged edition of William

Bird's *Magazine of honour* (1642) and Henry Whiston's *Treatise of nobility* (1664).

Not surprisingly, many were by or about Cambridge authors. Richard Ward's *Life of Henry More* (1710) was only to be expected, while Whiston had been at King's in the 1630s in the same years that the elder Worthington had been at Emmanuel. Two volumes of sermons were by a member of Worthington's own college, John Stoughton. Thomas Stephens of Christ's had succeeded Worthington as rector of Fen Ditton in 1665, and his collection of assize sermons preached at Bury St Edmunds *Ad magistratum* (Cambridge 1661) was also among Worthington's gifts. Henry Jenkes, who ended his days as Fellow of Caius in 1697, had been admitted to Emmanuel in 1646/7: the two books by him in Worthington's donation had been published in 1683 and 1684, after the elder Worthington's death, and Joshua Barnes' Ἀυλικοκάτοπρου (1679) was likewise published too late for him to have read. More frivolously, *The hermetick romance: or the chymical wedding* (1690) had been translated by Ezechiel Foxcroft of King's from the 'High Dutch' of C. Rosencreutz or Johann Andreae. Many of the books were of more historical than everyday use, and more likely to be consulted in a large library, but there were some that had only recently been published. Isaac Verburg's collected Cicero had been published in Amsterdam only in 1724; Maffei's *Istoria diplomatica*, a work on coins as well as inscriptions and manuscripts, only in 1727; and nine volumes of Paolo Pedrusi's account of the Farnese collections published in Parma between 1694 and 1724 was a gift of quite exceptional generosity[11] in a library that consisted so largely of more modest volumes. The first six volumes of the *Mémoires de l'Académie Royale des Inscriptions et Belles Lettres* (1717-29) were another valuable addition to the Library.

Scarcely surprisingly, many of Worthington's gifts proved

---

[11] That is, assuming that the gift plates were pasted into the correct volumes. None of these last three has Worthington's initials (the Farnese catalogue was rebound in the nineteenth century), and it may be that these books were bought with money raised by the sale of books given by Worthington.

to be duplicates, but although they seem to have been checked against the old library, it was still impossible to perform even so obvious an exercise with the Royal Library. The books were squeezed in among the current intake from Stationers' Hall and purchases from the Rustat Fund, in the classes in Rotherham's library on the east front which were distinguished by roman figures rather than by the letters of the alphabet used in the South Room: these had been considered to be full for several years, but extra shelves were added where possible and the classes extended so that they remained useful until they were dispersed at the end of the century.[12]

The impact of Worthington's gift is no longer easy to assess thanks to the books' having been reclassified, in some cases twice over. But despite the appreciable size of the collection, not all his books came to rest in the Library. Others found their way into the parish library of Bassingbourn, north of Royston and about twelve miles from Cambridge, perhaps through the agency of Gilbert Negus of Clare College, vicar of the parish from 1740 until his death in 1763 and one of the men most responsible for assembling the library there: the books from Bassingbourn are now divided between the University Library and Essex University Library.[13]

The collection that arrived in the University Library in 1727 was very different. On 2 May that year the University passed a Grace to thank George Lewis, archdeacon of Meath, for an assortment of oriental manuscripts and curiosities that was to become a celebrated tourist attraction. Lewis had formed his collection while chaplain to the East India Company settlement at Fort St George (modern Madras) between 1692 and 1714. Educated at Queens' College, he was ordained deacon in 1685 and priest in 1689, and came to be widely trusted in

---

[12] The last entry chronologically is for the *Nautical almanac* for 1792, but there are very few entries after 1788. The classes were entirely disbanded in the nineteenth century.

[13] Over thirty of Worthington's books can be identified among the Bassingbourn books at Cambridge, including a Hebrew thesaurus, the 1632 Paris edition of Bernard of Clairvaux and one anti-Quaker American book, Francis Makemie's *Answer to George Keith's libel* (Boston, Mass., 1694). The latest book was published in 1714.

India.[14] A gifted linguist, he was appointed with particular responsibility for the Protestant Portuguese-speaking[15] native population, but he was also sufficiently proficient in Persian: 'a very Worthy, sober, Ingeneous man, [who] understands the Persian Language very well, as also the Customs of the Country'.[16]

His chaplaincy spanned not only the transfer of management from the old East India Company to the new, but also the founding of the Society for Promoting Christian Knowledge, which from 1705 took the closest interest in the conversion and education of the population of the east coast of India; and he went out to the east just at the time when the need in England for copies of oriental texts, both religious and secular, was more urgently felt than ever before. A militant Protestant, ever aware of the threat of the Roman missionary press,[17] Lewis took the keenest interest in the education of the local population. So he had also charge of the library exported to Fort St George, and was closely involved in the beginning of the Danish missionary press at Tranquebar to the south.[18] His relations with Bartholomaeus Ziegenbalg and Johann Ernst

---

[14] There is no full biography of Lewis. Venn *Al. Cant.*, despite some hesitation, provides the most accurate summary of his career, although I have been able to add many details. The biography provided by Frank Penny in *The church in Madras . . . in the seventeenth and eighteenth centuries* (1904) p. 667 is inaccurate as to Lewis' life in England, but fortunately this does not detract from his account of Lewis' activities in Fort St George described elsewhere in his book. For a contemporary description of Fort St George, see Charles Lockyer *An account of the trade in India* (1711) pp. 3–29.

[15] Or rather, derivatives of that language. 'There is a kind of Lingua Franca or Jargon, call'd Portuguese, spoke in most of the Trading Towns on the sea coast, in which many of the Nations can so far express themselves, as to be able to buy and Sell' (Lewis to Henry Newman 1 February 1712/13, quoted in Shafa'at Ahmad Khan *Sources for the history of British India in the seventeenth century* (1926, repr. 1975) p. 329).

[16] H. D. Love *Vestiges of old Madras* (Indian Records Ser. 1913) 2 pp. 20–5, 108–11.

[17] See for example MS. Add. 4 no. 72 (Lewis to John Strype 3 March 1704/5) and another letter to Newman of the S.P.C.K. dated 1712, printed in *Propagation of the Gospel in the east* 3 (1718) pp. 41–2.

[18] In 1710/11 the S.P.C.K. sent out a printing press with type etc. in the care of J. Finck, a German printer, who was to have continued to Tranquebar after reaching Fort St George. Finck died on the voyage out, however, and on 9 June 1712 the authorities at Fort St George considered the matter. 'A Letter from M[r]. Sec[ry]. Wooley to this Board dated 17th Jan[ry]. 1710, and found in the chest of one Vink a Printer that came Passenger on the Jane, but was drowned in the Voyage, was read . . . Ordered that the Printing Press and all the materialls belonging thereto, be delivered to M[r]. Jennings & the Rev[d].

Gründler, the two promoters of the press there, were close, and in 1715 Lewis published a letter from them written in April two years previously.[19] The press was at work by June 1713, so that in September that year Ziegenbalg and Gründler were able to write to Henry Newman of the S.P.C.K., and report that Gründler had been to Madras to collect a fount of 'Malabar' type. Lewis had been particularly helpful, and had procured for them 'some Pieces of the Old Testament in Portuguese, viz. The Book of Job, the Psalms, the Proverbs, Ecclesiastes, and Isaiah, together with a Dictionary in Spanish and Portuguese'. With this and other help they were now able to contemplate an edition of the Old Testament in Portuguese, of which they hoped to send home a specimen with the next ship. They also hoped that Lewis, on his arrival back in England, would be able to present a favourable report to the Society of their endeavours.[20]

Besides these interests, Lewis was also, inevitably, prey to those in England who had no means of going to India for themselves. Arthur Charlett and Edward Bernard enterprisingly took advantage of his presence there to secure various orientalia for the Bodleian, Lewis' gifts to the Library arriving in 1698.[21] He had no difficulty in appreciating the needs of

Mʳ. George Lewis the persons mentioned in the said Letter' (Records of Fort St George. Diary and consultation book of 1712 (Madras 1929) p. 117). This reference seems to have escaped the main authorities: cf. V. Rosenkilde 'Printing at Tranquebar, 1712–1845' The Library 5th ser. 4 (1949) pp. 179–95, A. K. Priolkar The printing press in India: its beginnings and early development (Bombay 1958), ch. 3, and D. E. Rhodes The spread of printing; India, Pakistan, Ceylon, Burma and Thailand (Amsterdam 1969) pp. 17–18. The press eventually arrived at Tranquebar in August 1712, and to replace the unfortunate Finck a man able to print was found in the Danish colony there: Cf. Propagation of the Gospel in the east 3 (1718) pp. 42–4. The early reports in this collection, gathered into one volume in 1718 with many additions, have still not been superseded for the history of the early press in Tranquebar.

19 A letter to the Reverend Mr. Geo. Lewis . . . giving an account of the method of instruction used in the charity-schools . . . in Tranquebar (1715).

20 Propagation of the Gospel in the east 3 (1718) p. 65. The Library's copy of the Gospels in Tamil printed at Malabar in 1714 was presented in 1714 by Ziegenbalg and Gründler (Propagation of the Gospel in the east p. 116). On 22 January 1713/14 the University agreed to give £20 for missionary work in the east as recompense to Nathaniel Lloyd, Master of Trinity Hall and Vice-Chancellor in 1710–11 (Grace Book Θ p. 623).

21 A list of Lewis' gifts was published in the Philosophical Transactions of the Royal Society no. 246 (November 1698) pp. 421–44. Macray (p. 168) mistakenly attributes them to John Lewis.

Charlett and Bernard; but although he also gathered shells, nuts and butterflies for Sir Hans Sloane[22] and for James Petiver's *museum*, his letters to Petiver are tinged with acerbity and allusions to the urgency of other duties besides collecting specimens of natural history: Petiver's importunities to the surgeon at Fort St George, Edward Bulkley, met with rather greater success.[23]

Lewis left Fort St George on 21 January 1713/14.[24] Unlike his predecessor as chaplain, who had been forced to return home after allowing his commercial instincts to exceed the bounds of discretion and was thought to have taken back to England a fortune of £30,000, Lewis had proved a considerable success, trusted in London and India alike. Not the least reason for this achievement, in a period when the day to day affairs of the senior officers of the Company could be stormy, was that he had occupied a position that made it possible to avoid personality clashes, and that he had had the wit to restrict most of his own not inconsiderable trading to the eastern routes rather than the home run.[25] For most of the rest of his life, after an interval in London aiding the Company, he lived in Ireland. In June 1723 he was collated to the archdeaconry of Meath, an appointment he owed to the Bishop, John Evans, whom he had succeeded at Fort St George.[26] The two men had an additional bond: both were Welsh, Lewis having come from the diocese of Bangor and Evans having been bishop of that diocese between 1702 and 1716. Lewis was to outlive him

---

[22] Guy L. Wilkins 'A catalogue and historical account of the Sloane shell collection' *Bull. of the British Museum (Natural History) Historical Ser.* 1 (1953) pp. 1–48, at p. 37.

[23] For Lewis' gifts to Petiver see *Philosophical Transactions* no. 282 (November–December 1702) p. 1262; J. Petiver *Musei Petiveriani centuria nona et decima* (1703) pp. 25, 30 etc.; and Petiver's *Opera* (1764). Some of Lewis' letters to Petiver are in British Library MSS. Sloane 4063 fo. 143 and 4064 fos. 54, 57, and 99.

[24] *Records of Fort St George. Diary and consultation book of 1714* (Madras 1929) p. 8.

[25] Apart from the *Records of Fort St George*, some of Lewis' trading may be followed in *The Scattergoods and the East India Company* ed. Sir R. C. Temple, L. M. Anstey and B. P. Scattergood (Bombay and Harpenden 1921–35).

[26] H. Cotton *Fasti Ecclesiae Hibernicae* (Dublin 1849) 3 p. 129. For details of Evans' life, see (apart from *DNB*) H. B. Hyde *Parochial annals of Bengal* (Calcutta 1901) pp. 4–25, and Thomas Hyde *Syntagma* ed. G. Sharpe (Oxford 1767) 2 p. 474.

by six years, and he died in January 1729/30, three years after presenting his cabinet to Cambridge.[27]

His collection of oriental manuscripts was the most extensive to have entered the Library since that of Thomas Erpenius in 1632, for Moore had possessed no more than a handful and Nicholas Hobart's gift in 1655 had been modest by comparison. To these earlier collections the Library could now boast the addition of seventy-six oriental manuscripts, almost all in Persian characters though they included many in the Arabic language. They had been selected mainly for the sake of their subject matter rather than for their intrinsic beauty, though there was some fine illuminated work among them, while Lewis also included in his gift a scrapbook exhibiting many of the hands and languages of southern Asia.[28] Some of the manuscripts, such as a copy of the Gospels,[29] a recension of the compendium of Indian folk-lore known as the *Touchstone of knowledge*,[30] and a miscellany including a list of the Moghul emperors down to Aurengzeeb and examples of Aurengzeeb's poetry,[31] had been transcribed on Lewis' instructions. Besides copies of the Koran there were several Persian dictionaries, into Latin, Arabic, Turkish[32] and Hindustani.[33] Among a good collection of epics and other histories the most interesting has proved to be a volume written in 1690 containing a biography of Shah Isma'íl, King of Persia from 1499/1500 to 1523/4 (A.H. 905–30), though this had to wait until 1896 before it was published.[34] A copy of Hatifi's *Tímúr-náma* early attracted attention for the sake of its beauty,[35] as did a copy of the fifteenth-century poet Jámí's *Yúsuf ú Zuleykhá* transcribed in

---

[27] Hearne *Remarks and collections* 10 p. 233, quoting the *Northampton Mercury* for 26 January 1729/30.

[28] Add. 254. See Browne *Catalogue* pp. 285–6. Lewis' gifts were first catalogued in print in *Catalogus librorum orient. M.SS. nummorum, aliorumque cimelior. quibus Academiae Cantabr. Bibliothecam locupletavit, Reverendus vir Georgius Lewis ... 1727.*

[29] Add. 240, transcribed for Lewis in 1712.   [30] Add. 232–3.

[31] Add. 238, transcribed for Lewis in January 1713.   [32] Add. 194.   [33] Add. 224.

[34] Add. 200. Cf. E. Denison Ross 'The early years of Sháh Isma'íl, founder of the Ṣafaví dynasty' *Journal of the Royal Asiatic Society* 28 (1896) pp. 249–340.

[35] Add. 205; *Catalogus* p. 7.

1642.[36] Lewis' collection, however, also brought several literary texts that had not previously been available in the Library, notably poems by Nizámi[37] and battered copies of Háfiz,[38] as well as more modern writers such as the sixteenth-century poet Abú Turáb Beg[39] and Sá'ib (d. 1677).[40] The volume of lyrics of Rahá'i is still considered to be a rare text.[41] The books came from an assortment of sources. An explanation in Persian of some of the words occurring in the Koran, written in 1624, had once belonged to the Scottish orientalist and traveller George Strachan, who had acquired it in Isfahán the same year.[42] Most had provenances closer to Fort St George, however, and much more remarkable was a volume (MS. Add. 215) of panegyrics in praise of Aurengzeeb and Prince Muḥammad written on pink paper and bearing the bookplate of Aurengzeeb himself.

Besides the manuscripts there was a quantity of other material, more or less instructive, including a collection of oriental coins, weights, and a large slab bearing an inscription. The whole was contained in a cabinet standing about nine feet high fitted with shelves and drawers, the coins being stored in a drawer with concealed locks.[43] By the time that Samuel Dale saw it in May 1730 it also contained some suits of exquisitely painted miniature Deccani playing cards and a Chinese idol, both probably also the gift of Lewis.[44]

[36] Add. 202; *Catalogus* pp. 6–7.   [37] Add. 207.   [38] Add. 208, 217.
[39] Add. 220.   [40] Add. 209.   [41] Add. 218.
[42] Add. 252. On Strachan see D. McRoberts 'George Strachan of the Mearns, an early Scottish orientalist' *Innes Review* 3 (1952) pp. 110–28, and G. L. Dellavida *George Strachan; memorials of a wandering Scottish scholar of the seventeenth century* (Spalding Club 1956).
[43] Many of the contents apart from the manuscripts (which are still kept in the cabinet) were transferred to other university institutions in the nineteenth century; the coins are now in the Fitzwilliam Museum and the Chinese idol was moved to the Museum of Archaeology in 1887. A plan of the upper portion of the cabinet, containing the manuscripts, and an incomplete list of the whole of the contents, written out by Samuel Hadderton, is in the Library Archives (Luard 183).
[44] Add. 3466. There is no evidence that Lewis gave either the playing cards or the 'Chinese idol' (as Dale described it) save the circumstantial facts that they had never been recorded hitherto in the Library and that the cabinet was clearly made to contain at least the latter. Dale believed that the 'idol' was made of alabaster, but the *New Cambridge*

The contemporary printed catalogue (the first such list to be printed since that recording Matthew Parker's gifts in 1574) of the Lewis collection, as it has come to be known, lists the manuscripts (though it omits the scrapbook and two modern vocabularies), antiquities and *miscellanea* in the order in which they were arranged on the shelves or in the drawers. Potentially at least a useful collection of texts and linguistic aids, the gift had all the attractions of unfamiliarity; and the compiler of the catalogue, most probably Lewis himself, took care that other users of the collection should have some guidance beyond simply the titles of the books. Thus, for example, the plot of the 'Tales of a parrot', easily translated into Latin for the purposes of the catalogue as 'Psittaci historia', was summarized in thirteen lines, and to one recension of the story of Kalíla and Dimna was attached an exposition of the various versions. Jámí's *Yúsuf ú Zuleykhá* was described as 'Carmen Persicum de Amoribus *Josephi* & *Zulíche. Zulícham* vero volunt Orientales esse nomen uxoris Potiphar, quae Josephum ad illicitum concubitum sollicitavit', and of a poem by Nizámi it was explained, 'Hoc Poema propter styli elegantiam & numerorum concinnitatem in Persicorum praestantissimis habetur.' These presented few problems compared with the difficulty of describing some of the contents of the rest of the cabinet. The coins – Roman, Arabic, Turkish, Persian, Indian, Japanese and Siamese – were straightforward. That 'Ambrae Indicae fragmentum' was ambergris is perhaps obvious enough without the help of the cataloguer's crib on this occasion, but the cataloguer felt less confident with something that had only been known in England for about thirty years, and which he described as 'Bacilli eburnei duo, quibus Sinenses cibum colligunt, & in os ingerunt; unde à nostratibus nominantur.*Chop-Sticks.*' Long-winded perhaps, but the description was as clear as that of another item was

---

guide (1812) described it as 'boiled rice, which has the appearance and consistence of marble'. For the playing cards cf. R. von Leyden *Ganjifa; the playing cards of India* (Victoria and Albert Museum 1982) p. 49.

explicit: 'Nuces Indicae *Areka* dictae; e quibus minutim confectis, & cum foliis plantae Bêtlé commixtis, masticatorium conficitur; quo Indi Persaeque utuntur ad oris foetorem corrigendum & ad Stomachum corroborandum.' Lewis' selection for his old university was catholic in its interpretation of how oriental studies might be pursued, but on the other hand there was no other such collection easily available to students. In theory at least it was admirable.

Thus encouraged, there might appear to have been every reason for renewed interest in oriental studies in the University, and for serious scholarly achievement. In 1724 a second chair had been founded for the teaching of Arabic, to supplement the Sir Thomas Adams Professorship of 1666. The first to hold the new Lord Almoner's Professorship was David Wilkins, or Wilke, a German whose *Concilia* is still not superseded but who scarcely attended at Cambridge at all and whose claims as an oriental scholar are not impeccable. The University soon, and unwisely, allowed the two chairs to be held by one man, a practice which lasted until 1795, and in 1729 Leonard Chappelow became both Sir Thomas Adams Professor and Lord Almoner's Professor.[45] A more conscientious teacher than Wilkins, Chappelow taught for one term in each year and in 1735 was a contender for the Mastership of St John's.[46] To judge from his published work, however, his linguistic interests reached no further than Hebrew and Arabic; and although Cambridge produced several notable Islamic scholars no-one was appointed specifically to teach Persian until 1883.[47] Hopes for the future of oriental studies seem, indeed, to have been higher outside the University than in it. In 1729 the S.P.C.K. presented to the University Press a fount of Arabic type cut by Caslon in preparation for vernacular

---

[45] *Historical register* pp. 82, 89. See also Winstanley *Unreformed Cambridge* pp. 132–7.
[46] Baker–Mayor pp. 1022–3.
[47] The first to receive an official University appointment specifically for Persian was Charles Wilson, Professor of Persian at University College London, who taught under the auspices of the Board of Indian Civil Service Studies. (See *Historical register* pp. 132–3.) E. G. Browne was appointed University Lecturer in 1888 (*ibid.* p. 122).

editions of the Psalter and New Testament published in 1725 and 1727 respectively,[48] but it was hardly used at Cambridge: for many years the only person to exploit it was Chappelow in his contributions to the volumes of university verses published in 1738, 1748 and 1751.[49]

The conjunction of Lewis' gift and the foundation of the Lord Almoner's Chair was not however lost on the *Bibliothecarius* Samuel Hadderton, who in lamenting the death of George I in 1727 found opportunity also to allude, in his contribution to the collection of university verses assembled for the occasion, to the new cabinet of Persian manuscripts now in his care. He filled with his encomia of the late King more space in the volume than any other contributor, contriving to mention not only the Royal Library and the leading part taken by George I in providing funds to extend the building, but also the Rustat Fund and John Woodward's fossils, to provide a map of the colleges, and to report on these latest benefactions in their due places.[50]

The University declined to lend three manuscript Persian

---

[48] T. H. Darlow and H. F. Moule *Historical catalogue of the printed editions of the Holy Scripture in the library of the British and Foreign Bible Society* 2 (1911) p. 67. See also James Mosley 'The early career of William Caslon' *Journal of the Printing Historical Society* 3 (1967) pp. 66–81.

[49] In 1727 Chappelow also submitted a poem in Arabic for the verses on George I, but, the Press not then possessing the requisite type, it had to be set in Hebrew characters.

[50] Haud ignota loquor; MORI est bene nota supellex;
Moxque per *Europam* Nota futura magis.
Proderit *Europae*, Famâque ferente volabit;
Insignita volans NOMINE GEORGIACO.
Europae dixi? super & *Garamantas* & *Indos*
Fama volat properans dicere, LEWIS ait ...
Quis DOMINUS, nondum FREDERICO PRINCIPE, PRINCEPS?
ILLE habet híc Nomen, nec moriturus erit.
Cui quem conjunxi, quia Nomine jungitur, idem
Ipse habet híc Nomen, nec moriturus erit.
LEWISIUM dico; atque *Animum* fert *Principis Ille*.
Crede mihi, est Dignus qui comitetur EUM.
Jamque EBORUM PRAESUL, Tibi, GEORGI, consulit *Alter*
LEWISIOque suam jungere gaudet opem.
(*Academiae Cantabrigiensis luctus in obitum serenissimi Georgii I* (Cambridge 1727) G1^{r-v}).
Hadderton provided explanatory footnotes relating to both the Library and the professorship.

dictionaries from Lewis' collection to John Gagnier at Oxford so that he could embark on what would have been the first European translation of the *Zend-Avesta*;[51] but despite the existence of a printed catalogue there seems to have been very little demand on the collection at first. Almost inevitably, it was that part of Lewis' collection that consisted of curiosities rather than of manuscripts that attracted most attention: Cambridge was to become a centre for the study of Indian history and culture only in the nineteenth century. The manuscripts in the Lewis cabinet have proved, on the whole, to have only minor textual interest, but once in the Library they had to wait for many years before their true nature was discovered. For non-specialists the contents of the manuscripts hardly mattered. Novelty was everything, and this the Lewis cabinet provided in plenty. In 1730 one visitor at least scarcely noted the surrounding books, so distracted was he by the curiosities exposed to exhibition elsewhere:

Thrô the assistance of Mr Hough we had admittance into the Publick library, it now consists of 3 Galerys. We went first into that of the South at the end of which in a seperate appartment stands D^r. Woodwards 4 Cabinets of Fossils, and in the middle a curious one of American Cedar on the front of which on the Middle drawer is a Brass plate on which is engrav'd in large Letters *Bibliotheca Orientalis*. The upper part consists of shelves full of Books of the Oriental Languages some finley illuminated, and the Alphabets of divers of them. As Arabick Persian, Indian, Chinesse, Japonick, &c., and under is the Figure of a Chinese idol of Alabaster in a sedent posture. In a drawer on which the Inscription is are several sorts of Oriental Money both in silver and Gold, as likewise some of their brass weights. Here is likewise an Indian Proclamation & other writings. In another drawer is 2 boxes of Cards, one of which is on Boards finely painted containing 48 cards or 4 sets – and the other 96, or 8 sets on Tortois shell: each set contains 12 cards 10 of which are so many numbers, the other two a man on Horsback and the King on the Throne: these are distinguished by marks as suns, moons, swords, Helmets, fruits, folks, Billets etc. The Idol above mention'd is plac'd as in a chariot whereby it can be drawn out of the Cabinet for the better seeing it, the Back of which is made of a grey Stone, on wch is cut an Inscriptions in 4 Oriental

[51] Gagnier, Lord Almoner's Professor at Oxford, was prompted by the prize of £200 offered under the will of John King, Master of the Charterhouse: see the letter of William Whiston printed in Sidney Sussex College *Annual* (1906) pp. 40–1.

Languages viz[t]. 2 living and two dead or scolastick: on the breast of the Idol hangs a Medal by [a] chain about the Neck. On each side of the Idol are two open places in one of which a large Purpura triangularia Bonan. Recreat. Ment. et Oculi p. 151 n°. 275[52] which that author writes comes from the Persian gulfe. Also a porous fossil body call'd petrified Wood to me it seem a sort of Coraline Body, very much like the Tabula purpurea Imp. 631. but not in colour. . . There was likewise in that Cabinet a Book of writing on Palm leaves, cut with a graver, it resembled a file the leaves being strung upon a sort of cord . . . There are many other rarities in the collection which Mr. Hadderton the Sub-Librarian shewed us, which I cannot now recollect . . .[53]

The coins, playing cards, chop-sticks, Chinese statue and other miscellanea proved as diverting to generations of tourists visiting the Library as the cabinets of fossils acquired by the University from the executors of Dr John Woodward in 1728 and 1729. The fossils were housed in the Library for no better reasons than that there was no more appropriate place to put them, and that in 1731 Conyers Middleton added the title of first Woodwardian Professor of Geology to his others, being elected apparently solely on the strength of his friendship with the founder of the chair. He had become acquainted with Woodward shortly after his return from Italy in 1725, and had encouraged him in his plans to found a new professorship at Cambridge: the appointment as Professor, after so successful a suit, seemed in its peculiar way only just.[54]

So the library staff were placed in the position – now perhaps more commonly found in private collections than in university libraries – of having to show off much more than it had been the Library's original purpose to contain. The Woodwardian Professor (and, in Middleton's case, *Protobibliothecarius*) was, indeed, enjoined by Woodward in his will to

have the care and custody of all the said Fossils, and the catalogues of them, and that he do live and reside in or near the said Apartment so to be allotted for repositing the said Fossils as above-mentioned in the said University;

[52] F. Buonanni *Recreatio mentis et oculi* (Rome 1684).
[53] MS. Add. 3466 fos. 14[v]–16[r] (diary of S. Dale 31 May 1730: see also Sayle *Annals* pp. 96–7). On 17 May 1733 Dale managed to examine the Woodward collection more closely (Add. 3466 fo. 17[v]). [54] *Biographia Britannica* 5 (1760) p. 3097.

and that he be actually ready and attending in the Room where they are reposited, from the hour of nine of the clock in the morning to eleven, and again from the hour of two in the afternoon till four, three days in every week (except during the two months in the long Vacation, wherein he is allowed to be absent as above-mentioned) to shew the said Fossils gratis, to all such curious and intelligent persons as shall desire a view of them for their information and instruction; and that he himself shall be always present when they are shewn, and take care that none of the said Fossils be mutilated or lost.[55]

As an administrator Middleton proved no more effective than his supporters can ever have expected; but in one branch of his duties – so far as those duties can be said to be either defined, expected or understood – his period of librarianship was not without its achievements. Although, as we have seen in the case of the sale of his own trophies from Italy to Harley in 1725, and his tepid response to the chance to acquire Greek manuscripts from Mount Athos in 1727, he did not always act to the Library's best advantage, there were some gifts which came almost perforce. The death of Thomas Baker on 2 July 1740 brought a collection of manuscript notebooks central to the history of the University and renowned throughout his wide circle of acquaintances for their accumulation of antiquarian learning. Baker had been a close friend of Middleton, so close indeed that he was sometimes tarred with the same suspicion as to the strength of his Christian beliefs as Middleton himself on no better grounds than that he frequented Middleton's house and conversed with him.[56]

Tireless in his willingness to help the Library and those who sought information from it, for years Baker had acted as unofficial adviser, whether to enquiring scholars or to potential donors. An attempt in 1733 to persuade the Library to

---

[55] Clark *Endowments* p. 199. See also J. W. Clark and T. McK. Hughes *The life and letters of Adam Sedgwick* (Cambridge 1890) 1 pp. 166–88, and, for Woodward's contemporary reputation, *Cambridge under Queen Anne* pp. 365, 402, 404 etc. A brief account of Woodward's collection, with further references, is given in David Murray *Museums; their history and their use* (Glasgow 1904) 1 pp. 118–22.

[56] R. Masters *Memoirs of the life and writings of the late Rev. Thomas Baker* (Cambridge 1784) p. 113.

interest itself in some of the papers left by Thomas Rawlinson came to nothing in the face of Middleton's inaction and the University's lack of interest, but to Peter Le Neve Baker had been equally attentive. In 1729 Le Neve proposed giving his collection of prints and manuscripts to the Library, a suggestion that unfortunately miscarried; but here too Baker was eager to press the advantages to an owner anxious as to the future of his collection. His letter was written with the same balance of hesitation and suggestion that is still familiar in similar circumstances today:

> To your intended donation, I must not pretend to give advice: you can best judge how your books are to be disposed of. Only I may say, that in the Public Library there will be a convenient apartment for old Prints and MSS. as you will find in Dr. Middleton's printed plan or scheme. One thing further I dare venture to say, that they will be there taken care of, which is more than I dare say for that other place; and in a Public Library they will be of most public use.[57]

Despite such blandishments, however, Le Neve abandoned his scheme, no doubt discouraged by Baker's failure to answer his letter in reasonable time. The collection was sold at auction in 1731, its owner having died in 1729 leaving his manuscripts to Thomas Martin of Palgrave. But besides these and similar activities on behalf of the Library, Baker was also a close collaborator with Harley and Wanley in the creation of the Harleian Library, where he could exercise his lifelong pursuit of early printed books and the history of printing. So long as he was alive, these two loyalties, to Cambridge on the one hand and Harley on the other, could exist in comfort; but with his death no such dual existence was possible for the collections which, in the absence of work published in his lifetime, are his chief memorial. Twenty-three folio volumes of his notes and transcripts on the history of the University and colleges, including his unpublished history of St John's, were bequeathed to Harley, and nineteen to the University Library: the separation of the collection bore no relation to its contents.

---

[57] Quoted in Nichols *Literary anecdotes* 3 pp. 481–2.

With them came to the Library half a dozen books: Anstis' *Register of the Order of the Garter* (1724) because it was, in Baker's words, believed to be 'the only Copy in this University'; a copy of Burnet's *History of the Reformation* (1681–1715) copiously annotated by Baker and of especial interest because Baker's communications to Burnet had resulted in many of the corrections incorporated in the third volume; Wood's *Athenae Oxonienses* (1691), similarly annotated; Baker's transcript of White Kennett's preparations for a new edition of Gunton's *History of the church of Peterborough* (1686), of which Kennett's original, so swollen with notes as to be scarcely recognizable, is still among the manuscripts of the Cathedral; Kennett's *Register and chronicle ... from the restauration of Charles II* (1728), a gift from the author but bearing no notes by Baker apart from a few scattered on the flyleaves; William Wake's *State of the church and clergy of England* (1703), with substantial additions in Wake's own hand; and Maunsell's *Catalogue* (1595), interleaved and enlarged not only with Baker's notes on additional titles omitted by Maunsell (many of them culled from Samuel Harsnett's copy of the same work), but also with a wealth of supplementary notes on such topics as the history of printing in England and the early Bibles in the Harleian Library. Most of the rest of his library was bequeathed to his college.[58]

Baker had played as small a part as possible in the conflict between the factions surrounding Bentley, but the very reverse had been true of the man responsible for the next collection to reach the Library, John Colbatch, Fellow of Trinity, Professor of Moral Philosophy, ally of Middleton and butt of some of Bentley's least controlled invective. He died in 1748, and his

---

[58] Baker's will, dated 15 October 1739, was proved in the Vice-Chancellor's Court, and is now in the University Archives. It was printed in Masters' *Memoirs* pp. 133–7. A catalogue of his library survives in St John's College (MS. H.26, James 290). While most of his books are in St John's College library, many are now scattered; in 1740 the University Library already possessed a copy of *The institutes of a Christen man* (1537) that had formerly belonged to him and had passed into Moore's library. In 1805 Benedict Chapman, of Gonville and Caius College, presented Baker's much annotated copy of Chevillier's *Origine de l'imprimerie à Paris* (1694).

books are now divided between his college, the University Library, and the old Orwell school library (founded by Colbatch in about 1743), which in 1910 was given to the University Library by Francis Jenkinson. Colbatch was also rector of Orwell, and the parish received various school textbooks (some acquired by him in his teens), books of religious instruction, and a smattering of literature.[59] The books which came to the University Library were of a quite different nature. A few were of the sixteenth century, but most were more recent, with legal works, commentaries on Justinian, monuments of Jesuit scholarship, and commentaries on some of the later Church Fathers being particularly noticeable. Many of his books were of Spanish or Portuguese provenance, witnesses of the years at the end of the previous century when he had been chaplain at Lisbon. It was characteristic of the Library in the first half of the eighteenth century that no list was kept of this collection either, and that it can now be identified only by searches along the shelves, though many volumes have remained in the places first assigned to them in class Cc, that is immediately following the final class of the Royal Library, now Bb*.[60]

Both Baker's and Colbatch's collections were of some size, but other gifts caused less disturbance to the shelves. In 1715 Thomas Tenison, Archbishop of Canterbury, bequeathed to the University his interest in John Spencer's *De legibus Hebraeorum ritualibus* (Cambridge 1685), together with the related papers which he had 'caused to be prepared for the Press' for a second edition. The new edition was entrusted to Leonard Chappelow, Professor of Arabic from 1720, and was printed at the University Press in 1727.[61] A decade later, John

---

[59] Now class CCA–CCE.6. For Colbatch and Orwell see VCH *Cambridgeshire* 5 pp. 250–1.

[60] The University accounts for 1747–8 include payment of £1.10s.od. to 'Mr Mason' for bookplates for the collection, but Goodall was not paid for pasting Library bookplates into Colbatch's books until 18 October 1752 (Vouchers).

[61] *The last will and testament of Thomas Tenison, late Lord Arch-Bishop of Canterbury* (1716) p. 7. The annotated copy of the 1685 edition of Spencer's work now stands at Adv.a.44.11, next to his notes at Adv.a.44.12: cf. also MS. Add. 2610.

Browne, Fellow of Emmanuel College between 1687 and 1715 and rector of Wallington, in Hertfordshire, from 1715 until his death on 18 July 1736, bequeathed £100 to the Library in a will that also left a like amount to pay for a schoolmistress in his parish and £20 for the aged poor, besides £50 and some of his books to his college.[62] The money thus received by the University seems immediately to have been absorbed into the general funds, for I have found no hint of any particular thought given to its spending. In less workaday mood, William Thurlbourn, who was to superintend the sale of duplicates from the Royal Library, in 1739 presented the 1476 edition of Jerome's letters, and was also responsible for the gift of a copy on vellum of the *Livre des statuts & ordonnances de l'Ordre Sainct Michel* (1550). Of those that arrived after Colbatch's books, James Gibbs' *Bibliotheca Radcliviana* (1747), given by Dr Radcliffe's Trustees in 1748, can scarcely not have reminded the beneficiaries of Oxford's all too conspicuous success in completing its new library compared with the drawn out and unresolved arguments surrounding the needs of Cambridge. A donation the following year was somewhat less pointed: the gift in 1749 by the Earl of Pembroke of the volume of engraved reproductions prepared in 1746 of the numismatic collection assembled by his father could have no such embarrassing associations as Gibbs' volume.

While Colbatch's books slipped into the Library without fuss, the Lewis cabinet and the Woodwardian fossils had reminded the University that the Library was not solely a repository for books, and in April 1743 it received still ruder confirmation of the elastic functions expected of it. On 15 April Middleton wrote to Horace Walpole,

We have just received a *mummy*, a present to our University from Captain Townshend, who imported it from Constantinople; it draws a large concourse about it at present, and if its emblematic figures and hieroglyphics should inspire us with a resolution to understand and

---

[62] VCH *Hertfordshire* 3 p. 285; E. Shuckburgh *Emmanuel College* (1904) p. 192; university accounts 1736–7.

unriddle them, and make us learned like Moses, in all the wisdom of the Ægyptians, it would be of excellent use to us. The present however is very agreeable and very proper to the place.[63]

Townshend's mummy, like Lewis' curiosities, Woodward's fossils and most of the various other miscellanea presented to the University before the mid-nineteenth century, is no longer in the Library: it has been transferred to the Fitzwilliam Museum. To Middleton, with close links with antiquarian scholarship of all kinds in London, its arrival was naturally welcome, and happily coincided with the completion of his account of his own collection of antiquities. It came, moreover, from a benefactor of impeccable connections who was scarcely to be crossed, for George Townshend was nephew of Sir Robert Walpole and son of the man who had been instrumental in acquiring Moore's library for Cambridge.[64] Early in 1743, the year he gave the mummy, he was still serving in home waters, and was yet to go out to the Mediterranean where his controversial decisions in the face of the French brought opprobrium and court martial. But however enthusiastic Middleton might be to Horace Walpole, Walpole himself, ever independent in his judgement, seemed unable to comprehend why anyone should want something that appeared so incapable of explanation, and six days later he replied,

I believe the generality of your people are mightily pleased with their mummy – for my part I think it a most unnecessary present for a University – why is an old mouldy unintelligible bit of learning dug out of an Egyptian or Turkish tomb, of more value, than one seared up in a college cell? When I was at Cambridge, I could have directed a pick-ax to great treasures in Trinity Lodge, St John's or Christ-Church. Bentley only wanted to be embroidered with a few sphinxes and ibises, to be inestimable.[65]

---

63 Middleton to Horace Walpole 15 April 1743 (Horace Walpole *Correspondence* with Sir D. Dalrymple etc., ed. W. S. Lewis and C. H. Bennett (1952) pp. 17–18).
64 Lord Townshend announced his intention of giving the statue of George I by Rysbrack now standing in the Squire Law Library to the University in 1736. He died in 1738, and when the statue arrived in 1739 its cost was met by his heir (Willis & Clark 3 pp. 55–7).
65 Walpole *Correspondence* p. 19.

The University, uninfluenced by Walpole, was nonetheless
ready to welcome the gift, and thanked Townshend on 22
April in terms which fully expressed its simultaneous bewilderment and gratitude.[66] It was indeed a novelty, for the only
other similar curiosity available in Cambridge at the time was
the part of a mummy given to Trinity College by John
Laughton in about 1680. Outside Cambridge, the Royal
Society possessed one given to it in its early days by the Duke of
Norfolk,[67] but the study by Alexander Gordon (Secretary of
the Society of Antiquaries and of the Egyptian Society) of
mummies belonging to William Lethieullier and Richard
Mead had been public only since 1737.[68] With the assistance of
his friend William Heberden, Fellow of St John's and suitably
qualified in medicine,[69] Middleton fell to examining not only
the hieroglyphics, but also the composition of the Library's
new exhibit. They made more headway with the second than
the first part of their task, and in 1745 Middleton was able to
add an account of their investigations to the end of his account
of his own antiquities and curiosities.[70] But despite the fact that
guidebooks early in the nineteenth century alleged that the
mummy was over two thousand years old, Horace Walpole
was in fact closer to the truth than he realized. When E. A.
Wallis Budge of the British Museum, with Champollion's
work on the Rosetta Stone behind him, catalogued it in 1893
for the Fitzwilliam Museum he was brutally frank about the
hieroglyphics which offered such promise to Middleton. 'I am

[66] Grace Book *I* pp. 548–9. Epistolae Academiae 2 p. 653 (University Archives).
[67] N. Grew *Musaeum Regalis Societatis* (1681) pp. 1–3. For Laughton's mummy cf. Trinity
College MS. Add.a.106, fo. 85, and Gaskell and Robson *The Library of Trinity College,
Cambridge* p. 27.
[68] Alexander Gordon *An essay towards explaining the hieroglyphical figures on the coffin of the
ancient mummy belonging to W. Lethieullier. (An essay towards explaining the ancient
hieroglyphical figures on the Egyptian mummy in the museum of Dr Mead)* (1737). See also
Murray *Museums* 1 p. 123 and (on earlier collectors) pp. 50–5.
[69] On Heberden see Sir H. Rolleston 'The two Heberdens' *Annals of Medical History* N.S. 5
(1933) pp. 409–27, 566–83.
[70] *Germana quaedam Antiquitatis eruditae monumenta* (1745). This includes two plates of the
mummy.

unable to read any more than the first few words, and it is tolerably clear that the writer either copied a text which he could not read, or that he invented what is here written.' So far from being ancient Egyptian, he concluded that it was Roman and possibly no older than about the year A.D. 350.[71]

Meanwhile, in the eighteenth century, the mummy seems to have attracted no more scientific attention until 1779. In that year Rudolf Erich Raspe, author of the adventures of Baron Münchhausen and in exile in England following the discovery of thefts from the museum of the Landgrave of Hesse-Cassel, visited Cambridge with the intention of finding a niche as a teacher of history. He turned naturally to the University Library and Trinity College library for help in his investigations into the history of oil painting, and the effects of his visit are visible still in the damage wrought on the University Library's manuscript of Theophilus.[72] Richard Farmer, as *Protobibliothecarius*, was not in an easy position. It was not in his nature to be discourteous to visiting scholars; but he was sufficiently suspicious of Raspe to make his research difficult, and he was accordingly rewarded with a little of Raspe's spite in *A critical essay on oil-painting* published two years later. Librarians were, in Raspe's words, 'literary eunuchs': they have 'very often happened to keep the most instructive manuscripts in darkness for various reasons; either in consequence of their partiality to particular sciences and opinions, or by an effect of their torpid ignorance, or of their more mischievous and shameful jealousy'.[73] Raspe took offence too readily. But his diary records no difficulties in his examination of the mummy, which (being painted) was also an object of study. For this Farmer was 'unser dienstfertiger, gutherzieger Freund', who consented to anoint the mummy with lavender water in various places to watch the effect. Only when Farmer applied

---

[71] E. A. Wallis Budge *A catalogue of the Egyptian collection in the Fitzwilliam Museum* (Cambridge 1893) p. 63.   [72] See Oates *History* p. 341.
[73] R. E. Raspe *A critical essay on oil-painting* (1781) p. 36.

it to the mummy's right foot, where the paint had been worn away to powder, was he able to wash the colour away.[74] From this, Raspe concluded in his diary that the paint was laid on with resin or wax, but the small published portions of his diary impart less detail of the experiments than his subsequent *Critical essay*, where he revealed that the colours 'as perfectly resisted the dissolving power of spirits, nay, even that of double distilled lavender-water, and of alcohol or aether, which are known to be the strongest solvents of wax'.[75]

If the arrival of a mummy in 1743 was a new departure in the Library's collections, that of Roger Gale's coins in the following year was in a much more traditional mould. In 1738 Trinity College library was notably enhanced by Gale's gift to it of the manuscripts collected by his father Thomas, dean of York, which thus joined the Arabic manuscripts presented by Thomas in 1697.[76] On his death in 1744, however, Roger bequeathed his own collection of coins not to the college, but to the University: he also provided a catalogue compiled by himself.[77] They formed the second major portion of the University's collection, which had not been added to for some years, and were comparable in numbers only with those given by Andrew Perne in 1589. No separate list survives of Perne's collection, and when von Uffenbach visited the Library in 1710 he had found the entire collection, both Perne's and subsequent accessions, in disarray. 'We saw . . . a good number of ancient and modern coins, lying all covered with dust, without any order, in a deep, poor drawer, unlocked and left open. There were 20 and odd gold coins, with various silver

[74] O. Clemen 'R. E. Raspe in der Universitätsbibliothek zu Cambridge (April 1779)' *Zeitschrift für Bücherfreunde* N.F. 13 (1921) pp. 122–4. Raspe's diary, from which Clemen quotes, was then in Mitau (modern Jelgava) in Latvia.

[75] Raspe *Critical essay* p. 25.

[76] Gale announced to Bentley his intention of presenting the manuscripts in 1735; see William Stukeley *Family memoirs* 2 (Surtees Soc. 1883) p. 36.

[77] A further catalogue, in an edition of twenty copies, was printed in 1780. See *Reliquiae Galeanae* (J. Nichols *Bibliotheca topographica Britannica* 2 pt 1 (1781) p. x.

and copper.'[78] In 1733 Samuel Dale found the collection 'all out of Order', apart from those of the reign of Queen Anne – and this despite the fact that he was told that a catalogue of the collection had been made by 'one Mr Tomlinson'.[79] The provisions for the coins were hardly such as could be recommended to a prospective donor, and Gale's bequest seems perplexing, unless either some attempt had been made by the 1740s to tidy the cabinet or else he hoped that by his virtually refounding the collection the authorities would be moved to pay more attention to it.

Gale's bequest consisted solely of Roman coins, and came in a period that had seen a revolution in the study of Roman Britain with the publication in 1732 of Horsley's *Britannia Romana*.[80] Once again the Library seems to have owed its good fortune to the unobtrusive interest of Middleton, who could not fail to be sympathetic to Gale's interests when in 1735 he had shown Gale and Stukeley the collection of antiquities he had brought back from Italy.[81] Once in the Library, the coins were however placed with Perne's under the care of F. S. Parris, Master of Sidney Sussex College, who had no formal standing in the Library until he succeeded Middleton as *Protobibliothecarius* in 1750. So it was that when George North, the leading scholar of his generation on English numismatics, visited the Library later in 1744 he was disappointed to find that Parris was away in London with the key to all the collection in his pocket: North had to go away content with the collections only of Trinity and St John's.[82]

This incident alone might have been no more than an unfortunate coincidence, but he was under the impression that Parris was already the librarian; and when at the end of 1745 some joinery was required in Gale's cabinet, the work was

---

[78] *Cambridge under Queen Anne* p. 143.   [79] MS. Add. 3466 fo. 17^v.
[80] The whole university collection of coins was transferred to the Fitzwilliam Museum by a Grace of 30 April 1856.
[81] Stukeley *Family memoirs* 2 p. 36.   [82] Nichols *Literary anecdotes* 5 p. 429.

superintended by Charles Mason, Middleton's successor as Woodwardian Professor of Geology.[83] The collections of fossils and coins were certainly in the Library, but they were uncomfortable bedfellows and do not seem to have been regarded as of it. At a time, moreover, when the main part of the cataloguing was supervised by the University Registrary (John Taylor), aided by a single library assistant, Thomas Goodall, and joinery was ordered by the Woodwardian Professor, it seems difficult to discern much sense of responsibility in the two men officially entrusted with the Library, Thomas Parne and Conyers Middleton.

[83] Middleton resigned in 1734. For Mason's activities see Winstanley *Unreformed Cambridge* pp. 168–9.

7

NEW BUILDINGS AND OLD PROBLEMS

THE DEATHS OF BOTH *Protobibliothecarius* and *Bibliothecarius*, Middleton (of a 'slow hectic feaver') and Parne, within twelve months of each other on 28 July 1750 and 11 July 1751 respectively, brought into the Library in their place two men possessed of somewhat greater energy, at least so far as their statutory duties were concerned. Middleton, distracted by other interests, and a national figure, had come to take little part in the everyday organization of the Library, and despite the seniority of the position the election of his successor was marked by little excitement. The two final contestants were William Beaty, Fellow of Magdalene College since 1719, Senior Proctor in 1741–2 and rector of Westley Waterless near Newmarket since 1735, and a man several years his junior but much more experienced in every way, Francis Sawyer Parris, Fellow of Sidney Sussex College since 1728 and elected Master in 1746: he had also served as Vice-Chancellor in 1747–8. Parris was elected on 3 August 1750, and brought to his office some of the same qualities of determination that John Taylor had possessed fifteen or twenty years previously. His college was a small one: in 1752 there were but five fellows, and the number of undergraduates rose only to about forty;[1] though he was responsible for much of the everyday running of the college, and did much that would usually now be expected of a Bursar, his tasks do not seem to have been onerous. In the time thus available, he was able to continue the cataloguing of the Royal Library, working in close conjunction with Goodall.

---

[1] G. M. Edwards *Sidney Sussex College* (1899) pp. 180–1.

Stephen Whisson, Fellow of Trinity, who replaced Parne as *Bibliothecarius* in July 1751, won his place, by contrast, in a total final poll of 178 votes.[2] His most serious adversary, Henry Hubbard, Fellow of Emmanuel College, recorded the preliminary skirmishings in his diary, beginning only a few hours after Parne had died at six o'clock in the morning:

At 10 M^r. H. waited upon the Vice Chan: to ask him, as a Friend, whether He thought there was any Prospect of succeeding, if he should offer himself for the Place. The V. Ch: desired Time to consider of it, that he might consult some of the Heads, & said, M^r. Whisson, Trin: & M^r. Masters C.C.C. had already been with him. At Night he was still doubtful, but rather encouraged him to proceed. In the mean Time, M^r. Whisson & M^r. Masters, & M^r. Sturgeon of Caius, had been about to apply for it. However, at 8 that Night M^r. H. declared himself a Candidate; & the next Day visited for it.[3]

The older of the two men, Hubbard had been Tutor in his college since 1736, and in 1751 was scarcely unknown in the University, his support for a reform movement designed to improve behaviour among undergraduates earning him a lampoon in the anonymous pamphlet *A fragment* in that year.[4] No such distinction could be claimed for Whisson, who had been educated at Wakefield and had entered Trinity in 1734 as a sizar. He became a Fellow of his college in 1741, and in 1744 Taxor. Besides a series of livings – Babraham to the south of Cambridge from 1746 to about 1766, Shimpling in Norfolk from 1753 to 1771, and Orwell to the south-west from 1771 to 1783 – he also managed the less usual feat of being both *Bibliothecarius* and Senior Proctor in 1757–8. But the most

---

2 Thus Hubbard, quoted in Cooper *Annals* 4 p. 284. Luard 215(3) counted 174.
3 British Library MS. Add. 5852, p. 128.
4 For a brief portrait of Hubbard see F. H. Stubbings 'An eighteenth century Emmanuel tutor' *Emmanuel College Magazine* 41 (1958–9) pp. 43–5, quoting Sir Egerton Brydges in *Restituta; or titles, extracts and characters of old books in English literature, revived* (1814–16) 3 pp. 213ff.: 'He is a very corpulent and fat man, and was always in a state of perspiration; reckoned a good tempered, cheerful man, and merry companion, and always a severe disciplinarian; and was used to put in more *non placets* in the senate house, while I was in the University, than any other person besides.' Hubbard became University Registrary in 1758, though he never achieved his ambition of becoming Master of his college; Brydges also divulged that his sister was the third wife of Thurlbourn the Cambridge bookseller.

remarkable feature of his term of office was to be not so much in his outside activities (he never published a book) as in its length. He remained in his post for thirty-two years, a period of service unprecedented in the history of the Library and exceeded before the twentieth century only by his immediate successor John Davies. He served with four *Protobibliothecarii*, Parris, Law, Barnardiston, and Farmer, and yet once the Library extensions and alterations had been completed, and Moore's books finally arranged, his librarianship passed with scarcely a ripple.[5]

These changes in personnel took place amidst all the turmoil of building operations, as the younger James Essex and his employees transformed the room over the old porters' lodge of King's College into what became known as the Dome Room: 'a handsome square Room enlightened with a Cupola, lately fitted up with Doors of brass Wire-work for the Reception of Manuscripts and other valuable Books', as the standard guide to Cambridge *Cantabrigia depicta* remarked in 1763, noting at the same time that 'here likewise are preserved a Mummy, a *Chinese* Pagod, and many other Curiosities'.[6] In 1751, too, John Taylor gave up his post as Registrary, to be replaced by Lynford Caryl of Jesus College. His room in the Schools had once housed part of the Library's collection of early books, and with his departure all three officers of the University most closely associated with the building thus changed.

All these events, the completion of the Dome Room in 1752, the election of Parris as *Protobibliothecarius* in succession to Middleton in 1750 and the death of Thomas Parne in 1751, coupled with the election in December 1748 of the Duke of Newcastle as Chancellor of the University, contributed in 1752 to the overdue reopening of the question of the next stage in the Library's building plans. It was not one that was any more easily solved in the 1750s than it had promised to be in the 1720s, and, in Cole's words, 'it occasioned a great deal of

---

[5] For an account of Whisson, and particularly of his funeral, see Nichols *Literary anecdotes* 3 p. 657.   [6] *Cantabrigia depicta* (Cambridge 1763) p. 23. See fig. 3, p. 157.

Animosity and ill Temper in the University'.[7] James Burrough, the originator of the design for the Senate House arrangement later put into the hands of James Gibbs, was a popular figure. The University therefore turned naturally first to his proposals for the east front of the Library, entailing the demolition of Rotherham's range and the construction of a new building outwardly very similar to the Senate House. Burrough's proposed facade in 1752 differed little from that published in 1728 in Gibbs' *Book of architecture* save that he now omitted the urns from the roof (those planned for the Senate House still not having been put in place),[8] and the open arcade running the whole extent of the ground floor was now to be partly taken up with two small rooms for university offices.[9] His new plan would have replaced the old rooms on the ground floor of the old east front, which he proposed to deepen by an arcade terminating at each end in two small rooms that would have extended the north and south ranges by roughly equal amounts. The first floor was to be rebuilt, so as to make Rotherham's library two-thirds as wide again as previously. In other words, it was a scheme both economical and at one with the long-term plans for the development of the main university buildings round a three-sided court. But however economical and logical, the supporters of Burrough's scheme reckoned without the wishes of the Duke of Newcastle, who did not hesitate to exercise his influence in all possible matters in the University. On 25 October 1753 he announced to Edmund Keene, Master of Peterhouse, Bishop of Chester, and Vice-Chancellor for two years in 1749–51:

I have directed M[r]. Wright, to prepare forthwith a Complete Design, for Building a Wing to answer the Senate-House in front, and to the Regent-

---

[7] Willis & Clark 3 p. 65. British Library MS. Add. 5852 p. 137.

[8] The urns were not placed on the Senate House roof until 1889, when they were presented by Samuel Sandars, a benefactor with as keen a sense of inadequacies in university buildings as of those in the collections of the University Library.

[9] Burrough's plan was engraved by P. Fourdrinier at some time after the death of Burrough in 1764 (copy in University Library Map Room Views x.2(24)). See also Willis & Clark 3 pp. 62, 64–5.

Walk; – And, also, of a new front to the Library, and Schools, to front the Regent-Walk, with Arcades to Caius-College, and King's College, to join the Schools with the other Buildings. In the Building opposite to the Senate-House, I would propose, a Vice-Chancellor's Court, an appartment for the Librarian, at the End towards the Library; and for the Register, at the end towards S^t. Mary's Church. I must beg, that you would give immediate attention upon an affair, in which the Ornament, and Conveniency, of the university, and my own Credit, are so much concerned.[10]

Stephen Wright, the architect thus thrust upon the University, was a protégé of Newcastle, for whom he had just supervised work at Claremont. His earliest known connection with the family had been the completion of Wimborne House in Arlington Street, just south of Piccadilly, for Henry Pelham (the Duke's younger brother) after the death of William Kent in 1748.[11] His plan (fig. 9) for the new east front at Cambridge solved many of the problems associated with the site – so far as the floor plan was conceived – in the same manner as Burrough's; but his proposed façade was a radical departure from the Corinthian mass proposed by the local architect. The influence of Kent, in the treatment of the windows and of the arcade on the ground floor in particular, is so obvious as to have deceived the unwary, while Sir John Summerson has summed the matter up succinctly: 'The facade of the library is nothing but an expansion of the pavilion unit in the Horse Guards, the only pronounced novelty being the carving of a highly effective band of festoons under the main cornice.'[12] Wright's building has proved to be an excellent foil to the Senate House, and successful partly because it manages to be both formal and pretty at the same time. Like Burrough's suggestion, it involved as little demolition of old work as possible. The

10 British Library MS. Add. 32733, fo. 136. Quoted also in Winstanley *Eighteenth century* pp. 223–4.
11 Cf. Howard Colvin *A biographical dictionary of British architects, 1600–1840* (1978) pp. 932–3 and Peter Campbell (ed.) *A house in town; 22 Arlington Street, its owners and builders* (1984).
12 John Summerson *Architecture in Britain 1530 to 1830* (4th ed. Harmondsworth 1963) p. 188.

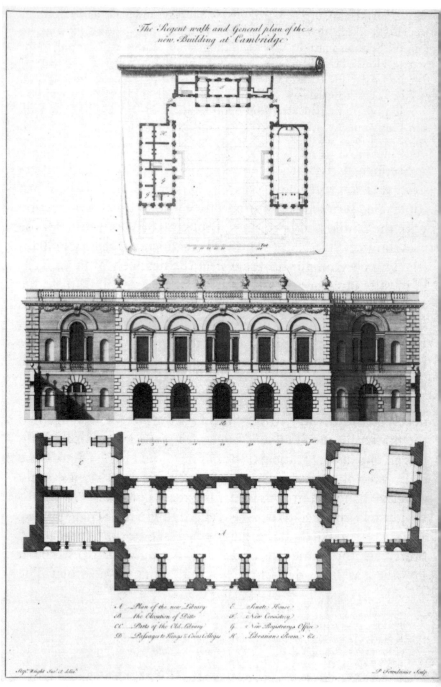

9   Stephen Wright's plans for the new east front, engraved by Paul
Fourdrinier, 1754. Size of original 468 × 312 mm.

arcade built out from the old line of the east front, at right angles to the Senate House, corrected the ancient alignment; two rooms were left on the ground floor; a new staircase was inserted at the south-east corner as the main entrance to the Library, replacing the old spiral staircase in the turret; and a large room on the first floor, the centrepiece and *raison d'être* of the project, was to link the old Regent House with the new first floor landing at the south. No drawings are known to have survived for Burrough's or Wright's designs for the interior of the East Room, as it became known, but where Burrough had planned façade. The consequent effect of great spaciousness is four could be accommodated thanks to Wright's generously planned façade. The consequent effect of great spaciousness is prominent in the illustration of the room published in Ackermann's *History of the University of Cambridge* published in 1815, but by the time that the Library was moved out in 1934 it had been completely obliterated by the insertion of smaller cases in all possible spaces including the wide central aisle. The room was provided with doors at the centres of the north and south walls, but they were placed there only after Wright had made his first drawings: initially he had proposed to insert them further to the west. Outside, the most noticeable point of his drawing of the east front is that it lacks the swags in stone that now form such a distinctive feature.[13]

As for the proposed south wing to face the Senate House, neither Burrough nor Wright proposed any plans for the façade on this occasion. Both may be presumed to have assumed that it would echo the Senate House, for Burrough's scheme for the Library differed little in principle from his earlier one of 1721–2, and the floor plan included in Wright's proposal shows a north wall that exactly matches the Senate House. However, it will be recalled that in his letter to Keene of October 1753, Newcastle proposed that the Librarian's room should be in the end of the wing nearer to the Library. In his drawing Wright placed the room on the ground floor in the

[13] Wright's drawing, then in the possession of Mr Charles Reilly, FRIBA, was reproduced in *The Builder*, 28 September 1907.

new east front – a rather more logical place – and a new Consistory in the south wing. This was corrected in the plan as published, but of course altered again when the wing was never built.[14]

Not unnaturally, the affair left Burrough disgruntled. William Cole, a sympathizer with him, called the new front 'absurd and ill-judged', and recorded that on Burrough's being asked what order it was he supposed it was the Duke of Newcastle's.[15] Once again he saw his ideas taken up by an outsider, denying him the opportunity to see a major building through to completion. Most members of the University, however, felt unable to gainsay Newcastle, and when on 11 June 1754 a Grace was passed authorizing the building to proceed, Burrough was among only sixteen who non-placeted it. Newcastle had further forced the issue by heading a subscription list with a gift of £500, and events moved so quickly that Paul Fourdrinier was able on 28 June to charge for printing 550 copies of Wright's plan.[16] By September, the foundations were sufficiently dug for them to be inspected by Newcastle, and on 30 April 1755 William Stephens provided the engraved inscription on copper to be inserted in the foundation stone.[17]

The laying of the stone provided an occasion for suitable celebrations in honour of the Chancellor. The Vice-Chancellor of the day being Stephen Goddard, Master of Clare, the proceedings began there:

Apr: 30. A Levee in Clare Hall Combination, & at about Half an Hour past 12, the Duke came to the Congregation, where all Masters of Arts were with their Hoods flourished: the Beadles in tufted Gowns, Coifs & Caps,

---

[14] The subsequent fate of plans for the south wing is no part of the history of the Library, but can be followed in Willis & Clark 3 pp. 69, 72–4.

[15] According to Cole, Newcastle obtained a knighthood for Burrough in 1754 in order to placate him. For details see J. Venn *Biographical history of Gonville and Caius College* 3 (Cambridge 1901) p. 127.

[16] On 4 September he charged three guineas for altering the plan, and ten days later he provided five hundred further copies (Vouchers).

[17] Printed in G. A. Walpoole *The new British traveller* (1784) p. 180. See also Willis & Clark 3 p. 67.

except Mr. Porteus, the Junior Beadle, who had on a Master of Arts Gown. From the Senate House a Procession to the laying the first Stone of the New Building, in this Order. First, the Junior Beadle, then the Syndics for the New Building, two & two, Juniors first: then the other two Beadles, the Chancellor, Vice-Chancellor, Heads, Doctors, B.D., Masters of Arts, &c. in Order of Seniority, Seniors first. When they came to the Place appointed for the Stone (which was the North Corner of the Front) the Duke performed the Ceremony, speaking a few Words in Latin at the same Time: the Vice Chancellor read the Inscription upon the Plate, & after That was inserted in the Stone, & Money, according to Custom put in, all returned to the Senate House, where the Orator (from a small Rostrum) made a long Speech; & the Chancellor adjourned the Congregation to Thursday 11 o'Clock.[18]

The volume of verses[19] composed in honour of the occasion was unusual in that these printed tributes were by custom reserved for national events, or for royal occasions such as births, deaths, accessions and marriages. Even George I, who had been so signal a benefactor to the University, had never received one on his visit to Cambridge, and public praise of his virtues (in this form at least) had to wait until his death in 1727. The verses presented to Newcastle in 1755, in a copy bound in dark blue morocco by Edwin Moor,[20] the most accomplished of the local binders, naturally could have little to say about a building that had reached only the foundation stone. Instead, the contributors concentrated on the merits of the Chancellor and the Hanoverian succession, and such sallies into architectural allusion as they attempted tended to be either general or inaccurate. These aside, the volume is of interest chiefly for containing a poem by the undergraduate Richard Farmer which contrived to include a disdainful reference to the 'Mausolean Pile' at Oxford, the recently completed Radcliffe Camera:

> See, *Learning* marks his chosen way
> With many a beam of early day;

---

[18] British Library MS. Add. 5852 p. 139.
[19] *Carmina ad Nobillissimum Thomam Holles Ducem de Newcastle inscripta, cum Academiam Cantabrigiensem Bibliothecae restituendae causa inviseret prid. kalend. Maias, MDCCLV.*
[20] The binding is reproduced in Maggs catalogue 966 (1975), no. 139.

And louring *Ignorance* gives place
To Science, with averted Face;
Whilst PELHAM bids the column rise,
And tell his bounty to the skies.
Now smiles old *Cam*, and scatter'd finds
His *Gothic* dust the sport of winds;
Nor envys *Isis*, who erewhile
Boasted her Mausolean Pile.
On Domes depend not PELHAM's name:
But be *They* founded on *His* fame!

But the person who was given the most scope was the Public Orator, John Skynner, Fellow of St John's, whose speech was annexed to some copies of the verses in honour of Newcastle and was also issued as a separate quarto pamphlet. He combed the records of classical antiquity for libraries with which to compare the new extension at Cambridge, to such effect that his speech might serve as a convenient starting point for an investigation of the subject. He was also careful to remind his audience of the graces received both from Newcastle and the King, and to emphasize that university studies were not, ultimately, solely for academe but for the glory of the country at large: 'peregrinentur, rusticentur'.[21]

It took three more years to build the extension. The old bricks (23,870 of them) had been saved in 1754, but in 1757–8 the University sold off the old stone to John Green, Master of Corpus Christi College, who thought that it would be of use in his college. He proved to be unlucky, for the clunch, exposed to the weather on all sides, began to rot, and so Green gave part of his purchase to William Cole. The main portion of the stone from Rotherham's entrance to the Schools was sold to Sir John Cotton, and now forms the entrance to the yard at Madingley Hall.[22] Cole also managed to scavenge some of the old wood

---

[21] Besides the official collection, Newcastle also received a volume from his protégé, librarian and (later) factotum James Marriott, Fellow of Trinity Hall. Marriott's *Two poems* (1755) bore a reproduction of a medal of George II on the title-page and an engraving of the new building on p. 10, the last in a rustic frame drawn by Marriott himself. The building was also illustrated in John Duncombe's *Poems* (1756).

[22] Willis & Clark 3 p. 18, quoting British Library MS. Add. 5834.

from the Library desks,[23] while he had already, in 1748 during an earlier fit of modernization under Parris when he was Vice-Chancellor, done what he could to rescue the old glass – with rather unsatisfactory results:

In *September 1748*, during my Absence on some Occasion from the *University* . . . the *Front* of these *Scholes* were thought to want Repair, at which Time all the old *painted Windows* were taken down to make Room for *Crown Glass*; & all those curious *Paintings*, tho' perfect & compleat, were taken away by the *Glazier*, to the no small Reproach of the *University* in thus defrauding the pious *Benefactors* & *Founders* amongst us of their just and grateful *Memorials*. There were also many other *antient Coats* in the *open Work* at the *Tops* of each *Window*; all which were taken away: & tho' I used all means I could think of to recover them, yet they were broken, dispersed or mislaid in a month after they were removed in such a Manner as I could not find them. *One large Pane* I had of the Gift of the *Vice-Chancellor*: Part of which composes *2 Gothic Windows* I made in the *Parsonage* at *Blecheley* in *Buckinghamshire*, one in the *House* itself, another in the *Hermitage* in the *Garden*: besides some which I put into the *East Window* of that *Parish Church*.[24]

None of the glass thus rescued, whether in his house at Milton (where he inserted Rotherham's device), Bletchley, or Burnham (where he became vicar in 1774), now survives.

For his part, Wright introduced his own craftsmen to work on the new building. Thomas Clark, the plasterer responsible for the panelled ceiling in the East Room on the first floor, with its elaborate cornice of fruit and flowers, and for the ceiling above the new staircase, had worked with Kent on the Horse Guards in Whitehall, and was in the midst of a much larger contract at Holkham, also originated by Kent. The carving in the doorways at each end of the room and elsewhere was the work of George Murray, who had also worked at Arlington

23 For some of Cole's activities on this occasion see Oates *History* pp. 43–4; W. M. Palmer *William Cole of Milton* (Cambridge 1935) p. 35; W. M. Palmer (ed.) *Monumental inscriptions and coats of arms from Cambridgeshire chiefly as recorded by John Layer and William Cole* (Cambridge 1932) p. 275 and pl. 45.

24 British Library MS. Add. 5820 fo. 186ʳ. See also J. W. Clark 'A description of the East Room of the University Library, Cambridge, as built by Bishop Rotherham, written by William Cole, M.A., in 1759' Cambridge Antiquarian Society *Communications* 10 (1903) pp. 419–26.

Street and the Horse Guards; the joiner was James Moss, later employed at Buckingham Palace, and the carpenters William Timbrell and John Spencer. The wrought ironwork in the new staircases was by Benjamin Holmes, who in 1742–4 had worked with Kent on Lady Isabella Finch's house at 44 Berkeley Square: his bill to the University dated 25 May 1758 (and paid nearly a year later, on 17 May 1759) amounted to £68.7s.8d., including £60 'for Iron Work to Grate Stair Case made to a Gothic Draping with a Gothic Truss at the Botham'.[25] Outside, the principal masons were Joseph Pickford[26] and William Atkinson: Pickford had worked with Kent at 44 Berkeley Square, with Kent and Wright at Arlington Street, and with Wright at Claremont. These two men were also responsible for the marble in the Grand Hall at Holkham.

It was estimated in 1754 that the new building, excluding demolition work and making no allowance for the second-hand bricks saved from the old one, would cost £7890. But the total far exceeded that, and by the end of the financial year 1758–9, when the final payments were made, it amounted to £10,176.13s.1¾d.[27] The best materials in fashion were used: Westmorland slates for the roof, and (to match the Senate House) facings in Portland stone, with the more familiar Ketton stone from near Stamford for the less obtrusive parts. The University saved where it could, partly by re-using the bricks, partly by allowing Pickford and Atkinson the use of the university crane to lift stone out of the barges at Garrett Hostel Bridge,[28] but the project had been badly costed. For the masons (excluding the carving) the figures were £4312.11s.5d. against an estimate of £3800, for the bricklayers £1225.4s.2½d. (estimate £800), and for the carpenters £993.4s.3¾d. (estimate

[25] Details of the costs are in the Vouchers for 1757–9.
[26] Not Pitchford as in Historical Monuments Commission *Cambridge* p. 12.
[27] Willis & Clark 3 p. 68 say £10,506.9s.8¾d.; the figure given here is based on the audited university accounts.
[28] The articles of agreement between the University and Atkinson and Pickford are now Luard 221³.

£680). Worse still, the cost of the joinery proved to be £1422.5s.3d., over twice the estimate of £700. Clark's work on the plastering also comfortably topped twice the estimate, at £532.15s.10d. instead of £240. The compensations were minor in comparison. The glazier was paid only £51.0s.8d. instead of £90, and further money was saved when the bill for painting charged to the account for the new building was a mere £5.15s.6d. compared with an estimated £60. The biggest comfort of all, but that minor enough, was in the cost of the stone ornamentation across the front of the building, estimated at £450: altogether the work cost £333.12s.9½d., including £159.10s.0d. for the festoons, the vases at £31, and the '4 Large Heads Representing the 4 Seasons with Drapery Ribbons &c' £32. Within the East Room itself, the extra bookcases proved to be unsuitable from the start. 'Mr Wright is much blam'd for his Classes,' wrote Philip Yonge, Master of Jesus College, to Newcastle on 13 October 1757, 'and it would have been well if he had talk'd with the Syndics and the Librarian about them; for he has made them very beautifull and very inconvenient.'[29] But although erected, the cases have not survived, and in 1787–90 the University employed a local Cambridge joiner, Charles Humfrey, to make a new set.[30] As for the architect himself, Wright's bill for his work in 1754–8, including twenty journeys from London, amounted to £508, or five per cent of £10,160, of which £100 was paid on account in August 1756 and nothing more until three instalments in May–November 1759, the final one being on 23 November.

By this time the Library was already open, the ceremony having taken place on 3 July 1758. Not everyone was enthusiastic. On seeing the building in July 1757, Charles Lyttelton, dean of Exeter and Bishop of Carlisle, had

---

[29] British Library MS. Add. 32875, fo. 75.

[30] Cf. Luard 249. The fiasco in 1757 must explain why the University went to considerable lengths in 1787 to draw up formal articles of agreement with Humfrey, complete with an illustrated schedule. The cases are now divided between the East Room of the Old Schools and the Bradshaw Room in the University Library.

complained of the façade (still, then, uncompleted) that 'tho' built of fine stone and much enriched with ornaments on the outside', it 'falls very short in Beauty when compared with the Senate House adjoining'.[31] And Thomas Gray viewed the proceedings twelve months later with distaste. 'That old fizzling Duke is coming here again (but I hope to be gone first) to hear speeches in his new Library,' he wrote to Mason on 20 June, 'with the BP of Bristol to air his close-stool. they have fitted it up (not the close-stool, nor the BP) but the Library with classes, that will hold any thing, but books: yet books they must hold, & all the bulky old Commentators, the Synopses, & Tractatus Tractatuums, are wash'd with white of eggs, gilt & letter'd, and drawn up in review before his Grace.'[32] On 13 October a bill submitted by Goodall to the Vice-Chancellor included payments of ten shillings to two men for moving books into the room, three guineas for himself for seven weeks' work at the same task, six shillings for three women to clean the new Library, and two shillings for cleaning the Royal Library 'where the old classes stood'.[33]

The work of raising the money to pay for the new building was far from complete, however. Newcastle had set an example with his initial contribution of £500,[34] and when this had been added to one of £2000 from George II and smaller sums from nine others the total raised in 1753–4 had produced an encouraging £3650. No money was taken out of the ordinary University funds until the very end, with the

[31] Lilian Dickens and Mary Stanton (ed.) *An eighteenth-century correspondence* (1910) p. 371.
[32] Thomas Gray *Correspondence* ed. Paget Toynbee and Leonard Whibley, with corrections and additions by H. W. Starr (Oxford 1971) 2 pp. 573–4. The Bishop of Bristol was Philip Yonge, Vice-Chancellor in 1752–4, who campaigned actively for the new library.   [33] Vouchers.
[34] On 25 October 1753 Newcastle wrote to Edmund Keene of Peterhouse, 'D^r. Yonge has begun the Subscription; about which, by the way, We have a Difficulty in our first Setting out. The Prince of Wales ought to be a Subscriber; the King, in that case, must subscribe so much more; – and it would be unreasonable to expect, that the King should subscribe 2000^l. for Himself, and 1000^l. for the Prince of Wales. – To avoid this, It is thought to begin with 1000^l. from the King, and 500^l. from the Prince; – that will necessarily reduce my Subscription to 500^l. also. But these may be augmented afterwards, if there should be Occasion' (British Library MS. Add. 32733, fo. 135).

exceptions only of the bequests of Sir Nathaniel Lloyd, Master of Trinity Hall, who had died in 1745 leaving £500 to the University, and Robert Tillotson of Clare College, who had left £30. Between them these two legacies produced £766.14s.0d. including interest, but even though this was realized in 1756–7 the outstanding debt in November 1758 was still between three and four thousand pounds. Newcastle thereupon doubled his contribution, and persuaded the King to add another thousand. Nonetheless, when the workmen's bills were settled in November 1759, money had to be advanced out of the university stock in the expectation that enough would eventually be raised: in fact, not quite enough was raised, and the University was forced to absorb the final deficit of a little over £200.[35]

As Gray realized, the University went to considerable expense to see that the bindings of the books were in presentable order for the opening of the new building in the summer of 1758. The occasion also witnessed an unwonted expenditure on new books, of a magnificence that, again, was presumably felt to be appropriate. In the few weeks before the opening, Thomas Merrill supplied Mark Catesby's *Natural history of Carolina* (1754), Eleazar Albin's *Natural history of birds* (1738–40), Réaumur's *Mémoires pour servir à l'histoire des insectes* (Paris 1734–42) and Flamsteed's *Historia coelestis Britannica* (1725) in the sciences, the typographical facsimile of the Virgil Codex Mediceus (Florence 1741) and John Martyn's edition of Virgil in the classics, four volumes of the *Biographia Britannica*, and two important additions to the infant cartographical collections: John Rocque's *Survey of London and Westminster* and, less expectedly, the *Atlas Russicus* published at St Petersburg in 1745. Thurlbourn and Woodyer's list, while no less magnificent or indeed fundamental to a large library, was

---

[35] Apart from the Audit Book, see Winstanley *Eighteenth century* pp. 225–7: his account is based on the Newcastle correspondence in the British Library. Clark *Endowments* pp. 455–6 provides a list of the contributors based on the Audit Book and on Cooper's *Annals* 4 p. 293, and calculates that the total raised was £10,254.14s.0d. – more than enough.

somewhat shorter, but included the Baskerville Virgil in a binding by Edwin Moor, William Cowper on the anatomy of muscles *Myotomia reformata* in the edition by Richard Mead, Griffith Hughes' *Natural history of Barbados* (1750) and the sumptuous edition published by Tonson and Watts of Montaigne's *Essais* edited by Pierre Coste (1724).

The dearth of regular funds beyond the modest amount sanctioned by custom (and varying greatly from year to year) did nothing to help the Library in its everyday affairs. The Worts Fund, though established under the terms of the will of William Worts in 1709, produced no income for the purchase of books until 1767, and even then only sporadically.[36] John Newcome's gift of £200 in 1758,[37] to be spent on theological books, followed by his bequest of £500 in 1765, were therefore all the more effective. Born at Grantham, Newcome had been Master of St John's College since 1734/5 and Lady Margaret Professor of Divinity since 1727, as well as dean of Rochester since 1744. He had been conspicuously generous in his contribution for the new East Front of the Library a decade before his death, and his Mastership had witnessed a complete change in his college's library, including in 1739 the decision to make a new catalogue and in 1741 the need to heighten all the dwarf cases following the bequest of Thomas Baker: in 1764 (perhaps taking its hint from the University Library) the Fellowship found it necessary to resolve again that the library should be recatalogued.[38] No friend of John Taylor, Newcome had had little influence in the University Library, and Taylor complained even of his final disposition of a library of far more than average interest. Taylor, Nichols records, 'inquired how he had disposed of his books; and though the account was a very good one, he received it with an air of

---

[36] Cf. the Audit Books for 1767 onwards, recording occasional receipts of £25 or £50. The first book in the Accessions Register listed as being specifically bought with the Worts Fund is Buffon's *Natural history* (1785), purchased that summer.

[37] For an example of the printed bookplate recording his gift in 1758 see J. Strype *Annals of the Reformation* (1725): classmark 5.39.5–.

[38] Baker–Mayor pp. 1035–6, 1041.

contempt; upon which one of the company said, *Then Doctor, do you not take care to do better*; upon which he sunk into seriousness, and said softly, *I wish I may*.[39] Neither Newcome nor Taylor left any books to the University Library. Taylor's went principally to his old school at Shrewsbury and to Anthony Askew, while the cream of Newcome's was divided between his native town[40] and St John's: as a result, the college received a collection of incunabula magnificent both in appearance (about twenty are in turkey leather bindings executed for Harley) and in containing a remarkable series from Italian presses beginning with Jerome's *Epistolae* printed by Sweynheym and Pannartz at Rome in 1468.

Newcome's gifts to the University Library were spent, over the next several years, entirely on theological books.[41] Defects in holdings of English publications were made good with the purchase of such books as Henry Stebbing's *Polemical tracts* (Cambridge 1727), David Wilkins' edition of the Coptic Pentateuch (1731), Picart's *Religious ceremonies* (1731–7) and Paolo Sarpi's history of the Council of Trent in Le Courayer's French edition published in London in 1736. Major works of foreign scholarship included Calmet's dictionary of the Bible (Paris 1730), Jacques Saurin's *Discours sur les événements les plus mémorables du Vieux et du Nouveau Testament* (The Hague 1735–9), and the extremely expensive – it cost sixteen guineas partly because of the binding – *Physica sacra* of Johann Scheuchzer (1731–5). Less predictable, perhaps, was J. G.

---

[39] Nichols *Literary anecdotes* 4 pp. 514–15, quoted in Baker–Mayor p. 1034. For the distressing last few days of Newcome's life see Gray's letter to Mason, 17 January 1765 (Gray *Correspondence* 2 p. 860).

[40] About 700 volumes went to Grantham, and were kept, in bookcases provided by Newcome, in the vestry of the parish church and so separate from the old chained library. See Edmund Turnor *Collections for the town and soke of Grantham* (1806) p. 28, and Angela Roberts 'The chained library, Grantham' *Library History* 2 (1971) pp. 75–90, especially pp. 81 and 88–9.

[41] The entries for the Newcome books in the Accessions Register begin with the date 17 July 1765; but Thurlbourn and Woodyer's first bill to mention the fund specifically was dated 12 September 1767. (William Thurlbourn and John Woodyer entered into partnership on 29 September 1756 (Advertisement in the *Cambridge Journal* 2 October 1756).)

Kalinsky's *Vaticinia Chabacuci et Nachumi* published in Vratislava in 1748, one of a number of books of linguistic scholarship bought in the first few years of the fund's life. The great majority of titles were of recent or fairly recent publications, the most pressing need being obviously to build on Moore's comprehensive collection; but he had not possessed the three-volume Arabic and Latin Bible published at Rome in 1671, which was now added, and in 1771 the five-volume French history of the Edict of Nantes, published in 1643, was also bought from Newcome's legacy. Elzevir's folio French Bible of 1669 duplicated Moore's large paper copy, but was kept nonetheless. The earliest book to have been bought with the fund appears to have been Vatable's polyglot Bible published at Heidelberg in 1559, purchased in 1771 for £1.11s.6d. and like the rest bought from John Woodyer, who succeeded Thurlbourn in 1768 at 1 Trinity Street. By 1790 the fund had enabled the Library to buy about 250 items in modest but essential and considered amends for what would otherwise have gone unrepaired.

The Library had too little money to buy seriously, but the position was made no easier by the inadequacies and slovenly administration of the Copyright Act of 1710. By the 1760s entry in the Stationers' Register, never comprehensive nor even representative since the early seventeenth century, had shrunk to a trickle despite its legal status. In 1760 thirty-three items were entered, in 1761 thirty-eight, in 1762 forty, in 1763 twenty-four;[42] and although the Universities Copyright Act of 1775, coupled with a fresh interest in the Register on the part of music publishers and a considerable expansion of the book trade in the last quarter of the century, brought some increase, the Register still did not contain more than a tiny fraction of the whole. The pattern, established in outline years before, was more pronounced than ever by the third quarter of the

[42] These figures include everything. Those listed in *Parliamentary Papers* 1818 9 p. 254 exclude various kinds of material and are consequently marginally smaller.

century, and the copyright libraries could do little about it. William Reading's complaint of 1724 had left the libraries in no more satisfactory a position than before.[43]

Rather than bother with the Register, the largest (and even most of the smaller metropolitan) booksellers preferred to run the risk of infringement of their property in almost everything, and the published exceptions – those that were actually entered in the Register – fell into if not a clear, at least to some extent a predictable, pattern. Titles involving large congers tended to be listed, such as the *Modern part of an universal history*, or the seventh edition of Philip Miller's *Gardeners dictionary*. Authors publishing their own works were naturally wary of their privileges, and those who were not necessarily so tended to obey the letter of the law. In this way the Register tended to acquire a disproportionate number of such titles. Not all were of such lasting interest as Horace Walpole's *Catalogue of the royal and noble authors*, entered in April 1758, or Charles Churchill's poems, twelve entries for which appear between November 1763 and September 1764, William Blackstone's *Commentaries on the laws of England*, the first volume of which, printed at his own expense at the Oxford University Press, was entered in November 1765, or Daniel Paterson's *Scale of distances of the principal cities and towns of England* (a single sheet and his first publication) the following April. Besides a smattering of sermons there were works on tax reform, cookery, popular medicine and accountancy, spelling books, ingenious systems of shorthand, and compilations such as Andrew Ducarel's *Repertory of the endowments of vicarages in the diocese of Canterbury* which could scarcely expect to be pirated. Thomas Burr took the precaution of entering his *History of Tunbridge-Wells* himself in June 1766, though the title-page proclaimed that it was sold by Hingeston, Dodsley and Thomas Caslon in London and E. Baker in Tunbridge Wells. Composers and publishers of music tended to enter more, as a

---

[43] See above, p. 31.

class, than the rest of the trade. In 1762, for example, besides Charles Wesley's *Short hymns on select passages of the holy scripture*, there were listed J. C. Heck's *Complete system of harmony*, William Riley's *Parochial music corrected* (with psalm tunes), Alessandro Besozzi's *Six solos for the German flute* entered by Edmund Chapman along with Tomaso Prota's *Sei sonate* and Dothel's *Six duetts for German flutes or violins*, all on 3–4 May, Thomas Call's *Tunes & hymns as they are used at the Magdalen Chapel*, Robert Bremner's *Rudiments of music* and Thomas Moore's *Psalm-singer's delightful pocket companion*.[44] The last two were from Scotland, and though Bremner's entry marked his departure from Edinburgh for London the number of books published in Scotland under quite ordinary circumstances and entered in the London Register was noticeable. Andrew Donaldson of Edinburgh, Francis Douglas of Aberdeen, R. & A. Foulis of Glasgow, Hamilton, Balfour and Neill of Edinburgh, Robert Taylor of Berwick, William Gordon of Edinburgh and John Newlands of Glasgow were among those whose books were entered in this period as a precaution against infringement of their copyright by southerners. Major London publishers entered little. Between 1758 and 1765, for example, John Nourse entered only *The handmaid to the arts* and two books of French grammar by Thomas Deletanville, all in 1758, Simson's *Elements of Euclid* in 1762, and Robert Orme's *A history of the military transactions of the British nation in Indostan* in 1763. Andrew Millar's total comprised Robertson's *History of Scotland* (1759), Hume's *History of England* (1759, 1761: the first volume was published in Edinburgh), Edward Barry's *Treatise on the three different digestions and discharges of the human body* (1759), John Home's tragedy *The siege of Aquileia* (1760: in production at Drury Lane, and so open to piracy), Sorel's *New and accurate chart of the cost of Africa* (1760), and Donald Monro's *Account of the diseases which were most frequent in the British*

---

[44] The proportion of music entered after 1776–7 was much greater than previously: see *Report from the Select Committee on the Copyright Acts* (*Parliamentary Papers* 1818 9) p. 254.

military hospitals in Germany (1764: a conger entry). Plays required some protection, but even so by no means all were entered, and other imaginative literature was entered only irregularly. In the same period *Rasselas* (entered jointly by the Dodsleys and William Johnston), Macpherson's *Ossian* (an Edinburgh book, from Hamilton and Balfour), Lyttelton's *Dialogues of the dead*, Gessner's *Death of Abel* (translated and entered by Mary Collyer), Lady Mary Wortley Montagu's *Letters* and Sterne's *Sermons* (vols. 3–4 only, by Becket and De Hondt) were all entered, but not Charles Johnstone's *Chrysal*, *Tristram Shandy*, Elizabeth Carter's *Poems,* Kames' *Elements of criticism*, *Sir Lancelot Greaves*, Walpole's *Anecdotes of painting* or *Castle of Otranto*, Johnson's Shakespeare or Percy's *Reliques*. Maps appeared from time to time, and so did children's educational games, such as Thorold Lowdell's *Royal alphabet* – several boxes of small letters on pasteboard – and even on occasion separate views, such as two copper-plates of the church and town of Halifax, entered by John Watson in October 1761. Equally serious in its consequences for the long-term development of the University Library and the other deposit libraries was the chaos surrounding entry of periodicals, which, aside from considerations of copyright, made any serious accessions policy next to impossible. Not only were scarcely any of these publications entered, whether journals, newspapers or books in parts, but also by the late 1750s even the few that did reach the Stationers' Register were entered at most only occasionally. A few parts of the *London Magazine* were entered in 1759 and early in 1760 by Robert Baldwin, for example, but none later; the issue of the *Lawyer's Magazine* for the Easter Term 1761 only; and the tenth number (again alone) of the *North Briton*, written by Charles Churchill, ever anxious in these matters, in 1762. So far as registration at Stationers' Hall was concerned, the position was even more perilous than it had been forty years earlier; though even then, while both the *Guardian* and the *Spectator* had been entered

273

neither had reached Cambridge complete: the Library had acquired both in 1716, but only in the duodecimo editions, as a binder's bill from Henry Crow makes clear.[45]

The consequences of all this for the Library will, in many respects, be obvious enough. But by no means all of what was entered and deposited at Stationers' Hall reached Cambridge. The onus, once the books were deposited, was on the copyright libraries to claim, and by the time that the first full surviving accessions book was begun in 1758 the Library had placed the task of claiming its books in the hands of the local book trade. As has already been explained, in the earlier part of the century the usual practice, in principle at least, was for parcels to arrive twice-yearly from the Stationers' Company, and for the Company's Warehouse-Keeper, Clerk, or Treasurer, to receive a gratuity for his trouble. The arrangement deteriorated in the 1740s. In 1751 the University paid arrears since 1737 to Thomas Simpson, the Treasurer of the Company, and in 1755 Parris paid the Clerk £1.11s.6d. for the previous three years. These irregular payments did however at least betoken some interest on the part of the Library authorities, if only, perhaps, in response to chiding from London. More seriously, on 13 July 1751 the Syndics, faced with a superfluity of unwanted books from London, resolved 'that such books as shall be judged proper for the Library be selected out out of those sent down from the Stationers company, and that the Remainder be sold and the money arising from thence be laid out in the purchase of such other books as are most wanted in the Library, at the discretion of the principal Librarian'.[46] The University abandoned direct dealings with the Stationers' Company on this score, and in 1758 the account of the local booksellers Thurlbourn and Woodyer included an item for carriage of two parcels of books from London. In that year and the following the University

[45] For more details of periodicals in the Stationers' Register and the consequences for the Library see Oates 'Copyright Act' pp. 67–8.
[46] University Archives *Minutes of Syndicates 1737–1834* p. 96.

also received £4.18s.od. in credit from the same booksellers in books, a sum that included £3.5s.od. for fifteen volumes of the *Modern part of an universal history* in boards from the Stationers' Company.[47] The same arrangement, with various booksellers, lasted until after the Copyright Act of 1814 even though neither Thurlbourn and Woodyer nor any of their successors could, in strict legal terms, claim to be the University's authorized agents within the meaning of the Act of 1710.[48]

It is impossible to establish with complete accuracy exactly how many of the titles entered and deposited at Stationers' Hall reached the Library, and it is equally impossible to discover how many reached no further than Thurlbourn and Woodyer's premises. The fact that, in principle, books had to be claimed from London certainly occasioned some wastage (though in the absence of any accounts in the Stationers' Company there is no absolute proof of this), while calculations are still further complicated by the fact that there was sometimes considerable delay between publication (and deposit) and arrival in the Library. In 1769, for example, a consignment of twenty-five volumes from London included nine published between 1753 and 1758, and such features persisted.[49] It has been estimated that in 1758–67 and 1771–73 about one-third of the books registered actually entered the Library, and that between 1766 and 1814 (the date of the next major copyright legislation) about one-sixth,[50] but the real figures may have been more modest still. In 1768, fifty-eight items were entered in the Stationers' Register, but no more than about twenty-two of them had arrived at the Library by the end of 1773. For 1769 the figures were respectively seventy-six and about twenty, for 1770 sixty-seven and about thirteen, for 1771 sixty-eight and about twenty-two, for 1772 sixty-two and about nineteen, for 1773 seventy-two and about twenty-one. The stark figures seem distressing enough, but the

[47] Vouchers 24 October 1759.
[48] Oates 'Copyright Act' p. 63 and note 5, pp. 72–3.
[49] *Ibid.*, pp. 65, 73.   [50] *Ibid.*, p. 64.

omissions are instructive, since they were either presumably (except for occasional accidents) refused deliberately, or were appropriated by Thurlbourn and Woodyer as cheap stock. Neither alternative reflects much credit on the parties concerned, but at least a passable picture emerges in this way of what the Library neither believed itself nor was held to be. Manuals such as *The universal directory for taking alive and destroying rats*, by Robert Smith, rat-catcher to Princess Amelia (1768) or Peter Gilchrist's *Treatise on hair* (1770; entered in the Stationers' Register in 1771) might not be expected to be acceptable to the Library authorities, and it might also be argued that *The Southampton guide* would offer little interest in Cambridge, but these were far from being the only classes of rejects. In 1768, besides Samuel Bentley's poem *The River Dove* and Joseph Priestley's *Rudiments of English grammar*, the Library could have received – and certainly did not keep – Sterne's *Sentimental journey*, Horace Walpole's *Historic doubts on the reign of King Richard the Third* and James Boswell's collection of *British essays in favour of the brave Corsicans*. Authorship seems to have had nothing to do with the process of selection (unless, again, the booksellers were tempted), for it was almost no time since the Library had retained Sterne's sermons (more respectable than his novels), Walpole's *Catalogue of the royal and noble authors*, and Boswell's *Account of Corsica*. John Russell's *Form of process in the Court of Session*, having to do with Scots law, may not have seemed relevant, but *The fruit gardener*, a work generally attributed to John Gibson, M.D., and being largely about the subject in the Clyde valley, arrived without mishap. Plays were rejected, but so were political pamphlets. Three years later, neither *Humphrey Clinker*, Percy's *Hermit of Warkworth*, nor the first edition of Paterson's best-selling road book ever arrived, though all had been both entered and deposited in nine copies at London. And although, as we have seen, music was periodically entered, the Library was so sparing of it that the only piece of sheet music to be accepted in these years was John Burton's *Ten sonatas for harpsichord, organ or piano forte* (1766).

Inevitably there were still difficulties about books published by subscription. The Library could not count on receiving them under the copyright legislation, but at the same time it could not always risk a subscription. So a few months after the publication of Baskerville's quarto Virgil in 1757 the Library bought its copy, bound by Edwin Moor, for twenty-five shillings from Thurlbourn and Woodyer, even though both Parris and Whisson, *Protobibliothecarius* and *Bibliothecarius*, as well as five colleges and Merrill the bookseller, had all subscribed. But on the other hand the University did subscribe to George Edwards' great illustrated *Gleanings of natural history* published by the author in two volumes in 1758 and 1764. The first volume arrived in April 1760, inscribed by the author and bearing the note that it had been 'coloured under the immediate inspection of the Author, and retouched by himself, and made to compare with the original Coloured Drawings'; Goodall, ignoring the fact that the first volume to arrive was strictly a subscription copy, followed Edwards' presentation inscription and entered it in the accessions register as a gift. And, scarcely surprisingly, there was wasted money. A planned edition of Meninsky's oriental dictionary, to have been published in four volumes by W. and J. Richardson, relieved the Library of six guineas in December 1770 but was never published. Nor was anything more heard of a quarto edition of James Beattie's *Essay on the nature and immutability of truth*, for which the University paid a guinea on 21 February 1774.[51] Subscriptions were sometimes placed through booksellers, rather than direct, both for foreign works such as Sir William Hamilton's *Collection of Etruscan antiquities*[52] and also for English ones. In July 1769, T. & J. Merrill charged £2.12s.6d. (plus two shillings for binding the first volume) for a subscription to Edward Lye's *Dictionarium Saxonico et Gothico Latinum*, published in 1772. The subscription to John Hutchins' history of Dorset was paid through Woodyer in April 1771, the two

---

[51] Printed receipts for both these projects are among the Vouchers.
[52] Subscribed to through John Woodyer, beginning with a payment of four guineas charged on 2 November 1769.

volumes arriving three years later; and the Library also subscribed to at least one other contemporary major contribution to British topography, Morant's history of Essex published in 1768: it was not so prompt with William Borlase's *Natural history of Cornwall*, published at Oxford in 1758, which it finally bought in 1781. In the case of the Morant, Cambridge was the sole copyright library to subscribe, while the only other to appear on the subscription list in Hutchins' work was the library of the Faculty of Advocates at Edinburgh, and in Lye's the University Library of Edinburgh.

But while the usual consequence for the Library of an inefficiently administered and widely ignored Copyright Act was that it had either to do without or to buy its English books through the trade in the normal way, this was not always the case. Many arrived as gifts. The Duke of Newcastle produced a copy of the latest edition of the Bible in Old Slavonic, published at St Petersburg in 1751, which he no doubt considered to be of more use at Cambridge than in his own library; the accounts for 1752–3 include a charge of half a crown for its transport from London. Hogarth gave his *Analysis of beauty* on its publication in 1753,[53] Edward Capell presented his edition of Shakespeare, published in 1767–8, and the Duke of Northumberland gave Thomas Percy's edition of the Northumberland household book in 1772, while the Library was also among the many recipients of the *Memoirs of Thomas Hollis*, in a characteristic binding. All the last four books ought, properly, to have come through Stationers' Hall; but to what extent these and other donors of English books gave them through ignorance, and to what through a desire to avoid the demands of legally established bureaucracy, is not clear. George Edwards was principally concerned to see that reliable copies of his *Natural history of uncommon birds* (1743 etc.)

---

[53] Now Rel.b.75.2. The Vice-Chancellor's letter of 28 November 1753 thanking him for the gift is now British Library MS. Add. 27995, fo. 10. See also J. Ireland and J. Nichols *Hogarth's works* 3rd series (1873) p. 99, and Ronald Paulson *Hogarth: his life, art, and times* (New Haven 1971) 2 pp. 185, 442.

were placed in the libraries he considered most appropriate, and like many another publisher of his own books ignored the copyright legislation, instead presenting copies to Cambridge, the Bodleian, the British Museum, the College of Physicians (of which he was Librarian), the Society of Antiquaries (of which he was a Fellow), and the Académie Royale in Paris. Besides authors whose books had not been deposited, but who gave their books, in January 1771 the London booksellers William and John Richardson presented their six-volume edition of Leland's *Collectanea*. The *Philosophical Transactions* of the Royal Society came regularly by gift;[54] from 1770 the Commissioners of Longitude presented their publications, beginning with a run of the *Nautical Almanac* from 1766; and in 1772 the Society of Antiquaries presented the first volume of its *Miscellaneous tracts*, published two years ealier.

Books published by the University Presses, to which it might be thought the libraries would be especially alert, posed similar problems. Many (but by no means all) Cambridge authors or editors presented their own works, and books of congratulatory verses by members of the University reached the Library with no difficulty; yet in 1769 the Library was constrained to buy from John Woodyer a copy of Francis Godwin's *De praesulibus Angliae* published in 1743: published by subscription, it had been subscribed for by two-thirds of the colleges and by Conyers Middleton himself, but only Sion College amongst the copyright libraries appeared in the list of subscribers. Baskerville's folio Bible of 1763, also published by subscription, arrived only when the Library bought a copy specially bound in red morocco from Thomas Merrill in the autumn of 1768 (the year in which it was remaindered) for six guineas. These two books were only untypical in that they were some of the few, certainly no more than a minority, to reach the Library from the Press during this period despite the

---

54 The American Philosophical Society, not of course affected by English copyright legislation, sent the first volume of its *Transactions* in December 1772 and annually thereafter.

fact that the close association of the two institutions allowed the University to acquire credit with the local booksellers by means of remaindered copies of *Suidas Lexicon*, rather than with cash. The arrival from John Archdeacon, the University Printer, of twenty-six volumes of the Statutes printed at Cambridge in 1762–6 broke with long-established practice, but the break was no more than temporary. It was not until 14 March 1786 that the Syndics of the Press agreed that 'one Copy of every Book whereof the whole or Part of the Expense of printing is defrayed by the University, be reserved for the Use of the public Library'[55] – a decision that was neither designed to include every book actually printed at the Press nor apparently even aware of the provisions of the Act of 1710. The Oxford press also presented complications. Not unnaturally, Oxford secured its legal position on publishing Clarendon's *Life* in 1759 by registering it at the Stationers' Company: as only the text was in question, the University entered and deposited only the octavo, and not the folio, edition. The work arrived at Cambridge later in the year, but Oxford also presented a copy of the folio edition to Cambridge. Blackstone's *Great charter and Charter of the forest*, printed at Oxford the same year, came as a gift from Blackstone himself, and Edward Huddesford presented his new edition (1760) of Edward Lhuyd on fossils, while the University presented two Delegates' books in the next few years, Thomas Hyde's *Historia religionis veterum Persarum* (1760) and the first volume of Clarendon's *State papers* (1767). Others had to be bought, yet the Library made no attempt even here to acquire the most important books as they came out: one of the few exceptions was the reprint, from the

[55] University Archives Pr.V.2, 'Orders for the Press' 14 March 1786. In 1586 Thomas Thomas (Printer to the University from 1583 to 1588) had also agreed to 'give unto thuniversitie librarie one perfecte copie or booke well and sufficientlie bounde of every impression that he shall prynt within Sixtene Daies after he hathe fynished the said bookes' (University Archives Pr.B.2(2), printed in John Morris 'Restrictive practices in the Elizabethan book trade: the Stationers' Company *v.* Thomas Thomas 1583–8' *Trans. Cambridge Bibliographical Society* 4 (1967) pp. 276–90, at p. 286. The agreement seems to have lapsed during the time of his successor John Legate.

original plates engraved at the end of the seventeenth century, of Martin Lister's *Historia conchyliorum* published in 1770, which was bought in December that year. The circumstances in which the decision was taken to purchase this last book were straightforward, since Oxford was unlikely to register a reprint of copper plates at the Stationers' Company, but more often publication and questions over whether to buy a particular book were nagged by doubt. It was not unknown for books bought in good faith to be returned later when a copyright deposit copy turned up, as happened with Alexander Dow's history of Hindustan: the Library bought a copy from Merrill on 9 August 1768, and paid for it on 8 November, but a few days later Woodyer, the rival bookseller, delivered a parcel of six items from the Stationers' Company including the same work, and the bought copy was returned to Merrill.

Whatever the practical difficulties that faced the Library when it chose to see them, the University's hold on privileges granted to it by Act of Parliament was becoming so slight that their slipping away might have caused little real change. The 1710 Act produced all too few books for the Library, and the Library responded with an uninterest that verged on somnolence. Yet this same legislation lay behind disputes within the trade itself that were of crucial financial importance and therefore of absorbing interest to all concerned. The debate over literary property, and the University's rights to free books from publishers, seemed to have little in common either in their matter or in the contrasting interest that either could arouse, but they were indissolubly linked in the 1710 Act. The point was made in a way more characteristic of the nineteenth century than of the eighteenth, and with more vivacity than the University had become accustomed to, by one of the most improbable figures ever to have been charged with the Library.

If public appointments within and without the University are considered appropriate criteria, then by far the most

10   Edmund Law (1703–1787), *Protobibliothecarius*. From a mezzotint
by William Dickinson after a painting by George Romney, 1777.
Size of original 455 × 355 mm.

eminent of those who held the office of *Protobibliothecarius* in the eighteenth century was Edmund Law (fig. 10), who was elected on 15 May 1760 following the death of F. S. Parris.[56] Law was one of the most remarkable pluralists of his generation; his career was crowned in 1769 with his consecration as Bishop of Carlisle, when he contrived not only a royal warrant and a dispensation from the Archbishop of Canterbury to hold the rectory of Greystoke in Cumberland (where he had first been instituted in 1739) but also to retain his Mastership of Peterhouse until his death in 1787. He was, moreover, a man in whom worldly success (to judge from his career in the church) and a reputation among his contemporaries for a love of books, were perfectly at ease. Admitted to St John's College in 1720, he took his M.A. from Christ's in 1727, having been elected to a Fellowship there the previous year. His scholarly reputation was founded in 1731 with his annotated translation into English of Archbishop William King's *Essay on the origin of evil*, and four years later with his contributions to the 1735 edition of Stephanus' *Thesaurus*. In 1743 he was appointed archdeacon of Carlisle, and moved from Greystoke to Salkeld. But, in the words of his biographer William Paley, 'Mr. Law was not one of those who lose and forget themselves in the country.' In 1745 the first edition of his *Considerations on the state of the world with regard to the theory of religion* was published (it was to go through seven editions in his lifetime), and in 1754 he returned to Cambridge to become Master of Peterhouse: the place was procured for him by Edmund Keene, previous Master and also Bishop of Chester, in an arrangement by which Keene's brother-in-law Venn Eyre received Law's former archdeaconry. Law was Vice-Chancellor in 1755–6. By the time of Parris' death he both

---

56 Grace Book *K* p. 326: Sayle (*Annals* p. 101) incorrectly gives the date as 1761. The following is drawn from Baker–Mayor 2 pp. 714–25; R. F. Scott (ed.) *Admissions to the College of St John the Evangelist* 3 (Cambridge 1903) pp. 331–3; Winstanley *Unreformed Cambridge* pp. 138–40; and William Paley *A short memoir of the life of Edmund Law, D.D.*, *extracted from Hutchinson's 'History of Cumberland'*, repr. with notes by Anonymus (1800).

commanded the necessary body of support and displayed sufficient scholarship to ensure his election as the new *Protobibliothecarius* in a contest against the less ostentatious Jonathan Wigley, former lecturer in Greek and Hebrew, and a collector of manuscripts, whose fellowship at Christ's had overlapped with Law's in 1736–40. It was, as Paley explained, 'a situation which, as it procured an easy and quick access to books, was peculiarly agreeable to his taste and habits'.[57] It was also one which (though like Conyers Middleton before him, he was to play little part in everyday administration) he was to render memorable by a single related publication. Middleton's pioneering study of Caxton had appeared during his term of office: Law's contribution, on copyright deposit, was similarly a milestone, and although it appeared only in 1770, the year after he had resigned his office, most of the arguments were drawn directly from his knowledge of proceedings at Cambridge.

For a few months in the middle of 1769 the Library was governed, in part, by a bishop. By the time of his consecration as Bishop of Carlisle on 24 February 1769, Law was, besides *Protobibliothecarius*, also Knightbridge Professor of Moral Philosophy (since 1764),[58] archdeacon of Stafford (since 1763), prebend of Lichfield (since 1763), prebend of Lincoln (since 1764), prebend of Durham (since 1767), rector of Greystoke and of course Master of Peterhouse. Many of the preferments were, in Paley's words, 'rather honourable expressions of regard from his friends, than of much advantage to his fortune',[59] but the score was a remarkable one

---

[57] Paley *A short memoir* p. 7.
[58] He had failed to be elected to the Lady Margaret Professorship in 1765: see Gray's letter to Mason, 17 January 1765 (Gray *Correspondence* 2 p. 860). Michael Lort, who found his Regius Professorship of Greek too restricting in that he was barred from college or other University offices, assumed too readily that Law would not hold the posts of Knightbridge Professor and *Protobibliothecarius* simultaneously: see British Library MS. Add. 35657 fo. 217 and Winstanley *Unreformed Cambridge* pp. 113–14, 117.
[59] Paley *A short memoir* p. 8.

nonetheless. He resigned from the Library on 4 October 1769, and from the 'Casuistical Professorship' on the same day.[60] But if his interest in the Library had been somewhat nugatory while he held a title to it, this was not apparent after he had resigned. In April 1769 the arguments for and against booksellers' perpetual copyright, that had rumbled long before 1710 and which the Copyright Act had signally failed to silence, came to a head and erupted with the decision in the Court of King's Bench in the case between Andrew Millar and Robert Taylor over the copyright of James Thomson's *Seasons*. The Court ruled that Taylor, a bookseller in Berwick, should compensate Millar for printing the work, which had been Millar's property since 1738.[61] Law could brook no such monopolistic tendencies. His *Observations occasioned by the contest about literary property*, printed at the University Press and published in 1770, was principally an attack on London booksellers, and involved matters of more interest to authors than to a copyright deposit library. But the first pages of his pamphlet were very pertinent to the libraries. Not only, considered Law, were the booksellers self-seeking in their arguments in favour of perpetual copyright, and in 'combining against the circulation of all copies that are not placed under their immediate protection'; they had also shown little willingness to co-operate with the clauses in the 1710 Act relating to the deposit of books at Stationers' Hall. 'Under the latter Act', he declared,

very few books of value have been obtained, the Booksellers being determined not to lose so many Copies of the largest Paper, as this Act requires to be delivered, and chusing rather to forfeit all the benefit of it, and trust one another, by never entering their Books in the Register of the Stationers-Hall; or when this method is not safe enough, entering only one Volume of each sett; that being deemed effectual to prevent any others of the trade from printing such sett upon them. And thus, when complete

[60] Vouchers 4 October 1769.
[61] See James Burrow *The question concerning literary property, determined by the Court of King's Bench on 20th April 1769* (1773).

setts of works have been claimed for any of the foresaid Libraries, or even offers made to purchase the remaining Volumes not entered as the Acts direct, the Bookseller has not only refused to part with them gratis, but even to sell the remaining Volumes to such claimants, unless those other Volumes, that had been delivered, were likewise paid for at the same time.[62]

This last sally was directed at Andrew Millar, who had recently turned off the University's agent charged with the task of collecting the final volume of Thomas Blackwell's *Memoirs of the court of Augustus*: Millar had been responsible for the third and last volume, published in London in 1763, following the appearance of the first two over the imprint of Hamilton, Balfour and Neill of Edinburgh in 1753–5. Had Law so wished, he could have furnished many more details of the difficulties besetting the Library as a privileged depository of copyright books. Publishers' willingness to run the risk of piracy, the lack of a proper deterrent against those who flouted the law, and the unrealistic provisions for the libraries to claim books due to them (which had then to be delivered within ten days) all contributed to the collapse of the Act by the mid-century. The Library was not interested in school books, manuals of domestic economy, or books of self-improvement, all of which appeared in the Register, while works of scholarly interest to the University formed a pitiful minority. The importance of this minor literature in the context of a national deposit library was realized only in the mid-nineteenth century as the Library's purposes were redefined. For the moment, however, no such modern concept existed in England. One of the purposes of the Copyright Act, like the Licensing Acts before it, had been to provide the universities and the other main libraries with not so much a complete archive of British publishing as the scholarly books necessary to their more local purposes. Its effect was very different. The number of books at Stationers' Hall to be claimed declined, and with it the number of those that held any interest for the libraries concerned. But it

---

[62] Law *Observations* pp. 3–4.

was to be another forty years before the matter was taken in hand.

Law resigned from his office of *Protobibliothecarius* in October 1769. The election of his successor had begun the previous January, when John Jebb, one of the most able men of his generation and an ardent promoter of university reform, was reported to have entered the lists.[63] But the contest lay in the end between two men of very different calibre, Joseph Thorpe of St Catharine's whose only previous university office had been as Junior Proctor in 1756, and John Barnardiston, Master of Corpus Christi College since 1764 and Vice-Chancellor in 1764–5.[64] Barnardiston was elected comfortably, and so joined Stephen Whisson, but a few months later the staff was again changed following the death on 22 November 1770 of Thomas Goodall: he was succeeded as Schools and assistant Library Keeper by John Marshall, formerly butler to the Master of Caius.[65] Barnardiston remained as *Protobibliothecarius* only until 1778, when he died, but Marshall remained to see a new century.

Barnardiston's arrival made little difference to the administration of the Library, and despite Law's outburst the funereal rate of accessions continued as before. As if in imitation of the modest effort put into purchases and into copyright deposit, donations proved to be similarly piecemeal, now as previously. The publication of *Cantabrigia depicta* in 1763, the first local guide book to treat the University Library at length, provided a certain *éclat* which over the next few years introduced a trickle of curious visitors: Christian VII of Denmark in August 1768,[66] the Corsican General Pasquale de' Paoli, in England after his defeat at the hands of France, in 1770,[67] John Wilkes in 1771,[68] and the Duke of Württemberg in 1776, and some, such

[63] *Cambridge Chronicle* 28 January 1769.
[64] R. Masters *History of the College of Corpus Christi with additional matter by John Lamb* (Cambridge 1831) pp. 251–2.
[65] Vouchers 1770–1; *Cambridge Chronicle* 23 November and 1 December 1770.
[66] *Ibid.*, 3 September 1768.   [67] *Ibid.*, 21 April 1770.   [68] Cooper *Annals* 4 p. 362.

as Christian VII,[69] left gifts. The strong affinities between England and Naples bore fruit in the gift by Charles III of Bayardi's *Prodromo delle antichità d'Ercolano* (Naples 1752)[70] and a succession of further books including, after his removal to Spain, catalogues of Greek and Arabic manuscripts in Madrid and the Escorial,[71] while in 1762 the young King Ferdinand sent a gold coin of the Emperor Augustus.[72] The gift of the Ibarra Sallust by its translator, the Infante Gabriel, brought to the Library in 1773 one of the most beautiful and impressive books printed in the eighteenth century.[73] The Library could not always (even had it wished to) look for such regalia. While William Burrell, formerly of St John's and now a successful lawyer and an M.P., added six 'Chinese Mss.' to Archdeacon Lewis' cabinet in 1772,[74] and in 1771 Richard Farmer passed on a bow and arrows brought back by John Byron from the south seas,[75] most donations were more mundane and – perhaps – of more immediate use. The University acknowledged these gifts when appropriate, but they were received into a library run with singularly little energy. While Farmer was prepared to deposit curiosities, and Thomas Gray (who in 1768 prompted William Taylor *How to give Algarotti's Opere* (Livorno 1764–5))[76] recognized something of the Library's position, its staff showed no inclination to search out gifts, pursue new publications, or improve its purchases. It was in danger of becoming all but moribund.

Once again, as had happened earlier in the century, the proof

---

[69] In 1771 he presented F. M. Regenfuss *Auserlesne Schnecken Muscheln und andre Schaalthiere* (Copenhagen 1758: Tab. b.55). See also *Cambridge Chronicle* 5 January 1771.   [70] Syn.5.75.3. See also University Archives *Epistolae Academiae* 2 709.

[71] University Archives *Letters 1613–1868* 12 April 1764; Grace Book *K* pp. 393, 395; *Letters 1613–1868* 9 December 1775; Grace Book *A* pp. 35–6. Copies of the books were also sent to the British Museum and the Bodleian: cf. *Archivo general de Simancas* Catálogo 17 (1947) pp. 247, 209.

[72] Grace Book *K* p. 360. He also gave the first two volumes of *Le pitture antiche d'Ercolano*, and promised more (Grace Book *K* pp. 360, 361, 374; University Archives *Letters 1613–1868* 19 October 1762; *Epistolae Academiae* 2 743).

[73] Most copies seem to have been given away by the Infante, to either individuals or institutions.

[74] Accessions Book 11 February 1772.   [75] *Ibid.*, 24 November 1771.

[76] Gray *Correspondence* 3 pp. 995–6; an exactly similar set is in Pembroke College Library.

that all was not quiescent came in a series of thefts. In 1772 it was found that the only surviving copy of a Sarum Breviary printed on vellum at Venice in 1483 had been stolen.[77] It proved to be, of its kind, an isolated case. The affair of Charles Burney was equally lamentable, if for different reasons. The son of the great Dr Burney, Charles came up to Caius in 1777, where he was described by William Cole as being 'very studious & industrious', and was unusual in coming into the Library virtually every day. His arrival at Caius, however, was shortly followed by various suggestive discoveries in the Library. Cole described what then happened:

Mr. Tyson of Benet calling on me this Day Thursd. Oct: 23.1777, told me, that he & the Master of Eman: being in the Library, found some Books ill used, & which could not have been returned in that Condition without the Schole Keeper's observing it: so concluded that it must have been done in the Library: whereupon an Order was given, that none under Mr. of Arts shd. be permitted to come there. Marshall the Schole Keeper accordingly acquainted Mr. Berney with the Order, who regularly came every Day & stayed till the Doors were closed. He however occasionally got Books in Mr. Tilliard's Name, & sending them back, on some Occasion, the Man observed that several Books were misplaced: & in searching for them that a great Number had been taken away, chiefly classical books of Elzevir Editions; whereupon he began to suspect Mr. Berney, & complained to Mr. Whisson, the Under Librarian, who advised him to be quiet, & contrive to get into his Chambers, & see if he could discover any of the lost Books: the Bedmaker said, it would be difficult, as her Master was very studious, & hardly 20 Minutes out of his Room at a Time except at Dinner Time: he got in at that Time & found about 35 Classical books in a dark Corner, which he had taken the University Arms out of, & put his own in their Place; & the Tutor being spoke to, he went into Hall the Day it was first discovered to him & then disappeared: & this Week a Box of Books belonging to the Library was sent from London, whither he had sent them. What further will be done is unknown. I pity his Father, who must sensibly feel the Stroke; as the young Man can never appear again in the University & so his views in this way utterly overturned.[78]

---

[77] It subsequently passed into the collection of Count MacCarthy, and later into the Bibliothèque Nationale: see Prothero *Bradshaw* pp. 101–2.

[78] On all this see Ralph S. Walker 'Charles Burney's theft of books at Cambridge' *Trans. Cambridge Bibliographical Soc.* 3 (1962) pp. 313–26, including a note by J. C. T. Oates. A list of his thefts was printed in 1808, no doubt at the behest of disaffected members of the University who sought to stop him taking a degree.

Burney completed his university education far from the scene of his teenage crimes, at King's College, Aberdeen, and was able finally to take a Cambridge degree only by royal mandate in 1808. He had stolen ninety-one volumes, all from the open shelves and all but three from the Royal Library. Burney's library later became celebrated, but the list of books stolen in 1777 betrayed little sign of being particularly attractive to the bibliophile in view of what else was available; if, on the other hand, he stole to pay his way (though it seems unlikely), the thefts were equally senseless. His sister believed, as she put it, 'the origin of that fatal deed to have been a Mad rage for possessing a library, and that the subsequent sale only occurred from the fear of discovery'. In any case, it seems that the offence was quickly forgiven by Barnardiston's successor Richard Farmer, who in 1792 was corresponding with him about some manuscripts he had allowed Burney to borrow.[79]

These unhappy events aside, the 1770s also saw two innovations that were out of the ordinary. The first was due more to Richard Farmer than to Barnardiston, even though it was begun while Barnardiston was still nominally in charge. The pictures in the Library had been left unattended for too long, and fashions had changed. On 12 July 1776, during Farmer's term as Vice-Chancellor, Joseph Freeman submitted a bill for attention to thirteen portraits including the sixteenth-century paintings of Edmund Grindal, John Whitgift and Queen Elizabeth as well as the more recent accessions, Isaac Whood's paintings of John Moore and of Charles, Viscount Townshend.[80] The bill was authorized by Farmer himself. On 10 September following, Christopher Sharp charged for further frames for drawings and other smaller pieces, and for stretching and pasting a copy of Magna Carta. These activities proved to be only a beginning in an operation that did much to change the appearance of the interior of the Library. Freeman did further work in October 1778, and cleaned and relined

[79] Percy A. Scholes *The great Dr. Burney* (Oxford 1948) 1 p. 348.
[80] Vouchers. See also Goodison *Cambridge portraits* p. 3.

Robert Peake's portrait of Charles I (now in the Old Schools)[81] in 1784. By the end of the century the Library presented an extraordinarily assorted gallery of illustrations. Besides the large portraits, the assemblage included a print of Sanderson Miller's and James Essex's Gothick tower at Wimpole (framed by Sharpe in 1777, and presumably the one published by Lord Hardwicke that year),[82] a specimen of Caslon's printing types and a chart illustrating different handwritings (both framed by H. Atherton in 1779), sheets setting out the succession of University Officers, John McArthur's map of Glasgow (received from the Stationers' Company in 1779, and one of the very few sheet maps to be acquired in the eighteenth century), and specimens of 'Indic Characters', framed by Atherton at the same time as he coped with a 'Warrant of the Empress of Russia' and mended an oriental fire-screen: he then went on to frame Capability Brown's altered and unfulfilled plan to transform the Backs.[83] Towering over all these distractions, Reinagle's portrait of John Nicholson was presented by its subject, and hung in place on the stairs at the desire of Farmer on 31 July 1790.[84]

The inspiration for all this came from Farmer, and, later, from Thomas Kerrich, but neither had anything to do with the other touch of modernity imposed on the Schools in the 1770s. In the winter of 1773–4 the University took delivery of a 'Large double tier' stove for the divinity school, supplied by the manufacturer and patentee Abraham Buzaglo of The Strand, and advertised as possessing properties ideally suited to the Schools: 'They cast an equal & agreeable Heat to every Part of the Room, are not attended with any Stench, or offensive Smell, consume less Coals by two Thirds than any Stove, cast more Heat, melt the Snow & Ice that lodge on Hot Houses,

---

[81] Goodison *Cambridge portraits* no. 17. The bill is in the Vouchers for 1783–4.
[82] A copy is kept in the Map Room, Views x.4 (102). See also Thomas Cocke *The ingenious Mr Essex, architect, 1722–1784* (Fitzwilliam Museum 1984) p. 36 and plate.
[83] On 17 November 1779 Joseph Freeman charged a guinea 'To making Alterations in M[r] Browns Plan & putting in the walks Rivers &c as in its present state'.
[84] Goodison *Cambridge portraits* 50; Vouchers 1789–90. See below, p. 311.

preferable to any Fleuse in Practice: require no Repairs for 100 Years ...'[85] Central heating had come to the Schools, if not quite to the Library on the first floor. In a period that, after the excitement of the new east front, could show few other improvements, it was a welcome relief.

[85] Quoted from Buzaglo's trade card in the Vouchers for 1774. See also J. C. T. Oates 'Hot air from Cambridge' *The Library* 5th ser. 18 (1963) pp. 140–2.

8

RICHARD FARMER

OF ALL THE University eccentrics whom Henry Gunning was able to recall in his *Reminiscences*, published in 1854, few were more minutely remembered than Richard Farmer, William Pugh and John Beverley. Pugh crowned his career as cataloguer in the Library by being sacked and subsequently losing his senses; Beverley, a less sympathetic figure, more successfully (but only slightly more competently) combined the duties of Esquire Bedell with other employment as a cataloguer; and Richard Farmer was at once *Protobibliothecarius* and Master of Emmanuel College.

John Barnardiston, *Protobibliothecarius* since 1769, died on 27 June 1778. The election of his successor lay between two members of Emmanuel, Richard Farmer, Master since 1775, and Francis Wilcox, Fellow of the college since 1767. Predictably, Farmer proved the stronger candidate and was elected with little difficulty. He brought to the post both new enthusiasm (not always directed as economically as it might have been) and fresh interests. As no-one who voted for him can have failed to be aware.

He had no taste for the prevailing pursuit in the university, the mathematics, nor ever paid any regard to it after he had obtained his first two degrees; but he cultivated the belles lettres with great assiduity, though with little appearance of regular study. His knowledge of books in all languages, and in every science, was very comprehensive.[1]

Isaac Reed wrote this in the light both of friendship and of shared interests in Shakespeare and in book collecting. His knowledge of Farmer, developed through extended visits to

[1] Quoted in [W. Seward] *Biographiana* (1799) 2 p. 581. For Reed's relations with Farmer see also his *Diaries 1762–1804* ed. Claude E. Jones (Berkeley 1946).

Cambridge rather than through local familiarity, chimed exactly with that of Samuel Parr, who as another visitor to Emmanuel also observed qualities that had nothing to do with the two men's complete antipathy in politics.

His knowledge is various, extensive and recondite. With much seeming negligence, and perhaps, in later years, some real relaxation, he understands more, and remembers more, about common and uncommon subjects of literature, than many of those who would be thought to read all the day, and meditate half the night. In quickness of apprehension, and acuteness of discrimination, I have not often seen his equal. Through many a convivial hour have I been charmed by his vitality.[2]

Reed and Parr might also have mentioned that he was lampooned and attacked in caricature, that his Shakespearean studies (supported by an enthusiasm for the playhouse at Stourbridge) were not universally appreciated, and that his ungainly and even gross behaviour inevitably attracted the attention of his enemies. For while to men such as Reed, George Steevens, Edmund Malone and Thomas Percy[3] Farmer's wide-ranging knowledge of English literature was both welcome and readily acknowledged, the minutiae of literary history and exegesis did not find such a ready audience in, for example, Peter Musgrave, the 'Cambridge Taylor', at a political meeting in Cambridge in 1792, when Farmer seems to have displayed little acumen. (Fig. 11)[4]

But while he became a by-word for his miscellaneous literary knowledge, Farmer's own output was slight, and confined almost solely to his *Essay on the learning of Shakespeare*,

---

[2] Samuel Parr *Aphorisms, opinions and reflections* (1826) p. 63.
[3] *The correspondence of Thomas Percy and Richard Farmer* ed. C. Brooks (Louisiana 1946). Various transcripts by Steevens from University Library books were sold with Reed's library in 1807.
[4] See, in particular, *The battle between Doctor Farmer and Peter Musgrave the Cambridge taylor* (1792) with a frontispiece caricaturing Farmer. The argument between the two men occurred originally at a meeting held in Cambridge on 6 July to pass a resolution supporting the King's proclamation of 21 May against riots and seditious publications: 'The address ... was moved by the Earl of Hardwicke, and seconded by Mr. Vachell; a few words in opposition were said by Mr. Musgrave, a reputable taylor and draper in the town, but the meeting did not seem to acquiesce in his opinion ... Mr. Yorke and Dr. Farmer spoke in support of the address ...' (*Cambridge Chronicle and Journal* 14 July 1792).

11 Grand Battle at Cambridge, 1792, between Doctor Bookworm [Richard Farmer], and Peter Musgrave, the Taylor!' From an etching by Richard Newton, 1792, prefixed to *The battle between Doctor Farmer and Peter Musgrave* (1792). Size of original 200 × 249 mm.

published in 1767, when he was still only thirty-two. His larger project, the publication of a history of his native Leicestershire enlarged from the earlier work by Thomas Staveley, had to be abandoned in the form he had planned, and after returning the subscriptions he had gathered in 1766, Farmer passed his materials on to John Nichols, into whose own history they were incorporated. With this his literary career came to an end, if appearance in print is to be the sole criterion. He was elected Master of his college, to which he was devoted, in 1775, and almost immediately served the first of two terms (the second was in 1787–8) as Vice-Chancellor. He held both the Mastership and the post of *Protobibliothecarius* (as well as, for many years, the living of Swavesey, nine miles north-west of Cambridge, on the edge of the Fens) until his death. But though he had reached the peak of his career at Cambridge, further preferment in the Church followed, with stalls in (successively) Lichfield, Canterbury and St Paul's Cathedral. Following his preferment to St Paul's in 1788, an increasing proportion of his time was spent in London, where he was able to give attention not only to the ornamenting of the cathedral with statuary but also (according to Gunning) to the stalls of old books in the churchyard and nearby.[5]

Farmer possessed a library celebrated nationally for its out-of-the-way curiosities and for its range, and by the time of his death it had become one of the most remarkable of its kind anywhere. Its dispersal at auction in May and June 1797 took thirty-five days, and King the auctioneer did not exaggerate when he described it as 'The most rare and copious Assemblage of Old English Poetry, that, perhaps, was ever exhibited at one View: together with a great variety of Old Plays and early printed Books, English and Foreign, in the Black Letter; many of which are extremely scarce.' Of it Farmer himself, when contemplating the production of a printed catalogue, had written,

This collection of Books is by no means to be considered as an *Essay* towards a perfect *Library*: the *Circumstances* and the *Situation* of the *Collector* made such an attempt both unnecessary, and *impracticable*. Here are few *Publications* of *great price*, which were already to be found in the excellent Library of *Emanuel* College: but it is believed, that *not many private* Collections contain a greater Number of really *curious* and *scarce*

---

[5] Gunning *Reminiscences* 1 p. 185; [W. Seward] *Biographiana* (1799) 2 pp. 592–8. On Farmer generally see, besides the article in *DNB*, E. S. Shuckburgh *Richard Farmer, an essay* (Cambridge 1884) and S. C. Roberts *Richard Farmer* (Arundell Esdaile lecture 1961). Many of Nichols' copious notes are gathered, with further references, in Edward L. Hart (ed.) *Minor lives; a collection of biographies by John Nichols* (Cambridge, Mass., 1971) pp. 17–40 etc.

Books; and, perhaps *no one* is so rich in the ancient *Philosophical English Literature.*[6]

Farmer also spoke no more than the truth, but he quite ignored one other aspect of his collecting. Not only did he feel able to pursue his interests to the complete exclusion of the University Library of which he had charge (it bought not a single fifteenth-, sixteenth- or early seventeenth-century English book during his librarianship, any more than it had under his immediate predecessors), but he also made the comparison not with the library of the University but with that of his own much smaller college collection. Despite his devotion to many of the curiosities in the University's possession, he failed to realize or acknowledge that the University Library might also have collected profitably in the fields that he made his own. The bibliomaniac took precedence over the librarian, who had never learned the lessons implied by Thomas Percy's requests in the 1760s to Farmer to borrow books on his behalf from the University Library.[7] It is galling, but unprofitable, to reflect that had Farmer chosen to channel only his Elizabethan and Jacobean literature into the Library, the University would now possess a collection in this field equalled even today by only one or two libraries elsewhere.

In view of the fact that the Library did not benefit in any way where Farmer's own interests might be at stake, much of this may appear unnecessarily removed and theoretical. His executors were faced with more tangible embarrassments, arising from his careless attitude to the books he was employed to preserve. It was not uncommon in the eighteenth, and for much of the nineteenth, centuries for the librarians and even

---

[6] Quoted from King's preface to the sale catalogue. On Farmer as a collector see L. J. Lloyd 'Dr Richard Farmer, 1735–97' *Book Collector* 26 (1977) pp. 524–36.

[7] *Correspondence of Thomas Percy and Richard Farmer, passim.* Percy borrowed the 1574 edition of Tottel's Miscellany in June 1762 and finally returned it to Farmer in the winter of 1766–7, but it is no longer in the Library. Among various books borrowed by Farmer for Percy was Wyat's *Seven penitential psalms* (1549), then thought to be unique: at the time the book was still on the open shelves as part of a pamphlet volume that has since been dismembered.

other members of the University to be reimbursed personally, on the strength of a private invoice, for books bought on behalf of the Library: this widespread practice was in addition to other regular arrangements with booksellers. Thus in 1788, for example, Farmer submitted a straightforward account for £15.8s.0d. listing subscriptions and other book bills paid by him personally on behalf of the Library: it included subscriptions for Woide's type facsimile of the Codex Alexandrinus (1786), G. B. de Rossi's *Variae lectiones Veteris Testamenti ex MSS.*, published at Parma in 1784–99, three guineas towards Boydell's as yet unpublished Shakespeare, edited by George Steevens, a guinea towards a setting of the Te Deum by James Kent that was never published in the form Farmer expected, and four guineas for Roesel von Rosenhof's *Historia naturalis ranarum nostratium*, first published at Nuremberg in 1758. All this was perfectly normal, for although von Rosenhof's book was entered in the Accessions Register only in October 1790 – and then as a donation – this may have been no more than a clerical slip resulting from some minor misunderstanding. But other similar transactions are more difficult to dismiss. In October 1791 Farmer received six pounds for one of the numbers of Boydell's Shakespeare and for a suitable portfolio in which to store it. On 9 November 1793 he submitted a bill for, and was paid for, not only a further subscription to the Shakespeare, but also one for the Boydell Milton and a payment of nine pounds for Harding's illustrations to Shakespeare. Besides this, Farmer also claimed four guineas for eight oriental manuscripts and a guinea for a manuscript of Priscian. Since all of these printed books had been published comfortably before 1797, by the time of Farmer's death in that year they should have been in the Library. But they were not.

He happily lent the Library's rarest treasures to friends and acquaintances. Gebhard Friedrich August Wendeborn was no more than an acquaintance, yet when he visited Cambridge during the Long Vacation in 1784 Farmer instructed the library assistants that what books or manuscripts he needed should be sent to his hotel.[8] More of this same casual attitude emerged during the attempts to tidy up his affairs after his death. In October 1797 his executors produced an accumulation of books to which the University clearly had a title, beginning with a manuscript volume on the history of the town and University that had been given to the Library in 1786 by Henry Turner, incumbent of Burwell and Newmarket. Farmer had inscribed a note about the donor on the front board, but as the book had never been listed in the Accessions Register it had not, so far, apparently reached the Library.[9] The executors' other offerings were less dramatic, ranging from the Rowley poems to the just published account of Lord Macartney's embassy to China, in three volumes with a folio volume of plates. Much of the rest of the list was taken up with odd numbers of part books and stray volumes from larger collections such as the fifth volume of the *Biographia Britannica* (for which the bookseller John Merrill had been paid in October 1794) and Alexander Dalrymple's *Oriental repertory*. As for his registered borrowings, half a dozen printed books could not be accounted for, including the Royal Library copy of the extremely rare *Compendious booke of godly and spirituall songs* (a paraphrase of the Psalms published at Edinburgh in 1621), the elder Samuel Pegge's *Memoirs* of Roger de Weseham (1761), three parts of the younger Pegge's *Curialia*

---

[8] G. F. A. Wendeborn *Erinnerungen aus seinem Leben* ed. C. D. Ebeling (Hamburg 1813) pp. 336–7; F. H. Stubbings 'Visiting scholar, 1784' *Emmanuel College Magazine* 60 (1977–8) pp. 20–1. In the 1950s, a group of University Library papers, including the Rustat Fund accessions register and the list of books bought with the Newcome benefaction were discovered to have been retained by Emmanuel after his death, and were returned to the Library (*Reporter* 1956–7 p. 1401).

[9] MS. Ff.3.33. M. R. James, following a pencilled note in Nasmith's catalogue of the manuscripts (see below, pp. 344–8), believed that it had once formed part of the gift of William Moore (University Librarian, d. 1659) to Gonville and Caius College even though the contents do not exactly tally with those described in Bernard's *Catalogi* (1697): see M. R. James *Descriptive catalogue of the manuscripts in Gonville and Caius College* 1 (1907) pp. xi, xx.

It may perhaps also be assumed that MS. Ff.3.34, a fragment of an eleventh-century copy of a commentary on Genesis attributed to Eucherius, Bishop of Lyon, arrived in the 1790s, since it is shelved between the two volumes known to have been among Farmer's effects: again, there is no record of accession.

(still, in 1797, in course of publication), a recently issued collection of poems by John Bidlake, and John Manwood's much older collection on forest laws. Two manuscripts were missing as well. It was presumed that Farmer had lent one of Moore's manuscripts, containing papers relating to various state trials under the early Tudors and now numbered Ee.3.1, to John Baynes, Fellow of Trinity College, who had unfortunately died ten years before.[10] The other was the well-known transcript (MS. Ll.5.10) of poems by William Dunbar and others made in 1622–3, and had most probably been borrowed by Farmer for the use of John Pinkerton in compiling his *Ancient Scottish poems*, published in 1786. Farmer, and his executors, were clearly responsible for the missing printed books, as they were for the books paid for by the University that had never been delivered up. But because of an omission in the University's rules, it was decided that 'The orders for the Library give no mulcts for M.S.S. lost – This loss must therefore be submitted to the Syndics of the Library.' Thus the two manuscripts were written down as being worth nothing. After various complicated calculations, involving the offsetting of Farmer's stipend of £50, his payments for an assortment of books (including, oddly, the de Rossi and one or two other books for which he had already received payment in his lifetime) and acquisition also of a number of other modern books from his library, the University ended up due to pay his executors £106.6s.3d. With the payment of this sum on 20 March 1798 the affair was almost, but not quite, closed. A few months later, Joseph Farmer, Richard Farmer's heir, applied for and obtained repayment of £25.18s.6d.[11] on the grounds that the oriental manuscripts, the Priscian, Harding's Shakespeare and half a dozen missing printed books had been returned, together with the Dunbar manuscript. The Dunbar is still in the Library, and the Priscian can be identified as

[10] MS. Oo.7.54 fo. 15ᵛ.
[11] The final audited accounts for 1797–8 record, mistakenly, £15.18s.6d. The details of Farmer's estates are derived principally from the Vouchers and the annual audited university accounts.

MS. Ff.3.35, a fine early twelfth-century copy that has escaped the attentions of modern binders. Neither the Priscian nor the oriental manuscripts seem ever to have been added to the Accessions Register. The Edinburgh *Songs* have been missing seemingly ever since, but the manuscript lent to Baynes found its way into the collection of Sir Thomas Phillipps, and was noticed in time to be withdrawn from the auction of part of his library at Sotheby's in 1893: it was bought from Phillipps' executor and put back in its rightful place after an absence of over a century.[12]

In spite of this disorder in his personal affairs, as *Protobibliothecarius* Farmer saw a period of expansion, reorganization and general improvement to the Library that could not have been envisaged a few years earlier. Credit for much of this is also due to John Davies, Fellow of Trinity and an enthusiastic and able botanist, who was elected *Bibliothecarius* on Whisson's death in 1783,[13] five years after Farmer had entered office. Davies emerged triumphant over five other candidates in an election that offered rather more excitement than the organized predictability of Farmer's. As was usual, the proceedings followed two stages, of nominations on one day followed on the next by an election between those two who had scored the most nominations. On 10 November following Whisson's death, the six comprised Robert Tyrwhitt, Fellow of Jesus, who had recently caused trouble in the University over a supplicat for a degree by royal mandate,[14] and who received eleven nominations; John Davies, with seven nominations; Adam Wall, Fellow of Christ's, older than most as he was in his mid-fifties, with six; Thomas Kerrich, President of Magdalene since 1775, with four; and Edward Mapletoft, Fellow of Christ's, and Samuel Vince, then still Samuel Taylor

---

12 Phillipps MS. 10239; Sotheby's 19–22 June 1893 lot 273.
13 On Davies cf. Sir J. E. Smith *A defence of the Church and universities of England against such injurious advocates as Professor Monk* (1819) p. 51 and Warren R. Dawson *Catalogue of the manuscripts in the Linnean Society of London* 1. *Smith papers* (1934) p. 35. Whisson's funeral is described in the *Gentleman's Magazine* 53 (1783) p. 981. See also Nichols *Literary anecdotes* 3 pp. 657–8.   14 Winstanley *Unreformed Cambridge* p. 90.

Lecturer at Sidney Sussex, with one each. Despite Tyrwhitt's early lead, Davies romped home the next day with 108 votes in a landslide victory over Tyrwhitt's thirty-six.[15] He remained *Bibliothecarius* until 1817, in a position that quickly became subservient to Farmer on almost all matters affecting the development of the Library.

Nowhere was this more true than in acquisitions: Farmer's handling of the sale of the manuscripts of his friend Anthony Askew, familiar from Askew's house fifteen or more years earlier, was, as we shall see, original in its inception and triumphant in its execution. It was he who at last again looked seriously at the early printed books, and remarked with satisfaction the success that followed a visit by George Nicol in the company of a Mr Braithwaite in 1784: it prompted Nicol to present the first volume of the de Spira Livy of 1470, bought in 1778 at the sale of Robert Hoblyn's books for a guinea and which now joined the second volume in the Library since 1715. Farmer preserved Nicol's note donating the book, and to Nicol's own remarks added a sprawling comment of his own; 'This *Edition* was not in the Collection of D[r]. *Mead* or D[r]. Askew: nor is it in the *King's* or any known Library in *England*. the *2 Vols* are worth at least 50£.'[16] It spoils a good story to say that within a few years both George III and Cracherode possessed the book that Nicol knew otherwise only at Lyon: that knowledge would certainly not have entirely suppressed Farmer's enthusiasm. Under his guidance the Library extended its interests to encompass a wider range of subjects, whether modern French scholarship, bibliography, illustrated books or even modern science: despite his known aversion to mathematics, Farmer was Librarian in a period when additions both in that subject and in the sciences stretching from conchology to engineering were prominent in the Library's book bills for the first time. He presided over the gift in 1787 of two complete sets of printed orchestral parts to thirty-four of Haydn's

[15] Luard 245(3).
[16] Letter pasted inside Inc. 1608: Farmer's comment is dated 23 October 1784.

symphonies, a donation which heralded the serious beginning of an organized collection of music.[17] For general supplies of suitable books, the Library turned for the first time in many years to fresh and untried booksellers. The near monopoly that Cambridge booksellers had enjoyed was broken, with the Library at long last (and as in the 1680s) taking advantage of the offerings appearing in London booksellers' catalogues. It is unlikely that Farmer himself was responsible for all these innovations: some reflected the University's interests and influence in such matters much more than his own, and some simply echoed fundamental changes in the book trade. But there crept into the affairs of the Library an energy and spirit of enterprise that it had not witnessed for decades. In some respects Farmer's reign merely coincided with external factors that neither the University nor, by implication, the Library, could ignore, while in others his hand was a distinctive guiding presence.

The spectacle of eighteenth-century Cambridge was not looked on with favour by the reformers of the next century, and with good reason. The University Library suffered under men who knew little about how to go about their work and who had still less energy either to learn or to reform. The successes of the century were on the whole modest, and they were most marked in the arrangement and cataloguing of the collection – in other words, in tasks executed by casual employees rather than by officers of the University. This was as true at the end of the century as it had been, with the single honourable exception of John Taylor, fifty years before. Reform of the University depended on the conjunction of individual pressure, college sympathy and the University's corporately expressed willingness to countenance proposed change; reform of the Library similarly depended on a combination of interests that had not, as yet, been established. There had to be both interest and action on the part of a well

---

[17] These were perhaps given by Humphrey Aram Hole of Jesus College, an accomplished 'cellist. (I am grateful to Mr. D. W. Williams for advice on this point.)

led, energetic and imaginative staff, and the University itself needed to have more power within a system so far dominated by the colleges.

Attempts at reform in the University towards the end of the eighteenth century failed when they were directed at the University itself. The suggestion put forward in 1773 by John Jebb, the Unitarian-inclined Fellow of Peterhouse, that the old Senate House examinations should be replaced by annual examinations of all undergraduates on a university basis was defeated, in part at least, by college interests. It was discussed solely by the Caput, and never reached the Senate; and it was opposed even by so dedicated an educational reformer as William Powell, Master of St John's, where a twice-yearly public examination of undergraduates had been enforced since 1765.[18] As late as 1822 J. H. Monk, the biographer of Bentley, could still remark that Powell's opposition was 'not only justifiable, but laudable: since their [i.e. Jebb's proposals'] practical result, had they succeeded, must have been, to take all direction of education out of the respective colleges, and to place it in those of persons nominated in an order following the cycle of proctors'. 'Several different schemes of reform', Monk continued, 'were subsequently proposed by Mr. Jebb, without success; all tending to reduce the whole University into the state of one vast and unwieldy college, but without making any effectual provision for its administration in this altered state.'[19] There was, as Monk realized, a very real difficulty, in that educational reform, however desirable in itself, could not be prosecuted in a university that still lacked a central administration and showed little willingness in some quarters to countenance one. The colleges' domination of all university affairs, most frequently in the guise of the Caput, persisted long into the nineteenth century, and in the same way obscured the definition and even advancement of the University Library.

---

[18] For the subsequent tale of intrigue against a reform with a wide measure of support in the University at large see Winstanley *Unreformed Cambridge* pp. 318–30.
[19] 'Philograntus' *A letter to the Right Reverend John, Lord Bishop of Bristol* (1822) pp. 37–8.

To a considerable extent the development of the Library in the last decades of the eighteenth century depended on men other than Farmer: on the attention of such able figures as Thomas Martyn (Professor of Botany from 1762 to 1825), Richard Porson (elected Professor of Greek at last in 1792), Samuel Vince (Plumian Professor from 1796) and Isaac Milner, the first Jacksonian Professor of Chemistry, elected in 1783. All pursued active careers at Cambridge, unlike some of their colleagues, and all, insofar as their interests can be traced through the current accessions, had an influence on the growth of the Library. Farmer's own bias towards bibliographical, antiquarian and literary interests combined with this concentration in the sciences to give a distinctive bent to what the Library chose to purchase.[20] Neither Steevens' edition of Shakespeare, published under Boydell's auspices, nor William Hayley's edition of Milton came under the Copyright Act, and it would have been astounding had Farmer not arranged for the Library to subscribe. The concerns of the Society of Antiquaries formed another focus of his interest. But besides these desiderata there was also one very great help to him, in that many of the major lacunae in the Library's collections of theological books published earlier in the century had already been made good. He was thus able to concentrate on new books and on less familiar topics with less danger of damage to the value of the Library as a whole. The blossoming of textual studies of the Bible, encouraged by Porson and Kipling at Cambridge and by Kennicott, Holmes and others at Oxford,

[20] For one example of Farmer's familiarity with modern books needed for the Library cf. a letter from Cole written in November 1780 pleading (unsuccessfully as it transpired) with Horace Walpole for a volume of Walpole's *Anecdotes of painting in England*. Farmer 'then expressed a wish that you would be so kind to your old Alma Mater as to give your works to the Public Library, promising them an eminent place in it. You have ever been so generous to me in particular, that I am the worst person that could have been employed on such a begging errand, but my esteem for Dr Farmer, and zeal to have your books in the University Library, give me a confidence and assurance that I should hardly have ventured on without them.' Walpole felt more bountiful towards his old college (King's) however, and claimed to have set aside a collection of his publications in his will: the will does not mention them, and the books never arrived. W. S. Lewis (ed.) *Horace Walpole's correspondence with the Rev. William Cole* (1937) 2 pp. 246–9.

that helped bring about the type facsimiles of the Codex Alexandrinus and of the Codex Bezae, was a phenomenon fully reflected in the Library's acquisitions. All this was well within the tradition established already. But in other respects there were marked changes. Works such as Athenian Stuart's *Antiquities of Athens*, Lavater on physiognomy, Curtis' *Flora*, Soane's *Sketches in architecture* and Smeaton on the Eddystone Lighthouse were on subjects that had never before been properly represented in the Library's purchases of current books. The Bodoni edition of *The Castle of Otranto* (1791), sandwiched in January 1792 between a commentary on the Bible and Joseph Fenn's course of mathematics (Dublin 1759) betokened yet different interests. April 1784 brought a consignment of Scandinavica from Merrill, ranging from saga literature to the first three volumes of the *Acta* of the Royal Society of Sciences at Uppsala: the Library was already receiving the proceedings of learned bodies at St Petersburg, Paris and Berlin. Cook's voyages (the account of the 1776–8 voyage came via the Stationers' Company in October 1784) were a *sine qua non*, but Marmaduke Stalkartt's *Naval architecture* (1781), bought from Merrill in April 1785, was less predictable: Merrill also supplied the grandly illustrated catalogue of the medals belonging to Jean Charles Hedlinguer (Augsburg 1782) – a book considered to be of sufficient value to lock away – and quantities of French scientific books on mathematics, physics and electricity, while his supplies of English books ranged over fifty and more years.

Farmer did not buy only from the local trade. He had a better knowledge of the London booksellers than most of his predecessors, and the Library began to take advantage, hesitantly at first, of the annual catalogues issued by many of the metropolitan trade. Peter Elmsley's assortment of 114 volumes sent in 1786 was entirely foreign (he had succeeded Paul Vaillant as the leading retailer of French books) and was an extraordinary array of all branches of learning, including the first twelve volumes of Grosier's *Histoire générale de la Chine*

(Paris 1777–83), the La Croix du Maine library catalogue, Racine's works (Paris 1783), Dezallier d'Argenville's *Conchyliologie* (Paris 1780), a volume of Karsten Niebuhr's *Voyage en Arabie* (Amsterdam 1780), works on inscriptions, medicine, astronomy, snake poison, entomology, the first volume of Pallas' *Flora Rossica* (St Petersburg 1784), even Nathaniel Halhed's *Grammar of the Bengal language*, published at Hoogly in Bengal in 1778. Elmsley became a regular supplier, in the latter years of Farmer's librarianship being responsible for quantities of catalogues and standard bibliographical reference works arriving at Cambridge, some at least for the use of Pugh in his cataloguing, which is described below. By the time his bill for 1795 was paid, Elmsley had been succeeded by David Bremner, but his remarks on having to wait nearly five years for the money (apparently as a result of Pugh's, or perhaps Farmer's, failing to produce the bill for Davies to deliver up for payment) are not recorded. No other bookseller outside Cambridge was used so much. In buying from Payne's catalogues in 1791 and 1794 the Library went through Merrill rather than direct. Benjamin White's firm, specialists in natural history books, was applied to for Moses Harris on English insects and the first English work on algae, Thomas Velley's *Coloured figures of marine plants* (1795). (It was White, too, who supplied at Martyn's request the first volume of Pallas' *Flora Rossica*, delivered by Elmsley in 1786: booksellers seem to have been in the habit of sharing each other's deliveries, so that the Accessions Register and the individual bookseller's bill are complementary in the discovery of who supplied what.) Finally, besides the constant trade in Cambridge with Merrill, Deighton, the Nicholsons and (briefly) W. H. Lunn, and the orders from the major London booksellers, there was always a trickle of arrivals from sources outside the normal run. George Adams, better known as a mathematical instrument maker, invoiced the Library for his own work on the microscope on 19 December 1788 as the result of an order from the Vice-Chancellor, Francis Barnes. Solomon

Lyon provided a small group of Hebrew books in 1791, and Martyn arranged for floras of Austria and Piedmont to arrive in 1795. George Nicol, who had so benefited the Library in 1784 with his gift of the Venice Livy, turned up again once only, in March of the next year when he provided Farmer with the first volume of Herbert's edition of Ames' *Typographical antiquities* and (at twelve guineas) one of the most lavish of all late eighteenth-century English illustrated books: the two-volume series of reproductions of drawings taken chiefly from the collection of Charles Rogers, published in 1778. The choices bear the stamp of Farmer's own interests, and it was not untypical of his librarianship that neither the Rogers nor the Ames was entered in the Accessions Register.

The beginnings of a formal collection of maps can be traced to 1794. Odd single-sheet maps had arrived periodically under the Copyright Act, such as Donn's county map of Devon (1765) and John McArthur's plan of Glasgow (1778). The Newcome account paid for Dupré's historical atlas *Révolutions de l'univers* (Paris 1763), and in July 1777, keeping abreast with affairs outside Cambridge, the Library bought Thomas Jefferys' *American atlas* (1776). But by the end of 1794 it possessed a collection of county maps,[21] perhaps supplied by William Folden of Charing Cross.[22] Hitherto the practice had been to place maps on the walls, sometimes (as in the case of the plan of Glasgow) mounted on canvas and rollers.[23] Capability Brown's proposals for the Backs, altered by Joseph Freeman, were framed and hung by Atherton in November 1779,[24] and in 1781 Atherton also framed a plan of the canals. But these decorative measures, undertaken in the course of a general attempt to tidy up the University's collection of pictures, were satisfactory only for as long as the collection was small. The arrival of the county maps in 1794 made some change

---

[21] 'To M^r. Burleigh for Carriage of County Maps', 5s. (Marshall's bill, 1794).
[22] A receipt from him for £36.9s.0d. is dated 8 December 1794.
[23] Woodyer charged seven shillings for doing this to the Glasgow map on 21 April 1779.
[24] Atherton also charged for 'Glazing Part of it again' in 1784.

imperative. On 23 August, Charles Humfrey charged for making a temporary case 'to keep the maps in', and almost exactly a year later, on 30 August 1795, he replaced this with new cupboards, followed at the end of October with another cupboard 'on the other Side' – of what it is not clear.[25]

Farmer's over-riding attention to his own and his friends' interests obscured his appreciation of what might have been done had he emulated his contemporaries elsewhere. The Bodleian Library, for example, launched into serious expenditure on early printed books in 1787 – not so much on English literature as on the more obviously desirable classics:[26] in this respect, the great riches of Moore's library may have helped to obscure the Library's needs. In the purchase of early printed books, Cambridge lagged behind. But in two essential matters, Farmer's librarianship brought care and attention to the manuscripts and early printed books on a scale and in a way that they had not often previously received. He began to segregate early printing from the rest of the Library in a systematic manner, and under his aegis, too, a massive programme of binding and repairs transformed the appearance of the books on the shelves. Between 1778 and 1797 something like 20,000 volumes were attended to by the binders, and many were labelled on their spines for the first time. Within weeks of his election, Farmer had organized a stream of commissions to local binders that between 1790 and his death in 1797 was to reach over two thousand a year. Most of this work was on the older books in the Library, and comparatively little needed to be done to the eighteenth-century volumes: among the few modern books to receive attention were *Sir Charles Grandison* (1754), repaired in 1780, and *Don Quixote*, repaired in 1783,

---

[25] Details of these activities are drawn from the Vouchers.

[26] Ian Philip 'The background to Bodleian purchases of incunabula at the Pinelli and Crevenna sales, 1789–90' *Trans. Cambridge Bibliographical Soc.* 7 (1979) pp. 369–75. T. F. Dibdin later noted, after inspecting the early printed books at Cambridge, that 'the Collection of the earlier and more precious Classics ... is miserably meagre and reproachful. The Auctarium at Oxford is 1001 degrees beyond the "Lock-up Recess"' (MS. notebook 'Horae Bibliographicae Cantabrigienses', in the possession of the Earl of Plymouth).

presumably the victims of popularity. At first the work fell to booksellers who had long been associated with the Library, John Woodyer, John Merrill (who bound the Baker manuscripts in 1784),[27] and John Deighton; but gradually other, new, names appeared on invoices, of E. Stephenson, James Jackson, John Nicholson (better known as 'Maps' (fig. 12)), John Bowtell, W. Cowper, Joseph Gee (father and son), and William Page.

By no means all were equally skilled. At first, many of the more valuable books were handled by Merrill, but from 1785 they were sent instead to Bowtell, a man of outstanding talents and, despite his distressing penchant for discarding earlier bindings wholesale,[28] more sympathetic to volumes under his care than many of his contemporaries. He passed a large part of his career in binding for the Library, and his nephew was to be a member of its staff for thirty-five years. His arrival as a binder acceptable to the Library was so dramatic that it prompts all the more strongly so far unanswered questions about his earlier career. In 1785 he was thirty-two years old, clearly thoroughly experienced, yet his biographer[29] was unable to advance much information about his previous employment beyond suggesting that he might have served his apprenticeship with Nicholson. Whatever his background, however, his first surviving bill to the Library, dated 20 September 1785, reflected the trust that was already placed in his work. Besides attention to the Library's catalogue, it also detailed repairs to a Koran (four shillings) and 'An illuminated Persian M.S. of Astronomy & Nat^l Hist. in folio bound in Blue Turkey and ornamented all over with variegated gold – 1.18.0'. The exact identity of this 'Persian M.S.' poses something of a problem, since (not for the last time) Bowtell's bill was less than exact in describing precisely what he had done. The only book in the

[27] Vouchers 1783–4.

[28] A. I. Doyle 'Two medieval calendars and other leaves removed by John Bowtell from University Library MSS.' *Trans. Cambridge Bibliographical Soc.* 1 (1949) pp. 29–36.

[29] A. B. Gray *John Bowtell: bookbinder of Cambridge (1753–1813); biographical notes with a further notice of his nephew John Bowtell the younger (1777–1855)* (Cambridge 1907).

12 John ('Maps') Nicholson (1730–96). From a painting by Philip
Reinagle, 1788. Size of original 231.2 × 146.7 cm.

Library that seems to match the descripton is the illuminated *Wonders of creation* presented by George Lewis' son in 1770 (MS. Nn.3.74), arguably the finest Persian manuscript in the building. This is still in its oriental binding, with the exception only of a spine of dark blue morocco decorated from head to tail with a dazzling display of binder's tools, the centre exhibiting the entire solar system with attendant stars and comets. If, as seems likely, this was Bowtell's repair, then it is a pity that he did not indulge his fancy more often.

The *Wonders of creation* proved to be an exceptional piece of work. Most of his tasks lay in the less exotic skills of rebacking or straightforward plain bindings in calf, or, for heavier books and particularly for manuscripts, the fashionable Russia. Bowtell's pre-eminence as the best binder of his generation in Cambridge was unquestioned. It was confirmed not only by the Library's entrusting him with the repair of manuscripts that, as a class, were the last to be tackled in this sustained onslaught (it has been estimated that between a third and a half of the manuscripts were repaired by him), but also by his being commissioned to prepare the widely trumpeted special presentation copies of the facsimile of the Codex Bezae published in 1793.[30] The Library's demands gave full scope to his talents. In September–November 1791, for example, 329 volumes passed through his hands. They included over forty manuscripts and a quantity of fifteenth- and early sixteenth-century books. Some needed only to be mended and lettered on the spines at fourpence apiece; of those requiring more treatment, most were clothed in half Russia, calf being reserved for modern books, which in these months included only a small batch of recently acquired music. Some volumes called for exceptional treatment. The volume of Livy (1470) that had been presented to the Library in 1784 by George Nicol came bound in red morocco, the clothing selected for it by Nicol himself. In rebinding its companion already in the Library, Bowtell was

---

[30] See below, pp. 337–42.

forced to depart from his usual style and materials, and to match the Royal Library volume: it cost the Library a guinea. For other reasons no longer apparent, the de Spira Augustine (1470), also from Moore's library, was bound in full calf. It was a feat of some skill to have repaired the book at all. Bowtell's bill, recording the work done on 4 September 1797 (four days before Farmer's death) described the book as having been 'washed & dried sheet by sheet & then neatly bound': the gilding and colouring of initial letters, handwritten headings, and even the paste-on cancels over errors in the manuscript index, are still in perfect condition, and make it difficult to believe that these repairs ever took place despite the explicit statements of Bowtell's bill. But neither it nor the Livy was as characteristic of his work on such volumes as the full Russia binding put on the *editio princeps* of *Suidas Lexicon* (1499).

So much work transformed the appearance of parts of the Library, and most of the repairs carried out in these twenty years remained sound long into the twentieth century. For the most part they grace books from the Royal Library, rather than the Old Library, and it has already been stated that few eighteenth-century books as yet required repair. The condition of Moore's books had, clearly, been something other than neat. Repairs were essential, but none of these binders was sensitive all the time to the inherent value of preserving old parts of books not obviously part of the text and not strong enough to be re-used. Bowtell's papers in Downing College contain many victims of what now seem unsympathetic attacks on volumes, and by no means all books were as fortunate as the copy of Pliny's *Natural history* rebound into the old covers in February 1780 for 4s.6d., or the collected works of James I (1619–20) presented by the author and rebound into its original velvet for 2s.6d. in September 1784, both repairs being by Merrill. It may be suspected that manuscripts fared better than printed books, for on the whole vellum pastedowns were preserved, while volumes previously unbound were simply stitched into a new binding, library labels and all: there was advantage in economy. The putative loss of medieval bindings is an indeterminable matter. It would have been astonishing if the work was not sometimes careless. In 1796 Bowtell charged a mere £4.15s.6d. for repairing and putting into half leather thirty-three folio manuscripts, and a few days later added a further thirty-eight given the same treatment for £3.18s.6d. These were not charges that allowed any great lavishing of time or thought. And yet, nevertheless, the programme (it was no less) that Farmer supervised must be accounted a very considerable achievement. He had found much of the Library in an appalling state. No attempt had been made to clean the manuscripts for years, and few books had title labels on their spines. Beginning by paying John Marshall and one Edward Bore ten pounds to take down and dust all the books in the Library,[31] Farmer had tackled both tasks, with lasting success.

The second major change under his direction lay in the cataloguing and arrangement of the books. In some respects this fresh expenditure was forced on the Library as the result of events already in train, and in others it displayed originality that cannot have been foreseen. As to the first, the completion of the East Room had been marred by unsatisfactory bookcases, and for many years the room was furnished partly with the old cases. On 5 July 1776 a syndicate was appointed[32] to complete the work and to publish a catalogue of the Library, but the move was an abortive one. By 1785 the situation in the Library appears to have become desperate, and it was forced to occupy, however temporarily, space on the ground floor of the Schools that had fallen into disuse and become a lumber room. Rough shelves were erected in part of the Royal Library the following March, and books from the East Room (consisting principally of post-1715 acquisitions) moved there by Marshall with the help of some temporary assistance. In September Charles Humfrey, the person responsible for most

---

[31] Vouchers 1777–8. [32] Grace Book Λ p. 40.

building work in the Library at this period, was dealing with the plastering of the walls where the shelves had abutted. Almost as if to catch up with events, a new syndicate was appointed on 23 March 1787,[33] charged with erecting new bookcases: this same body (headed by Farmer himself as Vice-Chancellor and including amongst its number John Chevallier, Master of St John's, and John Davies as *Bibliothecarius*) was also to see that the books were catalogued and was to arrange to print a catalogue. The work proceeded at a stately pace, but by the end of June the old floor of the East Room had been taken up and cleaned (this alone took eighteen man-days) and the books removed downstairs. On 1 November the syndicate was in a position to act formally, and to reach agreement with Humfrey on the furbishing of the room. According to the terms of an unusually detailed contract (the University was evidently unwilling to risk further disagreement over such things) Humfrey was to erect eight large double-sided cases, four to each side of the room, with returns to the windows, to a height of eleven feet, and four single ones for the ends of the room.[34] Almost exactly twelve months later (the final, crucial, items on Humfrey's bill are dated 31 October 1789), with a new floor laid, the bookcases were finished. In fact, so far from supplying simply new bookcases, Humfrey and his workmen had thoroughly restored the East Room (fig. 13), where they had found the earlier joists inadequate, had repaired the wainscot and done incidental plastering. For a building no more than about thirty years old, the extent of the work was astonishing.[35]

The East Room, at last fitted up, provided the surroundings for a thorough recataloguing of its contents. Much of

[33] *Ibid.*, p. 195.
[34] Luard 249; some of the cases, shorn of their returns, are to be seen in the Bradshaw Room of the present Library.
[35] The sequence of events can be followed in Humfrey's and Marshall's bills among the Vouchers. At one stage Wright's building itself was threatened with demolition, but Robert Adam's proposal for a new library was not adopted. See Arthur T. Bolton *The architecture of Robert & James Adam (1758–1794)* 2 vols. (1922) 2 pp. 173–80.

13   The interior of the East Room, showing Charles Humfrey's
bookcases. From Rudolph Ackermann *History of the University of
Cambridge* (1815). Size of original 200 × 263 mm.

Humfrey's work for the Library over the next few years was
related directly to this, whether making desks and stools for
Pugh, Beverley and Marshall or erecting separate shelves to
hold books identified as duplicates. The map collection
received special cupboards in 1795, and James Nasmith's work
prompted attention to the shelves for the manuscripts, while
both inside and outside the Library there was a variety of
repairs calling for attention. In addition to this, the University
came to acknowledge that the temperature in the Library, less
than comfortable, could be rectified. On 16 December 1790
fifteen pounds was voted for a fireplace,[36] five days after

[36]   Grace Book *Λ* p. 253.

Humfrey had already taken down some shelves in the Librarian's room so as to accommodate it. A further Grace on 10 October 1795 resolved that a fireplace was also to be installed in the ground floor.[37] These humane measures, supplementing (or perhaps replacing) the Buzaglo stove bought by the University in 1774, were however still inadequate. Years later Gunning remembered the building as being extremely damp, even to the extent that he could not recall any means of warming at all: his impressions may not, after the lapse of time, have been recalled with complete accuracy, but his memory of Marshall's finally losing the use of his limbs through rheumatism and being taken round Senate House Yard in a bath chair was vivid enough.[38]

Work on the Library's collections thus took place against a background of almost constant building work. To reorganize much of the Library was clearly beyond the capabilities of one man. As Library Keeper Marshall remained responsible for most everyday work, and he took on some extra as well; but most of the alterations that followed the appointment of the 1787 syndicate were executed, once again, by specially recruited staff who were responsible solely for cataloguing the collections affected, and for creating new reserved classes for rare materials. The old library, of pre-1715 classes, was relatively unaffected, insofar as the books were not (on the whole) reclassified. So, too, the Royal Library was left more or less alone, save that most of the very early printed books were extracted from it and placed in a new class. But the eighteenth-century collections, housed mostly in the East Room, were completely rearranged.

The four men appointed to do this were William Pugh, elected Fellow of Trinity in 1790, John Beverley of Christ's, Esquire Bedell from 1770 to 1827, William Williamson, and Solomon Lyon, a Jew settled in Cambridge. Pugh and Williamson were at work by the end of 1790, Beverley arrived

---

[37] *Ibid.*, p. 329.   [38] Gunning *Reminiscences* 2 p. 78.

a few months later, and Lyon was to work only for a couple of years in the mid-nineties. Temperamentally, it would have been difficult to find more disparate individuals. Of them, Williamson was the least odd. He worked regularly, at a salary of half a guinea a week, as an assistant whose tasks were not specified in his accounts (in fact he did most of the drudgery associated with creating new class-catalogues) between 1790 and 1798, and gave no trouble. Pugh and Beverley compensated amply for such normality. It is the misfortune of both men to have been so vividly remembered by Henry Gunning, who preferred a sting in his remarks. Both were eccentric to the point of outlandish, and both lacked the everyday graces required in the small society of eighteenth-century Cambridge.

Pugh had taken his B.A. in 1789, and was enlisted by Farmer soon after becoming a Fellow of his college – despite being (in Gunning's words) 'a man of unsocial habits, very slovenly, and altogether unprepossessing in his appearance'. Gunning also remarked that 'his acquaintance with various languages, and his habits of intense application', as well as his remarkable if shallow learning, made him particularly qualified to catalogue in the University Library.[39] All this was familiar to Farmer, but Pugh lacked three other prerequisites in a competent librarian: an orderly brain, a disciplined attitude to his work, and a neat hand. If Farmer did have any reservations at the beginning, he did not allow them to prevent Pugh from working on some of the least tractable parts of the collections. So to Pugh fell the task of writing the shelf-list of a new class for early printed books, itself the creation of Farmer, and the much more laborious one of writing out the new shelf-list of the pre-1715 Library, the modern 'stars' classes. The series of 'stars' class-catalogues, and the class-catalogue for the now disbanded class AB, in themselves tell much of Pugh's character and difficulties. The first are in use even today, their volumes

[39] *Ibid.*, pp. 56–7.

several times the bulk they need be as a result of Pugh's slovenly handwriting that could fit no more than about three titles to a folio page, and also because it was necessary to paste his work, sheet by sheet and fragment by fragment into large volumes of blank paper. The class-catalogue for class AB was even more idiosyncratic. Marshall arranged the books in this new, select, class, in 1795–6. It was designed to gather together the incunabula and other early printed books from the Royal Library open shelves, both English and foreign, and also to act as protection to a few later sixteenth-century items: the equivalent books in the stars classes were left on the open shelves apparently deliberately, since Pugh noted them as he catalogued duplicate copies.

His shelf-list for AB remained in use even under Henry Bradshaw's attempts to rearrange the incunables in his *museum typographicum*, but it was an odd document. That it followed no plan apart from the sequence imposed by the shelves which forced large books to be kept together was scarcely important: the list opened with the two copies of the Nuremberg Chronicle then in the Library, three of the finest Jensons, and Caxton's *Golden legend*. Much more unusual was Pugh's mode of research. He was ultimately dismissed from the Library in 1795 because, it was alleged, it had become his practice to read books through rather than restrict himself to essentials.[40] The AB class-catalogue offers abundant evidence of his methods. In one sense he had grasped the principles of incunable research, by verifying and quoting references to established authorities – Maittaire, Herbert's edition of Ames, Middleton and Bowyer, and De Bure. But he did not do so systematically. On other occasions he was punctilious in providing information he thought of interest: the entry for Bernardinus of Siena's *Chirche of the euill men and women* (Wynkyn de Worde 1511)

[40] 'It appeared, whenever he came to a work with which he was unacquainted, he was not content with looking at the title-page, but applied himself to reading its contents. Had he been paid according to the time he was shut up in the library, a good deal would have been due to him; but for the little he had done, he was considerably overpaid' (Gunning *Reminiscences* 2 pp. 57–8).

required over two pages in what was supposed to be a shelf-list, by the time he had copied out the title, preface and colophon, and quoted Herbert. Yet elsewhere Walter Hilton's *Scala perfectionis* (Wynkyn de Worde 1494) provoked the remark, 'Ames has not spelt the Verses right at end of 2^d. Book ... I must transcribe them': he did not do so. Sometimes he was perplexed. Of the sixteenth-century *Livre des statuts & ordonances de l'Ordre Sainct Michel*, printed on vellum and presented to the Library several years earlier by William Thurlbourn, he wrote 'See whether anything in Biblioth. Parisiana' – without looking. Faced with Andrew Chertesey's *Passyon of our lorde* (Wynkyn de Worde 1521) he added 'Q. whether is by John Michel mentioned by Maittaire, V.1. p. 674. I sh^d. think not, ∴ that is a mystery.' Some were noted as to be shown to Farmer. At other times he felt moved to add remarks intended less for himself than for posterity. 'Rd. Rawlinson's Copy. Be particular about it', he wrote against an edition of the Thirty-nine articles; 'This is the first Impression, & is valuable for the Story of Stephen Gardiner, the greater part of which is omitted in the other Impressions', he wrote of Foxe's *Actes and monuments*. He was also alive to the uses of *ex libris*. 'This book belonged to the Monastery of Stratford langthorne, in 1480 ∴ must have been printed before that time' was a contribution to the dating of Adolf Rusch's Bible (GW 4282) that still stands as a cornerstone to the history of an intriguing book. But Pugh was not always so alert. The Paris Bible of '1463' listed by Maittaire and dethroned by John Taylor in 1740[41] was listed simply as 'The famous Latin Bible' – an accurate, but inadequate, description. Nor was type identification his forte. The anonymously printed and undated Ovid (now Inc. 3315) drew simply 'Ed. vetus. Char. Goth.', a description that was soon improved by Lord Spencer following a visit to the Library in 1800: 'In the Characters used by

---

[41] See above, p. 101 and Oates *Catalogue* p. 19 and no. 2871.

Nicolas Ketelaer at Utrecht about the year 1473'.[42] For a subject of such complexity Spencer was very near the mark, as the book is now attributed to Ketelaer working jointly with de Leempt. On the other hand, however, when Pugh did attempt some type analysis, the results could be extraordinary. In view of the antecedents of Theodoric Rood, the first printer in Oxford and an emigré from Cologne, Pugh was almost right in linking the types of Rood's edition of Richard Rolle [1483] with those of Johann Koelhoff as exhibited in his Aegidius Romanus (1490), however wrong he was in stating that they both seemed to be 'in the same type'. The successes, and also the faults, of the AB class-catalogue, which marked so great an advance on previous attempts to catalogue a recalcitrant class of books, seem on the basis of the evidence presented in the volume to be those of Pugh alone: Farmer's contribution is both unrecorded and therefore inextricable.

The work carried out by Pugh on this and on the stars classes was not achieved without some cost to the well-being of the Library. He was not an easy companion with whom to work. In reckoning up his dues for 1794–5, Marshall felt moved to add an unaccustomed item to his bill, of ten guineas 'To Extra Worke done in the Library at the request of M^r. Pugh, such as looking out Duplicates for him, in order to save him the trouble, in writing the titles of Books twice over, which helped him to expedite his General Catalogue, &c. &c.' The following year he charged five guineas 'To comparing many thousand Titles of French and other Books, with the Bodleian Catalogue, by the desire of M^r. Pugh. which took up some months'. By then Pugh's luck was running out, and the authorities were becoming suspicious of his progress, but the memory rankled in the mind of a man who had been accustomed to sole responsibility for cataloguing, and who unlike his meteoric

---

[42] MS. slip pasted into the AB class-catalogue at AB.3.19^2. Spencer was also able to offer help on Inc. 2898 (AB.4.32), 'printed in the Characters used by Petrus Caesaris and *Johannes* Stol at Paris between the years 1473 & 1480'.

superior (Pugh was also paid more than Marshall) had worked steadily for the Library for many years. On 9 May 1797, the Syndics, having already sanctioned the payment to Pugh of £300 for his work since 14 July 1792, agreed to a further hundred on condition that he delivered to the Vice-Chancellor by the end of the month both an account of what he had already done and an estimate of the time it would take to complete an alphabetical catalogue of the entire Library. In itself, this last request showed little understanding of what was involved; but it had the effect (no doubt intended) of forcing Pugh to show his hand. His report was read out to the assembled Syndics on 31 May:

In July 1790 I began to arrange the Books in the new Room & to make Class Catalogues of them & finish'd July 1792. – after that I began to make class Cat^s. of the Books in the old Room & in 2 other Classes which contain a great quantity of Pamphlets formerly belonging to the new Room, & also of the first printed Books & finish'd July 1795 – At which time I receiv'd 500£ which I consider as a compleat payment. – Since which time I have been engag'd in making one general Alphabetical Catalogue of the whole Library, in order to which I have not only the fresh Trouble of examining the Books in the King's Library which are I believe equal in number to those in the two other rooms, but I am likewise under the necessity of re-examining the latter so as to have before me at one & the same time all other works of any given Author in which Room soever they are plac'd. Of this latter & principal work i.e. of the general Catalogue, I believe that I have accomplish'd one third, & that I may be able to accomplish the whole within three years from the present time.[43]

If Marshall's bills are any guide, the collaboration had not been a happy one. But Pugh's days were numbered, and Marshall was finally left in 1799–1800 to complete the work on class AB, not only labelling and writing in class-marks, but also continuing into new ground by cataloguing the adversaria and compiling an alphabetical index to the whole. Two years later, Marshall was still trying to clear up the muddle left by Pugh, and he recorded then that he had spent part of his time 'collating 28 Class Catalogues, in order to Ascertain, what

---

[43] University Archives *Minutes of Syndicates 1737–1834*, pp. 93–4.

Books M^r. Pugh had remov'd out of the King's Library into the new room'. Meanwhile Lyon, working on the Hebrew books, had also had his difficulties. He described his work simply as 'translating Hebrew title pages', but he did not find things straightforward. 'As the charge for the above', he wrote in 1796, 'cannot be computed to be the Nu^r of books, on acc^t of the difficulty of transcribing (when Each of them will take above an hour to find out that which is necessary by reading the preface; sometime a great Part of the book,) I have therefore charged according to my time and labour.' The account on this occasion was allowed not by Farmer, as was usual, but by John Davies and by none other than Pugh, who must have thoroughly understood Lyon's plight.

When dismissed from the Library, Pugh quickly found his position intolerable, and began to behave extremely oddly. Accounts of his activities vary slightly between the two main authorities, Henry Gunning and Adam Sedgwick, Gunning suggesting that the events described by Sedgwick as continuing over a period in fact occurred only on the evening after he had received his dismissal. Sedgwick's, more detailed, has however the ring of truth, as it was taken down by J. W. Clark in Trinity Combination Room in 1863:

Well, about his madness. For a long while he was very strange: he dreaded the society of every body: he never left his room for any purpose whatever: he would not let his bedmaker enter it: but would, at a stated hour every day, open the door a little, take in his breakfast, & slam it to again. One morning, very early, he was seen by the porter, walking across the court in a mistrustful manner, looking behind him, or to the right & the left, with the utmost circumspection; and so go in to the Bowling Green, which in those days was not closed with a grating as it is now. On his shoulders he carried a large white bundle. This he was seen to carry to the terrace overlooking the river, & then pitch it over. Someone made search for it and fished it up. On opening it, it was found to contain all his dirty linen, and everything else, which had become too foul to be endured longer: so he put them all in a table cloth, & pitched them into the Cam. This was not thought sufficient proof of insanity to warrant his being sent out of residence so he remained. Soon after the town was thrown into consternation by the frequent breaking of the lamps. Night after night several lamps were found broken: no one knew by whom: the mayor offered a reward: but still the culprit remained undetected. At last the porter of Trin: Coll: observed that Pugh was in the habit of going out after the gates were closed, & knowing he was mad enough for anything, stated his belief that he was the man. So a gyp was set to watch who when Pugh was out, followed him at a distance. He went down Jesus Lane, till he came to the end of the palings which fence in Jesus College, & then turned to the left along Jesus ditch. There he presently went down to the water's edge, & from the water flags & duck weed brought up a big stick. This he seized, and hurried back to the street. No sooner had he got there, than the frenzy seemed to seize him. He gnashed his teeth, and rushed along like a madman. Presently he saw a lamp: he made it, and with a loud oath, exclaimed, 'You are a Robespierre', & dashed it to pieces with his stick. So he went on with the others, crying out Danton, S^t. Just, & other names, till he had broken six or eight, when he returned to the ditch, hid his stick, and made his way back to College. After this he was requested to leave, & put under the care of a keeper. But he got cured, & returned to College, although he had still a somewhat insane look, behaved with perfect propriety ...

Notwithstanding his strange conduct, his judgment was considered extremely good. Greenwood, and other good scholars, preferred his opinion to that of most others in the Exam^n. for Fellowships. His memory was such that he could trust to it, when others had to refer to the book: as in the case of the Greek Tragedians.[44]

On his recovery Pugh was presented to the living of Bottisham, which he held until his death in 1825, but he never returned to the University Library's staff.

He died two years before John Beverley, with whom he had shared most of the recataloguing of the Library in the 1790s, and whose career in Cambridge was so extraordinary that in 1821 the Heads of Houses agreed to appoint a deputy to act for him as Esquire Bedell on condition that he removed himself completely from the city. Gunning's portrait of him is not sympathetic. The two men opposed each other in politics, but if even some of Gunning's tales have an element of truth (and there is no need to doubt them all), Beverley was not the most honourable man in the University. 'It was quite clear',

[44] Anecdote related by Adam Sedgwick in Trinity College Combination Room, 17 August 1863, and taken down by J. W. Clark (Cam.a.500.9³). See also Winstanley *Unreformed Cambridge* pp. 265–7.

remarked Gunning, 'that for many years he carried on the business of the University in the Senate-house, in perfect contempt of the statutes and of its approved usages.'[45] Many of his troubles arose from a constant want of money. 'It was well known that Beverley was always in difficulties, and that he never missed the opportunity of getting money from any available source': Gunning was alluding on this occasion to bribery and other unsavoury activities, but the same need for extra money brought Beverley to the Library. A member of Christ's, he had been elected an Esquire Bedell in 1770, and became an authority on the ceremonies of the University. His employment in the Library was thus by no means his first, or his only, career. But whatever his reputation outside, he possessed more self-control than Pugh, and was therefore a more useful, if a more humdrum, cataloguer. He also survived longer, his work on writing a new class-catalogue of the rearranged books in the 'new library' or East Room, and entering their titles in the four volumes of the interleaved Bodleian catalogue, not being complete until 1802. The last payment to him for work done in the Library was of ten guineas in 1806, for writing out a class-catalogue of duplicates identified in the recent recataloguing, now classes Pp* and Qq*.[46] And, like Marshall, he too had his own share of identifying where the Library's records needed to be corrected following Pugh's work, his account for May 1802 including charges for work both in the Royal Library and '17 Catalogues in the Old Library compared with the Bodleian to ascertain the Books removd out of the New Room by Mr Pugh'.

Yet despite all their shortcomings, these men set in order what had been disorder, produced shelf-lists that are still in use today, transformed the East Room, and, in identifying several hundred duplicates which the Library forbore to reject as yet,

45 Gunning *Reminiscences* I p. 152. On Beverley see also H. P. Stokes *The Esquire Bedells of the University of Cambridge* (Cambridge Antiquarian Soc. 1911) pp. 113–14.
46 Class Dd, consisting of music, had been begun by 25 September 1792, but by then Beverley had already written the new class catalogue for the general classes Ee–Oo. The class catalogue of Pp* and Qq* is watermarked 1804.

provided opportunities that could not be even guessed at in the last years of the eighteenth century.

Perhaps the most striking feature of all Farmer's librarianship was the attention paid to the manuscript collection. Of all the events during his term of office none was more remarkable nor so widespread in its consequences as his dramatic intervention in the sale of the manuscripts of Anthony Askew organized by Leigh and Sotheby in March 1785. It broke entirely with both tradition and precedent. Never before had the Library been so closely involved in bidding at an auction, never before had it sallied forth to buy manuscripts in such quantities; but never before had quite such circumstances arisen. On his death in 1766 John Taylor had bequeathed his manuscript notes to Askew, and the feeling was widespread that they should be preserved intact so far as possible. But the matter went beyond piety. In 1781 Oxford and Cambridge universities were awarded £500 each per annum in compensation for their loss of special privileges in the printing of almanacs. At Cambridge, by a Grace of 11 June 1782, it was established that this sum should be spent on the publication of works of scholarship, including new editions of classical authors.[47] Accordingly, in November 1782 the Press Syndics agreed to proposals for new editions of Aristotle's *Poetics* (by William Cooke, Regius Professor of Greek), Plutarch's *Moralia* (by J. Edwards of Clare College), and of Stanley's Aeschylus (by Porson): the first, which had in fact been originally advertised in 1780,[48] was published in 1785, the second in 1791, and the third underwent some modification as will be described below. In other subjects, the Syndics supported the publication of a new edition of Edward Waring's *Meditationes algebraicae* (1782), of George Atwood's *Treatise on rectilinear motion* (1784),[49] William Ludlam's

---

[47] S. C. Roberts *A history of the Cambridge University Press 1521–1921* (Cambridge 1921) p. 115.   [48] *Cambridge Chronicle and Journal* 22 April 1780.

[49] Advertised originally as to be published 'during the course of the winter' in the *Cambridge Chronicle and Journal* 18 September 1779.

Rudiments of mathematics and Richard Relhan's *Flora Cantabrigiensis*[50] (both 1785) and Agostino Isola's edition of Tasso's *Gerusalemme liberata* (1786).[51] The sum of £250 was granted to James Nasmith for his new edition of Tanner's *Notitia monastica* in 1784, to cover the cost of paper and press-work.[52]

The Press's record as publisher of works of scholarship had not been outstanding for several years previous to 1782, and the Askew manuscripts suggested (in the eyes of some people at least) a means to make further amends. For Farmer, moreover, they had all the advantages of personal acquaintance, since although Askew had taken his M.B. from Emmanuel in 1745 and had practised only briefly in Cambridge five years later, he had remained essentially a Cambridge figure.

Askew's printed books had already been sold, in a twenty-day sale organized by Baker and Leigh in February 1775. But his collection of manuscripts, together with Taylor's notes and adversaria, had been held over, delayed according to the auctioneers in 1785 by 'private motives alone'. For Farmer, and the Library, the second sale provided golden opportunities. On 17 January, two months before the sale, the Syndics passed a resolution to allow him and Michael Lort, formerly Regius Professor of Greek, to spend up to £500 out of the 'fund granted by Parliament', i.e. the annual compensation for the loss of the almanac privilege.[53] The two men went to work with a will.

The sale opened with the adversaria, and of the 312 lots sold in the first three days Farmer bought sixty-two, all but a couple for the University Library. His purchases included Taylor's own annotated copies of his editions of Demosthenes and

---

50 Published by subscription; proposals were circulated in the *Cambridge Chronicle and Journal* 21 June 1783.

51 Published by subscription; advertised in the *Cambridge Chronicle and Journal* 15 October 1785, and as 'this day published' on 25 March 1786.

52 University Archives Pr.V.2, 'Orders for the Press', passim. Only a few of the books actually printed by the Press figure in these minutes, such books as Robert Masters' *Memoirs* of Thomas Baker (1784) being financed from outside the University.

53 University Archives Pr.V.2, 'Orders for the Press'.

Lysias, and his *Elements of civil law*, as well as his notes on the Cambridge Suidas of 1705 – witness of a project announced at the end of his Lysias in 1741. A copy of the Stephanus edition of the Greek poets (1566) contained notes by Joshua Barnes, the editor of Euripides and Homer, and this too Farmer secured, together with a valuable series of collations of manuscripts in continental libraries entered in Stanley's Aeschylus of 1663, the work of Peter Needham,[54] and notes by Bentley in his own edition of Cicero's *Tusculanae disputationes* published at Cambridge in 1709. All this was in addition to volumes annotated and enlarged by Askew himself. Not surprisingly, Farmer here concentrated almost entirely on the classical books: Taylor's interleaved and annotated copy of the 1561 edition of *Piers Plowman* went to Richard Gough, and Dr James Sims took Minsheu's Dictionary in the edition of 1625 with manuscript notes. But Farmer did not obtain everything even in the classics. Taylor's annotated Harpocration of 1696 went to Charles Burney for £2.18s.od. (compared with twenty-seven shillings paid a minute before for David Casley's copy of the same work); Isaac Casaubon's copy of the 1537 Ruellius *Veterinariae medicinae libri duo* went to Richard Southgate for £2.3s.od. Taylor's own copy of his *Marmor Sandvicense* (1743) and his *Commentarius ad legem decemviralem* (1742) went to Gough, the *Marmor* at the considerable price of £5.10s.od.: it was almost certainly contested by Farmer, who had to pay high prices for many of his books including the highest in the first part of the sale, nine pounds for Taylor's annotated Terentianus Maurus *De literis* in de Colines' edition of 1531.

Apart from the British Museum, buying through Southgate, Farmer's chief rival at the sale seems to have been Gough; but while the prices realized in the first days of the auction may have caused mild surprise, those in the following

---

[54] On this and Needham's other notes for a projected edition of Aeschylus, and their relation to Askew's own work, see E. B. Ceadel 'The "Askew collations" of Aeschylus' *Classical Quarterly* 34 (1940) pp. 55–60. Needham's notes are now MS. Nn.2.32 and Adv.a.64.1, and Askew's (partly derived from them) MS. Nn.4.6 and Adv.a.51.1.

days, devoted to manuscripts, were quite different. Once again, Farmer carried off more of the Taylor materials – consisting this time of folio notebooks – than anyone else. He secured fourteen out of thirty-eight lots, with serious competition only from Isaac Gossett, who had bought modestly up to this point and who, after the appearance of Taylor's notes, retired altogether. But, in general, Gossett's needs did not conflict with those of Farmer, who was thus able to take away a series of Taylor's manuscript concordances to Greek authors for very small sums ranging up to thirty-five shillings for a four-volume index to Aristophanes: the exception was the index to Aeschylus, an obvious tool to add to Stanley's working papers already in the Library, and here Farmer was forced to pay no less than seven guineas. In this part of the sale, too, it was Farmer who paid the highest price when he was bid up to sixteen guineas for Taylor's manuscript on Terentianus Maurus: he secured all four lots in the sale relating to this author.

With Taylor's papers thus, as far as possible, salvaged, on the fifth day Farmer turned his attention to Askew's classical manuscripts, beginning with the Latin. They were, with justice, regarded generally as the centrepiece of the library. Askew's excursions to the continent and the near east had brought unusual opportunities for the acquisition of manuscripts. In 1814 George Dyer claimed that Askew 'brought into his own country a more curious collection of MSS both in the ancient and modern Greek language, than was ever possessed by an Englishman before' – an extravagant and easily disproved claim, but a pardonable one.[55] Others came from Richard Mead, whose own collection of Greek manuscripts he had purchased privately, and were therefore familiar to Lort, who had been Mead's librarian thirty and more years before.

[55] George Dyer *History of the University ... of Cambridge* (Cambridge 1814) 2 p. 382, quoted by F. H. Stubbings in 'Anthony Askew's *Liber amicorum*' *Trans. Cambridge Bibliographical Soc.* 6 (1976) pp. 306–21. I have relied on Dr Stubbings' article at several points in the following, but there is still no general account of Askew as a collector.

Almost all Farmer's successful bids brought gains for the Library. The Latin volumes, virtually all humanist copies of literary texts, have proved to be of less interest to textual critics than the Greek, though Gilbert Wakefield speedily made use of an ornate fifteenth-century Lucretius for his edition published at London in three sumptuous volumes in 1796–7. It had cost Farmer seven guineas at the sale, the first of the Latin manuscripts (apart from Taylor's notes) to be knocked down to him. Of all the prices realized, those for the Latin manuscripts were highest. The mid-eighteenth-century rise in the prices of early printed books and of manuscripts had to some degree levelled off since the sale of Mead's library in the 1750s, but even so the famous (and much esteemed) manuscript facsimile of the Vatican Virgil bought at Mead's sale for £3.13s.6d. now fetched twenty guineas. Farmer was prevailed on to bid seventeen guineas for a pocket Horace (now MS. Nn.4.7), but apart from this his bids were less extravagant than many. A Cornelius Nepos at four guineas (MS. Nn.3.11),[56] and a Juvenal at £2.15s.0d. (MS. Nn.3.45) were more characteristic. For the last part of the seventh day, a Monday, he left his bidding to Michael Lort, who secured a Plautus (MS. Nn.2.33) dated 1415 for £1.11s.6d. (it was the first manuscript by this author to enter the Library),[57] the second of two Sallust manuscripts for twenty-two shillings (MS. Nn.3.7), and the later of two Senecas for £1.13s.0d. (MS. Nn.2.35). The residue of the Latin manuscripts, sold at the beginning of the following day as a preamble to the last and most outstanding portion, brought at three guineas a fourteenth-century Virgil (MS. Nn.3.4) described as 'Codex vetust.' by Askew himself, who was responsible for the descriptions printed by the auctioneers.[58]

The *comble* of the sale, understandably reserved for the last

---

[56] Formerly in the library of G. B. Maffei of Volterra. The manuscript (lot 455) is not identified in J. Ruysschaert 'Deux bibliothèques romaines Maffei des XVe et XVIe siècles' *La Bibliofilia* 60 (1958) pp. 306–55 at p. 333 (no. 66).

[57] J. Hildyard (ed.) *M.A. Plauti. Aulularia* (Cambridge 1839) p. xv.

[58] *Gentleman's Magazine* 55 (1785) p. 285.

two days, was Askew's Greek manuscripts. Again, Farmer led the field, his main competition now being Wodhull (still), Lord Shelburne, Leathes and Southgate. His nineteen prizes included volumes of Aeschylus, Aristophanes and Euripides, Herodotus, Plutarch and Thucydides, Demosthenes, John Chrysostom and the Gospels. The thirteenth–fourteenth-century Aeschylus in the thirteenth-century recension of Thomas Magistros (at a guinea) completed his score, and was the more welcome as on 2 November 1782 the Press had agreed (as already mentioned) to proceed with an edition of Aeschylus by Porson, based on Stanley's edition, while in 1783 a notice in Maty's *Review* had announced that a 'scholar of Cambridge' was preparing this new edition.[59] But despite Farmer's encouragement (he secured all the relevant material in Askew's library), the project was in the end abandoned, and a fresh edition by Porson appeared instead in London in 1806. Askew, in cataloguing the manuscript, had not pointed out that the volume (now MS. Nn.3.17) was in fact made up of two separate manuscripts bound together. He himself had collated them as two entities in February 1744/5 when they had still been in the possession of Richard Mead, and they were used by Schütz, with other collations gathered by Askew, in his edition published at Halle in 1782–97; but it was left to Samuel Butler to do justice to the readings in his Cambridge edition of 1809–16, and he was followed by Charles Blomfield and subsequent scholars.

Like five other manuscripts from Askew's collection now in the Library, the first part of the Aeschylus came from the monastery of Dionysiou on Mount Athos.[60] The first portion of MS. Nn.3.14 (a volume consisting principally of Euripides) containing at the end the *Vita* of Aeschylus had, before it became detached, formed the opening of the first part of

[59] J. S. Watson *The life of Richard Porson, MA* (1861), pp. 38–40 gives an account of this plan that was never fulfilled. On 13 May 1797 the University Press Syndics agreed to defray the cost of Stanley's Aeschylus under the editorship not of Porson but of Samuel Butler (University Archives Pr.V.2, 'Orders for the Press').

[60] Stubbings 'Askew's *Liber amicorum*' pp. 316 and 321, quoting Mrs P. E. Easterling.

Nn.3.17. The same scribe had also been responsible for part of
Nn.3.15, a collection of plays by Aristophanes, all three having
been written perhaps in Thessalonica.[61] No such relationship
was as much as hinted at in the catalogue (it would have been
astonishing if it had), and Farmer took the Aristophanes and
Euripides at thirty shillings and fifty shillings respectively,
dominating the bids for these authors. The slightly later
Aristophanes *Plutus* and *Nubes* (now MS. Nn.3.3) cost
£1.11s.6d., a composite Aristophanes and Hesiod (MS.
Nn.3.16) ten shillings, and a fifteenth-century volume of
Euripides with Cato's Distichs, formerly the property of
Antonio Seripando (MS. Nn.3.13) was comparatively expensive at £3.10s.0d.: after belonging to Seripando, this last
volume had passed to the library of San Giovanni a Carbonara
at Naples, and had reached the collection of J. de Witt of
Dordrecht by about the end of the seventeenth century. The
sole Herodotus, dating from no earlier than the fifteenth
century despite Askew's epithet of 'perantiquus' fell to Farmer
at £3.13s.6d. (now MS. Nn.2.34), and was his last purchase of
the eighth and penultimate day of the sale.

The ninth, and last, continued the more or less alphabetical
progression through the Greek manuscripts, and Farmer's
energies remained undiminished. A late fifteenth-century
Plutarch, also from Seripando's library,[62] cost six guineas, and
the first of three copies of Thucydides one guinea: Wodhull
took the other two, both at higher prices. Askew's own notes
on the text of Aeschylus (MS. Nn.4.6) fell at £4.14s.6d., and
made the fifteenth-century Thucydides (MS. Nn.3.18) seem
all too easy at a guinea. If, as has been considered likely by
scholars from Porson onwards, the Cambridge Thucydides

[61] See A. Turyn *The Byzantine tradition of the manuscripts of Euripides* (Urbana 1957);
according to Turyn the same scribe also wrote Vatican Library MS. Vat. gr. 1333
(Sophocles and Pindar). Facsimiles from MS. Nn.3.14 are given in F. A. Paley (ed.)
Euripides, with an English commentary (1857–60) 3, opposite pp. xxx and xxxi.
[62] Now MS. Nn.2.39: given to Seripando by Giano Parrasio. On these two earlier owners
see G. Pierleoni *Catalogus codicum graecorum Bibliothecae Nationalis Neapolitanae* I (Indice
e cataloghi N. S. 8, Rome 1962), pp. ix–x and H. Omont 'Notes sur les manuscrits grecs
du British Museum' *Bibl. de l'École des Chartes* 45 (1884) pp. 314–50, at p. 334.

was the Clarendon manuscript used by John Hudson in his Oxford edition of 1696, it was one of the very few lots among the Askew manuscripts whose place in the hierarchy of copies of any author had been even approximately established by 1785: once again, however, Askew's description made no allusion to the textual history of the manuscript, which received detailed treatment again only when Richard Shilleto published his collations of the first two books in 1872–80, and pointed out that it was in the same hand as a copy of Herodotus in Archbishop Sancroft's library in Emmanuel College.[63]

Farmer missed a four-volume collection of homilies by John Chrysostom (sold to James Lambert, former Regius Professor of Greek, at £6.16s.6d.), described merely as 'vetustus', but the following lot, another collection also by Chrysostom and datable to the eleventh–twelfth century (MSS. Nn.1.21–2), was provided with no such estimate of its antiquity. He bought it at four guineas, and went on to take five of the next eleven lots. Most interesting among them was a fourteenth-century theological miscellany bearing the name of John Caravalla, whom Askew had brought back from Greece and found a place for as bedell and library keeper at the College of Physicians in 1773–4. It seems likely that a twelfth-century Gospels (MS. Nn.2.36) – one of the few of Farmer's purchases to bear much decoration – described in the catalogue as 'ex Monte Atho' had come to England at the same time. For it Farmer paid £20, the previous lot – also a Gospels and with the same provenance, dated 1159 – having gone to Southgate at £27.6s.0d. And finally, in the last minutes of the sale, he went on to bid successfully for Askew's *Liber amicorum* (now in Emmanuel College), recording his journey from Leiden through Göttingen and Leipzig to Vienna and thence to Constantinople and Mount Athos in 1746–7.[64] He also bought the last of all Askew's manuscripts, a Latin New Testament no

---

[63] R. Shilleto *Thucydides I, with collation of the two Cambridge MSS. and the Aldine and Juntine editions* (Cambridge 1872) p. vi.
[64] See Stubbings 'Askew's *Liber amicorum*' pp. 306–21.

longer identifiable with any certainty as ever having come to the University Library.

The sale was not, however, quite over. After Askew's manuscripts, and not describing them in the printed catalogue, Leigh and Sotheby put up half a dozen lots of orientalia. The prize, a folio Koran said to have cost 1600 rupees in India, fell to Hartley at fourteen guineas, but Farmer took two of the others, both Persian, Firdawsí's *Sháhnāma* at seven guineas and a late sixteenth-century illuminated copy of the Persian account of the creation, Mírkhwánd's *Rawḍatu'ṣ-ṣafá*, at six guineas.[65] Neither they nor any other of the Askew books were listed in the Accessions Register. The whole had been made possible by spending money from the University Press account, and Farmer's part in it was acknowledged in a Grace of 27 April 1786.[66] He had spent, according to Sotheby's receipt,[67] £284 on manuscripts and adversaria for the Library, excluding the orientalia which Sotheby's persisted in calling Chinese. The bill to the Press, as recorded by the Press Syndics in their annual report, was £298.12.6d.,[68] though the final university accounts recorded it as £312.5s.6d.: the disparity between the figures is not explained. This apart, there hangs over the sale, the largest exercise in buying manuscripts at auction in which the Library has ever indulged, only the puzzle of why Farmer and Lort, authorized to spend up to £500, spent so much less and allowed some desirable items to escape. By not adjusting their bids significantly during the sale (and they seem not to have done so) they lost £200 for books which could not be regained. It was the only cloud to mar an otherwise singularly cheerful few days for the Library. Otherwise, the pieces lost to rival bidders were on the whole negligible compared with what had been secured.[69] The most important of Taylor's

---

[65] Now MSS. Nn.1.20 and Nn.1.19.   [66] Grace Book *A* p. 181.
[67] Vouchers, 18 March 1785.   [68] University Archives Pr.V.3, 30 June 1785.
[69] Farmer bid successfully for manuscripts of Cicero's *De officiis* and *De inventione*, but bowed out in favour of the Marquis of Lansdowne; in return he received for the Library a bulky volume containing Gregory of Nyssa, Basil and John Chrysostom dating from the eleventh or twelfth century (now MS. Nn.1.23). See *Gentleman's Magazine* 55 (1785) p. 284n.

notes had at last returned to Cambridge, nearly twenty years after their compiler's death, while the stimulus provided by the first considerable acquisition of Greek manuscripts since 1715 both prompted further development of a supporting collection of printed books and provided for some of the needs of several generations of classical scholars who turned increasingly to the University Library. Porson was the first to exploit the collection seriously, directing his attention mostly to Euripides, Aeschylus and Aristophanes,[70] but Gilbert Wakefield, Peter Dobree, F. A. Paley, Thomas Arnold, Richard Shilleto and James Hildyard were only some among many who found occasion to refer to them at length over the next seventy years. As the chronicler of the auction in the *Gentleman's Magazine* tartly remarked immediately after the sale:

It is much to the honour of the University of Cambridge, that they have made so large a part of this collection their own. After having taken measures for putting their press on a respectable footing, they have paid a proper tribute to the memory of their late illustrious member [Taylor] by possessing themselves of all his MS notes; and you may congratulate the public on the approaching prospect of seeing them issue, with due honour, from the University-press, in new and correct editions of Aeschylus, Apollonius Rhodius, Pindar, Juvenal, Terentianus Maurus, and other classic authors. After so long an interval since anything more than Bibles and Common Prayers have proceeded from that press (for, I believe, Dr. Taylor's own works, printed there, were its last classic labours); we may hope the students of this university will give such specimens of their taste for, and proficiency in, the literature of Greece and Rome, as will show them not a whit behind the sons of their sister. Comparisons are invidious, and allowance must be made for filial piety. But whatever praise is due to the typographic part of the Oxford editions, many scholars of our own nation, and more on the continent, express themselves disappointed with the other requisites.[71]

In one respect the attention paid to the sale was an isolated phenomenon, occasioned by the conjunction of Cambridge associations that Farmer found impossible to ignore: of Askew,

---

70 Cf. P. P. Dobree (ed.) *Ricardi Porsoni Notae in Aristophanem* (Cambridge 1820). Dobree drew attention in his preface to the similarity between MSS. Nn.3.14, Nn.3.15 and Nn.3.17, while his remark on Nn.3.3 reflects Porson's own opinion: 'Codex satis recens, et saepe mendose scriptus, sed multas optimas lectiones exhibens' (p. x).

71 *Gentleman's Magazine* 55 (1785) p. 284.

a friend of many years' standing, and of Taylor, one of the most notable scholars of eighteenth-century Cambridge. Other names or occasions were easier to forget or forgo. But it was also a turning point in the history of the Library's manuscript collections; and although no collection of comparable size was to be added to the Library until the gifts of Claudius Buchanan in the first years of the next century, the Askew sale signalled a revival of interest in a much neglected quarry. The Askew collection aside, the volume of manuscript accessions under Farmer was not particularly remarkable, but it was an improvement. In 1786 an anonymous donor produced, together with a trio of printed books and a copy of Pozzo's medal of Middleton, three medieval manuscripts now numbered Dd.9.70–2 and a thirteenth-century glossed copy of St John's Gospel.[72] Among more modern collections, the Library missed the papers of William Cole, which went instead by bequest to the British Museum, the better to preserve for the time being their confidentiality,[73] but the University did manage to find thirty guineas for the papers on the history of the University compiled by William Richardson, Master of Emmanuel immediately before Farmer.[74] The Library also began to organize a repository of university lectures and exercises, including the Latin epistles to the University describing the adventures of Worts Travelling Bachelors and assorted formal lectures. The first among the latter to have been added for many years were the texts of the lectures delivered by the first and second Jacksonian Professors in natural and experimental philosophy, Isaac Milner and Francis

[72] They had been sent not to the Library but to Thomas Green, the Woodwardian Professor of Geology – a circumstance that does nothing to enlighten the mystery of their donor.

[73] His will is quoted in W. M. Palmer *William Cole of Milton* (Cambridge 1935) p. 29. In 1783 the University acquired Cole's annotated copy of Tanner's *Notitia monastica* for £5.5s.0d., in the belief that it would be of help to James Nasmith in preparing his new edition (published by the University Press in 1787); Nasmith however found it of very little use, and as the book was never entered in the Library's Accessions Register it is to be presumed that it was not intended for the Library. See also *Gentleman's Magazine* 57 (1787) pp. 619, 867 and 989.

[74] Nichols (*Literary anecdotes* 5 p. 158) states that Richardson bequeathed them, but the University paid this sum on 14 June 1782.

Wollaston: but despite Jackson's having specified in his will that copies of one of the lectures delivered by the professor during the year should be laid up in the University Library and Trinity College Library, his wishes have been generally ignored.[75]

The oriental collections were even more of an assortment. In 1794, among the copyright deposit books, arrived the first volume of Roderick Mackenzie's *Sketch of the war with Tippoo Sultaun*, published by the author at Calcutta the previous year, but this was no more than a freak, and such deposits never became usual. For the rest, with only the fewest of exceptions, the Library still relied (as it did for many years to come) on donations. The works of the poet Sa'dí, published in Persian and Arabic in Calcutta in 1791–5, were presented in 1797 by Richard Johnson, 'who, with his usual zeal for the encouragement of Asiatick literature, particularly interested himself in forwarding this publication', for which he had circulated proposals in 1788.[76] In 1778 Gilbert Bouchery, of Clare College, had given two Arabic manuscripts,[77] and a year later Sir James Marriott, a lawyer of national repute, gave two Turkish books, one a manuscript.[78] Robert Masters, the aged historian of Corpus Christi College, upstaged them both when he produced a Persian life of Alexander the Great originally acquired by Sir Busick Harwood, Professor of Anatomy, during his residence in India.[79]

None of these additions to the collections was so celebrated, and none so important to the history of scholarship or so reviled as Thomas Kipling's edition of the Codex Bezae, which broke entirely new ground. The manuscript had been studied in some detail since Mill and Bentley at the beginning of the century, by (among others) Ludolph Kuster, J. D. Michaelis, J. J. Griesbach and, particularly, by J. J. Wetstein in his *Prolegomena ad Novi Testamenti Graeci editionem* (Amsterdam

[75] Clark *Endowments* p. 214.
[76] Graham Shaw *Printing in Calcutta to 1800* (1981) nos. 181 and 277.
[77] MSS. Add. 257, 258.   [78] Moh. 872.c.3 and MS. Add. 259.
[79] MS. Add. 260. Gunning gives an account of Harwood in his *Reminiscences* I pp. 52–5.

1730).[80] This apart, it had been crucial to the beliefs of William Whiston, who thought it to have been written 'within 30 years of the death of John the Apostle': after publishing a translation based on both texts in 1745 he had proceeded to enlarge on the manuscript's textual eccentricities in his *Sacred history of the Old and New Testament*. But, while J. S. Semler had published the Latin text in 1778, no full edition had so far been attempted. In 1786 Carl Woide, assistant librarian at the British Museum, issued his facsimile edition of the New Testament after the Codex Alexandrinus, set in types cut in imitation of the Greek uncials by the London letter founder Joseph Jackson,[81] and so finally brought to completion part of a project for a complete facsimile first attempted in the 1640s.[82] The Codex Bezae presented an obvious next step. The parallel Latin and Greek texts, together with the less regular construction of the letters in both languages, admittedly posed more problems of interpretation and design for a punch-cutter. But whether or not Kipling himself at first appreciated this detail, the facts that it seemed that the scripts could be imitated typographically thanks to Jackson's skill, and that the prohibitive cost of an engraved facsimile could therefore be overcome, meant that a facsimile of the Library's most impressive and celebrated manuscript was for the first time a reasonable proposition. The importance of this technical saving is all the more clear if it is recalled that, although facsimiles of odd parts of Cambridge manuscripts had been produced hitherto, not least in Thomas Astle's *Origin and progress of writing* (1784) which included an approximation of some verses from the Codex Bezae, this was the first full facsimile to be attempted of any manuscript in Cambridge.

Thomas Kipling, Fellow of St John's and Lady Margaret Professor of Divinity since 1782 in succession to Farmer, could

---

[80] See also his edition of the Greek New Testament (Amsterdam 1751–2) and, for Wetstein's career, C. L. Hulbert-Powell *John James Wettstein, 1693–1754* (1938). The principal eighteenth-century scholarship is surveyed briefly in F. G. Kenyon *Handbook to the textual criticism of the New Testament* 2nd ed. (1912).
[81] On Jackson see T. B. Reed *A history of the old English letter foundries* rev. A. F. Johnson (1952) ch. 16.   [82] *Ibid.*, pp. 192–3.

produce no published work to demonstrate his suitability for editing texts of any kind. But on 24 May 1786 the Press Syndics agreed that he should proceed, and on 27 June they further agreed to defray the whole cost of paper and press-work. So far, there was no suggestion in the Syndics' minutes of a facsimile edition being prepared, though it seems unlikely, in view of the recent appearance of the Codex Alexandrinus New Testament, that Kipling was unmindful of such a possibility. On 1 February following, however, the Syndics agreed that 'the whole of Beza's Manuscript Copy of the New Testament, both Greek & Latin, be printed in a Facsimile Character, & that D^r. Kipling be desired to employ a proper Letter-Founder for that Purpose'. At the end of March they further decided that it was to be printed on 'a Folio Paper', that Kipling should choose that most suitable as well as the ink, and that the work was to be published at two guineas. By June 1788 the Press had accordingly invested in 108 reams of paper and had bought from Jackson, at a cost of £45.11s.0d., a specially cut fount of suitable type.[83] But that summer the wisdom of producing so elaborate an edition was called in question in the August issue of the *Gentleman's Magazine* by a correspondent calling himself simply 'Academicus'.[84] Richard Porson admired Kipling's

[83] University Archives Pr.V.2, 'Orders for the Press'. The paper was supplied by Wright, Gill, Son and Dalton of Abchurch Lane, London (Library Vouchers, 1787). The facsimile was printed on various papers in the end, and copies were bound in one or two volumes. In a few copies, such as that presented by Kipling to Peterborough Cathedral Library in 1811, the first leaf of the Preface, including an engraved facsimile of part of the text, is of vellum.

[84] This marked the reappearance of an argument in the *Gentleman's Magazine* in the latter part of 1787, when a correspondent had doubted whether it was right that the facsimile should be published at all, and had summoned Beza himself in his support: in 1700 Thomas Baker (*Reflections upon learning* p. 209) had been anxious to suppress, or at least conceal, readings in the manuscript so embarrassingly at variance with the received text, and had reminded the world that Beza's intention in giving it to Cambridge in 1581 had been that it should not be published. These objections were easily silenced in the October issue, and the project was kept before the public (no doubt at Richard Gough's instance) the following month with facsimiles of a few lines from the Codex Bezae and the Codex Alexandrinus (*Gentleman's Magazine* 57 (1787) pp. 572, 872–3 and opposite p. 952 (facsimile)). 'Academicus'' attack in August 1788 complained not of the morality in publishing the manuscript but of the fact that it abounded with absurd readings, and had been written by a man better skilled at calligraphy than Latin or Greek (*ibid.*, 58 (1788) p. 682).

scholarship, but this provided him with the opportunity to express his own views of the project:

> I entirely agree with your correspondent Academicus, that it will be of no use to print Beza's MS., at least in the expensive way that the University proposes. I also agree with him, that all the ends of its publication (except indeed the publisher's profit) would be as well answered by printing the text in common capitals, and giving only a facsimile of the most remarkable or difficult passages. But I must beg leave to differ from him concerning the value of the MS. It abounds, says Academicus, with absurdities. So does almost every ancient MS. A MS. may be, upon the whole, of great authority, and yet have many absurd readings. The greatest fault of our MS. is, that it is also full of interpolations. Yet even these are often curious, as they are supposed to be taken from apocryphal gospels.

After some discussion of the readings in the manuscript he then continued:

> But whatever Academicus and I may think about the matter, Beza's MS. will certainly be published in a short time. Almost half of it is printed off. I must own that if I could once perceive the use of such a work, I should readily grant that the University has pitched upon the fittest person in the world to be the editor. Dr Kipling (*quem honoris causa nomino*), is, without any question, furnished with every accomplishment necessary to get honour for the University, and money for himself.[85]

Notwithstanding criticisms, the facsimile was published by subscription in two volumes in 1793, and won a respectful review in the *Gentleman's Magazine*.[86] In Cambridge, however, opinion was far less favourable. As deputy Regius Professor of Divinity (for Richard Watson, Bishop of Llandaff), Kipling took a leading part in the prosecution of William Frend of Jesus College for his dissenting views; and this, coupled with several grammatical mistakes in his Latin introduction to the facsimile, prompted a series of attacks. Porson, who had previously merely had reservations about the form of the edition, was now sharply critical, in a review published in the *British Critic*. The *Monthly Review* was

[85] Richard Porson *Correspondence* ed. H. R. Luard (Cambridge 1867) pp. 23–4. See also *Gentleman's Magazine* 58 (1788) pp. 875–7.
[86] *Gentleman's Magazine* 63 (1793) pp. 732–3.

glowing in its appreciation of the production of the facsimile in 'most splendid form'. 'The paper is superfine; the types are admirably cut; the ink is of uncommon blackness; and the impression is scarcely paralleled. In all these respects it surpasses Dr. Woidé's publication.' The reviewer had not seen the original manuscript, and so was in some difficulty when assessing Kipling's editorial contribution (though he showed no such reservations when assessing the design of the type). He was unconvinced by Kipling's allegation that the book had been written in the second century, and in Egypt. Instead, his own belief that it had been executed in the west, 'not by a Greek, but by a Latinist', in the sixth century, was much closer to modern opinion. The review also contained a sting in its last paragraph: 'As to Dr. Kipling's Latin style, we shall only observe that it is rarely obscure, rarely elegant, and sometimes incorrect. It is such, however, as we find in most modern works of criticism; and neither Stevens nor Ainsworth will be required to make it intelligible.'[87] The onslaught by Thomas Edwards, Fellow of Frend's college, was much more distasteful. On 12 November he issued his *Remarks on Dr Kipling's preface to Beza*, a pamphlet which took full advantage of Kipling's imperfect command of Latin but was engendered as much by his involvement in Frend's trial and deprivation of his fellowship. 'We shall I hope', he concluded, 'be no more told, that the dignity of the University demanded the banishment of Mr Frend, unless the same persons will confess, that the literary character of our seminary more forcibly demands that a public vote of censure should be passed on Dr Kipling for the want of ability, integrity and accuracy, which he displayed in his preface to Beza.' But for all the criticisms, and for all Kipling's unpopularity, the two volumes remain, typographically, one of the greatest achievements of the University Press. And, despite Porson and Edwards, when Scrivener came to produce his own edition in 1864, he was able to be objective. 'I have

---

[87] *Monthly Review* November 1793 pp. 241–6. Stevens and Ainsworth were authors of popular Latin dictionaries.

found the text of my predecessor less unaccurate than some have suspected', he wrote; instead, for him, Kipling's fault lay more in that he had failed to take proper editorial account of the later insertions in the manuscript, and so had produced a distorted version. Kipling himself, denied a fair hearing, saw no such constructive discussion. His career at Cambridge came virtually to an end. In December 1797 he was nominated to the Mastership of the Temple, and in February 1798 he was installed as dean of Peterborough, a post in which he remained until his death in 1802.[88]

But despite the sour taste left in some mouths at Kipling's achievement, officially the University took very considerable pride in the edition. Two copies were immediately bought by the Library from Merrill at the full retail price, to be sent off to the Bodleian Library and the British Museum, done up in boards by Bowtell.[89] Then Bowtell was called on for his best. In November he charged six shillings 'for selecting an extra copy of Beza for the King of Denmark and another for the Duke of Marlborough by Order of Dr Kipling', five shillings for doing them up in stiff covers, and two shillings and sixpence for putting stiff covers on a copy sent to the Pope. In June the following year he charged six guineas each for two copies to be 'superbly bound in the best morocco' for the first two of these dignitaries, both erstwhile benefactors to the Library.[90]

Kipling's facsimile casts a great shadow over most other editorial work on the Library manuscripts at the end of the century, and affected even Porson. But at the same time as this megalith was being created at the Press, J. D. Carlyle of Queens' College, Professor of Arabic from 1795, was also

[88] On Kipling see, besides *DNB*, R. F. Scott (ed.) *Admissions to the College of St John the Evangelist* 3 (Cambridge 1903) pp. 698–700.
[89] Vouchers 1792–3, Merrill's and Bowtell's bills. The Library's own copy, 'on large superfine royal paper', was bound by Bowtell on 5 April, and is now 899.bb.383–4: the first volume contains one of the few known copies of Bowtell's label.
[90] Vouchers 1793–4. The presentation copies were described in the *Cambridge Chronicle and Journal* on 5 July 1794, and that for the King of Denmark is reproduced in A B. Gray *John Bowtell: bookbinder of Cambridge* (Cambridge 1907) opposite p. 359.

seeing through an edition of the part of the Arabic chronicles contained in MS. Dd.3.11 that related to Egypt. His edition of *Maured Allatafet Jemaleddini filii Togri-Bardii, seu rerum Aegyptiacarum annales 971–1453* was approved by the Syndics of the Press on 22 May 1790,[91] and was published two years later. Better considered as more in the nature of an exercise than as something with serious pretensions, it was dismissed by Stanley Lane-Poole in the *DNB* as 'a meagre work of slight historical value'; but however residuary its interest, it constituted one of the very few attempts in the eighteenth century to publish any of the Library's oriental manuscripts.

In the last quarter of the century, public attention was thus focussed on the collections in the Library, and particularly on the manuscript collections, to an extent that had not been usual hitherto. Through his friendships in the London literary world, Farmer made available for consultation and publication a variety of texts more or less obscure, usually in early English literature, while the Askew sale and his and Lort's efforts on behalf of the Library drew attention to a renaissance of classical studies in the University supported by the University Press. By no means all that was hoped for by the Press was achieved, especially in the classics, where hopes were highest, but the successful publication of a sumptuous and technically difficult facsimile of the University's most widely known possession at once demonstrated what could be achieved, contributed to scholarship on a European scale, and emphasized in the most public way possible a new outlook on the part of the Library itself. The low public profile which the Library, like the University, had preferred was no longer either realistic or even desirable.

In this context of expansion and increasing exposure to the worlds both of the University and beyond, the question of a

91 University Archives Pr.V.2, 'Orders for the Press'. Four years later the Press installed new Arabic type to print his *Specimens of Arabian poetry* published in 1796 (*ibid.* 20 June 1794).

new catalogue of the Library's manuscripts was inescapable. The old catalogue, dating from Parris' librarianship, had been obviously imperfect from its birth, had been added to by more or less competent glossators since, and was completely unfit for publication. The immediate import of the Grace appointing the syndicate to rearrange the books and to prepare a catalogue for publication had regard only to printed books, yet as a result of Farmer's repair programme the manuscripts were put in a better state than they had ever (in some cases) been before. Moreover, there was one person in the University whose competence was proven, who did not tax his fellows with eccentricities, and who was at leisure to be employed to catalogue the collection. James Nasmith, Fellow of Corpus and rector of Snailwell, two miles north of Newmarket, had finished his revised and much enlarged edition of Tanner's *Notitia monastica* in 1787. Tanner's original work having relied heavily on John Moore's manuscripts, Nasmith was thus familiar with many in the University Library. As a cataloguer he had proved himself with his catalogue of Matthew Parker's manuscripts at Corpus, published in 1777. Accordingly, on 30 June 1794, a Grace was approved arranging for Nasmith to prepare a fresh catalogue of the manuscripts in the Library, the cost to be defrayed from the University Chest.[92]

On 11 October 1796 (the same year as he was presented to the altogether more luxurious living of Leverington, north-west of Wisbech), Nasmith was paid a first instalment of £100. The work proceeded with an efficiency so rarely seen in such projects that it bordered on ostentation. Nasmith was paid a further £100 on 15 July 1797, and the work was finished on 22 November 1798. It had taken a mere three years, and Nasmith had provided the Library with a compact catalogue of its western manuscripts of impeccable neatness.[93] Fuller than any

---

[92] Grace Book *Λ* p. 309.
[93] MSS. Nn.6.42–5. According to Nasmith's note at the beginning of these volumes (bound together as one) he completed the work in 1794–6: the Vouchers suggest a slightly later period as he was paid in arrears.

previous catalogue of the collection, particularly in providing details of the contents of volumes, it naturally had both strengths and weaknesses. Nasmith kept to the shelf order, but for no very obvious reason introduced an additional sequence of numbers from 1 to 2604, and this attempt to facilitate reference simply led to confusion as, during the next sixty years, odd new acquisitions were crammed onto the same shelves regardless of the overall numbering scheme: when the mid-nineteenth-century catalogue came to be compiled on the same principles, the numbering of all but the earliest in the sequence was naturally automatically altered. At the end of his catalogue, Nasmith transcribed the series of descriptions of the adversaria prepared by Pugh, and so took the numbers up to 2703.

Numbering apart, Nasmith's descriptions of the manuscripts were themselves variable. He was careful, as his predecessors had been, to give formats and the materials on which the manuscripts were written, but he offered little on dates and that which he did was unreliable: he scarcely ever distinguished between different dates in composite volumes. His interest in the provenance of books was rudimentary, and usually restricted to copying out the more obvious monastic *ex libris*. On some kinds of books he lavished care, particularly in some of the literary, historical and Greek manuscripts: MSS. Dd.8.49 and Dd.8.23, two Greek Evangelistaria, had 134 pages of his handwriting devoted to them, and MS. Gg.4.4, a register from Bury St Edmunds, was catalogued in detail, in 938 parts, and took nearly ninety pages of description. But not everything drew such attention. Nasmith's achievement, in sheer speed, was extraordinary, and it is little wonder that on other occasions he skimped. Legal collections, commonplace books, and notebooks having no literary interest suffered particularly badly. He was weak on liturgies: among many similar mistakes, MS. Dd.5.2, a Psalter, was described as a breviary, and Dd.5.5, a fragment of a fourteenth-century breviary executed for Mary de St Pol, Countess of Pembroke, was described simply as 'Missale' – albeit 'nitide scriptus et pu[l]chre ornatus'. He made scarcely any reference to printed editions of the manuscripts. Whelock's edition of Bede, after the eleventh-century MS. Kk.3.18, was mentioned, but not Smith's of the Moore Bede (MS. Kk.5.16). On the Codex Bezae he simply repeated Kipling's conclusions despite the fact that they were by no means universally accepted. Gifted with little patience, and fully aware of the University's anxiety to see the job completed (he was working in the aftermath of the Pugh *débâcle*), Nasmith felt driven to remark at the end of the first description of all, a fairly comprehensive account of a fat miscellany of English literary pieces,

To endeavour to affix the names of their respective authors to the several anonymous poems contained in the MSS. of this library is a task to which I consider myself as altogether unequal. Were I to indulge conjecture, I should attribute the greater part of the contents of this volume to the prolific pen of Richard Hampole.

His remarks on this single volume characterized much of his approach to the remaining 2600 or so descriptions. He made little attempt to ascertain authorship beyond the most obvious literary pieces, and equally little to establish relationships with other similar texts. Of Dd.3.45, an incomplete copy of Raoul le Fevre's history of Jason in English, he simply remarked, 'There is no title to this MS. the frequent mention of Jason seems to point him out as the hero of the tale.' The Library possessed the version printed by Gerard Leeu at Antwerp in 1492, had Nasmith bothered to check. For much of the time he fell back on previous catalogues, without even properly examining what he had before him. 'Ascribed in the former Catalogue, and I suppose rightly to Dr Bates, though his name does not appear in the MSS', he wrote of Dd.1.9 – quite inaccurately, as Bates' name is plain to see.

Medical and other domestic books proved more recalcitrant, to Nasmith as to modern cataloguers. By no means all of MS. Dd.10.44, a fifteenth-century miscellany of medical works, has been identified even today: and faced with such difficulties Nasmith was, again, disarming: 'A book written on parchment in the fifteenth century', he wrote, 'containing a collection of Treatises in Physick, chiefly in English, to most of which no titles are prefixt, and which therefore can only be described from such knowledge of them as could be obtained from a cursory view of its contents.' As was his usual practice when faced with such miscellanies, whether literary, historical or medical, he then enumerated the sections separately so as to aid others, and in this his catalogue was a notable advance on previous work. He treated MS. Gg.1.1, a fourteenth-century miscellany mainly of French poetry, for example, with the fullest attention, to the extent that his naturally discursive style read even more than usually like an essay or article than a catalogue entry. A further example of his leisurely, but not inapposite, disquisitions, for MS. Dd.3.53, was included in the printed catalogue of the manuscripts published in 1856: like his successor, Nasmith also provided a full list of the 495 parts of the volume, and of the pendant, a fifteenth-century commentary on Chaucer's treatise of the astrolabe. His account of MS. Dd.4.4, a fifteenth-century compilation on farriery, was also completely accurate, and even constructively suggestive – although the manuscript's make-up eluded him just as it did Glover sixty years later in the printed catalogue.

There is no general title to this MS. and I am in doubt whether the whole be one continued treatise, or not rather a compilation from different writers on the subject without much regard to order or connexion. In one place we meet with, 'Practica Willelmi Marescalli Prioris Mertoniae' but as the said William seems to have been more of a conjuror than a phisician, and his receipt is rather a charm than a prescription, we must not ascribe it to the Prior, but should observe that Marescallus is not a surname but a title of office, the said William being Marshall or Farrier to the Prior . . .

And on MS. Ff.5.48, the volume containing the poem *The tournament of Tottenham* which William Bedwell had edited for publication in 1631, crediting it to Gilbert Pilkington, he seems to have been the first to express suspicions about the poem's supposed authorship: 'I see no sufficient ground for ascribing even the single poem ... to this Gilbert Pilkington, much less for making him the author of the miscellaneous contents of this volume', he remarked, recalling that he had 'several times' met with inscriptions such as 'Explicit q^d Gilbert Pilkington', 'whose titles plainly shewed them to have been written by persons different from those who placed their signatures after this manner at the Conclusion'. His opinion has since been generally accepted.[94]

If ever there was any hope, as seems likely, that this new catalogue might be printed, it was to be thwarted. The only existing recent printed accounts consisted in those published in Bernard's *Catalogi* of 1697, and this was incomplete even when it was published quite apart from relying on descriptions printed almost a century before that. There was no question of Nasmith's work not being an improvement on everything that had been done previously, but at the same time it was a disappointment, and was never published. Beleaguered by a cost-conscious university, and working too hastily, he had produced a catalogue whose deficiencies were only too obvious. On some of its faults he was candid, but others he let go unremarked. It did not much matter that the oriental manuscripts remained undescribed (descriptions of them were added gradually in the nineteenth century); but in failing, for example, to take much account of important examples of illustration his catalogue can have found little favour with Farmer's successor Thomas Kerrich, who joined the Library while Nasmith was still engaged on his work. Others added to Nasmith's descriptions in a piecemeal way: apart from the oriental descriptions the most useful additions were those by the Saxonist J. M. Kemble on some of the Anglo-Saxon and Middle English manuscripts. Despite Nasmith's labour, and apart from some pages in Dyer's *Privileges of the University*, published in 1824, little was made properly public until the appearance of the printed catalogue of manuscripts, compiled afresh by a body of scholars, in 1856–67.

[94] See Oates *History* p. 337.

All this activity brought with it one inescapable accompaniment. Under Farmer the cost to the University of running the Library soared. Building and repairs, cataloguing and binding had been deferred to the point where expenditure, when it came, was extraordinary. During the period from 1778 to 1797 the amount spent on the purchase of books remained (the Askew sale apart) fairly steady overall, and the number of bought volumes entering the Library, while veering wildly in some years as the result of particularly large orders (such as the arrival on 20 June 1786 of 114 volumes from the London bookseller Peter Elmsley) also remained reasonably constant. Likewise the salaries of Farmer (£50 p.a.) and Whisson and Davies successively (£35 p.a.) remained the same. But the overall cost of the Library in building, binding and cataloguing increased the annual bill to the University many times over, and none of this extra money came, as had that for the new East Front in the 1750s, from any appeal. The burden was supported partly by the incomes from a variety of funds whose first responsibility was for the purchase and repair of books. The estate of Ovington, a village between Watton and Shipdham in Norfolk, bought with Tobias Rustat's legacy in 1667, produced a net income of usually somewhat under £30 p.a. The University Press account could be raided on occasion, under exceptional circumstances, as with the Askew manuscripts, when it could be argued that the Press might gain from the editorial activity engendered by the purchase. John Newcome's legacy of 1765 brought a modicum to be spent on books, while, finally, the Worts Fund also brought in periodic sums at irregular intervals, including £100 in 1796–7.

In 1778–9, Farmer's first full year of office, the total audited expenditure on the Library, Schools and Registry (usually treated as a unit in the University's accounts) was £106.13s.4d., with an additional £4.16s.6d. from the Newcome Fund to cover a bill from Merrill. In the following year the total for the Library alone was £79.12s.8d., of which £59.6s.8d. was for binding and new books. The annual figure for both years included Marshall's bill as Library-Keeper, which varied slightly from year to year, but excluded the stipends of the *Protobibliothecarius* and *Bibliothecarius*, while in neither year did either the Worts or the Rustat Fund contribute in any way. The sums were modest, and the effort necessary to spend them equally so. But by the end of the century, and Farmer's death, there had come about a considerable change. Humfrey's bills to the University in the late 1780s, not only on the Library's account (on this alone in 1788–90 he received £827.3s.4d.), but also for work on the Anatomy and Chemistry Schools, drove up the totals in this part of the final accounts, while the proportion spent on the Library collections remained small: in 1785–6, for example, Humfrey was paid £320 for work on the Anatomy School, while the Library claimed only £70 of which Merrill received over half. Over the next few years, Farmer's binding programme quickly increased the Library's bills, but with the attack on the cataloguing of the printed books following the completion of the East Room, and Nasmith's work on the manuscripts, expenditure rose still more sharply. In 1790–1, the binding bills alone totalled £116.10s.10½d. (Bowtell's share was £75.14s.0d.), while Pugh, Williamson and Beverley between them received £59.7s.6d., and booksellers' bills and subscriptions combined amounted to £113.17s.7½d.[95] The respective figures in this year are contaminated in that Bowtell's bill also included some books sold to the University, and both Merrill and Nicholson, while predominantly booksellers, also charged for binding; but the tendency is clear, that an ever higher proportion was being spent in ways other than on the purchase of books. In the following year, Pugh received £180, in 1793–4 he was paid £130, and in 1794–5 £170 (and Beverley £94.2s.6d.). He received no payment in 1795–6, but in that year Williamson, Lyon, Nasmith and Samuel Ayscough (who

---

[95] Including six pounds for Boydell's Shakespeare and a guinea for Nathaniel Marchant's *Catalogue of one hundred impressions from seals* (1792). Marchant's two accompanying boxes of casts of seals arrived on 17 September 1796: there is no suggestion (*pace* Sayle *Annals* p. 106) that he presented them.

received £61.10s.0d. for transcripts of Baker's manuscripts in the British Museum) were altogether paid £206.7s.6d. Bills from the binders were even heavier, and helped to bring the total expenditure on the Library's collections to £558.13s.3d.[96] In a period of war, with escalating prices, associated fears for financial credit, and calls on the University for support of refugees from France and for the militia,[97] this expenditure on the Library needed to be all the more determined. By the time of his death, on 8 September 1797 after a year of illness during which he retired more and more from public life, Farmer had brought about changes in the Library's policies for selecting and buying books, of which the Askew sale had been an instance. But he had also set in motion, if not quite completed, a programme of tidying, binding and rearrangement for which previous generations had found no energy and with which his successors during the next half century were to rest content.

[96] Calculated on the basis of the audited accounts and the relevant (Library) parts of Marshall's bill. The total audited account for Library and Schools in 1795–6 was £950.8s.10½d. The figures for the following year were similar, if account is taken of £100 to Pugh, £13.10s.6d. to J. Baldrey for re-engraving the Royal Library bookplates, and £110 to Farmer's executors (of which £35.15s.6d. was received back, having been charged by mistake).   [97] Cooper *Annals* 4 pp. 445, 447, 451, 454–5, 458.

9

THOMAS KERRICH

FARMER'S DEATH WAS NOT UNEXPECTED. He had long been ailing, and as a consequence there had been plenty of time for those who wished to be candidates for his post of *Protobibliothecarius* to prepare their ground. But despite this opportunity there were only three nominations, and each in its way was peculiar. First in alphabetical order was John Davies, *Bibliothecarius* since 1783. To Henry Gunning, writing many years later, he seemed a candidate 'as a matter of course', after fourteen years in the Library:[1] while this may well have been the case, his candidacy also suggests that some opinion was beginning to express itself that the University had had enough of this dual control of *Protobibliothecarius* and *Bibliothecarius*, and that the office would be better vested in one person. Under Farmer, moreover, Davies had had ample opportunity to demonstrate his abilities. In theory at least, he was a serious rival when compared with the other two candidates. Philip Douglas, Master of Corpus since 1795 and Vice-Chancellor in 1795–6, was aged no more than forty and might have been supposed to possess just that cachet of academic honours looked for in the *Protobibliothecarius*. But, again in the words of Gunning, he

was a decided invalid, and confined himself very much within the precincts of his Lodge, and dared not for any consideration pass three hours in the Public Library, which at that time there were no means of warming, and it was so extremely damp that few persons could pass any length of time in it with impunity. He had, besides, lost one eye, and suffered so much from inflammation in the other that he was frequently confined for days together to his bed.[2]

[1] Gunning *Reminiscences* 2 p. 78.   [2] *Ibid.*

352

14   Thomas Kerrich (1748–1828), *Protobibliothecarius*. From an engraving by Georg Sigmund Facius after a painting by Henry Perronet Briggs. Size of original 297 × 241 mm.

Third, and finally, there was Thomas Kerrich (fig. 14),[3] President of Magdalene, and slightly older than Douglas. He had already tilted at the Library on the occasion when Davies was elected fourteen years previously. 'Mr Kerrich', remarked

[3] For other details of Kerrich's career, including his ecclesiastical preferments, see *DNB*.

Gunning with some composure, 'never courted popularity. I have heard him, after his appointment, repeatedly declare that he always considered himself one of the most unpopular men in the University.'[4] But unpopular or not, it was Kerrich who was elected on 21 September by a majority of 98 votes to Douglas' 70,[5] Davies having been already eliminated. 'The result of the election surprised many persons – no one more so than the successful candidate', recalled Gunning.[6] The election had, in fact, slightly misfired. Kerrich was not a Head of a House, as had been Farmer, Barnardiston, Law and Parris before him, and he owed his unexpected success to circumstances that the antiquary Samuel Denne, of Corpus and at the time living a little outside Cambridge at Wilmington, explained in a letter written a few days later, on 4 October:

You could not avoid noticing in the public prints, that the Master of Bene't was, by a decisive majority of thirty-one, foiled in his attempt to be the Principal Librarian of Alma Mater, *vice* the late Dr. Farmer; but perhaps you may not be fully apprised of the manoeuvres, that left him in such an unexpected minority, for, before the poll or ballot commenced, an opinion prevailed that it would be a close contest. The account I had from Fellow Currey was to this purport: It seems that the practice is for the Heads of Houses to put two persons in nomination: and, as they are generally partial to one of their own corps, the scheme is to start against him one who is not likely to be a formidable competitor. Mr. Davies, of Trinity, not coming under this predicament, his name was not returned to the Senate; but not being aware that he should be thus excluded the chance of a poll, he had applied to distant friends to come in and support him, nor was there time allowed to stop their progress. The consequence was, that they resented the trick that had been played off to the prejudice of their friend, and espoused Mr. Kerrich. Mr. Currey says, that our Master, from an indolence that is habitual to him, was too remiss at the beginning of the canvass; and he adds, that he is very much disappointed with his ill success, for, not aware how many there were upon the road on the solicitation of Mr. Davies, he and his managers had flattered themselves, that among the resiants he should secure so many votes, that a few outlyers would be sufficient; and, I understood, he had every vote in St. John's-college except one. His nuptial union with a niece of Mr. Mainwaring certainly gave him a great advantage in that Society.[7]

4 Gunning *Reminiscences* 2 pp. 78–9.   5 Thus Luard. Gunning gives 100 and 69.
6 Gunning *Reminiscences* 2 p.76.   7 Nichols *Illustrations* 6 p. 715.

Quite apart from such politicking, there was much in favour of Kerrich. As nominee for Whisson's place in 1783 he had been long associated with the Library, and in many ways he could be expected to continue in Farmer's footsteps. Both men had strong antiquarian leanings; both were part of a small group in and around Cambridge (including also William Cole) who collected paintings – and portraits in particular; and there are grounds for supposing that the culmination of years' work on the paintings in the University Library, the anonymous *Catalogue* of pictures there and in the colleges published in 1790, was from the hand of Kerrich himself.[8] Kerrich had, however, little of Farmer's interest in early literature. Instead, he devoted most of his not inconsiderable energies to the visual arts, as portraitist, engraver, recorder of ancient monuments and historian. As a Worts Travelling Bachelor in the early 1770s he had spent some time on the continent, chiefly in Rome, Paris and the Low Countries, being rewarded at Antwerp with a medal from the Academy there.[9] In 1775 he had been back in Cambridge, and in the following year occupied himself with making a catalogue of the prints in the University Library (most of them from John Moore's collection) with the help of Michael Tyson:[10] outside the Library, his artistic skills were put to use by Richard Gough, who included several of Kerrich's drawings of local monuments in his *Sepulchral monuments* published in 1786.

Kerrich's talents were recognized shortly after his election as *Protobibliothecarius* with his election to the Society of Antiquaries, and some of his best work as a draughtsman appeared in the pages of *Archaeologia*, occasionally alongside his own articles. His standards as an artist were high, and at a period when the demand for accurate drawings of objects of antiquarian interest was expanding at a rate unprecedented in England he was not an easy taskmaster. Few responded more sympathetically to this movement than Charles Stothard,

[8] G. R. Owst 'Iconomania in eighteenth-century Cambridge' Cambridge Antiquarian Society Proceedings 42 (1948) pp. 67–91, at p. 87.
[9] Nichols Illustrations 6 pp. 811–12.   [10] Nichols Literary anecdotes 3 p. 621.

draughtsman of the *Monumental effigies of Great Britain*, of the series of engravings of the Bayeux Tapestry issued by the Society of Antiquaries in 1821–3, and of many of the illustrations to Daniel Lysons' *Magna Britannia*; yet Stothard himself considered that he was only following the example set by Kerrich. 'Of his judgment', recalled Stothard's widow after her husband's premature death in 1821, 'my husband entertained the highest opinion, and always declared that to his just and candid criticism, during the progress of the work, he felt much indebted for much of its improvement. Mr. Kerrich, he would say, was a severe judge, but one who never bartered his severity for compliment, and whose praise was worth receiving, as it was the commendation of judgment without flattery.'[11] Kerrich's own writing was devoted to architecture and local antiquities, including a notable paper on Gothic architecture contributed to *Archaeologia* in 1812 that became a minor classic of its kind. But his most ambitious work, a study of the prints made after the sixteenth-century Dutch artist Maerten van Heemskerck, was published only posthumously, in 1829. Much of his own collection of prints, paintings, books and coins can still be studied as groups. To the Society of Antiquaries he bequeathed a series (of varying quality) of twenty-six paintings, mostly portraits of royal figures down to Henry VIII,[12] and his son followed his example and presented the collection of coins he had inherited to the same society. But when in 1873 Kerrich's son bequeathed his collection of works of art to the Fitzwilliam Museum the Cambridge authorities

[11] Nichols *Illustrations* 6 p. 815. Kerrich regretted that Stothard had to work on the Bayeux Tapestry: 'It is perverting him, & a worse artist would do it better – you would not set Grinling Gibbons to chop sticks for you, however delicately he carved in wood' (Kerrich to Francis Douce 27 May 1816, Bodleian Library MS. Douce d.36, fo. 138 ᵛ).

[12] Listed in *Archaeologia* 22 (1829) pp. 448–52 and in Nichols *Illustrations* 6 pp. 817–21. The pair of panels depicting scenes from the life of St Etheldreda, dating from about 1425, may well once have belonged to Ely Cathedral (M. Rickert *Painting in Britain; the middle ages* (2nd ed. Harmondsworth 1965) pp. 187, 249). For one of the other paintings, recovered by Edward Daniel Clarke from the Holy Land and given to Kerrich on his return, see E. D. Clarke *Travels in various countries of Europe Asia and Africa* 2i (1812) pp. 407–12, with a reproduction by Harraden.

responded with less than enthusiasm: as a result, only part of Kerrich's collection is now at Cambridge, notably a memorable picture by van Heemskerck of the artist himself at work in Rome in 1553,[13] a Virgin and Child by Joos van Cleve dating probably from the late 1520s, eight oil sketches by Rubens[14] and an important collection of books and prints. Kerrich himself bequeathed to the University in 1828 John Vanderbanck's portrait of Nicholas Saunderson, the blind Lucasian Professor of Mathematics, now hanging in the Old Schools.[15]

The effects of Kerrich's antiquarian and collecting tastes on the Library became obvious from the beginning of his term as *Protobibliothecarius*. Throughout his years of office the books selected for purchase, by Kerrich personally, tended frequently to be more appropriate to his own private interests than to any other lacunae in the Library's collections. Other fields of scholarship were – particularly in his first years – not so much neglected as forgotten by a librarian who seemed determined to use the collection to foster his own enthusiasm before all others. The first works to arrive in the Library on his orders were typical of what was to come. In April 1798 the entries in the Accessions Register included Samuel Lysons' glorious atlas folio on the Roman antiquities discovered at Woodchester, published the previous year, Daniel Daulby's *Descriptive catalogue of the works of Rembrandt*, published at Liverpool in 1796 and essential for any serious work on the Library's collection of several hundred of the artist's prints, and three earlier books, all equally critical in their field: Ciampini *De sacris aedificiis a Constantino Magno constructis* (Rome 1747), the Conte Malvasia *Felsina pittrice, vite de pittore Bolognesi* (Bologna 1678), and Carlo Dati's *Vite de pittori antiche*. That May Kerrich added to these foundations by purchasing (at seven guineas –

---

13 Given to the Museum in 1846 by R. E. Kerrich.
14 J. W. Goodison etc. *Fitzwilliam Museum Cambridge; catalogue of paintings* I (Cambridge 1960) nos. 103, 104, 228–31, 241–3, 240.
15 Goodison *Cambridge portraits* 30 and pl. 12.

rather more than the Library was accustomed to spend on most books) Bartsch's full-sized edition of Burgkmair's *Triomphe de l'Empereur Maximilien I*, published in Vienna and handled in England by Edwards of Pall Mall.[16] Von Heinechen's *Idée générale d'une collection d'estampes* (1771), a comprehensive general guide, was another, more obvious, gap in the Library that Kerrich filled in these same months.[17] His contacts with the Society of Antiquaries both prompted and encouraged many of the Library's acquisitions during his term, but he also remained constantly in search of books on art history, including in February 1801 the companion piece to the Burgkmair, the Vienna facsimile of Dürer's *Arc triomphal de l'empereur Maximilien I*[18] and in May 1817 the first edition of Vasari's *Vite* (Florence 1550), bought for three guineas. The inherent relevance to the rest of the Library of some of the more expensive items such as the Dürer and the Burgkmair has been to some extent obscured by the subsequent history of the print collection, transferred to the Fitzwilliam Museum in 1876, but Kerrich was also swimming with the tide of cultivated taste. His choices were informed, but they were not inspired. Equally apposite, though in a different way, was his acquisition of the Royal Library copy of the *Emblemata* of the Altdorf Academy (1597) from Leigh and Sotheby's priced catalogue for 1796, at the reasonable price of five shillings. The book came from the Knyvett library, and had been misguidedly discarded as a duplicate from the University Library in the 1740s. Whether his purchase on this occasion was fortuitous or deliberate, it neatly rectified an earlier mistake.

---

[16] This book later became a drug on the market, 'exceedingly common in our country, and of a very limited price' according to Dibdin. Thomas Edwards offered it at £10 in his 1815 catalogue, but at the auction of his books in 1828 an uncut copy fetched only thirty-three shillings.

[17] Apart from the Accessions Register, see Kerrich's bill to the University for these books, receipted on 14 January 1799 (Vouchers 1798–9).

[18] Price six guineas. Despite the Donations Register this was not a gift: see Kerrich's bill in the Vouchers for 1800–1.

The Library was not in a strong position to buy very liberally. Its income for books, part from the University Chest, part from the Rustat Fund, and part from the much less wealthy Worts Fund, was modestly supplemented by two bequests in the first years of the new century. On his death in 1805 Joseph Merrill, the local bookseller and binder, left over £3000 to various Cambridge charities, of which the Library was bequeathed £200, the capital to be invested.[19] Two years later, in 1807, John Mainwaring, Fellow of St John's and Lady Margaret Professor of Divinity since 1788, left £300 for divinity books, though the bequest was not paid until October 1814.[20] (Both bequests were invested in Consols, but produced dividends so small that they were quickly considered to be no longer worth listing separately in the university accounts.) With the money from these various sources attempts – sporadic and not always perfectly informed – were made to keep abreast of current scholarship. Among older books, serious efforts were made to improve the collections of classical authors,[21] mainly through Thomas Payne in London, who supplied not only the latest edition of Fabricius' *Bibliotheca Graeca* but even (in 1809) the Amsterdam edition (1713) of Bentley's Horace; the same firm, the only London booksellers to be used regularly at this period, was also responsible for Panzer's *Annales typographici*, the Somers *Tracts*, and the *Harleian Miscellany*. As previously, most of the Library's business continued to be conducted through John Deighton. Scott's edition of Dryden (1808), Cowper's poems, Malthus' *Essay on the principle of population* (1807), the Bells' *Anatomy of the human body* (1811), the new edition of Bentham's *Ely*

---

19 Cooper *Annals* 4 p. 483. The Audit Book records the sum of £200 received in the year ending 3 November 1806. By 1814–15 this produced £8.19s.3d. after tax.
20 Clark *Endowments* p. 463.
21 At the sale of Porson's books in 1809 the Library bought twenty-three lots for £22.17s.0d., charged to the Rustat account: the most expensive item was Schweighäuser's eight-volume edition of Polybius (Leipzig 1789–92). In 1809 the Library even sent a list of desiderata of classical texts to Payne, who supplied what he could (cf. Payne's bill in the Vouchers, 29 March 1809). Both this and the selection of books at the Porson sale were the responsibility of J. H. Monk.

(1812), Manning and Bray's work on Surrey (1809), Rees' *Cyclopaedia*, and Pitt's speeches all had to be bought, and helped to fuel the irritations that burst into a series of confrontations with publishers and Parliament over copyright deposit. The Library also bought Cuvier and Blumenbach on comparative anatomy, La Place on capillary action and, in a serious if somewhat random attack on astronomy and mathematics, a handful of works on calculus. In August 1816 the Rustat Fund allowed the purchase of fifty-one volumes of the *Annales de Chimie* – no doubt at the suggestion of Edward Daniel Clarke, Professor of Mineralogy, who was to have a decisive effect on the Library.

There were, however, still more pressing matters. The unhappy discoveries surrounding the tidying up of Farmer's estate[22] made all too obvious the dangers of allowing too easy access to the Library's treasures. It was essential to regulate the borrowing of manuscripts in a more formal way than by simple loans, and to abolish the abuses that had begun to creep into procedures. Accordingly, on 31 March 1798, the Syndics, headed by the Vice-Chancellor Robert Cory, Master of Emmanuel, ordered,

That all printed Books in the Classes that are locked up, which are taken out by the Vice-Chancellor, or under his Order, be returned before the expiration of his office, under the usual Penalties, to be paid by the Person or Persons to whom they are lent, or, in case of their failing to pay, by the Vice-Chancellor.

That no Manuscript whatever be taken out of the Library, without a Grace for its removal being obtained from the Senate.[23]

Problems persisted nonetheless, and two years later, on 22 March 1800, the Syndics felt it necessary to place still more restrictions on borrowing, by placing a limit to the number of volumes that might be in a member of the Senate's hands at any one time:

That no person be allowed to have in his possession, at one time, more than Ten Volumes belonging to the Library.

[22] See above, pp. 299–301.   [23] Luard 263.

That the Vice-Chancellor and the Librarians be empowered to dispense with the preceding Order in any particular Case, if they shall be unanimously of Opinion that sufficient reasons have been assigned for such dispensation.

That such dispensation continue in force no longer than to the end of the Quarter in which it shall be granted, but, upon fresh application, may be renewed by the same Authority.

That, for the purpose of allowing the Librarians sufficient time to inspect the Books at the end of each Quarter, (according to the Order dated 1748) all Books be kept in the Library on the Day appointed for their return, and the whole of the Day following.

That the above Orders be printed and hung up in the Library.[24]

These measures thus re-established on a formal footing the practice that had begun to emerge a few years earlier after a long period of desuetude, when George Travis, Archdeacon of Chester, and Robert Tyrwhitt had arranged to borrow manuscripts in the same manner.[25] So also, on 28 April 1802, a Grace was passed to allow Porson to borrow the Herodotus and Thucydides obtained at Askew's sale (MSS. Nn.2.34 and Nn. 3.18) with a fifteenth-century Thucydides that had once belonged to Benedetto Tagliacarne, the ill-fated secretary to the Republic of Genoa from 1514 (MS. Kk.5.19).[26] During the next several years similar Graces formed regular items of business. On 31 October 1807 it was even found desirable to agree that the Vice-Chancellor of the day should be able to borrow any manuscript relating to University affairs ('ad res Academicas spectantes');[27] but after this liberality the University reconsidered the matter in more general terms, and on 24 March 1809 decided that in future no manuscript could be borrowed by a private individual without his signing a bond.[28] The question of loans to institutions did not arise, and this system of bonds related to Graces still remained in regular practice at the end of the century.

Otherwise, Kerrich's term of office was less remarkable for its administrative innovations than for the additions to parts of

24 Luard 267.
25 Grace Book Λ pp. 318 (16 December 1794), 323 (10 July 1795), 335 (2 July 1796).
26 Grace Book Λ p. 413.   27 Grace Book Λ p. 517.   28 Grace Book Λ p. 533.

the collections that had not, hitherto, attracted much popular attention. Kerrich's own interests lay principally in western Europe and in Great Britain, the countries with which he was familiar from personal experience. At the same time there was an influential group in Cambridge whose energies were directed to classical archaeology, and in particular to the ancient Greeks. In time this was to have a permanent and visible effect on the Cambridge scene, in the design chosen for Downing College, in John Clement Mead's University Observatory, and, not least, in the University Library itself. But in 1800 this movement was no more than an embryo. The later fashion for Greece, popularized in different ways by Byron and Lord Elgin, had its origins in the 1790s, in men such as John Tweddell, Fellow of Trinity, who died at Athens in 1799, and John Marriott of St John's, who left for Greece in 1794.[29] The war with France virtually closed western Europe to English travellers, and the consequent shift of interest eastwards, coinciding with a revival of Hellenic studies at home by such scholars as Porson and Gilbert Wakefield in Cambridge (whatever their scholarly differences), wrought, literally, a change of scene. On 1 July 1803 the University received, and set up in the entrance hall of the Library as the only available public place, a fragment standing over six feet high of one of the two caryatids, dating from the first century B.C., that had originally been placed at the entrance to the inner Propylaea at Eleusis.[30] With it there also arrived part of an inscribed column that had been found in use as a mounting block in an Athens street.[31] Not surprisingly, these two pieces caused a stir, following as they did upon the arrival of the Rosetta Stone at the British Museum in 1802, and the probability of its decipherment with the publication of both Silvestre de Sacy's *Lettre au Citoyen Chaptal* and a response

---

[29] For the Cambridge background generally see R. W. Liscombe *William Wilkins 1778–1839* (Cambridge 1980) pp. 19–21.
[30] L. Budde and R. Nicholls *A catalogue of the Greek and Roman sculpture in the Fitzwilliam Museum Cambridge* (Cambridge 1964) no. 81.   [31] *Ibid.*, no. 132.

offering further suggestions by the Swedish diplomat J. D. Åkerblad. The first of the Elgin marbles arrived in England in August of the same year.

The Cambridge pieces, moreover, came from a man who had every claim to be one of the most successful (not to say resourceful) hunters after ancient remains of all kinds in the near east. They were presented by Edward Daniel Clarke (fig. 15), formerly Fellow of Jesus College, and his pupil John Marten Cripps. A polymath of quite extraordinary range, Clarke had entered Cambridge in 1786, from the grammar school at Tonbridge, as a chapel clerk. He took his B.A. in 1790, and (having given considerable attention to literature at university) within a short time of going down had formed the core of what became a notable mineralogical collection while tutor to Henry Thanet, later the Earl of Thanet, in the course of a tour round Great Britain. Between July 1792 and the summer of 1794 he was in England only briefly, and spent his time as tutor to Lord Berwick, travelling over Italy as far south as Vesuvius. An inveterate tourist, he returned to England with a further collection of minerals and the beginnings of one of antiquities, but with his sights already set on Greece. 'Inasmuch as Greece was the mistress of the fine arts, and Rome only her disciple,' wrote his biographer William Otter in 1825, 'inasmuch as Greece supplied the originals, and Rome the imitations; and the imitation never approached to the perfection of the original; the antiquities of Greece demand every investigation that the man of taste can appropriate to scenes of instruction and delight.'[32] The next years were however spent in Wales, with the Mostyn family, at the seat of Lord Uxbridge at Beaudesert in Staffordshire, and (in 1797) on an extensive visit to Scotland. In 1795 he had been elected a Fellow of his college, but this failed to keep him in Cambridge, and in 1799 he set out on an ambitious journey with T. R. Malthus, William Otter (later Bishop of Chichester) and a young man

---

[32] W. Otter *The life and remains of Edward Daniel Clarke* (1825) I p. 248.

15 Edward Daniel Clarke (1769–1822). From a posthumous marble bust by Sir Francis Chantrey, 1824. Height of original 781 mm.

also from Jesus, John Marten Cripps.[33] Only Cripps could stand the pace, and, leaving Malthus and Otter in Sweden, the two passed through Scandinavia, Lapland and western Russia down to Asia Minor, the Holy Land, Egypt and Greece. They came back both famous and possessed of vast collections of all kinds of curiosities. It was an expedition that might have been enough of a career for many men, but for Clarke it was merely a prelude. His hope of returning to the middle east was never fulfilled, yet while he attended to his spoils and compiled an immense record of his travels for publication, he also embarked on a career in Cambridge. Having finally returned in 1802, he was ordained in 1805, and from 1806 until his death in 1822 was rector of Harlton, a village six miles to the south of Cambridge. From 1810 he was additionally the rector of Yeldham in Essex. In 1808 he was elected Professor of Mineralogy, and proved an outstanding, if not very profound, teacher. An inveterate inventor, he also developed a self-igniting match, dabbled in botany, nearly blew himself up while experimenting in burning hydrogen and oxygen together, and in 1819 became one of the founder members of the Cambridge Philosophical Society. In 1817 he was elected *Bibliothecarius*, a circumstance to which we shall return.

Clarke was an avid writer, gifted with a style that added romance even to the most humdrum of occasions as soon as he was abroad. Of the various accounts of his discoveries, the first seen by the world at large was in a pamphlet[34] printed at Cambridge shortly after the arrival of the two-ton statue in the Library's front hall, in which he set out its past history, including recent accounts by Richard Pococke and Richard Chandler, who had seen it in 1739 and 1765 respectively: he did not mention that he had acquired it, in the face of competition from Elgin, by bribing Athenian officialdom with a telescope

---

[33] On the early stages of their journey, see, besides Otter's *Life*, Patricia James (ed.) *The travel diaries of Thomas Robert Malthus* (Cambridge 1966).

[34] *Testimonies of different authors, respecting the colossal statue of Ceres, placed in the vestibule of the Public Library at Cambridge, July the first 1803* (Cambridge 1803).

obtained from G. B. Lusieri, the man in charge of dismantling the Parthenon for Elgin himself.[35] Clarke was convinced that he had recovered a statue of Ceres, on the evidence, as he put it, of 'the Καλαθίον, or Holy Basket, which she bore on her head, and which, during the celebration of the Mysteries, was carried in solemn procession'[36] – a mistake encouraged, incidentally, by the peasants who had venerated the piece as having a benign influence on their crops even though it had apparently been buried up to its ears in a rubbish heap.[37] The column presented to Cambridge at the same time also grew in Clarke's eyes to something altogether more interesting than is supported by modern opinion, for he believed that he had found Euclid's gravestone: this amiable fiction passed with the statue of Ceres into the lore of Cambridge guidebooks.

Although Clarke held no official brief from the University it was his intention from the first that these spoils and his others should return with him to Cambridge. On 15 December 1801, just over three weeks after successfully extracting the monument from Eleusis, he wrote to Otter on the subject, triumphantly dating his letter from the 'Summit of Parnassus':

But what will you say to the acquisitions I have made for the University of Cambridge: the tomb of Euclid, and the colossal statue of the Eleusinian Ceres, from her temple in Eleusis, the known work of Phidias, and the gift of Pericles? We have freighted a ship from Athens, with antiquities; but it would fill a volume to tell you the difficulties I had to encounter. Lord Elgin had all his agents and artists in Athens, to pull down the temples, for materials to adorn a Scotch villa. Acquisitions for others were even prohibited; and I had to fight through the intrigues of a herd of rascally Greeks, the obstacles arising from a thousand causes, from expense, from bad air, from want of every necessary machinery, and last, and greatest, from *consular* chicanery, and *diplomatic* jealousy. But they are bound for England, and I breathe freely.

First of all, I have to thank Cripps, without whom I could have done nothing. And the expense of conveying to England the enormous statue of

---

[35] W. St Clair *Lord Elgin and the marbles* (Oxford 1967) pp. 102–7 summarizes Clarke's relationship with Elgin. On Clarke's Greek travels see his *Travels in various countries of Europe Asia and Africa* (1811–23) pt 2.   [36] *Testimonies* p. 16.

[37] Otter *Life and remains* 2 pp. 160–1. On the statue see also Dyer *Privileges* 2, supplement pp. 145–6.

Ceres, after I had obtained it, he has taken upon himself, by his own desire. The tomb of Euclid (you will hardly credit it) I bought of a consul, from under the very nose of the ambassador's chaplain, and his host of Gothic plunderers.

The removal of the statue of Ceres has been attempted by the French, upon a former occasion, without success. The Eleusinians also relate, that once being brought to the shore, she returned back to her station, by a miraculous flight, like the virgin of Loretto. — had, for once in his life, a flash of taste, and wrote to the ambassador to remove it, as I have since learned, but they gave it up in despair. At last come two *demi-semi-travellers*, from Jesus College, Cambridge, and whip it off in a trice . . .

After we returned from the Morea, I found the goddess in a dunghill buried to her ears. The Eleusinian peasants, at the very mention of moving it, regarded me as one who would bring the moon from her orbit. *What would become of their corn*, they said, *if the old lady with her basket was removed?* I went to Athens, and made application to the Pacha, aiding my request by letting an English telescope glide between his fingers. The business was done; the telescope, and the popularity of the English name at present in Turkey, determined the affair; and leaving Mr. Cripps in Athens, I set out for Eleusis, attended by a Turkish officer, the *Chogodar* of the Pacha. But how to move a statue, weighing sundry tons, without any wheeled machine, ropes, levers, or mechanical aid? – I made a triangle of wood, so – on which I laid the goddess, with her breasts upwards, and by means of cords made of twisted herbs, brought from Athens, and about sixty peasants, she vaulted into the Acropolis of Eleusis, and from thence to the sea-side, and at length into our little *Cassiot* vessel; moving the space of a mile, almost as fast as a snail.

Behold the goddess then bound for England, and touching at the Piraeus, to take leave of the Athenians.

The statue of Ceres is entire to the waist, being originally, as it is now, a bust; but of such enormous size, that I know not where the University will place it . . .[38]

The journey home was not without mishaps. Clarke's arm did not fall off, as local superstition had predicted, but the ship carrying these and other pieces was wrecked off Beachy Head and the cargo rescued only through the efforts of Cripps' father, who happened to live close by. A further accident, when a man fell off the scaffolding erected for the outsize statue, and broke his ribs, further marred the proceedings, but there could be no doubt of the delight that the booty brought

[38] Otter *Life and remains* 2 pp. 159–61.

in Cambridge, provoking William Pearce, Master of Clarke's college, to ecstasies. 'As for our master, he pulls off his gown and dances round it', wrote Clarke to Otter a few days after the so-called Ceres had been placed in the Library.[39]

Clarke was rewarded officially with the degree of LL.D., and Cripps with that of Master of Arts. The two pieces of sculpture that attracted most attention were moreover by no means the only ones they presented to the University. Their collection included a fragment which Clarke, with characteristic optimism, was convinced was part of the metope of the Parthenon (in fact it dates from the second century A.D.),[40] and a Roman piece representing Asklepios and Hygieia:[41] the last was thought by Clarke to be the initiation of Hercules into the Eleusinian mysteries – an identification which he found some difficulty in supporting as he could think of no other figure of Hercules draped in the same manner.[42] These, with further pieces found in western Turkey, Cyprus and other sites, formed the foundation of a collection that grew so rapidly within a few years that in 1809 Clarke was able to publish a catalogue of the *Greek marbles brought from the shores of the Euxine, Archipelago, and Mediterranean and deposited in the vestibule of the Public Library of the University of Cambridge*, a volume of some curiosity for reasons quite apart from its subject, for (except for the list of George Lewis' gifts of 1726 and the lost catalogue of Andrew Perne's coins) it was the first separately published catalogue of any part of the Library's collections. Besides the several pieces given in 1803, between then and 1809 Clarke's and Cripps' donation had been enriched by a number of like-minded enthusiasts, mostly young Cambridge graduates. Among these new benefactors were the Earl of Aberdeen, who had entered St John's in 1800 and soon afterwards departed for Greece to conduct his own

[39] *Ibid.*, p. 206. For an early account of the marbles see the *European Magazine* 47 (1805) pp. 350–1. They were removed to the Fitzwilliam Museum in 1865.
[40] Budde and Nicholls *Catalogue* no. 122.   [41] *Ibid.*, no. 123.
[42] E. D. Clarke *Greek marbles brought from the shores of the Euxine, Archipelago, and Mediterranean* (Cambridge 1809) p. 38.

excavations; the Rev. Bridges Harvey of Jesus, who produced an altar from Delos brought back by one of his ancestors;[43] Clarke's brother George, a captain in the Navy, who presented a fragment from the acropolis at Pergamon depicting a lively group of horses; John Spencer Smith; and the Rev. Robert Walpole of Trinity,[44] who in 1808 presented a torso of Asklepios carried back from Knidos and a comic mask from Stratonicea. To descriptions of all these gifts Clarke was able to add a brief note on a fragment removed from Egypt, about which he had already addressed the Society of Antiquaries, and some observations on the Rosetta Stone (of which he had given a cast to the Library) together with Porson's revised translation of the Greek text.

This great accretion to the Library quickly attracted attention. Flaxman was prevailed on by Clarke to draw the principal showpiece, the caryatid from Eleusis, and he contrived not only to recreate its mutilated face but even to produce a drawing of 'Ceres', 'restored from various authentic documents' seated on a throne and bearing a long staff in her right hand.[45] A further drawing by Flaxman, of a headless statuette of Pan, discovered at the foot of the Acropolis and also presented to the University by Clarke, graced the close of

[43] *Ibid.* frontispiece and opposite pp. 24 and 30. Clarke's views on the condition of his pieces are of some interest in the light of their generally unrestored state: 'No attempt has been made towards the restoration of any of the Marbles here described. They have been deposited in the Vestibule exactly as they were found. In this respect we have not imitated the example of the French: and it is believed, the Public will not dispute the good taste of the University, preferring a mutilated fragment of Grecian sculpture, to any modern reparation. Had Ceres gone to Paris, she would soon have issued from a French toilet, not only with a new face, but with all her appropriate insignia, her car, dragons, and decorations, until scarce any of the original Marble remained visible. Some of the Statues in the French Collection have not a cubic foot of antique marble in their composition. Even the famous Belvidere Apollo (a circumstance little known) was degraded by spurious additions, when placed in the Vatican' (pp. ii–iii). See also Francis Haskell and Nicholas Penny *Taste and the antique* (2nd printing New Haven 1982) p. 103.

[44] Editor of *Memoirs relating to European and Asiatic Turkey* (1817), which included letters of J. D. Carlyle (Sir Thomas Adams Professor of Arabic 1795–1804 and chaplain to Elgin's expedition) to the Bishops of Lincoln and Durham describing his fortunes in hunting for manuscripts. See also note 48 below.

[45] Otter *Life and remains* 2 p. 255.

Wilkins' *Antiquities of Magna Graecia*, published at Cambridge in 1807 but begun in the summer of 1803:[46] the book was further ornamented with an engraving on the title-page of the fragment from Pergamon, and it at once became one of the points of reference for the Greek revival in the arts, to be coupled with the earlier work of James Stuart and Thomas Major's *Ruins of Paestum*, now half a century old.[47]

At few times in the history of the Library has such widespread interest in a subject been so fruitful. And yet, despite the enthusiasm among many members of the University for Clarke's marbles, the rest of his collections were allowed to slip away from Cambridge. Clarke himself, even after his marriage in 1806 and the consequent end to his fellowship at Jesus, remained intimately involved in the University's affairs. In theory there should have been plenty of opinion in support of acquiring for the University any further parts of his collections. Porson was among the first to acknowledge the primary importance of the manuscript of Plato written in the year 895 and acquired by Clarke on Patmos: it remains still the earliest known copy of the first six Tetralogies. J. D. Carlyle, Professor of Arabic, who had himself taken part in Elgin's expedition in search of manuscripts at Constantinople,[48] might also have added his weight, except that he and Clarke had met in Turkey and fallen out publicly over the site of Troy:[49] Clarke returned home determined to prove that he was right in his opinion, and the quarrel was not patched up.

---

[46] R. W. Liscombe *William Wilkins 1778–1839* (Cambridge 1980) p. 33.

[47] In 1805 Clarke's other gifts in the entrance hall had been joined by a further donation, an Armenian inscription dated (according to the Donations Register) 1400.

[48] See above, note 44. The manuscripts collected by Carlyle himself on this expedition went – amidst some controversy – to Lambeth Palace: see H. J. Todd *A catalogue of the archiepiscopal manuscripts in the library at Lambeth Palace* (1812) pp. iv–v and MSS. 1175–1209, and *idem, An account of Greek manuscripts, chiefly Biblical, which had been in the possession of the late Professor Carlyle*; cf. also the anonymous review by C. J. Blomfield of Robert Walpole's memoirs (*Quarterly Review* 19 (1818) pp. 233–46).

[49] St Clair *Lord Elgin and the marbles* pp. 75 and 287.

The collections were phenomenal. At the end of 1801 Clarke had sent back to England seventy-six cases,[50] of minerals, inscriptions, Greek vases, over a thousand (by his own count) Greek medals and coins, and over six thousand plants. He had also accumulated an extraordinary collection of oriental and Greek manuscripts:

But I have such a collection of interesting manuscripts, that their mere names cannot be indifferent to you. –

In Greek, I have the Works of Plato; the Lexicon of St. Cyril; a volume of Greek Poems; and two works on Ancient Music.

In Arabic, the 'Arabian Nights,' or 'Elf Leela, O Leela'; the 'Delail il Hairat;' the 'Insarf,' or Arab Grammar; the 'Koran;' Arabic Poetry; and the famous Astronomical work of 'Olug Beg.' Also the History of Noureddin, Prince of Aleppo, during the Crusades; and Salaheddin, or Saladin, by Schehabeddin; a most valuable MS. in 4to.

In Persian, the whole of the Works of Saadi, the Persian Milton; containing, besides his Gulestan, or Garden of Roses, many works never translated; the Persian Prosody; the Persian Martial; from which it seems some of the Epigrams in the Latin Poet were derived; the works of Bidfai, or Pilpay; containing the Fables and Apologues known afterward to the Greeks under the name of Aesop; the 'Chosen History of Mohammed Kaveeni,' from the creation, to the time of the caliphs and scheiks; Tales, Poems, &c.

In Turkish, the Marvels of the Creation, a copy of which is in our Public Library, at Cambridge, as one of the most rare and ancient productions of oriental literature. I believe the Cambridge copy is in Arabic. Mine contains the course of the Nile from its sources, which the author places, with Ptolemy, in Africa, in the Lunar Mountains. The Rury Nameh, or Equinoctial Tables. Sentences of the Mohammedan Law; religious works, &c.

In Coptic, a copy of the Four Gospels, as preached by the earliest propagators of Christianity in Egypt; and some other MSS. the list of which is not now by me.

In Abyssinian, a copy of the Gospels, brought from thence by one of their bishops, a Negro, to Grand Cairo, with other MSS.

In Hebrew, a beautiful and useful MS. if I may not be allowed to say important. It is a copy, in folio, on vellum, of the Bible of the Karaean Jews, a sect become extremely rare; and established, under the protection of the late Empress of Russia, on a high rock, in the Crimea. You know they differ from the other Jews, in the superior purity of their traditions

[50] Otter *Life and remains* 2 p. 168.

and annals, and in having kept their copy of the Bible, from the books of Joshua, free from the interpolations and corrections of their Rabbis. Pallas succeeded in getting it for me, after I had left it in despair.

I have also a Greek copy of the Gospels, of the highest antiquity, on vellum, a MS. brought from Greece to the Crimea, at the first introduction of Christianity there.[51]

By the following March, at last heading towards home, he had bought a further collection of Greek manuscripts,[52] mostly theological works, and he had been able to add various Latin manuscripts on passing through Vienna a few weeks later.[53] He had not bought with the eye of an expert, but he had the sense to consult with those more knowledgeable on his return, among them Porson, Samuel Butler, Edward Maltby and Charles Burney, all of whom could advise on the classical texts. The manuscripts of the Gospels were inspected by William Pearce, dean of Ely and Master of Jesus College, and John Banks Hollingworth of Peterhouse.[54] It rapidly became clear that, whether expert or not, Clarke had brought back an unusually interesting collection. The discovery, however pleasing to the owner, presented insuperable difficulties for the University. Neither the Library nor the University felt able to buy it, and the collection, after nearly landing in the British Museum, was sold to the Bodleian for a thousand pounds in 1809: initially Oxford received thirty-two manuscripts, but Clarke added to it voluntarily, and the number stood eventually at over ninety.[55]

Few events could illustrate more dramatically the gulf between the two universities, one which had been apparent for some years, since the Bodleian had begun seriously to build up its collection of incunabula,[56] and which Cambridge seemed unwilling even to narrow. Only in 1805 Oxford had bought (for £1025) the d'Orville manuscripts, numbering about 570

[51] Ibid., pp. 176–8.   [52] Ibid., pp. 187–8.   [53] Ibid., p. 190.   [54] Ibid., p. 240.
[55] F. Madan A summary catalogue of the western manuscripts in the Bodleian Library at Oxford 4 (Oxford 1897) pp. 297–312.
[56] Ian Philip 'The background to Bodleian purchases of incunabula at the Pinelli and Crevenna sales, 1789–90' Trans. Cambridge Bibliographical Soc. 7 (1979) pp. 369–75.

items, many of them classical,[57] and in 1817 it paid the unprecedented sum of £5444 for the Canonici collection with a courageous loan from the Radcliffe Trustees and the University's bankers: the money was paid back by 1820.[58] The failure by Cambridge to acquire Clarke's manuscripts did not pass without causing some distress, but the University was impotent; and when Gaisford's catalogue of the collection was published in 1812 a reviewer in the *Museum Criticum*, probably Charles James Blomfield, the editor of Aeschylus, returned to the occasion and to upbraid Cambridge:

That learned body, with a spirit of oeconomy, which might have been exerted on a better occasion, declined enriching, at a moderate expense, its manuscript stores, the deficiency of which is the subject of constant regret with those of its members, who pay a critical attention to the languages of antiquity. On this, as on a former occasion, these Κειμήλια were eagerly purchased by the Curators of the Bodleian Library, who did not, it is to be presumed, accurately calculate the intrinsic value of certain quires of vellum, parchment, and yellow paper, disfigured by pot-hooks not easy to be deciphered, but were anxious to add to the literary treasures already deposited in that noble collection. On whose shoulders rests the blame of that ill-judged parsimony, which deprived us of the benefit of Dr. Clarke's offer, we are not disposed to enquire, nor will the public be much interested to know.[59]

It was to be far from the last occasion that collections of some importance were turned away ostensibly or actually for financial reasons. As M. R. James reflected at the end of the century when surveying the manuscript collections in Cambridge, 'At no time, I am sorry to say, have the University nor any of the Colleges spent any adequate sums on the purchase of MSS. ... Here we have bought timidly, and by twos and threes, instead of by dozens and hundreds.'[60]

Clarke valued his Plato[61] at £450, a tenth-century copy of Gregory Nazianzenus with scholia[62] at £40, and an eleventh-century illuminated copy of the Gospels in Greek at £60,

---

[57] Macray *Annals* p. 282.   [58] *Ibid.*, p. 299.
[59] *Museum Criticum; or, Cambridge classical researches* I (Cambridge 1814) pp. 128–9.
[60] Sandars lectures, 1903. Quoted in R. W. Pfaff *Montague Rhodes James* (1980) p. 208.
[61] Bodleian Library MS. E. D. Clarke 39 (*Summary Catalogue* 18400).
[62] MS. E. D. Clarke 12 (SC 18374).

believing that the last was somewhat older.[63] The prices were in line with contemporary trends, but in 1810 Richard Payne Knight secured a distinct bargain when Clarke charged him a mere £100 (and received a hundred guineas) for his collection of Greek coins.[64] Here, once again, since the Library already contained an important numismatic collection, there might have been found sufficient justification for adding to it. The University could have afforded it, while it would have been hard, though not impossible, to meet the cost of the manuscripts. In the financial year 1809–10 the University's total expenditure amounted to £20,424, of which £11,227 represented the cost of running the Press. As was customary, it ended the year with a balance in credit, which this year was £5205. Out of the total of £20,424, only £411 was spent on books and binding, a figure that was, again, typical even though the Library in a burst of energy thanks to J. H. Monk had spent £22.17s.0d. at the sale of Porson's books on 12 July. In contrast with what might have been done, and what was being done not only by Oxford but also by major private buyers with more freedom, such as Lord Spencer, William Beckford, and the Marquess of Blandford, the University's attitude was apathetic.

Clarke's ultimate belief that the University was unwilling to spend money on acquiring outstanding collections or single items was fully justified. But it was willing enough to accept gifts. In 1806 a small collection of Quaker books appeared from the Committee for the Sufferings of the Society of Friends:[65] the volumes seem to have been accepted readily enough, though the Library did not take the hint that there was room for further improvement in this field. It was much easier to accept, in 1810, the gifts of the Rev. Baily Wallis of Peterhouse, rector of St Mary Stoke, Ipswich, beginning with

---

[63] MS. E. D. Clarke 10 (SC 18372); Otter *Life and remains* 2 pp. 242–3.
[64] Otter *Life and remains* 2 pp. 244–5.
[65] Apart from the Accessions Register, a list of these is preserved in W. Sewel *Die Geschichte von dem Ursprung ... des Christlichen Volcks so Quäcker* (1742), Syn.3.74.1.

a trio of engravings by or after Dürer[66] and followed in November by a group of books including Jaillot's *Atlas nouveau* (1681), an extra-illustrated copy of Isaac Ware and William Kent's *Plans, elevations, and sections of Houghton* (1760) with notes on the sale of the house's paintings, and J. E. Smith and James Sowerby's *Exotic botany* (1804–5). The numismatic collections were advanced with gifts of medals commemorating the Battle of the Nile[67] and Boydell's Shakespeare,[68] a prize medal from Haarlem awarded to the Rev. Caesar Morgan of Christ's,[69] Pozzo's medallion of Middleton, and the gilt version of the same a little later.[70] The portrait of Conyers Middleton now hanging in the Library was presented by Mrs Heberden in 1802,[71] and a copy on canvas of a Babylonian inscription in 1804. In 1810 there arrived a picture purporting to be of the fourteenth-century Chancellor of the University Richard Ling, but dating from the late seventeenth or early eighteenth century,[72] and in 1817 'part of the Mulberry Tree, said to have been planted by W^m. Shakespeare at Stratford upon Avon'.[73] In 1802 Clarke added to the more scientific exhibitions with two thermometers showing the temperature according to three different scales, and in 1808 Kerrich elicited from Ralph Wedgwood a stylographic manifold writer with all the appropriate apparatus.[74] Faced

---

66 'St Eustace', 'Melancolia I' (a copy) and 'Knight, death and devil'.
67 Given by Alexander Davison, the friend of Nelson and agent for the sale of the prizes after the Battle of the Nile. See *DNB*.
68 Given by J. I. and J. N. Boydell and G. and W. Nicol.
69 Morgan had been awarded his prize by Teyler's Godgeleerd Genootschap for his essay *A demonstration, that true philosophy has no tendency to undermine divine revelation* (1786); the copy of this work presented at the same time stands at 8.18.10.
70 The first was given by Richard Harraden, the Cambridge artist, in 1810 and the second by Sir John E. Dolben in 1818.
71 Goodison *Cambridge portraits* 47; Donations Register 1800–65 p. 4.
72 Goodison *Cambridge portraits* 1.
73 Accessions Register February 1817. See also S. Schoenbaum *William Shakespeare; records and images* (1981) p. 57. It is (perhaps) worth adding that another piece of the same tree, 'formerly the property of Dodd the Comedian', was offered at Sotheby's auction of James Boswell's library in 1825 (Lot 3133), and was sold to Rodd for £3.5s.
74 Accessions Register 6 January 1808. For the career of the ingenious Ralph Wedgwood see Josiah C. Wedgwood *A history of the Wedgwood family* (1908) pp. 208–15. The manifold writer was a resounding success.

with the necessity for a new catalogue on the one hand (the old Bodleian interleaved one being full to overflowing) and annual accounts from the Library Keeper which inexorably repeated that Marshall had made treble entries for every book that entered the library from the Stationers' Company and from booksellers, it seems likely that Kerrich had some improvement in office procedures in mind: the manifold writer could not have helped Marshall's book-keeping without considerable rearrangement, but as it turned out the gadget was not even applied to the catalogue.

Besides these modest gifts, in one respect Kerrich's librarianship saw a series of unexpected successes. No major collection of oriental material had reached the Library since George Lewis' donation in 1726. Odd additions had filtered in, such as the Persian *Wonders of creation*, alluded to by Clarke in 1802 and the prize of the Library's Persian manuscript treasures. In 1794 the aged Robert Masters had given a manuscript Persian verse life of Alexander the Great, *Á'íné-i-Sikandarí*, brought back from India by Busick Harwood; and a sprinkling of books from the Indian sub-continent also found their way in. The *Wonders of creation* formed a principal attraction to passers-by in the Dome Room, together with half a dozen portfolios of now unidentified Chinese manuscripts presented in 1772 by the Sussex antiquary William Burrell.[75] Otherwise there was little new to show. Yet by 1824, the date of the publication of George Dyer's *Privileges of the University of Cambridge*, the Library had made major gains in its Syriac, Persian and Arabic manuscripts, and had laid the foundations of a collection of printed editions of native Indian literature. The manuscripts came from three main sources: from Claudius Buchanan, from J. L. Burckhardt, and from the library of Tippoo Sahib, and each in its way was outstanding. Tippoo Sahib, long the enemy to British expansion in India, was finally defeated and killed in May 1799. His property was subsequently auctioned off, with the exception of his library (most of which had been looted,

[75] See also J. Britton and E. W. Brayley *The beauties of England and Wales* 3 (1801) p. 96.

according to those who subsequently examined it), which was removed into the hands of the East India Company at Calcutta. From this residue a few manuscripts were extracted, for the Asiatic Society and for the Universities of Oxford and Cambridge. Like the Bodleian, Cambridge received a Koran of unusual quality, and as its part of the booty the Library also acquired a manuscript of the *Sháhnáma* of Firdawsí, dating from the late sixteenth or early seventeenth century, together with a finely illuminated copy of the works of Sa'dí.

The person who first sorted and catalogued these manuscripts, with the rest of Tippoo Sahib's library in Calcutta, was Charles Stewart; and on his return to England to teach at Haileybury College (still known then as the East India College) he set to work to prepare a full catalogue of the collection, which in 1809 was published by the University Press.[76] In Calcutta Stewart had been associated, as teacher of Persian, with the college of Fort William, whose staff also numbered a forceful and earnest Professor of Greek and Latin classics, Claudius Buchanan. Like Lewis' before him and Burckhardt's after, Buchanan's oriental manuscripts had been gathered in the course of his travels, and though his descriptive skills as a travel writer were inferior to those of Clarke, like Clarke he was quick to comment on when, where, and in what circumstances he acquired his treasures. Since many of his volumes were extracted from Jewish and Christian communities in an alien country, these remarks, like archaeological evidence, add measurably to the value and interest of his subsequent gifts to the University Library. Buchanan had attended the University of Glasgow, before coming up to Queens' College in 1791 at the age of twenty-five. In Cambridge, under the influence of Charles Simeon, he rapidly became identified with the emergent evangelical movement.[77] After his ordination in 1795 he served a brief curacy at St Mary Woolnoth in the City

---

[76] *A descriptive catalogue of the oriental library of the late Tippoo Sultan of Mysore* (1809).
[77] Much of the background to this is described in Ford K. Brown *Fathers of the Victorians; the age of Wilberforce* (Cambridge 1961).

of London, and in 1796 was appointed chaplain to the East India Company. Unwilling to take a passive part in Indian affairs, and much influenced by those who had sent him out east, Buchanan devoted his first years in India to familiarizing himself with Hindi and Persian. On the foundation of the College of Fort William in 1800 he was appointed Vice-Provost and given responsibility for teaching Greek and Latin. He remained with the Company until 1807, when he broke with it over its unwillingness to allow him to follow his missionary pursuits with the zeal that he wished.[78]

Whatever his intransigent attitude to those set in authority above him, however (and no-one doubted the sincerity of his beliefs), Buchanan either gave or caused to be given to the Library a succession of printed books and manuscripts that had no equal. In 1804 he announced his intention of presenting to the Library about a hundred volumes of oriental literature, printed in Bengal, and at the same time he gave £210 for four prize compositions on the general theme of Christian mission in India.[79] A Grace thanking him for these gifts and proposals was passed on 11 June, and in the following year he produced a further sum of £500 to encourage another prize essay on a rather larger scale.[80] But meanwhile there had been a hitch in the supply of the promised books. The University passed another Grace thanking him for his efforts on 16 March 1805,[81] just five days before he was constrained to write an apology from Fort William. 'Accounts have just been received here,' he warned, 'that the Ship on board which was the remainder of the Oriental Works for the University of Cambridge has been captured and carried into the Mauritius. A new set shall be prepared by next season.'[82] He was forced to

---

[78] Hugh Pearson *Memoirs of the life and writings of the Rev. Claudius Buchanan* 2nd ed. (Oxford 1817) I pp. 147–8 and 205. On the College of Fort William see M. A. Laird *Missionaries and education in Bengal 1793–1837* (Oxford 1972) pp. 57–8 etc.

[79] Grace Book *A* pp. 448–9 and Clark *Endowments* p. 380. Sayle's statement (*Annals* p. 108) that he presented nearly a hundred oriental books on 11 June 1804 is incorrect.

[80] Clark *Endowments* p. 381. Other prize money was offered at Oxford and elsewhere: cf. E. Stock *The history of the Church Missionary Society* I (1899) p. 97.

[81] Grace Book *A* p. 463. [82] Quoted in Sayle *Annals* p. 108.

write similarly to Eton College, to whom he also intended to present just such a collection as he designed for Cambridge.[83] A selection of sixty-five items was delivered safely to Cambridge in October, officially the gift of the College of Fort William but in fact due almost entirely to Buchanan in his capacity of Vice-Provost. The parcel, registered in the Accessions Book on 25 October, contained the core of the renaissance in printing native Indian literature. The Library had received an inkling of the activity in Calcutta with the arrival in March 1804 of William Carey's pioneering translation of the Pentateuch and Gospels into Bengali, the gift of the Baptist Missionary Society. The 1805 gift brought all that the Society's press at Serampore, under the management of Carey, had so far published, including his Bengali and Sanskrit grammars and the first printed versions of the classics of Bengali literature, many the work of pundits at the College of Fort William. From the Hindoostanee Press, established in 1802, a year after the Serampore press, came further contributions to the linguistic reformation and ordering that was part of the College's mission, emphasized again with the establishment of the Persian and Sanskrit presses in 1805 and 1807. The College subsidized the presses directly, in many cases taking large parts of the editions, and indirectly with its staff, and most of the books that came to Cambridge were from these new presses: among the few not to were John Gilchrist's *Oriental linguist* (1798) and H. P. Forster's Bengali dictionary of 1799–1802, both from the independent printer Paul Ferris.[84] Even this was far from all that Buchanan intended, and although no more printed books appeared, he wrote again in March 1806 to the Vice-Chancellor with a proposal to support two sermons encouraging oriental translations of the Bible, at the same time also enclosing proposals for translations on which he requested

[83] I am grateful to Mr Paul Quarrie for help on this point.
[84] For the background to this see M. Siddiq Khan 'William Carey and the Serampore books (1800–1834)' *Libri* 11 (1961) pp. 197–280; David Kopf *British orientalism and the Bengal renaissance* (Berkeley 1969); and Graham Shaw *Printing in Calcutta to 1800* (1981).

an opinion.[85] He was a tenacious and demanding benefactor, but he was to prove a generous one too.

If Buchanan had any influence in the gift of the manuscripts from Tippoo Sahib's library it was not made clear to Cambridge. So far, therefore, his name had been associated only with printed books. But in 1809 he presented from his own library a group of oriental manuscripts that proved to be of quite another order.[86] Between May 1806 and March 1807 he was on leave of absence from Calcutta, and he had travelled south in order, as he put it, to 'investigate the state of superstition at the most celebrated Temples of the Hindoos; to examine the Churches and libraries of the Romish, Syrian and Protestant Christians; to ascertain the present state and recent history of the Jews in the east; and to discover what persons might be fit instruments for the promotion of learning in their respective countries'.[87] Out of this journey, and a shorter one a few months later to visit Jewish and Syrian Christian communities in Malabar and Travancore, he fashioned most of his *Christian researches in Asia*, first published in 1811 and a considerable popular success.

Of some twenty-five Syriac manuscripts he was able to secure during these journeys, a badly damaged Bible dating from the end of the twelfth century was the obvious prize. It was given to Buchanan by the bishop of the Syrian church in south India after Buchanan had discovered it in a remote church, and it created an immediate stir. Buchanan himself sent a note of his travels off to England in January 1807, and his account of the Bible and sundry other manuscripts appeared in the issue for the following October of the *Christian Observer*.[88] Among the Hebrew manuscripts were a large Pentateuch roll

---

[85] Clark *Endowments* p. 382.
[86] The Donations Register for 1800–65 records eighty unspecified oriental manuscripts, but no more than about fifty can now be identified.
[87] C. Buchanan *Christian researches in Asia* 8th ed. (1812) pp. 68–9.
[88] *Loc. cit.*, pp. 654–62. For a further account of the manuscripts see Wright's *Catalogue* and F. C. Burkitt 'The Buchanan MSS. at Cambridge' *Kerala Society Papers* December 1928.

(MS. Oo.1.3), dating from the tenth century but amended and supplemented in various places by later hands, and another, somewhat smaller, roll of the Book of Esther, dating from the fifteenth or sixteenth century. Buchanan experienced some difficulty in procuring Hebrew manuscripts, for although he found little trouble in bargaining with the elders in the synagogue at Cochin, there was some antagonism towards a Christian removing even old and disused copies of the Law.[89] He overcame these difficulties, however, and went on subsequently to tour through other communities of Black Jews in the interior. 'I have', he remarked, in explanation of their interest,

procured a good many manuscripts, chiefly in the Rabbinical character, some of which the Jews themselves cannot read; and I do not know what to say to their traditions. A copy of the Scriptures belonging to Jews of the East, who might be supposed to have no communications with Jews in the West, has long been considered a desideratum in Europe; for the Western Jews have been accused by some learned men of altering or omitting certain words in the Hebrew text, to invalidate the arguments of Christians. But Jews in the East, remote from the controversy, would have no motive for such corruptions. One or two of the MSS. which I have just procured, will probably be of some service in this respect.[90]

Besides the need for manuscripts, Buchanan also sensed a dearth of Hebrew printed books, and he took steps to collect together some of those as well: his gift to Cambridge in 1809 included a dozen, dating from the sixteenth to the eighteenth century, but although there were amongst them an Old Testament printed at Hamburg in 1587 and an incomplete copy of the later part of the Old Testament printed at Paris in 1531, Buchanan's hopes were not so amply fulfilled on this account.

To these major collections of oriental literature, Buchanan was also able to add a modern manuscript of St John's Gospel in Ethiopic, found in the library of an Armenian merchant. The University, however, found three other items more attractive.

---

[89] Buchanan *Christian researches in Asia* pp. 249–51.   [90] *Ibid.*, p. 251.

A large Persian illuminated address to the Marquess Wellesley, Governor General of India in 1804 and largely responsible for the founding of the College of Fort William, was set up in a gold frame at the entrance to the Royal Library.[91] An Indian portrait of the Rajah of Tanjore, given to Buchanan by its subject in 1806, added further colour. But his most curious discoveries were represented by a series of copper plates that he had caused to have made, representing a series of brass tablets with both Christian and Jewish inscriptions, whose existence had been long known from the accounts of earlier travellers but which were recovered only in December 1806. 'It may be doubted', thought Buchanan, 'whether there exists in the world any documents of so great length, which are of equal antiquity, and in such faultless preservation, as the Christian tablets of Malabar.'[92] He was rightly proud of having arranged to have them copied, but even he was unwilling to venture a date.

On their arrival in Cambridge, the manuscripts were put into the hands of a man who, though originally a Hebraist, proved willing to tackle most of what Buchanan had amassed. Thomas Yeates, brought over especially from Oxford, did all that he could to publicize the collection. His first, brief, account appeared in the *Christian Observer* in January 1810, and he speedily pointed out that although Buchanan had collected them all in India, by no means all had been written there. 'Some', he alleged, 'were written at Antioch, Mesopotamia, and other parts of Syria, Asia and Africa.'[93] He drew attention to a link between the Pentateuch roll and Sephardic calligraphy in Spain,[94] though it seems more likely that the earlier parts were written by an Arab. He knew of only one comparable manuscript of the Syriac Bible, that listed by Montfaucon in the Ambrosiana, and dated Buchanan's to the seventh century.[95] This journalism was simply a prelude to a

---

[91] MS. Nn.6.45(2), fo. 61ʳ.   [92] Buchanan *Christian researches in Asia* p. 175.
[93] *Christian Observer* January 1810 p. 26.   [94] *Christian Observer* March 1810 p. 144.
[95] *Christian Observer* May 1810 p. 274.

much larger project, which appeared from the University Press in 1812 under the title of *Collation of an Indian copy of the Hebrew Pentateuch, with preliminary remarks: containing an exact description of the manuscript, and a notice of some others, (Hebrew and Syriac) collected by the Rev. Claudius Buchanan, D.D. in the year 1806*: he added to it a collation and description of the roll of Esther together with a text and translation. The whole book, an uncharacteristically prompt examination of a new acquisition, was supported with prefatory remarks by Herbert Marsh, the reforming Lady Margaret Professor of Divinity, and John Palmer, Professor of Arabic. Such, indeed, was the interest caused by the more important of the manuscripts that in July 1812 the University was prevailed on by Yeates and his associates to spend no less than a hundred guineas on a thirteenth-century Sephardic Pentateuch roll:[96] it arrived, unfortunately, too late for Yeates to include it in his study of the Pentateuch roll, and so in terms of scholarly interest was something of an anti-climax. But nothing could have expressed more clearly the enthusiasm of at least part of the University for the subject. Never before had the Library spent so much on a single manuscript, not even in the heady days of the Askew sale, and it was not to do so again for years to come.[97]

More than anything else, Buchanan was convinced of the need in India for missionaries from England, and for copies of the Bible in Syriac for the south. He was able to put the need for missionaries with some force to the new Church Missionary Society on his return to England in 1808, and proved a compelling preacher on the subject. The need for printed Bibles in Syriac was no less great, in the face of Roman Catholic expansion and despite doubts raised in the wake of the Vellore mutiny of 1806 as to the wisdom of printing the scriptures in

---

96 Grace Book *M* p. 63. Schiller-Szinessy no. 2 (MS. Add. 289).
97 Some idea of the relative magnitude of the price may be appreciated by recalling that on 3 July 1812, only the day before the Grace sanctioning the purchase of the Pentateuch, Leigh and Sotheby sold Samuel Guise's collection of 135 oriental (mostly Indian) manuscripts for £110.4s.6d.

native languages. Using his manuscripts as a basis, Buchanan embarked on an edition of the Gospels and Acts that was completed with the help of Yeates and Lee: it was printed (with types specially cut by Figgins) by Richard Smith at Broxbourne and published by the British and Foreign Bible Society in 1815, the year of Buchanan's death. After some dispute as to presentation a complete New Testament appeared in the following year, edited on slightly different principles by Lee alone, and the Old Testament was published in 1823.[98]

Yeates later readverted to his work on the Buchanan manuscripts in his *Indian church history*, published in 1818, but the first proper and reasonably full list of them was not made public until a series of articles in the *Classical Journal* in 1818–21 described the classical, biblical and oriental manuscripts of the Library. The articles were by George Dyer, who whenever faced with a difference of opinion tended to be swayed by the most recent. Nevertheless (and despite drawbacks such as a complete lack of any class-marks), his inventory, published in a revised form in his *Privileges of the University of Cambridge* (1824) remained the fullest available until the appearance of William Wright's catalogue of the Syriac manuscripts in the Library in 1901, and remains still the best easily available of some of the Hebrew part.[99]

On the death of the *Bibliothecarius* John Davies in 1817, the obvious candidate as his successor was Edward Daniel Clarke. With characteristic gusto, Clarke entered the election so eagerly that his printed circular offering himself as a candidate was dated before an election had even been announced. He had for years been active in the Library's interests whenever circumstances seemed to allow, and in 1815 had been instrumental in obtaining for the Library (there were no other

---

[98] Cf. Stock *History of the Church Missionary Society* I pp. 97–101; P. Cheriyan *The Malabar Syrians and the Church Missionary Society 1816–1840* (Kottayam 1935) esp. ch. 5; T. H. Darlow and H. F. Moule *Historical Catalogue of the printed editions of Holy Scripture* (1903–11) nos. 8977–9.

[99] Schiller-Szinessy's catalogue of the Hebrew manuscripts (Cambridge 1876 etc.) remained unfinished (see below, pp. 719–20) and lists only seven of Buchanan's gifts.

more suitable University premises) a group of Eskimo exhibits brought back from Hudson's Bay the previous year; it included sets of clothes for a man, woman and child, besides other odd sealskin items of clothing, a snow mask, a decorated barb from a harpoon, and, in the words of a list of these spoils, 'Two of their Images; the one representing a *Man*, and the other a *Woman*, in the *Esquimaux* Dress; shewing the first dawning of sculpture, and their inability to represent the human countenance, hands, or feet'. The University owed all these northern curiosities to Clarke's friendship with a young lieutenant in the Navy, Edward Chappell, who in fact gave them to the Library even though Clarke's name is recorded in the Donations Register.[100] So closely had Clarke become associated with the Library that to Charles Kelsall, one of the group of Cambridge Hellenists, he seemed to represent its epitome; in 1814 Kelsall addressed his proposals in his *Phantasm of an university* for a new Senate House, Library, and Museum to Clarke, the man to whom it would mean most.[101] Besides his interests in the more curious parts of the collection, Clarke had also proved his sympathies for manuscripts, if in a somewhat wayward manner, with the collections sold to the Bodleian Library in 1809. Overall, there could be no doubt that he possessed the imagination and breadth of knowledge, if sometimes only on a nodding acquaintance, that might be hoped for in a curator of a collection expanding rapidly and in ways not always understood thanks to the alarming success of copyright legislation described in the next chapter.

His official opponent in the election was an old friend, George D'Oyley, Fellow of Corpus Christi College from 1801 to 1813, when he had married, and since 1815 Rectoɪ of

---

100 For an account of the voyage of H.M.S. *Rosamond*, on which these were collected, see Edward Chappell *Narrative of a voyage to Hudson's Bay in His Majesty's Ship Rosamond* (1817), with a preface by Clarke and a list (pp. 253–4) of Chappell's gifts. Chappell's collection has since been transferred to the Museum of Archaeology and Anthropology.

101 C. Kelsall *Phantasm of an university: with prolegomena* (1814) p. 133. On Kelsall see David Watkin 'Charles Kelsall; the quintessence of neo-classicism' *Architectural Review* 140 (1966) pp. 109–12.

Uckfield in Sussex. The two men gained an equal number of nominations, four each, but by the election on 13 February D'Oyley had withdrawn to leave Clarke victorious. 'Yesterday', Clarke wrote twenty-four hours later, 'was one of the happiest days of our lives . . . In the morning at twelve our baby was christened. At two p.m. I was unanimously elected Librarian in the senate. In the evening, we had all our friends to a dance and supper, which went off in most gallant style till four. This morning, as soon as I was elected, the bells of St. Mary's and of St. Benedict's, fired off most jovial peals, and all was mirth and gratulation.'[102] Kerrich, on the other hand, viewed the prospect with mixed feelings, and before the final election wrote to his old friend and confidant on antiquarian matters, Edward Balme, 'The loss of poor Davies, & my anxieties about whom I was to have for a Colleague in his place you may conceive have kept me in a sort of fever: it is now settled that D[r] Clarke will be the man, & I am well contented: there is only one man, I know of, in the whole University I should have rather chosen for a partner – The Election will not be till next Thursday 13 of this month as perhaps you know, but both the other candidates have given up the contest. Clarke is good natured & liberal, & I think we shall agree very well – I fear nothing but his impetuosity.'[103]

More active than Davies in the everyday affairs of the Library, more respected in the University than Kerrich, Clarke was thus at last in a position to direct the affairs of the institution for which he had so long laboured. In 1817 he added to his gifts to the Library a manuscript description of a parish in Lapland by its pastor (MS. Ee.5.37), but he was to live only another five years, dogged by illness, and he was able to give but intermittent attention to his new post in a period when in any case he continued to conduct his scientific experiments, to teach, and to compile successive volumes of memoirs of his travels.

---

[102] Otter *Life and remains* 2 p. 343. I have been unable to trace the collection of Clarke's letters sold at Sotheby's on 19 July 1960, lot 462, to Mr Peter Kroger.
[103] Corpus Christi College, Kerrich papers 28. 85–6.

Clarke was faced with a library that was in danger of neglect. Neither Kerrich nor Davies had paid great attention to its everyday affairs for many months. Routines such as counter-signing invoices for payment, customarily the task of one or other librarian, had been left to the Library and School Keeper John Marshall and to his deputy James Tollworthy. Marshall, crippled with arthritis, finally died in 1819 after passing his last years in such discomfort that it would have been more fair both to him and to the Library had he been pensioned off. He had had the help of an assistant since 1798–9, but by October 1817 James Tollworthy (whose name appears in the accounts from 1812) was dead.[104] In Tollworthy's place the University appointed two men, Joseph Tollworthy and John Bowtell, nephew of the local binder, his namesake, whose duties were principally to catalogue books as they came in and to keep a register of books borrowed.[105] Both men were trained as bookbinders, and they continued to act in that capacity for the Library, by 1818 Tollworthy's bills being issued in the name of Tollworthy and Wootton. At first these two, of whom Bowtell was to remain into obstinate old age and his final dismissal in 1852, were employed only part-time, but on 16 March 1818 the Library Syndicate agreed to employ them full-time and by this means to extend the Library's opening hours from two to three o'clock in the afternoons.

On the same day that a Grace put this into effect, a further Grace was passed authorizing the payment of £500 out of the University Chest for a new 'class-catalogue', after the manner of Brunet's *Manuel du libraire et de l'amateur des livres*, first published in 1810 and of which a second edition had appeared in 1814.[106] This would have given the Library a catalogue arranged both by authors and by subjects, and a few days later

---

104 On 1 October his widow Elizabeth signed a receipt for £300 voted to her by Grace (Vouchers).

105 Cf. their invoice (Vouchers 22 October 1817). On Bowtell see A. B. Gray *John Bowtell; bookbinder of Cambridge (1753–1813); biographical notes, with a further notice of his nephew John Bowtell the younger (1777–1855)* (Cambridge 1907).

106 Later, the classified subject volumes of both the 1814 and the 1820 editions were used as checks of what the Library possessed, though not apparently for very long.

the Syndics resolved to approach Robert Triphook, the London bookseller, with a proposal that he should be employed to make the subject catalogue. Money to meet the additional expense that Triphook's labour would involve was not however forthcoming, and the bold plan for a subject catalogue on Brunet's model was perforce dropped.[107] Instead, in May 1818 John Bowtell began work solely on a new author catalogue to replace the old interleaved Bodleian one and the manuscript one of the Royal Library. By the end of November the following year he had completed the first two letters of the alphabet. He was paid twenty guineas for each letter, and by the beginning of November 1826 had finished his task, even down to adding a general title-page to each volume boldly emblazoned with his name.[108] His work survived in everyday use, expanded into several more volumes than the original, until the introduction of a printed catalogue in 1861.

Clarke's brief period of office was dominated by three topics: attempts to organize the Library by means of this new catalogue of the printed books; difficulties and arrangements over the Copyright Act of 1814, discussed below in Chapter 10; and, rather more immediately gratifying than either, the arrival of the Burckhardt manuscripts.

The Buchanan oriental manuscripts had provided an exciting collection, that offered fresh knowledge of a part of the world too little understood, and Yeates made rapid use of it. But Kerrich was to see further additions yet to the Library's shelves of oriental manuscripts – though it was Clarke, again, who was at the centre of the most numerous and most important single acquisition of Arabic manuscripts in the Library's history.

Jean Louis Burckhardt, born into a well-to-do Swiss family in 1784, had been drawn to England by Sir Joseph Banks and to Cambridge by Herbert Marsh, whose acquaintance he had

---

[107] Cf. Syndicate Minutes 16 March 1818, 13 April 1818, 12 May 1818. The Grace proposed at the second meeting, to employ Triphook, was never passed.
[108] Syndicate Minutes 26 November 1819, 21 March 1821; Grace Book *M* pp. 330, 368, 393, 425, 496; Grace Book *N* pp. 30, 145.

made at Leipzig. He arrived in Cambridge in 1808, in order to study Arabic in preparation for a venture planned under the auspices of the Association for Promoting the Discovery of the Interior Parts of Africa, usually referred to in less cumbersome terms as the African Association. Since its foundation by Sir Joseph Banks, Henry Beaufoy and a number of wealthy landowners in 1788, the Association had sponsored a series of journeys of exploration, undertaken usually alone, that had at last begun to extend knowledge of the northern parts of the African continent into the interior. Mungo Park's expeditions in 1795–7 caught the public's attention immediately, and three editions of his account of his journeys were issued in 1799, the year of its first publication. The young Burckhardt did not intend to explore these parts of West Africa again, but instead proposed to concentrate his efforts on reaching the northern parts of the Niger from the Mediterranean coast, beginning at Tripoli and traversing the Sahara with a caravan. It was a bold plan, and the bolder because he realized that in order to have a better chance of success he would have to travel in disguise, as a Moorish merchant. The African Association accepted his services in March 1808,[109] and he left England in March 1809. At Cambridge, where he threw himself with engaging determination into the task of learning his part, he stayed with Clarke, and the two remained fast friends.[110] Both men were instinctive explorers, intent on whatever life offered, and Burckhardt continued to correspond with Clarke for years afterwards. Probably through Sir Joseph Banks in London, Burckhardt also made the acquaintance of a member of the Association who remained another lifelong friend and correspondent, George Cecil Renouard, Fellow of Sidney Sussex College and curate of Great St Mary's, who had acted as British chaplain at Constantinople from 1804 to 1806, and was to be chaplain at Smyrna from 1811 to 1814.

---

[109] R. Hallett (ed.) *Records of the African Association* (1964) pp. 218–9.
[110] For a portrait of Burckhardt by Clarke's wife Angelica see the frontispiece to his *Travels in Nubia* (1819).

Burckhardt's final instructions from the African Association, delivered to him in January 1809,[111] proved to be very different from the plan he had proposed in 1808. Instead of approaching the northern Niger direct by the shortest route overland, he was first to go to Syria for two years in order to acquaint himself more fully with Arabic and Arab customs: only then was he to proceed to Cairo, where he could as a result expect to be received the more easily into a Muslim caravan crossing the desert from east to west. Burckhardt revelled in his mission. As it turned out, his travels began straightforwardly enough at Aleppo and Damascus, but from there he proceeded to the Euphrates and then, on a route that was as rewarding as the travelling conditions were harsh, to Petra (he was the first westerner to see it for centuries), south up the Nile, through much of Nubia, over the Red Sea to Mecca, and only then back north to Cairo to prepare for the main purpose of his expedition. No man had done so much; but still less had anyone ever contrived to report continuously and in detail on what he observed. Burckhardt's reports, in letters home to Banks and other friends, and in journals which were later published under the editorship of W. M. Leake and Sir William Ouseley, were voluminous.[112] But he never began the final lap of his journey, planned for so long. In Cairo he caught dysentery, and he died on 15 October 1817.

Throughout his travels Burckhardt had persistently sought out manuscripts wherever possible, though constant movement had not allowed him to accumulate as he might had he stayed in towns. In 1811 he sent back to Europe from Aleppo a consignment of Arabic manuscripts, enough to fill a 'large chest', bought at Aleppo and Damascus in the face of French competition: as Burckhardt explained to Banks, the French consuls in Syria were intent on acquiring such material for the

[111] *Records of the African Association* pp. 220–2.
[112] Besides his journals, the earliest account of Burckhardt's life remains the best: see William Leake's 'Memoir' prefixed to Burckhardt's *Travels in Nubia* (1819). Cf. also his *Briefe an Eltern und Geschwister* ed. C. Burckhardt-Sarasin and H. Schwabe-Burckhardt (Basel 1956).

Bibliothèque Nationale in Paris.[113] More were in his possession when he died, and with the exception of his European
books, which numbered only eight and were left to Henry
Salt, the Consul General in Egypt,[114] he left his entire library
to Cambridge.[115]

The manuscripts not already in England travelled back to
Cambridge via Constantinople, but meanwhile in March 1818
Clarke unpacked the first case of those already received with
the aid of John Palmer and Burckhardt's old friend Renouard,
Lord Almoner's Professor of Arabic since 1815.[116] The first
chest yielded eighty-eight volumes, besides various notebooks
and geological specimens; by the time everything had arrived
and been sorted out there were three hundred volumes in all,
and a quantity of miscellaneous pieces.[117] There was ample
cause for excitement. Clarke had already agreed, when the first
box was opened, that Palmer and Renouard should prepare a
special catalogue of so notable a collection, but as events turned
out the world had to wait longer than any of the three can have
envisaged before any kind of catalogue appeared. The collection was especially rich in history, literature and geography,
and ranged in date from the fifth century A.H. to the last years
of Burckhardt's life. It included an anthology of Arabic poetry
down to the beginning of the eleventh century (MS. Qq.51),
two copies of the celebrated collection of early Arabic poetry
Dīwānu'l-Ḥamāsa, first gathered in the early third century
A.H. (MSS. Qq.213, 296), and an important double manuscript dated A.H. 428 of Abū Ḥātim as-Sajistāni *Kitābu'l-
Mu'ammarīn* (or *Book of the long-lived*) with his *Kitābu'l-Waṣāyā*
(*Book of injunctions*, MS. Qq.285). There was a recent history of
Aleppo dating from A.H.1102, and an account of holy places

---

[113] *Travels in Nubia* 2nd ed. (1822) pp. xlvi, lxxxvii; Warren R. Dawson *The Banks letters;
a calendar of the manuscript correspondence of Sir Joseph Banks* (1958) p. 186.
[114] The two men were instrumental in acquiring for the British Museum a series of
Egyptian monuments: see E. Miller *That noble cabinet* (1973) pp. 201–2 and references.
[115] *Travels in Nubia* (1822) p. xcv.
[116] Sutro Library, San Francisco. Banks papers A 6/4.
[117] Now MSS. Qq.1–300 and Add. 273–82.

and shrines by one Shaykh 'Alī b. Abī Bakr al-Hiravī written out at the end of the seventh century A.H. (Qq.92). For many years the manuscript of al-Ya'qubi's history of the world since Adam, dated A.H.1096, was believed to be unique, and was edited as such by M. T. Houtsma in 1883.[118]

But despite such treasures, Renouard and Palmer never published even the briefest list. Palmer resigned from the Sir Thomas Adams Chair in 1819, and lived to the age of seventy-one in 1840 without publishing anything at all of any part of his profound and extensive knowledge.[119] Renouard's own energies were preoccupied by a plethora of other interests, and in 1821 he too resigned his professorship on being presented to a valuable living in Kent. It was the Library's misfortune that neither man was succeeded by an orientalist whose first interest was in Arabic literature. Instead, their successors leaned towards Hebrew, Persian, or the Indian languages, and thus neglected the possibilities offered by the Burckhardt collection. The manuscripts remained to be catalogued by Theodore Preston, Fellow of Trinity, over thirty years later. His *Catalogus bibliothecae Burckhardtianae, cum appendice librorum aliorum orientalium in Bibliotheca Academiae Cantabrigiensis asservatorum* was published in 1853, but it was a work unworthy of the collection. It was inadequate even by contemporary standards, and contained too many more or less ludicrous inaccuracies, which emerged only gradually under the eye of Henry Bradshaw and others.[120]

The conjunction of the arrival of Burckhardt's manuscripts with the presence in the Library of a man able to appreciate the spirit which had caused their collector to seek out such alien surroundings was one of the more pleasing circumstances of Clarke's few years of office. But his enthusiasm for the unfamiliar, his ever wandering imagination, and his reluctance

---

[118] A single further copy turned up subsequently in the John Rylands Library, MS. Rylands 46158.

[119] An account of his life is given in Sir R. F. Scott (ed.) *Admissions to the College of St John the Evangelist* 4 (Cambridge 1931) pp. 409–11.

[120] Preston was, nonetheless, elected Lord Almoner's Professor in 1855.

to set aside other distractions in favour of the needs of the Library, meant that he achieved less than he might have, in a position where it was easy to shine. Kerrich, always absorbed in his own collections of books, paintings and prints, paid no more heed to the Library than his official position demanded as a minimum, and with the bequest of the Fitzwilliam collection to the University in 1816 lavished on this new collection of *objets d'art* the time and attention that should have been spent elsewhere.[121] Whatever his new responsibilities as *Bibliothecarius*, Clarke proved unable to set aside his chemical experiments for more than brief periods. Two papers on antiquities unearthed at Sawston and Fulbourn, contributed to *Archaeologia*, the need to complete the publication of his travels, an article on the *lituus* (and associated correspondence on the subject with Richard Payne Knight), and the foundation of the Cambridge Philosophical Society, were all (and not the only) distractions from the Library, and were the more serious in one who was constantly prone to ill health. He complained of deafness, giddiness, headaches and failing sight. Yet he persisted with his experiments regardless of their danger until he finally collapsed, his last fortnight 'like a feverish dream after a day of strong excitement, when the same ideas chase each other through the mind in a perpetual round, and baffle every attempt to banish them'.[122] Delirious and incoherent, he finally died on 9 March 1822, and a few days later was buried in Jesus College chapel. For the second time in just over five years Kerrich was left without a *Bibliothecarius*; but this time the election was to produce a man of very different character.

---

121 The Fitzwilliam bequest almost immediately attracted offers of further books for the planned museum, including Young's *Night thoughts* with William Blake's illustrations and Thomas Thornton's *Sporting tour*, offered in October 1819 through Kerrich's agency (University Archives CUR. 30.1).   122 Otter *Life and remains* 2 p. 376.

10

THE NATIONAL STAGE: THE
COPYRIGHT ACT OF 1814

ALL THESE ADDITIONS to the oriental collections arrived
against a background of distractions at Cambridge that were to
have a much greater effect on the Library for most of its
readers. In 1805, the same year that Buchanan wrote from
Calcutta to announce that his shipment of books from the
College of Fort William had been captured at sea, there
appeared from the press of Francis Hodson in Cambridge a
pamphlet that proved to be the opening shot of a campaign
that was only temporarily halted with the passing of a new
Copyright Act in 1814. The pamphlet, *Enquiries and observations respecting the University Library*, was written by a man who
had no connection with the running of the Library. He was not
on its staff, not on the Library Syndicate, was not Head of a
House, and, indeed, had pursued a career that had little to do
directly with Cambridge. Basil Montagu had gone up to
Christ's College in 1786, was well acquainted with Wordsworth, Coleridge and the elder William Godwin, and in 1795
had left Cambridge in order to read for the bar. A philanthro-
pist of wide interests, he worked hard to clear John Beverley of
the debts incurred by his addiction to the bottle.[1] Besides a
long interest in bankruptcy and literary property, which
formed the mainstays of his legal business, between 1825 and
1837 he was also to produce a major edition of Francis Bacon,
while his own fine collection of Baconiana forms the
centrepiece of the Library's holdings.[2]

The spark which set off a protracted pamphlet war,[3] and

[1] Gunning *Reminiscences* 2 pp. 158–60.   [2] See below, p. 504.
[3] For a fuller account of much of this see J. C. T. Oates 'Cambridge University and the
reform of the Copyright Act, 1805–1813' *The Library* 5th ser. 27 (1972) pp. 275–92. The
following paragraphs rely heavily on this article.

was to involve the University in unheard-of expense as a result of fundamental alterations in the administration of copyright legislation was, ironically enough, a volume of law reports. Montagu first approached his subject not as a lawyer faced with an abstract problem, but as a reader – the plaintiff, rather than the barrister:

> Having occasion, some time since, to send to the university library for the seventh volume of the Term Reports, I was informed that it had not been received; because, as was supposed, it had not been entered at Stationers' Hall. – Recollecting that this volume contained the case of *Beckford* and *Hood*, by which it was decided, that an author, whose work is pirated, may maintain an action for damages against the offending party, although it is not entered at Stationers' Hall: – it occurred to me that the intention of the legislature, to assist in a regular augmentation of the library, was likely to be defeated, by the omission of authors to enter their works: – and the incomplete set, in the public library, of the Term Reports, which has not been continued beyond the sixth volume, although the work consists of eight volumes, has been a daily confirmation of my opinion. With the hope of rendering some assistance in exciting such enquiry as may tend, sooner or later, to meet this evil, this tract has been prepared; and is respectfully submitted to the consideration of the university.[4]

He then arranged his remarks as a series of six queries (with some subsidiary ones), and began by asking, 'Is it expedient that the author of every book, new printed in England, or reprinted with additions, should be compelled to deposit a copy for the use of the university library?'[5] The next two were on the existing law: 'Is it the intention of the legislature that a copy of every book new printed in England, or reprinted with additions, should be deposited by the author for the use of the university library?', and 'Supposing it to be the intention of the legislature that a copy of every book new printed in England, or reprinted with additions, should be deposited by the author for the use of the university library: are the acts of parliament so worded as to enable the university to enforce the execution of this intention?'[6] This was the half-way point, and the

---

[4] Basil Montagu *Enquiries and observations respecting the University Library* (Cambridge 1805) Preface p. [1].   [5] *Ibid.*, p. [3].   [6] *Ibid.*, p. 4.

remainder were on the university rather than the legislature: 'Does the university enforce it?' 'Ought the university to enforce it?' and, finally, 'Supposing that the existing laws are not sufficient to ensure to the public library a copy of every book new printed in England, or reprinted with additions: or supposing that the existing laws are sufficient, but that they ought not to be enforced – should an application be made to parliament to secure under any, and what, regulations a copy of every book so printed or reprinted?'[7]

To the last question Montagu responded with a footnote: 'Upon this subject the London booksellers may communicate valuable hints.' So far as he was concerned, the main query was the fourth, whether or not the University enforced existing legislation to acquire books. Montagu calculated that in 1803 there had been 391 works published in London: his figure, not so very different from the number of books entered at Stationers' Hall,[8] was patently a ludicrous underestimate, but his conclusions about what was actually in the University Library were alarming enough nevertheless. He could find only twenty-two works, not all of which appear in the Accessions Register: if he knew, he did not draw attention to the fact that at least one was a donation, and that several had been bought. But his figures spoke for themselves in all essential points. Part of the trouble was that in 1798 Lord Kenyon had handed down a judgement in the case of *Beckford* v. *Hood* that since an author's property was protected by ordinary common law, there was no absolute necessity to enter books in the Register, pay the attendant fee, or (therefore) to deposit copies for the copyright libraries. The effect was set fair to be disastrous for the Library, while in the same year out of 538 items entered[9] less than ten per cent were registered at Cambridge. The number of books entered at Stationers' Hall was a drop of over a

---

[7] *Ibid.*, p. 21.
[8] Partridge *Legal deposit* p. 315, quoting the return to the House of Commons recording entries in the Stationers' Register for the period 1709–1826, gives 372 for 1803.
[9] *Ibid.*

hundred compared with the total for the previous year of 651, but even this had been less than the peak of 670 reached in 1795[10] – when the Library had received only sixty-odd items. It had been possible to trace a decline in the number of entries at Stationers' Hall well before the case of *Beckford* v. *Hood*, and there was, therefore, a sense in which Kenyon's decision was not itself responsible for anything more than a continuing trend. But it gave powerful encouragement, and provided a focus of grievance in the next years.

And yet Montagu's pamphlet passed apparently un-remarked until 1807, when a much less tentatively phrased pamphlet appeared. This was the work of Edward Christian, 'Chief Justice of the Isle of Ely, Downing Professor of Law in the University of Cambridge, and Professor of the Laws of England in the East-India College at Hertford', and was aggressively titled *A vindication of the right of the universities of Great Britain to a copy of every new publication*. The brother of the more widely celebrated Fletcher Christian of *Bounty* fame, Christian had been educated at St John's and had taken a leading part in the litigation surrounding the foundation of Downing College in 1800. His edition of Blackstone's *Commentaries* had established his position as a legal writer since 1793. But as an individual he was only tolerated, not liked. Gunning, in common with many of his contemporaries, found him a ridiculous figure.[11] His pamphlet was sound enough, however. Like Montagu, Christian approached his subject as a disappointed reader. 'Till six or eight years ago I was supplied from the University Library with every book, which I had occasion to refer to or consult. Up to that time, the University Library was furnished from the Stationers' Hall with all the valuable modern publications upon law, as soon as they issued from the press.'[12] As a result of his disappointment at Cambridge, he enquired at Stationers' Hall as to possible

---

[10] Again, the figures are from Partridge.
[11] 'He died in 1823, in the full vigour of his *incapacity*' (Gunning *Reminiscences* I p. 220).
[12] Christian *Vindication* p. [3].

explanations, and was blandly assured that anything received there was sent on to Cambridge and the other libraries. A discussion with John Davies, in the Library, produced a similarly weak response, at least as recorded by Christian. 'He stated, that it had long been the general complaint of the University that no book of value was sent to the Library', and referred Christian to Montagu's pamphlet. Davies' staff were however much more forthcoming. Marshall, long familiar with the details of copyright accessions, could point to cases where the statement 'Entered at Stationers' Hall' had been printed in books that were never so entered, and he was also able to point out other more everyday annoyances. He won golden opinions from Christian as 'very obliging, attentive, and intelligent',[13] and told Christian that he had 'lately received the eleventh and twelfth volumes of a History, of which we have not any of the preceding volumes: and he says, that plates are seldom or never sent with books upon mathematics, surgery, botany, &c. without which the letter-press is of little or no value'. Marshall's assistant, the young James Tollworthy, lent even more colour to Christian's investigation when asked what kind of books the Library now received from Stationers' Hall: 'Horrid things, Sir, not worth putting up.'

In Christian's eyes, the case was clear. The relevant section of the 1710 Act ordaining that nine copies were to be delivered to the Company for disposal among the copyright libraries had nothing necessarily to do with another section of the Act concerning entry in the Stationers' Register. Admittedly, an Act passed in 1801 principally to cover Irish copyright[14] following the Act of Union had seemed to suggest otherwise, by linking entry in the Stationers' Register directly with deposit of two further copies for the King's Inns and Trinity College libraries in Dublin; but, as Christian remarked, 'If this was intended as an interpretation of the statute of Queen Anne,

---

[13] *Ibid.*, p. 13.   [14] 41 Geo. III c. 107.

it must be imputed to error or inadvertence.'[15] Thus far, he was seemingly on relatively sure ground. But other parts of his argument were by no means so well founded. Besides the ludicrous allegation that 'printing was brought into this country from abroad by Henry the Sixth, at his own charge and expence',[16] the connection between the rescinding of printing privileges granted by Henry VIII and the granting of privileges of copyright deposit was neither obvious nor constructive:

It became therefore reasonable and equitable that some provision should be made for the Universities; and surely a copy of every new publication, or of each edition of every work, which gave the author or editor a copyright, was a cheap compensation for the right which the Universities before possessed. Their previous right was to print at least one copy of every new book for each of its members, and all they got in exchange was a single copy for the whole during the continuance of the author's or editor's copyright of fourteen or twenty-eight years.[17]

The point was illogical, and his subsequent defence of poor students at the expense of poor authors was not one likely to appeal of itself either to authors, printers or publishers. Moreover, in suggesting, like Montagu, that the University had enjoyed copyright deposit to the full, and prior to Lord Kenyon's decision had received everything, he was misleading both himself and his public; such had been very far from the case.[18]

Christian had every right to be scathing about the provisions of the 1710 Act. He was not a man who easily understood the weaknesses of his fellows, but the intentions of the Act, so easily forgotten by many of the publishing trade in the eighteenth century when it so suited their purpose, sometimes seemed by the end of the century to have been forgotten altogether. In any case, it was clear that the universities were not being properly treated. Copyright, however provided for in the Act, was better protected by *de facto* publication and

[15] Christian *Vindication* p. 37.   [16] *Ibid.*, p. 5.
[17] *Ibid.*, p. 7.   [18] See above, Ch. 2.

occasional prosecutions on the part of injured bodies than by the burdensome arrangements provided by parliamentary legislation. The Act had become obsolete for most publishers' purposes, while so far as it applied to the universities it seemed to be next to useless. Christian produced figures to show recent accessions at Cambridge, but he might have gone further. In the last years of the century it was rare for the number of items reaching the Library from the Stationers' Company to climb far above a hundred, and from time to time they were much fewer. In the calendar year 1791, for example, there were less than fifty items, and in 1798 the total was a meagre forty-seven, received in July, followed by seven volumes of music in September. They were to fall still further. In 1801 it was calculated that the total number of new publications published in London alone (and therefore excluding a substantial portion of the trade), during 1800, was 693, at a total value of £230.5s.0d.[19] Yet in that year the Library received only just over fifty items, of which at least twenty-two were published outside the capital. In 1802 the figure was down to about thirty: it included a pocket guide entitled *A sketch of Hamburg*, published there in 1801 and having no apparent connection with the London trade at all.[20] Such quantities represented less even than what a reviewing journal could consider in a year. Apart from straightforward books, there were other difficulties elsewhere. Music appeared only intermittently, a handful in 1796, four items in 1803, six volumes in 1805: in 1810–11 there were no less than twenty-three volumes, but these were the first for several years. Maps arrived even less frequently. Among four broadsides of various kinds received at Lady Day 1800 was a 'Map of the Horizon', and in August 1803 there

---

[19] *Annual Register* 43 (1801) p. 29. No reliable figures exist for the number of publications issued in any one year during the first half of the nineteenth century (see further below, p. 438). Charles Taylor's abortive *Literary Annual Register* lists 928 titles for 1808, excluding music.

[20] Such foreign curiosities turned up from time to time; three arrived from Calcutta in 1803, and the Michaelmas 1801 consignment had included Thomas Dancer's *Medical assistant* published at Kingston, Jamaica, that year.

appeared a plan of Hereford together with J. E. Pellizer's *New system of the world*, but that was virtually all. The truth was that copyright in maps had never been properly legislated for in 1710, and that 'Hogarth's Act' of 1735 made no provision for the deposit of copies: what arrived in Cambridge was therefore due to no more than whim. Old and familiar problems also remained. In an effort to make up for what was not deposited, and to acquire some major scholarly works, there were inevitable mishaps. The consignment of books from Stationers' Hall in November 1808 included the fourth volume of William Mitford's *History of Greece*, which the Library had already bought from Deighton the previous September. But at least it arrived. Most books did not, and even those that did arrive were months late, making any proper attention to filling in gaps so discouraging that they were neglected virtually completely.

Of all this, however, Christian wrote only in the most general of terms. His concluding advice took the only line open to the University: that it or one of the other universities interested 'should commence an action in the court of King's Bench, as prescribed by the statute of 8 Ann. c.19'.[21] For various unavoidable reasons nothing was done publicly until 1811, with a solitary exception. In 1808 an attempt was made in Parliament to set matters straight, and in June that year John Villiers took up the libraries' interests by introducing 'A bill for the further encouragement of learning in the United Kingdom of Great Britain and Ireland, by securing to the libraries of the universities, and other public libraries, copies of all newly printed books, and books reprinted with additions, and by further securing the copies and copyright of printed books to the authors of such books or their assigns, for a time to be limited.' The Bill reached its second reading on 17 June, but on 4 July Parliament was prorogued, and Villiers was subsequently sent as ambassador to Portugal. Opposition to the Bill seemed to

---

[21] Christian *Vindication* p. 15.

be (on the whole) comparatively mild,[22] and Villiers was able to arrange an amicable meeting with the leading booksellers,[23] but it was the calm before the storm.

In January–February 1811 the University waded in of its own accord, in two notices published in the *London Gazette* for 15–19 January and in the *Monthly Literary Advertiser* for 9 February. It warned the trade that it had instructed its solicitors[24] immediately to commence legal proceedings against any printer or other party who failed to deposit his wares published after 1 February. Such was a smooth beginning. But the question of whom to prosecute was less straightforward. For its part, the University was hesitant to take on too powerful an opponent, while the booksellers themselves agreed to act jointly if any one of their number was threatened. In this way an attack on what appeared to be the first victim petered out. J. Johnson & Co. published William Jacob's *Travels in the south of Spain, in letters written A.D. 1809 and 1810* in 1811, but both the publishers and the printers (Nichols & Son)[25] passed on the University's demands, the printers to a committee of the trade. Much the same happened with Cadell and Davies, and with Andrew Strahan, the King's Printer. Finally, avoiding such giants, the University hit on Henry Bryer of Bridewell Hospital, Bridge Street, Blackfriars, and in July 1811 gave him notice that they intended to prosecute for failure to deliver Samuel Heywood's *Vindication of Mr. Fox's History of the early part of the reign of James the Second*, printed for J. Johnson & Co. and J. Ridgeway of Piccadilly. Besides Bryer's advantages as a smaller printer than

---

[22] Hansard 11 (1808) col. 918; Oates 'Reform of the Copyright Act' p. 281.

[23] For his account of it see *Parliamentary Papers* 1818.9 pp. 348–50 and, for Christian's, *ibid.* pp. 339–41. On this episode see also James J. Barnes *Free trade in books* (Oxford 1964) pp. 2–3 and (for the booksellers' meeting of 24 June at which they resolved to petition the House of Commons to adjourn consideration of the Bill), pp. 173–4, reprinting *Parliamentary Papers* 1818.9 pp. 93–4.

[24] R. and J. Dyneley, of Gray's Inn. For the full notice see Oates 'Reform of the Copyright Act' p. 281. Dyneley's bills for services are in the Vouchers. In 1810–11 the firm charged £13.12s.8d. and in 1814 it presented an account for £361.10s.6d.

[25] John Nichols was elected Master of the Stationers' Company in 1804.

some, the book had the merit of being one that, other things being equal, was unquestionably suitable for the University Library: it could not be dismissed as pamphleteering trash, and it had the added piquancy of having been written by a lawyer.

After considerable and inescapably ponderous activity behind the scenes, the case came finally to court on 7 January 1812, before Lord Ellenborough, Lord Chief Justice, and a jury vetted by the University's solicitors so as to eliminate anyone in the printing or bookselling trade.[26] Ellenborough himself had created a sensation as leading counsel for the defence in the trial of Warren Hastings, but for the University it may have been more germane that on graduating from Peterhouse in 1771 he had been elected a Fellow of his college,[27] and that he was the fourth son of Edmund Law, Master of Peterhouse, Bishop of Carlisle and *Protobibliothecarius* from 1760 until 1769. The University won its case against the Committee of Booksellers who undertook Bryer's defence, the penalty for the defendants being £5 together with the value of one copy of Heywood's book on best paper – £1.16s.0d. The finding was confirmed by the Court of King's Bench the following November.[28]

The decision was clear enough, but there were compensations and drawbacks for both the booksellers and the University. The University had proved its point, but at some cost in legal fees, while the trade was still protected by the knowledge that the University could enforce deposit only by individual prosecutions – even assuming that it could discover what had been published. As if to echo this ambiguous state of affairs, the number of entries in the Stationers' Register dropped to a tiny 271 in 1812, the lowest since 1785, and recovered only to a

---

26 Oates 'Reform of the Copyright Act' p. 283. The arguments produced at the trial are reproduced in *The Chancellor, Masters and Scholars of the University of Cambridge against Henry Bryer* [1812], and Lord Ellenborough's judgement in *The University of Cambridge against Henry Bryer* [1812]: copies of both pamphlets stand at Cam. c. 812.11.

27 He married in 1789, and so had to give up his fellowship.

28 E.H. East *Reports of cases . . . in the Court of King's Bench 1800–1812* p. 317, and Christian *Vindication* 2nd and 3rd eds, pp. 85–107.

modest 350 in 1813,[29] while the Library entered only just over eighty deposited items in its Accessions Register. To that extent the University's success was short-lived. But in one important respect its action promised to have much more prolonged consequences. It was no longer possible (or even thought desirable by the protagonists) to conceal the very real differences of opinion on the subject. On 16 December 1812 Davies Giddy, Member for Bodmin, presented a petition in the House of Commons from the booksellers of London and Westminster, and on 11 March following he further expressed his sympathy for their cause by persuading the House to appoint a committee to examine the Acts of 1710 and 1801. Nor was this all. In January 1813 the University of Glasgow produced a Memorial that at last began to strike at the root of the matter in a more direct manner than had either Montagu or Christian, both of whom had been too absorbed by legal minutiae to consider what the library might have as its purpose. Referring to the illustrated books that formed so large a proportion of serious modern publications, the Memorial (which was signed by the Vice-Rector James Couper) remarked with some force:

These costly publications are precisely those which Universities can least afford to purchase; but of which, at the same time, they stand in the greatest need. The possession of those magnificent productions of the British press, in which the refinements of elegant art have been so happily employed to adorn the noblest efforts of taste and genius, could scarcely fail to give to a University, in the eyes of students and of the public, that dignity and respectability which are so essential to its real usefulness.[30]

For John Britton, the antiquary, the question posed itself in very similar terms. His own heavily illustrated monographs demanded considerable investment. And while it had been asserted that conventional publishers might absorb the costs of what he and other opponents of copyright deposit termed a 'library tax', Britton felt particularly exposed as publisher of

---

[29] These figures are, again, all from Partridge *Legal deposit* p. 315.
[30] Quoted by [J. G. Cochrane] *The case stated between the public libraries and the booksellers* (1813) p. 15.

many of his own works: he calculated that his *Architectural antiquities* alone was liable to £440 of this 'oppressive' tax.[31] Furthermore, the Commons Committee unearthed statements from Longman's that over three years the cost to them would have been £5600, from White, Cochrane & Co. that their larger books would have lost £5289 over twelve years, and from Cadell and Davies that solely on the books then available the tax would be over £1000.[32] In detail these figures could be easily disputed, but the principle was clear: that it was thought to be an unreasonable expense for publishers to give away eleven copies of every book they published. The obvious solution, to price the rest of the impression so as to bear the cost of those eleven, was no solution at all, as Britton pointed out:

To prevent this tax from being oppressive, we are told that the price of books should be increased in proportion. This, however, is not feasible. The present price of books is complained of by all literary men, and those publishers who are in the habit of exporting books to the continent of America, inform us, that their correspondents complain greatly of the high price of English publications. It is a well known fact, that in France the expense of valuable works is very little more than half the price of ours; and in America they are republishing all our standard books, at a less price, and almost equally well. If, then, the export trade is endangered by the existing prices, will it not be entirely ruined by making them still higher? In Great Britain it would be a fatal step. In all cases the sale would be materially diminished, and sometimes entirely prohibited. In either instance the sphere of information would be contracted, and the sources of knowledge lessened.[33]

[31] J. Britton *The rights of literature* (1814) p. 56. Britton's sustained attack on legal deposit was summarized by T. E. Jones in *A descriptive account of the literary works of John Britton, F.S.A.* (1849) pp. 115–19. It began with a notice on one of the wrappers of his *Architectural antiquities* in December 1812 (quoted by Jones, p. 116), and continued long after the passing of the 1814 Act: 'In April, 1819, he renewed his remonstrances in a letter printed in the *Monthly Magazine*; and between the years 1825 and 1828, published two of his own works without letter-press, avowedly and expressly to evade the delivery of the copies. These were Robson's *Views of English Cities*, and Pugin and Le Keux's *Architectural Antiquities of Normandy* . . . He again publicly alluded to the harshness of the law, in his Prefaces to the *Picturesque Antiquities of English Cities* (1830), and the *History of Worcester Cathedral* (1835)' (Jones, p. 118).

[32] *Parliamentary Papers* 1812–13.4 p. 1030.

[33] J. Britton *The rights of literature* (1814) pp. 59–60. Cf. also Giles Barber 'Galignani and the publication of English books in France 1800–52' *The Library* 5th ser. 16 (1961) pp. 267–84, and, especially for later in the century, James J. Barnes *Authors, publishers and politicians* (1974) ch. 5.

It was easy to prove Britton's point. It had been done in the evidence before the Commons Committee,[34] while as Sharon Turner, the solicitor retained by the booksellers in defence of Bryer, had already pointed out in a pamphlet issued anonymously in 1813, in 1710

the price of an octavo was four shillings, and few folios cost more than half-a-guinea. Now the difference is great: and why? Because paper and print, like bread and meat, have so much risen in their prices. In the time of Anne expensive works with fine and numerous plates were comparatively unknown: now Nations are contending with each other who shall engrave and print the best; and if England allows herself to fall behind in the competition, the estimation of her press will sink in proportion. This is a very important national consideration, and well worthy the attention of the Legislature. The Parisian press is making such exertions in this respect, that one of its publications will cost 600 guineas.

Longman, Davies, and Cochrane all supported this view in their different ways before the Commons Committee. Evidence (or allegations) that higher prices would prevent some books from being published came easily to hand. In some cases the arguments were straightforward and economic: increased prices would mean ruinously depleted sales. John Nichols was even more obdurate: 'I have been five years employing myself in printing a second edition of a work (entitled, History and Antiquities of Hinckley, in Leicestershire) and it is at this moment ready for publication, but I will not publish it until this question is decided; and I shall be inclined rather to give them to my friends, than to sell them, if I must deliver these twelve copies.'[35]

The long arguments leading up to the Commons Committee had directed public attention to two aspects of university management which had emerged as being in clear need of reform. Although the copyright legislation affected other libraries apart from that at Cambridge, most of them attached to universities, it was Cambridge that had taken the lead.

---

34 [Sharon Turner] *Reasons for a modification of the Act of Anne respecting the delivery of books, and copyright* (1813) pp. 51–2.
35 *Minutes of evidence* p. 28, quoted with approval by Britton (*The rights of literature* pp. 57–8).

Christian's pamphlet remained at the centre of the dispute, while Christian himself kept it up to date, issuing a second edition in 1814 and even a third in 1818. Additionally, the University had been first to prosecute for non-delivery of its books. Quite apart from its victories over the publishers, however, Cambridge had laid itself open to public debate and criticism, even to parliamentary investigation, and it had taken the other universities with it. Ostensibly, the subject was the libraries only, but there inevitably entered into the picture the two spectres of university finance and education as well. It was the beginning of a movement that was to lead to the Oxford and Cambridge University Commissions of the mid-century.

Neither publishers, libraries, nor Parliament were able to equate the need of the universities with the trade's entire published output. As a consequence, the notional and theoretical requirements of the libraries as envisaged by their detractors provided ample scope for digression, sarcasm, and, only occasionally, serious contributions on what became a national debate on the purpose of the libraries: the relationship of their functions as centres of education and as repositories of the printed word under national legislation was seldom comprehended or even approached.

Villiers' Bill to reform the Copyright Act in 1808 had not progressed far through the Commons, partly because of the action of the booksellers. But it was before the House for sufficient time to be attacked with some effect by Sir Samuel Romilly. Ever the ally of the oppressed (on this occasion the booksellers and publishers), Romilly had helped to divert the Bill in its committee stage, but, more seriously, his speech on this occasion also expressed sentiments that suggested that the universities could not much longer remain in the private introspective seclusion they had enjoyed for most of the eighteenth century: the public at large also had some interest in their affairs. In the words of Hansard,

Sir S. *Romilly* regretted that it was now proposed to pass that part of the measure which was the most objectionable, or rather the only objectionable part of it. The system of copyright established in this country, made the public, instead of any individual, the patrons of literature; and this, with a view to independence of sentiment, and just thinking, was an inestimable advantage. It was certainly highly expedient that the libraries of the different Universities should be properly provided with books; but he was astonished that it should be proposed to lay a tax upon authors for that purpose, which the public at large did not bear. There were many works which cost 50 guineas a copy; and was it not monstrous that the authors and publishers should be taxed to the amount of 550 guineas, by being obliged to give away eleven copies? The fact was, that such works, from the expence attending them, were in no danger of being pirated, no person being able to enter into competition with them, or to deprive them of the benefit of copyright therein. It was for the interest of the public that the Universities should be supplied with books; but let that be done at the expence of the public, and not of individual authors.[36]

To the booksellers and others who appeared before the Commons Committee five years later, Romilly's supposition that it was so easy to make a distinction of this kind between authors and public would have seemed jejune. But in juxtaposing universities and public support he had struck a theme that was to become familiar.

There was one very real and tangible way in which the Library came to lose some of its old freedom. For years it had been the custom to reject many of the items that arrived at Cambridge, and to sell them to local booksellers: some were no doubt categorized as only waste paper. At Oxford, Sir Egerton Brydges stated in 1818, the Curators had followed a similar practice,[37] while in 1813 Cochrane expostulated that none of the copyright libraries had preserved all the books consigned by the Stationers' Company from booksellers and publishers.[38] In similar vein, Sharon Turner, speaking on behalf of the booksellers to the Commons Committee, also demanded that the libraries should preserve what they demanded, 'and neither sell, waste, nor give them away'.

Cochrane took his cue from Montagu's pamphlet of 1805,

---

[36] Hansard 11 (1808) col. 990.
[37] Sir Egerton Brydges *A summary statement of the great grievance imposed on authors and publishers* (1818) p. 14n.
[38] [J. G. Cochrane] *The case stated between the public libraries and the booksellers* (1813) p. 18.

and shifted the ground of the argument slightly. 'Let any man look at the list of publications at the end of Mr. Montagu's pamphlet, and put it to himself, if the cause of learning would be advanced by the preserving of such works, if the libraries would not be disgraced by the introduction of them? It will not easily occur to any one, how large a proportion of modern publications, plays, novels, romances, and poetry, constitute.' 'What *advancement of learning* can arise from . . . giving Sion College, (the library of the London Clergy), a copy of "Monro's Treatise on the Gullet", or Rees's Mystery and art of Cordwaining?'[39] Cochrane naturally made the most of his case, but in fact Montagu himself had in effect posed the same question, by refraining from defining what he considered to be 'a proper augmentation of the library', and by posing several supplementary questions to his first, in a footnote that assumed a greater significance as the debate developed and the 1814 Act took effect: 'If a copy of every book new printed were to be sent to the library of the University, ought they all to be preserved in the public library; or ought those considered of value to be preserved; and those considered of no value to be kept in a private room, or to be totally rejected?'[40]

Where Montagu timidly hesitated, Sharon Turner, an Anglo-Saxon historian self-taught in the sense that he had received no university education, saw no doubt at all:

The Universities are places for the instruction of youth. This instruction is conducted on a regular plan, and the whole time of the scholars is barely sufficient for them to go through their appointed exercise and necessary lectures, and private studies, with any degree of efficiency or credit. For the prosecution of these studies, the Universities print their own books; and to deluge the Universities with the publications that daily issue from the London press, can but operate injuriously to the students, by withdrawing them from their important and indispensable course of education, to waste their time in reading for amusement.

To the Teachers of youth, in these valuable institutions, the same remarks will equally apply. Whatever can seduce them from the perpetual

[39] *Ibid.* pp. 18–19.
[40] Basil Montagu *Enquiries and observations* (Cambridge 1805) p. 3.

prosecution of their dignified and important labours (for what human labours can be more dignified and important than the instruction and formation of the youthful mind?) is not benefit, but an injury. But is there a man of learning who will not confess, and with regret, how much of his time has been wasted by promiscuous reading? And to this the abundant possession of modern publications peculiarly leads.

If then solid classical learning, deep science, profound reasoning, extensive erudition, and patient and persevering habits of study, be worth preserving in our Universities, the delivery of all modern publications must be strenuously resisted.[41]

By the time the argument reached Parliament again, however, Turner's outburst had become virtually irrelevant. The question instead hinged on the very understandable reluctance of booksellers to part with property that they had been put at some expense to produce, in the knowledge that it could be destroyed or rejected by the libraries at the whim of people for whom, it had become all too clear, some of the book trade had little sympathy. Amidst attempts to curb the libraries' inclination to reject what had actually reached their hands, it was widely proposed that they might pay a part of the cost of the books, instead of receiving them automatically without any charge. The suggestion met with little favour among the libraries, while another clause in the Bill of 7 June seeking to force the libraries to keep all that they received drew a storm of abuse from the ever-ready Christian. In the second edition of his *Vindication*, published in 1814, he rushed headlong into the attack:

The next clause is the greatest insult that ever was attempted to be introduced into an act of Parliament. When it first appeared, there was such a burst of indignation expressed by all who were friendly to the Universities, that it was supposed that it was echoed on all sides to the patrons of the Bill, and that they immediately gave notice that it should be withdrawn. But to my great astonishment I find it printed a second time. In the first printed Bill, if a loose sheet was sold, the University offending was to be deprived of its privilege for ever. In the second, that penalty is removed, and nothing is substituted but what the common law inflicts,

[41] [Sharon Turner] *Reasons for a modification of the Act of Anne* (1813) pp. 54–5.

viz. fine, imprisonment and pillory. Quite sufficient for a man selling his own property!

We may burn, sink and destroy as much as we please, but our libraries might all be set in the pillory, if they unfortunately should sell a single pound of waste paper to the cheese-mongers.

What is the meaning of this dog-in-the-manger clause? The meaning is clear. It is to operate as argumentative slander, and to tell the House of Commons and the world, as far as a printed Bill can tell them, that the Universities only want a copy of every new book in order to convert it into a few despicable halfpence, by selling it again for waste paper.[42]

On the basis of the tiny number of books acquired by the University Library in the previous few years, there was no doubt that it could, with only a little help, have afforded to buy the copyright copies with very little difficulty, but Turner's interpretation of a university's purpose and needs for research was so limiting that it would have been in danger of constricting almost all scholarly advance. Christian, like many of those who pushed forward to offer their own views, was mistaken in thinking that the supply of books under the 1710 Act had been either 'constant' or 'ample', but he did calculate that 'the revenue necessary to purchase the valuable books, which I conceive we are at present entitled to, cannot be estimated, I apprehend, at less than £400 a year'. His figure was an under-estimate, while on the other hand virtually all that was available to Cambridge to buy books was the annual proceeds from the Rustat estates in Norfolk, which produced sums only intermittently until 1808. The £500 received annually since 1781 in return for giving up some of the University's printing privileges was (save for the Askew sale in 1785) devoted entirely to the Press, while Cochrane's suggestion that the profits from the Press could be devoted to the Library was unfortunately unrealistic.[43] So far as Cambridge was concerned, the University was in no position to allow to the Library a sufficient income to cover the cost of all the books published in Great Britain that would be desirable.

[42] Pp. 154–5. [43] [J. G. Cochrane] *The case stated* (1813) p. 22.

The twenty-one Members who formed the Commons Select Committee of 1813 included both the Members for the University, Palmerston and J. H. Smyth, as well as one each of those for Oxford and Trinity College, Dublin, while in the opposite camp were Sir Egerton Brydges, Member for Maidstone, a publisher in a small way as the owner of the Lee Priory Press, and a convinced supporter of the booksellers, and Andrew Strahan, Member for Aldeburgh. The Committee focussed its attention on the trade and, in the person of Thomas Frognall Dibdin, on authors. It heard no evidence from the University of Cambridge or from any of the other copyright libraries. Many of the views which the libraries could be expected to put forward had already been aired, if not always clearly, in the foison of printed effusions that had appeared in the preceding months, but on the other hand the substance of much of what had already been published on behalf of the trade was repeated to the Committee. While the booksellers, publishers and printers therefore put their case, not always with complete candour, the University held its peace until it could present two petitions in June, just before the Report was presented to the House.[44]

To the chagrin of the trade, the Committee found that, in the main, the provisions of the Copyright Act were 'proper to be retained'. Unimpressed by the booksellers' evidence,[45] it decided that 'continuing the delivery of all new works, and in certain cases of subsequent editions, to the Libraries now entitled to receive them, will tend to the advancement of learning, and to the diffusion of knowledge, without imposing any considerable burden on the Authors, Printers, or Publishers of such works'.[46]

[44] Grace Book *M* pp. 116–17 (8 June, against a suggestion that the University should pay one-third of the price of the books) and *ibid.*, pp. 121–2 (11 June, a more general complaint).

[45] Described by Oates ('Reform of the Copyright Act') as 'confusing and some of it disingenuous'. His summary of the Minutes of evidence is on pp. 288–91.

[46] *Parliamentary papers* 1812–13.4 p. 999.

The new Copyright Act,[47] which received the Royal Assent on 29 July 1814, was rushed through Parliament at the end of the session. It rode roughshod over the booksellers, showed little understanding of the everyday working of the trade or the libraries, and was the cause of repeated complaints. But there could be no doubt of its intention. The eleven libraries retained their status, and as a mild sop to the trade were to receive only items which they demanded. On demand, the requisite number of copies was to be delivered by the publisher to the Warehouse-Keeper at the Stationers' Company, while the Warehouse-Keeper was to distribute the books to the libraries within a month of their receipt. A penalty was laid down for failure on the part of either the publisher or the Warehouse-Keeper to comply, the offender to forfeit £5 for each copy not delivered or received, besides any legal costs and the value of the printed copies: prosecution was the responsibility of the libraries. Apart from the British Museum, which was to continue to receive copies on the best paper if an edition was published on several kinds of paper, the libraries were only now entitled to copies 'upon the paper of which the largest Number of impressions of such Book shall be printed for Sale'. For publishers, the copyright period was extended to twenty-eight years automatically, or until the author's death, whichever was the later. In order to provide some bibliographical guide – not least for the libraries – every work or subsequent edition with alterations was to be registered at Stationers' Hall within one month of publication, or within three 'if the said Book shall be sold, published, or advertized in any other part of the United Kingdom'; and at intervals of not more than three months the Warehouse-Keeper was to send lists of books entered to the libraries so that they could choose what they thought necessary. Finally, with an eye to convenience, but in a provision that was to have unforeseen

---

[47] 54 Geo. III c. 156. The deposit clauses are printed in Partridge *Legal deposit* pp. 308–11.

consequences, if a publisher found it easier he could deliver his books straight to the libraries or their appointed agents, this being deemed the same as if he had done so at Stationers' Hall.

The effect was dramatic. From 350 entries at Stationers' Hall in 1813, the figure climbed to 541 in 1814 and 1244 in 1815.[48] Accessions to the Library at Cambridge went up more than commensurately, partly because much more was now actually kept. Indeed, they proved an embarrassment: completely inadequate to cope with the flood of copyright deposit copies, all the Library staff could do for many years was to list them as they came in and then pick out those titles most obviously of interest. By the mid-century, the surplus of pamphlets and minor literature had accumulated with various purchases to form what became known as the 'heap' to Library staff, and remnants of it even survived to be transported to the new Library in 1934.

From May 1816 George Greenhill, Warehouse-Keeper at the Stationers' Company, supplied Cambridge with lists in alphabetical order of the contents of every parcel of copyright books despatched to the Library. In addition, as required by the Act, from November 1814 he had also sent a monthly list of books entered at Stationers' Hall, which at first Kerrich and Davies signed with a formal request for a delivery of all the books: they stopped signing in October 1815, but the Library continued to expect to receive everything, from which it could then make its choice in Cambridge. After some months of doubt as to the best course to take, in November 1816 the Syndicate established a sub-committee of four to report as required on which books should be accepted into the Library, the committee being designed to cover as wide a range of subjects as possible. The lists were then displayed for a week in

<hr>

[48] *Parliamentary papers* 1826–7.20 p. 509; Partridge *Legal deposit* p. 315. With these figures may be compared (in some despair at the incompatibility) the number of volumes, excluding periodical parts and music, received under the Copyright Act between 1816 (718) and 1847 (2904): *Parliamentary papers* 1849.45 pp. 202–3. The number of periodical parts received during this period (ranging from 195 (1816) to 4156 (1847)) was subject to wild fluctuations, partly because of irregular delivery.

the Library, in order to give other members of the Senate an opportunity to mark further books which they believed also to be appropriate. In practice, the Syndicate committee was quickly replaced by Kerrich and Clarke acting in the first place, with the Syndicate acting as a further check and referee.

In the first twelve months, from May 1816, of the scheme devised at Cambridge for selecting those books the Library wished to retain, almost 1500 items were sent up from London by Greenhill.[49] In sheer practical terms, the only proper course open to the Library was to be omnivorous – initially; for it was next to impossible to decide, on the evidence of titles alone, what was and what was not appropriate to an academic library.[50] The parcels arrived irregularly. Between May and December 1816 four appeared, including two in July and none in June, August, November or December; in 1817 there were seven altogether, with none in March, June, September, November or December; in 1818 there were none in February or March, but two in April.[51] In that the 1814 Act also forced more frequent deliveries as well as more books on the University it was clearly an immense improvement on the old system of deliveries made (in theory at least) twice yearly.

However infuriating for the booksellers and publishers, this also thrust on the Library an assortment of literature for which the authorities had no pressing desire, as Clarke and Webb each explained to the Select Committee in 1818. By dint of selection, Clarke, Kerrich and the Syndics reduced the figures to something more manageable, and in the five months from May to September 1816 extracted just over fifty per cent of everything sent up from London. For the most part their principles were simple. Novels, plays and music were virtually

---

49 Compared with 1178 items entered at Stationers' Hall in the calendar year 1816, and 1240 in 1817 (Partridge *Legal deposit* p. 315).
50 As was pointed out in a statement from the University of St Andrews to Parliament in 1818: see Philip Ardagh 'St Andrews University Library and the Copyright Acts' *Edinburgh Bibliographical Society Transactions* 3 (1956) pp. 179–211, at p. 196.
51 It was some time before books were entered in the Accessions Register under the same date as Greenhill's invoices: in 1816 the May consignment, for example, was entered on 7 June, and those of 13 and 27 July on 6 September.

all set aside, along with many periodicals, children's books, catalogues, the *Army List*, many pamphlets and minor sermons, and not a few poems. *Emma, The antiquary* and *Headlong Hall* were consigned to (in these cases temporary) oblivion, along with such Minerva Press products as Agnes Lancaster's *Abbess of Valtiera*, Catharine Smith's *Barozzi, or the Venetian sorceress* and the anonymous *Romantic facts, or which is his wife?*[52] Scott's poetry, however, acknowledged and widely popular, successfully forced an entry: the parcel on 13 July 1816 included the second edition of *The field of Waterloo*, and on the 27th there arrived the eleventh edition of *The lady of the lake*, the fifteenth edition of *The lay of the last minstrel*, and *The vision of Don Roderick*. Thomas Campbell's *Gertrude of Wyoming* finally arrived in its sixth edition, a further reminder that the Library had not yet acquired the knack of obtaining the original editions. But in any case, it certainly did not care for every popular author: in the same month it declined to accept into the main collections *The siege of Corinth* and *The story of Rimini*, with such lesser pieces in popular estimation as Shelley's *Alastor* and Wordsworth's *Thanksgiving ode*. Among its periodicals, the Library took the *European Magazine*, the *Quarterly Review*, the *Monthly Review*, the *Edinburgh Review* and the *Edinburgh Medical Journal*, but not the *Evangelical Magazine*, the *Christian Observer* (despite its strong Cambridge connections) or the *Monthly Theatrical Reporter*. In May 1816 it accepted the *Farmer's Magazine*, but did not two months later. Law books were gathered in wholeheartedly, as were medical works, while topographical works were restricted to such more important items as William West on Cranborn Chase, Joseph Aston on Manchester and Sir Cuthbert Sharp on Hartlepool. The sciences in all branches were also avidly collected, including veterinary science and agriculture, though

---

[52] A few years later taste – and Scott's reputation – had changed. *Ivanhoe*, entered in the Stationers' Register on 3 February 1820, appeared on a Cambridge invoice in its second edition on 1 April following, and was admitted straight into the Library. *The antiquary*, delivered to the Library in July 1816, was subsequently recovered from the castaways in the Law Schools following a decision on 25 May 1818 to allow second thoughts.

the Library's interest stopped short of such economic aids as Woolhead's *Average prices of corn* and many of the more obscure pamphlets advocating alterations in agricultural methods.[53]

The Act did not make everything more plentiful. Booksellers quickly realized that the easiest course to evade deposit was to omit to register titles altogether, as had been the overwhelming practice previous to 1814. The libraries, now with slightly more powerful legislation behind them, responded jointly. At a meeting at Sion College on 26 March 1816[54] they gathered for the first time, the College represented by its president and secretary, Cambridge by Christian and 'Mr Gatty', partner in the University's solicitors Dyneley and Gatty, the British Museum by Henry Baber (Keeper of Printed Books) and his assistant Joseph Bean, Oxford by Bulkeley Bandinel (Bodley's Librarian), the Irish libraries by Henry Joseph Monck Mason, of the King's Inns library, and the Scottish libraries by Alexander Mundell, the London solicitor for the universities of St Andrews and Edinburgh. Their main points of agreement were reached in straightforward manner:

That Evasions of the Act are such on the part of the Publishers as to demand prosecution.

That Prosecutions under the Act should be commenced at first only for Non-entry.

That only one Party sue under the 5th. section of the Act for not entering one individual publication and communicate the intention to each of the other Parties.

That four Prosecutions be commenced immediately against different

---

53 In 1818 both the Bodleian Library and the University Library provided returns of copyright books that had been 'rejected'. Between January 1815 and January 1817 Cambridge placed 486 titles in the Law Schools in the wake of the Syndics' decisions on 26 February 1816 to keep the books and on 17 November 1817 to catalogue them and make them available (*Parliamentary papers* 1818.15 pp. 75–88). Macray (*Annals* pp. 302–3) took full advantage of this printed return to ridicule the University Library not only for hesitating to show instant appreciation of an unfamiliar range of literature, but also for the minuteness of its return in listing even 'Turner's real japan blacking, a label': the Bodleian return is a much more hurried affair.

54 The following is based on Sion College Court Register D, Minutes of 22 April 1816, and E. H. Pearce *Sion College and library* (Cambridge 1913) pp. 306–8. I am grateful to Mr Oates for providing me with his unpublished notes on this matter.

Parties, and all four at the same time; viz. one for each of the universities of England, one for Ireland, and one for Scotland.

That [Sion] College should not prosecute, but be considered as exempted from the trouble and expence of prosecution from a readiness to give room and accommodation for the Meetings of the Persons present, and from Mr. Watts's having undertaken to receive communications, Post-paid, and to attend the Meetings.

That the following Booksellers be first prosecuted – Stockdale, – Cadell & Davies, for Bonney's Life of Bp. Taylor in particular,[55] – Murray – Dibdin, the Author – Ridgeway – Lackington & Co. for Dugdale's Monasticon in particular – Rivingtons – Sutor, for the Monthly Magazine.

That it appears that 8000 titles of Books are published in one year upon an average, and not above 1000 entered.

That Mr. Baber undertakes to communicate to the other Parties for what Publications the Trustees of the British Museum prosecute.

That means be established of Information respecting what books may be published out of London: and Mr. Mason agreed to endeavour to obtain such information respecting Dublin and the rest of Ireland, Mr. Bandinell respecting Oxford, Mr. Christian, Cambridge, and Mr. Mundell, Scotland.

That summer, however, in his position as link between the libraries, Watts learned from Baber at the British Museum that there was some evidence to suggest that the simple threat of prosecution might be enough. He therefore advised the other libraries to postpone the prosecutions to which they were committed, and to concentrate their attention on 'one book of value which has been sent to the British Museum, but is not entered. It is Murphy's *Arabian Antiquities* – which sells for 40 guineas – it is published by Cadell and Davies.'[56] This was an elephant folio of ninety-seven plates, with a preliminary text, and the subsequent events were concisely summarized in Dyneley and Gatty's bill for their services:

Novr 21   In consequence of letter from the Vice Chancellor, directing proceedings to be commenced for the non-entry of two[57] Costly

[55] H. K. Bonney *The life of the Right Reverend Father in God, Jeremy Taylor, D.D.* (London, for T. Cadell and W. Davies, 1815), delivered to Cambridge in Greenhill's parcel of 26 October 1816.   [56] Pearce *Sion College and library* p. 308.
[57] James Cavanagh Murphy *Arabian antiquities*, and John Shakespear and T. H. Horne *The history of the Mahometan Empire in Spain*.

works on Arabian Antiquities by Mr. Murphy published by Cadell & Davies Attending at Stationers Hall searching the Register for 13 months to ascertain that these books were not entered   6   8

Paid Search   1   —

Paid for 2 N^os of the Literary Advertiser for the purpose of examining them to find if possible the date of the publications   1   2

Attending at the British Museum to make inquiry on the same subject there when it appeared to be the opinion that the Books had been published more than 13 Months[58] and conferring with Messrs Baber & Bean the Librarians on the conduct of the Booksellers in disregarding the Act of 1814 and making Extracts from several lists there of publications within the last Year not entered   13   4

They then lost no time in going on to the next stage after the Stationers' Company and the British Museum:

22   Attending Mr Williams in the Strand the Publisher of a large work called *Cambria depicta* which he had omitted to enter conferring with him on his obligation to enter the same and insisting that he should enter it upon which he stated that he should consult the Committee of the Trade   6   8

Writing to the Vice Chancellor on our proceedings and Copy list for him of unentered new publications   6   8

And with this behind them they returned to Cadell and Davies:

26   Attending twice at Messrs Cadell & Davies and conferring with them this day on their obligation to enter Mr. Murphy's work which they stated had been advised to resist as to Book of plates but were now willing to deliver to the University if required   13   4

27   Writing to the Vice Chancellor on communication with Messrs Cadell & Davies   5   —

---

[58] The *Antiquities* was published in 1813, but the *History* only in 1816, and this statement was not therefore correct.

December 2   Attending Messʳˢ. Cadell & Davies on letter
              from the Vice Chancellor when they delivered
              the Books required   6   8

Prosecution had been avoided, at some cost to the University, but even in so straightforward a case the business was tedious and long-winded. The difficulties were multiplied elsewhere, and to be found for as long as patience allowed. The *Quarterly Review*, the *Monthly Literary Advertiser* and similar journals all contained lists of books published, but none complete and none in a way that could be very readily related to Greenhill's register or monthly lists. But the Library, and the other libraries with it, had entered the new era under the 1814 Act with an enthusiasm that took booksellers aback. According to Sir Egerton Brydges, who soon produced an aggrieved pamphlet offering *Reasons for a further amendment of the Act 54 Geo. III. c.156* in 1817, the libraries had claimed far more titles than had ever been envisaged. He expressed astonishment that the British Museum had taken a copy of every work entered, while almost the only consolation was that two libraries, the Faculty of Advocates' and Trinity College, Dublin, had declined to take music or novels. For the libraries, indeed, the Act, despite all the subsequent difficulties, had proved an immediate success. Brydges calculated that in the period 12 June 1815 to 31 March 1817 all of them had received at least 163 different titles with a retail value of twenty shillings or more, and that excluding novels. Whatever the opinions of the booksellers as to the cost, it was difficult to state in fairness that most of these were unsuitable for university libraries. Brydges therefore concentrated his attack on two fronts. First, that many of the most expensive books that had been demanded were luxurious reprints of early English literature. 'To extend the claims to Reprints of works of this class,' he remarked, 'must be a most wanton cupidity.' Second, the librarians concerned should have actually to name what they desired, and not simply issue 'a mere sweeping order'.[59] As Lackington & Co. explained to Brydges in some detail,

[59] Sir Egerton Brydges *Reasons for a further amendment* p. 23.

Neither at the passing of this Act was it contemplated that the whole Eleven Copies would be demanded of every Book entered at Stationers Hall, but that a *selection* would be made of such books only as were needed by different Libraries: no sooner however was the Bill passed into a Law, and the *Right* thus granted to Eleven Libraries to claim Copies, than so sweeping, so universal was the order given to demand every Book entered, that the Warehouse-keeper never now makes *written application* for such of the particular books needed by one or other of the Universities or Libraries as enjoined in the Act (Sect. 2, p.5 and 6.) but demands *every* Copy claimable of every Book entered; and so general is this order, that a *printed* circular, claiming for Ten out of the Eleven Libraries (and the eleventh Copy is always delivered upon entering the Book) is now invariably sent to Booksellers. A copy of this printed requisition is inclosed, and the two works named in it form cases of singular hardship upon the publishers in the selection made of the first, and abuse of the right to demand Books in the second: Of the first work, named "The Mirror for Magistrates," only 167 Copies were printed, and the greater part of the work had passed through the press prior to the Act taking place: no part of the Book having, however, been published, the Proprietors had no relief. The price of this Book is £12.12s. thus entailing a loss to them of £139.3s. The second Book named in the requisition is of a singular nature to prove useful in the *"Encouragement of Learning,"* namely a *"Treatise upon Greyhounds,"* and surely cannot prove eminently useful to the learned Bodies for whom it is demanded; but no Book is now exempt, from the *Child's Primer* of six pence in price, and intended for the instruction of infants, to the *Shooter's Guide*, or the verbal reprints of former ages.[60]

As one who had felt the force of the law, in being constrained to provide copies of the productions of his own Lee Priory Press, Brydges was quite ready to take up the cudgels on anyone else's behalf:

Upon these facts I am bound to ask, though some of the Public Bodies may affect to repel the question indignantly, what do they do with this indiscriminate mixture of expensive and useful Works, and contemptible trash? Where do they deposit them? Do they keep them in order? And do they bind them? If they do, would not the funds expended in paying the binder, the house-room, and the librarians for thus dealing with the mass of rubbish, be more generously and more usefully expended in paying some small portion of the price of the valuable works? If they do not, what becomes of the only alleged colour for their claim – that of public use?[61]

A. J. Valpy, deep in calculations for a new edition of Stephanus' *Thesaurus*, was equally acid:

[60] *Ibid.*, pp. 36–7. [61] *Ibid.*, p. 21.

They call for everything – and it consequently follows that they must receive a vast quantity of frivolous books, which are quite useless to them, and many others equally improper from their nature and tendency. Thus, among the former, they have lately demanded *Dr. Mavor's Catechism for the Use of Children under Seven Years of Age*; and among the latter, *a Work upon the Theory and Practice of Gaming* – another, *Upon the breeding and training of Greyhounds* – and a third, *Upon the flavouring of Wines and Spirituous Liquors !!!* – subjects, neither of which, it is presumed, are essentially requisite for students at the Universities.[62]

A petition to the House of Commons by various authors on 6 April 1818 sought to take a similarly firm moral line. Headed by T. D. Whitaker, the Yorkshire historian, and Archdeacon William Coxe, and including also Isaac D'Israeli, John Britton, William Frend, Mrs Barbauld, T. H. Horne and Sharon Turner, the petitioners remarked how much had been 'indiscriminately demanded' with 'astonishment and regret':

If they [i.e. books] be demanded and not deposited, then Authors and Publishers are burthened unnecessarily; and if all be deposited and read, your Petitioners think that if it be recollected how many multifarious Theories, Speculations, Discussions, and Doubts, are daily arising in society, and daily investigated in public by the press; an indiscriminate demand, and compulsory delivery, of every publication must tend to lead the impressible minds of the educating youth (who cannot yet have attained that solid judgment which time alone can create) to imbibe and nourish whatever spirit of change, desire of novelty, or projects of innovation, the conversations and incidents of the day may excite. Without this delivery no publication is purchased until it is wanted, and the expense of the purchase diminishes curiosity. But the delivery brings before the eyes of the educating youth of this country, and their instructors, Books that they would not have else noticed, and perhaps not have heard of – Books often highly useful and important in themselves, but not advantageous to the young and inexperienced mind.[63]

The booksellers and publishers, with their supporters, in fact, found that what they believed to be an unjust imposition in the first place was being even more unjustly exploited – and to no very obvious end. Despite their allegations, it was many years before Cambridge was to acquire, as they were published, anything approaching all the books and pamphlets

[62] Letter to Brydges, quoted in the latter's *A summary statement* (1818) p. 13.
[63] Copy in the British Library, shelf-mark 515.l.20.

published even in London: and it was to be longer still before the *omnium gatherum* policy was to be appreciated. Sir Egerton Brydges' tracts of 1817 and 1818 appeared amidst an orchestrated protest at the 1814 Act, and in March 1818 he was given leave to introduce a Bill to amend the legislation,[64] encouraged by a series of petitions from publishers and booksellers to the House of Commons.[65] Amid further suggestions that the libraries should pay a portion of the costs of the books, in April the Library Syndics at Cambridge issued a brief assortment of *Observations on the Copyright Bill*. For the most part it consisted simply of a selection of extracts from Christian's *Vindication*, the only printed defence of the University's rights to have appeared since Montagu's original outburst in 1805. The pamphlet (it comprised a mere eight pages) was signed by William Webb, Master of Clare College and Vice-Chancellor, and concluded with a series of observations that recapitulated the advantages of a copyright period of twenty-eight years, avoided all consideration of what the University Library was doing with its accumulated deposit copies, and insisted that the University's rights reached back to the charter granted by Henry VIII – a claim that the opposition had always found difficult to accept. This odd document was followed up with a *Further statement*, which unearthed Thomas Arundel's arrangements for the University to supervise the production of manuscripts in the early fifteenth century, among various other records exhumed from the University Archives by Webb. That any such privileges or duties, let alone the charter of Henry VIII, gave the University a right to modern books as they were published was at best dubious, and Brydges easily demolished the suggestions in a rejoinder dated only a fortnight after the Syndics' original *Observations*.[66]

Christian, however, by now treating his *Vindication* more

---

64 Cooper *Annals* 4 p. 519; *Journals of the House of Commons* 3 March 1818. A move to introduce a Bill in June 1817 was defeated by one vote.

65 The University also retaliated with petitions of its own: see Grace Book *M* pp. 246–8 and *Journals of the House of Commons, passim*.

66 [Sir Egerton Brydges] *Answer to the further statement, ordered by the Syndics of the University of Cambridge to be printed and circulated*, dated 20 April 1818.

like a legal textbook, to be kept constantly updated, than as a piece of polemic, duly reported the Syndics' beliefs in a third edition that brought the tale down to 20 April 1818, the very day of Brydges' rejoinder. At long last, for the first time since Christian had reported the opinions of Davies and Marshall in 1807, a member of the Library staff put in an appearance. One of the most noticeable features of the entire dispute had been that no librarian from any of the copyright libraries had stepped in. Instead, the arguments had been conducted by lawyers, amateurs and Members of Parliament, with only occasional interjections from the universities, with an abandon that had failed to reveal the exact nature of what had been received, at Cambridge or elsewhere, either before 1798 or since, what the University Library's funds for purchase were, or even how the University at large viewed the *fracas*. Yet Edward Daniel Clarke's remarks came as something of an anti-climax. He had been elected *Bibliothecarius* only a little over a year, and brought less command of the truth of the Library's position than Kerrich might have done; but the authority with which Christian endowed him, in the concluding paragraphs of the third and final edition of his *Vindication*, belied the weakness of Clarke's flawed claim:

He declares [wrote Christian] it is by far the cheapest way of advertising, let the price of the book be what it may, for it has fallen within his experience to make the observation, that as soon a book of credit appears upon a shelf of the Public Library, curiosity cannot be gratified by that book alone, and the consequence is, that it is seen soon afterwards upon the tables of the Senior part of the University, and that induces young noblemen and gentlemen of fortune again to purchase it for their Libraries in College, or to take it home to their friends, and thus the sale is far more rapidly promoted, than by spending the price of the book in advertisements in Newspapers.[67]

Brydges' Bill received its second reading in the Commons after some delays, on 17 April, by which time it had become clear to the House that the question was one even more

---

[67] Christian *Vindication* 3rd ed. (1818) pp. 198–9.

complicated than they had anticipated. In order to receive some guidance on the subject, on 20 April the House therefore referred the whole matter to a select committee, empowered to call whatever evidence it deemed necessary.

Chaired by Charles Watkin Williams Wynn, Member for Montgomeryshire and incidentally nephew to the Chancellor of the University of Oxford, the Committee first met on 27 April, and went speedily to work.[68] It became an altogether more wide-ranging investigation than that of the previous Select Committee. Apart from booksellers and publishers, it interviewed the printsellers Richard Harraden of Cambridge and William Cooke. It paid considerable attention to the practices of the printing trade, even enquiring into labour agreements and printing presses. George Woodfall, Richard Taylor, and Samuel Brooke, all major printers, gave evidence, and in order to gauge a little of the relationship of the University Printer at Cambridge with the University, both John Smith, Printer since 1809, and his foreman John Matthews were called upon. But the 1818 Committee differed from its predecessor still further, in that on this occasion a proper attempt was made to listen to both sides of the dispute. George Greenhill, of the Stationers' Company, gave evidence briefly as to the mechanics of the execution of the 1814 Act, and the Committee heard evidence from Oxford and Cambridge as well, besides that of Lancelot Sharpe, one of the governors of Sion College, and Henry Baber of the British Museum. For Oxford the witnesses were Thomas Gaisford and Joseph Phillimore, both appearing as Curators of the Bodleian, and Bulkeley Bandinel, Bodley's Librarian: as editor of the latest edition of Dugdale's *Monasticon*, which was to occupy much of the Committee's attention, Bandinel was in the piquant position of representing one side of the argument while having a vested interest in the other. Cambridge produced Christian himself, William Webb as Vice-Chancellor and Library

---

[68] For its Report, see *Parliamentary papers* 1818.9 pp. 249–54 and, for the Minutes, *ibid.* pp. 257–388.

Syndic, and Edward Daniel Clarke. Thomas Kerrich, although referred to periodically, did not give evidence, while John Villiers, author of the unsuccessful Bill of 1808, recalled the abortive negotiations with the booksellers, now ten years past.

Clarke's and Webb's evidence provides the most detailed account of the management of the Library in the early nineteenth century ever to have been published, but it is not a completely reliable document. Clarke had been *Bibliothecarius* only a short while, and Webb, though Master of a college, and Vice-Chancellor, as well as being familiar with Cambridge as a resident for a quarter of a century, had attended his first Syndicate meeting only in February 1816. Both men plunged headlong into their evidence, blissfully unaware of the extent of their ignorance. While Clarke was willing to state, apparently in the belief that he was telling the truth, that 'not a scrap of any kind has ever been sold', Webb clearly believed that many items were not at Cambridge simply because they had not been delivered. Their statements impugned the returns from Stationers' Hall, if correct, and if incorrect were a damage to the University's cause. By contrast with Clarke's verbose musings in place of clear answers, and Webb's misguided beliefs, Greenhill's evidence, clear, concise and forthright, placed the blame for missing copies squarely at the feet of the libraries, and the Committee preferred to follow Greenhill.

Clarke appeared both as an author and as a librarian, and not surprisingly a good deal of his discussions with the Committee turned on whether or not the presence of books on the Library shelves helped to encourage sales. Harraden, faced with the same question, answered strongly in the affirmative, so supporting Clarke. Not very relevantly, Clarke instanced the case of the eccentric William Davy, who had devoted the years 1795 to 1807 to printing, in an edition of fourteen copies, a *System of divinity, in a course of sermons on the first institutions of religion* in twenty-six volumes.[69] Davy's work, instantly memorable for containing more paste-on cancels (that is, slips of paper bearing revised texts, pasted over the original readings) than any other book, was, Clarke ambiguously remarked, 'known at the University': he failed to remark that Davy's book was not a copyright deposit copy at all, but was the gift of its author and printer. Clarke and Webb also explained something of the college libraries, the Library's finances (both topics had completely escaped previous attention), spoke of arrangements for visiting scholars to read as well as undergraduates, and went into some considerable detail, not without floundering, about the means whereby the Library coped with an influx of copyright literature that was larger than ever previously and whose miscellaneous nature so exercised critics such as Cochrane and the firm of Lackington. As for the books and other material not deemed worthy of attention, Clarke cheekily explained that, following a decision of 6 April 1818, the University would be happy if those who had sent them in the first place came and collected them again. 'Sometimes', Clarke remarked, 'we have received even the advertisements for patent medicines, and little scraps of paper, and children's books, and a great quantity of idle trash.'[70] As a

---

[69] On completing it, Davy had travelled round various libraries, presenting each with a copy. For some account of him see Macray *Annals* p. 337 and Cecil Torr *Small talk at Wreyland* (Cambridge 1918) pp. 32–4; at Cambridge, see also the letter pasted into the front of the first volume, Syn. 6.79.8.

[70] He omitted to add that a good number of children's books were in fact catalogued properly, but he did touch here on a complicated question. Part of the difficulty of course lay in the absence of a proper legal definition of a book. By 1911 it had been held to include the following: (a) newspapers (*Walter v. Howe* (1881), 17 Ch. D 708; *Walter v. Lane* (1900), A.C. 539); (b) single sheets of music, printed or in manuscript (*Clementi v. Golding* (1809), 2 Camp. 25; *Storace v. Longman* (1788), 2 Camp. 26, n.; *Hime v. Dale* (1803), 2 Camp. 27, n.; *White v. Geroch* (1819), 2 B. & Ald 298); (c) printed sheets containing legal forms (*Southern v. Bailes* (1894), 38 Sol.J. 681); (d) volumes of drawings without any letterpress (*Bogue v. Houlston* (1852), 5 de G. & Sm. 267; *Maple v. Junior Army and Navy Stores* (1882), 21 Ch. D. 380; *Life Publishing Co. v. Rose Publishing Co.* (1906), 12 Ont. L.R. 386); (e) Christmas cards with verses on them (*Hildesheimer and Faulkner v. Dunn* (1891), 64 L.T. (N.S.) 452); (f) sheets of drawing with no letterpress, except the names and prices of the articles illustrated (*Davis v. Benjamin* (1906), 2 Ch. 491); (g) road books (*Cary v. Longman* (1801), 1 East 358; *Cary v. Kearsley* (1802), 4 Esp.

rule, said Clarke, only some novels were retained, while when questioned specifically on the imitation of Dr Syntax's tours, *The life of Napoleon, a hudibrastic poem in fifteen cantos*, embellished by George Cruikshank (1815), Webb was driven to remark that 'Syntax's Life of Napoleon is, we presume, written by a man who called himself Dr. Syntax; and Dr. Syntax's Journey being a work of merit, that might render it proper to place this in the library.'

The 'idle trash' and other cast-offs could not be disposed of completely, and so in 1817 the Library authorities had hit on a novel solution. On 17 November, the Syndics agreed that cases should be set up in the Law Schools, on the ground floor below the South Room, where the rejects would be both outside the Library and yet within its control. Masters of Arts could thus examine them if they were so inclined, while the books were left in cheap boards rather than put into leather bindings, and a rough catalogue provided a modicum of control. The scheme had many merits, for Webb not least that the shelves were inconspicuous; and in any case, music had been stored similarly in the same room for many years. The notion of separating what was believed to be of some academic concern from a residue of the copyright intake was an original one. It has persisted to the present, in the modern distinction between the 'Upper Library' and the rest of the collections.[71]

168); (h) directories (*Kelly* v. *Morris* (1866), L.R. 1 Eq. 697; *Morris* v. *Ashbee* (1868), L.R. 7 Eq. 34; *Morris* v. *Wright* (1870), L. R. 5 Ch. 279; *Longman* v. *Winchester* (1809), 16 Ves. 269; *Lamb* v. *Evans* (1893), 1 Ch. 218); (i) tradesmen's catalogues (*Maple* v. *Junior Army and Navy Stores* (1882), 21 Ch. D. 369; *Collis* v. *Cater* (1898), 78 L. T. (N.S.) 6130); (j) sheets of advertisements (*Lamb* v. *Evans* (1893), 1 Ch. 218, 222); (k) telegraph codes (*Ager* v. *P. & O. Steam Navigation Co.* (1884), 24 Ch. D. 637); (l) commercial statistics (*Scott* v. *Stanford* (1867), L.R. 3 Eq. 718; *Maclean* v. *Moody* (1858), 20 D. 1154; *Trade Auxiliary* v. *Middlesborough* (1889), 40 Ch. D. 425; *Cate* v. *Devon* (1889), 40 Ch. D. 500); (m) statistics connected with sport (*Cox* v. *Land and Water* (1869), L.R. 9 Eq. 324; *Chilton* v. *Progress Printing Co.* (1895), 2 Ch. 29; *Weatherby* v. *International Horse Agency* (1910), 2 Ch. 297); (n) timetables (*Leslie* v. *Young* (1894), A.C. 335); (o) mathematical tables and calculations. Cf. E. J. MacGillivray *The Copyright Act, 1911, annotated* (1912) pp. 114–15. It seems superfluous to add that the Library has not pressed claims under all these heads.

71 The books not immediately accepted into the main part of the Library were at first shelved pell-mell, but in 1824 they were arranged with a letter of the alphabet and a

Clarke readily admitted to the Commons Committee that the 1814 Act produced more items than the Library strictly either needed or desired. On the other central point he remained adamant. 'We want books; we do not want money.' 'We have other interests besides the pecuniary situation; the ancient rights and privileges of our University, which are of incalculable value.' But his performance as a witness in defence of the libraries had not been notable for its command of the Committee, and he was only partially successful in his plea. The Committee heard its last evidence (when it cross-examined Christian on his *Vindication*) on 8 May. On 5 June Wynn presented his report, recommending that the British Museum should be the sole copyright library, and that the others should be given a fixed annual grant in lieu, or at least that the number of libraries should be reduced to five – the Museum, Oxford, Cambridge, Trinity College, Dublin, and the University of Edinburgh.[72] But five days later Parliament rose, the whole argument was shelved temporarily, and the Bill dropped. Brydges had won his point but not his case.

The Parliamentary Committee of 1818 produced a wealth of information on a topic for which there emerged no very satisfactory solution for almost a century, and its report was far from being the last word on the subject. A further petition to the House in March 1819 sought to reduce the number of copies deliverable to one for the British Museum alone;[73] but Brydges was no longer an MP, and the Commons were not interested. The debate thus meandered out of Parliament once again, leaving the libraries and the trade to arrive at a *modus vivendi* on their own. Robert Southey turned a journalist's eye

running number, A 1 etc. The Upper Library as now known dates from about 1866, and its creation involved the reclassification according to date and size of the residue of those books remaining after many of the novels had been removed into a new class Nov. in an operation begun in 1860 or 1861. The catalogue of the Upper Library (or Lower Library as it was called until its removal to the upper floors of the 1934 building) remained separate until the opening of the computerized microfiche catalogue in 1977.

[72] Hansard 38 (1818) cols. 1256–60. See also *Parliamentary papers* 1818.9 p. 253.
[73] Hansard 39 col. 1113.

to the subject in a long review of the matter, and, with the help of Valpy, came to a conventional conclusion:

It may be desirable that there should be one library which should receive every thing; one general receptacle, in which even the rubbish of the press should be deposited, for the chance that something may be gained by raking in it hereafter. The British Museum should be the place, as being a national and metropolitan library. But with regard to the University libraries, it should be remembered that their original and proper object is the collection of books which may assist the graver pursuits of the scholar, and which, because of their cost or scarcity, might otherwise be inaccessible to him. It cannot be necessary that they should supply the student with Dr. Mavor's Catechism for the Use of Children under seven years of age, with the newest editions of Dr. Solomon's Guide to Health, nor with the treatises upon the theory and practice of gaming, upon the breeding and training of greyhounds, and upon the flavouring of wines and spirituous liquors.[74]

The demise of the 1818 legislation did not mark any permanent decline in public interest. In 1821 *The Pamphleteer* still saw fit to include *Brief observations on the Copyright Bill* written by one 'M.A.' three years previously. The author, addressing his remarks to Henry Bathurst, Bishop of Norwich, proposed that each library should be compensated with the sum of £300 *per annum*, sufficient (he believed) to cover the cost of all 'useful' books, since the libraries could have no call for the residue of minor, non–academic, works worth an estimated £100 p.a. As evidence to the 1818 Committee clearly showed, production costs for books in England were significantly above those on the continent, and it was argued that the further burdens imposed by the copyright libraries made English books even less competitive. M.A.'s purpose was not to press for international copyright legislation to control the output of the continental press (which had produced besides cheap editions of fiction and poetry even Porson's *Adversaria*, Richard Payne Knight's *Prolegomena* to Homer, and a school *Gradus*), but simply to lessen the load for English publishers. His suggestions were, in economic terms, at least

74 *Quarterly Review* 21 (1819) p. 210. For Southey's authorship see H. and H. C. Shine *The Quarterly Review under Gifford* (Chapel Hill 1949) p. 65.

debatable. Few can have taken seriously his argument with reference to copyright deposit 'that the revenue itself suffers in a variety of ways by this check to publication, from decreased consumption of paper &c., and the consequent diminution of employment to artists and mechanics', since 'the duty on paper alone, of a work value 100 guineas, would repay Government for such a grant to these Libraries'.[75]

The Parliamentary Committee did nothing to relieve publishers or booksellers, and nothing to help the libraries in their legitimate complaints. The question of provincial publications, raised at the meeting of the library authorities at Sion College in 1816,[76] remained unresolved; publishers remained unwilling to replace imperfect copies or to complete works published in parts; and the libraries remained painfully aware that they were not – despite the 1814 Act – receiving even everything published in the metropolis.[77] Much of the difficulty stemmed from the fact that although proceedings at Stationers' Hall had been greatly improved, there were still many of the trade who preferred to run the risk of dispensing with these formalities. In the absence of any comprehensive trade list the libraries had no means of telling what, or even how much, was escaping. In 1816 they believed that eight thousand titles were published each year; yet the number of works entered at Stationers' Hall totalled only 2422 altogether.[78] It was hardly incumbent on the Stationers' Company to rectify the situation, since its role (so far as it related to identifying new titles) was a distinctly passive one: the Company was under no obligation to seek out those who did

---

[75] M. A. *Brief observations on the Copyright Bill* printed in *The Pamphleteer* 18 (1821), pp. 525–6. His point was not any stronger for repeating what Southey had claimed in the *Quarterly Review* in 1819, that 'It must be also remembered, that every English book printed abroad is a loss to the revenue of so much duty on paper. Hence, whatever intends to induce publishers to print English works on the continent, is an injury to the country at large' (*Quarterly Review* 21 (1819) p. 204).

[76] Sion College Court Register D, 22 April 1816.

[77] Quite apart from these perennial needlings, the Library also found cause to complain of printers delivering publications printed by half-sheet imposition in their uncut state, two publications thus appearing on one sheet: cf. Syndicate Minutes 29 May 1820.

[78] *Parliamentary papers* 1826–7.20 p. 509.

not register their new books with it. Matters were further complicated by virtue of the Company's being composed in very large measure of publishers and booksellers, who could be expected to comply with the hopes of the libraries only as much as seemed fit.

Greenhill's position was not an enviable one, and he understandably reacted with some asperity in 1818 to a suggestion that he should add to his duties by replacing defective copies of books that had passed through his hands. 'I beg to observe', he wrote, 'that I cannot undertake to send for imperfections that may be wanting in the books sent to the different Libraries being entirely out of my province – I would recommend you to request your bookseller in Town to do it for you or to write to the Publishers of the work desiring them to send the sheets wanting to the Hall and they shall be forwarded to you the first opportunity.'[79] In March and April 1819 Payne and Foss, the London booksellers, provided various parts of sets and of periodicals that would ordinarily have come through Stationers' Hall: their parcels included twenty-four numbers of the *Philosophical Magazine*, forty-eight issues of the *Naval Chronicle*, an assortment of Hansard's *Debates*, four volumes of the *Repertory of Arts*, the first fourteen parts of Dugdale's *Monasticon* in the new edition, and ten parts of Thomas Bateman's fundamental work on cutaneous diseases.[80] The position must have seemed scarcely better than before the passing of the 1814 Act.

Baldwin & Co. were still troublesome over Hansard's *Debates* in 1820, as were Lackington & Co. over Dugdale (which, having begun to appear before 1814, was arguably exempt). Others sought to hide behind a simple argument, that the Act intended only the first number or part of a periodical or book to be entered, and so delivered. In 1820 Longman accordingly hesitated to supply John Britton's *Cathedrals* and *Architectural antiquities*, or Dibdin's *Typographical antiquities*,

---

[79] Letter of 25 June 1818 (Vouchers 1817–18).
[80] For details, see the Accessions Register. Payne and Foss's bill is among the Vouchers for 1818–19.

while Hurst & Co. dallied over Neale's *Westminster Abbey*, and Murray over John Goldicutt's *Antiquities of Sicily*. Cadell & Davies, while willing to supply the later parts (comprising the Apocrypha) of Macklin's Bible, were unable to deliver many of the earlier parts as much of the work had been destroyed in a fire. The authorities at Cambridge were understandably unable to agree to proposals put foward by Rodwell & Martin and by Rivington that entry of part books should be delayed until the work was complete. And even in cases of probable hardship, such as James Sowerby's *Exotic mineralogy* (1811–17) and *Mineral conchology of Great Britain* (1812–: it ran in the end to 648 coloured plates) the University had no powers actually to excuse entry in the Register.[81]

Confronted by an intractable situation, and with old wounds kept open by the evidence presented to Parliament, the libraries, like the book trade, realized that their only hope lay in unity. Cambridge took the lead for a long time, and thereby earned the especial opprobrium of some of the trade, but with the meeting held at Sion College in 1816, the centre of operations had shifted, at least temporarily, to London.[82] By offering hospitality to a meeting of representatives of all the copyright libraries, the College adroitly avoided any responsibility for initiating active steps against recalcitrant publishers, but, more importantly, it was the closest library geographically to the Stationers. The first meetings produced little organized agreement, except to prosecute various publishers for non-delivery, and to compile lists of what was published in those provincial centres most convenient to the various libraries: the former fell in the end to individual libraries, as has been described above, and nothing further is recorded of the latter. But in the winter of 1818–19, faced with rumours that the booksellers intended to renew their battle after the bout brought to an end by the dictates of the parliamentary timetable, the libraries resolved on sterner

---

[81] Details in this paragraph are taken from a letter from Dyneley and Gatty, 26 June 1820 (MS. Add. 2594(2)). [82] See above, pp. 417–18.

action.[83] If the Stationers' Company could do nothing about books not entered, the only recourse for the libraries was to appoint a person able to look after their interests by concentrating on the rest of the current publications. On 3 February 1819 the Library Syndics at Cambridge agreed to appoint, with the other privileged libraries, 'a proper person to demand & collect Books not entered at Stationers' Hall'.[84] Greenhill was thus to continue as previously, and it was envisaged that the new man would be paid jointly by the copyright libraries other than the British Museum, which had indicated its preference to remain independent yet sympathetic.[85] The decision by the Syndics was straightforward enough, but it was taken only after prolonged investigations in London and elsewhere by John Hubbersty, Fellow of Queens',[86] whose surviving correspondence with successive Vice-Chancellors reveals an assiduous and determined man, assisted in much of his work by J. H. Monk. It was felt to be impolitic to proceed too quickly to an appointment of an agent for the libraries, who could clearly expect to meet opposition both from the book trade and, to a lesser degree, from Greenhill, whom some members of the University suspected of failing to send out books received from publishers.

The election of Christopher Wordsworth as Vice-Chancellor, however, brought a change of pace. On 4 December 1820 Hubbersty addressed to him a comprehensive account of proceedings so far, of which the main tenor was contained in a report on the views of Henry Baber of the British Museum – views now shared also by Greenhill:

> It is impossible to obtain the benefits we are entitled to, without having one or more person or persons (exclusive of Mr. Greenhill) fully qualified to enforce our rights, whose entire business it should be, to look after all

---

[83] Sion College Court Register D, 25 November 1818 and 21 January 1819.

[84] Letter from John Hubbersty to Sion College, *ibid.*, 15 February 1819.

[85] Hubbersty to George Neville, the Vice-Chancellor, 16 January 1819 (Library Archives).

[86] And an opponent of Milner. 'Described in the "Gazette", as "Fellow of Queens', Master of Arts, Doctor of Medicine, Barrister-at-Law, Recorder of Lancaster, a Cotton Spinner, and a Bankrupt"' (Gunning *Reminiscences* I p. 264). In 1824 he was appointed Deputy High Steward of the University.

Books published, & immediately after published or advertized for sale, to go round & make demands, & in cases of neglect or refusal, to have authority to take proper steps to enforce the delivery, except where the Case might be doubtful, which in that Case might be referred to the Syndics for their directions – The persons thus appointed ought also to collate & examine all Books when delivered previously to their being sent to the Library.

Baber added that the Library might by this means also receive new books more quickly – 'within less than two months after publication at the latest'. By the end of January, Hubbersty thought he had found a man suitable to act as agent, called Cochrane. An unsuccessful candidate for the post of Librarian to the Faculty of Advocates in 1820, Cochrane possessed the advantage of having been formerly associated with White's bookshop in Fleet Street: but in the event he refused, not least because he had had no success the previous August in eliciting any response from Kerrich when he had approached him on the subject of establishing an agency of the kind considered the preceding winter. In his place Hubbersty suggested Robert Durham, a man to whom he took increasingly and who showed every sign of understanding the libraries' needs: 'a person particularly fitted, he is by descent & education one of the trade, & for some years previous to the Death of Sir Joseph Banks was intrusted by him in the care & arrangemt of his Library'.[87] Since Banks' death, he had worked at a catalogue of his books, and he could further claim the esteem both of the Trustees of the British Museum and of the book trade. Durham was interviewed and approved at Cambridge, and by April was at work.[88]

His task as defined by the Library Syndicate on 5 March 1821 was one that presented a considerable challenge:

To assist in the recovery of the Books to which the University is entitled under the Copyright Act, who shall reside in London and whose duty in it shall be

1. To compile a complete List of all Books published whether in Town or Country, ascertaining the same from his own personal observation and

---

[87] Hubbersty to Wordsworth, 13 March 1821.
[88] On 15 May 1822 he was granted £80 for his twelve months' work to Lady Day 1822.

enquiries; by inspecting the News Papers; the Lists in the Literary Advertizers, and in the several monthly and quarterly Reviews, and by such other means as may offer for that purpose.

2. To note down the precise day of publication, so as to be able to bring proof thereof, with a view to ascertain all such cases as shall occur of neglect on the part of Publishers to enter their Books at Stationers Hall, within one month from the day of publication, advertisement for sale, or offer for sale within the Bills of Mortality, or three months in any other part of the United Kingdom.

3. To see that immediate demand be made in writing of all such parts of the above Lists as shall have been duly entered at Stationers Hall.

4. Regularly to communicate to the Vice Chanc^{or}. once every quarter at least, a copy of the List as above ascertained (art. 1), specifying distinctly such parts thereof as have been duly entered, demanded, received and forwarded to Cambridge – such parts as after being duly entered, and demanded, have not been received – and such parts as have not been so duly entered – with a request for farther instructions how he shall proceed in regard to these two latter cases of non-receipt and non-entry.[89]

The arrangement was not perfect, for aside from such initial needs as arming him with sufficient written authority to present to publishers, the Library's relations to Greenhill at Stationers' Hall and to the British Museum were still undetermined. It proved far from easy, let alone effective, for two collecting centres, the Stationers' Company and Durham's office, to attempt to see that everything was amassed for Cambridge, and although Greenhill provided for Cambridge a list of books entered at Stationers' Hall, Durham still found the task impossible to execute to everyone's satisfaction. Some attempt to supplement the Stationers' Register, by working through the periodic catalogues of recent publications in Bent's *Monthly Literary Advertiser*, had been made since 1817,[90] but it required no great effort to realise that Bent's compilations were by no means comprehensive. Indeed, the printed circular that Durham addressed to publishers pointing out that their new titles were to be entered in the Register was couched in such general terms that it was no very difficult thing for publishers still to enter only what they chose.

[89] Syndicate Minutes 5 March 1821.   [90] Syndicate Minutes 1 June 1817.

The Library's Accessions Register distinguishes Durham's deliveries to the Library from those of the Stationers' Company only between April and November 1822, though he continued to be paid for his work (and to despatch parcels of copyright books) until the financial year 1842–3. As part of continuing attempts to strengthen his hand, in June 1823 he was given power of attorney to demand books due under the Act.[91] It is perhaps some measure of the value the University set on his services that his annual stipend was £80, compared with £21 paid to Greenhill, but the arrangement was not entered into by all the other copyright libraries with the same enthusiasm: Durham was in fact employed only briefly by the British Museum, and by St Andrews only from 1824 to 1826,[92] when the complications of communicating with two collectors of copyright books brought his employment with that library to an end. Legal activities apart, in 1822 – the only year for which such figures survive – Durham collected nearly 140 items for Cambridge, of a very miscellaneous nature, compared with nearly three hundred retained from Stationers' Hall: the number entered in the Register was 1454, but many of these were as usual cast into the old Law School as unsuitable for a university library. There seems to have been no discernible pattern in what Durham, rather than Greenhill, supplied, save in one respect. In April 1822 his deliveries included a mass of odd numbers of journals and of parts of books: seven of Neale's *Westminster Abbey* (published by Hurst), four of Dugdale's *Monasticon* (at last elicited from the publishers), and six of Stephanus' *Thesaurus*: several had figured in the evidence presented to the 1818 Committee. The great increase in serious periodicals had also taken up a large proportion of Durham's time: for some, such as the *Annals of Philosophy*, the *Repertory of Arts*, and the *London Medical Repository*, the Library was now up to date, though the

---

[91] Grace of 11 June 1823 (Grace Book *M* p. 506). His register of claims for the years 1828–35 survives in the Library Archives.

[92] Philip Ardagh 'St Andrews University Library and the Copyright Acts' *Edinburgh Bibliographical Society Transactions* 3 (1956) pp. 179–211, at p. 198.

Medical Quarterly Review had earlier slipped a year and more in arrears. Not until separate invoices were instituted for periodicals in 1863 could there by any hope of keeping abreast of such material.

To this day it is impossible to measure exactly how much did not even reach Cambridge. But in the last years of the 1820s an effort was made to establish, by the only realistic means available, the gaps in the Library's resources. Bent's *Monthly Literary Advertiser* was, as had been noted, the principal yardstick against which to compare the success or otherwise of the arrangements with the Stationers' Company. Far from complete, it nevertheless contained the fullest available list of new publications, and on it were based the various cumulated volumes of the *London Catalogue of Books*. A cumulation for the years 1820–7 appeared in 1827, and in this volume an anonymous member of the Library staff entered the beginnings of a major survey. The results did not give much ground for optimism. Of 1198 books listed under medicine, surgery, physiology, and chemistry, the person checking the titles could find only 545 in the Library. The tale was an equally sorry one in other subjects, and there seemed to be no obvious solution. Publishers might or might not have produced copies of their books consistently. Robert Bampsfield's books on tropical dysentery and on diseases of the spine were both published by Longman, yet only the first could be found. Of J. R. Park's *Inquiry into the laws of life* and *Pathology of fever*, Underwood had supplied only the second. The third edition of William Lawrence's standard *Treatise on ruptures*, published in 1816 by J. Callow, had arrived, but the Library (like the British Museum) had missed the first two editions – it was first published in 1807 – and it still had no edition at all of his *Lectures on physiology* which had been published by the same firm. In other subjects, of four books by Chateaubriand published by Colburn, his *Recollections of Italy, England and America* and *Historical essay on revolutions* had arrived, but not *Travels in Greece* or *Political reflections on the true interests of the French nation*. None of John

Young's various catalogues of paintings in private collections, published by Hurst, was cheap, at prices between three and twelve guineas: the Library still lacked the volumes relating to the Grosvenor, Leicester and Miles collections, though it had acquired the Angerstein and Stafford catalogues. Cotman's *Architectural antiquities of Normandy* (1822) and John Britton's works were among many examples of illustrated books that had arrived, but even in the study of antiquities, to which Kerrich had given so much attention, there were still gaps. T. D. Fosbroke's most important works were in the Library, but not his *Wye tour* (published at Ross), or his *Synopses* of ancient arms and armour and of ancient costume, despite their also having been published by Nichols. Jeremy Bentham's *Rationale of reward* (1825) was safely at Cambridge, but not – according to this survey – his *Defence of usury* (first published in 1787 and reprinted in 1816) or *Chrestomathia* (1815). John Bramsen's *Travels in Egypt* (1820) was registered as not having come: to the bewilderment of the Library staff, this was in fact a republication of *Letters of a Prussian traveller* (1818), which with his *Remarks on the north of Spain* (1823) had come already: all were published by Colburn. Multi-volume sets posed a continuing problem. The first volume of John Bostock's *Elementary system of physiology* (published in three volumes by Baldwin), for example, arrived without mishap, but at the time of this survey of recent acquisitions neither the second nor the third had come: the Library eventually acquired the original edition of the third volume (1827) and the second of the second (1828). Similar difficulties arose over Robert Allan's *System of pathological and operative surgery*: the first two volumes, published by the University Press at Edinburgh in 1819–21, were in the Library, but it proved possible to acquire only the second part of the third volume, published in 1827 and by then in the hands of A. Balfour & Co.

The difficulties surrounding books published in parts have already been noticed.[93] Most such books prepared for the

93 P. 431 and n. 77 above.

cheaper end of the market, such as reprints of popular novels, devotional works, or books of self-improvement, escaped the Library's grasp altogether: in themselves they held little attraction for the library authorities, at Cambridge or elsewhere. More expensive plate books posed difficulties of other kinds. The Library subscribed to Gould's works; others arrived as deposit copies or were bought piecemeal; and in the case of John Sibthorp's *Flora Graeca* there was a rare chance to make good the opportunity missed on the first publication. The reasons for its not being acquired from 1806, when the first part appeared, may be manifold; but Sir James Edward Smith, President of the Linnean Society, recorded one when in 1819 he quoted John Davies, the late *Bibliothecarius*, who had told him 'two or three years after the first volume had appeared, that it was not then purchased, nor likely, as an Oxford work, to be so'. The work, published by John White, was edited by Smith from the papers of Sibthorp, who had been Professor of Botany at Oxford, but Davies' disregard for the other university was not perpetuated. The Library subsequently bought the entire work, which was completed only in 1840, but it had to make do with reprints of the first plates, which are watermarked 1816.[94]

The early nineteenth-century arguments surrounding the legislation for copyright deposit were often repetitive, illuminating only on rare occasions, frequently so blinded by partisan beliefs that logic could at best be perceived only murkily, and in so far that the question was not deemed by every party to be settled, inconclusive. But despite all this they deserve to be treated at some length because the controversy marked a turning point both for the book trade and for the universities' relations with the outside world. Much of the argument had pertained to the non-university libraries, particularly the

---

[94] Sir J. E. Smith *A defence of the Church and universities of England, against such injurious advocates as Professor Monk* (1819) p. 51. The 1816 plates are not recorded by William T. Stearn in his article in *Taxon* 16 (1967) pp. 168–78.

British Museum and Sion College, but much more had related to the universities. The concept of a university library that was also a national copyright library in the modern sense eluded every participant, whether bookseller, lawyer, independent observer or librarian. It proved to be not difficult to win admission that the British Museum should enjoy the privileges of copyright deposit, since it was self-evidently also the national library. But in the eyes of every party concerned, the two notions of a copyright library, receiving virtually every book or pamphlet issued by the press, and of a university library, were incompatible. The case for keeping a number of such libraries was fought on the grounds of legal precedent, and on a view of the purposes of a university that was related almost solely to the curriculum it followed. Questions put to the authorities representing Oxford and Cambridge (and particularly the former) in the 1818 Committee showed no sign of any sense that there might be some purpose in preserving the apparently trivial against a time when it would be treasured, and no-one attempted to contradict the view. To that extent the libraries collected only by default some of the material for which they are now sometimes most valued.

But if the modern concept of a university copyright library, as it emerged in the mid-nineteenth century, eluded those who took part in the debate in the first two decades of the century, other similar novelties did not. The universities, long virtually ignored by public opinion as to their internal arrangements, were easy objects of attack, but ironically it was the universities themselves that sometimes suggested the means. There was much in Edward Christian's *Vindication* that was foolish, but a reader outside Cambridge who perceived that he was reading the work of the Downing Professor of Law may be easily excused for supposing that what Christian described at Cambridge must most probably be true. And yet, if true in the sense that he assumed things to be for the sake of his argument, then Christian was being very much less than honest in some of his suggestions. 'Very few' graduates of Cambridge, he justly commented, 'are so fortunate, whilst they are resident in the University, as to gain affluent situations, or the means of purchasing valuable and expensive books.'[95] Nor could it be easily gainsaid that the purpose of the 1710 Act was 'to give encouragement to learning in all the Universities of Great Britain, by giving to the students, resident in them, the opportunity of becoming acquainted with every literary work, which could in any degree whatever contribute to the advancement of truth and science'.[96] And yet, as Richard Duppa, himself a member of the University of Cambridge, pointed out, undergraduates at Cambridge were not allowed to roam in the very library that Christian claimed as existing for their use.[97] The University Library was still reserved for senior members and for visiting scholars, despite the popular title of 'Public'. 'If the libraries', commented John Britton (with some justification under the circumstances) 'were open to every student, as they unquestionably *ought to be*, and, under certain liberal regulations, were also accessible to the literati, and to all persons of research, there would be some appearance of justice and fairness in the demands now set up.'[98] His remark about 'all persons of research', by which he meant visiting scholars, was wide of the mark, but the same could not be said of the Library's treatment of undergraduates. Senior members could borrow books on their behalf, but there was a gulf between that and equal access to the stacks.

The financing of the Library also exercised Britton, in common with many others. Something of the scale of money available to the Library at Cambridge to buy books only finally emerged in evidence before the 1818 Committee, which thus put an end to speculation. It was not of much relevance for Britton to allege that the university presses at Oxford and Cambridge produced profit amounting to 'as much, if not

[95] Christian *Vindication* p. 11.   [96] *Ibid.*, p. 28.
[97] [Richard Duppa] *An address to the Parliament of Great Britain on the claims of authors to their own copyright* 3rd ed. (*The Pamphleteer* 2 (1813)) p. 188.
[98] John Britton *The rights of literature* (1814) p. 61.

more, than £400 per year', and he was wrong in believing that Cambridge maintained a separate fund, raised by taxing students, for purchasing books. At Oxford there was such a system, where Cochrane reported that although nearly £2000 was collected in 1810–12 no more than a hundred a year was spent on modern books.[99] Britton commented on similar arrangements at the Faculty of Advocates and at the University of Edinburgh.[100] Cambridge was not to introduce such payments until 1825,[101] but in thus setting its own house in order – by internal taxes on its own members – remained more independent of outside influence than it might had the suggestion widely canvassed ten years earlier been taken up and the University been enabled by government grants to buy what it needed rather than receive books as a result of direct legislation on the trade. In 1814, reported Hansard, for example, Wynn 'was of opinion, that a sum should be rather granted from the public purse to enable them to purchase new works, than to impose upon publishers the tax proposed in this Bill. The sum for that purpose need not, in his judgment, exceed 2,500l. a year, to all the Universities.'[102] Wynn had the well-being of authors more in mind than the good of the university and other copyright libraries, and for the moment his suggestions progressed no further than being incorporated among the alternatives recommended by the 1818 Committee.[103] But in them lay the seeds of two later departures in copyright and university legislation: first, that the copyright privilege might be translated in some way into a cash sum, and second, that universities might receive a recurrent grant from the government. The first was to be put into practice in the clauses to compensate the six libraries that lost their copyright status in 1836, and the second has become a prominent feature

---

[99] [J. G. Cochrane] *The case stated* (1813) pp. 23–4.
[100] *The rights of literature* pp. 62–3.
[101] By Grace of 7 December 1825 (Grace Book *N* p. 107). See also below, pp. 454–5.
[102] He did not suggest that this sum would be full compensation for the loss of copies to all the libraries: such a figure would have been much higher. See Hansard 28 (1814) col. 752.   [103] Hansard 38 (1818) col. 1259.

of modern university administration. For the present, however, discussions on this last question foundered. A contributor to the *British Review* in the first weeks of 1819 remained a solitary voice advocating a more rational approach to the question in a truly national context, whereas the previous two decades had offered only parochialism and party strife:

It may be fit, that Universities, which had not adequate funds of their own, should be furnished with the means of procuring books: but let them be supplied at the expense of the public, rather than at the expense of a few meritorious individuals. The accumulation of books in their libraries, is an object of national policy; and, as such, should be provided for in the same way as the other wants of the state. The seats of learning might as well be supplied with book-cases at the expense of the cabinet makers, and with fuel at the expense of the miners of the United Kingdom, as with books at the cost of publishers and authors. Let them be provided liberally with all that can be useful to them: only let this provision be made on fair and equitable principles. We wish not to stint them in the supply of any of their wants; let tens of thousands, if it is thought fit, be lavished on them annually, but let whatever is given to them be raised by a general rather than by a partial tax. The existing mode is, no doubt, an easy way of furnishing them with books; it accomplishes the end without requiring from Parliament the arrangement of any scheme; all the trouble of details is thrown upon the publishers and the Stationers' Company. But it is worth while to be just, even at the expense of a little labour and a few exertions of wisdom. Parliament should consider what is best, rather than what is easiest.[104]

Finally, amidst this sorry tale of missing volumes and elusive titles, which seem always to form the routine of gathering in copyright copies, two more useful points emerge. First, as the book trade became more organized, and volumes systematically listing large numbers of current publications began regularly to appear, so the Library's hopes of what it might acquire increased. More information inevitably imposed fresh criteria. Second, while it had come to accept novels and minor literature almost despite itself, the Library's attitude to the national published output had in fact changed remarkably

---

[104] 'Claims of the public libraries to the gratuitous delivery of books' *British Review* 13 (1819) pp. 226–47, at pp. 231–2. The gist of the argument was also reported in *St James's Chronicle* on 11 February 1819. On the editor of the *British Review*, William Roberts, see *DNB* and Arthur Roberts *Life, letters and opinions of William Roberts* (1850).

within the term of one man, Thomas Kerrich. The mood in Cambridge in the 1820s was one of reform. J. H. Monk (Regius Professor of Greek) and Christopher Wordsworth (Master of Trinity College and Vice-Chancellor in 1820–1) were in the van of those who wished to reform the undergraduate curriculum.[105] Both took an active part in the attempts to improve the collections in the University Library. Their opponent on matters of the curriculum, William French, Master of Jesus and Vice-Chancellor in 1821–2, sat with them on the same sub-syndicate to consider copyright acquisitions. So too did John Kaye, Master of Christ's, Regius Professor of Divinity, Bishop of Bristol and likewise a reformer. In that undergraduates were not free to use the Library, the interest of these men in curriculum reform had little obvious connection with their willingness to see the Library expand into new fields at a rate previously unimagined. But their inclinations to transform the University were supported by others who never became Heads of Houses, and whose very appointments were innovations. Edward Christian, on whose pamphlet so much came to revolve, was the first Downing Professor of the Laws of England. Edward Daniel Clarke became first Professor of Mineralogy (a title founded by the University itself) in 1808, nine years before taking office in the University Library. In 1828 George Pryme began a thirty-five-year reign as Professor of Political Economy – a subject on which he had lectured since 1816 despite its not being a recognized subject within the University. William Smyth, Regius Professor of Modern History from 1807 until 1849, was similarly revolutionary in his attitudes, throwing open his lectures to all who would come, whether members of the University or not. And in John Lodge, *Bibliothecarius* from 1822 in succession to Clarke before becoming also *Protobibliothecarius* in 1828, the University had an officer who was more adventurous than any of his predecessors in extending the Library's collections in just that diversity of subjects which the times seemed to demand.

[105] Winstanley *Early Victorian Cambridge* pp. 65–72.

11

THE END OF THE OLD REGIME

THE EXTRAORDINARY, vituperative, and legally question-
able manoeuvres surrounding the appointment of Clarke's
successor as Professor of Mineralogy, and the rift between the
Caput and the Senate that took the University finally to the
Court of King's Bench, do not bear directly on the history of
the Library, and in any case occurred after the election of
Clarke's successor as *Bibliothecarius*.[1] But in some respects there
were parallels to be found between both events, for the man
who entered the Library in 1822 was not the establishment
choice. Clarke's death at the age of sixty-two on 9 March 1822
meant that the office of *Bibliothecarius* was again vacant after
only five years. Once again the development of the Library
was in jeopardy, since Kerrich could not be relied on to show
the energy necessary to carry through much needed change.
The University had weathered the crisis over copyright
legislation, and emerged puzzled but in a stronger position
nationally than ever previously thanks more to influence and
assistance outside Cambridge than to the acumen of resident
members. It had still to face a series of further crises: of lack of
space, shortage of money, and university reform. But it was to
do so with the aid of a man who had the sympathy and ear of
the reform party, and who proved to be, in his reserved way,
more effective and knowledgeable than either Kerrich or the
extrovert Clarke. For as long as he was alive, Kerrich was, as
Protobibliothecarius, nominally in charge of the collection. He

---

[1] J. W. Clark and T. McK. Hughes *Life and letters of Adam Sedgwick* (Cambridge 1890) 1
pp. 325–45; Winstanley *Early Victorian Cambridge* pp. 33–9.

died only in 1828, the head of a library whose management he had been content to let pass out of his hands and into those of the younger man, his junior in all respects. For the six years that separated the deaths of Clarke and Kerrich the Library was instead guided by a man who, though he did not hold the reins, began to lead it on the course it was to follow for the next half century.

The contest for Clarke's successor was eventually between James Clarke Franks and John Lodge (fig. 16). Born within twelve months of each other, both were members of Trinity. A theologian already of some promise, Franks had entered the college as a sizar in 1810, and by the time he was appointed a select preacher in 1819–20 had carried off the Hulsean Prize for divinity in 1813 and the Norrisian Prize in 1814, 1816, 1817 and 1818, besides the second Members' Prize for Latin in 1817. Lodge had won no prizes, had graduated in 1814 as twelfth wrangler, and had migrated to Magdalene in 1818, where he was elected to a Fellowship. In the poll for the Librarianship on 26 March 1822 Lodge obtained 139 votes to Franks' 113. He had the support of Kerrich and of John Haviland, Regius Professor of Physic (and, incidentally, of Henry Gunning, whose reminiscences have however little to say of the occasion) among the more senior members of the University, but he was also voted for by three of the most influential men in Cambridge in the next decades: William Whewell, Adam Sedgwick, and Joseph Romilly. He had enjoyed the friendship of Sedgwick since his undergraduate days, joining his mineralogical and antiquarian pursuits then and for many years later. Whewell and Romilly had been undergraduates with him at Trinity. On the other hand, however, Franks obtained the support of the majority of the Heads of Houses, including William French, Vice-Chancellor and Master of Jesus, William Webb of Clare, George Thackeray of King's, Francis Barnes of Peterhouse, and James Wood of St John's, all of them intransigent conservatives, while Christopher Words-worth (Trinity) and John Kaye (Christ's) alone could be

16 John Lodge (d.1850), *Protobibliothecarius* and Librarian. From a
mezzotint by James Egan after a painting by Frederick Walmisley
now in Magdalene College. Size of original 387 × 304 mm.
Cockerell's uncompleted east front can be seen in the background.
The plan by Lodge's hand is of Anderby church, Lincolnshire,
where he was rector from 1835 to 1850.

considered sympathetic to reform.[2] Less than three months after the election further evidence emerged of where Lodge's sympathies and support lay, when he was one of a deputation of three (the others were Sedgwick and Arthur Carrighan of St John's) who waited on the Vice-Chancellor to propose that the disputed election of Clarke's successor to the chair of Mineralogy should be referred to the Court of King's Bench.

Such a beginning might not be thought to bode much good. Lodge was still aged less than thirty, and could be expected to be associated with the Library for a considerable time. In fact the period between his election as *Bibliothecarius* and his resignation in April 1845 as both *Bibliothecarius* and *Protobibliothecarius* was marked by changes of which the University had as yet received barely a hint. In the late 1850s Henry Bradshaw was tart on the condition into which some of the early printed books had fallen,[3] but it was under Lodge that the collections expanded at a rate faster than the University could comprehend, undergraduates were at last given again some measure of access to the Library, and the buildings themselves were first threatened with wholesale replacement and then added to by one of the most masterly examples of neoclassical architecture in the country.

The first hint of upheaval came on 20 February 1822, a month before Lodge's election, when the Senate passed a Grace to petition the House of Lords to allow an exchange of land which would provide space for the enlargement of the Schools.[4] But although this initiative was taken before his arrival, nothing further was accomplished towards the expansion of the Library for several years. The changes came, first, within the Library.

It was to be a long time before any serious work was undertaken on the western manuscripts with any purpose of publishing a full description. Nasmith's work, so admirable in

---

[2] John Smith *The poll for election of Librarian of the University of Cambridge on Tuesday, March 26, 1822* (Cambridge 1822).
[3] Prothero *Bradshaw* p. 62.   [4] Grace Book *M* p. 412.

its own way, did not inspire the authorities sufficiently to bring them to the point of sending it to the press. Moreover, while the accessions of western manuscripts in the first half of the nineteenth century were modest, the additions to the oriental collections presented an altogether different and more demanding picture. The Burckhardt manuscripts were not properly described in print until Preston's catalogue was published in 1853, but abortive attempts to do justice to these and to other orientalia were made nearly thirty years previously. In May 1825 a Grace was offered to the Senate seeking to give authority to Daniel Wait of St John's, whose painstaking study of *Jewish, oriental and classical antiquities* had been published two years earlier, to prepare a catalogue of the oriental manuscripts.[5] But although the Grace was passed, nothing seems to have come of this scheme, and five years later the Vice-Chancellor requested Samuel Lee, Professor of Arabic, to catalogue the Burckhardt and other oriental manuscripts not already described elsewhere:[6] this, too, fell to the ground.

Those anxious for some change were rewarded with more success elsewhere. To the early years of Lodge's librarianship can be traced the modern history of the collections of those books that were not allowed to be borrowed because they were considered to constitute works of permanent reference. In February 1823 the Syndics compiled a list of thirteen dictionaries always to be kept in the Library,[7] which four years later was extended to include half a dozen further works of a more miscellaneous nature, among them an atlas, Cruden's concordance, Watt's *Bibliotheca Britannica* and Edmondson's *Complete body of heraldry*.[8] The Syndics' aims were modest, but the principle had been established. In May 1836 they added the *Encyclopaedia metropolitana* (in preference to any other), and even in February 1843, when a printed list of these books was produced for the first time, the tally ran to only thirty-two

---

[5] Library papers 7 May 1825. [6] Syndicate Minutes 15 November 1830.
[7] *Ibid.*, 17 February 1823. [8] *Ibid.*, 26 February 1827.

titles, finishing with the University Statutes and examination papers.[9] The practice of reserving books relating to particular subjects of study in the University, which was to figure prominently in debates over the arrangement and expansion of the Library in the second half of the century and to become familiar to students of history in the twentieth, seems to have had its origins in 1846, when the Syndics set aside sixteen titles for candidates for the prize offered by John Muir on Christianity and Hinduism:[10] the competition, won in 1848 by a Fellow of King's, was in practice open only to senior members, and there was no call for books to be reserved for other similar occasions in subsequent years.

In no area, however, were changes so apparent as in the accessions made to the Library. Among the principal subjects to which commentators on the Library as a place of copyright deposit returned repeatedly was, naturally, the money available for buying books. The University published no accounts, and as a result there was ample room for speculation and allegation. The truth, had they known it, was far from encouraging. Between 1797 (the year of Kerrich's election) and 1808 no money was available from the Rustat Fund for the purpose, although some was of course drawn from the general university funds. In 1808, for the first time in many years, an attempt was made to set the Fund straight. A report on the matter by the Library Syndics remarked that while available income had in the past been spent on books for the Library as determined by Rustat, 'it does not appear that this has been done by the consent & advice of the persons nominated for that purpose in M[r] Rustat's declaration, nor have the books been uniformly bound, or stamped with his arms, or registered in a Separate Catalogue'.[11] To set some of these matters right was a

---

[9] Printed notice in Library papers, 27 February 1843.
[10] Library papers 8 June 1846; *Historical register* p. 319.
[11] Rustat Audit Book. The Syndics noted that the advice and consent for buying books was required of the Vice-Chancellor, the Provost of King's, the Masters of Trinity and St John's, and the Professors of Divinity, Law, Physic, Mathematics, Greek and Oriental Languages, 'or by the advice & consent of any five or more of them'.

question of detail. New ledgers were bought, to record the Fund's accounts and books purchased. Two suitable binding stamps were engraved with the Rustat badge, to be impressed on the sides of all books bought with the Fund, and booksellers were instructed to identify in their bills which books had been ordered on the Rustat account.[12] There was, however, little enough money with which to operate. The Ovington estate in Norfolk, in which the Fund was invested, was leased at a rent of £360 per annum, but against this had to be set £40 rent payable annually to St John's College, Oxford, ten guineas payable each year to the University's agent, and (until 1816) a property tax of £36, quite apart from casual repairs. The managers of the Fund, having set it in reasonable order for audit, wisely spent cautiously at first. Out of a total outgoings in 1808–9 of £235.8s.5d. they spent £162 on books and bindings (including £22.17s.0d. at the sale of Richard Porson's library). The following year the respective figures were £293.19s.0d. and £211.5s.10d., and in 1810–11 £281.16s.7d. and £175.16s.0d. In 1811–12 no books at all were bought, and the Library benefited only by a small sum for binding and two guineas for Marshall's fee due in return for cataloguing the Rustat books already acquired. The following year took a turn for the better. With income from the estate and from the reserves at £1167.12s.5d., Deighton's bill alone totalled £302.11s.0d., while Payne and Foss supplied books to the value of £47.11s.6d. Yet between then and 1820 nothing approaching this sum was spent from the Fund. The accounts for 1814–15 record a mere £12 to Deighton, while expenditure actually on the estate (excluding unavoidable rents and taxes) amounted to over £40. In theory such parsimony ought to have yielded a reasonable fund for book purchases, since any sums not spent in a financial year were added to the Fund's capital. But although it was then and for many years after generally stated that the Fund produced about two to three

---

[12] Library Vouchers 1808–9: Bowtell's account for 29 April 1809.

hundred pounds a year for books and binding, this kind of sum was spent only intermittently. The Fund was used principally for books in foreign languages and for the more expensive English publications for which copyright legislation was ineffective. So in 1823–4 it enabled the Library to acquire not only Sir William Gell's *Itinerary of Greece* (1810), the five volumes of Edward Donovan's *Natural history of British shells* (1800–4) and William Godwin's life of Chaucer (2nd ed. 1804), but also Robert Morrison's Chinese dictionary and grammar, while foreign accessions were spectacular. Fourier's *Théorie analytique de la chaleur* (Paris 1822) suggested that there were new demands in the University, and was cheap compared with other titles, including François Solvyns' *Hindous* (four volumes, Paris 1808–12), Alexander von Humboldt's *Vues des Cordillères* (Paris 1810) or, more ambitious than any other book selected in the early nineteenth century, Humboldt's and Aimé Bonpland's immense *Nova genera & species plantarum* (Paris 1815–25), of which the first twenty-seven fascicles alone, with the plates coloured, cost £205.

For several years after 1827 money from the Rustat Fund used by the Library was in fact spent only on binding. Moreover, in 1822 the lease at Ovington fell in, and the effects of the post-war agricultural depression were made plain. In an attempt to reduce calls on the Fund, the University tried to lease the estate out at the old rent of £360 per annum, the tenant to meet all repair bills. The family of the former tenant refused the offer, and, the University failing to find anyone to take the estate at £310, the rent was finally forced down to £260 per annum. It stayed there until 1835, and even then climbed back only to £300.[13]

Fortunately, however, by then the Library could count on other funds. Expenditure on books, binding and necessary stationery, that for many years only rarely rose above £200 a year, increased suddenly with the election of Clarke in 1817

---

[13] Details from the Rustat Audit Book.

and then of Lodge in 1822. Both men struck out in new directions, brought fresh vigour to the ailing strength of Kerrich, and ensured that the habitually stolid pace of John Davies could never again be characteristic of the Library. In a burst of enthusiasm, binding and book bills for the financial year 1819–20 almost topped £500, but this proved to be only the beginning. The wisdom of raising money by a levy on members of the University (a practice already employed in Oxford[14] and the Scottish universities) had not escaped observers of the debate on the legislation for copyright deposit, and it could only be a matter of time before Cambridge attempted it. The Syndicate finally tackled the question of the shortage of funds for the Library in May 1825, and appointed a sub-syndicate with general powers 'to enquire what are the regular funds for the supply of Books for the Library and also to consider what would be the best mode of increasing the fund by contributions from Members of the University or other-wise'.[15] The committee, consisting of John Lamb, Master of Corpus, John Haviland, Regius Professor of Physic (both convinced reformers) and John Lodge, worked with a speed that suggests they were not unprepared for their task. On 3 June they reported to devastating effect.

The only regular funds appropriated to the supply of Books for the Library are the Rustat and Worts; the former may be averaged at £200 a year, and the latter has produced during the last two years £960. It is proposed to increase these funds by a quarterly contribution of 1s.6d. from each Member of the University (excepting Sizars) by which it is calculated that an annual sum will be received of about £1200. It further appears that the average expences of the Library independent of the purchase & binding of Books is about £650 which your Sub-Syndicate recommend to be defrayed as it now is from the University Chest.[16]

Besides those of the original trio, two further signatures were added to the report, of Christopher Wordsworth and of Thomas Le Blanc, the then Vice-Chancellor. No doubt suspicious of the speed at which the reformers were trying to

---

[14] Craster p. 34. [15] Syndicate Minutes 2 May 1825. [16] *Ibid.*, 3 June 1825.

move, the University rejected a Grace on 11 June that would have put the report's recommendations into effect. Instead, therefore, after pausing for the Long Vacation and hesitating for the Michaelmas Term, a second and similar Grace was put on 7 December, and passed by thirty-one votes to twelve after being non-placeted by the non-regents.[17] The results of the success were immediate and dramatic. Although by Michaelmas 1826 no payment had yet been received from King's College for its members, the Library had gained £938.5s.0d.: with King's contribution it could be expected to be £1181.5s.5d. The next twelve months brought in £1425.13s.11d., and in 1827–8 Library dues amounted to £1344.7s.0d. The levy meant more than a doubling of the book fund, and although one of the sub-syndicate's proposals, that all charges other than those for books and binding should be defrayed from the University Chest, was not accepted completely – the Library still paid for minor repairs to the fabric and furnishings – the Library had won a signal victory. Furthermore, besides this improvement in its financial fortunes, the Library could also look with some satisfaction on more strictly administrative matters. Thanks to improved accounting arrangements, which were imposed after a few years of somewhat casual attention to the University's audit records in the mid-1820s, salaries and stipends were at last separated under a different heading from general expenditure. From 1823, the Library was shown as a separate account for the first time, distinct from expenditure on the Senate House and the Schools. Financially and administratively, for better or for worse, it had achieved full recognition in its own right. And, equally importantly, the new arrangements concentrated attention on the book fund. No hint of the University's determination to increase the size of the Library's book stock

---

[17] Grace Book N p. 107, recorded on 20 February 1826 in the Syndics' Minutes: 'Placeat vobis ut singuli graduati et nongraduati [exceptis Sizatoribus] singulis trimestribus spatiis summam octodecim denariorum Academiae solvant in usum Bibliothecae Publicae erogandam.'

could be more clear. The emphasis could only be, for the present, on expansion.

Lodge seized on the advantage of an increased income for books, and set the style that was to characterize his term of office after he succeeded Kerrich in 1828 as *Protobibliothecarius* as well. In 1827–8 the Library overspent by fractionally under £200 in its new found freedom. £844.17s.8d. went on books (besides £150 covering a backlog of five years' subscription to Holmes' Septuagint), and £294.8s.6d. on binding. In 1828–9 the figures were £731.16s.1d. on books and £242.2s.3d. on binding. By the time of his resignation in 1845 Lodge had dealt with most of the major booksellers in London, a claim that can be made for none of his predecessors; but the likely tendencies of his interests, and his preferred methods of buying books, became clear in the six years that separated the deaths of Clarke and Kerrich. Lodge was during this time in virtual control of the Library, even though Kerrich was senior to him both in years and in his titular position, and in these years he gradually learned how to expand an already large library. On Lodge devolved responsibility for acquiring more books annually, with more money, than the Library had ever known. In the year ending Michaelmas 1829, his first full year in office as *Protobibliothecarius*, he reckoned to have spent £1053.0s.2d. on books and binding.[18] But although he was by then in name as well as in fact master of the Library, he had enjoyed much of the same power since Clarke's death. Kerrich's interests in these aspects of the Library had weakened still further in the last years of Clarke's term of office, and although the list of books bought for the Library naturally continued to place considerable emphasis on antiquarian topics, it gradually (and the pace was painfully slow) encompassed a larger proportion of other subjects.

Lodge was never afraid of quantities of books, even when (as in the case of the Heber sales of the 1830s) cataloguing could

---

[18] Vouchers 1828–9; as usual, the financial figures in these paragraphs are based on the Vouchers and the annual audited university accounts.

not keep pace. Within a few months of his election in 1822 he had ordered a set of the *Gentleman's Magazine* from 1731 to 1822. The *Historical Register* for 1716–30 came in 1824, and two years later forty volumes of the *British Critic*. But while this marked the beginning of periodical buying on a grand scale, supplemented more and more effectively by the copyright intake, it was by no means Lodge's only innovation. The auction sale in May 1823 of books from the library of Sir Henry Bate Dudley, journalist turned canon of Ely, suggested other opportunities. Though Lodge bought only sparingly at this sale, auctions became for much of the nineteenth century a major means of acquiring books: as a later Librarian, J. E. B. Mayor, was to remark,[19] judicious buying in this way could produce considerable savings. Lodge set the trend, and while paying especial attention to the more important local sales conducted by Elliot Smith (whose emporium just outside Trinity College was better known among undergraduates for its second-hand furniture), also began to tackle sales in London. He could not always find a great deal (the auction in Cambridge of Clarke's books in 1824 produced only what Elliot Smith's bill described as a 'Turkish almanack' at £2.10s.0d., for example), but once established, the habit could produce only beneficial results.

Besides buying generally at auctions, Lodge also began to spend on much earlier printed books. In 1818 the Library had bought a copy of Leonardo de Utino's *Sermones de sanctis*,[20] which replaced one found to be missing in 1748. Lodge followed this lead by venturing further among the lacunae in the Library's incunabula and post-incunabula. A copy of a Milan Julius Solinus offered by Payne and Foss in 1826 was returned, but in January that year the Library paid the same firm seven guineas for Constantinus Lascaris' *Erotemata* of 1495, the first book printed by Aldus. It was a fashionable acquisition from a fashionable bookseller. Besides these,

---

[19] See below, pp. 588–9.   [20] Inc. 612. See also Oates *Catalogue* pp. 24 and 49.

Lodge's account to the University for 1824–5 included eight guineas for the Aldine Herodotus of 1502 in a contemporary Italian binding, five guineas for a copy of Aldus' own Greek grammar, and smaller sums on Aldine editions of Oppian, Dante and Giacomo Sannazaro: the same bill also included a modern map of Germany at £2.12s.6d. In August 1826 Payne and Foss supplied the folio Aldine Aesop of 1505 in red morocco, at ten guineas, and the account from the booksellers Bohn in that year included further Aldines: Pindar (1513), Pontanus (1513–18), Dante (1515), an annotated Homer (1516), a Julius Caesar (1519: formerly the Duke of Grafton's copy), Justinus and Cornelius Nepos (1522: a 'very fine copy', in red Turkey leather, at £1.11s.6d.), Horace (1527), Aristotle's *Poetics* (1536: 'extremely rare', in blue morocco, £2.8s.0d.), besides half a dozen later Aldine imprints of more recent authors, among them Giacomo Sannazaro, Speroni degli Alvarotti, Machiavelli's *Arte della guerra*, and Judah Abravanel's *Dialogi di amore* in both the 1541 and 1545 editions. Bohn's bill, of which the Aldines formed only a small part, totalled £160.12s.0d. even after a five per cent discount.[21]

A few weeks before succeeding Kerrich in May 1828, Lodge paid the first part of the Library's subscription to Audubon's *Birds of America*, a far cry from Aldines and agreed following Audubon's visit to Cambridge in quest of subscriptions in March 1828.[22] By no means all the Library's purchases were so esoteric. In 1827 Lodge's choices included, besides twenty volumes of the *Farmer's Magazine* and Southey's *Letters written during a journey in Spain* to supplement the copyright deposits, the four-volume edition of Mrs Behn's plays (1724), and Defoe's *Tour through Great Britain*. In the same year Bohn supplied the first volume of the *Monumenta Germaniae historica*;

---

[21] These bills are among the Vouchers.
[22] For Audubon's signed receipt, see the Vouchers for 1827–8. He visited Cambridge in March 1828, and persuaded the University Library, the Philosophical Society, the Fitzwilliam Museum, George Thackeray (Provost of King's) and the heir to the Fitzwilliam title all to subscribe. (Howard Corning (ed.) *Letters of John James Audubon 1826–1840* (Boston 1930) I pp. 62–3).

Bossange (giving a discount of ten per cent) provided Guizot's *Histoire de la révolution d'Angleterre*, the first volume of which had been published in Paris the previous year, together with a collection of popular songs from Greece and volumes on travel; and Deighton sent in all so far published of Schleiermacher's edition of Plato, then appearing in Berlin, Winckelmann's collected works published at Dresden and Berlin in 1808–25, Louis Poinsot's *Élémens de statique* (1824), Griesbach's *Opuscula academica* (1824), Schlegel's complete works in ten volumes (1822–5), and Wieland's in forty-nine (1818–23): the firm's consignments of older books contained few earlier than the mid-eighteenth century, but did include such standard works as Stukeley's *Palaeographia Britannica* (1743–52), Ducarel on Norman coins (1757), the first three volumes of Brequigny's *Table chronologique des diplômes* (Paris 1769–83), as well as Johann Breitkopf on playing cards (Leipzig 1784) and a collection in two volumes of type specimens issued by the Propaganda press at Rome in the latter part of the eighteenth century. As an accompaniment to the English translation published in 1827 by Hunt and Clarke, Lodge also picked out Jean Pierre Abel Rémusat's version of a 'roman chinois', *Iu-kiao-li, ou les deux cousines* published in Paris the year before. The British and Foreign Bible Society gave Bibles or parts of Bibles published from Haarlem to Serampore, from St Petersburg to Colombo, and in languages as unfamiliar to Cambridge as Lettish, Estonian, Wendish and Amharic, besides Chinese, Hindi and Malay. Howell and Stewart, booksellers in Holborn, supplied a total of 104 items for £73.4s.0d. after discount, mostly in theology. Bossange's list included nineteen volumes of Buffon's *Histoire naturelle*, Thierry's *Lettres sur l'histoire de France*, published that year, and Thomas Stevenson's recent German editions of classical authors, besides J. Kolderup-Rosenvinge's *Leges regis Canuti Magni*. Lodge himself obtained for the Library the first volume of a large paper copy of Joseph Pettigrew's *Bibliotheca Sussexiana*, at seven guineas, and the first six volumes of Jacob

Sturm's *Deutschlands Fauna* at three guineas, besides paying out a further small sum for incidental expenses at auctions. Elliot Smith, the local auctioneers who in the University's financial year 1826–7 also charged £105.11s.1d. for joinery and repairs about the Library, including six large new bookcases to receive some of the current accretions, within the same period sent in twenty-eight lots from the auction of Sir George Lee's books and fifty-seven from another – a total expenditure of £53.4s.2d. Lodge was one of Elliot Smith's most faithful customers, but despite the great range of his attack he paid less systematic attention to the London booksellers. In 1827, for example, the year in which all this activity took place, he ignored Payne and Foss's catalogue of Aldines issued in April, ignored their major catalogue of manuscripts later in the year, and obtained only fourteen titles out of nearly 6700 offered in their main annual catalogue of printed books. But what his list from Payne and Foss lacked in quantity, it made up in price and quality. Among the books chosen from their catalogue (all on historical, antiquarian or linguistic topics) were both G. B. Passeri's *Picturae Etruscorum in vasculis* (Rome 1767–75), 'very neat in russia, gilt leaves', at ten guineas and his *Novus thesaurus gemmarum veterum* (Rome 1781–3) at four guineas, as well as the octavo edition of François Anne David's *Antiquités étrusques, grecques et romaines*, with Pierre d'Hancarville's notes (Paris 1785–8), at three guineas, and François Valentijn's *Oud en nieuw Ooost-Indien* (Dordrecht 1724–6) at six guineas. Here at least Lodge, prompted clearly by Kerrich's interests, was buying at the top end of the market.

The auction in February and March 1827 by Evans of Pall Mall of the library of the Rev. Henry Drury, an original member of the Roxburghe Club, Fellow of King's from 1799 until his marriage in 1808, and since 1801 assistant master at Harrow, offered further chances to improve the University Library. Sir Thomas Phillipps had made two separate attempts to buy Drury's manuscripts privately, without success, and in the end was to obtain sixty-nine at the sale,[23] but Lodge paid

[23] Munby *Phillipps studies* 3 pp. 53–4.

little attention to them. Instead, he turned to the printed books and, bidding through Payne, acquired several dozen volumes, principally of travel and published in the late eighteenth and early nineteenth centuries: most cost only a few shillings.[24] In many ways the Drury sale was remarkable for what Lodge did not buy, rather than for what he did. There is no evidence to suggest that he placed bids on Drury's celebrated collection of early printed books that then proved to be pitched too low; but in those lots that he did obtain he could count considerable success. Of the most expensive books thus acquired for the Library, Mabillon's edition of Bernard of Clairvaux (Paris 1719) was knocked down to Payne at £3.15s.od., Nathaniel Salmon's *Hertfordshire* (1728) at 31s.6d., Sir William Gell's *Geography and antiquities of Ithaca* (1807) at £2.9s.od., and Joseph Desormeaux' *Histoire de la maison de Bourbon* (5 vols., 1772–88) at four guineas. These were very far from being the most expensive books in the sale, and they represented only a tiny (and atypical) proportion of what Lodge obtained. His concentration, on this occasion, on works that were at once cheap and central to their subject, besides in many instances adding important books to the Library that the Copyright Act had failed to supply, was thoroughly sound, while at the same time his flutters with the fashionable Aldines a few months earlier hinted also at a sense of what the Library still lacked among early editions of the classics. The Library's buying policy in Kerrich's last years of office, just before Lodge took over completely, was as eclectic as it was astonishing, but under Lodge's aegis it was to change again, and as dramatically, within an even shorter time.

Meanwhile, however, gifts of all kinds continued to spice the collections, and Lodge marked them by beginning a new separate register in which to record them.[25] William Bankes, elected Member of Parliament for the University in 1822, celebrated his election by presenting over the next months

---

[24] A full list of the Library's purchases is in the Accessions Register.
[25] The new Donations Book contains entries from 1800 onwards, but it is watermarked 1823, the first pages being composed retrospectively.

virtually a complete set, many of the volumes on large paper, of Angelo Mai's elephant folio illustrated edition of the *Iliadis fragmenta antiquissima*, and besides these western books he also provided Arabic–Turkish and French–Armenian dictionaries The gifts of Richard Sheepshanks, whose later devotion to the development of the University Observatory is beyond our scope here, included a group of books printed at the Convent of S. Lazzaro near Venice, while from John Palmer, late Professor of Arabic, there came in 1824 half a dozen Arabic and Turkish manuscripts. Two Burmese books arrived from Captain T. Coe, of the Royal Navy, in the following year, and from E. D. Clarke's library the Rev. C. F. Bromhead, Fellow of Trinity, produced Linnaeus' *Flora Suecica* (Stockholm 1745): the volume, purchased by Clarke amongst a group of books from Daniel Naezén's library, was particularly valuable on account of the added marginalia by Daniel Solander[26] – a naturalist better known for his work with Captain Cook in the Pacific Ocean.

The bequest of Peter Paul Dobree in 1825 was altogether more numerous. Regius Professor of Greek since only 1823, when he had succeeded J. H. Monk, he had long been associated in many people's minds with Porson, whose notes on Aristophanes he had edited in 1821 and whose transcript of the Gale manuscript of Photius in Trinity Library he had used for his own edition the following year. Besides following so literally in Porson's footsteps, Dobree had also spent not a little time in studying Greek inscriptions, of which Trinity and the University Library provided so convenient a starting point. But he left comparatively little published work behind him. At the time of his death he was still in his early forties, and much of what might have appeared later existed so far only as notebooks and marginal annotations. By his will, Trinity College Library received a thousand volumes, while the University Library received all those containing his annotations, as well as his notebooks: the nature of the collection had

much in common with Taylor's notes, salvaged from the
Askew sale in 1785. The printed portion of his bequest to the
Library comprised some 140 volumes, and by the time that his
notebooks and loose papers had been bound up according to
the terms of his will there were a further forty-two manuscripts.[27] Dobree had paid especial attention to the text of
Demosthenes, but this was far from being his only preoccupa-
tion; when in 1831–5 James Scholefield, his successor as
Professor of Greek, published three volumes of his manuscript
marginalia he left out those in some volumes (such as
Montfaucon's *Bibliotheca Coisliniana* (1715)) altogether, and
was so selective that he courted criticism.[28]

The Dobree books formed one of the few collections to
come to the Library in the 1820s, but sheer numbers were not
everything. The Library's collections of ephemera might be
said to date from the gift in 1828, by the festival committee, of
an album containing the programmes for all the concerts given
at the York Festival in September that year, together with the
admission tickets.[29] More conventional in its nature, but less so
in the manner in which it came, in 1829 the Master and Fellows
of Trinity agreed to part with one of the college library's two
copies of John Dee's *General and rare memorials* (1577: they
parted with the Lumley copy),[30] while the next few months
also saw Noah Webster presenting the first edition of his
Dictionary (New York 1828),[31] Dawson Turner giving an
album of his wife's etchings, and the Board of Ordnance
producing four of their new maps.

There could, meanwhile, be no doubt of the Library's need
to find more accommodation. The University had agreed to
the purchase of new shelves in December 1815,[32] ominously

[27] Now MSS. Pp. 7.1–42, formerly MSS. A 1–42. A catalogue of them was drawn up by
J. B. Hollingworth in 1825–6 (MS. Pp. 6.33, prefixed by a transcript of part of Dobree's
will; for another copy of the same portion of the will cf. Luard 338).
[28] On Dobree see, besides Venn *Al. Cant.*, George Pryme *Autobiographic recollections*
(Cambridge 1870) pp. 150–3. Pryme and Hollingworth excised Dobree's 'severe or
sarcastic observations on living authors' before passing the books on to Trinity and the
University Library: see also Luard's remarks in his *Catalogue of adversaria* (Cambridge
1864) p. 66.   [29] Now MR 450.c.80.2.   [30] Now Sel.2.82.
[31] Now LE.34.9.   [32] Grace Book *M* p. 172.

463

soon after the passing of the new Copyright Act, and in June 1816 the Syndics had agreed to two new bookcases being set up in the Royal Library.[33] On 20 November 1820 Clarke and Kerrich had asked the Syndics to provide yet more space, on this occasion for folio volumes (a reflection of the kind of acquisition that Kerrich had encouraged),[34] and the Syndics returned to the request almost exactly twelve months later, when they asked the Vice-Chancellor to order that suitable cases should be erected down the centre of the north room in the space later to be occupied by the Library's general catalogue.

Furthermore, as long as the University offices and, particularly, space for teaching took up most of the ground floor of the Schools, there was little room to expand into other rooms, while the growth of the Woodwardian collections of geological specimens served yet further to emphasize that the old buildings were no longer adequate.[35] The need was obvious enough. Besides the expanding Woodwardian collections, added to further by Clarke, other departments were also in difficulties. James Cumming, Professor of Chemistry, had an ·inadequate room near Queens' College, 'miserably dark and confined, and totally unfitted for the preparation and exhibition of his experiments', that by 1831 was also used by William Smyth, Regius Professor of Modern History. There was no lecture room set aside for the Professor of Mineralogy; and although Adam Sedgwick as Professor of Geology had a room in the Schools, it was damp and poorly lit. William Clark, Professor of Anatomy, occupied a room handed over by the University Press for the purpose in 1716 and now, a hundred years later, simply too small.[36] In 1828 neither James Scholefield, Regius Professor of Greek (who used a room in

---

[33] Sydicate Minutes 7 June 1816.   [34] *Ibid.*, 20 November 1820.

[35] Clark and McK. Hughes *Life and letters of Adam Sedgwick* 1 pp. 233–4, quoting Sedgwick's report of 1 May 1822. In 1842 five cabinets were removed from 'a small room under the Public Library' to underneath the new Cockerell Building; the history of the Woodwardian Museum is chronicled in the *Cambridge University Gazette* (November–December 1869) in a series of articles by H. G. Seeley.

[36] [G. Peacock] *Observations on the plans for the new library* (Cambridge 1831) pp. 8–9; *Historical register* pp. 221, 231–2.

Trinity College) nor Charles Babbage, the newly elected Lucasian Professor of Mathematics, was provided with any lecture room at all. 'Without some provision for lecture-rooms and for Collections, in addition to what Cambridge now possesses,' wrote Whewell, 'she will have the mortification to see herself left behind in the cultivation of such studies as are above-mentioned; at a time when her Professors are as zealous as they have ever been, and are not charged with incapacity; when her Students are daily growing in activity and intelligence; and when her scientific possessions are such as to offer no mean foundation for future times to raise into complete collections.'[37]

But in 1791 the University had rejected plans by Sir John Soane for an administrative and teaching building to face the Senate House, and with that decision it remained – for the moment – content.[38] No further serious proposal to erect a south range of a new court bordered on the north and west by the Senate House and Library was put forward until the end of the nineteenth century. In truth, so far as the Library was concerned, the only realistic solution lay not so much with the University as with King's College. In 1822 the college, encumbered with buildings that had become unsuitable, was in the midst of considering the extending of its buildings to the south, beyond the Gibbs Building and towards St Catharine's, so creating a third side to the area bordered by the Chapel and the Gibbs Building of 1724–49. By the end of October 1823 the college was in a position to proceed, the last legal hindrances to the repositioning of King's Lane in its present line having been removed.[39] In anticipation of likely events, the University had by this time already entered into negotiations with the college, with a view to acquiring the old court, or western

---

[37] Statement to the Senate, 9 December 1828, quoted in Willis & Clark 3 p. 100.
[38] Soane's plans are now in the University Archives (P. xxx.1–7) and the Sir John Soane Museum, London. For Adam's slightly earlier proposals see Arthur T. Bolton *The architecture of Robert & James Adam (1758–1794)* (1922) 2 pp. 173–80. The notion of building a block to face the Senate House was raised again in 1892 and 1920 (*Reporter* 1919–20 pp. 657–9).
[39] Willis & Clark 1 pp. 348–9; A. Austen Leigh *King's College* (1899) pp. 243–7.

17 The old court, King's College. From an engraving by J. and H. S. Storer, 1830. Size of original 87 × 130 mm.

part of what is now the Old Schools. Though nothing was said of it officially, the consequent removal of King's promised more than simply extra space. The court was the source of serious distraction to those in the Schools. 'Dogs and King's were in a manner identical', recalled one Kingsman much later, in remembering also the rough games, rowdy behaviour, 'small college loafers' and freedom of speech amongst old Oppidans from Eton, all of which could make the area seethe with noise. There were the inevitable and feeble complaints: 'Occasionally a casement from the Schools would open, and a voice protest; – "Non possumus procedere propter" – that "Propter" would be the last word heard.'[40]

The buildings (fig. 17) – or rather, the land and the buildings, for some of the structures were fit only for demolition – on

[40] W. H. Tucker 'Life in the old court, King's College, Cambridge, 1822–25' *Etoniana* 1923 pp. 500–1.

466

which the University cast its eyes dated back in part to 1441, when Henry VI himself had laid the foundation stone of his new college in the south turret of its gateway. In fact this gateway, facing Clare College, was never completed while it remained a part of King's, and in its unfinished state reached only just as far as the second floor. The range to the south of the gate, fronting Mill Street (the end of the present Trinity Lane) had however been finished, as had the entire south range facing King's Chapel and abutting the University Library itself at the Library's south-west corner. To the east, the court was directly overlooked by the Royal Library in the Library's west range. Thus far, therefore, all could be said to be in reasonable order. The tenements forming the top two floors of the range to the north of the gateway did not present an insuperable challenge, and the remainder of the buildings so far described were sound enough to be converted with comparatively little difficulty. But the north side of the court was an altogether different matter. Never completed, most of it was of a later date, and the buildings were distinctly shoddier: it included among an assortment of squat components the kitchens, buttery and hall, running along Senate House Passage between the north range of the Schools and the roadway. In the published illustrations of its external appearance, facing out towards Trinity Hall and in towards the court (the two published respectively in Ackermann's *Cambridge* (1815) and the Storers' *Illustrations of Cambridge*) the effect is distinctly picturesque.[41] But the acquisition of the court as a whole would inevitably commit the University to the further expense of some rebuilding.

So hemmed in was it by legislation, however, that the University could do little without parliamentary sanction: both the University and any college which might be involved in the scheme to expand the University's central buildings needed authority to sell land, even to each other. The Library's eyes turned naturally to King's, as the only immediately

---

[41] On all this, with reproductions of some of the relevant illustrations, see Willis & Clark I pp. 321–33.

adjacent landowners, but for the University as a whole the problem was a more complicated one. As the petition presented to Parliament in 1822 explained, not only was the Library too small, and the lecture rooms of the professors 'too few in number inconveniently situated and ill adapted for the proper delivery of public Lectures', but the University also needed an observatory[42] and a place in which to display the pictures, books and other objects bequeathed by Richard, Viscount Fitzwilliam, in 1816.[43] The Library's need for more space was only one among the University's several difficulties, and for some years its needs and those of many of the professorships were conterminous in the financial, political and architectural debate that preoccupied the University from 1822 until 1837, when the foundation stone of a new library building was eventually laid.

Neither side moved with undue speed in the initial negotiations concerning the land belonging to King's. There was little point in doing very much until the college had moved into its new buildings south of the Gibbs Building, and February 1823 saw simply a polite exchange between the Vice-Chancellor (on behalf of the Library Syndics) and George Thackeray (Provost of King's) to record the fact that the college would be glad to treat with the University, 'being aware how important an addition it [i.e. Old Court] would be to the Public Library'.[44] Wilkins' new buildings for King's were begun in April 1824, and although they took a little short of four years to complete,[45] the college felt able meanwhile to press ahead. For its part, the University clearly had the needs of the Library more in mind than anything else when considering the expansion of the Schools building, for despite the pleas

---

[42] The observatory on top of Trinity Great Gate, completed in 1739, was dismantled in 1797 after years of neglect. Robert Woodhouse, a notable innovator in Cambridge mathematics, was appointed Plumian Professor of Astronomy in 1822.

[43] Grace Book M pp. 412–24. The Act allowing the transfer of the land received the Royal Assent on 24 June 1822.

[44] Letter from Thackeray, 24 February 1823 (Luard 333(1)). See also Syndicate Minutes, 17 February and 26 May 1823.   [45] Willis & Clark 1 p. 565.

contained in its petition to Parliament in 1822, little further reference was made to the needs for lecture rooms or museums. The proposal that a syndicate should be appointed to treat with King's came from the Library Syndicate, and the composition of this new syndicate offered further confirmation of how little those professors in the experimental sciences who had most to gain took an active interest in the proceedings, though George Peacock's and William Whewell's subsequent fulminations in 1831[46] on the need for more space in these subjects were not rhetorical flatulence. Apart from the Vice-Chancellor, the Syndicate given powers on 24 November 1824[47] to negotiate with King's comprised Thomas Turton, Lucasian Professor of Mathematics, George Peacock of Trinity (future Lowndean Professor of Astronomy and Geometry), Joshua King of Queens' (future Lucasian Professor and President of his college), Lodge and Kerrich as the two librarians, and John Haviland, Regius Professor of Physic and an inveterate administrator. At first all proceeded smoothly, if slowly. But when in April the following year Charles Humfrey submitted his valuation of the site of King's Old Court for a sale to the University there was at least some ground on which to argue. Humfrey, familiar with the position and with the University, took a practical view of his brief, and produced a figure based solely on how much the site and buildings would fetch at public auction, taking into account also that the building materials recoverable from the site would be worth £1400 or £1500. The other possible figure, 'its value to the University connected as it is with an already existing academical establishment of great and unquestionable public utility and importance', he thought wrong in principle as a mode in which the two bodies should conduct their negotiations. Given this, it was not surprising that King's considered his figure of £6300–£6500 too low,[48] despite the Syndicate's adding £1000 to the

---

[46] [G. Peacock] *Observations* (Cambridge 1831) pp. 12–14; [W. Whewell] *Reply to 'Observations on the plans for a new library'* (Cambridge 1831) pp. 3–6.
[47] Grace Book *N* p. 54.   [48] Humfrey's valuation is Luard 333(9).

upper figure.[49] Thackeray was quick with a reply, and, only the day after the Syndicate had communicated its offer to the college, rejected it outright.[50] The college was in a commanding position, and knew it; and all that the Syndicate could do was to apply to another valuer. It chose the second one with a touch of genius, for instead of approaching another local man it agreed on Joseph Stannard of Norwich, already employed by King's as chief contractor for the new building.[51] But Stannard's figures were even less likely to be agreeable to the college. He estimated the building materials at £1573, but, like Humfrey, had some difficulty over the land, preferring in the end to ignore the somewhat intangible value of it to the University as opposed to any other possible purchaser. Compared with other freehold property in Cambridge, however, he concluded that it was worth no more than £4344 – a total of £5917 in all.[52] In near despair, on 30 June the Syndics were finally driven to asking the college on what terms it wanted to part with its property.[53]

The college went to Thomas Chapman, of the Middle Temple, an 'eminent London surveyor', who produced a figure of £14,525 as a valuation to an 'indifferent purchaser'. Chapman also added, however, that if a neighbouring college (or, by implication, the University) had no other means of procuring further premises so conveniently situated this sum might be raised to £18,000.[54] Such figures were, predictably, unacceptable to the Syndics, whose own unofficial valuations had been only about one-third of these, and on 16 March the Vice-Chancellor wrote to the college stating that the Syndicate proposed to recommend that the University pay £12,000. Thackeray did not reply until 13 June. Chapman stood by his valuation, but suggested that by a 'liberal abatement' the figure might be reduced to £13,125. And with that, no doubt with some relief on both sides, the Syndicate agreed. It reported on 3

[49] Letter to the Provost of King's, 21 April 1825: draft at Luard 333(10).
[50] Luard 333(11).   [51] Willis & Clark 1 p. 565.   [52] Luard 333(14).
[53] Luard 333(15).   [54] Luard 333(17).

July, and deferred a Grace on the subject until the Michaelmas Term. So far the negotiations for the purchase of King's Old Court had taken three and a half years, but all that could be said was that the first phase had now been completed. The Grace was rejected on 2 November 1826, and a second Grace to purchase the court at a lower figure of £12,000 was rejected by an only marginally smaller majority on 20 March 1827. Four days later, the college showed its displeasure by issuing a notice to the University to quit the land on which the arches supporting the Dome Room at the south-west junction of the Library had stood since 1752.[55] But the deadline passed peacefully, and instead it was to be two years before the Syndicate felt strong enough to recommend once again that the figure should be £12,000. The Grace to put this into effect was passed on 3 April 1829 after a vote had been forced on the issue once again.[56]

The various delays had been caused by a multitude of arguments, but two were crucial. King's could not move completely out of its old court until the new buildings were ready in February 1828; but more seriously, the Regent House, faced with a topic on which its members could easily believe themselves knowledgeable, once again found itself unable to agree. And if there could be so much controversy over acquiring the land on which to build, how much more provocative the question of exactly what to build there promised to be.

[55] Luard 333(18–25).   [56] Grace Book *N* p. 245; note at the end of Luard 333.

12

'DOCTRINAE ET SCIENTIAE
INCREMENTA'

BY THE TIME OF Kerrich's death, on 10 May 1828, the difficulties inherent in two men, *Protobibliothecarius* and *Bibliothecarius*, running an establishment such as the Library had become absurdly clear to many members of the University. What had begun in 1721, as a sop to Middleton after his unsuccessful battle with Bentley, had worked reasonably well throughout the eighteenth century partly because for much of the time the two officers found little enough to occupy them, and partly because one or the other had tacitly retired, content to accept a salary in return for only a modicum of labour. Under Kerrich's eye all this had been laid aside. The Library was more active in its acquisitions, larger in size, and more frequented by readers than it had been; and whereas Middleton, Parris, Law and Farmer had also all held outside appointments, Kerrich's sole official appointment was to the Library, while in Clarke and (especially) Lodge the University enjoyed the services of men possessed of energy and imagination, in sympathy with the new mood of the University as a whole. New curricula, new examination procedures, and new interpretations of the University's function in the national community implied also new management. Old arrangements, like everything else, came under scrutiny, and like so much else were found wanting.

Lodge was the natural candidate as Kerrich's successor, so much so that even before the election a Grace had been passed deferring the election of his own successor as *Bibliothecarius* until 25 November following should he be elected *Protobibliothecarius*. His only opponent in the contest for Kerrich's place on 22 May was William Crawley, ten or eleven years his junior, who had followed him from Trinity to a fellowship at Magdalene in 1824: like Farmer's election in 1778, it had all the appearances of a staged arrangement, and Lodge was duly elected.[1] But although the Library Syndics agreed on 17 November 1828 to recommend to the University that the offices of *Protobibliothecarius* and *Bibliothecarius* should be amalgamated, their proposal met with only partial success. James Geldart, Regius Professor of Civil Law, found it impossible to countenance the Syndicate's proposal, and as a result it was thrown out by the Caput. Instead, on 6 December a Congregation agreed that Lodge should be constituted sole Librarian, at a salary of £210, that being the combined total of the two salaries formerly paid.[2] He remained still an administrative anomaly, but in practice the Syndicate had got its way.

Among all the changes that were to follow, none was more dramatic than the long awaited extension to the Library. The University acquired the site necessary for the expansion of the Library's buildings in 1829, but no new building was available to readers, staff or books until 1840. The interval, which spanned the most active years in Lodge's term of office, was taken up with one of the most extraordinary series of delays in the history of the University. It was not the longest by any means, but the events surrounding the preliminaries to accepting the architect, and the treatment of the architect once selected, have with justice passed into the folk-lore of architectural history. It gave plenty of opportunity for ill will to be nurtured in the University, for several architects to be understandably vexed, and for the Library itself to suffer in the general disorganization that the delay helped to provoke.

Nothing in the first weeks, when the University was, after prolonged negotiations with King's,[3] finally able to determine what it stood most in need of, suggested that there might

---

[1] Grace Book *N* pp. 206–7, 209. Crawley lived, incidentally, until 1896, when he died aged 93.
[2] Grace Book *N* p. 232. The other principal documents connected with this are described under Luard 359.   [3] See Luard 333.

develop quite such an imbroglio. On 6 May 1829[4] a Syndicate was appointed to report on what to do with the now derelict Old Court. Besides Lodge, Joshua King, and George Peacock, all of whom had been members of the negotiating syndicate, the New Building Syndicate (known subsequently as the 'first syndicate', for reasons that became painfully obvious) also included Whewell, who had already expressed himself with some vigour the previous December on the subject of teaching space in the University. Whewell had then suggested that the natural sciences should be concentrated on a site in Queens' Lane, pointing out that if the University became possessed of any other site there would be no difficulty in finding a use for it.[5] Six months after his remarks, the University had such a site, in King's Old Court, and into that space combined with the Schools the Syndicate appointed to report on its use proposed to compress virtually everything except anatomy and chemistry – two subjects, it was felt, better taught elsewhere than in a building that also housed the University Library:

They consider it necessary that provision should be made, not merely for a large increase of the accommodation of the Public Library, but likewise for four additional Lecture Rooms, for Museums of Geology, Mineralogy, Botany, and, if practicable, of Zoology, for a new Office for the Registrary, for an additional School for the Professor of Physic, and for other purposes connected with the dispatch of the ordinary business of the University.

That they consider the extent of ground, now the property of the University, including the site of the present Library, as amply sufficient for all these objects.

That they consider it expedient to make application to four Architects, for complete plans, elevations and estimates to be forwarded to the Vice-Chancellor, on or before the 1st of November next: and that the Syndicate should be authorized to give the necessary instructions; to offer the sum of 100 Guineas to each of the three Architects whose plans shall not be adopted; and to make a further report to the Senate before the end of next Term.

Thus, not only was King's Old Court to be demolished, but so was the Library as well. Even with wholesale rebuilding the

---

[4] Grace Book *N* p. 247.   [5] Willis & Clark 3 pp. 98–101.

Syndicate was optimistic in its calculations of what could be fitted into the space; but in recommending also that there should be a competition among four chosen architects – a seemingly fair way of approaching the subject – it heaped trouble on the University.[6] These suggestions, however, were passed by the Senate on 6 July, and the Syndicate forwarded a series of instructions to each of the four selected architects: Decimus Burton, C. R. Cockerell, Rickman and Hutchinson, and William Wilkins, former Fellow of Caius. The firm of Rickman and Hutchinson was already familiar to the University as the architects of St John's New Court, then in course of construction, and Wilkins' hand was to be seen in Corpus, King's, Downing, and Trinity, but the work of neither Cockerell nor Burton could be examined in Cambridge in 1829. The instructions, which involved the demolition of both the Schools and the Old Court of King's, left the exact style of the new building to the discretion of each of the architects, but described in some detail the required internal arrangements of the rooms. In general, the Schools and offices were to be on the ground floor, and the Library on the floor above:

The Library to occupy the whole of the first floor, above the Registrary's Office, Schools and Museum, so as to form a complete square; the front of the present Library (that is the first floor), to be extended towards King's Chapel and Caius College, over the Schools and Museum: a projecting Room towards Senate House Lane on the first floor opposite the West end of the Senate House, for the use of the Librarian and Syndics: the Cross Library to be retained, either supported entirely on arcades, or with a passage through the centre: this may be extended also towards Senate House Passage, if practicable and consistent with the other objects described above, so as to form a Reading Room: the Books to be placed on projecting cases as in the Library of Trinity College, which must be so constructed as to admit hereafter of the addition of galleries.[7]

In short, no simple extension was envisaged, such as might have been built over the land newly acquired from King's. It was an ambitious, even grandiose vision that made concessions

6 Report dated 6 July 1829, Grace Book N pp. 256–7: Luard 368 (1).
7 Willis & Clark 3 p. 104.

to the past only in the arrangement of the shelves in a more economical manner than the wall cases of the recently completed King's Library in the British Museum. For the first time the Library was also to have a separately designated reading room, rather than the old arrangement where tables and chairs had been simply scattered round the building. But in their determination to push ahead the Syndics recorded only what had been already accepted by the University, and omitted three crucial points. The decision to omit any recommendations on the style of the building avoided argument before there was anything to argue about; the lack of any proposed budget seems more odd, but again had the effect of avoiding disputes within the University for the time being; and, finally, though it was tacitly assumed that the entire library would have to be moved, it was only explained to the architects in private that while they were expected to submit plans for an entire building, construction should be so ordered that one part might be erected first, and completed for occupation, before the next was begun. The implied decision of the Syndics, to defer discussion of style and cost until later, however well-intentioned, was to prove disastrous. By late November the four architects had submitted their plans. Both Cockerell and Rickman sent in two designs. But whereas both of Cockerell's – one considerably more ambitious than the other, and reviving the old hopes of a south pavilion to answer the Senate House – were Grecian in inspiration,[8] those of Rickman were in violently opposed styles. He took advantage of the committee's decision not to pontificate, and submitted both an Ionic proposal of no very great inspiration and a Gothic extravaganza which – however much more sympathetic to Rickman himself – fortunately did not distract the Syndics.[9]

[8] Cf. David Watkin 'Newly discovered drawings by C. R. Cockerell for Cambridge University Library' *Architectural History* 26 (1983) pp. 87–91, with plates.
[9] Two of Rickman's designs, from the RIBA drawings collection, are reproduced in D. Watkin *The triumph of the classical: Cambridge architecture 1804–1834* (Fitzwilliam Museum Cambridge 1977) plates 7 and 8.

In a report that was remarkable not least for its extreme brevity (it ran to thirty-nine words in all) the Syndics announced on 25 November that they recommended one of Cockerell's designs.[10] George Peacock, Fellow of Trinity and a member of the Syndicate, himself acknowledged later that 'It was perhaps unfortunate that the Report did not state more expressly, that the conclusion of the Syndicate was comparative and not absolute. Nothing indeed could be further from their intention, than to recommend to the Senate the adoption of Mr. Cockerell's plan, without most material alterations.' As he must have known, the Syndics were in fact constitutionally powerless to express to the University any more than a preference. But if his words were an admission that they might have produced a slightly less reticent report, his next remark was a rueful understatement, written in retrospect two years later.

It was extremely improbable that any plan could have been proposed in the first trial, which would satisfy all the wishes and wants of the University, where so many different objects were to be combined, so many difficulties to be overcome, so many conflicting interests and claims to be reconciled, and where the instructions as might be expected, required more to be done, than was practicable under the circumstances of the situation or under the imposed conditions.[11]

The members of the University, unable to examine the proposed design for themselves, reacted tempestuously. Rickman's Grecian design found its own advocates, and only in February 1830 was the matter advanced, by the decision to appoint a syndicate to enquire into the means at the University's disposal for the proposed development.[12] This Syndicate reported in May, and although their exact findings have not been preserved it seems that Cockerell's plan proved to be prohibitively expensive. On the other hand, he had

[10] 'That they unanimously agree to recommend Mr Cockerell's Design (No. 1) for the New Library and other Public Buildings, as being, in their opinion, upon the whole, best adapted to answer the purposes which the University have in contemplation' (quoted in Willis & Clark 3 p. 106).

[11] *Observations on the plans for the new library, &c. by a member of the first syndicate* (Cambridge 1831) p. 16.

[12] Willis & Clark 3 p. 107; Library papers 23 February 1830.

meanwhile received word that this first plan required some modification, and he had therefore circulated in private a less ambitious version of the second, rejected plan submitted to the original Syndicate.[13] This was the olive branch the University needed, and on 31 May a further Grace was carried, appointing a further (known as the second) syndicate to consider the whole matter with respect both to the first syndicate's report of the previous November and to the funds available. In reply to a circular issued by the Vice-Chancellor in June, all four architects agreed to submit revised plans prepared in accordance with a slightly more detailed specification that stipulated both the style (Grecian) and the cost of the new building.[14] Only a portion of it was to be erected for the present, the northern range, which would contain a new room for the Library on the first floor connected by a temporary arrangement with the old library, that was to remain intact. The cost of this reduced first phase was to be £25,000. In the end, Decimus Burton was distracted by other work; but in order to avoid one of the first syndicate's mistakes, the plans of the other three contestants were all made available for the University's inspection at the end of October.[15] Thus, at last, the whole dispute was brought into the open, and on ground that had been at least reasonably prepared. With what seemed even at the time to be sheer perversity, on 10 December 1830 the second syndicate issued a brief report recommending the design of Rickman and Hutchinson. Even more serious, however, was the cost, estimated in February 1831 at £30,000: had the syndicate's proposal been effected, it would have committed the University to deducting £500 a year from the Library fund for the next thirty years.[16]

The report proposing the adoption of Rickman and Hutchinson's plan was never put to the Senate. Instead, the

---

[13] [W. Whewell] *Reply to 'Observations on the plans for the new library, &c. by a member of the first syndicate'* By a member of both syndicates (Cambridge 1831) p. 9.
[14] [Peacock] *Observations* pp. 19–22.   [15] Willis & Clark 3 p. 111.
[16] Library papers 15 February 1831; Willis & Clark 3 p. 113.

debate was carried out of the Senate House and onto the printing press, in a series of pamphlets by or on behalf of the various architects, and not all of them cast much light on the argument. Unable to judge the matter on either aesthetic, personal or financial grounds, the University was in no condition to come to a decision, and the only official proceeding between February 1831 and March 1834 was the reappointment in February 1832 of the syndicate to consider ways and means to raise sufficient funds.[17]

In the light of all the work for which Wilkins had been responsible at Cambridge by 1831, it is not without interest that he apparently found no advocate to support his submission. Peacock remarked that he had 'followed very strictly the instructions of the Syndicate, and the arrangements of the interior of his building as well as its exterior, shew the hand of a great master of his art. The portico in front of his building, with all its accompanying decorations, would be nearly unrivalled in this country for propriety and good taste.'[18] Whewell, as a member of the second syndicate, acknowledged that it had 'many claims' to 'some intelligent and active advocates'.[19] But it was left to Wilkins to defend his own plans for himself, unaided by the printed effusions of anyone within the University, and by the time he did so he wrote with a faint heart.[20] No such reticence affected George Peacock, a member of the first syndicate whose recommendations had been overturned by the second, or William Whewell, a member of both. Cockerell's building, 'an unusual combination of a minor Greek Doric order with a major Roman Corinthian order',[21] dominated on the east front by a magnificent double

---

[17] Library papers 8 and 22 February 1832.
[18] [Peacock] *Observations* p. 51. Wilkins' designs are now in the University Library (see Watkin *Triumph of the classical* plate 4 (wrongly captioned Trinity College) and pp. 33–4). The illustrations annexed to his *Appeal to the Senate* (Cambridge 1831) are reproduced in R. W. Liscombe *William Wilkins 1778–1839* (Cambridge 1980) plates 92–4.   [19] [Whewell] *Reply* p. 20.
[20] William Wilkins *Letter to the members of the Senate of the University of Cambridge* (Cambridge 1831); *An appeal to the Senate, on the subject of the plans for the University Library* (Cambridge 1831).   [21] Watkin *Triumph of the classical* p. 35.

portico protecting a double staircase rising up to the Library on the first floor, and on the ground floor leading through to a courtyard accessible also from the west, was innovative and accomplished. The inspiration lay partly in Baldas Longhena's design for S. Giorgio Maggiore at Venice and in the university at Genoa.[22] Had it been built, the library would have become one of the major sights of Europe. Cockerell's surviving finished watercolours of the interior, views taken from the junction of two of the ranges, echoed ancient Rome in the barrel vaults of the ceilings, while David Watkin has also pointed out the links in the vestibule itself with Palladio's chapel at Maser and Michele Sanmicheli's Capella Pellegrini in the church of San Bernardino at Verona: the reference was ultimately to the Pantheon.[23] But although in many respects a work of genius, Cockerell's plans offended the Syndics' instructions in failing to 'provide for that close connexion of the Museums and Lecture Rooms which they conceived to be the first of conditions',[24] while it also went dramatically beyond the Syndics' plans for the old library to be connected temporarily to the new building during the various phases of construction. Peacock was unmoved by such difficulties. He concentrated much of his initial attack on the Rickman and Hutchinson proposals for lighting in the Library (where they were undoubtedly inept), on the unimaginative waste of space and loss of opportunities not only at the junctions of each range but also in the untidy creation of irregular tiny light wells where inspiration had failed. 'There is a total want both of simplicity and of symmetry in the internal arrangements, a most extravagant waste of space, and a consequent failure in providing the quantity of accommodation which the extent of the building admits of, and which the University requires.'[25] His pamphlet earned an immediate rejoinder from Whewell in

[22] [G. Peacock] Remarks on the replies to the Observations . . . &c. (Cambridge 1831) p. 69.
[23] Watkin Triumph of the classical; idem, The life and work of C. R. Cockerell (1974) p. 189.
[24] [Whewell] Reply p. 14.   [25] [Peacock] Observations p. 31.

favour of Rickman and Hutchinson, and a series of observations on Peacock's strictures by the architects themselves. With the debate in danger of lapsing into trivia, a contribution by an outsider who had sat on neither syndicate was a sorely needed fillip. Henry Coddington, Fellow of Whewell's own college and only slightly less catholic in his accomplishments than Whewell himself, opened his *Few remarks* with zest: 'It is a trite observation that a large body of men, with a democratical constitution, cannot compete, as to active improvements, with an individual, or even with an equally large body which is directed by the judgment of one individual.' He poured ridicule on some of the more foolish allegations and suggestions that had been put forward, and touched on one subject for the first time, which had nothing to do with either the style of the building or the arrangement of the floor area:

I beg leave most earnestly to call the attention of my readers to the circumstances that neither Messrs. Rickman and Hutchinson nor their defenders have ever ventured to say a word on this subject [of ventilation]. I affirm boldly that it is of at least as great importance as the lighting, because though it may be awkward to have to get a candle to look for a book in the middle of the day in the University Library, that is a trifling evil in comparison of the book falling to pieces in your hands when you have found it. If the zeal of the Author of the Reply had led him to pay a visit to the new King's Library at the British Museum . . . he would have found that, though amply lighted, it is almost untenantable in consequence of the confined state of the air in the lower part, and that the books are in many places nearly destroyed by a current of dry 'heated air' such as is ordered by the 8th article of the 'Instructions'.[26]

The matter of ventilation, now recognized as crucial to proper conservation practice, was among several points returned to by Peacock in one further pamphlet,[27] but the University had argued itself to a standstill. The irreconcilable and not always constructive disputes between the powerful

26 [H. Coddington] *A few remarks on the 'new library' question*. By a member of neither syndicate (Cambridge 1831) p. 17.
27 [G. Peacock] *Remarks on the replies to the Observations on the plans for the new library, &c.* (Cambridge 1831).

advocates of Cockerell on the one hand, and the second syndicate on the other, combined with a widespread distaste for the proposed financial measures to bring about another stalemate. Peacock and Whewell were agreed on the folly of committing so much of the Library's income for the next several years to the new building, where it might otherwise have been spent on books. As Peacock pointed out, for two years already the Vice-Chancellor had deducted £500 from the annual income of nearly £1500 received under the 1825 capitation tax, while of the special funds only the Manistre Fund (see p. 493) was available for general purposes: the Worts Fund had come to be used for major works of natural history or for other expensive items, and the Rustat for books that could not be borrowed from the Library. In this context, the Syndics' proposals would wreak serious damage:

Those persons who like myself have experienced the full benefit of possessing the power of an immediate reference to the most valuable literature of the day, whether domestic or foreign, and who can procure, through the watchful exertions of the Librarian, whatever works may be required for a specific enquiry or research, would feel most sensibly the inconveniences which would result from the proposed appropriation of this fund to purposes foreign to its original destination: and it is no sufficient answer to say, that this diversion of the ordinary supplies of the Library, would be temporary only. For in what manner are the wants of the Members of the Senate, many of whom are now residing in Cambridge, expressly for the purpose of enjoying the assistance derived from this Library, to be supplied in the mean time? The lapse of a few years, which may appear trifling to a permanent institution, may comprehend the whole period of activity of those very persons whose interests in this question, are the most deeply concerned.[28]

His proposal to raise the necessary money instead by increasing the levy on members of the University and borrowing the remainder met with some sympathy from Whewell:

I see nothing unjust or unreasonable in throwing such a charge on any part of a person's University career when it can conveniently be borne: for to supply the means of being acquainted with all that is best in literature for

---

[28] [Peacock] *Observations* pp. 58–9.

those who have access to the University Library, is not to minister to *their* wants, so much as to provide for the general usefulness and credit and dignity of our whole system. Students are sent here in the expectation that they will here find a body of well-taught, well-read, intelligent and cultivated instructors and friends: and this they will find, so long as the present active interest in all that ancient and modern literature has produced, in any country, or any subject, is fostered and fed. That this should be the character of our academic body, is an advantage of inestimable importance, and one to which none but very short-sighted or very selfish persons among those who ask to derive the benefits of the place would, I am persuaded, grudge to contribute.[29]

It was therefore against a background of financial crisis that Lodge declined to accept the proposal in May 1832 to increase his salary to £300 a year. Admiration was widespread for the manner in which he ran the Library, and for the increase in book stocks under his auspices, but perhaps he wisely recognized that Whewell's and Peacock's argument for books in favour of building would be better understood if the University's resources were not allowed to dribble away on salaries. In any case, he was the only person between 1831 and 1834 who publicly expressed an opinion on the proposals to extend the Library's premises. In 1833 he was elected Senior Proctor for the academical year, and on 4 November he delivered a speech at the election of the Vice-Chancellor which Joseph Romilly noted as 'very good indeed, especially the part about the Library'.[30] Most of the speech was, in fact, about the Library. Lodge contrasted the splendour of some of the designs for a new building with the Library's true plight – the books in confusion, old books muddled with new ones, small with large, subjects in disorder, and, above all, the collections overcrowded to such an extent that no proper organization was feasible. It was an eloquent plea, and marked a new departure for the University in that a Librarian spoke out for perhaps the first time in public – and in print – on the condition of the collections and the implications of the University's

---

[29] [Whewell] *Reply* pp. 26–7.
[30] J. Romilly *Romilly's Cambridge diary 1832–42* ed. J. P. T. Bury (Cambridge 1967) p. 41.

policies: he was able to do so, however, as Proctor, not as Librarian.

Per antiquam igitur bibliothecae famam – per vestrum in literas et scientiam amorem – per tantos in prelum academicum, in speculam astronomicam, in musea chemiae et anatomiae sumptus et labores – oro et obtestor, ut ea ingeniorum nutrix, illud scientiae armamentarium vestrae solicitudinis tandem particeps sit – ut bibliotheca, si non luxu exornata, eâ tamen decentiâ, si ita dicam, sit instructa, ut digna habeatur, quae κειμήλια tanti pretii conservet, et in eam amplitudinem extensa, ut illi librorum incremento sufficiat, quod assidue postulent doctrinae et scientiae incrementa.[31]

Lodge's diatribe had its effect. After hesitating in uncertainty for two and a half years, the University appointed a syndicate in March 1834[32] to confer with the original architects and to report by the summer. Whewell, again, was a member of this attempt, and the Vice-Chancellor Joshua King was also familiar with the earlier debates, but two new men were now introduced: H. H. Hughes of St John's and Henry Calthrop of Corpus. The solution they attempted was simple, and reflected the decision implied by the months of inaction: that the University had been 'compelled to abandon the intention of building a New Library', and that the competing architects should all accept the original fee agreed for plans not accepted.[33] With this Cockerell could not agree, and although Burton, Rickman and Wilkins all accepted their palliatives, he remained adamant despite Whewell's being despatched as an emissary to soothe his ruffled pride: the Syndics felt unable to recommend to the University that it should accept Cockerell's proposal for the whole business to be submitted to independent arbitrators.[34]

This unsatisfactory state of affairs, dishonourable to the University, galling for Cockerell, and disastrous for the Library where Lodge later reckoned that the current rate of

[31] J. Lodge *Oratio Procuratoris Senioris in Senaculo habita, pridie non. Novembris* (Cambridge 1833) pp. 4–6. On Lodge and his stipend see also below, pp. 498–9.
[32] Grace Book *N* p. 448.
[33] Report of the Syndicate, 31 May 1834 (Library papers).
[34] Cockerell to Joshua King 9 May 1834; King to Cockerell 19 May 1834 (Luard 420).

accessions of nearly five thousand volumes a year would fill the shelves available within three years,[35] was resolved by Cockerell's original champion, George Peacock. In a pamphlet published early in 1835 he rejected a proposal merely that the old court of King's College should be fitted up with bookshelves, and suggested instead the the northern range only of a new library should be erected for the present: although he mentioned no architect by name, the implication that it was Cockerell who had been wronged was a clear hint that his opinion had not changed. On 4 March another syndicate was appointed to collect subscriptions for the new building to be erected by whichever architect was finally selected.[36] Whewell meanwhile had retired from the fray, and by the end of the month was able to write with equanimity to his sister not only that subscriptions were increasing 'very prosperously', but also that 'I am now become a peaceable person, and shall be content with any plan which the majority of the University will agree, so that we may but get the buildings erected.'[37] Headed by Lord Camden, Chancellor of the University, and the Duke of Northumberland, High Steward, who subscribed £500 each, the subscription list grew rapidly, and in November the Syndics announced that they had collected over £20,000.[38] The University agreed readily to the same special syndicate's proposals that the site should be properly cleared (the old gateway of King's being left in place for the present), and that a third competition should be held in the following spring, for which plans were to be submitted by February. Those revised proposals that had been received were exhibited to the University in April to a lukewarm reception from Romilly, though the architects by now were equally

---

[35] [G. Peacock] *Observations upon the report made by a syndicate* (Cambridge 1835) p. 9.
[36] Grace Book *N* p. 489.
[37] Mrs Stair Douglas *The life and selections from the correspondence of William Whewell* (1881) p. 172.
[38] Apart from those printed with the official Appeal, lists of subscribers were also published in the *Cambridge Chronicle and Journal* on 20 and 27 March, 10 and 24 April, 15 May and 5 June.

disillusioned: 'Rather disappointed with Cockerells: dont like Rickmans; Burton sent none; & Wilkins's is not exhibited because he had pettishly said he would send none, but afterwards changed his mind: – his plan is worthless.'[39] On 11 May 1836 Cockerell's plan was chosen by a majority of sixty votes to nine for Rickman's and none for Wilkins'.

It was not, however, until 29 September 1837 that the foundation stone of what became known as the Cockerell Building was laid, at a small private ceremony when it was noted not irrelevantly that the stone – from Whitby – was 'peculiarly cheap as well as good'.[40] The interval was partly taken up with a wrangle with Cockerell over the estimated cost of the building and preliminary reports on whether any of the existing structures might be incorporated. Structural work, by Messrs J. & C. Rigby of London, was completed by March 1840. So, at long last, the University was within sight of possessing a sorely needed extension to the Library and, on the floor below, space for the geological and mineralogical collections as well as a lecture theatre.[41]

The new library remained to be fitted with bookcases and other furniture, however, and only in November 1844 could the Syndics turn their attention to transferring the manuscripts to a fresh home.[42] Almost inevitably, costs were higher than had been estimated, and at first only the eastern portion of the new library room was fitted up;[43] but when the Syndics inspected the uncompleted work, reaching only halfway along the room and still without a gallery, they rightly proposed a further method of raising the necessary money to avoid the 'inconvenience and disadvantage that would arise if the work were to be suspended, and the Room left for any great length of time in an unfinished state and unfit for use'.[44]

[39] Romilly *Cambridge diary* p. 100.   [40] Willis & Clark 3 p. 120.
[41] Fuller accounts of the events of 1829–40 are to be found in Willis & Clark 3 pp. 101–21; Watkin *Cockerell*, ch. 11, with an appreciative account of the building's appearance; and R. W. Liscombe *William Wilkins 1778–1839* (Cambridge 1980) pp. 196–9.
[42] Syndicate Minutes 18 November 1844.
[43] Grace of 6 July 1840; Syndicate Minutes 29 June 1840.
[44] Syndicate Minutes 15 June 1841; Library papers 22 June 1841.

18 Cockerell's new building, viewed from Gonville and Caius College. Only the north range, nearest the college, was completed. From John Le Keux *Memorials of Cambridge* (1841–2). Size of original 98 × 138 mm.

While the Syndics laboured to complete even one wing, and the University scraped together enough to meet the bills from Cockerell and the contractors, no such embarrassments hindered the artists, who depicted what they hoped to see with all the licence they could command. Le Keux' *Memorials of Cambridge*, published in 1841–2, reflected the slow progress of the building neatly: the illustration of the Gate of Honour of Gonville and Caius College shows the north wall of the old library before the view was hindered by the Cockerell Building, while the same book also included an impression of what the whole of the new library would look like when completed (fig. 18) – no longer a fourteenth-century miscellany crouching behind an eighteenth-century facade built to a height in keeping with the Senate House, but instead what might have been a nineteenth-century masterpiece of confident display, 'the gleaming triumph of Cockerell's intellect'.[45] Le Keux' dream remained imaginary, however, as hopeful and unfulfilled as Frederick Walmisley's portrait of Lodge painted in 1838, which also showed Cockerell's proposed colonnade on the east front.[46] The *Cambridge University almanack* for 1839 joined in the celebrations by publishing a conceit that contrived to depict the north range in course of erection, the western part still finished only to halfway up the walls of the ground floor while the eastern part was entirely finished: by this means the engraver, E. Challis, could show the inside not only built but even fully furnished with book cases, books, and busts atop the cases. Challis's engraving (fig. 19) was based on the work of Cockerell's assistant, and the interior (fig. 20) subsequently underwent various modifications: the ceiling, for example, was different from the diagonally ribbed vault eventually erected, and so were the bookcases with their slate shelves, whose lines became more and more obscure as pressure on available space increased at the end of the nineteenth century. The conversion into what is now the Squire Law Library, following the University Library's exodus in 1934, has still further obliterated the details of Cockerell's designs for the fittings. But despite modern intrusions, the effect of this new room for the Library, a fragment of what might have been created, is of a majesty found in no other library at Cambridge save Wren's at Trinity College. Inspiration for details of the ceiling has been linked with sources as diverse as Thomas Donaldson's published work on the temple at Bassae (1830) and Borromini's Sant'Ivo in Rome, while the Ionic columns at each end were likewise evolved from the temple of Apollo Epicurius.[47] But quite apart from the classical allusions, the building gains in grandeur from the fortunate incapacity of the University to proceed further. The destruction of the Schools would have been a tragedy, and the

---

[45] Watkin *Cockerell* pp. 193–4.
[46] The portrait is in Magdalene College; a mezzotint of it was published by the Cambridge printseller J. Dimmock in November 1839: see p. 448.
[47] Watkin *Cockerell* pp. 194–5.

19   The Cockerell Building under construction. From the *Cambridge University almanack*, 1839. Size of original 266 × 419 mm.

hesitation in November 1835 over what best to do with the old gate of King's leading out to Trinity Lane betokened some sympathy for earlier buildings even when they threatened to stand in the way of university development. Instead the gate and the untidy assortment each side of it remained, a picturesque anachronism, suffered at first almost by default, while the attempts to reconcile the new Cockerell Building with the older parts of the Library soon brought anguish for Syndics and Library staff alike.

As was fully realized, the completion of the first part of the new library presented a unique opportunity to reorder completely the contents of the entire straggle of buildings, and to arrange in proper subject order the accumulations of printed books that by 1840 only suggested intermittently any scheme of classification. The chaos (it seems to have been little less) that resulted from the attempt to carry out such an operation with a hopelessly inadequate staff exercised the Syndics to the full, and led to the enforced retirement of John Bowtell. But matters were rendered still worse by the occupation of the East Room of the old library by the collections destined for the Fitzwilliam Museum.

Richard, Viscount Fitzwilliam, had died unmarried in 1816, leaving his pictures, books, antiquities and other works of art to the University, together with a sum to pay for the erection of a suitable museum 'with all convenient speed'.[48] Basevi's building was however not begun until 1837, and not opened until 1848. Meanwhile the collections were housed first in the old Perse Grammar School, which was fitted up by William Wilkins, the school itself being rehoused. But in 1834 the Perse trustees wished to reoccupy the old buildings, and although this immediately prompted the establishment of a syndicate to consider more permanent accommodation for Fitzwilliam's bequest, the collections remained for the time being in their old home. Such an arrangement could presume on the goodwill of the trustees only for a brief period, and in 1842 the collection was again moved – into the only building that seemed the least bit appropriate, the University Library. Among the signatories of the report recommending this step was Lodge; but while the East Room offered one great advantage in being already fitted up with shelves for Fitzwilliam's books and manuscripts, it had an even greater drawback in that it was already full of books belonging to the University Library. The printed report spoke of the Library Syndics' having 'kindly expressed their concurrence and their readiness to afford every facility in carrying the proposed measure into effect', but three of the five Fitzwilliam Syndics had also signed the minutes of the relevant Library Syndicate meeting, and Lodge himself was a fourth: the Library Syndics merely recorded their decision in their minutes with the proviso (repeated in the printed report) that any expenses should be defrayed out of the Fitzwilliam funds, and that the Library staff should be adequately compensated for any additional work that might result.[49]

[48] The relevant portion of Fitzwilliam's will is printed in Clark *Endowments* pp. 487–8.
[49] Library papers 10 March 1842 (Report); Syndicate Minutes 10 March 1842; Willis & Clark 3 pp. 199–200, 202–3.

20 The interior of the Cockerell Building, first floor, *c.* 1860.

The decision had been, to some extent, forced on the University; but while it coped conveniently with the problem of housing the Fitzwilliam collections as the Museum itself was gradually erected between 1837 and 1848, it was no help at all to the Library, which suffered severely from the upheaval in the East Room. The decision was taken in Lodge's time, but for his successor Joseph Power the collections were a hindrance to his attempts to reorganize the Library on a more rational footing. With an eye on the progress made in building the Museum (which was structurally complete by the end of 1847), in November 1847 the Library Syndicate – headed now by Robert Phelps as Vice-Chancellor, and still including two of the signatories to the 1842 report recommending the removal of the Fitzwilliam collections to the Library – therefore appealed to the Senate for relief from the 'great and growing inconvenience'. A syndicate to supervise the removal of the collection was appointed the following March, and within two months the room was clear.[50] The Library was free to tackle its own internal difficulties once more, but the effects of the episode lived on for twenty years.

It was left to Power, Lodge's successor, to meet them. Lodge's principal legacy was in his additions to the books in the Library. He had accomplished astonishing feats in the 1820s, which contrasted strangely with what had gone before, but this was only a beginning. Little of the transformation he wrought in the Library would however have been possible without a dramatic rise in the available income. No benefaction designed to produce a regular dividend had come to the Library since that of William Worts in 1709, which by the first years of the nineteenth century constituted with the Rustat Fund the sole regular source of funds for purchase. An account has already been given of the origin and success of the Library Subscription Fund, raised by levying a toll on each member of the University except sizars. It lasted until 1866, when instead

---

[50] Syndicate Minutes 15 November 1847; Grace Book O pp. 12, 13.

the University instituted a capitation tax of seventeen shillings per annum, from the proceeds of which the Library received a grant of £2500.[51] Besides this step in regularizing the relationship between the Library and the University at large, the Library in 1829 also received a windfall that made yet more adventurous purchases possible, and which formed no mean addition to its income. John Manistre, Fellow of King's between 1768 and 1791, died as rector of a Dorset parish in 1826, leaving £5000 to be invested in trust for Mary Hare Gowan. She died childless in 1829, and the University Library thereupon became the beneficiary under Manistre's will, which had also specified that in this event the money was to be spent on the purchase of books.[52] By mid-July 1836, the dividend on 7½ years amounted to £1158.15s.0d., or nearly ten per cent of the total received in the same period from the Library subscriptions. In 1836–8 the sum spent on books from the fund was £624.0s.6d., leaving a balance at Michaelmas 1838 of £676.4s.0d. At Michaelmas 1844 it stood at only £172, evidence not of an ailing interest rate but of the Library's determination to spend its income as it was received and not to allow this part of its wealth to accumulate.

Lodge was thus in a strong position. The sale of the second part of the van de Velde library at Ghent in August 1833 provided just the kind of opportunity that he was to welcome, and marked a completely fresh attitude to ways in which the Library's stock could be extended. J. F. van de Velde, theologian, University Librarian of Louvain, Rector of his university and persistent champion of its existence even after its temporary demise in 1797, had died in 1823, leaving an outstanding theological library collected despite (and during) his enforced exile from Louvain. He had assembled it partly for the preparation of his *Synodicon Belgicum*, published posthumously between 1828 and 1839.[53] The auction catalogue of

---

[51] Grace Book Σ pp. 89–90. See below, pp. 624–5.
[52] Clark *Endowments* p. 453 (giving the wrong date for Manistre's death); Luard 363.
[53] On van de Velde see the Belgian *Biographie nationale* 27 (Brussels 1930–2) cols. 543–55.

the first part of his collection was published at Ghent in 1831, and the second in 1832; and since the sale was not scheduled until August 1833 there was ample time to plan the best way to apportion bids among the fourteen thousand-odd lots.[54] It seems doubtful whether the hundred pounds sanctioned by the Cambridge Syndicate on 3 June 1833 was as much as Lodge may have hoped for, and in view of the Library's activities at the sale there also seems to be sound reason to suppose that he regarded the figure as no more than a basis for negotiation. But with permission to spend this nonetheless considerable sum of money, Bowtell, the Library Keeper, was despatched to Ghent. He was away for over a month, and returned having bought 451 lots for a total of £193.18s.7d. By the time his various expenses had been added to this, and £24 added for freight across the North Sea alone, the total was £267.13s.0d.[55] It was far more than the Syndics can have envisaged, as regards either the size of the final account or the quantity of books Bowtell and Lodge had obtained.

Out of over 450 incunables in the sale, only one, a commentary on the Psalms published in 1480,[56] was in their selection. Instead their additions consisted by and large of late seventeenth- and eighteenth-century theology, books characteristic of van de Velde's library generally and invaluable in that many of them were works of major scholarly importance in their fields which the Library had failed to obtain previously. In church history the Library thus at last secured Quirini's edition of Cardinal Pole's letters (1744–57), the revised edition of Ughelli's *Italia sacra* (1717–22), Cocquelines' collection of papal bulls (1739–44), Ripoll's collection of Dominican documents (1729–40) and Michael à Tugio's of Capuchin (1740–52). Especial attention was paid to liturgies, beginning with Eusèbe Renaudot's collection of eastern practices (1716)

[54] The title-pages of the catalogues mention 14,435 lots, but the numbering of the entries was inaccurate, and the last is described as 15,354.

[55] Details of his expenses, and a list of the lots bought at the sales, are in a separate notebook in the university accounts for 1832–3 (University Archives).

[56] Inc. 652. Many others from van de Velde's Library were acquired later in the century.

and including Muratori's great *Liturgia romana vetus* published in 1748, as well as a varied selection of more recent, post-Tridentine, works: a Carthusian Collectar of 1738, a Carmelite Lectionary of 1752, a Sens Ceremonial of 1769, a Tours Ritual of 1785, and a Roermond Ritual of 1599. Van de Velde had possessed an unusually good collection of lives of the saints, and these too caught the eyes of Lodge and Bowtell: among them came one of the few early printed books in this part of the sale, a copy of Erasmus' life of Hieronymus Stridonensis published at Cologne in 1517. And, theological topics apart, van de Velde's library also produced Leibniz's *Collectanea etymologica* (1717), by then a rare work, Châtelain's *Atlas Historique* (1713), the plates illustrating *Splendor magnificentissimae urbis Venetiarum clarissimus*, Giuseppe Bianchini's *Dei gran Duchi di Toscana* (1741), Ant. Sander's *Grand théatre sacré du duché de Brabant* (1734), Butkens' *Trophées du duché de Brabant* (1724–6), and the sole volume published of Bayardi's *Catalogo degli antichi monumenti dissoterrati dalla discoperta città di Ercolano* (Naples 1755).

No record survives of how carefully the catalogue was checked before the sale, or of the extent to which the books bought by Bowtell represented Lodge's real hopes.[57] The quantity proved on its arrival to be more than the Library could cope with; but thanks no doubt partly to hasty preparation several of the volumes bought proved to be duplicates and had to be shed. Yet the sale was, in general, a vindication of Lodge's belief that the Library could answer the needs of contemporary Cambridge in a reasonable fashion only if it responded to contemporary opportunities. He was limited solely by what the Syndics would allow him to spend.

Three months after the van de Velde sale, the Syndics agreed to pay the cost of the books additional to what they had

---

[57] Since Deighton also attended the sale, there would have been ample opportunity to make arrangements for him to receive anything not wanted by the Library. In 1835 Deighton issued a catalogue of English and foreign theology that contained much from the van de Velde collection, including outstanding sections dealing with Luther and Melanchthon.

originally sanctioned, and the whole was charged to the Manistre Fund.[58] Lodge repaid their indulgence by advancing further proposals, but he was more careful on other occasions to suppress his enthusiasm for buying books enough to keep within the Syndics' limits. For the sales following Richard Heber's death on 4 October 1833 he extracted £200 from the Syndics in November 1834, and a further £100 the following March;[59] part only went on the Heber books, and the total spent, including expenses, came to only £251.8s.7d. – well within the boundary.[60] But even more than the van de Velde sales, those of Richard Heber's books brought to the Library such quantities of material that they remained unsorted for years even after J. E. B. Mayor was moved to comment on what still remained to be done as late as 1866.[61] This was, however, of little concern to Lodge. At the same meeting in November 1834 when he secured the Syndics' agreement to expenditure at the Heber sales, he also presented his account for £226 spent by him personally on 1243 volumes for the Library.[62] Part of the Syndics' willingness to make so much available on this occasion was due perhaps not to any innate awareness of how much the Library might gain, as to more practical economic considerations. In preparation for an excursion to Spain, Lodge had in May 1834 obtained

---

[58] Syndicate Minutes 18 November 1833.

[59] Syndicate Minutes 17 November 1834 and 2 March 1835.

[60] One of the most notable acquisitions at the second Heber sale in June 1834 was a collection of ninety volumes of eighteenth-century editions of French plays, formerly in Garrick's library: most are now shelved at XIV.19.1–.

[61] [J. E. B. Mayor] *Statement made to the Syndics of the Library* (Cambridge 1866) p. 7. The Heber purchases are now widely scattered through the Library, and cannot all be identified from contemporary records. Samuel Sandars later noted (in his copy of Cooper's *Memorials of Cambridge*) that they included 421 tracts on the history of Belgium, 181 of an archaeological nature collected by the Abbé Barthélemy (now mostly at Mm. 58.21–41), 1300 political tracts of the seventeenth and eighteenth centuries, and a 'considerable number' of scientific interest; he appears to have taken his information from the 1865 annual report, which also mentioned that the scientific tracts came from Bishop Thomas Dampier's library, and alluded to a large collection of sale catalogues.

[62] Syndicate Minutes 17 November 1834. Lodge's note of the titles bought is among the Vouchers for 1834.

permission to draw up to £500 from the general funds of the Library to spend on books. In fact he spent none of it, and so was presumably able to gain some advantage for his subsequent demands: miscellaneous auction sales in London by Sotheby's and by Southgate, including a few purchases at the sale of the library of the historian Alexander Chalmers, came during the financial year to £65.10s.6d.[63]

Notions of the appropriate way for the Library to behave, of what it should collect and how much it might spend, had indeed altered dramatically. Besides the long-standing dealings with Deighton, the Library was now buying in quantity from Bossange, Barthés and Lowell in Great Marlborough Street, who supplied chiefly French, Spanish and Italian books, and from J. B. Baillière in Regent Street, to whom it went for mathematics, medicine, natural history and other sciences. The Manistre Fund enabled the Library to buy the twenty-seven volumes of *Descriptions des arts et métiers* of the French Académie Royale des Sciences (Paris 1761–88), and to meet some of Robert Willis' demands for books on mechanics, architecture and archaeology (including in 1837 Jacques François Blondel's great *Architecture françoise* (Paris 1752–6) and his *Cours d'architecture* (1771 etc.)). The Manistre Fund was not restricted, and it could encompass patristics and genealogy as well as J. S. Henslow's requests for Moriz Seubert's *Flora Azorica*, Joseph Hooker's *Flora Antarctica* and Philippe de la Peyrouse on the flora of the Pyrenees.[64] Both the University Library and the Philosophical Society were among the few subscribers to Sarah Bowdich's *Fresh-water fishes of Great Britain* (1828). Following Audubon's *Birds of America* of a few years previously, it subscribed repeatedly to Gould's expensively illustrated works, in May 1833 alone paying £13.12s.0d. for the first four parts of the *Birds of Europe*, while in the next month the Syndicate approved the purchase of Michele Tenore's *Flora Napolitana* in thirty-seven numbers at a cost of

---

[63] Vouchers.   [64] Cf. the Manistre account book 1837–52, *passim*.

£46.5s.0d.:[65] the cost was met from the Worts Fund. In June 1838 Lodge wrote to Thomas Worsley, the Vice-Chancellor,

to mention that Deighton & Bowtell are going to the Continent for a month or so, to hunt for books at Brussels, Antwerp, Frankfurt, & I hope also at Nuremberg, & Würtzburg. As this is a favourable opportunity for the Library obtaining many books which are wanted, perhaps you would have the kindness to allow them to purchase to the amount of £100 on the Library account, & 100£ on the Manistre or Rustat fund. – I hope also they will be able to get 200£ on the Worts' trust, of which the Masters of Pembroke, Christ's, Jesus & King's are the sole trustees. – As Bowtell is aware of what are the deficiencies in the Library, I should be sorry if this occasion were lost.[66]

The decision in 1839 to spend £300 from the Manistre Fund (which at that stage contained over £600) on books imported from Paris by Deighton,[67] and a similar one in the financial year 1840–1 to spend over £100 from the Rustat Fund on books imported by Bossange from Spain, were further moves in the same direction.

This apparent willingness to buy on a scale greater than ever before was not arrived at without some difficulty, and even rancour. While George Peacock could write of 'the flourishing state of our Public Library', 'a subject of pride and constant interest to every resident and to many non-resident, Members of the Senate',[68] and of Göttingen (whose achievement was trumpeted in the *Quarterly Journal of Education* in 1831 also)[69] as a model to be imitated, there were frustrations as well. In view of the obvious increase in the work and responsibility connected with the Librarianship it was only just that Lodge's

<hr>

[65] Syndicate Minutes 3 June 1833; Bossange's account is in the Vouchers for 1833–4.
[66] Lodge to Worsley 29 June 1838. This seems to have been part of an experimental new policy of allowing the Library's more trusted suppliers to select books on the Library's behalf: in February the same year the Syndics agreed to allow Lowell not more than £400 for purchases of Italian books for the Library during his forthcoming trip to Italy (Manistre account book 1837–52).
[67] Syndicate Minutes 18 November 1839 and University Accounts p. 170.
[68] [Peacock] *Observations* (1831) p. 59.
[69] 'The Göttingen library' *Quarterly Journal of Education* 2 (1831) pp. 215–26. It is noticeable how much Göttingen's reputation was founded on past achievements rather than current policies.

stipend should be increased, and on 21 May 1832 the Vice-Chancellor gave notice that a Grace would be offered on the 23rd. As we have seen, such was, however, far from Lodge's wish. Sorely hurt by the opposition to the proposal expressed at a syndicate meeting a few days earlier by one of its members, Gilbert Ainslie, Lodge felt the delicacy of his position with characteristic sensitivity. Ainslie, Master of Pembroke, had been Vice-Chancellor in 1828–9, and although not averse to some changes he was a man who preferred the *status quo*: he openly said that he could find a person to discharge the Librarian's duties for £50 a year, a clear insult to Lodge. The proposal by the Syndics that was the cause of the Vice-Chancellor's notice suggested that Lodge's stipend should be increased from £210 to £300, the additional amount to be paid out of the Common Chest. Lodge might have withdrawn to allow the public events to take their course, and receive his increase gracefully and with content. A less sensitive man would certainly have done so. But instead he took Ainslie's remark to heart, and requested the Vice-Chancellor to withdraw the Grace, taking refuge in an appeal to public needs. 'Such however, as I have been informed,' he wrote, 'is the low state of the Funds of the University, that I do not feel myself justified in accepting the kindness offered me, till such times, at least, as means can be found for increasing those funds, and for carrying into effect those important objects connected with the welfare and dignity of the University, which have been long in contemplation.'[70] The Grace was consequently withdrawn, and there could be no doubt of Lodge's sincerity, whatever its cause. But, even more serious than Ainslie's unkind remarks, at the same meeting that it had recommended an increase in his stipend the Syndicate had also limited Lodge's annual expenditure on books without reference to the Syndics to £400 a year. In the face of such decisions, Lodge was sorely tempted to resign. It was not surprising that Romilly, his closest friend and

---

[70] Quoted in the Syndicate Minutes. See also Luard 403. The stipend of Bodley's Librarian at this time was £400. (Craster p. 28).

confidant, remarked that John Graham (Master of Christ's, and the then Vice-Chancellor) and Ainslie were 'most awkward people to have to deal with'. However much Romilly might fulminate in the privacy of his diary, call Ainslie a 'beast' and the Syndics 'rascally', Lodge himself had to come to terms with the Syndics.[71] It can have been small comfort to him that the episode simply reflected the always difficult path for reformers of more imagination and foresight than the committees set to control them. The Syndicate kept as tight a rein as it could on Lodge's expenditure, but ten years later relations could still be strained. 'This Ev^g Lodge called on me to pour out his indignation ag^t the V.Ch. (Archdall) for his conduct to him as Libr^n: – the V.C. wont allow him to buy any books, & wont pay the standing bills!!', noted Romilly on 18 January 1842:[72] Romilly's own feelings were expressed on this occasion in the ambiguity of exclamation marks. Nonetheless, within just over a month the Syndics granted a further £200 as usual, and the accounts for the year 1841–2 included some £500 from the ordinary funds spent on the purchase of books besides £228.4s.0d. from the Manistre Fund: the figures for the following year were over £700 and £112.10s.6d.

Quite apart from Lodge's plans and hopes for the Library, the University could not afford to take advantage of every opportunity. On the death of the biblical scholar and Wesleyan Adam Clarke in 1832, his son J. B. B. Clarke approached the University with an offer to sell some of his father's most prized possessions. Clarke's collection of manuscripts numbered about six hundred, and less than half were European: the remainder was a mixture mostly of Hebrew, Persian, Arabic, Armenian, Syriac, Singhalese and Pali. Among the latter were ten Hebrew manuscripts that Clarke had bought in 1823 from the family of Jan van der Hagen, a minister of the Reformed Church in Amsterdam who had in turn bought them in 1726

[71] Romilly *Cambridge diary* p. 14.   [72] *Ibid.*, p. 230.

after the death of another minister of the same church, Cornelius Schulting. The group was thus not least of interest for having been kept together for over a century. Clarke's son considered them 'among the most ancient in Europe': they included five of the Pentateuch and three of the Targum; and since Kennicott had failed in his attempt to consult them there was indeed some incentive for them to be collated. The price asked, six hundred guineas, was however more than the Syndics felt able to justify when they considered the matter in January 1833,[73] and in 1834 the manuscripts were bought instead by the British Museum, which thus began its own programme of building up its collections of Hebrew manuscripts by purchase.[74]

This was not yet the end of the matter for Cambridge, however. In June 1835 J. B. B. Clarke again wrote to the University, offering to sell his father's remaining European and oriental manuscripts for £2,500.[75] It was an extraordinary collection. A man of much wider tastes than his published work implied, Clarke had lavished a fortune on his collection, and had put together one drawn from over much of the world that was in some respects well ahead of its time. Apart from the oriental manuscripts, which formed just over half the total and which by themselves would have been cause for comment, and the collection's remarkable historical and heraldic portions, it contained a notable accumulation of Icelandic manuscripts, a copy of Seneca from St Albans, a composite volume of Aesop, Seneca and Horace dated to the eleventh century on a then unidentified palimpsest believed to be of the fifth or sixth century, and a Wycliffite Bible that had commanded Clarke's particular attention. It also included one of especial interest for Cambridge, a book of prayers written in Italy and given to Lady Margaret Beaufort by Giovanni Gigli, Bishop of

---

[73] Syndicate Minutes 14 January 1833.
[74] Now British Library MSS. Add. 9398–407. See Esdaile *British Museum Library* p. 297.
[75] Library papers.

Worcester.[76] Clarke's son, anxious to place the manuscripts as one lot, had by December 1834 compiled a detailed catalogue of them:

I have frequently thought that such an unknown Individual as myself was not the one most fitted to be the Possessor of such a Collection: it would be a most notable addition to even the best and most extensive MS. Library in any Country, whether Public or Private: and it is possible that the following three united circumstances may shortly separate them and their present owner, – a want of Time to *use* them, an inability to *encrease* them, and my being apparently born only to occupy heavy curacies.[77]

The price was however far beyond the University's means, and the Syndics' Minutes do not even record that the matter was discussed. Clarke's approach to Sir Thomas Phillipps in March 1836 through the bookseller Cochran also failed;[78] the collection was finally dispersed at auction by Sotheby's in June 1836 and at a further sale in May 1838.

Somewhat less dramatically, the question of the future of the core of Walter Whiter's research on English philology posed similar problems for the Syndics. At the same meeting as that in which they declined the first of the Clarke manuscripts, they also rejected Whiter's adversaria. The sums involved were nothing like as great, but the valuation placed on the books and manuscripts by Dawson Turner was heavy enough, at £200. Whiter[79] had died in his mid-seventies in 1832, having been a Fellow of Clare from 1782, and he was still remembered by many members of the University.[80] His papers included his own annotated copy of his pioneering *Etymologicon magnum* (1800), a work remarkable for its comments on Romany, and his *Etymologicon universale* (1811–25): both books had been

---

[76] Now British Library MS. Add. 33,772.

[77] J. B. B. Clarke *A historical and descriptive catalogue of the European and Arabic manuscripts in the library of the late Adam Clarke* (1835) p. xi.

[78] Munby *Phillipps studies* 3 pp. 97–8; notes by Munby in his annotated copy of the catalogue of Phillipps' manuscripts (original in the Bodleian Library; photographic copy in Cambridge University Library); Phillipps subsequently bought Phillipps MSS. 10340–62 from the special catalogue issued by Baynes and Son of Paternoster Row in 1836 (a copy of this catalogue is bound up with the Library copy of Clarke's *Historical and descriptive catalogue*); another Clarke/Phillipps MS. (Phillipps 9516) is now in Yale University Library. [79] See *DNB*. [80] Gunning *Reminiscences* 2 pp. 69–71.

printed by the University Press, and there was therefore some cause to hope that Whiter's notes against further editions would be put to practical use in the University. The Syndics on this occasion were rescued from embarrassment by John Hookham Frere, whose offer to subscribe £120 towards the cost was gratefully accepted the following July, the balance being paid out of ordinary Library funds.[81]

As one sensible step in administrative improvement, Lodge reintroduced (for the first time since the eighteenth century) printed bookplates to record the names of donors. But despite his anxiety to buy books, he attracted few donations of consequence, while as will be explained later one collection that did arrive was unusual to the point of being offensively eccentric. The advent of fifty-three miscellaneous foreign and English guide books in April 1832 displayed in the donor William Whewell a characteristic understanding of the wider purposes of the University Library as they were developing, while the name of Robert Willis, Fellow of Gonville and Caius, who in the following July gave three of Rameau's theoretical works on harmony, was to become familiar to every generation since 1886 as the instigator of the standard history of the University buildings. One of the most curious manuscripts to come to the Library for some years was the gift of the Rev. Robert W. Johnson, of Packwood, Henley in Arden. Johnson had matriculated at Magdalene in 1833, and no precise record now survives of the year in which he presented a manuscript copy of *The benefits of Christ's death*, ascribed variously to Antonio Paleario or Benedetto da Mantova, in the translation made by Edward Courtney, Earl of Devonshire: an exceptional example of English calligraphy, it had been the very copy prepared for Edward VI, who had himself added to its interest by writing his name in the book twice over, perhaps when he gave it to his uncle the Duke of Somerset. Whether or not it was already in the Library when S. R. Maitland gave a

---

[81] Syndicate Minutes 3 July 1833. Whiter had for many years been rector of Hardingham in Norfolk.

hasty account of it in the *British Magazine* in 1840 is not clear, but it caught the attention of Churchill Babington fifteen years later, and so was published for the first time.[82] The collection of paintings which hung in the Library was added to when in May 1833 Mrs Esther Raine, of Richmond in Yorkshire and sister of one of the sitter's closest friends, gave John Hoppner's portrait of Richard Porson.[83]

Welcome in their different ways as these and other private donations were, they were overshadowed in 1836 by the decision of Basil Montagu to present his extensive collection of works by Francis Bacon. Apart from his interest in copyright deposit, described earlier, and his legal work on bankruptcy, Montagu had between 1825 and 1834 seen through to publication by his friend William Pickering an ambitious edition of Bacon's works for which many thought him unsuited: it nevertheless held the field until Spedding's appeared in 1857–74.[84] But however much Spedding, Macaulay and others found in Montagu's edition to snipe at, the Library gained as a result an outstanding collection created before large author collections became fashionable. To the printed books, Montagu added his own manuscript notes, which, however, have not proved of lasting importance.[85]

Such donations were straightforward – and welcome – enough. Few gifts received by the Library have on the other hand been so extraordinary as the cabinet of books presented by the Rev. Robert McGhee in June 1840. McGhee had entered Trinity College, Dublin, at the age of seventeen in 1835, and five years later his aversion to Roman Catholicism had reached such a pitch that he assembled two almost precisely identical collections of books – or 'documents' as he called them – to prove that the teaching of popery, and particularly that at

[82] MS Nn. 4.43. See *British Magazine* 18 (1840) pp. 256–60; A. Paleario *The benefit of Christ's death*, with an introduction by C. Babington (1855); Benedetto da Mantova *Il beneficio di Cristo* ed. S. Caponetto (Florence 1972) p. 507.

[83] Now in the Old Schools. Goodison *Cambridge portraits* no. 33.

[84] Montagu was introduced to Bacon's writings by Sir James Mackintosh (*Memoirs of the life of Sir James Mackintosh* ed. R. J. Mackintosh (1835) I pp. 151–2).

[85] Now MSS. Add. 4326–38. The Syndics resolved that 'a Compartment of the Library' should be appropriated to Bacon's works, but this has never been done.

Maynooth, was thoroughly subversive. He sent one each to the universities of Oxford and Cambridge. Even in the Anglican stronghold of nineteenth-century Cambridge, committed by statute to upholding the rights of the Established Church, the Syndics found McGhee's collection of thirty-one volumes of evidence a difficult meal to digest. His conditions were strict. Not only were the books always to be consulted in the presence of the Librarian (since they were more than simply works of reference): 'they shall never be taken by any person out of the Library on any pretext unless they might be required by the Vice Chancellor and the Heads of Houses to be produced before them as evidence of some facts which they prove or unless they might be required to be brought before a Committee of either House of Parliament'.[86] Such conditions might be regarded as no more than eccentric, but together with the books came a cabinet in which to house them, ornamented with a brass plate that made explicit what might otherwise have been passed over, describing the contents as 'Documents on the crimes of the Papal apostacy'. The quandary in which the Syndicate thus found itself was recorded not in its minutes, but privately by one of its members, G. E. Corrie, Norrisian Professor of Divinity since 1838:

The Vice-Chancellor explained that we had to decide on accepting the proffered books. Then burst forth all kinds of expressions against the idea of collecting books for such a purpose, and a proposition that they should be rejected. It was argued that the books were common and to be met with anywhere, and so it were useless to accept books which might be had for asking for. On this I observed that some of the books could not be had for any price. Among others selected as common was a Macnamara edition of the Bible with annotations. I observed that the very *existence* of the *edition* lying before us had been denied. Then it was proposed we should accept the books, but reject McGhee's regulations respecting their use. The object of this was evidently designed to make Mr McGhee refuse us the books except with his stipulation. But this idea was negatived.[87]

---

86 McGhee's manuscript list and conditions are kept in the cabinet; see also Syndicate Minutes 8 June 1840.
87 *Memorials of the life of George Elwes Corrie* ed. M. Holroyd (Cambridge 1890) pp. 144–5.

It took until the following year to obtain McGhee's consent to the Syndics' final decision, to alter his original plate (which was however kept) for a less provocative replacement, but as so frequently, the books which caused most bother to the authorities at their arrival caused least stir once on the shelves. By 1850 McGhee had left Dublin and had become rector of Holywell-cum-Needingworth, a tiny parish on the Ouse just outside St Ives, and when in that year a meeting was held at Huntingdon on the subject of 'papal aggression' the audience learned with some astonishment that there was printed proof of McGhee's allegations about Roman canon law to be seen less than fifteen miles away. His collection thus came once again, briefly, to the attention of the University, but even under the enforced aegis of G. E. Corrie, the then Vice-Chancellor and the staunchest of supporters of the Church of England, McGhee's gift remained little more than an idiosyncratic bywater. Emotions and disputes in Cambridge about Roman Catholicism were spirited enough in the mid-century, but they were of a different kind from the torrid atmosphere of mistrust at an over-powerful clerisy in Dublin.[88]

Lodge had shown more energy, more understanding and more willingness to work at the Librarianship than almost any of his predecessors for nearly two centuries. Rarely can any librarian have received such plaudits as those heaped on him by Whewell in the midst of the debate on the new buildings for the Library in 1831:

I have no hesitation in saying that the character and conduct of our present Librarian (I hope he will excuse me for thus openly referring to him, as it is for a purpose of public good) are strong *public* reasons for not diverting from the uses of the Library any large portion of the funds which now contribute to its increase. There is a benefit of which we cannot be too strongly aware, in the perfect conviction which every one now feels, that every shilling which is at present devoted to the Library is spent in the best

[88] Cf. R. J. McGhee *A key to the documents of the crimes of the papal apostacy as lodged in the Bodleian Library at Oxford, and in the University Library at Cambridge* (1840); *An account of the documents on popery presented to the libraries of the universities* (n.d.); *The Church of Rome: her present moral theology, scriptural instruction, and canon law* (1852); Macray *Annals* p. 340.

manner that the most conscientious impartiality, the most unwearied activity, the most extensive acquaintance with ancient and modern bibliography, and with the wants and condition of the existing Library, can enable any one to devise. These are qualifications which I hope our Librarians may always possess. But we cannot be confident that we shall always enjoy them in the same degree; and if we were now to deprive ourselves in any great measure of the advantages which the Library receives from its present administration, we cannot be sure that on restoring the fund thus diverted to its original use, it will be applied in a manner equally meritorious; to say nothing of the almost irreparable chasm in our literary possessions which the interruption would occasion. The day will come (may it be far distant!) when the funds of the Library will be distributed from other hands: and he must be a sanguine person who hopes for a plan of operations so much *more* energetic and extensive than the present, as will be required to recover the ground which, by a temporary deficiency of means, must be lost.[89]

But whatever his apparent energy in promoting the Library's cause, in private Lodge became a hypochondriac, and prone to frequent bouts of depression. In the end, genuine ill health forced him to accept a deputy, and he was prevailed on eventually to resign. There were few who were more privy to his ailments than Joseph Romilly, and none more sympathetic. As an ally for the Library, Romilly's place was finally sealed when in 1844 he was officially appointed Deputy Librarian *pro tem.*, while as a friend both in and out of health Romilly met Lodge for many periods almost daily. His treatment of Lodge's real or imaginary ailments was at times unusual. 'To cure Lodge's head ache took him a walk of 6 miles in the pouring rain with the wind blowing a hurricane: both got sopped to the skin',[90] he recorded on 28 February 1833. Seven months later Lodge's headaches still persisted, and he had passed an unhealthy summer: 'Lodge still but poorly from a rheumatic headache he had lately. – In the Long Vacation he had a smallish attack of cholera.'[91] In 1840 Lodge was 'lumbaginous',[92] but by the next year matters had become considerably more serious. Romilly recorded that the morphine he had been prescribed had induced a headache, and that

[89] [Whewell] *Reply* p. 27.   [90] Add. 6816, 28 February 1833.
[91] *Ibid.*, 28 September 1833.   [92] Add. 6820, 22 January 1840.

the leeches applied to him had induced erysipelas.[93] In the summer of 1843 Lodge sought relief first in the north of England and then in a sally to the continent cut short at Ostend through sickness. Romilly, who had been acting as Deputy Librarian and corresponding with him every day, sought him out immediately on his return to Magdalene: 'Most happy finding him much better than his own report of himself: – he complains of physical weakness, resulting from his disturbed rest: – he has however a bright eye, a clean tongue, a good pulse (tho feeble), & no yellowness mixt up with the natural red of his Complexion.'[94]

He was able to show the Queen the chief treasures of the Library when she visited it on 26 October 1843,[95] but within a few days Romilly had again been left in charge. As Lodge became more and more depressed, it became clear that only a complete change would allow an escape from the melancholy round of hypochondria and genuine illness. Leaving Romilly as his deputy, he left for Germany in June 1844, and while Romilly coped with a visit from the King of Saxony to the Library,[96] the Librarian himself tottered from Ostend to Cologne to Wiesbaden,[97] where he was laid up with a sharp attack of what he believed to be gout. It proved impossible to go on to Switzerland, and Lodge returned via Strasbourg (where he alarmed his cousin Annette, who was accompanying him, by a 'bilious attack') to Leamington and then Harrogate. The English spas proved more efficacious than those on the continent, and he returned to Cambridge on 2 October in much better health. But what Romilly diagnosed as

---

[93] *Ibid.*, 1 and 2 February 1841.   [94] Add. 6822, 13 June 1843.

[95] *Ibid.*, 26 October 1843. See also *Victoria and Albert at Cambridge; the royal visits of 1843 and 1847 as they were recorded by Joseph Romilly, Registrary of the University* (Cambridge 1977).

[96] On 21 June.

[97] Add. 6823, 1, 4, 6, 8 and 18 June, 4, 8 and 11 July 1844. Lodge's travels had not, however, always been those of a valetudinarian. On one occasion, visiting the libraries of Melk and Göttweis, he was able to produce his friend T. F. Dibdin's accounts of the two monasteries in *A bibliographical, antiquarian and picturesque tour in France and Germany*, and translate them for the benefit of the respective communities: his zeal at taking so unwieldy a book so far, and producing it when required, so flattered Dibdin that he dedicated the second edition, of 1829, to Lodge.

hypochondria two days later transpired to be in reality something altogether different: his cousin Annette had set her affections on him, and he felt unable to return them. Indeed, her feeling induced in Lodge only acute anxiety and yet further depression. So, despite the fact that term had begun, he left Cambridge again, this time for Boulogne until the end of October, when he left for the family home at Hawkshead after spending a few days prostrate in bed at Cambridge suffering from little more than despondency.

The Library Syndicate could hardly ignore such absences. Lodge did not return until the end of November, and meanwhile on 18 November a sub-syndicate was established to consider the matter, while Romilly became officially Deputy Librarian.[98] There was only one honourable course open to Lodge, and he took it. In December 1844 he resolved to tender his resignation. The meeting of the sub-syndicate that was to have considered it was a fiasco, since only two members, Whewell and Romilly, turned up,[99] and so matters dragged on into the spring. Lodge alternated between the Library and his bed, but with the Librarian a sick man, Bowtell ailing from another illness, and the transfer of books to the new Cockerell Building in turmoil the final announcement to the Syndics that he wished to resign on 25 March 1845 met with both sympathy and relief. He attended his last Syndicate meeting on 13 March, 'so weak & exhausted when he got to Sidney Lodge that he had to be supported upstairs by D[rs] Graham & Archdall'.[100] Romilly's attempt to rally him with a bottle of madeira met with less than success, and in order to meet the administrative needs of the University Lodge's resignation was finally dated 9 April.[101] He died on 27 August 1850.

---

[98] Add. 6823, 18 November 1844.   [99] *Ibid.*, 6 December 1844.
[100] *Ibid.*, 13 March 1845.   [101] *Ibid.*, 9 April 1845.

13

JOSEPH POWER AND THE
DISTRIBUTION OF
RESPONSIBILITY

LODGE'S RESIGNATION was delayed for a few days in order
to allow the University to correct the anomaly that it had failed
to correct in 1828, and to amalgamate the two offices of
Bibliothecarius and *Protobibliothecarius* into one office, of Librarian. The Grace to allow this having been passed without
incident on 9 April,[1] the way was paved for Lodge's departure
and the election of his successor. The event had been long
expected, and before the middle of March all the candidates
had declared themselves. At the beginning of the month
Romilly had received a letter from the Rev. George Williams,
vicar of Newton, enquiring for instructions on how to apply
for the librarianship and adding that he was acquainted with
nearly a dozen languages. 'Pretty well!' remarked Romilly.[2]
Despite the precaution of writing in good time, Williams was
not among the seven candidates from whom the final two
nominations were drawn. Lodge's own choice was Mynors
Bright, Fellow of Magdalene and later celebrated as editor of
Pepys' diary, who addressed a circular letter to the electors as
early as 25 February. Bright was quickly followed by Joseph
Edleston, Fellow and Bursar of Trinity and nominated by
Whewell; Charles W. Goodwin, of St Catharine's, a lawyer
and Egyptologist and one of the most able of the candidates;
Joseph Power of Clare, nominated by Sir H. J. Fust the Master
of Trinity Hall; W. N. Griffin, Fellow of St John's and Senior
Wrangler in 1837; J. M. Kemble of Trinity, the most learned
Anglo-Saxon scholar of the century, living in London after his

---

[1] Grace Book *Ξ* p. 406; Add. 6823 p. 23 *bis*. [2] Add. 6823 p. 16 *bis*.

marriage and nominated by the Master of Magdalene; and J. J. Smith, nominated by Benedict Chapman, Master of Caius. Three of these, Bright, Goodwin and Griffin, withdrew before their names were put to the vote. Nominations on 16 April showed Power and Smith in the lead, followed by Edleston and Kemble.[3]

The University's choice lay, as was statutory, between the first two. John James Smith, Fellow of Caius and an active reformer, was a man of antiquarian tastes whose stormy Vice-Presidency of the Cambridge Camden Society had ended with his resignation.[4] He had entered Caius as a pensioner in 1823, and graduated in 1828, when he had also been elected a Fellow; from 1830 to 1837 he had served as dean of his college. Besides his interest in the Camden Society, he had also been instrumental in founding the Cambridge Antiquarian Society in 1839, which published his pioneering *Survey of college plate* in 1845. His opponent, Power (fig. 21), was all that Smith was not. Smith's energy was never in doubt, whereas Power was inclined to a more comfortable pace. Where Smith courted unpopularity for his outspoken views and manner, Power enjoyed a wide circle of friends. Or, as the wits put it, it was a choice between 'Power without work, or work without Power'.[5] Born in 1798 at Market Bosworth, Power had entered Clare College as a pensioner in 1817 and graduated as tenth Wrangler in 1821. In 1823 he had been elected Fellow, but migrated to Trinity Hall, where he remained a Fellow from 1829 until 1844 when he returned to Clare. He never married, barely stirred from Cambridge, and although he produced no full-length separate book he contributed a number of papers on mathematical subjects to the *Transactions* of the Cambridge

---

[3] Add. 6823 p. 25 *bis*. On 18 April 1845 W. B. Donne commented to J. W. Blakesley, 'I am sorry for Kemble's defeat but not disappointed for I never expected him to be nominated. There is so much in our friend to frighten a university from its propriety, that I should have been surprised at his success. He would, I believe, make an excellent librarian, but he would never look like one' (quoted in Peter Allen *The Cambridge Apostles* (Cambridge 1978) p. 213).

[4] James F. White *The Cambridge Movement* (Cambridge 1962) pp. 40, 113.

[5] Quoted by Romilly, 9 March 1855 (Add. 6834).

21   Joseph Power (1798–1868), Librarian.

Philosophical Society. At the time of his election, however, Romilly noted not his achievements in mathematics, but his 'corpulence' and 'somnolence':[6] his unkind observation was prompted by a witticism emanating from Smith's committee room.

The polling on 9 April was a protracted affair.

The Election of Librarian began at 9: Drs Webb & Graham sat one on each side of the V.C; Birkett & Mills were umpires for Power, Eyres & Prowett

6 Add. 6823 p. 26 *bis.*

512

for Smith: – Mr Hunt & I attended officially. – At $3\frac{1}{2}$ there was an adjournm^t for 4 hours: – the n^{os} then were 259 for P, 179 for S. – Dined in hall. – Polling resumed at $7\frac{1}{2}$: – at $\frac{1}{4}$ to 10 (with the consent of both parties) the polling closed: Sharpe (of Qu) tendered a vote for S. after this, – he having been in the S[enate]. H[ouse]. all day! – Final n^{os} P 312; S. 240.[7]

Besides the all but unanimous support of his two colleges, Clare and Trinity Hall, Power also received the majority of votes in Peterhouse, Pembroke, Corpus, King's, Queens', Catharine Hall, Jesus, Magdalene, Emmanuel, Sidney and Downing; and although Smith had slight majorities in the two largest colleges, Trinity and St John's, opinion there was not overwhelmingly persuaded of his merits. All but three of the Heads of Houses who cast their votes did so in favour of Power. Among them he received the votes of William Hodgson of Peterhouse, and George Archdall of Emmanuel, each Vice-Chancellor twice over in the previous few years, and of Henry Philpott of St Catharine's, Vice-Chancellor in 1846–7, while the sentiment of those who had sat on the Library Syndicate was clearly on his side.[8] Unlike Lodge before him, Power therefore came into office with an assured base of senior opinion in the University in his support.

Power remained Librarian for nineteen years, until he retired in 1864. The voluble complaints of his successor, J. E. B. Mayor, and the radical nature of the reforms that Mayor and (a few years later) Henry Bradshaw felt it necessary to introduce, have perpetuated the impression current among his contemporaries in 1845, that Power was too much enamoured of a life of leisure to bring himself to that pitch of activity that the Library seemed to demand. That his librarianship did not, in the event, pass without incident, need cause no surprise. The Cockerell Building was occupied by the end of the 1840s, further space was acquired in 1856 with the requisitioning of the Divinity School, and the continuing discussion on other means of

[7] Romilly's diary, 17 April 1845: Add. 6823 p. 25 *bis*.
[8] Henry Gunning *The poll on the election of Librarian of the University of Cambridge* (Cambridge 1845).

extending the Library punctuated the fifties and early sixties as it had the thirties and forties. These were predictable extensions of what had already passed. But Power's achievements were more than this. Under his aegis the Library staff was increased from four (including himself) and a boy in 1845, to seven in 1864, reaching a peak briefly in 1858 of nine. The Syndicate itself underwent much needed reform in 1853, to the accompaniment of criticisms of its unwieldy constitution in the Cambridge Commissioners' report of 1852. And in 1856 there appeared the first volume of a printed catalogue of the Library's manuscripts, the first published account since 1697 and the first ever to treat them in a separate publication. In administrative matters Power also showed himself well able to amass the necessary detail in his more than adequate account of the Library submitted to the Commissioners.

The body responsible in practice for approving and seeing through all these changes was the Library Syndicate, on the one hand charged with the Librarian and staff, and on the other able to accomplish little without reference to the Senate supported by written report – though in fact few of the Syndicate's recommendations were ever rejected. By a Grace passed in 1751, the Syndicate was to consist of the Vice-Chancellor, the Heads of Houses, all Doctors regardless of faculty, the Public Orator, the entire body of professors, and the current proctors, taxors and scrutators. In fact this unwieldy group never met. But although the quorum was only five, the theoretical composition was clearly ludicrously inept. The Cambridge Commissioners in their 1852 *Report* thought that the number of those eligible to attend exceeded seventy, and briefly summed up the other objections: 'its members are not selected for their special fitness for their duty; they are not elected or changed periodically'.[9] In fact, however, the Commissioners had been pre-empted by those anxious for reform from within at Cambridge, in the work of

[9] Cambridge University Commissioners *Report* p. 131.

the Statutes Syndicate; it was in response to this rather than the Commissioners that the Library Syndicate itself proposed its own reform at the end of November 1853. In place of the old body there was to be a much smaller one consisting of the Vice-Chancellor and sixteen others elected by the Senate, of who four were to retire in rotation every year. At least two meetings were to be held every term, and the Syndicate was to report annually to the University on the state of the Library and its finances: the series of printed annual reports dates from February 1855, just over a year later. Of the eighteen who signed the report[10] that effectively ended the old Syndicate, five remained to become the first members of the reformed Syndicate agreed by Grace on 8 February 1854: William Whewell, Henry Philpott (Master of St Catharine's and a born administrator), H. W. Cookson (Master of Peterhouse and an able philologist, though regarded by Romilly with some justice as a timid man), W. H. Bateson (Public Orator, Fellow of St John's, and generally considered a liberal), and G. G. Stokes of Pembroke, Lucasian Professor since 1849 and destined to fill the same chair until 1903. Besides these, the new body was composed of several who were already familiar with the Syndicate's proceedings, and of some new blood: they were J. T. Abdy of Trinity Hall (Regius Professor of Civil Law from 1854), Robert Willis of Caius, engineer and historian of architecture, J. A. Jeremie (Regius Professor of Divinity), Henry Bond (an outstanding Regius Professor of Physic), and several less established figures including William Collett, author of the catalogue of early printed books in Caius Library, Francis France of St John's, John Roberts of Magdalene, a lawyer and classicist, Charles Hardwick of St Catharine's, whose career as a scholar of Christian archaeology and contributor to the catalogue of the manuscripts in the University Library was cut tragically short in the Pyrenees in 1859, F. J. A. Hort of Trinity, the authority on the New

10 Library papers 28 November 1853.

Testament and one of the Syndicate's youngest members, William George Clark of Trinity, later founder of the *Journal of Philology* and of the Clark Lectures in English literature, and J. E. B. Mayor, a young classicist of St John's, subsequently University Librarian. If successful reform is constituted of a judicious mixture of old and new, then the new Syndicate, ensured of fresh blood with each annual election, offered a fair measure of hope.

Contrary to its later experience, when pleas for more staff fell on the ears of the University with monotonous regularity, Cambridge had not, in the first part of the century, been troubled with importunities. It was generally agreed that the new Cockerell Building would require further hands to run it, and particularly so if undergraduates were to be more freely admitted. But despite the prodigious increase in the number of books under Lodge, a third Library Keeper was added only in December 1842, when Charles Nathaniel Wootton began his long career after some training in a lawyer's office.[11] He joined John Page, who after several years as an assistant with Stevenson's the local booksellers[12] had arrived in succession to Richard Rowe in 1840 and was to serve until his death in 1855, and John Bowtell, who had joined the staff to manage the Library when there was otherwise only the crippled John Marshall apart from the Librarians Kerrich and Clarke. Bowtell himself, set in his ways, a venerable if not patriarchal figure in the Library by 1845, when he was aged sixty-eight, was allowed to employ his grandson John Dearle as an aide. Dearle's career was all too brief. In 1846, convicted of selling several library books as waste paper, he was sentenced to transportation for seven years.[13] With Dearle's dismissal, the staff apart from Power himself therefore consisted of only

---

[11] Grace Book Ξ p. 298; University Archives, University papers 1840–3 no. 872.

[12] University papers 1840–3 nos. 197, 198

[13] Luard 530; University papers 1843–7 no. 830; Add. 6824, p. 28 (Romilly's diary 8 May 1846); *Cambridge Chronicle* 4 July 1846. The circumstances of Dearle's thefts were fully recorded by Wootton in Add. 2594(4). The sentence was later commuted to imprisonment.

three people. His dishonesty, which attracted unwelcome curiosity, had however called attention to the lack of any proper supervision in the Library or provision for checking missing books. Dearle's crime was discovered early in May, and on 4 June a specially appointed sub-syndicate recommended not only that the Library should be checked annually and a proper register of borrowers maintained,[14] but also that the Senate should be asked to approve at least one more Library Keeper.[15] The first two suggestions were passed without further ado,[16] but the last was not so easily understood by the whole University: after being delayed until the Michaelmas Term it was acquiesced in only after a formal vote. John Smith, son of the clerk of Great St Mary's church and with four years' experience behind him as an assistant in Elijah Johnson's bookshop in Trinity Street, was appointed fourth Library Keeper, at an initial salary of £63 p.a., in December 1846.[17]

Bowtell was clearly in his last years, however. The relic of another age, fixed in his ways but deserving of every sympathy after his long service with the University, he found it impossible to accustom himself to the expectations of a new generation. The inspectors of the Library in 1846, appointed from the University at large, discovered that considerable numbers of books were missing, but found that their task had been made immeasurably more difficult by the removal of books into new classes in the Cockerell Building. Shelf-lists had not been properly amended to show new locations, whole pages had been torn out of the shelf-lists and rewritten with little regard for what had been there previously, entries had been erased with a knife, and old class-marks on the books themselves had been removed in similar fashion.[18] These last

[14] The Grace confirming this was passed on 4 July (Grace Book Ξ p. 466). Two registers of loans, arranged alphabetically by borrowers' names, survive in the Library archives. The system was discontinued by Grace in November 1847 (Grace Book Ξ p. 561).
[15] Syndicate Minutes 4 June 1846.   [16] Grace Book Ξ p. 466.
[17] Grace Book Ξ p. 493; University Archives, University papers 1843–7 nos. 939, 941. In 1851 Page received £78, Bowtell £160, and Wootton £73.10s.
[18] Syndicate Minutes 22 February 1847.

were particularly tiresome. While obviously resulting in a neater appearance than a succession of old entries crossed through in pen, the erasures made it extremely difficult to trace the movements of individual books, and when in Michaelmas 1849 the Library inspectors (consisting as in 1846 of senior members of the University) found that their recommendations on this point had been ignored they were understandably incensed.[19] The culprit was John Bowtell, who, alone, had replaced most of the books into the new building, besides continuing to catalogue the current intake and to administer (more and more haphazardly) the instructions to binders. A Herculean task even for a young man, and too much for an ailing one, by 1851 the Library reorganization had reached such a state of disorder that some intervention was necessary. While the inspectors complained yet again, and with even more vehemence, of further erasures, Smith and Wootton (whose duties of aiding and supervising readers did not normally cause them to help in compiling the catalogue) were enlisted to make good the damage so far as possible. By November 1851 they had made some progress:

The Records of ye Inspectors of 1846 present Lists of many thousand Volumes, which at that time were not to be found in ye places assigned to them in ye Class-Catalogues: and a great part of them have been removed into ye New Library without having their new places marked in ye general Catalogue. Instances of this were particularly numerous in those portions of ye Library, which have been examined by ye present Inspectors: and it has been a work of great labour to trace ye Volumes reported as missing in 1846 to their new places, and to correct ye Catalogues accordingly. Thus in Class Oo alone it was necessary to trace 230 Volumes in this manner, and many thousands in ye Classes A*-S*. The whole of ye Class-Catalogue and ye general Catalogue also to a great extent, have now been properly corrected. Mr Wootton, to whose willing and laborious cooperation during and since ye Inspection great credit is due, is at present occupied, with ye assistance of Mr Smith, in correcting ye general Catalogue. This is a labour, which requires ye Inspection of every page. It is estimated that at least 15,000 corrections still remain to be made.[20]

[19] Syndicate Minutes 14 February 1850.   [20] Syndicate Minutes 14 November 1851.

As in 1849, the inspectors published a list of the missing books, which now numbered over two hundred volumes, most printed within the last fifty years. Smith's and Wootton's work deserved the praises of the inspectors, but Bowtell remained intransigent. The inspectors also found it necessary to fault his practice of 'constantly and unnecessarily removing Books from place to place', and to recommend that henceforth this should be done only with the Librarian's express permission. Every user of the Library had suffered through Bowtell's increasing incompetence, but the inspectors and the Syndicate met his work with more patience even than was called for in view of his years. The break finally came only in November 1852, when the Syndicate decided to remove him from office and to grant him an annual pension of £100.[21]

Part of the reason for Bowtell's prolonged misdemeanours after being warned by the Syndicate lay in the nature of his office: he could be removed from his place only by Grace. Power was more profuse on the relationship of the staff to the Senate than was perhaps called for in his report to the 1852 Commissioners, but no more so than might, under the circumstances, have been expected. He wrote with Bowtell in mind, and in some perplexity. Apart from the irregularities discovered by the library inspectors in November 1851, to which he alluded, Bowtell's presence had not, finally, been conducive to the good order of the collections. 'I do not think' wrote Power, 'that sufficient provision is made for the prompt cataloguing of new books: it might proceed more quickly if there were greater unanimity among the assistants, and if the Librarian were armed with greater authority.'[22] 'Our small staff of five persons is economical to the utmost', he continued, and he went on further to appeal for more staff: Trinity College, Dublin, he pointed out, had four clerks constantly

---

21 Syndicate Minutes 1 November 1852; Grace Book O p. 329. Bowtell died at Great Yarmouth on 13 November 1855, aged 78.
22 Cambridge University Commissioners *Evidence* p. 57.

employed solely on a quantity of incoming publications that was smaller than that at Cambridge.

Power's plea for one, or two, extra assistants was not attended to immediately. Instead, on Bowtell's departure the Syndicate sought to amend matters by recommending a Grace to give him authority to appoint a Secretary, removable at will, to assist him at an annual salary of seventy guineas[23] – less than half what Bowtell had been receiving. Their further decision, to appoint a sub-syndicate to consider the duties of the Library Keepers and the arrangements for binding books (for which, in Bowtell's last years,[24] responsibility had fallen solely on Power) was less than Power had hoped.

Oscar Heun, who joined the staff as the Librarian's Secretary (the term seems to have been introduced solely to indicate that he was Power's appointment, rather than the University's) in 1852, was a native of Leipzig, and proved in some respects to be an appointment of outstanding discrimination. Instructed at first 'to place his services at the disposal of the Librarian . . ., to assist persons consulting the Library, especially with regard to Books in foreign languages, but to have no authority over the Library Assistants',[25] he rapidly vindicated the somewhat anomalous nature of his place. His connections with Germany provided an easy entry to the German book trade, to the great advantage of the Library, while his readiness to toil at the task of reducing the catalogue into order won ready admiration. In December 1853 his position in the Library was regularized and recognized with the Syndicate's decision to appoint him Principal Assistant, charged with the direction of Page, Wootton and Smith.

With that, however, Power could not remain content. Page was an ailing man. In February 1854 he was given leave to attend the Library for a reduced period each day,[26] and a year later he was dead. Conditions in the Library were far from

[23] Syndicate Minutes 1 November 1852.
[24] Ibid., 15 November 1852; Cambridge University Commissioners Evidence p. 55.
[25] Library papers 24 November 1852.   [26] Syndicate Minutes 13 February 1854.

comfortable. No artificial heating existed in the old library, and in 1852 the Syndicate had expressly allowed Wootton and Smith to pursue their cataloguing in the new building. In March 1854 the Syndicate, again remarking the 'extreme cold', and the 'injurious effect thereby produced on persons consulting the Library and on the Library Assistants, who are detained there during a great part of every day', reported that they wished to arrange for a hot-water central heating system to be installed.[27] They easily secured the Senate's approval, and at the same time also gained permission to employ a further assistant, at the modest salary of a pound a week, to paste together the new catalogue then under consideration. So Robert Fynn joined the staff (he was joined ten years later by his son of the same name), the first of a succession of 'boys' who formed the core of the Library's junior assistants until the social revolution of the mid-twentieth century rendered the title no longer acceptable. The Syndics felt able to go further, however, having secured Fynn's appointment in 1854. In optimistic, and even bullish, mood after the satisfactory account they felt able to give of the new catalogue in their first printed annual report, issued in February 1855, the following month they proposed the addition of yet another assistant in addition to one to fill the vacancy caused by Page's death.[28] The stay of William White, the new assistant, was all too brief, since at Christmas 1856 he accepted a post in the library of Christ's College with a view to preparing a catalogue of the collections there instead. Furthermore, while Dennis Hall, Page's successor, quickly proved able to shoulder responsibility, and gave distinguished service for many years, in other respects the staff did not present a tidy arrangement. White's resignation after only a few months was overshadowed by the complete breakdown of Heun in the most distressing circumstances. Already ill in December 1855, when he was given leave to recuperate away from Cambridge,

[27] Library papers 27 March 1854; Syndicate Minutes 27 March 1854.
[28] Library papers 9 March 1855: the Grace was passed on 14 March. On the new catalogue see below, pp. 533–5.

521

by the following March he was seriously deranged. 'He had far too much work to do,' commented Romilly, '& did it with intense energy: – he had the delusion of think⁸ he was going to be married & bought several white waistcoats: then he purchased a gun: – then he subscr⁴ £100 to some charity: – poor Fellow! they have found it necessary to confine him.' The University met his medical expenses, and he resigned from the Library the following October after enjoying a brief respite. A few months later Romilly could only record that 'Poor Heun (who did such admirable work in the Library) is quite out of his mind: he complains of the Police for not protect⁸ him from the annoyance of people who look through his green eye-shade into his heart: – he is making a tin covering over the breast to guard himself.' In the end he recovered some of his health, enough to be employed briefly by Quaritch in London, but the Library had broken him and he had little to offer the world save as a teacher of German.[29] Meanwhile White's post had been filled early in 1857 by Alfred Hart, whose sole task, of transcribing titles into the catalogue, was to come to an end in 1861 and so to end his employment as well: the Syndics hoped that the money thus saved would pay for the printing of the catalogue henceforth. While White and Hart were employed almost wholly on the catalogue, and Fynn became the first binder actually to work at repairs regularly within the Library (the Syndics bought a quantity of binding equipment in 1859),[30] other needs were equally manifest. A further report therefore reached the Senate in May 1857, one of what had become almost an annual series. Its recommendations, that two further assistants should be employed – a porter, and a foreign clerk to deal with modern continental books and to assist in the preparation of the new catalogue – were agreed within a week, but the report concealed many of the Syndics' private fears. Continuing increases in accessions, the fact that the more

[29] Syndicate Minutes 5 and 11 December 1855 and 20 October 1856; Add. 6836 (Romilly's diary) 11 March 1856; Add. 6837 (idem) 12 February 1857; Heun to Bradshaw 20 February 1860.   [30] Syndicate Minutes 13 April 1859.

liberal admission of undergraduates had not only brought more people into the Library to be supervised but had also greatly increased the number of books borrowed, and the even more pressing need to clear the mass of periodicals and pamphlets that had been accumulating for years in the various store-rooms, coupled with the need to prepare the new catalogue of printed books, rendered this increase of staff essential. For all his energies, Heun's work on catalogue revision had proved to be less than expected; and the Library could ill afford to employ experienced staff on duties that could equally well be undertaken by newcomers.[31] However, the Library had at last acquired its first porter (his duties were also to include pasting on book labels and noting the absence of the other assistants) in July 1857 with the arrival of Henry Hancock. It took a little longer to find a foreign clerk, the Syndicate reporting in February 1858 that they had still failed to secure one, and only in the following June was Otto Charles Marcus, of Bonn, appointed, for four months in the first instance and indefinitely the following December.

Insofar as his duties lay primarily in dealing with modern foreign accessions, Marcus (who had some experience of the book trade, including a year with Williams and Norgate, who specialized in foreign books) was the obvious successor to Heun. But in administrative terms rather than everyday practicalities Heun was replaced as principal assistant by a man neither foreign nor in the least professionally experienced in the book trade. Unlike his predecessors, he was also a graduate of the University. In November 1856, the month in which he was first appointed to the Library, Henry Bradshaw was twenty-five years old (fig. 22).[32] Descended from a prominent Lancashire family, Bradshaw was born in 1831, and lost his father in 1845. From Eton, where he was captain of the school,

31 Syndicate Minutes 27 May 1857; Library papers 28 May 1857.
32 The standard life is by G. W. Prothero A memoir of Henry Bradshaw (1888). See also Roy Stokes Henry Bradshaw 1831–1886 (Metuchen, N.J., 1984), a selection from his publications with an introduction and bibliography.

he passed in February 1850 to King's, and three years later, having completed the requisite period, he was elected Fellow of his college. Although there was no need for him to do so, since as a Kingsman he could have taken a degree without examination, he sat for the classics tripos the following summer, where he was less successful than had been hoped. Rather than remain at Cambridge, he had thereupon taken a post at St Columba's College, the school-cum-college a little outside Dublin founded ten years before by William Sewell and designed to offer both a public school education in Ireland and the means for training clergy to preach in the tradition of the Oxford Movement to the Irish people in their own tongue.[33] The college was then under the charge of George Williams, also a member of King's, who became a lifelong ally and friend. But when in 1854 Williams was elected Vice-Provost of King's, Bradshaw was left with few congenial friends in Ireland who could share his intellectual tastes, save J. H. Todd of Trinity College, Dublin,[34] who had been instrumental in the founding of St Columba's and remained its most influential supporter until his death in 1869. Bradshaw left the college in April 1856 with few regrets at the time, but returned to England with no definite prospects. If he had an eye on the University Library, it was more probably that of a scholar anxious to read in it than of one contemplating membership of its staff. As an undergraduate he had questioned Heun on the Irish books in the Library[35] – he had inherited a celebrated collection of them from his father – and had by 1855 already laid the groundwork of his knowledge of the early printed books to the extent that he could write to Heun from St Columba's:

It would be a charity to rescue, from the dust in which it lies buried, a copy of Wynkyn de Wordes 'Noua Legenda Anglie'. fo. Lond. 1516. It by rights belongs to K★.10.38, but it is lying (or was when I left) on the top of

[33] Cf. Lionel James *A forgotten genius; Sewell of St. Columba's and Radley* (1945).
[34] Cf. G. O. Simms 'James Henthorn Todd' *Hermathena* 109 (1969) pp. 5–23.
[35] Bradshaw to Heun 7 February 1855.

22   Henry Bradshaw (1831–1886), Librarian. From a photograph by Hills and Saunders.

the bookcase next the staircase leading up to your room, so that, when I wanted it, I could not find it for some time. I should not ask you to do this, but I see the Bibliographers seem to look upon it as de Worde's chef d'oeuvre –

    There are also two of Thomas Churchyards books in the Library. Any of his are extremely difficult to buy – & the Cambridge library has a very small share of them. Bb.10.41 is his Fortunate Farewell to Essex and

N*.4.58, is his 'True Discourse Historicall' (of the different English officers serving abroad) –

Of all Barnabe Rich's tracts, wch are very uncommon there is but one at Cambridge – bound up with several other things in Dd.3.49. & called A New Irish Prognostication, 1624. But of all those small publications on Ireland, perhaps the most curious (& unquestionably one of the rarest) is Derricke's Image of Ireland – of w^h. there is a collation in M^r. Grenvilles Catalogue – It is in the same case with the *Rich*. Dd.3.19.

These four, I should think, or certainly the last, it would do no harm to put aside.[36]

The gradual discovery of rarities too easily mislaid, and the proper ordering of the early books in the Library, were to occupy the rest of Bradshaw's life, and his reference to the Grenville catalogue was more than incidental. In 1855 two volumes had appeared of Payne and Foss's catalogue of the great collection of Thomas Grenville, bequeathed to the British Museum in 1846 (a third and last was published in 1872). They became a new shibboleth of rarity, but they also heralded the beginnings of a fresh spirit in cataloguing large private libraries. It was typical of Bradshaw to refer to the most recent reference book, and for much of his career he was absorbed directly or indirectly in the preparation of bibliographies or catalogues designed to meet new standards set by the scholarly world. George Bullen's '1640 catalogue', of books in the British Museum printed in the British Isles down to 1640, was published in 1884, two years before Bradshaw's death; J. W. Holtrop's catalogue of the incunables in the Royal Library at The Hague appeared in 1856; and the first instalment of M. F. A. G. Campbell's more ambitious bibliography of incunables printed in the Low Countries in 1874. Apart from his work on the manuscripts – western and oriental – at Cambridge, and despite encouragement from Holtrop to prepare a full bibliography of English fifteenth-century books, Bradshaw was to produce little himself. But his contributions to the works of others were crucial, and were characterized by the same readiness to seek out and evaluate books (whether at Cambridge or elsewhere), and to compare them with existing

[36] Bradshaw to Heun 24 February 1855.

authorities, that marked his correspondence with Heun when he was not even in a position seriously to contemplate an appointment in the University Library.

Whatever Heun may have thought of being offered advice by a young graduate exiled in Ireland, by the summer of 1856 Bradshaw had become something of an authority on the Library, not only capable of proffering criticism but also expected to have explanations for its shortcomings. 'The University Library', wrote the London bookseller C.J. Stewart to him in August,

ought to have both Lesley's edition of the Mozarabic Missal. *Roma* 1755. 2v 4°, which is valuable for the Notes, & the one of Angelopolis which you mention. I send my Catalogues regularly to the library, the Liturgical one lacks those books in it, but I never receive an order unless some book is expressly recommended by say Professor Willis or others. How is this? It is surely the duty of the librarian to fill up the gaps in the library as he can. In Mr Lodge's time years ago I supplied a great deal.[37]

In August Bradshaw was in a poor position to cheer Stewart with regular orders, but following Heun's resignation (it cannot have been unexpected) he seized the opportunity to present himself as a candidate for the vacancy. His letter of application to the Vice-Chancellor, of 31 October, was brief and to the point, but it was enough – as George Williams wrote excitedly five days later:

My dear Brads,

All goes *swimmingly*. I *took* your note to the Vice Chancellor this morning – he was only elected yesterday – in order that I might speak to him of your qualifications &c. It was altogether unnecessary, as he seemed quite to have made up his mind, and did not apprehend any kind of difficulty. He was extremely kind and nice. Your note was all that was required; and he promised to bring it before the Syndicate next Monday, & with great delicacy proposed to have the Meeting at his own Lodge, rather than in the Library, which is so public. He had understood that *you wished* the name of the office to be changed, & he thought there would be no difficulty in that, & that the Syndicate were quite competent to do it. I told him that I did not think you had suggested this, or cared much about it, but he thought it would be better.

Well, now I have something more to communicate, which I trust will

37 C.J. Stewart to Bradshaw 20 August 1856.

also please you. I last night received a note from the Vice Chancellor asking me to allow him to nominate me 'to the *Council* & Senate' on the *Press* Syndicate. I told him this morning that I would *rather* serve on the *Library* Syndicate – if there was a vacancy . . . This Evening I have a note from him proposing to nominate me on the *Library* Syndicate! Now is not that thorough? I thought it might be a comfort and support to you to have me on; and of course, it will be a pleasure to me to stand in any relation to you; and as you were one of *my Masters* at S. Columba's, I trust you will not object to my being *one of yours* on this Syndicate: and will we not work Messrs Wotton & Co?'[38]

In the end there was no change of title for the present, and on 10 November Bradshaw was appointed Principal Library Assistant, entrusted like Heun before him with the charge of the other assistants under the authority of the Librarian and the Syndicate. In appointing him, and deviating so far from tradition as to appoint a man avowedly more familiar with the old books than with the new, more anxious to pursue bibliographical research than to attend to the everyday needs of the Library's management, the Syndics were taking a risk. Whatever their feelings of satisfaction (expressed in the following Annual Report), Bradshaw had been placed in a library whose two over-riding needs were for a new catalogue and for the proper arrangement of books that had been stowed away with little regard to the future in the Divinity School on the ground floor. When Romilly first met Bradshaw the following March he was impressed with the manner of a man 'who seems to be heart & soul in his work'.[39] But besides pursuing books wrongly borrowed from the Library, checking booksellers' bills, and supervising the other assistants, Bradshaw proved himself a still less traditional assistant with his discoveries among the Library's manuscripts – of part of Bishop Bedell's Irish Bible once in the Library of Trinity College, Dublin, and now MS. Dd.9.7, and of the tenth-century Book of Deer (MS. Ii.6.32). Not unnaturally, many of his interests remained in Ireland, and in 1857 he was still

---

[38] George Williams to Bradshaw 5 November 1856. See also J. C. T. Oates 'Young Mr. Bradshaw' in D. E. Rhodes (ed.) *Essays in honour of Victor Scholderer* (Mainz 1970) p. 280.
[39] Add. 6837 (Romilly's diary) 11 March 1857.

contemplating the donation of his Irish books inherited from his father to the Royal Irish Academy, rather than to the University Library which became their ultimate home.[40] More seriously, he was not an easy employee. Unwilling to behave conventionally, by his continued absence from the Library in the early months of 1858 Bradshaw forced his friend and supporter George Williams to protest. On 30 June he sent in his resignation, explaining later that he was 'far from well most of this summer, and indeed for many a year past'.[41]

Bradshaw's difficulties were more profound than mere physical illness. Never a great administrator, a man in whom the contradictory extremes of laziness and desperate activity were habitual, possessed of what has been described as 'a monumental capacity for procrastination',[42] he was temperamentally unsuited to what was formally demanded of him, and had not yet found his niche. Before proceeding to the appointment of his successor in December, the Syndics felt it necessary to record what they expected from the Principal Library Assistant: 'to provide for the distribution of the books in proper classes; to examine and correct the accounts for books purchased and for binding; to revise the lists of books sent to be bound; to take care that the binders execute the work committed to them in a satisfactory manner; and also to ascertain that the Collector of Books under the powers of the Copyright Acts sends from time to time to the Library copies of all books, which the University has the power to claim'.[43] In these respects, Bradshaw's successor, the Rev. Alfred William Hobson, an M.A. who had graduated from St John's in 1845, proved admirable.

A major problem was that there so far existed no means of employing Bradshaw in the tasks to which he was most suited, and in which the Library had most to gain. There was, therefore, an element of ingenuity in the formal report from the Syndics on 1 June following, proposing that he should be

---

40 J. H. Todd to Bradshaw 30 March 1857   41 Syndicate Minutes 5 October 1858.
42 Oates 'Young Mr. Bradshaw' p. 279.   43 Syndicate Minutes 15 December 1858.

employed at the nominal sum of twenty pounds per annum to rearrange and supervise the repair of the manuscripts and early printed books.[44] The Grace sanctioning his appointment for two years in this capacity was passed on 9 June, thereby giving Bradshaw virtually free rein to pursue the subjects that had proved dearest to him. He began work on the 15th.[45] Taking advantage of his new position, he also began to set his stamp on the acquisition of early printed books, and rapidly became the acknowledged master of much more pertaining to the Library's collections than simply their reorganization and repair – much of his work with William Blades on Caxton was done during this period[46] – but the arrangement could in truth be no more than temporary. Romilly noted that Bradshaw had a 'sleepy discontented look always';[47] but having secured their objective with the appointment to a newly invented post, the Syndics reported in 1861 that Bradshaw's work had been 'carried out in a highly satisfactory manner', and proposed to increase his salary for two years to £150.[48] Bradshaw was, according to Romilly, 'disgusted' – whether at his salary or at having nothing to do with the administration of the Library he did not record – but he accepted, with a bad grace. A complaint to Quaritch brought a predictable crumb of comfort. 'I am astonished to hear that your Bibliographical knowledge is not better appreciated in Cambridge, and that you have not met yet with such an appointment as would be in harmony with your taste and extensive acquirements.'[49] A further report by the Syndics at the end of the two years fully vindicated their action, and established Bradshaw formally at an increased salary of £200 per annum (the figure, incidentally, that Hobson had attained after only fifteen months).

---

[44] Library papers 1 June 1859; Syndicate Minutes 1 June 1859. See also below, pp. 552–3.
[45] Add. 4593 fo.2.
[46] The later relationship between the two men is discussed in Robin Myers 'William Blades' debt to Henry Bradshaw and G. I. F. Tupper in his Caxton studies; a further look at unpublished documents' *The Library* 5th ser. 33 (1978) pp. 265–83.
[47] Add. 6840 7 July 1860.   [48] Library papers 18 May 1861.
[49] Quaritch to Bradshaw 26 July 1861.

We cannot pass unnoticed the very important assistance which Mr Bradshaw has afforded, not only to members of the University, but also to strangers from a distance, who wish to make use of the Manuscripts or of the older part of the Library of Printed Books for literary purposes. We believe that the presence in the Library of an Officer deeply versed in so important a department of bibliography, not commonly studied, reflects credit on the University.[50]

Bradshaw's position in the Library marked a new departure. But as will have been plain from the above account of the Library's staff in the 1850s and early 1860s, by no means the least of the difficulties with which Power had to wrestle was the future of the Library's catalogue of printed books. Charles C. Babington, in his evidence to the University Commissioners in 1852, spoke of the desirability of transferring the old books belonging to the Botanical Museum (principally the collection of John Martyn) to the University Library,[51] and it was several times suggested that the Library and the Fitzwilliam Museum might come to some amicable agreement on the purchase and maintenance of large works on art history. But such projects demanded reasonable catalogues. Power himself was not alone in recognizing the desirability of a union catalogue of books in the college libraries, though he was realist enough to know that it was impracticable.[52] No attempt was made at such a catalogue, and instead there appeared from among the colleges a thin series of inventories of separate collections of treasures of early printing – none challenging Horne's remarkable achievement in the two-volume catalogue of Queens' library published in 1827.

Within the University Library, and regardless of the rest of the University, there existed two main difficulties, of which the second was realized only gradually. A paper prepared in 1852 on the future management of the Library not only recommended 'that all new Books of any importance whether

---

[50] Library papers 20 May 1863.
[51] Cambridge University Commissioners *Evidence* p. 450. The Botanical Museum sold to the University Library Martyn's copy of Pliny's *Historia naturalis* (Venice 1491) in 1865.
[52] *Evidence* p. 60.

English or Foreign . . . be catalogued and placed on the shelves within a week or ten days after reception', but also had an eye on past misdemeanours: 'That the numerous Books which now stand on the shelves either not catalogued at all, or incompletely so, as well as the costly Books recently locked up, by order of the Syndicate, and others which may hereafter be added to them, be catalogued and collated as the Syndicate has directed, with as little delay as possible.'[53] The great backlog that had accumulated over the previous thirty-odd years – the legacy of increased copyright deposit and of Lodge's willingness to buy on a larger scale than ever before – was one thing, however. The catalogue itself was quite another. The rearrangement of the Library's collections consequent on the opening of the Cockerell Building, and the chaos that accompanied the Fitzwilliam Museum's temporary sojourn in the East Room, combined with Bowtell's failing powers to produce near anarchy in the catalogue. Originally the work of Bowtell himself, it had marked a distinct improvement on the old eighteenth-century catalogue, but by the 1850s it was both showing its age after years of wear, and was also proving to be disarmingly incomplete, quite apart from containing more inaccuracies than were acceptable. In 1853 Francis Bashforth of St John's insisted that a new catalogue, based on re-examination of every volume in the Library, was necessary, and reminded the University that some libraries had found salvation in writing a description of each book on a separate slip of paper that could then be arranged in a series of volumes: by using an anastatic or autographic process, he suggested, it would be easy to produce extra copies of the entries for future use.[54] These several considerations combined to lead to the Syndics' decision in February 1854 to appoint four of their

---

[53] Library papers 24 November 1852.
[54] Francis Bashforth *Observations on some recent university buildings* (Cambridge 1853) p. 28. Bashforth also seems to have been the first to propose that pigeon holes should be provided for new issues of periodicals, so as to make them available to readers more quickly, and that a stamp ('Like that of the Post Office envelopes') would be a better means of marking books than the easily removed bookplates (*ibid.* pp. 28–9).

number to report 'whether any & what steps should be taken to make a fresh Catalogue or Catalogues, systematic or otherwise'.[55] Whatever they had in mind in the last phrase, at the end of March their formal report to the Senate recommended that a new alphabetical catalogue should be constructed, and that – since the existing Library staff could copy out the titles of the books – the only requisite increase in staff was for one person to paste the slips of paper bearing the entries into the catalogue.[56] Strengthened by the addition of J. E. B. Mayor to the sub-syndicate in May 1854, Power and the Syndics secured the services of Robert Fynn, and that summer caused the rules governing the new catalogue to be printed: based on the British Museum rules of 1839, the fifteen Cambridge rules were easily fitted onto two sides of a quarto sheet.

For a while it seemed to be proceeding smoothly. By the time that the Syndics produced their first printed annual report,[57] in February 1855, the new scheme had been in operation for almost twelve months, and they not unnaturally adopted a tone of some self-confidence: 'They now have the satisfaction of reporting that considerable progress has been made in execution of the work: since March 1854, when it was commenced, 9779 slips have been copied and pasted in 16 volumes, 6931 being titles of books, and 3388 cross references. Amongst these titles are included newly arrived Pamphlets and a part of those which had been for a long time accumulating in the Store-rooms.'[58] Not surprisingly, the Syndics were oversanguine, and in their next report, dated 30 March 1856, they were forced to admit 'This work has since continued to advance, although with somewhat less rapidity than was anticipated, owing partly to the ill health of the principal library assistant': production had fallen to 8451 slips. Their remedy, put forward after fourteen more months of unsatisfactory progress, was to appeal for more staff; but the

---

[55] Syndicate Minutes 27 February 1854.   [56] Library papers 27 March 1854.
[57] Again, Bashforth was to the fore in pressing for such a regular formal account of the Library: the Observatory Syndics already did so (Bashforth *Observations* p. 29).
[58] Annual Report 1855.

catalogue sub-syndicate clearly believed that the Library staff could be better organized, and they added one final sentence to their unpublished report to the Syndics: 'The whole question of the best mode of compiling a Catalogue is so extensive and so difficult as to require deliberate consideration before the transcription of the Old Catalogue is commenced.'[59] The old catalogue, dating from the beginning of the century, had thus still to be tackled seriously. Although Heun had begun to revise it, almost everything remained to be done, and the Syndicate told no more than the truth when at the end of May it applied to the Senate for two further staff and spoke of its apprehension that unless immediate action was taken, 'serious inconvenience may result from the decay of the only copy that had any claim to completeness.[60] Not for the last time, the temporary increase in staff which the Syndicate pleaded for, and was granted, proved to be a fantasy: the post of foreign clerk was indeed short-lived, but on the other hand the Library in time possessed not one but several porters to attend the front door.

There was presumably – since it was plain to any reader – no need for the Syndics to comment on two of the most obvious drawbacks to the procedures followed since 1854: first, that a catalogue composed of separate manuscript slips pasted into volumes in alphabetical order, with due space left for future additions, threatened to become unmanageably bulky, and second, that Hart's transcriptions were neither accurate nor clear.[61] The obvious solution, and one that had been suggested but not adopted at the British Museum as recently as 1850, was to have the entries printed. After the Syndics had inspected a specimen of a printed slip for the catalogue, they agreed on 22 May 1861 to a year's trial of the method.[62] The catalogue

---

[59] Syndicate Minutes 27 May 1857.   [60] Library papers 28 May 1857.
[61] Letter from Dennis Hall to E. Atkinson (Vice-Chancellor) 16 February 1863 (Luard 1835–69, no. 86★). For some of the background see also *Report of the Commissioners appointed to inquire into the British Museum* (*Parliamentary papers* 1850. 29), especially the evidence of J. W. Croker (paras 8718 etc.) and Panizzi (paras 9339 etc.).
[62] Syndicate Minutes 8 and 22 May 1861.

approved then has remained in use ever since, and was begun, with some sense of occasion, with the entry for the first volume of William Blades' life of Caxton, published that month. But the abortive attempt to produce a new catalogue in manuscript, followed by what proved to be the more successful and lasting expedient of a printed one, had left the Library with three principle catalogues, the contents of none of which could be easily defined. It was an easy matter to reduce three to two, but the depressing prospect of two catalogues, either of which might contain what was sought, was not to be relieved for many years, since the early nineteenth-century catalogue was not finally abandoned as a reference of last and sometimes desperate resort until the twentieth century. Nonetheless, its incorporation into the new printed catalogue became an immediate goal.

The man most competent to organize this major enterprise, involving the recataloguing of most of the Library, was Dennis Hall, who could offer both imagination and the requisite practical experience. On 16 February 1863, with the new printed catalogue approaching its second birthday, he wrote to Edward Atkinson the Vice-Chancellor:

I replied some time ago, to the inquiry of the Syndics about the 'progress made in incorporating the old catalogue', and stated that, in fact, this 'incorporation' had never even been seriously commenced. Mr Heun began to copy a few titles here & there in a very random & irregular way, but even these amounted altogether to only 100 or 200; since which nothing has been done – i.e. for more than 6 years. And, as we have now adopted the system of *printing* the titles, I presume that the old ones, when copied & corrected, are also to be printed. The annual cost of printing the *new* titles is about £70, the number of fresh titles being about 3000 during the first year since we began printing . . .[63]

Constitutional demands required the Syndics to remark in their annual report that the incorporation of the old and new catalogues had made no progress.[64] Having pressed for and obtained the increase in staff that had been estimated as

[63] Luard 1835–69, no. 86*.   [64] Annual Report 4 March 1863.

sufficient for the project, they had by now little option but to insist that the work was carried through by those already employed in the Library. The recommendations in May 1863 of yet another sub-syndicate, this time of Charles C. Babington, George Williams and H. R. Luard, (see fig. 27a) were too vague to have much impact, though they did confirm that the form of the new catalogue was to be of moveable printed slips and suggested that £500 a year should be set aside towards its cost.[65] But by the end of the year the issue had taken a wholly different turn, and for unexpected reasons.

A report by the Council of the Senate (which had been invested with many of the powers of the old Caput) pointed out that the annual income of the Library had increased, thanks both to the unlooked-for productivity of the Library Tax, and also to improvements in the Library's other resources. As a result, it seemed 'to warrant the conclusion that the Library may be efficiently and satisfactorily maintained and administered without any charge being imposed upon the other resources of the University'; and the Council therefore recommended that the Librarian's stipend should henceforth be charged to the Library Subscription Fund rather than the Chest.[66] In this the Council took a somewhat specialist view of the Library's income, for both the Subscription Fund and the Worts Fund had performed consistently over several years. Nor did it see any need (if it remembered) to remind the University that when in 1856 the Library Syndicate had sought and obtained the Senate's approval to transfer from the Chest to the Library account the cost of insurance, salaries and wages, coal, and capital expenditure such as bookcases, it had done so on the express understanding that the Librarian's stipend should be excluded.[67]

The new recommendations in 1863 had little apparently to do with the delays and difficulties that confronted improvement to the catalogues, but the two were soon dragged together. Only twenty-four hours' notice of a discussion of the

[65] Syndicate Minutes 6 May 1863 etc.   [66] Library papers 16 November 1863.
[67] Library papers 21 February 1856; the Grace was confirmed on 27 February 1856.

report was allowed (it was issued on 18 November, though dated the 16th, and the discussion was on the 19th), and it inflamed J. E. B. Mayor, who immediately caused to be printed a counter-attack that was all the more forceful for the rapidity with which it had been composed. Amidst so much that demanded extra expenditure, whether new buildings for readers and books, more accessions, or replacement of over-worked staff (Hobson had been forced, through ill health, to name a substitute only that month, and was unable to continue full-time), Mayor was moved to sarcasm at the Council's foolishly worded report. 'It is strange,' he wrote, 'that the library tax, bearing as it does, a constant relation to our numbers, should astonish a mathematical university by its unforeseen productiveness, at a time when the complaint is every where heard that those numbers do not advance according to reasonable expectation.' But this was mild, and he reserved most of his rhetoric for the last third of his short pamphlet, the part that dealt with the catalogue:

Indeed the calls of the immediate present are now so imperious, that we seem to have abandoned all hope of overtaking past arrears; the librarian has postponed, apparently to the Greek kalends, the compilation of that new catalogue, which, if we may trust the 'ordinationes', was commenced in 1854 and proposed in 1857.

I think that the council were bound, before asking us in any degree to cripple our existing resources, to enquire why that work remains in abeyance, to which three of the assistants were expressly appointed. If it is found that the work cannot be efficiently done with the present staff, we may perhaps discover a more profitable investment of the subscription funds than that suggested by the council. Those who are acquainted with the management of a library do not need to be reminded that the catalogue is always the main difficulty, involving great expense, patience and skill. Already the promised catalogue has been delayed nearly as long as the capture of Troy; every time we search for a book we are led a chase through two alphabets: let us not, by accepting this hasty report, render it impossible for the syndicate ever to make good its engagement.[68]

Mayor's paper, much of which was echoed by Hobson in a private letter a few days later,[69] had been written in answer to

---

[68] J. E. B. Mayor *To the members of the Senate* (1863).   [69] Luard 1835–69 no. 98c.

the demands of a moment, however much he had already contemplated the subject; and a rejoinder by J. B. Pearson of St John's on 2 December[70] seemed therefore all the more welcome for its folly. It gave Mayor just the opportunity he needed, and a week later he penned a long reply to the Vice-Chancellor, which was reprinted as a pamphlet for the use of the Library Syndicate.[71] Pearson's ill-judged and ill-informed suggestions were easy prey. There could be no argument over whether or not to abandon the old catalogue and incorporate the books listed there in a new one, since it was both so tattered and so crowded that it was no longer in proper alphabetical order – and thus the cause of duplicates having been bought needlessly. Pearson's proposal that both catalogues should be continued concurrently, 'taking the old Catalogue as the Catalogue of books to be found in the Library previous (say) to the year 1853', the date at which the new catalogue was commenced, provoked Mayor to particular scorn:

By all means accept the existence of the two catalogues as a fact, in the same way in which you accept any other abuse and nuisance as a fact, viz. by getting rid of it with all convenient speed. If however Mr Pearson thinks that the old catalogue contains the titles of all books to be found in the library before 1853, he is doubly mistaken. Some, at least, of such books were transferred to the new catalogue by Mr Heun, and many later accessions have been entered in the old catalogue. But it appears from what follows that what Mr Pearson hankers after is a catalogue, not of the library as it existed at the end of 1852, but of all books, no matter when acquired, published before that date. It is needless to insist on the objections to this project. It would leave no known place for undated books; it would separate two editions of the same book, and even two volumes of the same series; it would saddle us for ever with two concurrent catalogues, each receiving continual accessions; nay Mr Pearson even threatens such of us as shall then be alive with another epoch (1875), when we shall have to hunt through a third catalogue. Why not a fourth and fifth, and so on to infinity?

The same question has faced every large library since, and still allows no easy reply, but Mayor's views were quite

---

[70] Cam. d. 863.12.   [71] Library papers 9 December 1863.

properly influenced by the appalling condition of the old catalogue. He went on to suggest in detail how recataloguing might be induced to show some progress; and to oppose publication of the catalogue because it would serve no useful purpose, would offer an invitation to theft, would be difficult to correct, and would require more detail (and so compete with Brunet and other similar compilations) than the straightforward finding list that the University itself needed. The arguments had much in common with the evidence heard by the British Museum Commissioners in 1848–9. Mayor claimed to have consulted most of the recent authorities on librarianship; he quoted Augustus de Morgan on the speed at which books could be catalogued, and (with approval) S. R. Maitland's introduction to the catalogue of the early printed books at Lambeth setting out his principles for publishing catalogues and bibliographies; and he estimated that if his scheme of employing four 'editors' (drawn from the Library's staff) was employed, there could be two identical catalogues of most of the printed books in the Library by 1872.

Rarely, if ever, had the internal management of the Library been subjected to such public, detailed and lengthy scrutiny by an outsider. Mayor was no longer a Syndic, having come to the end of his term in 1862, but he remained committed to the improvement of the Library as he saw it, and impatient of obstacles in his way. The degree to which he thought of his diatribe (ostensibly on the subjects of a stipend and a catalogue) within the wider context of the Library's general well-being emerged in his remarks on security – 'Probably there is no large library in the world less protected than ours' – and on Bradshaw's work with the early books, on the need to compile a catalogue of duplicates that could be offered for exchange, on the seemingly endless proliferation of newly concocted classes (Sm[all] and Sc[hool] books being the latest), and in his final suggestion that plans should be displayed of the Library's arrangement. Less than three months later Power had resigned, and Mayor had succeeded him as Librarian. The question of the new catalogue had not been settled by Mayor's pamphlet, but he was a man convinced of what he wanted, and one who had the energy to pursue it.

The main catalogue of printed books inevitably attracted most publicity within the University, as the largest and most unwieldy single item that challenged all readers' ingenuity and patience. But it was not the only catalogue. The music which had been received under the Copyright Act, or (occasionally) bought, had for the most part been unceremoniously dumped on shelves on the ground floor for half a century or more. But the expenditure of over £50 from the Rustat Fund for music from the library of Thomas Attwood Walmisley following his death in 1856 suggested that the Library had taken a fundamental decision to treat the subject more seriously. Walmisley had dominated Cambridge music for twenty years, and done much to improve music in the college chapels, and the Library responded.[72] In June 1856 the Syndicate accepted Hall's offer to prepare a catalogue of the music 'for a sum not exceeding £12'.[73] By February 1858 they could report good progress, that the more important material had been found, that a class catalogue had been prepared, and that Hall was about to begin an alphabetical catalogue.[74] When he finished his work in 1861 he estimated that the class catalogues contained over 17,000 separate titles or pieces of music.[75] He was rewarded with £25 rather than £12, having set the collection on its feet.

The project to compile a new catalogue of the manuscripts in the Library was however of somewhat longer standing than either Hall's work on the music or the labours of the staff generally on the catalogues of printed books. It had proved impossible to publish the descriptions of them prepared by

[72] The purchase from Walmisley's library included full scores of *Elijah* and *St Paul*, Haydn's *Seasons*, *Fidelio*, *Il seraglio*, Beethoven's symphonies and Masses in C and D, works by Spohr, Cherubini, Hummel and Corelli, and four volumes of Bach, for whom Walmisley had a particular admiration.
[73] Syndicate Minutes 16 June 1856.   [74] Annual Report 17 February 1858.
[75] *Memorandum to the Syndicate 6 February 1861*, Luard 1835–69 no. 74d.

James Nasmith in the 1790s,[76] and the only printed accounts that had appeared since were neither authoritative nor complete. George Dyer had broken new ground in 1824, in *The Privileges of the University of Cambridge*, but he was far from comprehensive; Gustav Hänel had ignored the University Library in his *Catalogi* of the manuscripts of a large part of western Europe in 1830; and despite its title C. H. Hartshorne's *Book rarities in the University of Cambridge* (1829) had scarcely mentioned the existence of a manuscript collection at all. The standard reference to the collection therefore still remained Bernard's *Catalogi*, over a century and a half old, woefully incomplete even for its time, and desperately in need of replacement. Moreover, even within the Library the staff seem to have been shy of using Nasmith's handwritten catalogue, since it bears noticeably few signs of wear. If any further support was needed for a new catalogue, the demands of a generation who had become accustomed to different ways of looking at manuscripts, and who brought requirements and interests scarcely envisaged even fifty years before, could not easily be ignored. The popularizing work of men such as J. O. Westwood, who in his *Palaeographia sacra pictoria* (1843–5) reproduced several of the Library's main treasures, had begun to draw general attention to the illuminated manuscripts at Cambridge. Joseph Ritson and Robert Jamieson had explored the collection for ballads and early popular literature, and the Maitland Club, the Camden Society, the Chetham Society, and the Percy Society had all published major manuscripts from the Library. Biblical, classical and historical research brought ever new demands for proper and convenient documentation of the relative textual importance of each manuscript, essential if discussions and discoveries were not to be in danger of being buried and virtually irretrievable. And yet the sole attempt at a separate printed catalogue was the work not of the Library staff, but of a private individual. When

---

[76] See above, pp. 343–8.

James Orchard Halliwell's *Manuscript rarities of the University of Cambridge* was published by Thomas Rodd in 1841, its author was only twenty-one years old, yet already a Fellow of both the Society of Antiquaries and of the Royal Society. The rumours of his thefts of scientific manuscripts from Trinity College became general only in 1845;[77] and although the University Library continued to buy his privately printed editions of English literature there could be no question of his continuing the work he had begun on its manuscripts. Halliwell had in any case declined to proceed further, preferring to leave his uncompletd work (and his scheme for a union catalogue of manuscripts in Cambridge) to more proper authorities. Despite its title, his modestly sized book was in fact a systematic catalogue, fuller than anything previously published, of the western manuscripts in classes Dd to Ff. But it never gained wide acceptance even within the library that had most to benefit, and no mention was apparently made of Halliwell's work when the question of a new catalogue of manuscripts was raised in the 1850s.

Halliwell's catalogue apart, there also existed one other separately published recent guide of a more specialist nature. The *Index to the Baker manuscripts*, published under the auspices of the Cambridge Antiquarian Society in 1848, covered Thomas Baker's collections at both Cambridge and the British Museum, and was the work of four men, J. J. Smith, Charles C. Babington, C. W. Goodwin and Power; but it had never been conceived as a unit of a larger whole, and had in fact been compiled simply to meet the needs of the society. In no sense could it be called a catalogue.

In October 1849 the entire collection of manuscripts was moved to the Cockerell Building, into premises that were neither adequate as regards available space nor suitable as regards the shelves onto which they were bundled. But whether the space was adequate or not, the wish to display the

---

[77] Cf. D. A. Winstanley 'Halliwell Phillipps and Trinity College library' *The Library* 5th ser. 2 (1948) pp. 250–82.

manuscripts in the newest part of the Library seems also to have suggested the need for a new catalogue. On 11 December 1850 the Senate approved a Grace to the effect that a catalogue was to be made at the expense of the University Press, and by the end of February sufficient agreement had been reached for the Press Syndics to consider the principal proposals as to the standards thought desirable. The five signatories to the discussion paper were headed by Churchill Babington, and two of the other three were also to be contributors to the catalogue finally published: Charles Hardwick (the main instigator of the project), William Wayman Hutt of Caius, the son of a local bookseller, and William R. Collett, whose catalogue of the early printed books in Caius had been published in 1850. They proposed that the language of the catalogue should be Latin, as had been those of James, Bernard and Nasmith before them (and, incidentally, as the Bodleian Quarto catalogues still were), and that so far as possible each description of the manuscripts should include eight particulars: the material on which it was written, its size, the number of pages (and columns and lines to a page), the style or styles of handwriting, its probable age, traces – if any – of the original owner and its subsequent history, its present condition, and, lastly, whether it had been published or its text collated.[78] The *incipits* and *explicits* of each text were to be quoted.

By no means all the entries in the published catalogue conform with these ambitious standards. But the chief recommendation to be challenged was that descriptions should be in Latin, a language not only traditional for catalogues of this kind but also still and for many years later the medium of communication between several Cambridge scholars and colleagues in Scandinavia. English carried the day, however, with one exception. By 1852 Preston had finished his catalogue of Burckhardt's oriental manuscripts. His catalogue followed similar ones for those of the British Museum and the Bodleian,

---

[78] Luard 1835–69 no. 31**.

and on his own admission was modelled on Dozy's catalogues of Arabic manuscripts at Leiden, published in 1851. For these, quite apart from other, linguistic, reasons, Preston pleaded that his work at least should be published in Latin. Its appearance in 1853 did not affect the larger project to catalogue the western manuscripts, and Preston's half-hearted suggestion that the English manuscripts should be described in English and the classical in Latin found as little sympathy as he expected.[79]

At first it was suggested that, as in the past, the task of describing the manuscripts should be the responsibility of one man; had the University agreed to this it might have saved itself much anguish. The person proposed, the antiquary Joseph Stevenson, had learnt his trade in the British Museum, the Record Commission, and the Cathedral Library at Durham, and had already more than demonstrated his industry in a long list of publications. In 1849 he had moved from Durham to Leighton Buzzard in Bedfordshire, and his new-found proximity to Cambridge (aided by the new railway lines) must have seemed to some an ideal opportunity. To others, however, it seemed that the only appropriate method lay in a team approach, where each member could offer his own particular knowledge: on these grounds, and (so Bradshaw was told) on the grounds that Stevenson was not a member of the University, it was decided that a multitude was better than an individual.[80]

By the end of 1851 eight people had been found to tackle the four thousand-odd western manuscripts in the Library. Charles Hardwick, who became editor, headed the list, and was followed by Churchill Babington, H. A. Woodham of Jesus (author of a short work on university and college heraldry for the Cambridge Antiquarian Society), John E. Cooper (who had signed the original document, but who did not in the end contribute formally), Preston (almost *ex officio*, since his interests were oriental), W. R. Collett of Caius, C. W.

---

[79] Letter from T. Preston 30 January 1852 (University Archives Pr.B.4.1).
[80] Memorandum by Bradshaw, 'Further suggestions on the MS. Department of the Public Library', Add. 6419.

Goodwin of St Catharine's, and J. Goodwin. By the time the first volume was published in 1856 the team had changed considerably. Despite alterations, however, the work pressed ahead at first with extraordinary rapidity. Hardwick was apologetic for the lack of obvious progress in his report to the Vice-Chancellor in November 1852, but the team had by then already been through all the manuscripts and had seen one sheet of the final catalogue off to press. The project slipped more seriously into arrears over the following twelve months. Neither C. W. Goodwin nor J. Goodwin was resident, and their absence caused delays to work on the legal and medical manuscripts. Cooper left Cambridge in 1853 to become rector of a Norfolk parish, his place being taken by C. B. Scott of Trinity, F. J. A. Hort, and W. W. Howard of Sidney Sussex. In addition, Woodham had relinquished his work on the heraldic manuscripts to Charles C. Babington, who as it transpired could offer too little expertise. Indeed, so depressed had Hardwick become by June 1854 that he placed his resignation in the hands of the Vice-Chancellor on bringing to completion his own work on the Anglo-Saxon, Anglo-Norman and early English items. The response of the Press Syndics allowed no such retreat, however. Instead, they appointed Hardwick formally as General Editor, gave him authority over the other cataloguers, and told him to procure further contributors as he thought necessary. They were determined that their intentions should not be frustrated, and while ordering twice-termly reports on progress, also announced that printing was to begin at the start of the following Michaelmas Term and was to proceed at the rate of not less than a sheet a week. Printing began as planned soon after the opening of term, and though it proved – not unexpectedly – impossible to maintain the pace set by the Syndicate at first, this had been remedied by the following summer: on 1 June Hardwick was able to report that it was 'not improbable' that the first volume, describing class Dd, would be completed by the end of the Easter Term.[81]

81 Details from University Archives Pr.B.4.1.

Unwilling to disappoint the Press Syndics, he did not then mention publication, and the preparation of an introduction setting out the history of the collection occupied the next several months. With Romilly's help, it was finished on 1 January 1856, and as the first serious contribution to the earliest history of the Library fully deserved Romilly's praise when three weeks later he read what Hardwick had written.[82]

With the pace now established, the second volume appeared in 1857, and the third in 1858. The project remained prey to the vagaries of contributors' careers and interests, but so much had been accomplished between 1851 and 1856 that the alterations to the lists of contributors at the front of each volume were happily few. H. R. Luard had joined the team that tackled the theological manuscripts before the publication of the first volume. The scientific and medical manuscripts had been initially the province of J. H. Webster, until his practice as a doctor at Northampton forced him to withdraw: his place was taken by John Glover, chaplain of Trinity until he became college librarian in 1858, and who latterly also worked on the historical collections.[83] And in the third volume appeared for the first time the name of Edward Ventris, priest-in-charge of Stow cum Quy since 1825, who collaborated with Glover and Luard on the historical portion and with Professor Abdy on the legal.

All this had been accomplished not, as might be expected, by the Library Syndicate, but by the Press Syndicate, who undertook it in 1851 when the Library was still encumbered with debts from the new buildings, whereas the Press was eager to find projects in which to invest sums from the Government Annuity Fund, established since 1782 with the annual sum paid to the University in compensation for the loss

---

[82] Add. 6836 (Romilly's diary) 14 December 1855 and 21 January 1856.

[83] Glover added further to the variety of his achievements by working with W. G. Clark on the Cambridge Shakespeare in 1863 and editing a volume for the Rolls Series in 1865. He was succeeded in the Wren Library by William Aldis Wright in 1863, on being presented to a living in the Isle of Wight. (R. Sinker *Biographical notes on the librarians of Trinity College* (Cambridge 1897) pp. 75–6).

of their restrictive privilege to print almanacs. By the end of the 1850s, however, the Press Syndics had become concerned at their over-enthusiastic expenditure from the fund, and sought to trim demands on it.[84] By the time that the third volume of the manuscripts catalogue was published in 1858, editorial and production costs of the three main volumes and of the Burckhardt catalogue had reached over £1600. In order to disembarrass their funds, the Press Syndics therefore proposed that the Library Syndicate should meet the editorial costs, both those already incurred and those still to come.[85] Financial considerations thus conspired with the death of Hardwick in a climbing accident in the Pyrenees in August 1859 to cause a delay before the publication of the fourth volume. The interval was marked by a long memorandum[86] from Bradshaw on the errors so far made in the preparation of the catalogue. He was bitterly critical of the decision to distribute the entries among several amateur compilers without any proper professional supervision, 'which last is especially a Librarian's work, and requires considerable experience, and I do not hesitate to say cannot be done satisfactorily by an amateur'. Again he adverted to the especial importance of the one man whose '*business*' it is to provide descriptions, as opposed to casual workers who could offer only their leisure time: such an arrangement would not only have benefited the scholarly world and the Library, but would also have saved money. The mistakes and omissions in describing some of the most important manuscripts in the Library only confirmed his view. Of Bedell's Irish Bible (Dd.9.7) 'not a word is said even of what language the book is written in, nor any reference to any work on the subject'. The first (and subsequently discarded) description of Ii.6.32 (the Book of Deer) had claimed that the script was Anglo-Saxon, and had failed to recognize the importance of the Gaelic. And even after the description of the Cambridge Juvencus (Ff.4.42) had been revised so as to mention the Welsh

---

[84] S. C. Roberts *The evolution of Cambridge publishing* (Cambridge 1956) pp. 23, 34–5.
[85] Library Syndicate, printed paper dated 30 November 1858.   [86] Add. 6419.

547

and Irish marginalia, the catalogue still persisted in calling them Breton.[87]

The fourth volume, when it appeared, brought descriptions down to the end of class Oo and thus the end of the main series of western manuscripts. It was not published until 1866, Luard having taken over the editorship. By then Charles C. Babington had ceased to supply descriptions of the heraldic manuscripts, after some criticism of his work, and two new principal contributors had been enlisted for the few 'monastic cartularies &c.' as the acknowledgements put it: Thomas Bendyshe and George Williams, both of King's, the one a barrister, a journalist of unusually eclectic interests and a man whose opinions many found perverse, and the other a more conventional figure in that he had been Vice-Provost of his college in 1854–7 but whose travels had implanted in him sympathy for the Orthodox church and made him an accepted authority on the Holy Land. Bradshaw's work on several of the manuscripts was also acknowledged, and the printing of a series of corrigenda to the entire catalogue in the fifth volume, published in February 1867, provided a further opportunity for some of his more important discoveries to be aired. Meanwhile with the publication in 1864 of a much slimmer volume describing the printed books with adversaria in the manuscript classes, the achievement of Luard and Churchill Babington, the entire project (at least as regards western manuscripts) was complete. The fifth volume contained full accounts of the Baumgartner papers, only recently acquired,[88] of the Baker manuscripts (a labour of devotion by J. E. B. Mayor), and everything else that so far existed of the new numbering scheme of the series of Additional manuscripts, down to MS. Add. 337. For several years a manuscript index

---

[87] For Bradshaw's work on the Juvencus see his paper 'On the oldest written remains of the Welsh language' repr. in his *Collected papers* (Cambridge 1889) pp. 281–5, and his remarks in the Appendix, pp. 454–5 etc. See also Oates *History* pp. 342–6 and J. C. T. Oates 'Notes on the later history of the oldest manuscript of Welsh poetry: the Cambridge Juvencus' *Cambridge Medieval Celtic Studies* 3 (1982) pp. 81–7. [88] See p. 595.

had been available to the curious in the Library, and later in 1867 this was put into a more permanent form with the publication of Luard's *Index*, prefixed by an account of those manuscripts Luard considered most interesting or important: his preface was none the less impressive, as the first modern attempt of its kind, for failing to mention some of the most noteworthy volumes in the collection.

That the catalogue of manuscripts thus published between 1856 and 1867 still remains unrevised and the fullest account to have been printed is perhaps a dubious accolade. But there is no doubting its achievement in the nineteenth century. No other large library in the country could boast so full a description of all its western manuscripts, and for historians in particular it presented an obvious boon in, for example, the detailed account of the thousands of letters and documents preserved in the Library. By no means all manuscripts were described equally well. Apart from the different talents and knowledge of the various contributors, not all manuscripts had been sufficiently studied for their places in their subjects to be properly established. Classical texts had commanded more attention than literary or medical; and while many of the latter remain little explored even today, the work of the Early English Text Society under the enthusiastic direction of F. J. Furnivall (and the more discreet guidance from a distance of Bradshaw) was to transform knowledge of Middle English texts within two decades. Many of the more serious omissions were discovered in time to be included in the corrigenda of the final volume: Luard, for example, had failed to recognize that MS. Dd.5.5 had been prepared for Mary de Saint Pol, Countess of Pembroke, the foundress of Pembroke College, and dated the manuscript wrongly to the fifteenth century; the erased inscription in MS. Ff.4.11, a copy of Stephen Langton's commentary on Ecclesiastes, had defeated first attempts to decipher it, but by 1867 it had been identified as recording the gift of the book to Balliol College by the founder of the college library, William Gray (this manuscript too had been wrongly dated, as fifteenth- rather than early thirteenth-century);[89] the detailed description of MS. Ee.3.60, a fourteenth-century register from Bury St Edmunds, was riddled with misreadings; Chaucer's *Man of Law's tale* had not been recognized in MS. Ee.2.15;[90] the textual interest of MS. Ff.5.31, a copy of the Golden Legend dated only a year after its author's death, had been missed; and it remained to be pointed out that a portion of MS. Ee.4.35 (a poetical miscellany), described simply as '"Fabula", i.e. a story' was a well-known poem that also appeared in MS. Ff.2.38.[91]

Nevertheless several old ghosts had been laid to rest. One of the most notorious absurdities, which the Library had insisted on parading to foreign visitors, occurred in MS. Nn.4.1, a Flemish Benedictional once the property of the Abbot of Les Dunes, near Ostend, and still in its early sixteenth-century blind-stamped binding. In 1799 I. K. Baldrey, a local printseller, had published a reproduction of one of the illuminations, describing the volume as a missal and attributing the decoration firmly to Giulio Clovio, contemporary of Raphael. Thirty years later, the volume by then identified as a book of hours, J. D. Passavant saw it, and despite the attribution at the end of the volume to Clovio thought it 'aus der altniederländischen Schule'; Waagen, similarly sceptical, also pronounced it Flemish, and in the printed catalogue the fashionable eighteenth-century attribution to Clovio had been finally terminated with a damning exclamation mark.[92] Other

---

[89] See now R. A. B. Mynors *Catalogue of the manuscripts of Balliol College Oxford* (Oxford 1963) p. 378; the manuscript (one of two copies of the same gloss given to Balliol by Gray) was at Cambridge by 1556/7.

[90] An omission speedily noticed by the reviewer of the second volume of the catalogue in the *Athenaeum*, 5 September 1857 p. 115. The first volume had been reviewed in the same journal on 7 March 1857, p. 305.

[91] Bradshaw's own annotated copies of the catalogue are now Adv.c.77.39– and Adv.c.77.52; Luard's (identifying those responsible for each entry) is Adv.c.87.1–.

[92] J. D. Passavant *Kunstreise durch England und Belgien* (Frankfurt am Main 1833) p. 205; G. Waagen *Treasures of art in Great Britain* (1854) 3 p. 452. A copy of Baldrey's engraving is in the Manuscripts Department. The cult of Giulio Clovio is discussed in A. N. L. Munby *Connoisseurs and medieval miniatures 1750–1850* (Oxford 1972) pp. 24–6 *et passim*.

errors had crept, more seriously, into works of reference. With some hesitation, for example, Thomas Tanner had included an entry on Thomas de Drayton in his *Bibliotheca Britannico-Hibernica* on the basis of an inscription in one of John Moore's manuscripts, now MS. Gg.2.18, described in Bernard as 'Memoriale Johannis de Draytone Monachi': the book was nothing other than a copy of the Golden Legend, given to Winchester in the thirteenth or fourteenth century by a monk of that name,[93] and although some of these facts were only discovered later, the new printed catalogue did kill off an author who had never existed and establish the true identity of the text.

Although Hardwick and, later, Luard, attempted to impose some uniformity on the descriptions of a miscellaneous and varied collection, and had before them the instructions laid down in 1851, the finished catalogue lacked the discipline that had once been promised. It set new standards in England in many respects, but in others it was less organized than work already appearing on the continent.[94] Descriptions of illustrations were frequently inadequate, and of rubrication barely existent; bindings were seldom mentioned save on the few occasions – such as the copy of the Golden Legend just mentioned – when they were especially decorative; and despite the 1851 instructions details of provenance were recorded only at whim. It fell to Bradshaw not only to correct collations, but also to establish which had come from Richard Holdsworth's library in 1664.

Bradshaw was elected University Librarian within a few days of the publication of the last volume. In the previous ten years he had come to know the manuscripts better than anyone before him, and although he barely figured in the list of contributors Luard did no more than justice when in February

---

[93] Thomas Tanner *Bibliotheca Britannico-Hibernica* (1748) p. 233; Ker *Medieval libraries* p. 316.

[94] Cf., for example, J. Mangéart's *Catalogue descriptif et raisonné des manuscrits de la Bibliothèque de Valenciennes* (Paris 1860).

1867 he presented the report on the fifth volume to the Library Syndics:

It is believed that now every M.S. in the Library and every book with M.S. notes or Adversaria has been examined and catalogued. And the Editor also hopes that the defects and errors which have been observed or pointed out in the earlier volumes of the Catalogue will be found to be remedied by the Corrigenda. For this purpose no pains have been spared – many of the MSS. have been again completely gone through, and any deficiencies or errors which have been discovered have been corrected . . . The Editor cannot speak of this part of his work without mentioning to the Syndics the very great assistance he has received from M^r. Bradshaw, to whom many of the most important corrigenda are due, and who has brought together the scattered MSS from different parts of the Library in such a way as to make the arrangement and cataloguing of the additional MSS. a comparatively easy task.[95]

Bradshaw had not been alone in his unease at the state of many of the older books in the Library, and in Luard had a sympathetic and powerful ally. 'The bindings of the greater part of the MSS', wrote Luard in a memorandum to the Syndics in 1858, 'are in a most disgraceful condition: the backs or sides often being loose – many leaves in the same state – & in some instances so as to seriously endanger the preservation of the MS. Again the material of the leather is such as to make it impossible to handle many of the MSS. without everything w^h. which it comes in contact being soiled . . . Many leaves are often misplaced by the carelessness of the binder, and parts of the same treatise are sometimes bound in two separate volumes & placed in separate shelves.' As for the lettering on the spines, in some instances it seemed ignorant and in others ridiculous. The twelfth-century Winchester Pontifical (MS. Ee.2.3), for example, was lettered 'Missalia', and 'Romish Devotion' also caught Luard's eye, while there was even a copy of the Canterbury Tales labelled as Piers Plowman. And so inadequate were the shelves that not only were volumes crammed in haphazardly, but also the whole of class Dd.13, including the handsome copy of Cicero, written out in the mid-fifteenth

---

[95] Syndicate Minutes 12 February 1867.

century by Theoderic Werken for William Gray, was simply kept on the floor. The need for the shelves to be enlarged as appropriate, the manuscripts to be dusted periodically, and for them to be thoroughly examined preparatory to repairs was obvious, and there would be no better opportunity than now, when the work could be done under the superintendence of those preparing the catalogues.[96] To execute Luard's recommendations, and to put the manuscripts in order, were Bradshaw's first tasks. Some errors were beyond recall, and there remain several instances of two volumes of the same work being placed apart in the collection. Nor, despite Luard's apparent understanding of the subject, were the manuscripts always repaired with the sympathy which he seemed to imply in commenting, 'Of course all MSS notes, marks of ancient ownership, or old class marks in the covers, or *outside*, if such there be, will be carefully preserved.' In too many cases, the contents, boards and pastedowns went three different ways.

Two years later, this wretched picture had begun to alter for the better, and Bradshaw had even begun to tackle the early printed books in the Library to the same purpose. When asked to give an account of himself he emphasized first the practical aspects of his work, collating and organizing the work of the binder:

The Manuscripts (except those in Archdeacon Lewis's Cabinet) have now been all brought together, and have been placed upon the shelves, according to their labels. The same has been done for the printed books in Class AB.

A great number of volumes which require binding have been carefully collated for the purpose, & several have been partly bound; and if the Syndics will allow the books to go out of the Library to Nutt's or Wiseman's as they did formerly, the work will progress much more satisfactorily, and I feel sure that there will be no greater risk than there is at present.

The greater portion of the manuscripts require to be lettered properly, being now labelled 'Tracts MS.', if not something more likely to mislead. This part of the work cannot be done on the premises, because (1) Fynn

---

[96] Memorandum to Syndicate 18 May 1858: Luard 1835–69, no. 70*.

says he cannot do this part of the business, and (2) there is no way of supplying the Library with the ordinary appliances for this kind of binders work.

Further – the Old Library, known as the Star-Classes (A★ to S★), and occupying the upper story of the West, North and South rooms, is still in the condition in which I found the Manuscripts, and Class AB; that is, the books are *stowed away* on the shelves, so that the Class marks do not in any way point to the places on the shelves.

A great deal may be done towards remedying this, without much disturbance, if the Syndics think fit. Even apart from this, there is work enough to occupy me some time longer.[97]

The very fact that this work was being done by a person naturally of an enquiring mind, and increasingly well informed, had its corollary, and it was one that was only confirmed by the publication of the catalogue of manuscripts and the attendant publicity thus given to the collections.

There is still the same crying need in the Library of some one whose duty it is to be on the spot, and to be able & ready to give information so as to render the older portion of the Library more available to enquirers than it has been hitherto. Every year the want is more and more felt, and the experience of the last five years here compels me to say what had come better from any one else, were there any one else in the Library to make the representation.[98]

The printed report of the Syndics which two years later, in 1863, ushered in the Grace to increase Bradshaw's salary to £200 added little to his own estimate, save that it reported further progress, placed officially before the University the need to arrange and make proper provision for the incunabula and other rare books, and gave due acknowledgement to Bradshaw's achievement as guide to the collections – a task which involved a concept of librarian that was not yet familiar in Cambridge.[99] By then Bradshaw was the established authority on the older books in the Library, and had proved himself not only by the help he had given to enquirers but also by a series of discoveries of his own. Investigation into the Book of Deer had brought him the acquaintance (and later friendship) of Lord Lindsay, whose curiosity about Bradshaw

---

[97] Memorandum by Bradshaw, 15 June 1861: Luard 1835–69, no. 78(4).
[98] *Ibid.*   [99] Library papers 20 May 1863.

was aroused not least by the fact that Haigh Hall had once been in the possession of the Bradshaw family;[100] he had been of crucial help to F. H. Scrivener in preparing an edition of the Codex Bezae;[101] his attack on Simonides' claims to have written the Codex Sinaiticus had both been damning and had carried the tone of authority;[102] and he had contributed fundamentally and immeasurably (literally, since the details are still not all clear) to William Blades' life of Caxton published in 1861–3.[103] These were by no means all, but among the multitude of other topics that his position in the Library had forced on him none was to engage his interest more than the history of the liturgy, for which he had already some sympathy. F. A. Paley's challenge in the course of a long account of Cambridge manuscripts in the young Sir John Acton's newly founded journal *The Home and Foreign Review* in 1862 was well placed, well timed, and well aimed, when it stated that – Maskell, Daniel Rock and Lingard apart – 'probably there are but few now, among even the Catholics of this country, who have ever made any researches into the extensive department of medieval Church-offices, or who have a conception of their variety, or the changes they have undergone in name, matter, and arrangement according to local uses, and before the general introduction of the Roman uniformity'.[104] In all these different subjects, Bradshaw's professional obligations and his own private interests merged indistinguishably. By the end of 1863 he had made the acquaintance of F. J. Furnivall, who was to found the Early English Text Society in 1864 and the Chaucer Society in 1867, and in 1864 he began seriously to collate versions of the Canterbury Tales in preparation for an edition that was never to be finished.[105] By 1867, the date of Mayor's resignation as

[100] Lindsay to Bradshaw 20 December 1860.
[101] F. H. Scrivener (ed.) *Bezae codex Cantabrigiensis* (Cambridge 1864).
[102] Prothero *Bradshaw* pp. 95–8.   [103] Myers 'William Blades' debt' pp. 265–83.
[104] *Home and Foreign Review* I (1862) p. 473.
[105] On Bradshaw and Furnivall see D. S. Brewer 'Furnivall and the old Chaucer Society' *Chaucer Newsletter* I ii (1979) pp. 2–6, and Donald C. Baker 'The evolution of Henry Bradshaw's idea of the order of the *Canterbury Tales' Chaucer Newsletter* 3i (1981) pp. 2–6.

Librarian, he had also identified the long 'lost' Vaudois manuscripts brought to Cambridge in the seventeenth century by Samuel Morland and established their true date as fifteenth- rather than thirteenth-century,[106] had begun to tackle the oriental manuscripts with the help of a smattering of the principal languages, and on his election to the Roxburghe Club in 1866 had embarked on an edition of the English version of Guillaume de Deguilleville's *Pélerinage de la vie humaine* – which he felt obliged to relinquish on his election as University Librarian.[107] His work on John Barbour, centred on the mistaken belief that two Library manuscripts contained hitherto unknown poems by the author of *The Bruce*, had been presented to the Cambridge Antiquarian Society in 1866, and published in its *Communications*: the attributions were not disproved in print until the year of his death, and it was characteristic of Bradshaw that his own projected edition was never completed, the poems instead being published in Heilbronn in 1881–2.[108] In the case of Barbour he was mistaken, but the discoveries were made in the course of a systematic survey of the early English poetical miscellanies in the Library. This class of manuscripts tended to present particularly recalcitrant problems of codicology and identification, but the work had an especial relevance to the demands of Furnivall as well as both English and, increasingly, German, philologists, besides his own work on the early English printed books.

---

[106] The most convenient summary of this is J. H. Todd *The books of the Vaudois. The Waldensian manuscripts preserved in the library of Trinity College Dublin, with an appendix* (1865). See also Oates *History* pp. 283–8, and Bradshaw *Collected papers* pp. 1–15.

[107] Edited from MS. Ff.5.30. It was finally published as a Club book, edited by W. Aldis Wright, in 1869.

[108] C. Horstmann (ed.) *Barbour's Des Schottischen Nationaldichters Legendensammlung nebst den Fragmenten seines Trojanerkrieges* 2 vols. (Heilbronn 1881–2). The attributions of MSS. Gg.2.6 and Kk.5.30 were easily disproved by E. Köppel 'Die Fragmente von Barbour's Trojanerkriege' *Englische Studien* 10 (1887) pp. 373–82 and P. Buss 'Sind die von Horstmann herausgegeben schottischen Legenden ein Werk Barbour's?' *Anglia* 9 (1886) pp. 493–514. Bradshaw's error was so respectfully pointed out by W. W. Skeat (*The Bruce* EETS 1870–99 pp. xliii-l) that a casual reading might suggest that Bradshaw had not been misled at all.

His first official responsibilities had been to the manuscripts; but it was the needs of the printed books that had caused him to write to Heun in 1855.[109] The identification in 1863 of the unique Paris copy of the vellum Sarum Breviary printed in Venice in 1483 as the same that had once belonged to the Library was a minor triumph of detective work.[110] It was a result of Bradshaw's gradual piecing together of the Library's history, and also of his self-imposed task to bring together all the incunables for proper study and protection. 'Real bibliographers are very scarce in this country,' he wrote to J. W. Holtrop in The Hague in March 1864, 'and the study of Incunabula is never carried out in a satisfactory way.'[111] Besides the organization of the Library's early printed books, he had also embarked on a course that was eventually to have a profound effect on incunable studies. Blades' work on Caxton, following what Bradshaw termed a 'natural history' method in grouping together books according to their types, had differed in its approach from Holtrop's own catalogue of the Royal Library at The Hague, published in 1856, though Bradshaw realized that he saw in both books the results of the same method: 'It is not until you get a book like his [Blades'] Caxton or your own *Catalogus*,' he explained to Holtrop, 'where a large number of books is ranged simply and methodically according to their *natural* order, and in print (this last is most important) – that you can really set to work upon a proper basis.'[112] By analysing the contents of a series of major sales of incunabula from the Low Countries in the next twenty years Bradshaw was able at once to advance his own studies and to create a collection in some respects unmatched in Britain.

[109] See above, pp. 524–6.
[110] Prothero *Bradshaw* pp. 101–2; George Williams to Bradshaw 19 May 1863.
[111] Bradshaw *Correspondence* I p. 26.
[112] Bradshaw to Holtrop 21 March 1864, *Correspondence* I p. 49.

14

THE COPYRIGHT AGENCY

FEW EVENTS IN POWER'S LIBRARIANSHIP were of more lasting importance than the alterations to arrangements for copyright deposit, which not for the first time involved co-operation between the privileged libraries, and the results of which remain intact even today.

It could scarcely be claimed by any party that the legislation botched together in 1814 worked to anyone's satisfaction, while it failed singularly to assuage the argument over what seemed to many to be the rapacity of the libraries. In emphasis of his opinions, as well as to save expense, John Britton announced in 1826 that he planned to issue only the plates of George Fennell Robson's *Picturesque views of the English cities*, and to publish the related letterpress as a separate work: in this way he would avoid the need to deposit copies.[1] John Nash's *Royal Pavilion at Brighton*, published without any accompanying letterpress, escaped the Act by a singular design.[2] The *New Monthly Magazine*, in 1826, had every sympathy with such ruses, and made sport of the ludicrous situation where pictures of an amalgam of Chinese pagoda, Turkish mosque and Moorish seraglio had to be paraded without explanation. Furthermore, it seemed to the magazine that Oxford and Cambridge, amply provided with funds, were in the iniquitous position of preventing access to their books to much of the

---

[1] In fact Britton never wrote the accompanying text, and instead the project was extended to *Picturesque antiquities of the English cities* (1828–30), published by Longman in conjunction with Britton and J. Le Keux. See T. E. Jones *A descriptive account of the literary works of John Britton* (1849) pp. 42–3, and John Britton *Picturesque antiquities* pp. ix–x.

[2] *New Monthly Magazine* 18 (1826) p. 504. On applying for Pugin's *Examples of gothic architecture* in 1831, Durham was informed that only the prints were sold, and the letterpress was given away (Claims ledger 1828–35).

population of the country, since the universities were forbidden to dissenters and Roman Catholics: only the Scottish universities were open to the entire population.[3] But it was a half-hearted plea at best for Scotland, and while the defence for the English universities was more vocal so too was the attack on them. Robert Maugham, founder of the Law Society, raised again the question of the relevance to current educational needs of taking all publications:

The works which are esteemed in these ancient colleges are those which have long maintained their rank as standard productions. The great bulk of modern publications are not introduced, and cannot, perhaps, with propriety be introduced into the course of study pursued at the Universities. A large part of the system of education is confined to ancient authors, and to subjects which do not admit of modern improvement. Indeed, the general plan of instruction is opposed to whatever is novel and speculative. Nothing is adopted but that which has been long tried and established, and we cannot conceive, therefore, why the heads of colleges require those valuable but modern works, which they do not permit to be used . . .

Now, however agreeable to the eye are splendid editions, and however suited to the taste of the affluent, we exceedingly question their utility, not only to the student, but to the professed author. Fine plates and bindings are adapted to the literary idler and looker-on, but can scarcely stimulate any one to intellectual exertion. These splendid trappings are for holidays, and not for days of learned labor. They tend, like great luxuries in general, more to enervate than invigorate . . .

Antiquarian works are of course expensive, but we are not aware that the Universities profess to induct their pupils in the knowledge of antiquities, the study of which may safely be left to the Antiquarian Society. So also botany and zoology may be effectually studied without the aid of magnificent plates, which, indeed, are rather calculated to excite a taste for drawing, and to encourage a love of show and splendour, than to induce philosophical and studious habits. We can see no advantage to public education in attracting the pupil to quit the hard study, which can alone render him eminent in society, for the purpose of gratifying his taste in examining splendid folios, and admiring the productions of the arts of drawing and engraving.[4]

These were not all new arguments, but Maugham put others still more boldly: that the universities did not enjoy a

[3] *Ibid.* [4] Robert Maugham *A treatise on the laws of literary property* (1828) pp. 197–9.

monopoly in producing authors, and that the need to preserve everything was not proved. 'We think it bad morality, on the coldest application of the doctrine of expediency, to do an act of positive injustice, for the sake of preserving something which may become *curious*.'[5] To Maugham the so-called 'Library Tax' was both a tax upon industry and a restraint upon the press, 'a direct invasion of that great palladium of our rights, A FREE PRESS'.[6] It was a criticism that echoed the mood of the time, but the argument was not pursued in such terms. In one of the less hot-headed contributions to the debate, a correspondent of James Silk Buckingham's *Parliamentary Review* attempted a more balanced view. The Copyright Act, despite its declared intention, did not advance learning, since its provisions for the deposit of eleven copies (to Britton an 'imperious impost') militated against the production of expensive books. It thus prevented the spread of learning, while being also more accurately a tax on knowledge than a 'Library tax'. To Buckingham's correspondent there were only two advantages in copyright deposit: it provided for good university libraries, and it preserved books from the danger of complete loss. But the universities were no longer, as they had seemed more obviously two centuries before, the country's sole centres of learning. Learned societies had founded their own libraries, and for most specialists there were more accessible sources than the universities' collections. To guard against the 'bare possibility' of a work being lost, the British Museum and one other public library (only) should be sufficient. 'More than that is clearly an injury to the author or the public, or both, and as clearly a *discouragement of the cause of learning*.'[7]

Such was the background to the 1836 Act, under which six libraries were compensated for the loss of their free copies: Sion College, the Universities of Aberdeen, Edinburgh, Glasgow and St Andrews, and the King's Inns, Dublin.[8] The reduction

---

[5] *Ibid.*, pp. 200, 201.   [6] *Ibid.*, p. 205.
[7] *Parliamentary Review* 1834, pp. 717–18. The correspondent was 'C.R.D.' of Oxford.
[8] Partridge *Legal deposit* pp. 77, 320–1.

of the list of eleven libraries to just five, the British Museum, Oxford, Cambridge, the Faculty of Advocates, and Trinity College, Dublin, brought some satisfaction for the publishers. It was the work principally of James Silk Buckingham, M.P. for Sheffield since 1832 and a man sympathetic to radical views. He was supported by Thomas Thompson, M.P. for Hull and a former Fellow of Queens' College, and William Ewart, educated at Christ Church, M.P. for Liverpool and later instrumental in promoting the public library movement. Buckingham's speech in the Commons introducing the Bill on 28 April presented a full historical survey of the question, including copious quotations from the 1818 report. He had, he claimed, directed his attention to the question from the time that he first took his seat, and he could see no reason why ten of the eleven privileged libraries should continue to receive books at the expense of publishers and authors. Only in the case of the British Museum was he – reluctantly – willing to make any concession, while the other libraries could, he suggested, be compensated financially from public funds. The ensuing debate, in which Buckingham's Bill was seconded by John Bowring, M.P. for Kilmarnock, promised little comfort for the universities. Both members for the borough of Cambridge, Thomas Spring Rice (doubly influential as Chancellor of the Exchequer) and George Pryme, Professor of Political Economy, supported the Bill. From his vantage as Member for the borough, rather than the University, Pryme was a regular campaigner for university reform. His willingness to give up the copyright privilege was not universally supported in Cambridge at the time, and seemed even more extraordinary in 1853 to Francis Bashforth,[9] author of one of the sanest pamphlets to be published on the nineteenth-century library: but in 1836 Pryme could also adduce the testimony of Lodge himself, having 'been assured by the librarian of the University, they had a great many books transmitted to them which

---

9 Francis Bashforth *Observations on some recent university buildings* (Cambridge 1853) p. 23.

were not worth a place in the library, and that many works of great value never reached them until a very long period after the time of their publication'.[10] In a debate notable for the single-mindedness of its purpose, no-one protested at the proposal that the universities should be compensated for their loss with sums of money. The mood was summed up by Spring Rice: 'It would be better, and more convenient for the universities, that they should each have at their disposal a sum of money for the purchase of really useful works, than that they should have thrown upon them an indiscriminate mass of publications, many of which were worse than useless.'[11]

But whatever the views of the two Members for the borough of Cambridge, those of the Library Syndicate, like those of Oxford, were the exact opposite. The Bill dated 10 May 1836 proposed not only that the British Museum privileges should be ended in favour of an annual grant sufficient to buy new books at their wholesale price, but also that the libraries of Oxford and Cambridge should each receive a flat rate of £500 a year from the Treasury in lieu of books, and the other libraries lesser sums. The compensation proposed for the two English universities was in fact not ungenerous, if set beside the wholesale value of books entered at Stationers' Hall in 1833–5: these figures amounted in each year to approximately £233, £203, and £248 respectively, excluding music and, of course, ignoring all those books not so entered.[12] The Syndics' response was rapid. By the end of the month they had decided that the best reply was to petition the House, and on 3 June, amidst all the excitement of work at last getting under way on the new library (Cockerell's design was finally chosen on 11 May) the Senate approved a petition against the provisions of the Bill as they affected Cambridge.[13] It was not a document of any great originality or special merit. As on the previous occasions when the University had

[10] Hansard (1836) vol. 33, col. 463.   [11] Hansard (1836) vol. 33, cols. 440–64.
[12] *Parliamentary papers* 1836. 47 p. 71.
[13] Grace Book N pp. 547–8. The petition is recorded in the Syndics' Minutes for 3 June.

considered the question, it opened with a reference to Henry VIII's licence to the University to print books, and on the subject of copyright deposit as it appeared to would-be reformers it was distinctly bald. 'That, in the judgement of your Petitioners, it would be extremely difficult to assign *Any* sum which would be an adequate compensation for a Privilege so valuable to the University, and so important to the interests of Literature: That, the sum named in the Bill abovementioned is considered by your Petitioners as by no means an Equivalent for the Right which they at present enjoy.' But however inadequately argued, the petition had its desired effect. Buckingham's Bill was amended in Committee and when brought before the House again on 14 July the names of both Oxford and Cambridge, as well as the British Museum, were omitted from the list of libraries that were to lose their right. The privileges of the Faculty of Advocates at Edinburgh and Trinity College, Dublin, were restored at a later stage, and so, when the Bill received the Royal Assent on 20 August the number of copyright libraries had only been reduced from eleven to five.

The escape had been a narrow one, and the Library's privileges were not seriously challenged again until the Copyright Commissioners' report of 1878. In practical terms the passing of the short-lived Copyright Act of 1836 (6 & 7 William IV, c. 110) provided much more of a disturbance to the University than did its successor of 1842 (5 & 6 Victoria c. 45), but the latter, the so-called Imperial Copyright Act, was the more important legislation, which further emphasized the distinction between the British Museum and other libraries. The 1842 Act repealed the Act of 1710 as well as those of 1801 and 1814, and ordained (so far as the British Museum was concerned) that one copy of each publication, on the best paper, should be delivered there without further ado within one calendar month, or within twelve months if published in the British dominions. The other libraries were entitled to a copy 'upon the Paper of which the largest number of Copies of such Book or Edition shall be printed for Sale': but they had either to demand them in writing within twelve months of publication through an officer of the Stationers' Company, that officer to deliver the copy or copies for the use of each library within one month, or publishers might deliver copies direct to the libraries, such deliveries being deemed the same as if they were to the Stationers' Company. The libraries might also claim through an authorized agent. Moreover, entry in the Stationers' Register was no longer a prerequisite of copyright, and this procedure was made quite separate from the depositing of so-called 'copyright copies'. If prosecuted successfully for failure to deposit, a publisher was to be fined not more than five pounds plus the value of the book he ought to have delivered.[14] Under the 1842 Act there was no stated limit to when publishers might be prosecuted, but in fact thanks to other quite separate legislation this was limited to an absurdly short six months; and so when a few years later the libraries began to take a more active interest in their entitlements their hands were seriously tied. Moreover, if as frequently happened a work was scarcely advertised, its existence could easily escape the notice of the library authorities in the absence of any communication with the Copyright Office of the British Museum (itself markedly ineffective and lazy until Panizzi turned his attention to it), while the difficulties were further exacerbated by the lack of any trade journal that recorded the national published output: both the *Publishers' Circular* and the *English Catalogue* were notably deficient in their registering of metropolitan as well as provincial publications.

This lack of proper bibliographical control makes it difficult now to present plausible details of the numerical extent of the difficulties apparent by 1850, the year a Royal Commission began its investigations into the University of Cambridge. For their Report, published in 1852, Power provided a long account of the Library, including an analysis of the copyright

---

[14] The text of the relevant part of the Act is printed in Partridge *Legal deposit* pp. 325–6.

intake from 1844 to 1850 expressed in terms of volumes, which when set against even the figures of the *Publishers' Circular* alone suggest a little of the problem. In 1844 Cambridge received 2508 volumes, excluding music and periodical parts, where the *Circular* listed approximately 2880 publications for London alone; in 1846 the respective figures were 2682 compared with a nationally (rather than London) based figure of about 3060; and in 1849 3160 against about 3690.[15] Both the *Publishers' Circular* and the *English Catalogue* listed Scottish and Irish publications only very thinly, and pamphlets hardly at all, so that in fact the University Library as well as the other libraries at Oxford, Edinburgh and Dublin were losing much more than these figures suggest.

By no means everyone was convinced, or even imagined, that this was unsatisfactory in a library whose first responsibility, in the eyes of outside protagonists in arguments over copyright deposit as well as of Cambridge itself, was to the University. Joseph Power himself took a conservative view, and admitted in his evidence to the Commissioners that 'I have taken upon myself to deprecate the sending of infantine publications, of which we used to receive a great number, and which served only to swell out the lists inconveniently, and to embarrass us at the Library.'[16] On a very rough calculation, Power estimated that the books received in 1850 were worth a little over £1360,[17] but against this had to be set, as the Commissioners realized, other factors such as the cost of their management:

Of the books which are received, the greatest part are of little worth, or are better suited for a popular circulating library than for one which is designed for a repository of the permanent literature and science of all nations. The cost also incurred for binding this vast multitude of books, for arranging and collecting pamphlets and periodicals, for entering them in the catalogues, and for payment of the expenses of the agent for collecting them at Stationers' Hall, is probably not much less than 600l. per annum; and inasmuch as the books which are derived from this source are

[15] Cambridge University Commission Report (1852) *Evidence* p. 55.
[16] *Evidence* p. 56.   [17] *Ibid.*, p. 55.

received very soon after publication, they form a principal attraction of those who use the library less for literary objects than for amusement, and thus increase unduly the labours of the Librarians. Of the books which are removed from the Library, under the privilege conceded to every member of the Senate, a great majority belong to this class.[18]

So that the Library did not miss valuable books, some of which were bound to escape notice, Power suggested that the libraries other than the British Museum should be put on the same footing as the Museum and that their books should equally be deliverable without printed notice: the Commissioners somewhat unrealistically expected that the libraries would return what was not wanted, and so 'free those libraries from all trivial or worthless publications and from the serious expenses which they entail; and would further tend to confine the circulation of the books which are received into them to a class of readers who have a real interest in literature as a dignified and important occupation'.[19] The principle of a copyright library of deposit for the national literary output, as distinct from a university library enjoying (by virtue of its age) free books, can scarcely be said to have been understood, let alone followed. It was left to Francis Bashforth to point out the relevance of the 1849 report of the Select Committee on public libraries, which had obtained information on copyright deposit practice in other countries, and to remind the University of Panizzi's questions at the hearings on the British Museum, 'What is trash?', 'Who is to judge of it and to discriminate?', 'Are novels trash?'[20]

In presenting his evidence on copyright deposit, Power mentioned that only one work in his experience, Gould's *Birds of Australia* (begun in 1840, and still not complete when he wrote) had, children's books apart, deliberately been allowed to escape the net: the University had subscribed to it, and it had also frequently to meet the cost of colouring plates in other expensive books. He explained briefly the operation of the 1842 Act, and the part played in it by the Library's agent Mr

[18] *Report* p. 128.   [19] *Ibid.*, p. 129.
[20] Bashforth *Observations on some recent university buildings* pp. 25–7.

Greenhill;[21] but he gave no hint of any difficulties with Greenhill, and in 1850 at least all seems to have been well. It was not to be so for long. Panizzi's pursuit of recalcitrant publishers, his astonishing successes in increasing the British Museum's copyright intake from 9834 in 1850 to 13,934 in 1852 (the first year of prosecutions) and 25,818 in 1855,[22] coupled with a gradually increasing awareness of the purpose of a copyright library, led to predictable strains. Power knew that important books were escaping, but he did not elaborate. Nor did he (scarcely surprisingly) acknowledge that the lack of several recent novels was, even as he was assembling his evidence for the Royal Commission, exercising no less a person than James Cartmell, Master of Christ's and Vice-Chancellor in 1849–50. Though no longer Vice-Chancellor, on 7 February 1851 Cartmell wrote to Greenhill listing thirty-three works, all but one of them novels, published in 1845–51 but none of them yet in the Library.[23] The list included Mrs Gore's *Peers and parvenus* (1846: Colburn), Frances Trollope's *The Robertses on their travels* (1846: Colburn), Eugène Sue's *Martin, or memoirs of a valet de chambre* (1847: Appleyard), and three works by G. P. R. James: *Henry Smeaton* (1851: Newby), *Dark scenes of history* (1849: Newby) and *The stepmother* (1845: Saunders & Ottley). Other publishers involved included Moxon, Churton and Shoberl. In due course almost all the books arrived safely, though not the Sue; and the expected 31s.6d. three-decker by Lady Dalmeny *The Spanish lady's love* turned out to be a one-volume chromolithographed elephant folio. The exercise proved to be thoroughly worthwhile, and several more similar attempts were made to fill in the gaps of previous years, not always with equal success. Despite the attempts of Greenhill, the Library still lacked the first edition of G. P. R. James' *The woodman* (first published in 1849, with a second edition the same year) and of Thackeray's *The*

---

21 The Stationers' Company was served by successive members of the Greenhill family. In 1849 George Greenhill resigned, and in the same year Joseph Greenhill became Treasurer of the English Stock.

22 Partridge *Legal deposit* p. 327; Edward Miller *Prince of librarians* (1967) pp. 202–7.

23 The following is based on lists of books inserted in the Accessions Register for 1839–48.

Kickleburys on the Rhine (first edition 1850, second edition 1851), as well as such novels as *The golden calf, or railway frauds* (1849), the revised 1849 edition of *Crichton Armsworth* to add to the 1837 edition already in the Library, and Catherine Gray's *The gambler's wife.*

Such a situation was clearly unsatisfactory, but, as was to become clear over the next few years, novels (other than those published in parts) were in fact collected fairly efficiently. They were advertised widely and, most importantly, they were actually wanted (despite occasional protestations) by both the staff and the readers in the University Library. Such could not always be said of items published outside the main publishing centres of London, Oxford, Cambridge, Edinburgh and Dublin, nor of much which appeared to have only transient interest and whose significance was often discovered only subsequently.

Major illustrated works offered difficulties of a quite different kind. If Power believed that Gould's *Birds of Australia* was the only English work to which the Library had subscribed in recent years, he was mistaken. The considerable sums expended on Gould's other projects alone belied, and were to continue to belie, his statements. But Greenhill's tasks were complicated in other ways as well. The 1842 Act distinguished between the British Museum, which was to receive the best issue of each new book, and the other libraries, which were empowered to demand only copies 'upon the paper of which the largest number of copies of such book or edition shall be printed for sale'. No specific allusion was made to books with coloured plates in the section providing for libraries other than the British Museum. By the middle of the century the Library had reached a compromise on the question of illustrated books coloured by hand, and in several cases paid for colouring to be added.[24] So Greenhill's bill for the half-year to Michaelmas 1855 included four guineas for exchanging four parts of

---

[24] Bashforth *Observations on some recent university buildings* p. 23.

Edward Churton's folio *Monastic ruins of Yorkshire* for the superior coloured proofs, and payments for colouring the latest parts of G. B. Sowerby's *Thesaurus conchyliorum*, L. A. Reeve's *Conchologia Iconica*, the *Botanical Magazine*, Sir Joseph Hooker's *Botany of the Antarctic voyage of H.M. discovery ships Erebus and Terror*, and Henry and Arthur Adams' *Genera of recent mollusca*.[25] As the publishers were now receiving, via Greenhill, payment for their additional expense entailed in colouring books, the Library had gone some way towards meeting one of the principal criticisms levelled at copyright legislation forty years earlier.

Other similar books still eluded the Library's claim, however, and their purchase fell on the Rustat Fund, which was generally used to buy modern foreign books, particularly of the more expensive kind. In the mid-1840s, besides paying for Cuvier's *Histoire naturelle des poissons*, the latest parts of the *Acta sanctorum*, a dozen and more journals, Louis-François Cassas' immense *Voyage pittoresque de la Syrie* (Paris 1799), and the third and concluding volume to François Levaillant's *Histoire naturelle des perroquets*, by A. Bourjot Saint-Hilaire (Paris 1837–8), the Fund was also charged with Britton's new edition of John Carter's *Ancient architecture of England* (London 1837), S. R. Meyrick's edition of Carter's *Specimens of the ancient sculpture and painting now remaining in England* (London 1838), William Swainson's *Exotic conchology* (London 1841: the 1821 edition had never been acquired), and J. R. Planché's new editions of Joseph Strutt's *Royal and ecclesiastical antiquities* (London 1842) and *Complete views of the dress and habits of the people of England* (London 1842).

The Royal Commission reported in 1852, but it could provide no means to modify the existing arrangements for copyright deposit. Meanwhile matters began to come to a head, not only in Cambridge but also in the other libraries. Panizzi's successes drew attention to how much was being lost,

---

[25] Vouchers 1855. Trinity College, Dublin, also bought coloured plates when necessary (Dublin University Commission, *Parliamentary papers* 1852–3. 45 *Evidence* p. 179).

and also, by implication, to Greenhill's weakness.[26] In the summer of 1854 Greenhill met the reformed Library Syndicate, who requested that he should supply them with a list of publishers known to be defaulting, but only on 5 April 1855 did he finally provide this document, naming Parker and Blackwood amongst others. A further list followed on 5 May, Greenhill at the same time complaining of the illness that dogged him throughout what turned into negotiations over whether or not he ought to be allowed to retain his connection with the libraries. All but one of the names on his second list were of London publishers, the outsider being no more provincial than the specialist oriental printer and publisher Stephen Austin of Hertford. In London the culprits were Collins of Paternoster Row, C. J. Skeet, Vizetelly, R. Griffin & Co. of Warwick Square, J. D. Potter of Poultry, Craddock & Co., J. Gilbert of Paternoster Row, George Berger of Holywell Street, Wildy & Sons, Bagster, and William James of Paternoster Row. As a survey of the position, Greenhill's paper was unsatisfactory, and palpably incomplete even among London publishers. Power, acting with the consent of the Syndicate, decided to take some of Greenhill's work upon himself, and to write to four of those firms for which Greenhill provided lists of books he believed not to have been correctly delivered. The list was very different from earlier ones, not mostly of children's books or novels, but of books in which, in many cases, the University Library ought clearly to have an interest. Wildy, the legal publishers, had not delivered Frederick Prideaux' *Handbook of precedents in conveyancing* (1853), James Deane's *Acts for amendment of laws of wills* (1852), or C. J. Bunyon's *Laws of life assurance* (1853). At the other end of the trade, Gilbert, rather less specialized, still owed a sixpenny pamphlet *Wine, temperance and trade* as well as C. J. Sturt's popular handbook *Female physiology* (1854). The list

[26] The following is based on a parcel of papers marked 'Copyright Act' in the Library archives.

from Potter was more serious. They published much of their work in connection with the Admiralty, and some of the muddle appears to have arisen simply from divided responsibilities; the result was that Greenhill's list included eleven items, one of them a map of Sebastopol and only recently demanded, but also including the fifth edition of Henry Raper's *Practice of navigation* (in fact a reprint: the Library already possessed the third of 1849), the Admiralty tide tables and charts for 1853, a history of the harbour at Belfast from 1613 to 1830 (1852), and a two-shilling volume of *Arctic despatches* (1854). Austin had not provided the *Haileybury Observer* or the *Monthly Miscellany of Western India*, two short-lived journals now of extreme rarity. Nor, according to Greenhill, had he sent E. B. Cowell's *Prakit grammar* or half a dozen oriental texts, some of them claimed originally in 1853 and including Edward B. Eastwick's *Bāgh o Bahār* of 1852. C. J. Skeet emerged as the most varied in his defaulting. The *British Chess Review*, begun in 1853, had still not begun to reach Greenhill, and the arrival of the *Chess Players' Chronicle* had been only intermittent; and the two-volume *Life of a collegian* (1853), Lady Lytton's *Behind the scenes* (1854), *Alice Offley, or the pervert and the soldier* (1852), E. Colburn's *Evil star* (1853) and *Lights and shadows of English life* (3 vols., 1855) were among the fiction whose absence had been noticed.

To all these publishers Power wrote on 14 May, requesting answers within five days. The replies he received were disturbing. It was not to be expected that each and every one of the publishers concerned would immediately post off the books listed by Greenhill, but it quickly emerged that Power was acting in several cases on false information based on records kept imperfectly by Greenhill. Potter simply referred him to the Admiralty for most of his books, but remarked with a panache that would scarcely have encouraged his authors (however much it may have perplexed Power), 'Gribble's *Lights in the Red Sea* you have had, but can have another copy, as the book is useless.'[27] Skeet wrote an abject, even spineless, letter of apology,[28] but both Wildy and Austin claimed that they had already sent copies.

Wildy's books were not, however, to be found at Cambridge, and there seems to be some hint in Austin's letter that the firm's own book-keeping was a little short of perfect. Power meanwhile had discovered that Potter had already delivered the second edition of Johnson on the compass and the history of the harbour at Belfast, and that at least one of Austin's books had arrived from Greenhill as long ago as August 1853.[29] Such were not circumstances in which it would be easy to pursue, still less prosecute, publishers who might or might not be breaking the Act, and in reply to Power's protest to Greenhill on 19 May Greenhill fled to Hastings, replying on 23 May that 'I have been so unwell lately as to be ordered here for a short time to recruit & I shall not be in town till Tuesday next.' In due course he returned, and went about gathering the books from the recalcitrant publishers; but, writing to Power on 15 June, he could only offer the somewhat weak observation about those who claimed that they had already sent in their books, that they ought to be able to demonstrate the fact by producing his receipts. Such was true enough, but it was not sufficient on which to base stronger legal proceedings.

There the matter rested until January 1858, when the Syndics again examined the problem, and asked one of the Library assistants, Dennis Hall, to report. He reported on 28 October to devastating effect. He had examined the *Publishers' Circular* (only) from July 1857 to April 1858, two or three months at a time, forwarding lists compiled from it of books not yet arrived three or four months later. So he sent the July–September 1857 list on 16 February 1858, October–December in April, January–February 1858 in June, and March–April on 25 October. His first list contained seventy-six omissions, only

---

[27] Potter to Power 17 May 1855.   [28] C. J. Skeet to Power 17 May 1855.
[29] Power to Greenhill 19 May 1855 (draft).

twenty of which had dribbled in subsequently; the second listed 119, of which sixteen had subsequently arrived; the third 118 (thirty sent since); and the fourth 130, of which three had turned up in the three days between his sending it and the compilation of his report. He noted that these figures were based on one published source only, but nonetheless he identified four particular evils: firstly, the delay of seven or eight months after publication in the case of many books, meaning (as Hall saw it) that books of a temporary interest were of little value when they did arrive; second, that it was frequently the case that the Library had to make do with second or later editions or impressions; thirdly, that periodicals were imperfectly and irregularly delivered; and fourthly, perhaps most seriously, that 'the attention required for the scrutiny of the Publishers' Circular as now carried on, is more than sufficient to employ one's whole time' yet the net result of nine months' work was sixty-nine omissions received, leaving a balance of 374 remaining, in Hall's phrase, 'unreconciled'. Hall therefore recommended that a person on the Library staff should be deputed to deal solely with copyright claims, and that he should travel down to London twice a month to liaise with Greenhill and cope with the publishers, Greenhill's tasks thus being reduced to an absolute minimum.

It was clearly time, however, that Greenhill's work ought to be reconsidered – not only by Cambridge but by the Bodleian, the Faculty of Advocates and Trinity College, Dublin, as well. From this stage each library became progressively more involved with the others, as they sought to agree on how to interpret the 1842 Act, how physically to collect the books, and what to do about Greenhill, whose position was fully supported by the Stationers' Company.

Oxford had been worried in ways similar to Cambridge,[30] and the question was raised by Bandinel, the aged Bodley's Librarian, in correspondence with Panizzi in December 1858.

---

[30] The Bodleian position is described in Craster pp. 61–4.

In his evidence to the Royal Commission on Oxford, H. E. Strickland had commented on the lack of provincially published books received under the Act, and had suggested then that 'the Library might easily employ an agent, at a small salary or commission, in each of these [six or more] towns, to collect the local literature and forward it to Oxford'. Panizzi offered better than this, in a letter to Bandinel on 21 December 1858:

It seems to me that Mr Greenhill, whom you cannot get rid of, should make out lists of the books he receives, & deliver lists & books to your agents here and have some remuneration for his trouble.

Your agents here to whom the books should be sent by Mr Greenhill . . . should be the receiver of our books [i.e. the British Museum's] under the copyright act and his assistant, whom the Trustees would, I hope, permit to undertake the business. They would draw up lists of what they receive for all those who have a right to publications, whether from Stationer's Hall or collected as I shall presently say, and forward the parcels. There ought to be a person whose business should be to claim and collect what is not delivered at Stationer's Hall. I have one of our men in view for that also.

The advantage of this arrangement would be that you would know precisely what to claim, and thus receive as much as we do.

I think the whole expense would not exceed £200 a year.[31]

Here, in essence, was the beginning of the concept of what much later became the Copyright Agency, the libraries all acting together in their joint interests, supporting a staff in London, and using the bibliographical knowledge of the British Museum as a basis for knowing what to claim. But the agreement between the four libraries outside the British Museum proved difficult to establish. Henry Wellesley, Principal of New Inn Hall, sent a copy of Panizzi's letter to W. H. Bateson, Master of St John's and Vice-Chancellor of Cambridge, on 10 March 1859, enquiring also whether Cambridge would be disposed to co-operate. Greenhill, meanwhile, was continuing to report on an unsatisfactory state of affairs in London. At the end of March he supplied another

---

[31] Panizzi to Bandinel 21 December 1858 (copy at Cambridge).

list, which eventually found its way to the special Copyright Act Syndicate, once again naming Wildy & Sons as persistent evaders or ignorers of the Act, and adding the names of Hope & Co. of Great Marlborough Street (publishers of children's books, novels, and religious works) and Hughes & Butler of St Martins le Strand, who handled Trübner's guide books and also published Welsh books. The patience of the authorities, in Cambridge at least, was running out, and they began seriously to consider prosecuting Wildy and Hughes.

Hall's calculations could not, moreover, be ignored. Where the University had once been aware only that it was missing many books, it now knew more exactly the extent of the damage. Out of fifty-one books listed on a single page of the *Publishers' Circular* for December 1857, for example, twelve are still not in the Library today: if reprints (not claimable under the Act) and so-called new editions are included the number is seventeen. Some of the forty-four remaining may of course have been bought or given since, but this only depresses the number of copies not delivered. Of a sample taken a year later, in November 1858, the proportion is even greater. Many were, admittedly, children's books, whose value in a research library has been recognized only comparatively recently, but they included as well various illustrated editions of the English poets, quantities of yellow-backs, Colburn and Holley's *Permanent way and coal-burning locomotive boilers of European railways* (a work published in New York which had somehow found its way into the *Publishers' Circular*), a new and revised edition of W. L. Rham's *Dictionary of the farm*, religious and tractarian pamphlets, Brannon's guides to Bournemouth and to the geology of Purbeck, and the first edition of Ballantyne's *Martin Rattler*.

The existence of the Copyright Agency subsequently tended to ensure that there was little discrepancy between what each library received, but in the 1850s the experience of Cambridge was not equally shared elsewhere. The comparative success of Trinity College, Dublin, in acquiring books made J. H. Todd, the librarian, reluctant to enter into a scheme involving more than Greenhill alone. Todd's letter to Wellesley of 4 April 1859 was, indeed, a curious one. He grasped somewhat less firmly than the authorities at Oxford or Cambridge the purpose of the Copyright Act, and, not having organized any survey such as that carried out at Cambridge, dismissed as of no value the thirty volumes not received in 1857 which they had traced through the *British Catalogue*. But then, oddly, he went on to complain that the library did not receive more than half of the books published in Wales, Scotland, or Ireland, only the 'worst half' of published music, and, like the other libraries, only irregular supplies of periodicals.[32]

On the other points he was however more sympathetic. He preferred an independent agent acting in London for the four libraries rather than one based in the British Museum, who might, he feared, have divided loyalties; and he also proposed the logical step of the libraries' co-operating over cataloguing, buying catalogue entries from the British Museum and furnishing the Museum with entries for books not catalogued in London. His second proposal, though widely canvassed in library circles in one form or another during the next decades, was a century ahead of its time. It was not welcomed by Panizzi when Todd put it forward and, having little to do with the current difficulties, was for the moment ignored.

The Faculty of Advocates, on the other hand, welcomed Panizzi's proposal, and on 31 May a meeting was held at the British Museum of the representatives of the four libraries: Wellesley from Oxford, Philpott (recently Vice-Chancellor) from Cambridge, Todd from Dublin and Samuel Halkett from Edinburgh. In Philpott, Cambridge had as forceful a man as Wellesley, and the two men together were responsible for

---

[32] In 1853 Todd estimated that since he had been appointed Assistant Librarian in 1834, the copyright deposits had more than trebled, thanks principally to increased staff, and he added, 'I am of opinion that we now receive nearly all that we can legally claim.' At Dublin, children's books, school books, and 'the inferior class of novels' were simply stored away in boxes (Dublin University Commission, Parliamentary papers 1852–3.45, *Evidence* p. 173).

most of the subsequent negotiations. The four libraries agreed to follow Panizzi's proposals for British Museum staff to gather the copyright books, and the plan put to Greenhill (with the blessing of the Cambridge Copyright Syndicate) was straightforward: first, that an agent should be appointed with constant access to the British Museum list of copyright accessions, who would each month send a list of books to the Stationers' Company, those not having arrived already to be claimed forthwith; second, that in addition to his duties laid down under the Copyright Act, Greenhill was to be asked to mark up these lists with the books received; and third, that each of the libraries was to pay Greenhill £25 per annum.

Greenhill, scarcely surprisingly, was not impressed. The proposed fee represented a drop in salary, and there followed a spirited series of letters of greater or lesser animosity between him and the authorities at Oxford and Cambridge. To Wellesley he wrote in July:

I beg to acknowledge the receipt of a copy of the resolutions prepared by a meeting of Deputies from the several Libraries entitled to books under the Copyright Act, and to express my great regret that, connected as the Stationers' Company is, by the Act of Parliament, with the Libraries in question, it did not occur to those gentlemen to ascertain from the Company's officer what he might be permitted, & what he would be willing to undertake . . . No officer of the Stationers' Company could possibly act with any agent in the way suggested, and it might not be in his power to accept a less gratuity than has been hitherto paid, as that has been very inadequate to the labour performed, I having agreed to it only for the purpose of getting rid of agents formerly employed . . .

In effect, he was fighting for his livelihood with two men determined to push a much needed reform as far as they possibly could. He visited Cambridge and discussed the matter there, and he examined the lists of copyright accessions at the British Museum – apparently for the first time. Meanwhile, Wellesley having opened the question with the Stationers' Company at large in November, the Company appointed a committee which reported in January that the libraries' proposal was unrealistic; instead, they proposed that Greenhill himself should obtain lists from the British Museum. The rumpus continued for nearly two years, from the winter of 1860 to the summer of 1862, but the outcome was never seriously in doubt. While the Bodleian was willing to try to continue with Greenhill for another twelve months from March 1860, Power in Cambridge was beset by continual reports from his assistants on the repeated failures in the daily working of copyright deposit. The earliest edition of *Adam Bede* received at Cambridge was the sixth, a year after the novel's first publication; Greenhill had never bothered to reply to letters enquiring after the publications of the Dublin booksellers Hodges, Smith & Co.; and Bohn's edition of Pepys' diary was incomplete, lacking the first three volumes. To such omissions Greenhill pleaded ill health. But the Faculty of Advocates now took the lead, and on 20 March 1860 began the process of separating itself so far as it could legally from Greenhill and establishing its own agent in London: Greenhill was offered the post, but declined, and his agreement with Edinburgh was terminated on 31 December. In his place was appointed Gregory W. Eccles, a member of the staff of the British Museum, who began work on 1 January and who kept his ledger of books claimed and supplied with an orderliness that had been so absent in Greenhill's work. If the Copyright Agency can be said to have been founded, rather than to have emerged gradually, the beginning of its records under Eccles marks its date of birth.

Greenhill's dismissal by the Faculty of Advocates provoked in him a fresh spirit of activity, and in February 1861 Power was able to report to the Vice-Chancellor that he had latterly had no cause for complaint. Although Jarvis' Act, which necessitated prosecution within six months for evasion of the Copyright Act, prevented a couple of prosecutions, the number of volumes delivered by Greenhill increased markedly. To Edinburgh, however, Greenhill was vindictive, and on 30 May the Curators of the Advocates' Library were forced to recommend that legal proceedings should be taken against him. This unhappy course was fortunately avoided, for the spectacle of the person who was empowered by law to act with power of attorney in prosecuting publishers for three of the copyright libraries himself being prosecuted by a fourth could only have been risible for the book trade at large.

Such remained the position for the summer of 1861 and for the whole of 1862. But in March 1863 Alfred Hobson, principal assistant at Cambridge, raised the matter yet again and opened what was to prove to be the final battle in the long campaign. In a letter addressed not to Power or to the Library Syndicate, but to the Vice-Chancellor (now Edward Atkinson) he rehearsed much of what had by now become tediously familiar: delays in delivery, failure to acquire books, and general negligence. But he wrote secure in the knowledge that the Faculty of Advocates had broken away successfully, while Greenhill's behaviour (quite apart from his inefficiency) was no longer such as could be tolerated.

As if on purpose to prevent us from taking any steps to rectify these evils by any efforts of our own, Mr Greenhill *refuses to answer any letters of inquiry.* During my first year in the library [1859], I wrote to him 6 or 7 times, but never received a single line of reply. He has, now & then, I believe, written to Mr Power, but even this has been of scarcely any use to us in the Library. After writing to Mr Greenhill several times, without effect, I told him I should represent the matter to the Vice Chancellor & Syndics – which I did, now about 3 years ago as I have already mentioned. Since that time I have not written to him more than a few times – finding it utterly useless. One consequence of this refusal to communicate directly with me, has been that I have often had long & useless correspondence with publishers & others – as a specimen of which I enclose letters from the Secretary of the Chetham Society – from Mr Bohn – & from Mr Bell. We have had to buy several volumes of the Chetham Society's Publications (at 12/– a volume, tho pub^d at only 5/– the vols having become scarce) which have thus been lost to us through Mr Greenhill's conduct.

Hobson, fortified by the support of the higher authorities, now pressed on, and wrote immediately afterwards to Halkett in Edinburgh, who supplied a full account of how the Advocates' Library had fared since Greenhill's dismissal. Scarcely surprisingly, Greenhill had proved as obstinate as the

1842 Act allowed. Since the summer of 1861, however, he had apparently accepted the position, Eccles (at the British Museum) having persuaded most publishers to lodge the Edinburgh copies at the Museum and needing to go to Stationers' Hall only on odd occasions. For Hobson this was encouraging, and on 6 April (events at last gathering speed after so many years) Eccles agreed that, if asked, he would act for two or more of the libraries on a similar basis to that for Edinburgh at an annual charge of from sixty guineas to £80 to each library, depending on how many joined in the scheme. Coxe at Oxford was at first reluctant to make the final break, relations between Greenhill and the Bodleian having been apparently somewhat more amicable than between him and Cambridge, but on 26 March 1863 the Senate at Cambridge voted to give notice to Greenhill.[33] Oxford followed on 16 May, and Trinity College, Dublin in July.

Eccles took up his new duties at Michaelmas, operating from 36 Hart Street, Bloomsbury Square, as the Museum proved to be over-full. Amidst further opposition from Greenhill, which he found more effective than when the Advocates had appointed him their agent, the disorderly state of Greenhill's work came gradually to light. Greenhill opened his attack by printing a circular cunningly implying to publishers that he was the sole authorized agent to collect books. This was in direct contradiction to the form issued by Eccles in September, quoting the Copyright Act, and on 10 October the four libraries were compelled to send out another printed statement to the effect that Eccles had indeed been appointed their agent. On 2 October Eccles visited Stationers' Hall and brought away a cart-load of books, including periodicals dating from as far back as 1842. Another load arrived on 13 October, again containing old periodicals but also with several months' accumulation of music and numbers of odd copies of books. The mess was gradually sorted out, but a principal difficulty

[33] Luard 684.

remained even after Greenhill had been pensioned off amidst a welter of acrimonious correspondence. The obstacle was the 1842 Act, which had laid down that books were to be delivered either to Stationers' Hall or to an agent of the four libraries, collectively or individually. The implication on a cursory reading of the Act, was that the normal method was via Stationers' Hall; but the libraries based their case on the proffered alternative. Eccles pointed out that the coincidental introduction of a Bill in November 1863 by the publisher Adam Black to strengthen authors and publishers in protecting their property, would be an opportune moment to revise this part of the Act as well. Black's Bill was, however, submerged following the appointment of a Select Copyright Committee, and this vexatious point was not to be resolved for several years more.

Greenhill had served as the four libraries' agent for just over forty years, and he was to continue as Treasurer of the English Stock at the Stationers' Company until February 1883, when he retired after sixty-four years with the Company. The proven incompetence which provoked the libraries to dismiss him was however extenuated by two circumstances. In 1843, when he was appointed as agent, the clauses concerning copyright deposit in the 1842 Act and its predecessor of 1814 had been, to a great extent, an embarrassment. None of the copyright libraries had yet come properly to terms with the fact that the Act meant what it implied, and that all books were of equal importance in the eye of the law, whatever the wishes of the more selective readers at Oxford, Cambridge, Edinburgh or Dublin. Not until Panizzi provoked the country into creating a national library which would be fully comprehensive in its coverage and record, rather than selectively representative, was it ever likely that the other four libraries would realize the extent of their obligations. The Act provided for some selection, in making the libraries outside London claim their books rather than receive them as of right like the British Museum. As a palliative to the publishers, the principle of selection was less than effective, since the libraries naturally concentrated on the more expensive books and exercised their right to choose in the case of children's books, school books, popular literature and other cheap or apparently insignificant productions rather more than in that of large or expensive books. On the University's part, responsible selection was impractical and even dangerous. It was attempted in the knowledge that the information available was insufficient, while the attendant risks of missing what was valuable – judged only by the University Library's own idiosyncratic standards – were in the end found unacceptable. Power and his successor J. E. B. Mayor both sought to shelter behind policies of selection, in the face of imminent congestion, but they could only do so at the expense of the Library's interests. In order to be effective as a copyright library, the University Library had to be comprehensive. It was not a conclusion that was easy to accept. Panizzi's work forced the Library to re-examine its entitlements, and it did so with gusto. But the corollary, of a yet greater and more varied intake of which only a small minority could be said to be of immediate academic importance, was not altogether welcome. In part, Greenhill was the victim of these conflicting ideals. He had been appointed in an age which disappeared rapidly in the early 1850s, and, lacking the capacity to adapt to new attitudes or to comprehend the increasing bibliographic control imposed on current publishers' output, could only be sacked. He was replaced by an arrangement which proved satisfactory for only a short time, as the University soon found itself in difficulties with Eccles too, and the opposition of the publishers at large was not muffled effectively until 1911; but the Copyright Agency has survived ever since.[34]

[34] In a form that has, of course, undergone several modifications. The modern arrangements respecting its operation are set out in *Reporter* 23 January 1980 pp. 238–9.

15

NEW DIRECTIONS

WHILE THE PROVISIONS for copyright deposit became gradually more effective, attention was not distracted from purchases of foreign books, of sets of periodicals, and, gradually, of early printed books. Whatever the fears of some members of the University about Power's fitness for his post, he proved no less willing than had Lodge (with Romilly as his active deputy) before him to do everything possible to build up the Library's purchases of new foreign works.

During Power's librarianship most business was conducted either through J. and J. J. Deighton in Cambridge, Barthés & Lowell of Great Marlborough Street, or H. Baillière of Regent Street, part of a wide-flung family of booksellers with a branch in New York which from about 1845 enabled them to supply American books to Cambridge: the Library's preference at first was for works of medicine and natural history, but it gradually ventured further, into (from 1849) poetry by N. P. Willis, Mrs Sigourney and Longfellow, Robert Dale Owen's *Hints on public architecture* (New York 1849), Charles Edwards Lester's *Gallery of illustrious Americans* (New York 1850) and Jerome B. Holgate's *American genealogy* (Boston 1852).[1] Eventually Henry Stevens won the task of supplying transatlantic books on what became a considerable scale. The Library's increasing demands in the 1860s for books in Hebrew and oriental studies were met by Frederik Muller of Amsterdam. But besides these regular agents there came to be a multitude of others, unearthed and acknowledged by the exertions of a group of men, not all of whom were on the

---

[1] All these were charged to the Manistre Fund.

Library staff, anxious to build up the collections in several different directions: Heun, Bradshaw, Mayor and H. R. Luard. Thanks to them the names of new suppliers began to appear at the heads of invoices. Following Bradshaw's visit to Sweden in the early autumn of 1862 books arrived from Gleerup in Lund; and by the end of 1862 Baillière was driven to complain more generally, 'Is it not very strange that I cannot sale any Books now to the University Library; formerly I use to Get orders But now nothing comes – There is *something* wrong in the kingdom of Dennemark.'[2] The change had in fact been considerable. In March 1856 a small notice inserted in *The Athenaeum* reminded the trade of opportunities:

The Librarian of the Cambridge University is DESIROUS of RECEIVING CATALOGUES of SECOND-HAND BOOKS, and also of approaching Book Auctions. They should be directed (postage paid) to Mr D. HEUN, Principal Library Assistant, University Library, Cambridge.[3]

Heun had approached the question of book acquisition, so far as it related to his own country, with fanatical zeal. In 1854, greatly daring, the Syndics tackled the catalogue of the library of Gottfried Hermann which was auctioned in Leipzig following his death six years earlier. The sale of the books of the successor of Bentley, and to many eyes in Cambridge of Porson as well, had an obvious fascination that seemed to amount to necessity; and thus goaded the Library laid plans to bid at a sale more distant than usual. To its great advantage, the books were to be sold in Heun's home city. A sub-syndicate of W. H. Bateson, W. G. Clark and J. E. B. Mayor recommended that the formidable sum of £350 should be made available, £150 for the adversaria and £200 for other desiderata. Heun's excursion proved to be a most gratifying success. He returned with over sixteen per cent of the 8472 lots, including several of Hermann's annotated copies of his own works, for a total of

[2] H. Baillière to Bradshaw 7 November 1862.
[3] *The Athenaeum* 8 March 1856 p. 282.

only £214.[4] While in Germany, however, Heun also organized, with the balance remaining, further orders of books
from several other booksellers. Only his illness and resignation
prevented his initiative from being developed into a permanent policy. The episode had reminded the Library authorities
of the spectacular achievements possible in the auction rooms,
while at the same time booksellers continued to supply other
needs. Among the retail trade in England, Quaritch produced
runs of the *Almanach de Gotha* in November 1854 and of the
London Gazette from 1768 to 1818 in 1861; Williams and
Norgate a run of the *Annalen der Chemie* for £17 in June 1857;
Macmillan & Co. (still in Cambridge, since 1845 at Stevenson's
old shop at 1 Trinity Street) 258 volumes of the *Journal* of the
Asiatic Society of Bengal for £29 in August the same year; and
Joseph Lilly a series of Roxburghe, Bannatyne and Maitland
Club volumes for £152.5s.0d. in January 1858. Even Joseph
Greenhill, Treasurer of the English Stock at the Stationers'
Company, whose formal task was to collect books delivered
under the Copyright Act, supplied books on occasion,
including in 1852 seventeen volumes of the *Illustrated London
News* which he had unearthed for £13.18s.0d. to make up the
Library's set.[5] Further opportunities to acquire books of
obvious interest came in collections offered privately. From
the estate of the aged William Webb, Master of Clare since
1815, the Library was able in 1856 to buy several volumes of
pamphlets relating to the University,[6] and two years later it
bought for £50 eighty-six editions of Horace from Churchill
Babington; two years later again, the Syndicate agreed to
purchase 112 private Acts of Parliament of the reign of George
I from William Salt, a banker who had devoted twenty years

---

[4] Annual Report 1855. Many of the adversaria are catalogued in H. R. Luard's *Catalogue of adversaria* (Cambridge 1864) pp. 39–54, but there are many more annotated volumes from Hermann's library that were simply placed on open shelves. Heun's marked copy of the sale catalogue, recording the lots bought for Cambridge, is Adv.c.83.37.

[6] Syndicate Minutes 7 April 1856.

of his life to a study of the subject[7] and whose devotion to the history of his native county led after his death in December 1863 to the establishment of his library as a public collection in Stafford: Cambridge was also to benefit several years later, when in 1873 a further collection of private Acts arrived as a gift from his widow.[8]

More and more, however, the Library was coming to look for its purchases of earlier books in what was offered at auctions. The sale of the books of Thomas Galloway, F. R. S., by Sotheby's in February 1852 prompted George Peacock (by now Professor of Astronomy and Geometry, and dean of Ely) to recommend various mathematical works, and in this manner the Library at last obtained the 1543 edition of Copernicus *De revolutionibus orbium coelestium*, for two guineas.

The sale of William Pickering's library offered an opportunity of an altogether different kind. In April 1854 the Library had bought the three folio volumes of John Donne's sermons from William Straker for five guineas.[9] Their purchase marked a new departure, for until this time little attention had been paid to improving the collections of major sixteenth- and seventeenth-century English authors. The first two Pickering sales seem to have passed without any active response from the Library, but the third, at the end of October, produced a quite different effect. It was not ideally timed, since it began on the very day that the Syndicate agreed to appoint Hardwick, Collett and Mayor to examine Sotheby's catalogue. Nor were the Syndics particularly alert to the results, since they did not adopt the report of their subcommittee until the following February. Mayor and his colleagues could however report considerable success. They had missed the first day's proceedings because of the unfortunate timing of the Syndicate meeting, but for an outlay of £66.4s.6d. they had secured about eighteen hundred titles.[10] Among them were Samuel

---

[7] Syndicate Minutes 13 June 1860; Salt to Power 11 June 1860.
[8] B. F. Watson to Bradshaw 26 November 1873; Bradshaw to Watson 29 January 1874.
[9] Vouchers 1855.   [10] Syndicate Minutes 30 October 1854, 5 February 1855.

Daniel's *Certaine small poems* (1605), the 1634 edition of Herbert's *Temple*, John Foxe's rare *Syllogisticon* (1580?), Thomas Fuller's *Andronicus, or, the unfortunate politician* (1646), Robert Hegg's *Legend of St. Cuthbert* (1663), an extra copy of Thomas James' *Ecloga Oxonio-Cantabrigiensis* (1600), several Miltons including a 1680 *Paradise regained, Eikonoclastes* (1649), *Tetrachordon* (1645) and *Pro populo Anglico defensio* (1651), poems by Quarles, L'Estrange's translation of Quevedo's *Sueños y discursos* (1678), Jeremy Taylor's *Discourse of the liberty of prophesying* (1647), Blundeville's *Art of logike* (1599: no longer in the Library), and John Philpot's *Trew report of the dysputacyon had at london* ('Basil' 1554). Besides many dozen sermons and tracts there were a bundle of sixty-five pamphlets on the liturgy and a small group of accounts of trials. The Library moved dramatically in a double sense out of its traditional collecting domain with lot 1907, which brought a series of play quartos: the 1633 edition of *The dumbe knight*, the 1632 *Rival friends*, the 1640 edition of Henry Glapthorne's *The Hollander*, and the 1633 edition of Thomas May's *The heire*. And in lot 2729, a folio volume of eighteenth-century poems that perhaps caught attention because of the Oxford University verses on the termination of the War of the Spanish Succession, the Library secured a collection whose true significance was only realized over a century after it had been secured for twelve shillings: Sotheby's catalogued the better-known poems, but failed to connect any of them with Jonathan Swift, and the extreme rarity of many of the forty-three pieces in the volume was not properly understood until the appearance of David Foxon's catalogue of *English verse 1701–1750* in 1975.[11] By no means every bid had been successful, however, and only two-thirds of what the Syndics had allowed was spent. The Library, after hesitating over several books by Donne and various emblem books, had finally not bid for them. But among those which it had

---

[11] The volume is now Syn.3.71.4.

attempted, the 1596 *Faerie Queene* had been lost at two guineas against the Library's two pounds; a 1668 *Paradise lost*, advertised as the first edition, went for thirty shillings, ten shillings more than the Library's bid; George Wither's *Preparation to the Psalter* (1619) and advertised as 'very rare' went to Stevens for £2.19s.od., nearly six times what Cambridge had hoped to pay; and Joseph Haslewood's edition of George Painter's *Palace of pleasure* (1813) was sold to Straker at £2.18s.od., well beyond the Library's bid of 7s.6d. The Library was unsuccessful too in its attempts at books by George Herbert, James Shirley, Henry Vaughan and Francis Quarles.[12]

Despite these disappointments, however, the Pickering sale could be accounted a resounding success, and henceforth the Syndicate regularly gave permission to Power or his advisers (chiefly Mayor, and later Bradshaw) to venture into the auction rooms. In 1866, writing by then as Librarian, Mayor explained the advantage, having in the previous year alone bought through Puttick and Simpson 577 volumes and nearly sixteen hundred prints and engravings for an outlay of only £41.

Never was it so advantageous to buy from sales as now; there are no rivals, no Hebers in the field. Good standard books fetch only the price of waste paper; and the auctioneers' commission in many cases does not cover their expenses. To buy from sales you need, 1. promptness; 2. a practised judgement of books and their prices; 3. a certain method. My method has been, for nearly 20 years, to mark in the catalogue all valuable books which are not in the library for which I buy; to affix a moderate price to each, bidding highly only for lots which have a special interest for the library in question, or which are unique, the collection perhaps of a lifetime.[13]

Mayor's further statement, that in order to save ten per cent commission he dealt directly with the auctioneers, rather than

---

[12] Details from the Library's annotated copy of the sale catalogue; Sotheby's bill is in the Vouchers for 1855.

[13] J. E. B. Mayor *Statement made to the Syndics of the Library* 7 March 1866 (Cambridge 1866). See also p. 648.

through an agent, was not entirely correct, since even in the London sales the Library had frequently resorted to third parties. Boone, for example (his name was perhaps suggested by Bradshaw), had secured a number of valuable lots for Cambridge at the sale of John Britton's library in May 1857, including Britton's own working copy of Dibdin's *Specimen of an English De Bure* (1810), his heavily grangerized copy of Gough's *English topography* (1780) – bought over Bohn at £4.14.0d. – and his uncompleted manuscript life of Lady Margaret Beaufort,[14] a work which was superseded a few years later by the publication of C. H. Cooper's *Memoir*, edited posthumously by Mayor himself.

For the sale of Dawson Turner's manuscripts in June 1859 the Library applied to C. J. Stewart, and secured a selection of lots that seems now sadly unadventurous in their blinkered insistence on local Cambridge interest: they did however include transcripts of the papers of John Covel, Master of Christ's College from 1688 to 1722, and a group of letters from John Strype on which the Library was prompted to bid £25 following the recent and much larger donation of the greater part of Strype's papers the same year by J. P. Baumgartner of Milton Hall. The Library secured virtually everything it bid for at the Turner sale, and with a little more fortitude and imagination might perhaps have secured much more. The one serious disappointment, in fact, was the Covel collection. Sir Frederic Madden was determined to get the original letters for the British Museum, and succeeded, leaving Cambridge only with the transcripts. 'The Covel Correspondence produced much higher prices than I had expected,' he wrote in his diary, 'but I was determined to have them, and I think the Cambridge people have acted ill in not stopping the bidding of their agent (Stewart) after I had given up to them the other Mss they wanted.'[15] Since by this stage in the sale the only lot

14 MS. Oo.6.89.
15 Madden's diary 6 June 1859, quoted in A. N. L. Munby *The cult of the autograph letter in England* (1962) p. 56.

Cambridge had wanted (and secured) was an eighteenth-century notebook about various books in Cambridge libraries, it is difficult to understand Madden's confidence in his own magnanimity unless he had already arranged matters with Stewart or the Library before the sale. In any case, with Sir Thomas Phillipps too short of money even to bid, Madden and the Museum carried nearly all before them. Cambridge was not a serious contender, either financially or in what it hoped to achieve, and manuscripts came a poor second to the quest for printed books. Indeed, apart from the Dawson Turner purchases, virtually the only other worthwhile manuscripts to be bought under Power's aegis consisted of a handful in Hebrew, offered by Nathan Coronel in the 1840s. The prize among them was a fourteenth-century French Ashkenazic volume containing as endpapers some ninth- or tenth-century fragments described by W. H. Lowe thirty years later as 'in all probability, the oldest specimen of the Talmud Babli in existence'.[16] This was an isolated incident, however, and in their almost complete uninterest in the acquisition of manuscripts of any kind Power and the Syndics proved themselves wholly within what had become virtually a Cambridge tradition. Rightly or wrongly, the chance to buy printed books in much larger quantities seemed to offer a more appropriate excitement.

The Dawson Turner sale, a relatively minor episode in the eyes of the Cambridge authorities, came only a few weeks after the auction in Paris of the library of the French classical scholar and *savant* Jean-François Boissonade, an affair which seemed to be of rather greater importance: for this, and for a sale by Van Voorst in Antwerp the same year, the Syndics set aside £150 each, compared with £82 for Dawson Turner.[17] Faced with a much wider variety of books than in the Pickering sale, the Library bought seriously from among Boissonade's law books,

---

[16] MS. Oo.6.70 (Schiller-Szinessy no. 79); W. H. Lowe *The fragment of Talmud Babli Pᵉ Sachim of the ninth or tenth century in the University Library, Cambridge* (Cambridge 1879) p. xiii.   [17] Syndicate Minutes 2 March 1859.

and even acquired two important *typographica*, A.-F. Didot's *Essai sur la typographie* (1851) and Didot l'aîné's *Spécimen* of 1819. But the classical texts held most attraction, and prompted extensive purchases, including the Library's third copy of the *editio princeps* of Plotinus (Basel 1580): most were of rather less interest in themselves. The Plotinus, at eight francs, was cheap compared with the many books advertised as bearing the annotations of Boissonade himself, but the Library bought several such adversaria, paying most for a copy of Grangaeus' edition of Juvenal (Paris 1614) – though Luard was unable to agree that the notes were by Boissonade at all.[18] Altogether, for the sum of £33.0s.6d., the Library acquired 188 lots, comprising many more titles.[19]

Ranging in date from 1519 (a copy of Francesco Filelfo's *Epistolae familiares*) to the mid-nineteenth century, with most falling into the last hundred years, the Boissonade purchases offered a more familiar selection of books than those from the Pickering sale: the Library had been filling its gaps in classical scholarship and other modern works of learning for years, and had paid especial attention to adversaria since the Askew sale of 1785. It was much more difficult to become accustomed to the suggestion of Henry Bradshaw, whose notions of what the Library should buy were not always met with whole-hearted enthusiasm or even grudging tolerance.

'Our library authorities very rarely consent to the purchase of anything except what they choose to call modern useful or scientific books', complained Bradshaw a few years later, in 1865, on declining a group of Low Countries incunables for the Library which he also considered too steeply priced for his own pocket.[20] However understandable his querulousness on this occasion, his verdict on the Librarian and the Syndics ought in fairness to have been delivered tongue in cheek. Quite apart from such episodes as the Pickering sale, where the

---

[18] Luard *Adversaria* p. 13.
[19] The annotated Boissonade catalogue stands at 8880.c.43.
[20] Bradshaw to Another (perhaps Nijhoff) 9 November 1865.

Library had taken a serious interest in English books of the sixteenth and seventeenth centuries, the authorities had shown themselves to be not wholly immune to Bradshaw's pleas for the acquisition of earlier books still. In March 1857 he and Mayor were authorized to buy extensively out of the latest catalogue from Thomas Kerslake of Bristol, and the two men were thus able to add a long series of recusant books to the Library.[21] His influence was to be seen in the purchase of a Sarum Missal of 1534 from Charles Dolman of New Bond Street in 1857, for £31.10s.0d., and of Zacharias Ferrerius *Hymni novi ecclesiastici* (Rome 1525) for seven guineas from C. J. Stewart in 1858.[22] A few months later David Nutt, of the Strand, supplied a quantity of liturgical books from his catalogue.[23] If such sums were to be spent regularly, it could not be long before there would be no more funds available, and in this lay a serious threat to Bradshaw's hopes. Many of the more important and obvious fifteenth-century books seemed in any case to be beyond the Library's grasp, and attainable, if at all, only by alternative methods. In view of this, it seems at least possible that when Thomas Boone, an old friend, wrote to Bradshaw in November 1859, there was some connivance between the two men:

Amongst the many rarities you so kindly shewed me the other day in Cambridge, I do not recollect seeing a single specimen of Block Book, and having now a copy of one of extreme rarity, there being but 3 known, I thought you might like to possess an example in exchange for one of your triplicate! Caxtons &c.

The volume in question is the 'De Generatione Christi' described by Sotheby Principia Typographica Vol. 2. p. 72. Two other copies only are known, one in the Royal Library at Gotha, the other in the Museum, which last besides being cut close and laid down has 2 Leaves in Facsimile, whereas ours has ample Margins and only 1 Leaf in Facsimile.

The other two copies being in Public Libraries, ours may be looked upon (in the view of acquisition) as a *Unique Book* and affords an opportunity for exchanging some of your many duplicates for so desirable

---

[21] Syndicate Minutes 18 March 1857. The invoice listed 139 items for £77.5s.0d.
[22] Vouchers 1858.   [23] Vouchers 1859.

a volume, as may never again occur. I forget the name of the Caxton of which there are 3 copies in Bp Moore's bequest?[24]

The Syndicate had been given power to exchange duplicates in March 1857.[25] Nothing however came of this proposal to exchange a block-book for one of the Library's three copies of Caxton's *Royal book*, even though Bradshaw was granted permission to pursue negotiations. Of the opportunities – even need – for such transactions, he had no doubts: 'the only way open to us of completing the collection of specimens of early typography; and the number of duplicates wch. we possess offers unusual facilities'.[26] There was therefore rather more satisfaction in the successful exchange three years later of one of the same three Caxtons for a copy of the St Albans *Nova rhetorica* of Laurentius de Saona, a work of more interest to Cambridge since it had been written there during Laurentius' sojourn in the 1470s, but which Bradshaw valued as much (if not more) for the sake of the type in which it was composed. The copy came from the Bodleian, and had been the high point of a sale of duplicates in May 1862: it had been acquired for £110.5s.0d. by Boone, who paid Cambridge an additional £100 as part of the exchange agreement.[27] The irony of the outcome was not realized until many years after, when it was discovered that not only had the Bodleian rejected Laud's copy, but that in retaining Tanner's it had kept a book that had once belonged to John Moore and which Tanner had failed to return after borrowing.[28] This transaction with Boone proved to be only the first of several exchanges involving the Library's incunables,[29] and the extra cash on this occasion allowed further purchases. With the additional money, Bradshaw was free to concentrate his attention on early printed books. Among them, Ulrich von Richtenthal's

---

[24] Thomas Boone to Bradshaw 24 November 1859 (MS. Add. 2591).

[25] Luard 601.   [26] Note by Bradshaw at the end of Boone's letter (note 24 above).

[27] Bradshaw to Edward Atkinson 19 November 1862: Bradshaw believed the price to have been £105.10s.0d.

[28] See above, pp. 66–7; Craster pp. 47–8; J. C. T. Oates 'The sale of a duplicate' *Bodleian Library Record* 3 (1950–1) pp. 175–6.   [29] Oates *Catalogue* p. 26 n. 4.

Concilium zu Constanz, printed by Sorg in Augsburg in 1483 and sold at Sotheby's in January 1863, arrived from Stewart in February. It was followed by the 1508 Statius from Deighton at a modest twelve shillings. By the summer Boone had produced a Bamberg Missal of 1506 and a Ratisbon Missal of 1515, both in contemporary pigskin, as well as a copy of Johannes de Verdena *Sermones Dormi secure* printed at Lyon in 1488; Deighton had supplied two more, including (at twelve guineas) a volume containing two works in Spanish by Pedro de Alcalá, printed at Granada in 1505–6; and there had arrived from Stewart a copy of the polyglot Pentateuch printed at Constantinople in 1547 – this last rather battered internally but none the worse for having belonged to Colbert. All these, and a number of others, were recorded by Bradshaw in a small notebook, until, at the end of the year and with a balance of £22.12s.6d., he noted the purchase from Ellis of a Passau Missal printed in Venice in 1522.

The exchange provided an all too rare occasion for Bradshaw to spend the Library's money as he wished. For the rest of his life, many of the books he bought for himself ended up in the Library eventually, as he strove to make an appropriate compromise between his own interests as a collector, the wider interests of the Library in which he was employed, and the task of persuading the Syndics to spend ever more heavily on early printed books. One of the few casualties of Bradshaw's practice of buying for himself, where in retrospect it might be argued that the Library had a superior claim, was the loss to the Library of a copy of Tate and Brady's Psalter printed at Tranquebar in 1717. It was offered in the second of Sotheby's sales of the books of Philip Bliss in August 1858, a sale where the Library seems to have bought nothing[30] to Bradshaw's eighteen lots, and was knocked down at twelve shillings despite a note in the catalogue to the effect that Henry Cotton knew of only one other copy. Bradshaw's prize does

---

[30] Despite the Syndics having given Bradshaw permission to spend up to £50 over the vacation if necessary.

not appear to have arrived at the Library among all his many donations, but this was an isolated and uncharacteristic misfortune. At an anonymous sale in March 1857,[31] for example, while the Library's purchases included a volume of *The weekly-journal: or, Saturday's-post* (1716–18), Bradshaw carried off a trophy for his Irish collection, Thomas Bray's *Statuta synodalia pro unitis dioecesibus Casel et Imelac* (1813), encouraged by the auctioneer's note that it was 'next to an impossibility to procure a copy of this work, which was printed for Priests only . . . No other copy than the present (it is said) has appeared for public sale.' Bray's book came to the Library within a few years as a gift, modest in that it was certainly not the most valuable of his donations; the final result, here as so often, was that Bradshaw was supplementing the Library's purchases out of his own purse.

Thanks not least to three or four individuals, donations arrived at the Library with ever more regularity and frequency. Because of its nature, it was almost inevitable that one collection was remembered above others. The correspondence and papers of John Strype and of Simon Patrick, Bishop of Ely, already alluded to, were made over to the Library by John Percy Baumgartner, of Milton Hall, in 1859–61, having originally been collected by Samuel Knight, the biographer of Erasmus and Colet, and with them came a mass of Knight's own papers.[32] These apart, the only donations recorded by Sayle in his *Annals* were of the manuscript of William Boyce's Installation ode for the Duke of Newcastle in June 1749 (given by Walmisley in 1851),[33] Richard Lepsius' monumental *Denkmäler aus Aegypten und Aethiopen* (given by the King of Prussia in 1852 and subsequently), and the manuscript of a work on Emanuel Swedenborg presented in 1854 on condition that it was never published.[34] The Donations Book records a rather more active period, notable also for repeated gifts by

---

[31] 6 March 1857 and following days: C. J. Stewart to Bradshaw 17 March 1857. The books were from the library of the dissenter John Wilks, an attorney of Finsbury Square: see *DNB*.   [32] MSS. Add. 1–88.   [33] MS. Nn.6.38.   [34] MS. Nn.6.35.

Charles C. Babington, J. E. B. Mayor and George Williams. Thirty-one items arrived from James Orchard Halliwell in 1848, including a number of sixteenth- and seventeenth-century Italian books and his own edition of the Lincoln *Morte Arthure* (1847), while in 1857 the widow of George Cornelius Gorham presented 227 tracts, pamphlets and other papers relating to the controversy surrounding her husband's beliefs in baptismal regeneration. Among the individual benefactors who produced books in a less wholesale manner were Sir Thomas Phillipps, who added to the parts of the printed catalogue of his manuscripts first given in 1840, Dr Martyn Price of New York, who presented his influential *Institutes of medicine* (New York 1854) in 1855,[35] and Henry Hazard, who gave runs of the *Cambridge Chronicle* and *Cambridge Journal* in 1859. The Rev. Arthur Brook, vicar of East Retford, added to the incunables in 1860 with the gift of a 1493 Thomas Aquinas.[36] The following year Charles C. Babington presented Robert Southey's copy of Pehr Löfling's *Iter Hispanicum 1751–1756* (Stockholm 1758), bought by Southey out of a Longman catalogue in 1826; Leonard Jenyns supplemented the collection of eighteenth-century editions of Italian literature given by him in 1852 with the manuscript of an unpublished poem *The sentimental naturalist*, the work of his great-uncle Leonard Chappelow, nephew of the former Professor of Arabic of the same name;[37] while through H.M. Ambassador at Constantinople were acquired various Arabic newspapers published in Beirut the year before, to accompany a collection presented by Lord John Russell in 1859 simply on the grounds that Russell thought that they 'might be an interesting addition to the University Library'.[38] Equally curious, in 1860 the Library received from J. S. Henslow a copy of *Robinson Crusoe* in Maori published at Wellington in 1852 and the compilation

---

[35] He also gave the eighth edition in 1867 and the ninth in 1870.   [36] Inc. 1969.
[37] MS. Nn.1.33. On Chappelow's friendship with Mrs Piozzi, who scribbled her remarks on the poem in the manuscript, see James L. Clifford *Hester Lynch Piozzi* 2nd ed. (Oxford 1968).   [38] Donations Book.

of *Maori mementos; being a series of addresses, presented by the native people, to Sir George Grey* (Auckland 1855). The Chancellor of the University, Prince Albert, sent not only William MacGillivray's *Natural history of Dee Side and Braemar*, edited from the manuscript in the possession of the Queen, but also Andreas Schleiermacher's *Bibliographisches System der gesammten Wissenschaftskunde* (Braunschweig 1852) – a manual of library classification in which the Library staff seem to have taken little positive interest. The University could not well refuse this, but in a rare act of ingratitude the Syndics did decline to accept a pretty little volume by George Asplen of Corpus Christi College, *A lively sketch of a trip to Killarney and the south of Ireland*, published in 1858: ironically, two copies arrived among Bradshaw's Irish books in 1870, and slipped safely into the Library. All these were from private individuals. One of the few manuscripts to be given (the Baumgartner papers apart) came through the generosity of the Society for Promoting Christianity among the Jews, who in 1853 presented a seventeenth-century Pentateuch roll written in a Chinese hand.[39] Maps of the United States arrived from the U.S. Coast Survey, and of France (both the 1:80,000 and 1:320,000 series) through the French Embassy. American legislation arrived both from Washington and from several of the individual states, and from about 1840 the Smithsonian sent a steady flow of donations leavened in 1855 with the gift by James Lenox of David de Vries's *Voyage from Holland to America 1632–1644* (New York 1853). Other offerings came from the universities of Utrecht, Leiden and Kiel, even from as far away as Bombay, and from Melbourne, where the State Library, government and university all sent regular parcels. From 1855, all gifts were recorded in the printed annual reports.

Not everything, however, was gain. In 1855 Whewell became Vice-Chancellor for a second term, and within a few

---

[39] MS. Add. 283 (Schiller-Szinessy no. 6).

weeks exerted his position to take upon himself to rearrange the pictures in the Fitzwilliam Museum. The results were not entirely happy, and in protest against his high-handed action five members of the Museum's Syndicate resigned.[40] To rearrange the Library was altogether too large a task – in most respects. But for years it had been used as a repository in which to hoard all manner of museum objects, of which some had little more than curiosity value and others were of obvious scholarly importance. When Andrew Perne had given his collection of coins to the University in the sixteenth century they found a place in the Library well established by contemporary conventions of collecting. By the mid-nineteenth century, not only had conventions changed, but the erection of the Fitzwilliam Museum also meant that for the first time the University had a museum in name rather than the *ad hoc* arrangements in the Library. The University Library therefore began to divest itself of some of the special collections that had come to seem inappropriate, and the process began under the guidance of Whewell. In April 1856 the Syndicate (chaired by Whewell) requested a Grace to transfer the old university collection of coins to the Museum, where they could be added to the coins and medals already there.[41] The Grace was passed easily, but later in the summer further changes were made that were far more obvious to a casual visitor.

The Library Syndicate Minutes for 16 June record simply that the Vice-Chancellor was authorized to spend whatever was requisite 'for the necessary repairs of the Pictures belonging to the Library'. Nothing was recorded as to moving them out of the Library permanently, and yet on 17 July Whewell descended on Romilly in the Registry, offering to send him the pictures he planned to turn out, including Vanderbanck's portrait of Nicholas Saunderson, bequeathed

---

[40] Winstanley *Early Victorian Cambridge* pp. 139–47.
[41] Syndicate Minutes 21 April 1856; Library papers 26 April 1856; Grace of 30 April 1856 (Grace Book *II* p. 74).

by Kerrich in 1828. Scarcely surprisingly, Romilly acceded joyfully, noting also in his diary that Whewell planned to demote Reinagle's vast portrait of 'Maps' Nicholson from its 'too honourable place' on the Library staircase, where it had hung since Farmer's day.[42] When the pictures arrived on 23 August, Romilly found that among the assortment of twenty-two paintings and framed prints he had acquired from the Library there were also the celebrated picture (executed long after its subject's death) of Thomas Hobson the carrier, and the old painting still in the Registry depicting the duties of the Proctors and other university officers.[43] He despatched two of them straight to be 'restored & beautified', and Whewell got his way: neither Saunderson nor Thomas Hobson is now in the Library, and Nicholson himself was saved only because the picture was too large to be accommodated elsewhere. Whewell's autocratic methods had, perhaps, little to recommend them, but the removal of the coins to the Fitzwilliam Museum, and the beginnings of a general tidying up of the Library with the removal of some of the pictures were practical, logical, and even necessary. Other objects were also to find new homes round Cambridge during the next decade, in attempts to impose some logic on the University's accumulations.

In the face of Power's opinion that the Library could usefully gain by being put on the same footing as the British Museum with regard to copyright deposit, his seemingly contrary admission that he deprecated the sending of 'infantine publications', his expressed disappointment at the difficulty in cataloguing so many books, his repeated belief that a reading room was indispensable, and his wish for an extension to the Library, the Cambridge Commissioners arrived at the most obvious conclusion: 'That the privilege which the Copyright

---

[42] MS. Add. 6836[2]: 17 July 1856; Gunning *Reminiscences* 1 p. 200.
[43] MS. Add. 6836[2]: 23 July and 25 August 1856; a list of the pictures dated 1856 is in the University Archives, C.U.R. 20.1.21(5).

Act gives to the University might be advantageously commuted for a money payment, to be expended in the purchase
and binding of such works recently published as might be
deemed to be worth preserving.'[44] By no means the least of the
considerations that led them to this was the nature of the
buildings in which the books were housed, and particularly of
the Cockerell Building:

The cost of providing space and fittings for the reception of books supplies
another argument against the accumulation of such as possess a temporary
interest only. The portion of the New Library, with its fittings, but
exclusive of the Geological and Mineralogical Museum beneath it, was
completed about fifteen years ago, at an expense of about 20,000*l*; it was
designed to afford space for about 80,000 volumes, and the accumulation
of books which has taken place since that time have already nearly sufficed
to fill the space which it provided. If future additions to the building are to
be made in the same style (and the locality is one that demands no small
amount of architectural decoration), it would involve an expenditure of
250*l*. for every 1000 volumes. This consideration alone renders necessary
the exercise of great vigilance and caution in the selection and purchase of
books, in order to see that their intrinsic value, whether for the purposes of
reference or study, is sufficient to justify the large expenditure required for
their reception and preservation.[45]

The most obvious way to achieve savings without damag-
ing the book funds was to erect a cheap building, and the first
proposal to emerge after the Commissioners' Report was made
public suggested just that. Thomas Smith was, however, no
genius, and his plan for an extension to the Library can have
commanded little serious consideration. He proposed a continuation at first floor level along the line of the south side of
King's Old Court, linked to the old South Room of the
Library by a bridge and to the Law School below it by a
passageway from the gallery at its west end. The room was to
be lit by five plain sash windows on the south, and two on the
west overlooking Clare College, while the ground floor was
open to the court through a series of round-headed arches. At
an estimated cost of £554.10s.0d., his plan, presented to H. W.
Cookson and to Robert Willis, the Jacksonian Professor, had
one merit only; but the advantage of its extreme economy was

---

[44] Cambridge University Commission *Report* p. 129.   [45] *Ibid.*, p. 128.

no compensation for a poverty-stricken and completely undistinguished design. It did not provide the answer the University sought, and fell from the drawing board already dead.[46]

But if the Commissioners took a gloomy view of the future of the Library, Francis Bashforth, Fellow of St John's, took one even more so. In his view, even if Cockerell's proposed court were finished, there would at best be only room for ten years' expansion.[47] His proposals, to build bookstacks to a much more modest and utilitarian design, and to convert part of the Cockerell Building into a reading room, were not taken up, but his pamphlet, printed only a year after the Commissioners' Report had been published and (so far as the Library was concerned) ignored in most respects, was a salutary reminder. With the Cockerell Building still not paid for, and the Library expanding at an alarming rate, it seemed to Bashforth that Cockerell's plans for wholesale remodelling should be entirely abandoned. His pamphlet, on these points at least, met with tacit agreement in the University, and the reformed Library Syndicate turned its attention instead over the next few years to the possibilities offered for expansion in the existing buildings. Their decisions were partly influenced by two other bodies. In February 1853 a Museums and Lecture Rooms Syndicate had been appointed to look into the whole question of teaching accommodation, including the rooms below the Library;[48] and in 1854 the Worts Trustees agreed to make over £7000 of Old South Sea Stock available for an extension, subject to a contribution from the Library Subscription Fund for the same purpose.[49] Besides these developments, by the end of 1858 the Building Fund for a new library stood at £3688.5s.6d., of which £2000 had been given in trust by Thomas Halford of Jesus College in 1842 and £50 came from Power's own pocket.[50]

[46] Smith's plans and accompanying letter dated 21 January 1853 are now in the Map Room, MS. Plans 675–7.
[47] Francis Bashforth *Observations on some recent university buildings* (Cambridge 1853) p. 11.
[48] Grace of 2 February 1853; Winstanley *Early Victorian Cambridge* pp. 268–89.
[49] Syndicate Minutes 13 and 27 February 1854.   [50] Clark *Endowments* pp. 457–60.

Uncertainty about regular Library expenditure caused the Library Syndics to feel compelled to put off the Worts proposals initially, however, and they did not return to the subject for over eighteen months. Moving therefore with some care, they reported formally to the Senate only in February 1856, and appealed publicly for funds towards a new building – without specifying whether they had in mind an extension to the Cockerell Building or to the original Schools.[51] Nonetheless, by this time it had become clear to everyone that Cockerell's scheme would never be completed, and there was a pragmatic air about the Syndics' next move. The rooms at the northern end of the Arts School and the western end of the Divinity School, for many years used as stores for music, novels, and, more recently, newspapers, were accessible only through a door at the north-west corner of the Schools court and so were not directly under the supervision of the Library. By erecting an iron spiral staircase down to the ground floor from the northern range of the Library this area could be brought under better surveillance. The Grace approving this simple measure also allowed the Library to take in the rest of the Divinity School[52] – a room used only as a storeroom for tables, platforms and other paraphernalia employed in ceremonies in the Senate House.[53] By the following March, with the windows enlarged to admit more light and with proper access from the other smaller rooms in

---

[51] Syndicate Minutes 21 February 1856 (printed report). The Minutes of the Worts Trustees are in the University Archives, Char.II.6.

[52] Syndicate Minutes 20 October 1856; Library papers 27 October 1856; Grace of 29 October 1856.

[53] When the Queen and the Prince Consort visited Cambridge in 1843, Adam Sedgwick had to prepare a way through this room at unexpectedly short notice. 'Since the building of the New Library this place of ancient theological disputations has been converted into a kind of lumber-room, and was filled, from end to end, with every kind of unclean thing. You would have laughed to see this dark and dismal chamber, just lighted enough to show its horrors. Mops, slop-pails, chimney-pots, ladders, broken benches, rejected broken cabinets from the Library, two long ladders, and an old rusty scythe, were the things that met the eye, and everything was covered with half an inch of venerable dust' (J. W. Clark and T. McK. Hughes *The life and letters of Adam Sedgwick* (Cambridge 1890) 2 pp. 61–2).

the north-west corner, the new room was ready for occupation.[54] Much of the space was filled almost immediately with runs of periodicals and Parliamentary papers, and a collection of books described in the next annual report of the Syndics as 'light reading',[55] consisting principally of English poetry, biography and fiction. In expansive mood, the Syndicate then moved on to consider the remainder of the ground floor. The need for a room where readers could be brought especially valuable books remained, and their thoughts on this turned to the East Room which, cleared of the bookcases, would have been a reading room of great beauty. Two possibilities offered themselves: first, that the lectures, examinations and other activities customarily conducted in the Arts and Law Schools (on the ground floor of the west and south ranges respectively) might be exiled to a temporary building to be erected in the old Botanic Garden, or second, that the south range of the Library should be extended westward, towards Clare College and across the south side of the old court of King's – a project which would add two rooms each about a hundred feet long to the Library and would leave an ample residue in the building fund.[56] Neither scheme progressed very far, and by March 1860 the Syndicate viewed the situation with some desperation as they urged the appointment of a special syndicate to examine the subject.[57] This further syndicate's recommendation, that the ground floor should be made over to the Library and new lecture rooms built, met with decided opposition, and had been (temporarily) abandoned by April 1862:[58] the Arts School was finally vacated for the Library only in 1903, and the Woodwardian Museum of Mineralogy beneath the Cockerell Building, dismissed as inadequate for its purpose in 1853,[59]

---

[54] Romilly's diary 9 January 1857 (Add. 6837); Syndicate Minutes 4 February and 1 April 1857; Annual Report 7 March 1857.   [55] Annual Report 17 February 1858.
[56] Library papers October and November 1858.   [57] Annual Report 7 March 1860.
[58] Grace of 25 October 1860; Library papers 15 November 1860 (report); Romilly's diary 25 April 1861 (Add. 6840²); Library papers 27 March 1862; Romilly's diary 4 April 1862.
[59] University Archives Min.VI.65, p. 23 (printed report 31 December 1853).

became available the same year.[60] Motives for preventing the Library from taking over the Arts and Law Schools were various, part financial and part practical. There was everything to be gained by building a proper extension, as George Williams, one of the most able defenders of the Library's real interests, explained:

The old Divinity School which has been already annexed to the Library is very ill suited for the purpose, and is calculated to hold not more than 10,000 volumes: some of which are suffering from damp and mould, owing to insufficient ventillation; a defect which it would be very difficult to remedy. The other Schools which it is proposed to appropriate would certainly be neither more capacious nor more commodious than the Divinity School; while the Lecture Room is so small that its value for Library extension would be scarcely appreciable.[61]

Even if all three rooms, including the small lecture room under the East Room which had been used to teach Divinity since 1795,[62] were added, there would still be room for no more than about five years' expansion. Williams had, therefore, persuaded Thomas Smith, Curator of University Buildings, again to draw up plans in 1858–9 for an extension to the west, in a style close to the fifteenth-century south wing, and to survey the south wing with a view to adding a third storey. The whole project would, he calculated, be well within the University's ability to pay from the accumulated Building and Worts Funds.[63]

Williams dated his pamphlet 28 March 1862, and within less than seven weeks a yet further syndicate was appointed, specifically to consider additional buildings for the Library.[64] It acted with a determination that had not always been customary in such matters, as if to compensate for the several years' debate that had preceded it. The Syndics' choice of architect fell not on Anthony Salvin, whose plans for new

---

[60] *Reporter* 1903–4 p. 1126; but see also *Reporter* 1883–4 p. 924.
[61] G. Williams *University Library extension. A letter to the Vice-Chancellor* (Cambridge 1862) p. 5.   [62] Willis & Clark 3 p. 68.
[63] Williams *University Library extension* pp. 8–10.
[64] Grace of 15 May 1862, Grace Book *P* p. 237.

lecture rooms in Free School Lane had been before the University since 1854,[65] and whose work was inescapable to passers-by in the town since he had been responsible for the rebuilt front of Trinity Hall and had only recently completed the first stage of Whewell's Court at Trinity, but on George Gilbert Scott. To Scott had been due the successful restoration of Ely Cathedral, under the guidance of the Dean George Peacock – the same man who had taken so active an interest in the Cockerell Building in the 1820s – who died in 1858. Scott had since been retained as architect of the new chapel at St John's,[66] but he had still not completed any major building in Cambridge. In choosing him the Syndics could have found their encouragement in a sentence in Scott's *Remarks on secular & domestic architecture, present & future*, of which the second edition appeared in 1858: 'I must say that I think it would be difficult to conceive anything more noble than an extensive library, carried out with true feeling, and in a style founded on that of the best period of our art.'[67] He presented his preliminary plans on 22 November, less than eight months after the Syndics had been appointed. They provided for a third storey to the south range, and a continuation towards the west returning at the south-west corner to the old fifteenth-century gateway of King's – 'one of the architectural gems of Cambridge'.[68] The southern range of King's Old Court had been pulled down several years before, and by 1862 the site was covered with little more serious than a patchwork of single-storeyed buildings prettily (and wholly unsuitably) roofed in pantiles (fig. 23). Scott quickly proved his sympathy for the task by designing a building which was in a style not far removed from the original buildings as recorded in the Cambridge University almanack of 1822, which had depicted

[65] *The Builder* 11 January 1862 p. 31.
[66] Historical Monuments Commission *Cambridge* pp. 214, 246; Alec C. Crook *From the foundation to Gilbert Scott; a history of the buildings of St John's College, Cambridge, 1511 to 1885* (Cambridge 1980) p. 92.   [67] *Remarks* p. 201.
[68] G. G. Scott to the Syndics 22 November 1862, printed in Library papers 10 December 1862.

23   The west face of King's College Old Court. From a photograph by
William Kingsley, *c.* 1850.

King's old buildings from the south-west. His design was
restrained, even plain along the southern face, where the
building could in any case be viewed only in sharp perspective.
It provided for a first-floor room high enough to permit a
gallery, while the westernmost end, somewhat more decorative, was rounded off with a turret at the corner. The whole
was castellated to marry with the older parts of the Schools.
The cost was not impossible. Scott estimated that the southern
side of King's old court could be built for £11,500 or £12,000
and a third storey added to the old south range for an extra
£3800 or so, a total of £15,800. After the University had paid
King's a small sum for 'several small Pieces of Ground which
will be required for the erection of Buttresses, a Turret, and a
Bay Window' on the side facing the chapel,[69] the Library

[69] Library papers 11 June 1863.

Building Syndicate recommended that the University should accept a tender of £14,500 – agreeably less, despite various alterations, than Scott's first estimate. The oriel window on the first floor overlooking Clare College gateway was an after-thought, and not included on the original plan.[70]

The contract for the work was awarded to Messrs Jackson and Shaw of Westminster, who were by this time already at work on Scott's chapel at St John's and who therefore had an edge on their rivals in costing the work for tender. By the end of April the foundations of the new wing were virtually complete. George Williams laid the foundation stone on 21 May, and apart from the unavoidable delays in winter the building went steadily forward. Central heating was installed in April 1867, and the work finished at the end of the following September – though the building had been pressed into use for examinations six months before the builders had left.[71] While this new work was being done, an opportunity was also taken thoroughly to restore several of the older parts of the Schools, including the main staircase on the east front, the windows, much of the east court, and the great gates in the old gateway of King's. Williams had hoped – and even proposed in a printed pamphlet in December 1864[72] – that the new building would be continued round to the old gateway, to provide a Divinity School on the ground floor and a council chamber on the first. Had his proposal been accepted, much acrimony over the use of space might subsequently have been avoided, since the extra buildings would have freed space more convenient to the Library. There was much support for his hopes, but his sympathizers wielded insufficient influence to carry the day. Scott had taken on himself to prepare estimates for a western range, and pleaded repeatedly for the University to dip further into its pocket. Work on the south range was well advanced

[70] Library papers 2 February 1864; Luard 709 (contract, specification and plans). Most of Scott's plans are in the University Archives, P. XXXI.1–40.

[71] Weekly letters from William Cooper, for the contractors, to the Vice-Chancellor, date between 23 April 1864 and 5 October 1867. See also Willis & Clark 3 pp. 123–4, and Grace of 28 March 1867.   [72] Library papers 6 December 1864.

when on 1 July 1865 he wrote to James Cartmell the Vice-Chancellor, 'Is it not wasteful to erect a wall to the end of the building where it is so patent that an extension is contemplated?'[73] Like Scott, a petition organized in the following November spoke of the consequent unsightliness, quite apart from inconvenience to the University.[74] Besides Mayor (by now Librarian), Bradshaw and R. L. Bensly, the signatories included J. B. Lightfoot, John Couch Adams, both Churchill and Charles C. Babington, E. W. Blore, J. T. Abdy, H. R. Luard, and the young J. W. Clark: much of the support came, not unnaturally, from St John's, Mayor's own college. This well-meaning effort had however no effect against a financially cautious University, and Scott had to bow to the majority. 'I am grieved to hear', he wrote the following April, 'that my hopes, so long entertained, are destined to be disappointed and that the Library is to remain a shapeless fragment. I will give orders for the condemnatory wall and hope for better times.'[75] Until the erection of the Hancock Building (so named after Edward Grey Hancock)[76] in 1887–90 to Scott's design, the western face of the Library thus offered a distinctly bizarre series of contrasts (fig. 24).

   None of these developments – new buildings, a greatly increased stock of books, a leap in expenditure, and an expansion of the Library staff – was however so fundamental that it conflicted in principle with the Library as it had existed since the fifteenth century. Imperfectly understood and inefficiently pursued though its purposes had been on many occasions and even for long periods, in one respect it had remained little different. The rules promulgated in 1751 began with the simple regulation, repeated from earlier similar codes 'That no person be allowed the use of the library but members of the university senate, and bachelors of law and physick'.[77] Undergraduates and Bachelors of Arts were thus not merely

[73] MS. Add. 2594 (10).   [74] *Ibid.*
[75] Scott to Cartmell 23 April 1866 (MS. Add. 2594 (10)).
[76] Clark *Endowments* pp. 460–2.
[77] *Statuta Academiae Cantabrigiensis* (Cambridge 1785) p. 424. Cf. Oates *History* p. 296.

24   The west face of the Scott Building, with the Cockerell Building
      and the old entrance to King's College. From a photograph taken
      c. 1880.

not expected to have any need to use the Library: they were
excluded. As long as undergraduate study aimed at a modest
level of competence in a few restricted subjects this mattered
little for most men, and although one or two colleges such as
Trinity (which boasted an undergraduate library from as early
as 1700) made some provision for undergraduate members and
B.A.s, for many there was no such library at all. On occasion
the University Library allowed exceptions, as in the case of
Charles Burney – 'very studious & industrious: insomuch, that
he was admitted into the Public Library, tho' an undergraduate'.[78] But Burney's behaviour gave the authorities an excuse

[78] Note by William Cole, British Library MS. Add. 5864 p. 318; see Ralph S. Walker
'Charles Burney's theft of books at Cambridge' *Trans. Cambridge Bibliographical Soc.* 3
(1962) pp. 313–26, at p. 313.

to withdraw even this selective privilege in 1777. Undergraduates did not gain free entry into the building for a century, and it was half a century again before they became commonplace.

By May 1814 the Syndics had however relented from the position entailed on them by Burney's reprehensible conduct, and undergraduates and Bachelors were at least tolerated, up to a point: 'That no person *in statu pupillari* . . . be allowed to examine the Catalogue or take down books, unless in company of a Master of Arts, or a Member of the Senate, or Bachelor of Law and Physic'.[79] But although the Syndics found it necessary in 1833 to remind undergraduates of this regulation, and to add that those *in statu pupillari* who entered the University Library should do so in their academical dress,[80] in 1828 they had recommended to the University that Bachelors of Arts should be allowed to use the Library and to borrow books on the counter-signature of their tutors:[81] the Syndics' far-reaching proposal, opposed by Dr Geldart in the Caput in December that year, received the approval of the University on 18 March following. So far would the mood of the University allow, but no more. In March 1831, two years after admitting Bachelors, a Grace proposing that Samuel Matthews, organist of Trinity College and a Bachelor of Music, should be allowed to use the Library was withdrawn before it could be put to a vote, and even when the proposal had been amended to cite the example of Thomas Tudway (later Professor of Music) in 1684 it was thrown out by the Caput.[82]

Such was the technical position, still based in the 1830s on rules adopted in the middle of the previous century, which themselves incorporated earlier regulations. Bachelors of Arts and undergraduates had been admitted under the wing of Masters of Arts before the reforms of 1829,[83] and by 1848,

---

[79] Library papers 25 May 1814.   [80] Library papers 3 June 1833.
[81] Library papers 17 November 1828; Grace Book *N* pp. 242 and (when the Grace was passed on 18 March 1829) 243.   [82] Luard 392. See also Oates *History* p. 457.
[83] [E. S. Appleyard] *Letters from Cambridge* (1828) p. 123.

with the rules for undergraduates still unchanged, the provisions of 1751 were in practice set aside whenever it seemed appropriate. As Power explained:

Strictly speaking Members of the Senate and Bachelors of Law and Physic are the only persons who are privileged to search the Catalogues and to take down books from the shelves, but that privilege is by courtesy extended to Bachelors of Arts, to Masters of Arts who have ceased to be members of the Senate, and to persons who have taken an ad-eundem degree from Oxford or Dublin. Undergraduates can only use the Library when accompanied by a member of the Senate or a Bachelor of Law or Physic, and are not at liberty to take out Volumes in their own right though they frequently obtain them through a Member of the Senate, or Bachelor of Law or Physic, the latter being responsible for them.[84]

As there were inevitably occasions when no senior member of the University other than the Library staff was available to come to undergraduates' aid, in 1834 a bell was placed at the door of the Library to be rung before they entered: it seems that one of the Library Keepers, thus alerted, acted as the necessary cicerone while these few intrepid undergraduates ventured in, unhindered either by the catalogue (which they were forbidden to consult) or by the need to read (since they could not take books off the shelves).[85] This arrangement was both absurd in that it was clearly beyond the spirit of the 1751 rules, and foolish in that it took no official account of the mood for reform in undergraduate courses. It was merely a convenient means of meeting criticism that had been voiced since at least 1828. 'Access is granted to any, – directly to members of the senate, indirectly only to members *in statu pupillari*', remarked one observer that year, a little before the admission of Bachelors of Arts, adding, 'Yet why not, may I ask, directly to all? Since all contribute by a recent grace to its support.'[86] Demands on other libraries in the University, which presented a somewhat patchwork quality, are not easy to estimate, but

---

[84] Return to the Home Secretary 20 November 1848; Luard 542; *Parliamentary papers* 1849. 45 p. 203.
[85] Syndics' orders 17 November 1834 and 27 May 1844 (Library papers).
[86] [E. S. Appleyard] *Letters from Cambridge* (1828) p. 122.

the example of Trinity College, the largest of the colleges and blessed with an undergraduate collection, is not irrelevant. Describing the scene in the cloister below the library there just before it opened for the Easter Term J. M. F. Wright wrote – not necessarily with grotesque exaggeration:

Immediately the doors flew open in rushed the torrent, fifty perhaps wanting the same identical book. Such was the eagerness displayed by all, that some tripped up in ascending the lofty stairs, others stumbled over them, caps and gowns flying in most irreverent unacademical confusion. 'But necessity has no law,' and 'cares not a fig for fine feathers.' Books many wanted I, but being short-legged and weak-muscled, brought up just in time to meet them on the way out of the Library.[87]

The demand, however, was for a strictly limited number of textbooks, not for the universal range of the University Library where few undergraduates had, strictly speaking, any need to roam. The changes, when they arrived, came as a result not so much of undergraduate pressure (though that played a part) as of changes to the curriculum and of reformed teaching methods and practices.

Meanwhile, to senior members of the University unwilling to countenance the shattering of their prerogative to read in peace, and to critics anxious not to admit more readers into an already overcrowded building, George Peacock was ready in 1831 with a proposal. Like several others, he saw the extension and rebuilding of the Library as the means to promote reform, but even he was not prepared to allow undergraduates direct access to the shelves:

If proper Reading Rooms were provided in the New Library, I can see no reason why the Undergraduates generally should not be allowed to consult books, whilst the privilege of taking them to their own rooms should be confined to Graduates. It would require two rooms, in one of which the catalogues would be placed, and an additional Library Keeper, for procuring the books which might be asked for, and for replacing them afterwards in their proper places in the Library.[88]

Peacock's plea, unheeded in 1831, was taken up in print again by a correspondent to the *Cambridge Chronicle* in 1842, who

[87] [J. M. F. Wright] *Alma mater; or, seven years at the University of Cambridge* (1827) I p. 183.
[88] [G. Peacock] *Observations* (Cambridge 1831) p. 62 n.

pointed out that three-quarters of the resident members of the University were excluded from the use of the Library.[89] But others, such as V. A. Huber, Professor of European Literature at Marburg and author of the fullest study of the English university system as a whole so far to have appeared in the nineteenth century, were not convinced that undergraduates should be able to consult whatever they wished anyway:[90] his view, however, was not shared by an increasingly powerful faction in Cambridge.

In 1840 the *Cambridge Portfolio*, a miscellany of university topography and history edited by John James Smith of Caius, remarked of the Library, 'There remains now but to give facility of access to Undergraduates; a concession which promises so well that it is to be hoped the completion of the new building will be the date of its bestowal.'[91] Smith became, as Fellow of his college, an industrious pamphleteer with a penchant for printing open letters in the interest of reform; and six years later he returned to the attack in a tract ostensibly about the new Botanic Garden. In his eyes the Library and the museums had one feature in common: neither was accessible to those who had real need to use them. 'The *Public* Library too is shut against a number of Members of the University, who, nevertheless, expressly contribute to the funds of the Library.' But there was a further unfairness beyond the oft-repeated complaint that undergraduates were liable to the so-called library tax. Complete strangers, he pointed out, could be admitted without so much as an introduction from a Master of Arts, and once inside had frequently to be left unattended while the inadequate staff were otherwise distracted; 'and thus strangers enjoy a licence which those who contribute to the support of the Library may not indulge in'. 'Indeed,' Smith continued, 'the students themselves, as they begin to feel the want of books, owing to the improved and advanced state of study, are also beginning to ask the question, why the Library

[89] University Archives, University papers 1840–3, no. 842.
[90] V. A. Huber *Die englischen Universitäten* (Cassel 1840) 2 p. 438 n.
[91] J. J. Smith (ed.) *The Cambridge Portfolio* (Cambridge 1840) p. 446.

is called *Public*, when the larger number of those who constitute the University . . . are excluded virtually by the rules of the Institution.' Like many in Cambridge, he recognized the great strides taken by the Library in other matters, and appreciated how much had been done with how few staff: 'Together with many others, I can bear witness to the improvement going on in this establishment, both as to the order and security of the books; an improvement which has been promoted by zeal and judgment, against the great disadvantage of want of hands.' The answer, for Smith, seemed to lie in two specific needs. First, there must be some increase in staff; and second, he could see no reason why undergraduates should not be served with whatever books they demanded, and even be allowed to borrow on a limited scale: the second of course depended on the first.[92] But his suggestions, although they attracted sufficient attention to be printed verbatim in the local press,[93] brought no immediate reform.

Cockerell's building, even had it been completed, made no provision for any general reading rooms, either for undergraduates or for anyone else, and with only one wing completed in any case the Syndics were forced to compromise. In February 1849 a sub-syndicate composed of the Vice-Chancellor H. W. Cookson of Peterhouse, Henry Philpott (Master of St Catharine's), G. E. Paget, W. H. Stokes (the Senior Proctor), and Joseph Power, was appointed to re-examine the Library's rules generally. The inclusion of Philpott and Paget, later Regius Professor of Physic, was astute. Forthright in their willingness to promote reform, and at the same time respectful of earlier traditions, both men enjoyed the confidence of the University, and the sub-syndicate took a much needed step forward. Besides amending various borrowing regulations as they applied to those already entitled to use the Library, and dealing with the rules applying to casual visitors, it also

[92] J. J. Smith *Address to the Senate on the subject of the new Botanic Garden, etc.* (Cambridge 1846) pp. 12–15.   [93] University Archives, University papers 1843–7, no. 827.

proposed that undergraduates should be admitted during the last hour that the Library was open each day, without any need for formal supervision by senior members or Library staff. It was so small an advance that the full Syndicate did not feel it necessary to propose a Grace; and in any case the established practice within the Library remained – enshrined from 1 May in properly endorsed rules – that undergraduates 'shall not be permitted to examine the Catalogues or to take down Books from the shelves'.[94]

For many in Cambridge the problem seemed to be one not only of staff, but of space. Adam Sedgwick, thinking of teaching and other undergraduate facilities generally, re-marked a few months later in speaking of public lecture rooms ('defective in number and unworthy of the University'), 'Our new scheme of Undergraduate-study will make these defects seem more grievous than they were before, and induce us, I trust, before long, to complete a second side of the new quadrangle of the Public Library.'[95] Whether he had in mind some modification of Cockerell's plan so as to incorporate a reading room, or simply the great increase in the number of books assumed for extended curricula, his plea for some further action was clear. In the event, restrictions on the use of the Library by undergraduates were all but abolished before there was either a reading room or adequate new buildings.

The position was made no easier by the state of the college libraries, which in itself was not a matter for the University. For much of the century the extent to which they met the needs of triposes was considered with disarming irregularity. They figured in few of the many accounts, serious or satirical, of student life, while the findings of the Cambridge Commission in 1852 revealed a panorama that varied dramatically from college to college as regards not only size but also access and provision of modern textbooks. For the Commissioners,

---

94 Library papers 26 March 1849.
95 Adam Sedgwick *A discourse on the studies of the University of Cambridge* 5th ed. (1850) p. cccxlvi.

Trinity College seemed almost a model. Placed under the control of the Stanhope librarian, a senior member of the University whose sole business it was and who was assisted by an under-librarian, well used (in 1850 five thousand books were borrowed by a society of something over fifty Fellows and 502 undergraduates), regularly inspected for losses, and blessed with a selection policy for new books that had student needs particularly in mind, it bore little resemblance to most others in the University, which remained the preserves of Fellows.[96] By contrast, Peterhouse, with an undergraduate population of forty-two, did not expect junior members of the college to remain in the library unless accompanied by the Master or a Foundation Fellow; and at Queens' the tone of J. E. Dalton, the Vice-President, seemed distinctly chilly: 'Under-graduates occasionally obtain books by application to individual Fellows: but it is generally the case that they are referred to the College Tutors, who obtain for them from the Library the books which they need.' At Magdalene, Mynors Bright saw fit to mention undergraduate admission in the same sentence as he reported that a fire was kept alight in the library: the college had also overcome problems of security in a courageous manner, to the advantage of its fifty undergraduates. 'Keys are given to those of them who are deserving, and who are desirous of the privilege, and they are allowed in the daytime to sit and read there. This is a privilege, which is found to be of great benefit, and of which the undergraduates gladly avail themselves.'[97]

But while access to their college libraries was at least possible for most undergraduates, few colleges could boast a collection that had much regard to their everyday needs. Exceptions apart (and there were, admittedly, several), the Commissioners

[96] Cambridge University Commission *Report* (1852) pp. 133–4. Whewell's report as Master on the library, submitted under protest, is printed in the *Evidence* p. 425; the Commissioners went out of their way to placate him. On the college library in the nineteenth century see P. Gaskell and R. Robson *The Library of Trinity College; a short history* (Cambridge 1971) pp. 33–8.

[97] *Evidence* p. 315 (Peterhouse), 358 (Queens'), 413 (Magdalene).

remarked bluntly, 'there is generally . . . a considerable deficiency of modern books for the use of Students'.[98] Even at Trinity, where Whewell noted that 'the Library is well supplied with modern and other books, connected with the usual subjects of academical instructions and study, especially Classics, Mathematics, English History, and the history of the English Language',[99] the Commissioners commented that its deficiencies included law, physics, and the natural sciences.[100] St John's, second in size only to Trinity, was confessedly 'not well supplied with books of Modern Literature', though Ralph Tatham, the Master, was careful enough also to point out with some justice that 'it cannot be said to be defective in those books which relate to the usual branches of Academical instruction and study'.[101] Of the seventeen college libraries in the mid-nineteenth century only these two, Trinity and St John's, earned from the Commissioners any remarks as to their usefulness for modern student needs. Others were by no means ignored, since several possessed ancient collections deserving some mention, but their provision of modern books was passed over in silence in the final Report. Instead, the evidence had to speak for itself. After several years of attempts to repair the deficiencies, Peterhouse still lacked a proper stock of modern books suited to the curriculum. Pembroke was strong on literature, the classics and theology, but contained few modern books on mathematics. Queens' was 'tolerably supplied', and had spent heavily on both books and accommodation (though Dalton, the Vice-President, could only guess at the entire stock as being somewhere between five and twenty thousand works). St Catharine's, too, could state that it had devoted some effort to improving the stock of modern books in recent years. King's, also, could claim the same, while Caius pleaded want of space as an excuse for not purchasing many new books (because of the Bursar's accounting methods, the college claimed also to be unable to estimate how much was

---

[98] *Report* p. 133. [99] *Evidence* p. 425.
[100] *Report* p. 134. [101] *Evidence* p. 402.

spent on the library annually). But the absence of comment on the subjects either of modern books or of expenditure by several others suggests – at the very least – that the various authorities may not always have been anxious to parade possible failings.[102] By the end of the 1850s few colleges had found it necessary (or, in some cases, possible) to extend their library buildings. King's had already acquired a new building as part of the Wilkins scheme in 1824–8, and Corpus had rehoused the Parker Library in suitable magnificence in 1823. St John's was able to expand conveniently into the ground floor beneath the old library from 1858 onwards, and Queens' did similarly. Caius remodelled and extended in 1853. But while Trinity inserted more bookcases to ever more depressing aesthetic effect in Wren's building until an annexe was completed in 1897, Pembroke added a new library, by Alfred Waterhouse, only in the 1870s, and Christ's did not extend the old library until the 1890s: no other college seems to have needed to add very materially to arrangements dating in most cases back to the times of their foundations. On the other hand, however, two of the best college libraries, at Trinity and St John's, belonged to the two largest colleges, which in 1851 contained over 47% of all undergraduates: the potential pressure on the University Library was not therefore as great as might otherwise appear in a University which boasted next to no departmental or specialist library provision. By the end of the nineteenth century the Library was seriously overcrowded with both books and readers, but any fears that senior members of the University may have had in the 1840s and 1850s that it would be prey to an unmanageable number of newly privileged undergraduates were gradually dispelled, as regulations became ever more lenient.

Power himself, entrusted with upholding the regulations of the University, showed no willingness to encourage change. In his evidence to the University Commission he returned several

---

[102] *Evidence* pp. 315 (Peterhouse), 324 (Pembroke), 358 (Queens'), 360 (St Catharine's), 349 (King's) and 329 (Caius).

times to the want of space in the Library; and like Peacock thirty years previously he believed that a reading room would answer undergraduates' needs justly. Such a room would also, he believed, encourage library users to consult books in the Library itself, rather than borrow them, 'so that the University library might become, not as at present, the *last*, but the *first* resort of a student, wishing to consult any particular work'. On undergraduates in particular he remained loyal to the rules laid down by the Syndicate in 1849, but his tone suggested that the official view was not universally held. 'I am by no means of opinion', he stated, 'that the undergraduates ought to be admitted to the privileges enjoyed by graduates of consulting the catalogues, and taking down the books from the shelves; but I would go to the full extent of accommodating them in the reading-room with any volume they may name and require.'[103] In general the Commissioners concurred with Power's views; but though they made no recommendations on the compromise enshrined in the 1849 rules, within little over two years of their report both these regulations and Power's opinion had been set aside. The new rules for the Library promulgated in November 1854 not only lengthened the time that undergraduates might use the Library from one to two hours, but also swept away all restrictions as to both the catalogue and the shelves. In time the period was extended to three hours, and from 1875 it was possible for undergraduates to enter in the mornings as well, on the recommendation of their tutors.[104] And so, for the first time since 1472, the Library was accessible on virtually equal terms to every member of the University. Hindered by chronic overcrowding and a severe shortage of staff, and given no encouragement by those who were content to use these as excuses, it was a reform that was long overdue even within the nineteenth century.

[103] *Evidence* p. 58.
[104] The Library's 'Rules and orders' were published annually in the *Cambridge University Calendar*, q.v.

16

TURBULENT YEARS:
J. E. B. MAYOR

FOR POWER, the many changes in the 1850s made his place as Librarian far from easy, while the activities on the one hand of J. E. B. Mayor, acting from outside the Library, and on the other of Henry Bradshaw within it, obscured his position as Librarian. By 1862 gossip spoke of his resigning, so that when the incumbent of Fornham All Saints, near Bury St Edmunds, died in February after holding the living for twenty years, there was inevitable speculation. Fornham was one of the wealthiest livings in the gift of Clare College, and to have relinquished both the librarianship and the considerably poorer living of Litlington, near Royston, would have enabled Power to effect an honourable retreat. Robert Potts of Trinity College even went so far as to solicit Romilly for his support in applying for Power's post, only to be rebuffed by Romilly's confession that he would prefer to see the Library's principal assistant A. W. Hobson in the place. Fornham however went elsewhere, and further embarrassments were thus prevented.[1] Power's resignation came instead two years later, on 13 February 1864.[2] He was to live only another four years, and died as rector of Birdbrook, in the north of Essex, on 7 June 1868, 'a man of most friendly spirit, remarkable for the simplicity and cordiality of his manners, and the versatility of his talents'.[3]

It was some indication of the altered status of the Library within the University that there were no less than three

---

[1] Romilly's diary (MS. Add. 6841) 14 March 1862.
[2] Library papers 13 February 1864.
[3] [J. M. Chapman] *Reminiscences of the Rev. Joseph Power, M.A.* (privately printed 1868) p. 4.

obvious candidates, all of whom could demonstrate their suitability for the post, while two were already part of the Library staff as well. To Romilly, Hobson still seemed the obvious choice, until he discovered that Hobson (who had been forced to absent himself because of ill health) intended neither to offer himself nor to remain in Cambridge, but to retire to Kent.[4] Others, including Richard Shilleto whom he had recently helped with Thucydides manuscripts,[5] expected Bradshaw to apply, and some even said that this was Bradshaw's intention.[6] Bradshaw enjoyed the high admiration of Romilly, but to George Williams, his friend and supporter in Library matters, he had seemed twelve months earlier 'excellent in the departmt of M.SS.', yet 'without system & method', and 'unfit for general superintendence as Librarian'.[7] Williams knew Bradshaw all too well, but it was no small achievement even to be considered at the age of only thirty-three. There hung no such question, however, over Mayor (fig. 25) who on 16 February offered himself as candidate in a printed circular, promising in particular that he would take an active part in the formation of the new catalogue.[8] Despite even an extraordinary plea from H.W. Cookson, the Vice-Chancellor, to put his name forward as an electoral dummy,[9] Bradshaw refused to stand against Mayor. Instead R. L. Bensly, of Gonville and Caius and lecturer in Hebrew, was set up as required for the election, and Mayor was duly elected on 26 February: by 10.30 a.m., half an hour after polling was due to begin, he had already been admitted to the post, much to the astonishment of Romilly who had expected at least the proprieties of a tussle.[10]

As should already have become clear, Mayor was in no sense a traditionalist in Library matters. His term of office added

[4] Romilly's diary (MS. Add. 6842) 15 February 1864.
[5] Shilleto to Bradshaw 16 February 1864.
[6] Romilly's diary (MS. Add. 6842) 18 February 1864.
[7] Romilly's diary (MS. Add. 6841) 13 February 1863.
[8] Library papers 16 February 1864.   [9] Cookson to Bradshaw 22 February 1864.
[10] Romilly's diary (MS. Add. 6842) 25 and 26 February 1864.

25   J. E. B. Mayor (1825–1910), Librarian. From a photograph taken in 1906.

further confirmation to the evidence of his determination to break with many of the old ways. Born in Ceylon on 28 January 1825, the son of a missionary, he had been educated at Christ's Hospital (where he claimed to have profited little except in learning how to write) and at Shrewsbury, entering St John's College in 1844. In 1848 he had graduated as third classic, and the following March was elected Fellow, but he remained in Cambridge only a few months before taking up a post as assistant master at Marlborough. He taught there until 1853, when he returned to St John's. His edition of Juvenal, first published in 1853, was prepared at Marlborough, and by the time of his election he had edited biographies of Nicholas Ferrar (1855) and Matthew Robinson (1856) in a series devoted to Cambridge in the seventeenth century, Roger Ascham's *Scholemaster* (1863), Cicero's Second Philippic (1861), and the original statutes of St John's (1859), apart from contributing to the catalogues of the manuscripts in the University Library. The first volume of his edition of Richard of Cirencester for the Rolls Series appeared in 1863, and offered still further proof of the great range of his erudition and capacity for sheer hard work. Besides all this he had been involved with Lightfoot and Hort in the foundation of the *Journal of Classical and Sacred Philology*, which died after only five years and was to rise again in 1868 as the *Journal of Philology* under the joint editorship of W. G. Clark (the Public Orator), Mayor and W. Aldis Wright, Librarian of Trinity College.

Neither Lodge nor Power had achieved such academic distinction outside the Library, and Mayor came to his new post anxious to secure its recognition as one of the most important in the University. He came also, in Romilly's words, as 'a very lively & a most zealous & indefatigable bookworm'.[11] Where Power had been content to let the reins of control slip into the hands of the Syndicate, and the daily management of the Library into the hands of others, Mayor was only too eager to seize them himself. His election was preluded by a decision of the Council interpreting the university statute on the office of Librarian as meaning that the Librarian could not be a member of the Library Syndicate[12] – a decision which barred Mayor from a body on which he had sat in the past to so much effect. Furthermore, a correspondent from St John's College signing himself merely J. E. B. (M.A.), not impossibly Mayor himself, wrote to the *Cambridge Independent Press* the following day in satirical vein, suggesting that before proceeding to the election of a new Librarian, 'the Senate ought to weigh matters carefully, whether the money the Librarian receives could not be better spent for the use of the Library, inasmuch, as the Library Syndicate has '*de facto*' taken the place of the 'Librarian' of olden times. All that is required is a competent person to report to the Syndicate before they meet.'

[11] Romilly's diary (MS. Add. 6840) 10 July 1860.
[12] Library papers 19 February 1864.

Mayor won a place for himself at Syndicate meetings – at least on occasion[13] – but he was never reconciled either to their proceedings or to the University's wishes respecting the Library. Their differences became public in 1866, when the Syndics' twelfth annual report recommended that the Library subscription, unchanged since 1825, should be increased from 1s.6d. to 2s.6d. a quarter. To Mayor, this seemed to skirt round much more serious problems, and in a pamphlet addressed to the Syndics only a week later he proposed a more thorough-going examination of the needs of the Library:

That a sub-syndicate be appointed to take evidence and report upon the income, expenditure and work of the library during the last four years; to examine all bills, to visit the library, to see the work intended for the proposed addition to the staff; to report upon the present state and probable cost of the catalogues, and to take evidence upon the past action of the syndicate.[14]

For a Librarian to non-placet a Grace supported by his own Syndicate has become a rare occurrence, yet to such lengths was Mayor prepared to go. His flysheet opposing a Grace to appoint a syndicate to revise the capitation tax concentrated on two points: first, the needs of the Library and the relation of Library expenditure to the University Chest, and second, the foregone conclusion in appointing a syndicate five of whose eleven members served on the Council. Indeed, the Council's overweening intentions seemed only too evident to Mayor, who used the opportunity to complain also of the last elections to the Library Syndicate, which had increased to seven the numbers of those who served also on the Council, out of a total of sixteen. 'If the Council,' remarked Mayor, 'in addition to its one statutable function of revising graces, is to control the action of syndicates, it is plain that we should relieve individual members of the Council of the labour of serving on those syndicates. Is the senate aware that of four names added to the library syndicate last November, no less than three are found

13 Syndicate Minutes 7 March 1866.
14 [Mayor] *Statement made to the Syndics of the Library, by the Librarian, 7 March 1866* (Cambridge 1866) p. 16.

also among the council?' The Grace was duly carried on 14 April, however, and led only to yet more differences. The special syndicate's report recommended that the library tax should be subsumed in a general capitation tax, and that the annual charge of £900 towards the building fund should be transferred from the Library funds to a general building fund controlled by the Chest. In itself, the proposal seemed simple enough; but (if the printed flysheets that were the result are a true guide) it provoked more indignation, misunderstanding and even outrage amongst a small group of protagonists than any other controversy over the Library since the 1830s. As quickly became apparent, it was not £900 per annum that was at stake, but the very bases of the Library's finances in relation to the other needs of the University. H. W. Cookson was not on entirely firm ground in the flysheet that he issued on 29 May in defence of the recommendations, but his paper had the advantage of expressing more concisely, at an early stage in the debate, what was not always clear later on:

When the resources of the University are considered, I think it must be acknowledged that the Library has been treated with great liberality and consideration for the last forty years. If some charges have been placed upon its funds in later years which were formerly borne on its behalf by the chest, it must be remembered that this was not done until the income of the Library funds had been very largely increased, in consequence of the great increase in the proceeds of the Library Subscription, in the income of the Worts and Rustat funds, and of the accession of the benefaction of Mr Manistre. This treatment will be more apparent if it be borne in mind that during the same long interval, almost all the scientific Professors were left to provide apparatus and assistants at their own expense; and the Museums of Natural and Physical Science were left to be supplied chiefly by the professors themselves, by their friends or through private subscriptions in the University.[15]

Neither Luard (now University Registrary, following the resignation of Romilly in 1862) nor Mayor believed that the Library would gain from the special syndicate's recommendation, but while Luard was content – at first – to issue a flysheet that took up less than a page of print,[16] Mayor allowed his pen

[15] Library papers 29 May 1866.
[16] 'On the proposed increase of the Capitation Tax' (Library papers 30 May 1866).

the liberty of a pamphlet on the running of the Library. Cookson was no longer Vice-Chancellor, but he could still provoke Mayor's wrath by his allegations. 'As the master of St Peter's college "thinks it must be acknowledged that the library has been treated with great liberality and consideration for the last forty years," I may be allowed to state certain facts which make it impossible for me to make any such acknowledgement.' He rehearsed the amalgamation of the offices of *Protobibliothecarius* and *Bibliothecarius* in 1828, the chaos of the East Room consequent on its being cleared to receive the Fitzwilliam collections, the vast accumulation of arrears, the charges on the building fund, the discouragement following the suppression of Bowtell's post of Library Keeper, the setting of an under-librarian's stipend at the level of that of a transcriber in the British Museum, the attempt in 1863 to transfer the Librarian's salary from the Chest to the Library subscription fund, the tiny number of staff despite Power's attempts at improvement, an estimated 60,000 volumes in need of repair at a cost of £10–12,000, the charging of mutilated and defaced books to the Library fund instead of the Chest as hitherto, the expenses – eventually forced on the Library – of the catalogue of manuscripts, the cost of the new catalogue, and the urgent need for a reading room: all seemed to Mayor to denounce Cookson's allegations. 'The library has many other wants, but if these had been taken into account, we should not have been asked to consent to a measure which will ultimately diminish its resources.'[17] Cookson's reply twenty-four hours later was scarcely less frank. After tackling a selection of Mayor's points he simply concluded, 'The remainder of Mr Mayor's paper shows what a large amount of work an able and zealous Librarian will find, but it does not prove that the University could have done more for the Library than it has done, or that it has acted with any want of liberality towards it.'[18] The Grace was confirmed on 31 May,

[17] Untitled pamphlet by Mayor, 30 May 1866 (Library papers).
[18] Library papers 31 May 1866.

and Mayor was to remain in his office less than a year before tendering his resignation. The power he sought to bring to the Librarianship eluded him, but he was foiled not so much by the Library Syndicate as by the needs of a university faced with greater and more various calls on its resources than ever previously, in which the Library was only one department, its buildings only one need among calls for new lecture rooms for the arts and museums for the sciences, and its funds therefore even more subject to public scrutiny. 'In politics, whether public or academic,' wrote his biographer H. F. Stewart, 'his instincts were conservative.'[19] It was inevitable that his devotion to the interests of the Library as they had become defined should clash with the administration of a reformed university.

The Library could not have had a more convinced defender, but at the same time there was little evidence of Mayor's innate conservatism in the enthusiasm with which he attacked its faults and the vigour with which he pressed for reform. Both inside and outside the Library he seemed to rebel. The University Orator, W. G. Clark, spoke with the knowledge of one who was a member of the Library Syndicate when he contributed to the discussion of the Syndicate's proposal to increase the Library subscription: he 'had heard it said that the Library Syndicate had not proper control over the Librarian, and it was true that the relations between the Syndicate and the Librarian were very unsatisfactory, and no one desired more to see them put on a better footing than the Librarian himself. Then it had been said that the Librarian had been extravagant – this was a charge which could not have been brought by anyone who knew the facts: the University had never had a servant so economical.'[20] Mayor made enemies easily, but Clark, joint editor with him of the *Journal of Philology*, was not among them.

---

[19] J. E. B. Mayor *Twelve Cambridge sermons* ed. with a memoir by H. F. Stewart (Cambridge 1911) p. lxi.
[20] Press report, University Archives album of University papers 1864–6, no. 1625.

The tone that characterized Mayor's brief reign as Librarian was set within a week of his election, with the appearance of a printed notice at the entrance of the building:

Graduates are requested to come in person for the books they require, in order to save the time of the assistants, who are now liable to be called off at any moment from their proper duties. Those who are unable to come themselves, will greatly promote the work of the library by sending their orders between two o'clock and four, and at no other times.[21]

But it was to prove easier to arrive at a correct assessment of part of the Library's difficulties, the egregious demands made on a small and over-taxed staff, than to correct them. In response to A. W. Hobson's request to be allowed to nominate a deputy for his work during his illness, on 18 November 1863 the Syndicate had appointed in his place Robert Lubbock Bensly, Hobson's own choice.[22] There was already sufficient evidence of Bensly's talents as a scholar. He had entered Gonville and Caius in 1851, and had graduated in 1855. His talents lay not so much in the classics, in which he took his degree, as in the oriental languages (and especially Syriac), where he was to make his career and reputation. From 1855 to 1860 he had studied at Bonn and Halle, and on his return to Cambridge he was appointed college lecturer in Hebrew, having won a University Tyrwhitt Hebrew scholarship in 1857. But although Bensly did not remain long in the Library as understudy, and Hobson returned to take up much of the administration, Power's departure coincided with Hobson's decision to leave the Library and Cambridge. He resigned on 30 March 1864.[23] The loss to the Library was compounded within a few days by the dismissal as from Michaelmas of O. C. Marcus, the foreign clerk. Hobson's health had long posed at least the possibility of his resignation, but there was no such preparation for the Syndicate's peremptory decision to cast off a servant whose devotion and efficiency had been well proven, and Marcus was understandably dismayed.[24] The two events

[21] Library papers 5 March 1864.   [22] Syndicate Minutes 18 November 1863.
[23] Letter of resignation to the Vice-Chancellor, Library papers 30 March 1864.
[24] See his letter of 14 April (Library papers).

provided the Syndicate, however, with an opportunity to revise the staff structure slightly, and in May they issued a report proposing that Hobson's post of principal library assistant should be replaced by an under-librarian, at £150 per annum, and that Marcus' post as foreign clerk should be abolished, to be compensated for with an additional assistant at £80.[25] When their proposals were put to the University, the first was accepted with no difficulty, but the second was carried only after a vote. The Library was, indeed, in some embarrassment. In 1866, after Marcus' death, Mayor wrote of the 'not wholly groundless jealousy of his position' felt by the other assistants,[26] but even in their report the Syndics were forced to speak well of what he had done. The summer of 1864 saw too the organization of printed testimonials in his favour that could not comfortably be ignored.[27] Indeed, the Syndics' desire to break with the past seemed almost wanton, in the face of Power's affirmation of his work as foreign clerk, that he 'gave great satisfaction, not only in that particular department, but also in the purchase of such English Books as could not be procured under the Copyright Act of Parliament. His long experience in the Book Trade enabled him on very many occasions to obtain books for us, English and Foreign, at more reasonable prices than we could have purchased them without his assistance.' Only one solution was possible to what had every appearance outside the Library of being a ludicrous situation, and on 19 October Marcus was re-engaged as an additional assistant. It was, fortunately, easier to elect Hobson's successor. On his resignation, J. R. Turing, curate of Great St Mary's, had applied for the post, citing his experience in Trinity College library, but on 2 November Bensly became the first to hold the title of Under-Librarian.

There had, however, been so far no net increase in the staff, and Mayor was to have only modest success in this respect. The same month that saw Bensly's election also brought permission

---

[25] Library papers 11 May 1864 (reissued on 23 May).
[26] [Mayor] *Statement made to the Syndics of the Library* p. 4.
[27] Copy in Library papers, 1864.

to appoint a boy at not more than ten shillings a week. By the time of their next annual report,[28] the Syndics were also able to announce that the Library had engaged a young B.A. of St John's, G. R. Crotch, to begin a new alphabetical catalogue of the printed books for a period of three months in the first instance. Crotch had the still unusual distinction of having graduated in Natural Sciences, in 1863, and through his friendship with Bradshaw was to have an indirect influence on the development of historical bibliography based on systems of classification hitherto more generally applied in natural history. But although his initial term of appointment was several times renewed, and in April 1866 he was appointed to catalogue periodicals for a full year (and so produce the Library's first formal catalogue of such material), Mayor seems to have seen no reason to mention him in his otherwise extremely detailed statement on the conditions of the Library made to the Syndics on 7 March that year.

Meanwhile the death of Marcus had brought other changes for which Mayor had clearly much greater enthusiasm. Scarcely surprisingly, his relations with Marcus had not been easy, and he hesitated before committing himself on a successor. As an aid principally in cataloguing the accumulated backlog of books, Mayor found in the person recommended to him by Frederik Muller, the Amsterdam bookseller, a member of staff who fully met his exacting standards. J.H. Hessels had worked for Muller, and came reputedly able to work for fourteen hours a day. His stay in the Library as a formal member of staff was only temporary, since it lasted a mere seven months before he left to pursue his interests in the early history of printing undistracted by the mundane routines of a large library. His position was described in the Minutes of the Library Syndicate as that of 'private secretary' to Mayor – a post reminiscent of Heun – but whatever his title he won the admiration from Mayor that was not easily given. 'Mr. Hessels

---

[28] 8 March 1865. On all these appointments see also Syndicate Minutes 2 November 1864.

is a man of high spirit and a scholar; he gives me twice the time to which I am entitled.' 'Mr. Hessels' work may shew what a man of rare energy, from the best school in the world, can achieve in seven months, under the difficult conditions of our library, where it often takes half an hour to find a place for a book.'[29] In addition to his work as assistant charged with foreign accessions, Hessels had in fact also both catalogued books and classified and prepared for binding several thousand items; but he chose not to remain. 'It is a pleasure to me to do the work; but in my country assistants in public libraries are regarded as gentlemen; it is amazing how they are slighted here.'[30] He was succeeded on a rather longer-term basis on 9 December 1865 by Charles Bielefeld, a man who came with experience of the book trade both in England and in France and Germany, and who was to remain until he resigned in the first weeks of 1870.

But Mayor's searching gaze was applied most to the contents of the Library. Amidst all his rearrangements there were some articles of university property that could, clearly, be dispensed with altogether. In the course of their eleventh annual report, issued in March 1865, the Syndicate proposed briefly that the marbles and antiquities presented by Clarke and others half a century before should be removed to the Fitzwilliam Museum, so as to create space for an office at the foot of the staircase leading up to the Library.[31] The Fitzwilliam authorities agreeing to this, and the University giving its formal blessing by Grace on 24 May,[32] the pieces were transported down the road together with a bust of Clarke by Francis Chantrey presented to the University by a group of subscribers in 1824. The consequent building operations required a proper clearance of the vestibule, so the Syndics next sent some rhinoceros horns to the Museum of Comparative Anatomy[33] – a decision which did not demand ratification by

---

[29] [Mayor] *Statement made to the Syndics of the Library* pp. 9–10. [30] *Ibid.* p. 9.
[31] Annual report 8 March 1865. [32] Grace Book *P* p. 532.
[33] Syndicate Minutes 24 May 1865.

the University. Their willingness to pursue the rationalization of some of the Library's collections was further prevailed on in June 1866 with the removal of the standards of weights constructed by W. H. Miller, Professor of Mineralogy, in 1834 after the destruction of the old ones in the burning of the Houses of Parliament. These actions marked a far from complete tidying, for the Library still possessed the ethnographical prizes brought back by H.M.S. *Rosamond* in 1815, the collection of curiosities kept in the Lewis Cabinet, post-mortem casts of the faces of Charles XII and other celebrities, and similar detritus besides, but there was much sense in rejecting what the Library could not possibly look after properly or display adequately. More and more it was being defined as a collection of books, as its other incidental offices of university museum, art gallery, and scientific repository were displaced by more specialist institutions. Not all that was done in the name of rationalization in the next twenty years could be claimed to be so necessary or so sensible.

The increasing thought given to all aspects of the Library extended even to donations. The last years of Power's term of office had seen the emergence of a small group of people within the University like-minded in their view that the Library could both benefit from, and would give a welcome to, gifts of books of all kinds. Luard, George Williams, Churchill Babington and Mayor himself were among the earliest to realize this, and they set a trend which, with the publication of lists of donations and donors in the annual reports, could only be emulated by others. Robert Potts overcame any discomfort he may have felt at failing to raise much enthusiasm for his candidature as University Librarian, and bought heavily at the sale of Romilly's library following his death on 7 August 1864, presenting his purchases to the Library. The books, containing a high proportion of Spanish, Italian and French literature, included the Brussels 1625 edition of Cervantes' *Novelas exemplares* and several works by Rousseau, among them an 1764 *Nouvelle Héloise*, Giovanni

Sivrac's Italian translation of Horace Walpole's *Castle of Otranto*, published by James Edwards in 1795, and Uvedale Price's *Dialogue on . . . the picturesque and the beautiful* (Hereford 1801): none was of especial rarity, but when set among Potts' other gifts to the Library show him as a benefactor of persistence and even imagination. Others responded to the Library's first official appeal for specific donations, contained in the Syndics' annual report of 8 March 1865, and added to the infant special collection of Cambridge books, while among the continuous arrivals of university calendars, reports on astronomical observations, government publications and private printings of all kinds, a few were of more than ephemeral interest. In May 1866 James Finn, British Consul at Jerusalem from 1845 to 1862 and author of histories of the Jews in Spain and in China, presented a Sephardic Pentateuch roll dating from the fifteenth or sixteenth century, which had been given to him ten years or so previously by the Jewish community in Morocco as a mark of gratitude for support he had given Jews in Jerusalem:[34] he was also able to add a collection of Samaritan Pentecost prayers, purchased at Nablus. George Williams' annual gifts of foreign newspapers were varied in 1867 with the arrival through his offices of a complete set of the books, in both Greek and Arabic, printed at the press established by Cyril, Patriarch of Jerusalem. And F. W. Maitland's long association with the Library (culminating in his election as Sandars Reader in 1906) was begun in July 1866 when, while yet a schoolboy at Eton, he presented his grandfather S. R. Maitland's annotated copy of the Oxford edition of Strype.

It was inevitable, given the rapid expansion of the Library in the previous few years, that attention had at last to be given to the many books which had long ago been discovered to be duplicates. Unwilling to waste space or money in providing for unnecessary books, in 1855 the Syndicate requested Power

---

[34] MS. Add. 333. For some account of his work at Jerusalem see his posthumously published *Stirring times, or records from Jerusalem consular chronicles of 1853 to 1856* 2 vols. (London 1878).

to prepare a list of duplicates found in the course of compiling the new catalogue, and they repeated their request two years later.[35] The suggestion may well have come from Mayor even then, since he sat on the Syndicate, but it was not long before he was able to execute the Syndics' wishes himself. In 1857 the Syndics had in mind other libraries in Cambridge as suitable customers to buy or exchange unwanted books,[36] and several were disposed of in this manner, but Mayor was to prove both more determined and more adventurous. Acting with characteristic zeal, he pressed further and took the opportunity to develop the collections in ways that had not, perhaps, originally been envisaged, as the Library had not sold large numbers of books since the auctions of duplicates from the Royal Library in 1742. Furthermore, in searching auction catalogues Mayor and the Library's other advisers had persistently sought large lots, of pamphlets as well as more substantial books, and by no means all needed to be kept. The result was a series of heavy sales from the Library. Many of the books sold to Henry Stevens of Vermont and at auction during Mayor's brief librarianship could be said never to have entered the collection; they had been invoiced and paid for, but never catalogued. The inadequacies of the Library's catalogue had in addition made it all the easier to buy duplicates accidentally. Besides what was therefore a simple tidying operation to dispose of unwanted purchases, Mayor now turned to the books already on the shelves, in an attempt both to make space for additions and also to raise money for further purchases. There was little resemblance between his renewed attack and Bradshaw's painstaking negotiations with Boone over the Caxton and St Albans books of a few years earlier. Unwanted purchases, many of them bought at auction only very recently and dating from the seventeenth century onwards, appeared anonymously at a series of general sales held by the London auctioneers Puttick and Simpson between June 1864 and

[35] Syndicate Minutes 5 February 1855 and 18 February 1857.
[36] Annual report 7 March 1857.

August 1865.[37] Into the same sales went also books that had failed to find buyers through Henry Stevens, whose efforts to supply the Library with modern American titles in return for virtually a free run of the Library's less valuable duplicates, taken usually on a sale or return basis, dominated Mayor's efforts to rationalize the collections in 1864–5. The results at Puttick's were not particularly encouraging. Scarcely anything fetched more than two or three shillings, and many only sixpence – the minimum possible. Labbé's *Nova bibliotheca* (probably after Stevens had failed to find anyone interested) was knocked down at a shilling, fifteen volumes of the *Historical Register* (1716–30) at two shillings, and Linnaeus' illustrated *Hortus Cliffortianus* (Amsterdam 1737) at a shilling. Of the thirty lots offered on 4 August 1865, the last in the series, only three fetched as much as 3s.6d., and – the fashion for early scientific books not having properly emerged yet – the first edition of Newton's *Principia* a mere sixpence.[38] The copies offered were not, perhaps, in exciting condition, but the returns were distinctly modest. Nevertheless, by March 1865 the exercise had rid the Library of 1230 items that it regarded as useless, and a further fifty-four had been disposed of privately to Mayor, Bensly and other members of the Library staff. A year later the total had risen to 1473, a figure which excluded those selected by Henry Stevens in a series of transactions that was of rather more benefit to the Library and considerably more interest.[39]

Stevens was already well familiar with the Library. His name seems first to have occurred in invoices in 1853, when he sold thirty-one American books to the Library, including

---

[37] Puttick and Simpson 18 June 1864: lots 1118–67, 1326–45, 1365–401, 1437–42. 30 August 1864: lots 1078–107, 1294–303, 1338–45, 1389, 1391–8, 1450, 1451 (withdrawn), 1464. (Information from the auctioneers' printed letters to Mayor, 11 June and 24 August 1864, and marked sale catalogue for 30 August 1864.) 6 March 1865: lots 1106–19, 1367–72, 1415–17. 21 April 1865: lot 929. 4 August 1865; lots 1547–58, 1695–707, 1748–52. (Details from Register of duplicates sold, 1864–5, though not every book was recorded there.)

[38] Details, again, from the Register of duplicates sold, 1864–5.

[39] Annual reports 8 March 1865 and 28 February 1866.

Thomas Betton's translation of Regnault's *Elements of chemistry*, Benjamin Johnson's report to America of the Great Exhibition, Edward Everett's collected edition of Daniel Webster, a collected Edgar Allan Poe, and catalogues of the libraries of the American Antiquarian Society, the Library Company of Philadelphia, and of Harvard.[40] Among sundry other advantages, the prices charged to the Library compared favourably with those that might have been exacted by other dealers.[41] His position at Cambridge was further consolidated by his friendship with Adam Sedgwick. Nonetheless, his connection with the Library was sporadic, even in need of explanation on occasion. In 1856, when passing a bill – for thirteen volumes of the statutes of Virginia (New York 1823) and sixteen volumes of Samuel Hazard's *Register of Pennsylvania* – that seemed more than usually large, Power noted on the invoice for the benefit of the Vice-Chancellor that 'Mr Stevens explained the large amount of these charges as being occasioned by the scarcity of these works. He has been about two years in finding them, and his former charges have been extremely reasonable.'[42] For years he had been supplying the British Museum with American books, following Panizzi's invitation to 'sweep America for us', and his connections with the Bodleian Library were scarcely less intimate. By 1858, thirteen years after his first approach to the British Museum, the collection of Americana there numbered 30,000 volumes, and it was to reach probably 100,000 by the time of his death in 1869.[43] 'I am dosing the British Museum & the Bodleian Libraries with American books to their hearts' content', he wrote in 1846.[44] His connection with Cambridge, formed

[40] Office copy of invoice dated 4 November 1853 in the Clements Library, University of Michigan.

[41] This is clear if Stevens' prices are compared with those listed in Sampson, Low's *American catalogue of books* (1856). The Library paid 12s.6d. for Regnault (36s. in Sampson, Low's catalogue), 3s.6d. for Johnson (5s.), £2.12s.6d. for Webster (£3.13s.6d.).   [42] Stevens' bill for 28 December 1855: Vouchers 1856.

[43] Arundell Esdaile *The British Museum Library* (London 1946) p. 208.

[44] Stevens to Francis Parkman, 18 November 1846, in J. Buechler (ed.) *The correspondence of Francis Parkman and Henry Stevens, 1845–1885* (*Trans. American Philosophical Soc.* new ser. 57, pt 6, 1957) p. 17.

somewhat later, was conducted on a rather lesser scale, but proved to be of considerable advantage to both parties nonetheless.

Realizing that he had a new Librarian to deal with, he wrote to Mayor in April 1864, seven weeks after his election, in an attempt to revive flagging orders from Cambridge.

Having supplied the British Museum and the Bodleian Libraries for the past fifteen years with the greater proportion of their American Books; and having on hand a large stock of Historical and other standard works of this class, I shall be happy to treat with you for an American order, large or small, for the University Library. The stock which I have on hand being mainly duplicates of the books supplied to the British Museum & Bodleian, I shall gladly, in these war times, put the prices *very low* that is for half price or less. Being the European Agent for many of the U.S. Government Publications for gratuitous distribution, I doubt not, I can place some works in your library as presents that would be deemed desirable. If you are disposed to consider these matters, & perhaps treat with me, I will some day next week, or whenever convenient for you come down to Cambridge . . .[45]

Mayor's reply was encouraging, and the two men moved quickly on to discuss not so much outright purchases as exchanges for Cambridge duplicates, in a scheme where at first Stevens hoped for more than Mayor had mentioned. 'I hope Mr. Bradshaw will part with some of *his* (he seems to know them so well I cannot use any other pronoun) Caxtons, Wynken de Words and other very rare early English books. I can help him to others perhaps equally rare & so mutually benefit ourselves, that is our Libraries. I have many rare books on hand.'[46] However high his hopes, the outcome of Stevens' next visit to Cambridge a few days later put the matter in Mayor's perspective. Stevens could not, in the eyes of the Cambridge librarians, offer overwhelming reasons for their disposing of Caxtons, while Mayor himself was far more anxious to dispose of more recent flotsam. But in two days at Cambridge, spent largely in reading the Library catalogues, Stevens established for himself what he needed to know, and went away with some idea of the likely extent of the duplicates

[45] Stevens to Mayor 14 April 1864. [46] Stevens to Mayor 17 May 1864.

among the existing collections. He returned to London anxious to proceed with all possible speed. 'My orders at present are large but in these days of high exchange & war, there is no certainty how long a time may elapse before they are countermanded. I ought therefore to lose no time.'[47] It did not concern Mayor that the American Civil War had cost Stevens dear, both in lost book sales and also in his ill-fated association with the Unionist General Frémont. By the spring of 1864 Stevens was under severe financial pressure, and was forced to take measures to stave off his creditors.[48] Nor did Stevens explain that his current large orders were not least the result of having returned in January from a visit to America with the agency for a new library at Hartford, Connecticut. The first librarian of the Watkinson Library, a free reference library created under the will of David Watkinson, had been appointed only in January 1863, but by the following August had prepared a detailed guide to his needs.[49] For Stevens, nothing could have been better timed than Mayor's readiness to dispose of unwanted duplicates, many of which could not fail to appeal to a new reference library, while at the same time he was also able to channel numbers of the Cambridge books to other libraries in America and to the British Museum.

His first selection was not numerous, but it gave some hint of his seriousness of purpose: a run of the *London Gazette* from 1768 to 1818, Bayle's dictionary, Graevius' *Thesaurus*, and the ten volumes of Pearson's *Critici sacri*. Together they covered only part of the cost of the books Cambridge took from Stevens, and he was therefore able to press his hopes with all the more resolve:

I shall be glad if you will this week report me the prices &c. of some more of those we have spoken about. To give you a better idea of what I can use I have jotted down on the enclosed slips a few hundred volumes, of most

---

47 Stevens to Mayor 23 May 1864.
48 Wyman W. Parker *Henry Stevens of Vermont* (Amsterdam 1963) p. 256.
49 Marian G. M. Clarke *David Watkinson's library; one hundred years in Hartford, Connecticut* (Hartford 1966) ch. 1. By the time that the Watkinson Library was opened to the public in August 1866, the librarian, J. H. Trumbull, had succeeded in obtaining 12,000 of the intended 25,000 titles, from Stevens, Edward G. Allen and others.

which you have, no doubt, duplicates. The list is brief, but no doubt will be understood by you. Of the *Fathers* I can (till the order is counter-manded) use any of the good editions, & so of the four great Polyglot Bibles. I can take also almost any of the English topography or county or town histories. When I have given only the name of the author, it means all his works – no matter how many: as in the case of Dugdale – Camden &c. If you will report from day to day what works you find, with price & condition, I shall give an early answer. – I have no idea how much you can turn out. I am ready to take £500 or £1000 worth at once & give you good standard books in Exchange at low cash prices.[50]

With the exceptions of De Bry, the 1662 *Lawes of Virginia*, Simon Grynaeus *Novus orbis* (he specified the 1537 edition) and one or two others, Stevens had listed not so much Americana or obvious books for private collectors as more general needs, from the Complutensian Polyglot to the 1557 edition of Thomas More: his list also included the 1476 and 1486 Bibles, the major sixteenth-century theologians, Du Cange, Galen, Grafton's *Chronicle*, Grotius, Hardwicke's *State papers*, Holbein, Inigo Jones, Ben Jonson, Leibniz, Lydgate, Montfaucon, and William Prynne, besides the topographical books mentioned in his letter. The visit to Cambridge of the Prince and Princess of Wales in the first week of June distracted Mayor from the course set him by Stevens, who by the summer was pressing him even more, both to accept new American books as selected for him and to determine which other duplicates he wished to exchange:

I sent you the other day another box of American books, chiefly historical. Some of the sets are imperfect, & were sent only as samples. In all cases I can make the sets complete if ordered. As I mentioned to you when I was in Cambridge *time* is of importance with me just now, and therefore I shall be glad to settle with you at your earliest convenience. Exchange is so high now that I am afraid that my orders for old books will be suspended or countermanded. I am desirous of shipping as soon as possible any duplicates I may receive from your library, so as to have the orders executed before I can hear to the contrary.

In selling you the American Books, of course I should greatly prefer to receive the money, but am willing to take books in exchange for the

[50] Stevens to Mayor 23 May 1864.

greater part. The list which I sent you a short time since will serve to let you know what sort of books I can use.[51]

The deadline set by his American customers, 25 June, came and went without the countermand Stevens feared, and when he wrote on 19 July there was a little less urgency in his enquiry as to whether the Library had a spare set of Montfaucon. He could also offer a complete set of the records of the US government from 1789 to 1863 in about 1500 volumes, similar to a set made up for the Bodleian a little earlier.[52] With the arrival of the Long Vacation Mayor at last had the leisure Stevens so desired. That summer Stevens paid a second visit in search of duplicates, and returned to London so well satisfied that he felt able to write to Coxe at Oxford in a state almost of rapture.

I spent three weeks in the library at Cambridge, and as you say found heaps of sport. I have relieved the library of nearly *three tons* of duplicates and am able to supply it with many standard American and other books in exchange, and particularly to complete their broken sets. Such *sport* is a godsend to the Library and I only hope my venture in their 'Pp. and Qq' preserves (store of Duplicates cast out 100 years ago) will strengthen me.[53]

The prices he paid were fixed by Mayor and his staff, and after some repairs the books were shipped off to America, leaving Stevens to write to Mayor two days after his letter to Coxe, 'I have had *3 tons* of your duplicates – & I think 5 more will fill me for the present.'[54] His trawl had reached many corners of the Library other than classes Pp★ and Qq★. Besides the unwanted purchases of recent auctions (including a volume containing Roger Ascham's *Toxophilus*, 1571, and *Scholemaster*, 1570, at £1.10.0, and Wolfgang Lazius' folio *De gentium aliquot migrationibus*, 1572, at a shilling), the Library sold many of the books that had been in it for two centuries. Not all Stevens' wants that he had listed in May could be provided for by any means, but the Library ejected the 'stars',

[51] Stevens to Mayor 11 June 1864.   [52] Stevens to Mayor 19 July 1864.
[53] Stevens to H. O. Coxe 20 October 1864 (Bodleian Library archives).
[54] Stevens to Mayor 22 October 1864.

or old library, copy of More's 1557 *Workes*, almost certainly bequeathed by Richard Holdsworth in 1649, preferring to keep the copy from John Moore's library given by George I in 1715. The Royal Library copies went of Rymer's *Foedera*, Wharton's *Anglia sacra*, Plot's *Natural history of Staffordshire*, Thorton's *Nottinghamshire*, Leycester's *Cheshire*, the *Works* of James I, the first edition (1694) of George Fox's *Journal*, dictionaries of John Baret (1580), Cotgrave (1611), Robert Estienne (both the 1543 and the 1573 editions) and Calepinus (1667), besides seventeenth-century editions of many of the Fathers. The stars classes, containing still earlier gifts to the Library, lost books on a similar scale, including besides the More mentioned above copies of both the 1617 and 1627 editions of Minsheu's *Ductor in linguas*, the 1694 dictionary of the French Academy, the 1611 edition of Florio's *Queen Annas new world of words*, Henry Holland's *Herωlogia anglica* (1620), bound up with Verheiden's *Effigies* (1602), and the first edition of Thomas Fuller's *History of the worthies of England*. The provenance of the books mattered as little to Mayor as it did to Stevens. It was enough simply that the books were duplicates, and therefore as unnecessary to Cambridge as they were desirable to Stevens and his major American customers.

Among Americana alone he could count in his selection nine parts of De Bry's voyages, for which he paid £15, Moore's copy of De Laet's *Novus orbis* (1633), the original edition of Hernandez' *Materia medica* of the New World, the *Lawes of Virginia* he had specified in his list of desiderata, Richard Hakluyt's edition of Peter Martyr Anglerius *De orbe novo* (1587), a 1626 *Purchas his pilgrimage*, and the account published in 1633 of Thomas James' search for a north-west passage. After a small sum had been deducted for imperfections and over-estimates of some books' value by Mayor, Stevens received 554 items for £215. Many of the books were sent immediately overseas, salted with various others including duplicates obtained in like manner from the Bodleian Library. While Stevens also had the Peabody Library at Baltimore in mind[55] for those that proved unacceptable to libraries in the north-east, his eyes were fixed first on the Watkinson Library, to whom he sent two long on approval invoices in October 1864 and January 1865. Of the 581 titles offered, the Watkinson took seventy-six before the same invoices were submitted to Trinity College, also in Hartford, and elsewhere.[56]

The end of the year found the Library nevertheless still in debt to Stevens. Besides the credit gained for duplicates, and for some books sent to Cambridge on approval but returned, it had paid sixpence short of £80 in cash between July and December, making a total of £361.6s.6d. Against this was set a debit of £456.18s.0d, the accumulated total of five invoices principally for American serials and other multi-volume works, and including one bill for £284.6s.0d. alone to cover nine or ten cases of books.[57] By February 1865 Stevens was ready to reopen negotiations, but he hesitated at first to write until he could report the fate of the duplicates sent across the Atlantic the previous autumn. At last his hope for more business overcame the lack of news. 'I have not heard much from America', he wrote to Mayor on the 20th, 'but things are moving, & hence I am willing to go on and relieve you of a few more cart-loads of old Books.' Only one duplicate title, the twelve volumes of the Royal Library copy of the *Tractatus universi iuris* (Lyon 1549) found its way into Stevens' hands that spring, but once again the Long Vacation brought better sport. Many of the more expensive duplicates which he wanted had already been found, but there remained more than enough. In 1864 he had taken few classical authors, but now he found dozens, the earliest amongst them being two copies of Aldus'

---

[55] Stevens to J. Trumbull 14 December 1864 (Watkinson Library archives).
[56] Stevens' invoices are now in the archives of the Watkinson Library which, since 1950, has been housed and managed with Trinity College Library. Although the Cambridge bookplates and class-marks were removed from the books before they were sent overseas, sufficient indications remain for ex-Cambridge books to be identified on the shelves in American libraries and elsewhere with no great difficulty for an eye familiar with the older collections at Cambridge. [57] Stevens to Mayor 29 October 1864.

1521 edition of Livy at seven shillings for the two. The Royal Library copy of Plantin's 1575 edition of Virgil, with commentaries by Vaillant de Guelle and Scaliger, went for 2s.6d., and Heinsius' Hesiod of 1603 for a shilling, while the 1537 edition of Hesiod was valued at 7s.6d. Camerarius' Homer (1541), again a Royal Library book, was charged at 2s.6d. The Royal classes could also count the loss of Labbé's *Nova bibliotheca*, editions of Strabo published in Paris in 1620 and Amsterdam in 1707, the 1631 edition of Selden's *Titles of honor* and the 1590 edition of Camden's *Britannia*, as well as Timothy Bright's *Treatise of melancholie* (1586) and the first edition of George Ruggle's *Ignoramus*. For some reason the second edition of this last, the most famous of the Cambridge college plays, was also disposed of from the stars classes, despite the fact that it was not a duplicate at all. Few books fetched significant prices, and only two were valued at as much as £5. Of these, the sale of the first part of the Blado Homer of 1542–50 from the 'stars' classes was a mistake. It left the last two volumes of the four volume set, published in 1549–50, still in the Library as a reminder of what had once been there. Understandably, Stevens had paid especial attention previously to books of direct interest to American history, but he managed this time to add a little more. Neither Joseph de Acosta's *De natura novi orbis* (Cologne 1596) at seven shillings nor two copies of Georg Horn's *De originibus americanis* (The Hague 1652) at two shillings each were excessively priced, and in fact quickly proved to have been significantly undervalued by Mayor as Stevens' exhortations to American historians and librarians to buy Americana in languages other than English took rapid effect.[58]

His second selection, amounting to £90.3s.6d. at Mayor's figures, brought the exercise to a close, though Stevens remained at the end of September as anxious as ever to continue. Writing to Dennis Hall preparatory to agreeing a

---

[58] Cf. for example Henry Stevens *Bibliotheca historica . . . to be sold by auction by Messrs Leonard & Co.* (Boston, Mass., 1870) preface pp. ix–xi.

final valuation, he was worried only that Mayor might have valued some of the books over-optimistically:

Some of the books are priced very reasonably, while others seem to me dear, especially as I can go into the market and buy them for considerably less. However this dont matter provided I can sell them. I have now got them all carefully catalogued, & shall at once see what I can do with them among my customers. I have no doubt I can sell a large proportion of them – and as many more as you may send – provided they are put at moderate prices.[59]

Overall, these further duplicates seemed to Stevens to lack the sparkle of his first selection, despite his invitation to Dennis Hall. He was, therefore, less sanguine to Mayor, to whom he described them as

Rather a hard lot, being so over loaded with Theology and classics, the two classes of books just now the most difficult to sell. However, if anybody can sell them I can: and another fortnight will enable me to judge. If I cannot move a considerable proportion of them I can send them to Puttick's, but I think I can sell them. I am a little startled at some of your prices. I say nothing of the Cheap ones, but for some few of them you have marked, I think, too high. I suppose you found a precedent. No matter, if they sell all right, if not they will find their proper level at auction.[60]

By this time Stevens' affairs were less bound up with the libraries at Hartford. Instead, much of this second batch was offered to the British Museum and to the State Library of New York at Albany, which was pursuing a vigorous purchasing policy under John V. L. Pruyn; one or two others may have been offered to Henry Huth.[61] The prices paid by the British Museum and others, subject to a mark-up of several hundred per cent in many instances, showed Stevens at his most enterprising. For Cambridge, meanwhile, it proved more convenient to settle the balance in cash rather than further

[59] Stevens to Dennis Hall 27 September 1865.
[60] Stevens to Mayor 27 September 1865 (Stevens letter books, Clements Library, University of Michigan).
[61] Copies of Stevens' invoices (to the British Museum, December 1865, and to New York State Library, 27 January 1866) are in his day books at the Clements Library. Some of his dealings with Huth are documented in the Stevens papers at the University of Vermont, Burlington, and the University of California, Los Angeles.

duplicates, and Stevens' bills of both 15 June and 10 July were paid conventionally at the beginning of October.

To meet his bills was one matter, however, and to set the Library straight after disposing of so much was another. In his letter to Coxe, Stevens had alluded to classes Pp★ and Qq★, assembled half a century before in the course of arranging the East Room; but by no means all his books had been drawn directly from this part of the Library. Where comparison with other copies in the Royal, stars or other classes had suggested that it would be more appropriate to dispose of these, they had been sold instead. Resulting gaps in the shelves were then filled with the copies from Pp★ and Qq★. Moore's collections and the classes that had once constituted the Library before 1715 had already been extensively raided for the new theological classes in the Cockerell Building, and were by these alien additions still further confused. Books bought from the Rustat Fund replaced copies that had formed part of the Library's central collections, and the copy of Rymer's *Foedera* presented by the Duke of Somerset, Chancellor of the University from 1689 to 1748, took the place of that given by George I simply because the departure of Moore's copy left a space that had to be filled.

By the time of the next annual report, Mayor could write that the Library had disposed of 1240 duplicate volumes to Stevens alone, and that 1139 new volumes had been procured from him.[62] The supervision of the operation had been placed in the hands of Mayor and Bradshaw jointly,[63] but however appreciative Bradshaw could be of the Library's history, he had not prevented the departure of books which had a strong claim to remain. His influence may perhaps be seen in the fact that so few early sixteenth-century books and no incunables were disposed of in this way, but Mayor was usually unsympathetic to claims either of history or of future effects:

The exchange with Mr. Stevens was a drill for our whole staff; teaching us how to receive, despatch and invoice large masses of books; giving

---

[62] Annual Report 28 February 1866.   [63] Syndicate Minutes 11 May 1864.

quickness and a sure eye in the weary labour of collation; opening to me new fields of literature, not only in the books received, but also in those sought by Mr. Stevens. The most interesting discovery was a presentation copy of Lycidas, with an entire line and two other corrections in Milton's hand. This had been standing in the open classes, inviting the curious collector. Every duplicate sold has passed about six times under my eye; the copy kept by us has in every case been collated throughout, often by me; no book has been sold that differed at any point from the copy kept, or that contained any autograph or note of interest. One fifth of our books were transferred at once to the British Museum; the rest have gone for the most part to American public libraries; a few, put into auctions, after being re-backed, brought less than the sum allowed us for them. Most of the books sold were of an unsaleable class, in bad condition; many imperfect; some rotten, worm-eaten or otherwise damaged. Mr. Stevens would have lost by his bargain, if he had received no money.[64]

The reasons for the Library's comparatively sudden concentration on American books were varied, but prompted chiefly by comparisons with other national libraries, the need to extend the range of the Library, Mayor's eye for a bargain, and the interest aroused by the American Civil War. By no means all the books obtained from Stevens were found to be of immediate use: their justification emerged only later. But at one stage it seemed that they would be very pertinent indeed. In 1864 Henry Yates Thompson (better known in his later life as a princely collector of medieval manuscripts), who had graduated from Trinity College two years earlier, offered to endow a readership tenable at Harvard, the Reader to present a biennial course of lectures at Cambridge in England on the history and political institutions of the United States. He did so in the knowledge that there was no opportunity at Cambridge for future political leaders to gain any such extraneous information, and he felt the more discomforted by general

[64] [Mayor] *Statement made to the Syndics of the Library* pp. 14–15. Stevens' overall profits cannot be computed exactly, partly becaue not all the books he took away proved equally marketable, but the following suggest something of the proportionate profit he expected given the right conditions: Graevius' *Thesaurus*, 12 vols., sold by Cambridge for £3.0.0, went to Trinity College, Hartford, for £7.17s.6d.; Cardanus *Opera*, 10 vols., sold for £1.0.0, went to the Watkinson Library for £3.10s.0d; Arringhi *Roma subterranea*, 2 vols. (Rome 1651), sold for 12s., went to Trinity College for £1.5s.6d. and Lazius *De migrationibus* (Basel 1572), sold for a shilling, cost Trinity College 10s.6d.

ignorance of North American affairs in Britain after passing the latter part of 1863 observing the Civil War at first hand. The offer provoked a bitter controversy in Cambridge, and gained little from the support accorded it by Charles Kingsley, Professor of Modern History: Kingsley's allusion, in a flysheet supporting the proposal, to the large additions of Americana recently arrived in the University Library, was more to the point than most of the rest of the dispute, but his encouragement was fatal. Unpopular in many quarters for his political views, and suspect as an historian, Kingsley's well-meaning remarks were ridiculed by E. H. Perowne and others, and when Yates Thompson's proposal was put to a ballot on 17 February 1866 it was rejected: the fact that it was turned out with the help of the entrenched Church of England clergy from around Cambridge, brought in to vote against transatlantic republicanism (as it seemed) made the defeat no easier for liberals to bear. The episode did not, as it transpired, turn on the adequacy of the University Library, despite Kingsley's plea; but inasmuch as the Library did not actively seek American books on the same scale until many years later the incident was not, perhaps, without its effect.[65]

The proceeds from the sales of duplicates to Stevens went almost entirely towards the cost of new American books, and as we have seen had to be supplemented in the end by cash payments, while the sums received at Puttick and Simpson were negligible. At the same time as energies were being concentrated on American books, the totals expended on book purchases as a whole (but particularly on continental and

[65] Although an attempt was made to revive Yates Thompson's offer in 1907, no formal post existed until the Pitt Professorship of American History and Institutions was established in 1944 thanks to the initiative of the University Press. For the episode of 1864–6 see the papers gathered in Cam.b.865.1; *Charles Kingsley; his letters and memories of his life* edited by his wife (London 1877) 2 pp. 227–30; F. W. Maitland *The life and letters of Leslie Stephen* (London 1906) pp. 175–7; and Henry Yates Thompson *An Englishman in the American Civil War* ed. Sir C. Chancellor (London 1971), especially pp. 14–16. Kingsley's career at Cambridge is discussed by Owen Chadwick in 'Charles Kingsley at Cambridge' *Historical Journal* 18 (1975) pp. 303–25, though his remarks on the effect of Kingsley's lectures on undergraduate demands of the University Library (p. 311) should be compared with Max Müller's introduction to Kingsley's *The Roman and the Teuton* (London 1875) pp. xi–xii.

antiquarian books) were less in the financial years ending November 1865 and 1866 than they had been since 1859–60, when (according to the official accounts) the Library spent only £743.7s.2d. altogether on books. In 1864–5 and 1865–6 the figures were respectively £975.1s.3d. and £983.18s.1d.: in neither year was the Rustat Fund drawn on, it having provided over £1669 in the years 1860–4 for books and binding. Expenditure from the Library's general funds after the particularly unimpressive performance in 1859–60 rose in 1861–2 to £1113.3s.4d. before slipping nearly 12½% over the next three years. In 1865–6 it rallied modestly, and then fell in 1866–7 to £765.2s.2d., less than 69% of the 1861–2 figure. This last sum, moreover, was supported by only £143 from the Rustat Fund, which was thus allowed to accumulate for Bradshaw's sortie into the Enschedé sale in December 1867.

At a first glance the figures might suggest some falling off of purchases, but this was very far from the case. While it seems likely that in some respects there were indeed fewer new foreign books to show, Mayor's eye for cheap second-hand books did not desert him. 'Last year we received from Puttick 577 volumes and nearly 1600 prints and engravings, for £41', he reported in 1866. 'Never was it so advantageous to buy from sales as now; there are no rivals, no Hebers, in the field. Good standard books fetch only the price of waste paper; and the auctioneers' commission in many cases does not cover their expenses.'[66] But his enthusiasm proved within a few weeks to be more than the available funds or the Syndics would allow. He had spent the entire budget for books in the financial year November 1865–November 1866 within the first six months, and on 2 May the Syndics commanded that with the exception only of serials or continuations of works already partially received by the Library, all expenditure on purchases and binding should cease.[67] Mayor was to remain less than a year longer in office.

---

[66] [Mayor] *Statement made to the Syndics of the Library* p. 13. Many of the prints he mentioned, which related to Cambridge and Ely, turned out to be duplicates, and were subsequently disposed of.   [67] Syndicate Minutes 2 May 1866.

Most of the Library's modern foreign books (and with one or two notable exceptions it was able to buy few early printed books during the latter part of Mayor's term of office) came from four principal sources: Deighton, Bell & Co, Barthés and Lowell, Baillière, and (to a much lesser extent) Williams and Norgate. Thanks mainly to the interest of Bensly, works of oriental scholarship were also supplied by Muller in Amsterdam, and occasionally by Asher or Quaritch in London, while Bradshaw was responsible for the Library's orders for Scandinavian books to C. W. K. Gleerup in Lund. But of all these, the local booksellers Deighton, Bell enjoyed the lion's share, supplying in 1866–7 (the year of transition from Mayor to Bradshaw) everything from the 1867 *Bradshaw* to a set of the *Allgemeine Literatur-Zeitung* for 1809–45 at £12 plus £1.16s.od. freight charges from Germany. In 1866–7 the firm presented a total of 128 invoices for monographs, continuations and periodicals, an overwhelming number of which had been published in Germany. Despite an approach in 1865 from the Berlin firm of Asher & Co. shortly after it opened premises in Bedford Street, Covent Garden, the Library still preferred to use the local firm for most German purchases, on an agency basis when necessary: Asher sold the Library a mere three items in 1866–7, for a total of eight shillings. Thus, quite apart from books and serials supplied in the ordinary way, in the same year Deighton, Bell also handled the Library's orders from catalogues issued by Joseph Baer of Frankfurt, Benzian of Berlin (specialists in Hebrew books), Besold of Erlangen, Brockhaus of Leipzig, Butsch of Augsburg, Calvary of Berlin, Graeger of Halle, Hartung of Leipzig, R. F. Haupt of Halle (at whose sale of the library of the theologian and orientalist Hermann Hupfeld the University Library bought ninety-eight pounds' weight for a total of £10.8s.6d.), Heckenhauer of Tübingen, Kirchhoff & Wigand, Köhler, Liman, and List & Francke, all of Leipzig, Schletter of Breslau, Schmidt of Halle, Wagner, and Weber. According to their normal practice Deighton, Bell added a 10% surcharge, or more if circumstances seemed to warrant. Indeed, so complete was the firm's hold that only one invoice from a German bookseller was filed in the accounts for 1866–7, recording a single book supplied by Ferdinand Steinkopf of Stuttgart, almost certainly on Bradshaw's recommendation.

The total number of volumes added to the Library from all sources in 1865 was 15,932, 76% of which came under the Copyright Act, 2401 by purchase, 1139 by exchange, and 250 as donations. It was a tenfold increase on the total for 1846, twenty years earlier, when 1048 volumes had arrived as copyright copies and 387 had been purchases, while in 1825 the total from Stationers' Hall had been only 621.[68] But while the number of books regularly arriving in the Library had no precedent, the accessions under Lodge and Power had in their time proved no less overwhelming. As Mayor lost no opportunity to remind the University, the rump of the Library's purchases at the van de Velde and Heber sales still remained to be catalogued when he was elected Librarian. He was very far from exaggerating when he estimated in 1866 that since the introduction of the library tax in 1825 the number of books had 'far more than doubled'.[69] Apart from the problems of space that these increases brought with them, leading to the erection of bookcases in places never intended for them and producing in the East Room more an effect of a crowded lumber room than the noble open prospect originally intended, Mayor was thus also faced with a paramount need to arrange and record a large backlog of accessions. His solution was practical, simple, and accepted until the advent of a computerized catalogue in 1978. From June 1861, when the printed catalogue slips were introduced, until June 1865, 11,519 titles had been entered in the new catalogue, a figure which could in no sense be thought to equate with the number of accessions. Crotch had meanwhile begun to recatalogue the books already in the Library, weeding out duplicates and setting aside books considered too trivial for the new printed

[68] Figures given by Mayor in a flysheet (Library papers 30 May 1866).
[69] [Mayor] *Statement made to the Syndics of the Library* p. 6.

catalogue. But many of even the copyright books had never been catalogued beyond being assigned a number and set on the shelf in the unembarrassing obscurity of the ground floor. Mayor would have no truck with such a situation, especially as it also meant that what he dismissed as 'small tracts of no interest or value' had as a result of the Library's expansion come to occupy some of the more accessible shelves in the Library. Several of the old stars classes, relegated to shelves erected along the walls above the eighteenth-century cases holding the Royal Library in the West Room, were therefore moved back down onto the shelves accessible without the need of a step ladder, and much of the minor literature received under the Copyright Act was banished upwards in their place.

It took ten minutes to reach a 'star' book, and some of them could only be reached by poking them down with a stick . . . I always trembled for Mr. Wootton's neck, as he stood on tiptoe on the top of a ladder in CAM; access to every book is now safe, but it took us a year to procure oak of sufficient length for our purpose. Many books in the south room had rotted away; skirting now protects them from the damp wall. In the royal library, the tops of the cases, before treacherous nests of vermin, are now safe platforms, convenient for many uses; the cases themselves, for 150 years supposed to be full, have yielded space for about 9000 books from the star classes. Partly in this way, partly by the sale of duplicates, partly by the removal of rare and Cambridge printed books, the star classes now afford the very retirement we require for the inferior copyright books, which, once classed and catalogued, cause no further trouble or expense; they stand in rows one behind another, safely locked up.[70]

In this was the real beginning of the modern 'Upper Library', chiefly of English books seemingly of less interest to the current academic needs of the Library when first acquired, and so called now because most of it is housed in the tower of the new building occupied since 1934.[71] Books which previously had been only roughly arranged were now given proper class-marks, beginning in 1864 at shelf 140 so as to

---

[70] *Ibid.* pp. 11–12.
[71] In the years just before the move to the new building it was known as the Lower Library, since it was consulted in the Goldsmiths' Room on the ground floor of the Cockerell Building.

accord with a soon disbanded plan to impose a uniform numbering system on the entire Library in place of assorted letters, stars, and roman and arabic numerals. In order to save space the books were arranged by size, without serious regard to subject matter, and although within a few years the scheme was modified so as to proceed year by year, the class-marks from 1870 onwards beginning with a date rather than the former numbers (which had by then reached 150), the system has remained very similar ever since. Access to the newly arranged books was put on an orderly footing for the first time, with the beginning of a handwritten catalogue on slips, each entry of which formed a leaf in a volume: the expense of printed slips here did not seem to be justified. By November 1865 Mayor could speak of this too with some satisfaction: 'Inferior books, down to the smallest farthing tract, are catalogued by Mr Hall on slips, which are kept in alphabetical order, so that we have now (for the first time) a catalogue of every publication received, without incurring any large expense for books which could in many cases be bought new for less than the cost of printing their titles.'[72]

Few aspects of library administration brought Mayor more gratification than the innovations he was able to cause in the Library's purchasing policies, and the amends he made to the catalogues. He estimated that when he first tackled the uncatalogued books in June 1864, he was faced with about two wagon-loads, but two years later he still estimated that it would take himself and two assistants a further three years to complete the work. The new assistants were not forthcoming, however, and despite his heroic efforts he was never to eliminate the heap completely. It was inherited by Bradshaw, and grew steadily.

Though he was reluctant to admit it openly, Mayor can scarcely have expected to remain in the Librarianship for long.

---

[72] 'To the Syndics of the Library' 18 November 1865, p. 4 (Library papers). But compare Bradshaw's remarks in his letter of 18 January 1868 to J. Winter Jones (*The Library* new ser. 5 (1904), pp. 431–4.

He did not give formal notice of his intentions to the Syndicate until January 1867, a month before his resignation took effect, but he had offered a clear enough hint ten months before:

My time has long been deeply pledged for literary work, the work for which I live; I am in disgrace at this moment with printers, publishers, schoolmasters, the syndics of the Press and the Master of the Rolls; and now of late three persons have died or been disabled, to whose labours I must succeed. Why then did I seek a new and engrossing occupation? If this library, like the Bodleian, had been for nearly 300 years governed by known scholars under wise laws, if it had had printed catalogues the growth of 250 years, if the staff had been adequate and well paid, I would not have accepted office here. The wants of the library drew me to it. I thought I saw the way to bring things straight, and I felt bound to try. Nothing could be done by evading responsibility. All who had undertaken a responsibility which was not theirs had been fairly crushed. Mr. Heun lost reason; Mr. Bradshaw, health; Mr. Hobson, life. I had encouraged one and all of them to come.[73]

Of his literary obligations there could be no doubt. Only the first volume of his Richard of Cirencester had been completed for the Rolls Series, he was long overdue to the Press with his edition of Thomas Baker's history of St John's College, work for the Cambridge Antiquarian Society for a project on Cambridge under Queen Anne was no farther advanced, and Juvenal had progressed hardly at all. There was every incentive to retire from the Library so as to meet promises given long before. He was further provoked by the discouraging reception given to his proposals for the reform of the Librarianship itself, put in February 1865: his pamphlet, addressed to the Syndics alone and entitled *Notes on the statute and ordinances affecting the library*, had been almost totally ignored in some of its most important recommendations – that the Library should be subject to an annual thorough-going visitation and reported on along lines similar to the annual report of the British Museum, that the Librarian should be given far greater freedom to buy books at his own discretion, and that a new set

---

[73] [Mayor] *Statement made to the Syndics of the Library* pp. 15–16. Heun's collapse is described in Romilly's diary (MSS. Add. 6836–7) 11 March 1856, 12 February 1857. See also above, pp. 521–2, 527–8.

of rules should be printed codifying decisions otherwise recorded only in the Syndics' Minutes. Sufficient support for his proposals could be found in the standard handbooks on librarianship by Christian Molbech of Copenhagen, F. A. Ebert of Dresden and Julius Petzholt, while the current practice both at the British Museum and at Oxford seemed to Mayor to be preferable to the overburdened machinery at Cambridge. Too literal interpretation of the Grace of 7 December 1853, which had established the reformed Syndicate and vested in it 'all matters concerning the purchase of books and binding' and even 'ordinary repairs and cleaning' proved a millstone that Mayor was unwilling to carry, and that he could not cast off without resigning.

Bradshaw had been privy to many of Mayor's proposals long before they had been put to the Syndics,[74] and as his heir presumptive was also among the first in the University to hear of his final decision to resign. Mayor was able to be more candid to Bradshaw than he could in his printed letters of intention, and it was clear to both men that his literary work was only one reason for his departure. The bitterness of the argument over capitation tax still rankled, and Mayor could not willingly submit to the Syndics' insistence on keeping control of book expenditure. In November 1866 he had made his decision:

My dear Bradshaw

It seems right that you should now know what I had not intended to communicate to any one in the library until I should announce it publicly.

Macmillan, to whom my tenure of the librarianship involves a loss of at least £100 a year, appeared to have a right to my confidence from the first. In May 1864, when I ceased the printing of Juvenal, I told him that I would relinquish the library and return to his service when I thought I could in justice to the university and without dishonour.

When Bielefeld, to my surprise, applied for Marcus's vacant post, I told Bell that if ever, after my retirement, Bielefeld repented of his choice, I should be glad to receive him again.

Clay [the University Printer], who has had just cause to complain of me,

---

[74] Mayor to Bradshaw 24 October 1864, addressed from The Priory, Kenilworth.

has also known for a year or more, that I considered library work incompatible with publishing engagements. Pierotti[75] for more than a year, and the iibrary since, have not left me time to clear off more than a few sheets for the Ant. Soc. and the Baker catalogue; the last of which I should never have completed, if my power to purchase and to bind had not been taken away.

I need not speak of archd. Cotton's or Lord Romilly's claims upon me. Maitland's and Cooper's deaths,[76] the last more particularly by making my collections useless, seem to call me to devote what time I can to the history of the church and of learning. Nor do I think the prospects of classical learning in England so bright, that any man who has read carefully and extensively can be willing to remain silent for life, while 'science militant' carries all before it. I cannot make up my mind to put my collections into Macmillan's hands, that he may employ some drudge to put them into shape.

For these reasons, and because I was sure from the first that to place the librarian's office on a firm basis I must be able to say 'Whatever is done, will not affect me', I told the subsyndicate appointed to draw up the paper I gave you this morning, that I purposed to resign office at Christmas. However, as that would be inconvenient, and some time will be required for drawing up the various forms mentioned in the report, I think now of holding on till Feb. 26, on which day three years I was elected.

. . . I do not act from transient pique, and the university will probably be inclined to take a more favorable view of my services than it does now, or indeed than they deserve; all which will tend to procure a hearing for the wants of the library.

Hessels, if he is willing to continue with me, will be invaluable as a corrector of proofs and library helper in many ways: I hope too to study Dutch systematically with him, so as to speak and write fluently. If he will not stay, his residence in England will at least have made him more useful to a foreign employer.

I think my exact observance of the statutable term of residence will prove the folly of the statute; I confess that, not having left Cambridge for eight days consecutively for near three years, I am hungry for a summer abroad.

In talking of myself I have left myself no room to speak both of your generosity in leaving the field open to me in 1864, and of the ready help

---

[75] G. Pierotti, whose *Jerusalem explored* translated by T. G. Bonney (1864) had involved Mayor in considerable labour.

[76] S. R. Maitland (d. 19 January 1866), former librarian at Lambeth; C. H. Cooper (d. 21 March 1866), the first two volumes of whose *Athenae Cantabrigienses* were published in 1858–61: a third volume, with additions by Mayor and others, was published only in 1913.

which you have given me all along. Without you I should have thrown up my post in disgust long ago; now I hope by my retirement to do more for the library than I have done by any work in it.

I am ever very truly yours
John E. B. Mayor[77]

To the Syndics, not all of whose support he enjoyed, he was briefer: 'The work which I set before myself at the commencement was twofold; to clear away arrears and to establish a methodical system on the one hand, and on the other to obtain a recognised sphere of activity for the librarian.'[78] In case they might see fit not to understand the implications of the last phrase, he drew attention to his pamphlet issued now nearly two years previously, marking for their especial consideration Winter Jones' telling remarks about his relations as Keeper of Printed Books at the British Museum with the Museum Trustees: 'I may remark here, that if I were not allowed to purchase books generally without the previous sanction of the Trustees, it would be hardly possible for me to carry on the business of the department at all – certainly not with any efficiency.'[79] And, finally, came his official letter of resignation, addressed to the Senate on 26 February 1867 and – so habitual had it become – printed for circulation. It would not have been appropriate to give the whole truth to the world at large, and Mayor did not attempt to do so. 'Engagements of long standing, the pressure of which has, by no act of mine, been of late greatly increased, make it impossible for me any longer to devote to the business of the library either the time or the undivided interest which are necessary to an honest discharge of the duties of your librarian.'[80] It was, indeed, three years to the day since his election.

Mayor's break with the Library's administration proved to be complete; for although he was to be elected Professor of Latin in 1872, and was to die only in 1910, short-tempered in

[77] Mayor to Bradshaw 11 November 1866 (Library papers).
[78] Library papers 26 January 1867.
[79] J. Winter Jones to Mayor 3 November 1864.
[80] Library papers 26 February 1867.

his infirmities,[81] at the age of 85, he was never again a Syndic. Official recognition from the Syndicate of his contributions had to wait until after his death, more than forty years after three of the most turbulent years of the Library's history. By 1910 the bitterness had been virtually forgotten, and in Francis Jenkinson the University had a Librarian of quite different stamp. In the words of the Syndicate's annual report for 1910, 'With Professor Mayor's tenure of the office the organization of the Library on modern principles may be said to have begun.'[82] It would not have been delicate, at that juncture, to recall what M. R. James was to remember in 1926 besides his 'purest enthusiasm for learning', 'a want of sense of proportion (and humour) which could hardly be exaggerated'.[83]

---

[81] So remembered by Sir Geoffrey Keynes (1887–1982).

[82] *Reporter* 41 (1910–11) p. 270.

[83] M. R. James *Eton and King's* (London 1926) p. 182. A full obituary was printed in *The Eagle* 32 (1911) pp. 189–225: this also reprints tributes from *The Athenaeum*, *Blackwood's Magazine* and *The Times*.

17

BRADSHAW IN COMMAND

THERE CAME INTO THE ROOM, solidly, quietly, and imperturbably, a short, stoutly built, plump, clean-shaven man, in a serviceable suit of grey. His hair, cut very short, bristled over his big round cranium. I fancy that he had small side-whiskers. His head was set rather low on his shoulders and thrown slightly backwards by his upright carriage. Everything about him was solid and comfortable; he filled his clothes sturdily, and his neat short-fingered hand was a pleasant one to grasp. His small eyes were half-closed, and a smile half-tender, half-humorous, seemed to ripple secretly over his face, without any movement of his small but expressive lips.[1]

Henry Bradshaw was Mayor's chosen and obvious successor. Since standing aside for Mayor in 1864 his reputation in the University and in the learned world at large had become ever more firmly established, while his knowledge of manuscripts and printing history, based on research pursued with no less excitement and spasmodic energy than before, now carried with it the *gravitas* of accepted authority. In June 1866 he had been elected to the Roxburghe Club; as Dean of King's College for two terms of office he had taken a central part in the college's reform, leading to the arrival in October 1865 of its first non-Etonian undergraduates; and he enjoyed the respect of both H. O. Coxe, Bodley's Librarian, and Winter Jones of the British Museum. When in the early weeks of 1867 the fifth volume of the Library's catalogue of manuscripts was published, it included a long appendix of corrigenda to earlier volumes which encapsulated something of the contribution Bradshaw had made to manuscript studies so far, besides affording a well-timed reminder to the University of the only

[1] A. C. Benson 'The leaves of the tree. IX. Henry Bradshaw' *Cornhill Magazine* new ser. 30 (1911) pp. 814–25, at p. 818. Benson was recalling Bradshaw in 1874.

possible candidate for the Librarianship. Nevertheless, he did not face the final months of Mayor's term with equanimity. As heir presumptive he contemplated with dismay the prospect of interruption to the work which he had come to love. His planned monograph on Colard Mansion, the Bruges printer associated with Caxton, was never completed despite a protracted visit to Bruges in October 1866: whether it might have been had he not been elected Librarian is a moot question. More seriously, he recognized that Mayor's resignation was his own Rubicon. 'In the Library I am nothing whatever – I receive a salary on the express stipulation that I tell the world that I have no *status* whatever in the place.' If he was not elected to succeed Mayor, he had decided to abandon Cambridge for Oxford, 'an unworked field for true bibliographers' as he described it to J. W. Holtrop of the Royal Library at The Hague.[2] It was therefore not surprising that his relations with Mayor were not invariably amicable. Four days before Christmas 1866 Mayor felt himself bound to protest:

May I ask you to abstain from remarking upon what you consider my neglect of duty in the presence of my friend Hessels? It is an affront to him which he is not in a position to resent. Any suggestions which you may have to make to me personally I shall thankfully receive, as I hope I always have done. You know when to find me in the library, more than half an hour in the week. I believe I have not spent less time and thought upon the work of the library this year than any other during which I have been at the head of it. The principal work on which I have been employed you and Luard alone are acquainted with; I should be sorry to think that you deliberately judged it unfavorably; but if I did think so, that would be a further confirmation of the resolution which I have already communicated to you.[3]

Within hours of the official notice on 27 January declaring the Librarianship vacant, Bradshaw had produced a twelve-line printed circular for the University.[4] His sole opponent was Robert Burns, Fellow of Trinity College and a pioneer in the

[2] Bradshaw to Holtrop 4 March 1867 (Bradshaw *Correspondence* 1 p. 131).
[3] Mayor to Bradshaw 21 December 1866.
[4] Library papers 27 February 1867. Printed in Prothero *Bradshaw* p. 153.

archaeology of ancient Rome. Burns was, however, no more than a man of straw, and he withdrew immediately, leaving Bradshaw to be elected Librarian from 8 March.[5] Among all those who wrote to offer their congratulations, none spoke more appropriately than Coxe, who unconsciously echoed Romilly's remark on Bradshaw's 'discontented' look seven years previously: 'My very best congratulations to you. May you be happy! & not be bothered overmuch by Curators or Syndics or whatever your Masters may be called.'[6]

Anxieties about the Syndicate apart, Bradshaw seemed now in his element, able to press the Library's interests as its acknowledged and official head. Where before he had been subject to two masters, Mayor and the Syndics, only the Syndics now remained to admonish and order, or to be cajoled, as occasion demanded.

Bradshaw's election to the Librarianship at last made it easier to take advantage of opportunities to build up the collections as he wanted, and to devote especial attention to the fifteenth-century printed books. Over six hundred incunabula were acquired between 1867 and 1886, the great majority at a series of auctions of continental collections formed in the aftermath of the French Revolution and Napoleonic wars. Bradshaw's interests were not conventional, and neither was his approach. Rather than concentrating his search on established collectors' pieces (where, in any case, the prices were beyond Cambridge's purse), he sought to bring together two related assemblages: first, an outstanding group of incunabula from Cologne, the city in which Caxton had learned to print and which had dominated the export market to England, and second, a definitive collection of fifteenth-century printed books from the Low Countries – not only of Bruges, the site of Caxton's first press, but also of the uniquely complicated series

---

[5] Grace Book Σ p. 170.
[6] Romilly's diary 9 July 1860; cf. J. C. T. Oates 'Young Mr. Bradshaw' in D. E. Rhodes (ed.) *Essays in honour of Victor Scholderer* (Mainz 1970) pp. 276–83; Coxe to Bradshaw, undated letter [March 1867].

of printers (by no means all of them were named) whose surviving output presented exactly the kind of intellectual challenge to identification that best suited Bradshaw's methods of organization.

The auction of the Enschedé family library at Haarlem in December 1867 provided an occasion that had just such an appeal for Bradshaw, despite the patronizing assumption by Thomas Watts, Keeper of Printed Books at the British Museum, that Cambridge would not bid for the rarities.[7] Like others who sought to buy the more interesting books at the sale, however, Bradshaw was disappointed. Although armed with £100 from the Rustat Fund, he secured only six lots and spent a fraction of what the Syndics allowed. The level of prices, predictably high for one of the most renowned collections in the Netherlands, surprised even J. W. Holtrop, who wrote of 'prix exorbitants',[8] as well as Henry Stevens and Thomas Watts.[9] Bradshaw seriously under-estimated the competition, and as he also miscalculated the time it would take for his instructions to get from Cambridge to Haarlem via The Hague he was too late to bid on some lots at all. Some of those he most wanted went instead to the Royal Library in The Hague,[10] and at the end of January he had to face the further disappointment of learning that one lot which he had been told by Nijhoff was secure had in fact been bought on behalf of the town library at Haarlem.[11] On this his bid had arrived too late, and in this lot alone he had missed a volume containing two books printed by Bellaert at Haarlem and one by Gerard Leeu at Gouda. Finally, therefore, he had to rest content with only one quarter of what he had hoped to buy: his purchases included two pamphlets printed by Zel at Cologne, the first printing of the Dutch Old Testament from the first press at

[7] Watts to Bradshaw 10 December 1867.
[8] Holtrop to Bradshaw 24 April 1868: David McKitterick 'Henry Bradshaw and J. W. Holtrop; some further correspondence' *Quaerendo* 11 (1981) pp. 128–64, at p. 154.
[9] Henry Stevens to Bradshaw 15 January 1868; Watts to Bradshaw 17 January 1868.
[10] Nijhoff to Bradshaw 30 December 1867.
[11] Nijhoff to Bradshaw 26 January 1868.

Delft (the one really satisfactory acquisition, and described in the catalogue as 'très-bien conservé), two Dutch *Horae*, and a copy of the *Devote ghetiden van den leven ende passie Jesu Christ* printed for the Collacie Broeders at Gouda in 1496 and in an unusually fine contemporary stamped binding.[12] The results were respectable enough, but galling, and it must have been with some sense of irony that Bradshaw was able shortly afterwards to buy from Quaritch one of the Dutch *Horae* (also printed for the Collacie Broeders) which he had missed at Haarlem. Thanks also to Quaritch[13] he was able to examine one of the most intriguing lots of all, the only known copy of *Dat liden ende die passie*, the first book from Jacob Bellaert's press at Haarlem: Quaritch had bought it on commission for W. H. Crawford, and Bradshaw did not live to see it auctioned again and pass into the hands of Samuel Sandars, who gave it to the University Library in 1892.[14]

The Enschedé sale was a lesson to Bradshaw to be more prompt, and with these disappointments behind him he concentrated in 1868 on booksellers' catalogues. In this way he added about sixty items to the Library – more than had entered the building in a single year since 1715, and more than had been bought within twelve months than ever before. His own gifts almost doubled the number. The purchases came from Asher in Berlin, Tross in Paris, Kockx in Antwerp and Lilly in London (from whom had come one or two of Bradshaw's own books in 1866). It was Tross who supplied copies of Thomas Aquinas *Catena aurea* from Zainer's press at Augsburg, undated but with the rubricator's date of 1475, the three-volume *Speculum* of Vincent of Beauvais from the monastery of SS Ulrich and Afra at Augsburg, and Ratdolt's *Missale Brixiense* (1493), all in early bindings and each an outstanding copy. Normally Bradshaw took little interest in the early

---

[12] Cf. G. D. Hobson *Bindings in Cambridge libraries* (Cambridge 1929) p. xvii. For further details on the Enschedé sale see W. Hellinga 'The Enschedé sale was most disappointing' *Quaerendo* 5 (1975) pp. 303–11 and Bradshaw *Correspondence* 2 pp. 376–85.
[13] MS. Add. 4559 p. 93. [14] *Reporter* 1891–2 p. 1050.

Italian presses, but Macmillan's shop provided an irresistible opportunity in August, the middle of the Long Vacation, to add Bessarion's *Adversus calumniatorem Platonis* from the first press in Rome. As has already been stated, his usual concentration was on the German presses, especially at Cologne (and particularly Ulrich Zel), and on those in the Low Countries: the arrival of an unrecorded edition of Hugo de Sancto Caro from Antoine Caillaut's press at Paris was partly at least the result of its being bound up with a book from Govaert Bac at Antwerp. To add to three Hebrew incunabula – two from Soncino and one from Lisbon – given by Hirsch Lipschütz of Cracow, the Library also bought from him two others from Rabbi Eliezer's press at Lisbon; they formed a useful appendage to the rather more considerable purchases of Hebrew manuscripts from Lipschütz, who received £100 from the Rustat Fund in 1867–8 and another £210 from the same fund the following year.[15]

Bradshaw's sombre note of 1859, that exchanges of duplicates offered the only way for the Library to obtain specimens of early typography, had thus, within a decade, been proved inaccurate. Further, and much more important, auctions were to come, but he did not let slip opportunities for exchange when they seemed especially worthwhile. At the beginning of June 1869 the Syndicate sanctioned the exchange with A. J. Horwood of a copy of Albertus Magnus printed by Machlinia for the Library's copy of the rather more common *Abbreviamentum statutorum* of Lettou and Machlinia together: Horwood's books were sold in 1883, and the volume passed into the collection of Pierpont Morgan.[16] The exchange involved breaking up the volume containing one of the Library's three copies of the *Statutes*, but rather less trouble than the negotiations for a German volume containing four texts, much annotated by Ulrich von Ellenbog, father of a

---

[15] Rustat Audit Book. The totals from the fund spent on books in these years were £438.14s.4d. and £309.14s.6d. respectively. See also below, p. 721.
[16] I am grateful to Paul Needham for drawing my attention to this.

fifteenth-century prior of the Benedictine house of Ottobeuren into whose library the volume later passed. For this and three other books, in 1870, the University Library provided (with a small sum from the Rustat Fund) a Caxton *Doctrinal of Sapyence* and *Speculum vite Christi* (both duplicates from Bishop Moore's books, and both of which F. S. Ellis, who engineered the transaction, passed on to Henry Huth), and Wynkyn de Worde's printing of Walter Hilton's *Scala perfectionis*. 'Ellenbog's book', as the volume became known, was later to provide crucial evidence for Robert Proctor in elucidating the press of the monastery of SS Ulrich and Afra at Augsburg.[17] With it Ellis also provided the Carmelite *Tabulare* from Thierry Martens' press at Alost (for which Bradshaw had telegraphed in June 1869), a slightly imperfect Greek New Testament lectionary of the thirteenth century,[18] and Colard Mansion's French Boethius of 1477 – the last a superb copy, decked out with inserted paintings executed a little later, perhaps in Ghent,[19] which, valued at £200 by Ellis and Bradshaw, was one of the most dramatic prizes of Bradshaw's librarianship.[20]

Compared with the prices paid to Lipschütz for Hebrew manuscripts in 1868–9, the sum allotted by the Syndicate[21] to the sale of the library of Jean de Meyer at Ghent in November 1869 was not immoderate, and was perhaps influenced by Bradshaw's demands of the previous months. The cataloguing was of an exceptionally high standard – it was the work of Ferdinand Vanderhaeghen – and the incunables offered (in a catalogue of 1265 lots) provided Bradshaw with an opportunity unequalled since the Enschedé sale. For the De Meyer books he was more prompt. On the arrival of the catalogue from

---

[17] Robert Proctor 'Ulrich von Ellenbog and the press of S. Ulrich at Augsburg' in his *Bibliographical essays* (1905) pp. 73–88.

[18] MS. Add. 679 (not 720, as Oates *Catalogue* p. 26).

[19] Inc. 3835. Cf. Georges Dogaer in *Le cinquième centenaire de l'imprimerie dans les anciens Pays-Bas* (Bibliothèque Royale Albert Ier, Bruxelles 1973) p. 223.

[20] Details of this transaction are set out on the invoice preserved in Inc. 128 etc., 'Ellenbog's book', which was itself valued at a mere three pounds.

[21] Syndicate Minutes 13 October 1869.

Boone in mid-October, he worked through the fifteenth-century books and rearranged the appropriate entries country by country, town by town, and printer by printer, the books from each press being arranged finally in chronological order. More for his own convenience than for others', he had this re-organized list printed before going over to the continent with G. W. Prothero, a second-year undergraduate from King's,[22] and examining the books at Ghent for himself. When eventually published as a pamphlet, the second of the *Memoranda* that constitute the major part of Bradshaw's published work, the success of his method and diligence was plain. Against forty-four entries in his *Classified index* he was able to put 'At Cambridge (this copy)', and since Cambridge already possessed copies of twenty-one others, some sixty-five out of eighty-six entries in all were now available at the University Library. Fr.-J. Olivier, writing from Brussels, thought the prices realized 'fort inégale comme prix',[23] and Boone's bill of £191.5s.0d. was almost twice as much as the Syndics had agreed to spend: it was met from the Rustat Fund.[24] Bradshaw had shown his colours, and demonstrated his determination to create as near definitive collections as possible of fifteenth-century printed books from the Low Countries and from Cologne. The justification for such an attempt was set out by implication in the final version of the *Classified index of the fifteenth century books in the De Meyer collection* published the following April,[25] which built on Holtrop's classified catalogue of the incunables at the Royal Library in The Hague (1856) and his subsequent *Monuments typographiques des Pays-Bas au quinzième siècle* (1865–8). Holtrop himself died on 13 February 1870, and thus did not live to see Bradshaw's work, 'the first fruits of my attempts to follow in his footsteps'. It was the vindication of the method, of

---

[22] MS. Add. 4561 f. 40. Prothero's biography of Bradshaw was published in 1888; for his career see *DNB*.
[23] Olivier to Bradshaw 30 November 1869.   [24] Rustat Audit Book.
[25] Reprinted in Bradshaw's *Collected papers* (Cambridge 1889) pp. 206–36.

classifying printing types and assigning them to their presses, that had occupied him for a decade, worked out on the shelves at Cambridge and expounded in nearly six years' correspondence with Holtrop. Vanderhaeghen's cataloguing, good though it was, was not equal to Bradshaw's analysis of the books once he had them back at Cambridge: besides assigning several books to other presses, Bradshaw also added a series of notes by way of appendix, including a major analysis of the presses at Zwolle, a suggestive essay on Veldener's career, and a more personal account of the discovery that a 1484 Dutch *Plenarium* long thought to have been printed by Gerard Leeu at Gouda was in fact printed by another press working there at the same time. In these appendices emerged something of the relish Bradshaw experienced in unravelling seemingly minor points; they were, indeed, written with a sense of mission made the more acute by the news of Holtrop's death, 'to shew that if only a rational method of pursuing such researches be once adopted, results may be expected which will fully compensate for the long and patient work by which alone they can be obtained'.[26] Based as it was on only one collection, his pamphlet made only modest claims for itself, but as an example of a method it is a classic of historical bibliography.[27]

The De Meyer sale proved a resounding success for Cambridge, but hard on its heels followed a much greater challenge. Bradshaw received the *Catalogue of a bibliotheca typographica*, describing a quite outstanding collection of chiefly fifteenth-century books to be offered for sale by Sotheby's in the second week of February 1870, when he was still absorbed in analysing the De Meyer books. It presented somewhat more problems than the De Meyer collection, containing as it did a much more diverse assortment of books, while the inaccuracies and occasional sheer sloppiness of its compilation made the task of rearranging the entries in order

---

[26] Bradshaw *Collected papers* p. 207.
[27] For a more extended analysis of Bradshaw's work on the De Meyer incunables see Bradshaw *Correspondence* 2 pp. 283–5 and 388–91.

of presses all the more difficult. Nonetheless, Bradshaw compiled a preliminary index within a few days,[28] and his excitement was enhanced by the realization (thanks to a hint from Blades on the whereabouts of the imperfect copy of Caxton's *Quattuor sermones*) that these books could only be from the library of Senator F. G. H. Culemann of Hannover. 'This greatly adds to the interest of the collection, and further accounts for the large number of Lübeck & other similar books which are found here', he noted on 4 January.[29] In fact the books had been consigned anonymously by F. S. Ellis who had bought the collection *en bloc* and was himself responsible for the descriptions.[30]

Bradshaw had given the Library's commissions for the De Meyer sale to Boone, an old friend, but he was now dead, and early in January, a few days after Bradshaw had visited his shop at 15 Piccadilly, Bernard Quaritch (fig. 26) wrote to offer his services. He was, as usual, direct:

Sotheby's Catalogue of the sale of Febr. 7/10 contains many very curious books, such as you doubtless will try to secure. I believe it will be in your interest to charge me with your commissions. I am aware Sotheby's will take them free of charge, others may buy for you at 1/– per lot, – my charge is 10%, the same as is charged by all other respectable booksellers in London. By employing me, you secure however the advantage of neutralizing me as a buyer for myself. I require, when I receive commissions always a clearly fixed price. An auctioneer will *never* try to buy for you at a minimum price, I always endeavour to buy as low as I can.[31]

Quaritch secured Bradshaw's orders, and so began a long association with the Library as its customary agent. Supported by the agreement of the Syndics to spend up to £500 from the Worts Fund, Bradshaw placed his bids on over 120 lots,[32] and met with astonishing success. The Library acquired ninety lots after imperfect copies had been returned. 'I have succeeded

---

[28] MS. Add. 4561, fos. 126–33, 137–58; MS. Add. 4562, fos. 3 etc.; MS. Add. 4321.
[29] MS. Add. 4562 fo. 25.
[30] Note in Francis Jenkinson's copy of the sale catalogue.
[31] Quaritch to Bradshaw 4 January 1870.
[32] MS. Add. 4562, fos. 71 etc. His annotated copy of the catalogue is now Adv. c. 77.66.

beyond all expectation in getting the books I wanted', he wrote to Ferdinand Vanderhaeghen. Besides a useful group of books in Low German from Lübeck, the Library added two books by the printer of the Mainz *Catholicon*, German, Dutch and French editions of Bernhard von Breydenbach's *Itinerarium* (an imperfect copy of a German edition was returned), a copy of part of Mentelin's Bible of 1460 apparently made up of proof sheets, and an Eggestein Bible in a binding with bosses dated 1469. Nearly two dozen came from Cologne, and slightly more from Low Countries presses: these last included one of the sale's high spots, the unique copy of a Dutch edition of *Reynard the Fox* printed by Leeu in Antwerp which had already been the object of some curiosity in the learned world and for which Bradshaw was prepared to bid up to £20. He secured it for eight guineas. Five Hebrew incunables were added, to join the gifts of Hirsch Lipschütz of two years previously. In many cases Bradshaw won unexpected bargains. The Mentelin Bible reached only £4.17s.6d., where he had been prepared to bid to £15, and a Utrecht Eusebius a guinea where he had set a limit of £12. But while only a few of his bids proved unsuccessful, they included a token £5 for the first book printed at Lisbon (sold at £11.15s.0d.: the Library acquired what is perhaps the same copy in Samuel Sandars' bequest in 1894) and £50 on a Dutch block-book printed on vellum, for which Quaritch paid £120 for stock. Lot 216, Gerard Leeu's Jordanus (1487), on which Bradshaw set £25 but Quaritch paid £52 on his own initiative, came to the Library despite the price, but the block-book was beyond its means. A vellum leaf of the 42-line Bible at £9.15s.0d. instead of £5, bought by Quaritch and offered to the Library at the higher price, was also manageable, and so joined the three leaves of the 36-line Bible which the Library had secured at £4.15s.0d. Lot 644, a copy of Ludovicus Pontanus and others by the Dutch Printer of the *Speculum*, reached £82.10s.0d., almost three times what Bradshaw had bid, but it too was secured from Quaritch after the sale, for

26 Bernard Quaritch (1819–99), the Library's principal agent at
auctions from 1870 and founder of the firm of booksellers.

£86.10s.od.: to the cautious Samuel Sandars, who took the closest interest in the sale, it seemed a long price.[33] Wolfram von Eschenbach's *Parsival* and *Titurel*, printed by Mentelin, were rescued afterwards in the same way.[34] The final total, again somewhat over the limit set by the Syndics, was secured by charging the balance to the General Fund.

Two major sales in the course of one winter, involving about £700, or not so very much less than the year's total expenditure from the General Fund on the purchase of books (in 1869–70 it was £759.3s.1od.)[35] did not dampen Bradshaw's enthusiasm for improving his *museum typographicum*. Tross, Nijhoff and Kockx added further to the collections, and F. S. Ellis presented the Culemann copy of Durandus *Rationale* printed by Georg Husner at Strasbourg. But while he managed to sell several books to Bradshaw personally, including the Ghent Boethius of 1485 and three leaves from the 1457 Psalter for which the Library's bid at the Culemann sale had been inadequate,[36] Ellis failed to arouse Bradshaw's interest sufficiently to buy an imperfect block-book: since he had already plundered it to perfect a better copy, he had no objection to Bradshaw's pulling it 'all to bits'.[37] Olivier had failed similarly to provoke Bradshaw in November 1869, shortly after the De Meyer sale, in offering a block-book Apocalypse which, though incomplete, appeared to Olivier to be still in its original binding and otherwise in excellent condition.[38]

With the exception of the Inglis sale at the end of July, for which Bradshaw had inadequate time to prepare himself, and where he bought only one book through the agency of Hessels (though he was able to buy a few lots subsequently in the

---

[33] Sandars to Bradshaw 16 February 1870.
[34] But on the other hand, after bidding successfully on lot 186, a German Bible printed by Sensenchmidt and Frisner, Bradshaw allowed it to be bought by Dr Ginsburg: the Library finally acquired the Huth copy among A. W. Young's gifts in 1933.
[35] Annual Report 30 March 1870.   [36] MS. Add. 4562 fo. 130.
[37] F. S. Ellis to Bradshaw 30 July 1870.
[38] Olivier to Bradshaw 30 November 1869.

trade),[39] the following year, 1871, passed off more quietly. It proved to be impossible to spend the £200 allocated from the Rustat Fund in June for incunables, and nothing came of proposals which would have involved heavy expenditure in other areas: neither the zoological and anatomical portions of the library of the Czech physiologist J. E. Purkyně nor the mathematical library of Augustus de Morgan was obtainable for Cambridge despite the Syndics' hopes,[40] and de Morgan's was instead bought by Lord Overstone and given to University College, London. Nijhoff's auction at the end of January 1872 was of rather more appeal to Bradshaw. Advertised as the collection of G.-H.-M. Delprat, historian of the Brothers of the Common Life and a man closely interested in Huguenot history, the catalogue in fact also acted as a vehicle for several duplicate incunables from the Royal Library at The Hague. Had Bradshaw been a less irregular correspondent, and not allowed the seven months before the sale to slip by without writing to M. F. A. G. Campbell, Holtrop's successor, who was responsible for consigning the books, it might, perhaps, have been possible to come to some arrangement between Cambridge and The Hague which would have pre-empted auction of the books for which Bradshaw was now forced to bid. His reaction to hearing from Henry Gosden, Quaritch's assistant for the sale, that many of the lots bore the stamp of the Royal Library, is not recorded: Gosden was under the impression that they had been released in 1838, whereas they had in fact been entrusted to Nijhoff only in 1871.[41] Sceptical about the condition of many of the books, Gosden was also puzzled at Bradshaw's determination to get one lot (he was willing to bid up to £50), a poor copy of the Dutch *Speculum* printed by Veldener at Kuilenburg: he could not know that Kuilenburg was virtually the only Dutch town with a press in the fifteenth century of which there was no specimen at

[39] Bradshaw to M. F. A. G. Campbell 20 January 1872. See also Bradshaw *Correspondence* 2 pp. 424–5. [40] Syndicate Minutes 31 May and 14 June 1871.
[41] Henry Gosden to Bradshaw 30 January 1872.

Cambridge,[42] and that the lot therefore had an overwhelming attraction for Bradshaw. He secured it for rather less than Bradshaw feared, to the subsequent regret of other booksellers who realized that they had let an important book go,[43] and obtained over twenty other lots including the Enschedé–Royal Library copy of Jacob Bellaert's edition of the Dutch *Somme le roy* printed at Haarlem in 1484 (Cambridge had already bought another, imperfect, copy in 1864), and Veldener's *Passionael* (1480) in contemporary stamped calf.

The Delprat books were charged to the Rustat Fund. Bradshaw had been allowed £150 for them, the same sum to which he was restricted (from the Worts Fund this time) for the sale of the library of Jules Capron in 1875.[44] The Capron books presented a more serious challenge than had the rather battered copies at the Delprat sale three years earlier. Capron was a more conventional bibliophile, with an eye and a purse able to command the best, and Olivier's expectations for the sale were obvious from the introduction to the catalogue: 'Un assez grand nombre sont véritablement précieux, plusieurs uniques ou inconnus ailleurs, la plupart d'une valeur hors ligne.' Rather than rely on reports, Bradshaw inspected the books himself before entrusting the bidding, once again, to Quaritch. The fourteen lots brought back to Cambridge fitted gaps which Bradshaw had long been anxious to fill,[45] including the Dutch *Somme le roy* printed by Barmentlo at Hasselt in 1481, Leempt's Dutch Albertanus (the first incunable printed at 's Hertogenbosch that Bradshaw acquired), a second book printed by Conradus de Paderborn at Louvain to join the Inglis copy of the *Speculum ecclesiae*, and a Maestricht Breviary printed at Cologne in about 1504, the only printed service book of that use which Bradshaw had ever seen. Prices were high at the sale (Bradshaw overstepped the Syndics' limit by

---

[42] Bradshaw to Campbell 23 May 1870: Bradshaw *Correspondence* I p. 147.
[43] Gosden to Bradshaw 7 February 1872.
[44] Syndicate Minutes 24 January 1872 and 17 March 1875.
[45] Bradshaw to Campbell 11 October 1875: Bradshaw *Correspondence* I p. 191.

over £50), and discomforted Campbell, who, trying to buy for The Hague, complained that book collecting had become a fashion, even speculative, with prices buoyed up by English and American dealers.[46] Nonetheless, thanks chiefly to the Capron sale and a particularly useful catalogue from Kockx in Antwerp, more incunables entered the Library than were to arrive in any subsequent year until 1884.[47]

The coincidence that brought under the hammer a series of major collections of incunables of just the kind that most interested Bradshaw had enabled him to buy for the Library with more system than had ever been applied to any part of its collections. But while the Culemann sale had, perhaps, been the scene of his greatest triumph, where he was most able to take advantage of special knowledge and where the Cambridge authorities had put most money at his disposal, from a point of view on the other side of the North Sea there was a yet more celebrated collection still in private hands. François Vergauwen, Belgian Senator, President of the Societé des Bibliophiles Flamands and owner of probably the most important private library of its kind in Belgium, died in July 1881. Bradshaw never met him, but was fully aware of his treasures, many of which were referred to in Campbell's *Annales de la typographie néerlandaise au XVe siècle* and Holtrop's *Monuments*. Campbell compared it with the Spencer Library in England and the Westreenen van Tiellandt collection in the Netherlands, and even a year before the books were finally auctioned held back from publishing a second supplement to his *Annales* until he could report the outcome of the sale.[48]

---

[46] See his outburst in the *Nederlandsche Spectator* (17 April 1875), transl. in Bradshaw *Correspondence* 2 pp. 444–5.

[47] Tross's Bill from Paris for April 1875 included one of Bradshaw's rare Italian purchases, Johannes Regiomontanus *Kalendarium* (1476), the first book printed by Ratdolt (Inc. 1737).

[48] *Nederlandsche Spectator* 1 March 1884 (translated in Bradshaw *Correspondence* 2 p. 468); Campbell to Bradshaw 5 April 1883 (David McKitterick 'Henry Bradshaw and M. F. A. G. Campbell; some further correspondence' in T. Croiset van Uchelen (ed.) *Hellinga Festschrift/Feestbundel/Mélanges; forty-three studies in bibliography presented to W. Hellinga* (Amsterdam 1980) pp. 335–8 at p. 337).

More importantly for Belgium, to whom the family had unsuccessfully offered the collection,[49] Vergauwen had paid especial attention to the history of his country, and to Flanders in particular, with devoted emphasis on Low Countries incunables. As Olivier explained in the preface to his catalogue of the two-part sale in March–April 1884, 'Les Incunables ne sont point de pures curiosités d'amateurs: Ce sont de véritables monuments historiques et littéraires. On sait combien les origines de la Typographie sont intimement liées à l'histoire intellectuelle, morale, sociale même, de l'Europe.' The importance Bradshaw himself attached to the sale is evinced by the extensive notes he made on the collection – he viewed the books in person – and in his persuading the Syndics to allocate £500 from the Rustat Fund. The sum expended was finally £551.6s.4d., most of which was taken from the accumulated reserves in Consols.[50] Among the ninety-odd volumes that came to Cambridge as a result of the sale, Bradshaw secured several items that were the only copies recorded, and he took especial pleasure in having bid successfully (via Quaritch, as usual) for those most relevant to his typographical researches. Thanks to going in person to Brussels he had discovered a packet of fragments undescribed in the catalogue, including several from a Ghent *Horae* whose importance emerged, with his encouragement, shortly afterwards in W. M. Conway's *Woodcutters of the Netherlands*. The fragments were something of a bargain at 225 francs, and it was characteristic of Bradshaw's methods that he paid particular attention to unfamiliar items, or to lots whose interest was more typographical than bibliophilic. The Library's funds would not permit serious hope of securing obvious treasures such as Colard Mansion's printing of Jean Boutillier's *Somme rurale* (sold to Margand of Paris for 10,100 francs, the equivalent of £404); and a volume in contemporary calf containing two works including the earliest dated book from Utrecht was, at

[49] *Nederlandsche Spectator*, 1 March 1884 (see n. 48).
[50] Syndicate Minutes 30 January and 23 April 1884; Rustat Audit Book 1884.

1020 francs, the most expensive lot to come to Cambridge. For 310 francs Bradshaw was able to add to the five items from the Culemann sale printed by the Dutch Printer of the *Speculum*, the so-called Costeriana that he believed, for reasons he had set out in a Memorandum issued in 1871, to have been produced at Utrecht.[51] Among the Belgian books, besides the fragments of the *Horae* were two outstanding successes: St Augustine's *Manuale* from the first press at Alost, where Johannes de Paderborn and Thierry Martens had set up their equipment in 1473 and so become the first printers in the modern geographical Belgium, and a *Sammelband* from the Premonstratensians at Grimberghen near Malines containing five works from the press of the Brothers of the Common Life, the first press in Brussels, and catalogued as having been printed in Cologne.

The Vergauwen sale proved to be the last opportunity Bradshaw had for buying incunables on such a scale. He approached no other task with more devotion and sustained energy than he brought to analysing and financing the series of auctions that offered so much from the presses of Cologne, Belgium and the Netherlands, or to examining his purchases once they were at Cambridge. Other auctions in England usually passed him by, even though the economic depression of the late 1870s and early 1880s brought a series of spectacular collections on to the market. At the sales of the Sunderland library in 1882 the University Library purchased only one book, albeit an unexpected one: but the Subiaco Lactantius was bought more on the prompting of H. R. Luard than on that of Bradshaw. A grant from the Syndicate enabled the Library to buy the Sunderland *editio princeps* of Terentianus Maurus the following year, but apart from these – and despite Quaritch's vast purchases for stock at the sales – Bradshaw made no serious attempt to buy anything further. It was also probably at

---

[51] Inc. 3295; cf. Bradshaw's 'List of the founts of type and woodcut devices used by printers in Holland in the fifteenth century', repr. in his *Collected papers* (Cambridge 1889) pp. 258–80. But see also Wytze and Lotte Hellinga *The fifteenth-century printing types of the Low Countries* (Amsterdam 1966) I pp. 7–8.

Luard's suggestion that the Library bid for Dionysius Paravisinus' *editio princeps* of Constantinus Lascaris, lost at a Sunderland sale for £57 to Quaritch, and lost again at the Syston Park sale in 1885 thanks to a commission of twice the sum the Library was prepared to pay from the American banker Brayton Ives.[52] The Library finally obtained Lord Crawford's copy in 1887 with the help of Samuel Sandars. Bradshaw could not dictate everything the Library should buy, and when, bowing to pressure from both Luard and Sandars, he had to acknowledge to Quaritch the safe arrival of a German block-book Apocalypse after the Syston Park sale, he did so with a bad grace despite its being the first the Library had ever acquired: 'There are many people who no doubt would be glad to see a block-book in the University Library; but for my own part I must confess that there are many books in your stock that I would much sooner buy for the Library, and sooner recommend to be bought, even at a higher price than this.'[53]

With the dramatic exception of the Vergauwen sales, the only auctions latterly at which Bradshaw's successful bids for early printed books ran to double figures were those of A. J. Horwood, in 1883 (where he even bought two duplicates for no apparent reason, including one of a book he had presented to the Library himself in 1868), and of the Wodhull books in 1886. At the Horwood sale he concentrated, as usual, on the Low Countries and the lower Rhineland. He missed only one lot, a large quantity of fragments, and out of notional bids totalling £124 had only £52.4s.6d. to pay even after Quaritch's commission.[54] Only three lots cost him more than five pounds. Among them was a volume[55] containing the earliest work from the Cologne press of the Printer of the Augustinus *De fide*, bound up with Gerson *Opus tripartitum*

---

[52] Bradshaw bid up to £100 through Quaritch, but Quaritch was also handling Ives' bid and obtained the book for him at £105.
[53] Bradshaw to Quaritch 30 December 1884.
[54] Inc. 988, 1014, 1029, 1049, 1059, 1077, 1082, 1139, 1162, 1164, 1178, 1183, and 1194.
[55] Inc. 1176 etc.

from the Brothers of the Common Life at Marienthal (the only representation of the press in the Library) and a Gerson manuscript, and the first book from Johannes de Paderborn's press at Louvain. Besides this, Beriah Botfield's copy of Petrus de Crescentiis *Liber ruralium commodorum* (1474) was knocked down at exactly half Bradshaw's limit;[56] but in simple financial terms the best bargain of all was perhaps a volume of four Cologne quartos[57] at twenty-six shillings where Bradshaw had been prepared to pay £30. The Wodhull sale, two and a half years later in January 1886, came when he was heavily overworked, distracted by arguments over the Library's ridiculously inadequate buildings and tired from a row in the Council of the Senate as a result of which he had tried to resign from it. The Syndicate authorized Bradshaw to bid up to £15 each on two late manuscripts of Thucydides that had once belonged to Anthony Askew,[58] but both were lost resoundingly at £47 apiece to another of Quaritch's customers. Despite other responsibilities, however, he found time to make an analysis of the Wodhull incunables.[59] His bids on printed books were more successful than those on the manuscripts, and (reminded by his correspondence the previous autumn with Talbot Baines Reed) he obtained Edward Rowe Mores' *Dissertation upon English typographical founderies* (1778) at £4.10s.0d. together with fourteen incunables which bore the firm stamp of his selection, five coming from Germany and eight from the Low Countries. Two were from Gerard Leeu's press at Gouda, and of the four from Johannes de Paderborn's at Louvain the 1475 Justinian was a particularly satisfactory purchase at £5: Bradshaw had been prepared to bid up to £20, and it was the Askew copy.[60]

---

[56] Inc. 3696 – not, however, the first book printed at Louvain as claimed by Sotheby's cataloguer. [57] Inc. 453 etc. [58] Syndicate Minutes 20 January 1886.

[59] Bradshaw's analysis is now MS. Add. 4323.

[60] The Library's purchases at the Wodhull sale are set out in Luard's annotated copy of the auction catalogue. To the eleven listed in Oates *Catalogue* must be added Inc. 2902 and Inc. 3764; Lot 1654 was disposed of subsequently (cf. Oates *Catalogue* 3708, bought in 1901). Bradshaw lost two books printed by Zel (Augustinus *De vita christiana* (1467) and the *Gesta Romanorum* (c. 1473)) to Quaritch and Stevens; the 1481 edition printed by

Years before, Bradshaw had built up the collection of incunables at his own expense, and he had continued to add to his own private library even while also buying for the University. The annual report for 1884–5 recorded his present of four more from the Low Countries, and that for the following year (published after Bradshaw's death) the gift of 129 liturgical books – by no means all dating from the fifteenth century – and seventeen other incunables. Since there is some evidence to suggest that he died even while these last donations were being added to the Library, some may in fact have come from his executors.[61] A rare *Missale ordinis Eremitarum S. Pauli*, printed in Brünn and given to Bradshaw by Luard at Easter 1884, was passed on to the Library the following year; but most others are recorded simply as being from his library, including a rare Cologne *Nocturnale* (bought from Quaritch in 1878), a volume of three pieces from Amerbach's press that he had kept as a souvenir from the Culemann sale, and the *Breviarium Upsalense* printed by Johannes Fabri in 1496: although very seriously imperfect it remained the only fifteenth-century Swedish printed book in the Library until 1916.

Partly, no doubt, to mark the confirmation of his connection with the Library, and partly, perhaps, as an example to others, a year after he had been elected Librarian Bradshaw presented over fifty incunables to the Library. Not only had no librarian ever given so much before, but this was also to prove the first of several major gifts on his part. More incunables followed in 1870, when he also presented his unequalled collection of Irish books, and a miscellaneous supply of other donations meant that his name was rarely absent from the lists of benefactors published in each annual report. In all the Library's history, only his pupil and successor at one remove,

Gerard Leeu of the *Dialogus creaturarum moralisatus* to Stevens (Bradshaw had presented the 1480 edition to the Library in 1870); Wynkyn de Worde's edition of Lyndewode *Constitutiones provinciales* (1496) also to Stevens; and Aquinas *Secunda secundae* (Mentelin) to Ellis. Wodhull's collection of Baker, Leigh and Sotheby catalogues, on which Bradshaw put a sporting bid of five pounds, went to the Liverpool collector Joseph Mayer.   [61] Cf. Oates *Catalogue* p. 33.

Francis Jenkinson, has shown equal dedication and conviction. Circumstances favoured Bradshaw. He was, in buying both incunables and early Irish books, more knowledgeable than almost all his suppliers, and since he did not interest himself in the traditionally fashionable fifteenth-century presses he faced less competition, with accompanying lower prices. His purse was not particularly long (he had once been forced to sell part of his library, a course of action which he regretted for long after), but in the years before he had full control over the Library's expenditure, as Librarian, he was in effect buying early printed books for Cambridge out of his own pocket. Hardly surprisingly, he concentrated his efforts on his own chosen fields of interest, a feature fully reflected in the books presented in March 1868. Most important among this gift was a magnificent copy in contemporary stamped calf of Bartholomaeus Anglicus *De proprietatibus rerum*, printed at Cologne in 1472 and now recognized as crucial to any study of early printing in England as the first book to be printed by Caxton.[62] Over half Bradshaw's gift were Cologne imprints, and of these two-fifths had been printed by Ulrich Zel, the city's first printer: the group of a dozen titles from Zel's press comprised rather fewer volumes, since five were contained in one volume – still in its sixteenth-century stamped binding – that Bradshaw had obtained from Muller through Deighton, Bell in April 1866.[63] Other books he had bought abroad while on his travels: among them were copies of Dictys Cretensis *Historia Troiana* and Aretino *De studiis et literis* from Tross in Paris in January 1866, and of Rolewinck and Thomas Aquinas found at Bruges in October. Bernhard von Breydenbach's *Itinerarium* in German, printed by Anton Sorg in Augsburg in 1488, had been supplied by Weigel of Leipzig in sixteenth-century stamped pigskin. By contrast with the Cologne

---

[62] Bradshaw disagreed strongly with Blades' distaste for associating this book with Cologne, and preferred (correctly) to concentrate on Veldener's very similar typeface: see his marginal comment on William Blades *Life and typography of William Caxton* (1861–3) 1 p. 52 (Adv. b. 77.18). Cf. P. Needham 'William Caxton and his Cologne printers' in *Ars impressoria* (*Festgabe S. Corsten*) (Munich 1986) pp. 103–31.

[63] Inc. 380 etc.

imprints, there were only three Italian books in all, but the half-dozen French works included a volume (since broken up)[64] from the Pinelli library containing a rare copy of Richard Fitzralph's work printed by the first printer at Lyon, bound up with two other provincial tracts. The remainder, all from the Low Countries, pointed to Bradshaw's greatest interest. In October 1866 he had boasted to J. W. Holtrop of his copy of the Utrecht printer G.L.'s *Wech der sielen salicheit*[65] bound up – though he did not mention it – with Otto von Passau's *Boeck des gulden throens*.[66] St Bonaventura's *Sermones* printed by Pieter van Os at Zwolle in 1479, had been supplied to Bradshaw by Muller in April 1866, the date that the same firm also provided a volume containing works by John Cassian and St Jerome printed by the Brothers of the Common Life in Brussels.[67] Four months earlier, in January, the London bookseller Boone had sold him a tiny Psalter printed by Leeu in Antwerp at the modest price of £2.12s.6d., and this too came with Bradshaw's first major donation. Besides these, there arrived a handful of puzzles, characteristic of Bradshaw's curiosity about what could not easily be placed, for which existing reference books were no help and around which, in some cases, there is still an aura of doubt. They posed exactly the kind of questions that he adored, but it was left to Victor Scholderer in 1960 to remove a copy of Gerson's *De pollutionibus nocturnis* away from its allotted place in Holland to the other side of the Elbe, in Germany.[68]

The University Library had not received so many incunables since George I had given Moore's library in 1715. Though less numerous than his 1868 donation, Bradshaw's further gift in 1870 was of equal quality. In 1870 the Culemann sale yielded leaves from the 42-line and 36-line Bibles, among much more, to which Bradshaw added a broadside *Cisianus zu*

---

[64] Inc. 3179, 3267, 3290.   [65] Bradshaw *Correspondence* 1 p. 119.
[66] Inc. 3330, 3332.   [67] Inc. 3854, 3861.
[68] Inc. 3669. See Victor Scholderer 'The printer of Leo I, *Sermones* (Proctor 3248)' *Papers of the Bibliographical Society of America* 54 (1960) pp. 111–13, and Bradshaw *Correspondence* 1 p. 119 and 2 pp. 355–6.

dutsche in an early state of the 36-line Bible type (the unique recorded copy), and some fragments of the 1457 Psalter: the Library could scarcely afford the complete copies, even when they became available. Even more than previously, Bradshaw's selection voiced his attention to the Low Countries, though it also included a superb copy of the Jenson Cornelius Nepos (1471) in a contemporary Italian stamped binding. To an incomplete set of Bernard of Clairvaux' sermons printed by Pieter van Os at Zwolle, acquired by the University Library at the De Meyer sale in 1869, he was able to add the *Somerstuck*. From Olivier, in Brussels, he had secured in November 1869 what became the third book to enter the Library from Jacob Bellaert's press, the first in Haarlem. His copy of Petrus Berchorius *Liber Bibliae moralis*, the earliest dated book to be printed by Pafraet, the first printer at Deventer, came in its original binding, as did a handsomely illuminated Latin and Dutch Boethius from the first press at Ghent that possessed the additional attraction of containing in its binding several copies in fragments of an indulgence from the press of Arend de Keysere,[69] to whose modest output as the only fifteenth-century printer at Oudenarde Bradshaw was able to add Hermannus de Petra's *Sermones* (1480) at the Capron sale in 1875. Overall, Bradshaw's gifts were the more valuable in that they so logically complemented his purchases on the Library's behalf at the Enschedé sale in 1867, the De Meyer sale in 1869, and the Culemann sale in 1870.

Bradshaw's further gifts were equally unparalleled. When in 1845 his father had died, he left a considerable collection of Irish books which Bradshaw augmented as time, energy and money permitted: Boone in London, and Charles Hedgelong in Dublin were especially important to him in developing an interest in Irish history, literature, language, and, by extension,

---

[69] Bradshaw bought the Boethius (Inc. 4003) from F. S. Ellis in April 1870 for £18. See also Bradshaw *Correspondence* 1 p. 147 and 2 pp. 400–1, and Bradshaw to Ferdinand Vanderhaeghen 24 April 1870, announcing his acquisition of the Boethius the day before (J. Machiels 'Henry Bradshaw's correspondentie met Ferdinand Vanderhaeghen' *Archives et Bibliothèques de Belgique* 43 (1972) pp. 598–614, at pp. 604–5).

type design, that had been part of his childhood and that lasted until the end of his life. Outside the book trade, and most important of all, was J. H. Todd, to whom Bradshaw owed much of his bibliographical and palaeographical knowledge.[70] Todd's death on 28 June 1869, at the age of only sixty-four, helped to mark for Bradshaw the end of an era. The sale of his books followed in Dublin on 15 November and the following days under the auspices of John Fleming Jones. With Boone's help, Bradshaw bought extensively, concentrating his attention principally on Irish history. It would not have been in Bradshaw's nature to let such an opportunity slip for the University Library: he saw no difficulty in buying side by side with the Library, each collection thus complementing the other. Through Boone, therefore, and with the aid of the Worts Fund, the Library obtained nineteen lots, including several standard works on Irish history annotated with additions or corrections. Bradshaw was also anxious to acquire several modern manuscripts, especially those of John O'Donovan, editor of the *Annals of the kingdom of Ireland*, and of his friend Eugene O'Curry, Professor of Irish History and Archaeology at the Catholic University of Ireland, whose magisterial lectures in that capacity had appeared in 1860; but in this he met with only imperfect success, partly because by the time they came to be offered some of the Library's money had already gone to pay for a fourteenth-century *Legenda aurea*.[71] One of the relatively few other books falling outside the field of Irish history, a Würzburg Missal printed by Georg Reyser in the late 1490s, proved to be lacking two leaves when examined, and was reduced to half price: it was the only early printed book to attract Bradshaw's attention. He was, subsequently, however, able to make good some of his disappointments at the sale. For only three of the Library's purchases had

---

[70] Todd's contribution to Trinity College, Dublin, has been described most recently by G. O. Simms (*Hermathena* 109 (1969) pp. 5–23) and in R. B. McDowell and D. A. Webb *Trinity College, Dublin 1582–1952* (Cambridge 1982) pp. 276–8.

[71] Lot 1832: MS. Add. 618. Bradshaw's working copy of the sale catalogue is at Hib. 5.869.21.

it had to pay as much as £11. On the other hand, Trinity College, Dublin, challenged by piety as well as by need to bid as high as possible on a few key books of its own Librarian's collection, over-reached itself. A heavily annotated copy of Harris' edition of Sir James Ware (1745) reached the astonishing price of £450; a collection of transcripts relating to the history of the college obtained £55;[72] and O'Curry's transcripts of Irish martyrologies fetched equally high prices despite the fact that the transcript of the Martyrology of Tallaght taken from a Brussels manuscript of the seventeenth century had been used as the basis for an edition (albeit a misleading one) in 1857.[73] A transcript of the Martyrology of Donegal,[74] for which Trinity College bid £57.10s.0d., had already been published under Todd's care in 1864. Bradshaw seems to have been especially anxious to secure the volume containing the copy of the Martyrology of Tallaght,[75] but he lost it at the fierce price of £56 to Trinity College. He also hoped to buy a rather earlier manuscript of much greater original interest. The Sarum Consuetudinary and Troparium from Dublin, dating from about 1360, offered as lot 1451, was already well known as the subject of a series of articles by Todd in the *British Magazine* in 1845–7, and appealed strongly to Bradshaw on both liturgical and musical grounds,[76] but it was knocked down at over £70. All these seemed irretrievable, until in August 1870 Todd's brother wrote from Dublin to say that the College had declined to take the Ware, and had returned all the other books and manuscripts bought at the sale: in inviting offers from Cambridge he dropped the agreeable

---

[72] MS. Add. 707.

[73] R. I. Best and H. J. Lawlor (eds.) *The martyrology of Tallaght* (Henry Bradshaw Society 1931) p. xvii.   [74] MS. Add. 709.   [75] MS. Add. 708.

[76] MS. Add. 710. See W. H. Frere *The Use of Sarum* (Cambridge 1898–1901) pp. xlix–li; H. E. Woolridge and H. V. Hughes *Early English harmony from the 10th to the 15th century* (1897–1913) I plates xlvi and xlvii; [R. J. Hesbert] *Le tropaire-prosaire de Dublin* (Monumenta Musicae Sacrae 4 (1966)); and John Stevens in Iain Fenlon (ed.) *Cambridge music manuscripts 900–1700* (Cambridge 1982) pp. 78–81. The story is recorded that when Sir Charles Villiers Stanford appealed to Bradshaw for advice on the *Angelus ad Virginem* in his opera *Savonarola*, Bradshaw answered his enquiry from this manuscript. See also below, p. 763.

hint that he thought the original bids absurdly high. Bradshaw bought everything offered, including a notebook relating largely to the life of Trinity College kept by Anthony Dopping, Bishop of Meath and Fellow of the college from 1662.[77]

In November 1869, the month of the sale of Todd's books, some special pleading was called for to justify the University Library's diversifying seriously into bidding for Irish manuscripts, but by August 1870 the position had changed completely. Bradshaw's success at the sale was clouded by the news of the death of William Boone, one of his closest friends in the book trade, whom his father had known when he was only just getting established, and who had never lost his especial interest in the Bradshaw family collection of Irish books. He collapsed just after returning from attending the sale at Dublin, where he had executed the bids of the University Library. With these two linked episodes, the sale of Todd's books and now Boone's death, recent in his memory, Bradshaw therefore finally turned his back on his original scheme to present his Irish library to the Royal Irish Academy,[78] and instead offered it to Cambridge on 30 March 1870. The offer came in a long letter addressed to the then Vice-Chancellor Edward Atkinson, Master of Clare College and a man who on more than one occasion showed unusual understanding of the Library and its collections.

My dear Sir,
    There is a matter which has been in my mind for some time past, and which I should be glad if you could bring before the Library Syndicate before they separate for the Vacation.
    I have a considerable collection of books, pamphlets, and other printed papers relating to Ireland. The basis of it is the Irish portion of my father's library, that portion of it in which, as coming himself from the North of Ireland, he took most interest, and which, at his death in 1845, he left to me. For several years I did a good deal to increase the collection, especially

[77] MS. Add. 711.   [78] J. H. Todd to Bradshaw 30 March 1857.

in the matter of pamphlets and printed papers; though it is still of course very far from having any claim to completeness.

It would give me sincere pleasure if the Syndics would accept this collection as a gift to the Library. More than forty years ago, when public libraries were less plentifully supplied than they are now, literary men used to come to my father's house to work at these books when engaged upon writing upon Irish affairs, and from the time that I was a child, they have had a particular interest for me. Although I have been able to give but little attention to them for some few years past, yet I have by me a mass of bibliographical notes on the subject, collected during the last twenty years; and if I could feel that these books and papers were deposited in some more permanent resting-place than my own library, I should more readily try to put my notes in order so as to turn them to some practical use.

There are about 1000 bound volumes; and of the pamphlets and other printed material there are, speaking roughly, about 2700 in octavo, 700 in quarto, and 500 in folio, including proclamations, broadsides, and fly-sheets. These, with a number of original signed petitions to the Houses of Parliament (chiefly ranging from 1809 to 1819 and relating to the so-called Catholic Claims) and a few other manuscripts, amount in all to about 5000 pieces. There are necessarily many duplicates in such a collection, and many also will be already in the University Library; but after making all due allowance for these, there must remain a considerable number which the Library does not possess, and which it would be difficult either to find elsewhere or to bring together again.

I should not wish to impose any terms whatever upon the Syndicate, if they should think fit to accept the books. I have no views about the sacredness of duplicates, or the necessity of keeping such a collection intact. My whole wish is to enable the University to enrich its library with a class of books with which, though possessing some very precious things of the kind, it is on the whole but poorly provided at present; and I should therefore prefer that any suggestion which I might be inclined to make concerning their arrangement, should be made by me as the Librarian to whose charge they would be confided under the control of the Syndicate, rather than that the gift should be hampered with conditions such as in many cases serve to hinder the very object for which the collection was formed.

It will not be easy for me to forget the liberal manner in which the University, at the suggestion of the Library Syndicate, enabled me for more than seven years to pursue the studies which I had most at heart, and the confidence implied in the fact that no report of my work during that time was ever demanded of me. I hope that the confidence was not wholly misplaced; but I cannot express strongly enough that the freedom of those seven years of work, as it has produced results which I could not have foreseen, so it has given me a sense of debt to the University which nothing can remove.[79]

The collection stretched chronologically from the sixteenth to the nineteenth centuries and was, even then, one of the best of its kind. With the addition of a second Irish library that Bradshaw amassed between 1870 and his death in 1886, presented by his family, and further purchases and donations subsequently, by the time that the catalogue was published in 1916 under the auspices of Charles Sayle, it was probably unparalleled.[80] But despite his hopes of putting his notes in order, Bradshaw published next to nothing either about his collection or about the history of printing in Ireland. The text of his lecture on the latter, given to the Library Association at Dublin in 1884,[81] has not survived. Meanwhile his notes continued to accumulate, whether on John Bale or on Irish printed letter-forms, and it was left to Talbot Baines Reed in 1887 to use Bradshaw's accumulated wisdom in the pages of his *History of the old English letter foundries* as a result of a brief but exhaustive exchange of letters that cheered the last weeks of Bradshaw's life.

Thanks to Bradshaw's personal generosity, the Library thus on the one hand added (in his incunables) to a traditional strength, albeit in a new way, and on the other began to extend its horizons, to look beyond the established and general accumulations of printed books to the acquisition of major new special collections. The Todd sale and Bradshaw's Irish books formed two parts of the same acquisitions policy, and marked the beginning of a progress that gradually brought the University to accept Bradshaw's arguments for a national, rather than simply a university, repository of special collections as it was already of copyright deposits. It was a policy, however, that had perforce to be modest when there were no

[79] Library papers 4 May 1870.
[80] [C. E. Sayle] *A catalogue of the Bradshaw collection of Irish books in the University Library, Cambridge* 3 vols. (Cambridge 1916).   [81] *Library Chronicle* 1 (1884) p. 163.

appropriate gifts. Despite the impression given now by the heady list of rare fifteenth-century books to enter the Library over the next few years, money was not plentiful. In November 1876 the contribution from the University Chest towards the running of the Library was raised from £2500 to £3000, but for most of its major purchases the Library continued to rely on the Worts and Rustat Funds. The decision to close the old hand-written catalogue, and incorporate entries in it into the new printed one – a scheme involving the entire recataloguing of most of the books in the Library – entailed a sharp rise in expenditure on printing, so much so that in November 1871 the Syndicate successfully applied to the Worts Fund to meet the cost of all foreign periodicals.[82] Oriental acquisitions, discussed separately below, drew heavily on both the Worts and the Rustat Funds, and neither for these nor for western purchases was much distinction made between the two funds save in the case of expensive botanical works, that were still, as hitherto, charged to the former.

In 1870, hard on the heels of the Culemann sale, Bradshaw had set an example by giving to the Library most of his collection of early printed books. From then until his death no-one gave more. In 1869 his donations included the first prayer book of Edward VI, the *Comes* of a ninth-century Gospel Book from north-eastern France,[83] and a quarto notebook by Jean Matal, friend of Antonio Agustín, on the libraries of Rome in the 1540s.[84] He was still using his own purse to buy manuscripts for the Library in the last years of his life: in this way the Library received a terrier of the old west fields of Cambridge,[85] and a fourteenth-century Collectarius from the Bramston sale at Puttick and Simpson's in 1885.[86] The unique

[82] Syndicate Minutes 8 November 1871. The Worts Trustees agreed on 8 March 1872.
[83] MS. Add. 563.
[84] MS. Add. 565. See A. R. A. Hobson 'The *Iter Italicum* of Jean Matal' in *Studies in the book trade in honour of Graham Pollard* (Oxford 1975) pp. 33–61, and idem 'Jacobus Apocellus' *Trans Cambridge Bibliographical Soc.* 7 (1979) p. 279–83.
[85] MS. Add. 2601. See F. W. Maitland *Township and borough* (Cambridge 1898) and C. P. Hall and J. R. Ravensdale (eds.) *The west fields of Cambridge* (Cambridge 1976).
[86] MS. Add. 2770 (Bramston sale, 24 June 1885, lot 646).

collection of eighteenth- and early nineteenth-century street ballads collected by Sir Frederic Madden came to the Library only after Bradshaw's death, bought from his executors in June 1886, and proved to be one of the most prescient acquisitions of the late nineteenth century. It had represented something of an embarrassment for Bradshaw, however. At the sale of Madden's books in July 1873 the collection, consisting of sixteen thousand-odd sheets arranged printer by printer and bound up in twenty-six volumes, had fetched £443 on Quaritch's bid. The sale occurred during the Long Vacation, and Bradshaw seems to have ordered them from Quaritch in the hope of persuading the Syndics to accept them even at this considerable price. Once they were in Cambridge, it became clear that neither would the authorities accept them nor could Bradshaw conscientiously recommend them. The ballads were too late to interest friends who might have helped by their enthusiastic support, such as F. J. Furnivall, and Bradshaw felt – willingly or no – obliged to keep them.[87] In making himself responsible for the bill at a time when the collection seemed to have no appeal or interest for the Library, and so leaving them to be available after his death, Bradshaw once again, albeit unwittingly, set an example to the Library's well-wishers.

But while not everyone could match his standards, the donations received during his librarianship formed a significant addition to the collections of manuscripts and early printed books. The gift by E. W. Blore, Fellow of Trinity College, in 1880 of many of his father's and grandfather's papers[88] was especially rich in the genealogy and local history of Derbyshire and Rutland, but also brought many of the records of Edward Blore, one of the century's most successful architects, who had died the previous year: they added a field to the Library's collections of manuscripts that had not been represented before, but their significance was discovered only with the revival of interest in the architecture of the Victorian

---

[87] Bradshaw to Quaritch 12 August 1873; Bradshaw to F. J. Furnivall 22 August 1873; Quaritch to Bradshaw 3 September 1873.   [88] MSS. Add. 3874–956.

country house almost a century later. By contrast, few books gave Bradshaw greater pleasure than the twenty-three volumes relating to Hendrik Niclas and the Family of Love, given by the Master of Jesus College G. E. Corrie in 1884. By then in his nineties, Corrie possessed a library of which he was justifiably proud enough in 1880 to issue a catalogue of the scarcer books contained in it, while years earlier a series of papers in the publications of the Cambridge Antiquarian Society on the early history of various college libraries had witnessed to interests shared with Bradshaw, the first serious historian of the University Library itself. The Family of Love collection had been the subject of a paper by Bradshaw's protégé J. H. Hessels in *Notes and Queries* in 1869, and a separate catalogue was published in 1880 to stand alongside the other list of the same year. In the spring of 1884 Corrie presented part of this collection to the Library, and after analysing the printed catalogue Bradshaw felt prompted to ask for more: Corrie offered no objection, and as a result Bradshaw could regard the University Library's collection of publications relating to the subject as complete.[89]

However valuable each of these gifts was in itself, they were modest in comparison with those in some other libraries, and Bradshaw cast envious eyes at Oxford. There, since the arrival of Richard Gough's bequest in 1809, the Bodleian could point to the libraries of Edmund Malone and Francis Douce, quite apart from smaller collections given or bequeathed by others. By contrast, mourned Bradshaw, 'None of the great collectors of modern times have thought fit to deposit their treasures with us; and hence it is, perhaps, that our library has never acquired that unfailing tradition of a learned staff which the accession of

---

[89] Bradshaw's annotated copy of the 1880 list is now Adv. d. 77.22. See also Syndicate Minutes 23 April and 7 May 1884; Bradshaw to Corrie 5 November 1884; Annual Report 1885 (*Reporter* 26 June 1885, pp. 959–60); and M. Holroyd (ed.) *Memorials of the life of George Elwes Corrie* (Cambridge 1890) pp. 317–18. Corrie's books were sold at Sotheby's at a sale beginning on 18 May 1886 – after Bradshaw's death. Bradshaw's notes on the Family of Love are now Add. 6434, but the Library's collection of these works was not in fact quite complete.

such gifts from time to time naturally develops, and of which Bodley's library affords so notable an example.'[90] Corrie gave his books to the University Library not least as a result of Bradshaw's special interest and obvious ability to appreciate them, but in 1882, the year in which he spoke these words, Bradshaw had in mind another collector, of more varied tastes.

On Samuel Sandars (fig. 27d), Bradshaw's influence was profound, even definitive. The founder of the Readership in Bibliography that bears his name died in 1894, bequeathing the best part of his books to the Library.[91] In his lifetime he was a regular, sympathetic, and painstaking benefactor who allowed his own inclinations to be so guided by Bradshaw and, later, by Francis Jenkinson, that his collections became doubly valuable to the Library when eventually they came to Cambridge. Sandars' family was originally from Derbyshire, but by the time he entered Trinity College from Harrow in 1855 the family was in Essex, scarcely fifteen miles from Cambridge, and his father had been Conservative Member of Parliament for Wakefield for eight years. In 1860 he took his degree and, having been admitted to the Inner Temple the year before, began his career in law; he was called to the bar in 1863. In February 1868 he joined the Cambridge Antiquarian Society, which besides attracting archaeologists and historians of architecture then also provided a platform for Bradshaw to report his most recent investigations into early printing. The first surviving letters between the two men, in the early summer of 1868, deal with preparations for an account by Sandars of the history of the University Church, eventually published by the Society in 1869. Sandars' anxiety for detail – as an archaeological study his account has still not been altogether superseded – and his growing familiarity with the British Museum may have suggested to Bradshaw that this

[90] Address at the opening of the fifth annual meeting of the Library Association (Memorandum no. 7, 1882), repr. in his *Collected papers* (Cambridge 1889) pp. 371–409, at pp. 387–8.

[91] See Francis Jenkinson's anonymous obituary in the *Cambridge Review* 8 November 1894, pp. 54–6.

(a)

(b)

(c)

(d)

27 (a) H. R. Luard (1825–91), University Registrary. From a photograph by Fradelle and Young, London.

   (b) Solomon Schiller-Szinessy (1820–90). From an engraving by I.
Fischer.

   (c) William Wright (1830–89), Sir Thomas Adams Professor of
Arabic. From a photograph by Elliott and Fry.

   (d) Samuel Sandars (1837–94). From a painting in the possession of
the family.

young barrister had more to offer than amateurish ramblings; but he seems to have spurned Sandars' first proffered gifts to the Library. The Donations Register therefore records nothing as having been accepted before December 1869, when a single sheet of *c.* 1700 is listed together with a volume of pamphlets relating to Cambridge. They were pleasant enough, but gave no hint of what was to come.

Bradshaw was able to add little to Sandars' work on the architecture of Great St Mary's; but when, with that behind him, Sandars cast round for another subject and hit on a survey of books in Cambridge printed on vellum, there was more scope. Sandars' inspiration came from Bradshaw's own short addendum to Van Praet published in *Le Bibliophile Illustré* in 1863;[92] but to this theme, the most obvious of pursuits for an aspiring book collector in the generations brought up on Dibdin, Bradshaw was able to add a variation which transformed Sandars' plodding care. Van Praet's assiduous search for vellum in French libraries, coupled with Dibdin's rhapsodies, may have first awakened Sandars' interest, but the idea of devoting a volume to such books in Cambridge germinated with Bradshaw. Sandars' instincts as a collector inclined towards the conventional. He had a Victorian's love of colour, and tended to believe that all books in need of repair should be clothed in morocco by Bedford or, later, Zaehnsdorf. As a collector, Sandars' importance (which came to be recognized well beyond the confines of the Library) lay not in the sums of money he spent: these were relatively modest, concentrated in the last thirteen or fourteen years of his life, and did not compare with the continuously high figures expended by such men as Lord Amherst or Lord Carysfort. But he was one of a small number of collectors in the 1880s seriously committed to collecting liturgical books. The reasons for his interests in this field are not far to seek. First, as Van Praet had reminded the world, they were frequently on vellum, either entirely or (for the leaves of the canon of the Mass) in part. Secondly, they could

[92] September 1863, p. 105; November 1863, p. 123.

be colourful, especially if prepared for some special patron. The popularity of books of hours as an art form had been demonstrated in the 1840s in the colour lithography of firms such as Day and Son, and artists and writers led by Owen Jones, Henry Shaw and Henry Noel Humphreys, whose work provoked a host of imitators and acolytes, while the link with sixteenth-century printed decoration was epitomized in Mary Byfield's decorations in the Pickering prayer book of 1853. The accompanying craze among amateur artists for illuminating and copying was another expression of the same phenomenon. Among contemporary collectors, Sandars' taste had perhaps most in common with that of Sir Thomas Brooke, part of whose somewhat grander collection of liturgical manuscripts found a home in Keble College, Oxford.[93]

Sandars had proved himself a skilful ecclesiologist in his work on Great St Mary's and in this too he was in sympathy with his mentor. Bradshaw's knowledge of the history of the liturgy, culminating in the edition of the Sarum Breviary he undertook with Christopher Wordsworth and Francis Procter, and commemorated in the society named after him, left an unmistakable mark on the Library in his purchases of early books and, after his death, in the creation of a special class *Rit.* or ritualia. In Sandars he had a ready pupil, and during the last months of 1869 and the first of 1870 began to change him from a magpie collector of curiosities into something of a specialist. The list of books Sandars offered in January 1870 was not significantly different from earlier ones: all were modern books, and besides some sermons on ritualism most were on topography or of local interest, including an account of the history of rowing in Cambridge published in 1852, and guidebooks to Aix la Chapelle and Strasbourg. But the same letter also brought evidence of careful if not very informed reading of Sotheby's *Catalogue of a bibliotheca typographica*, the

---

[93] Cf. *A catalogue of the manuscripts and printed books collected by Thomas Brooke, FSA* (1891) and M. B. Parkes *The medieval manuscripts of Keble College, Oxford* (1979), especially pp. xi–xiii, giving further references.

Culemann catalogue which so engrossed Bradshaw. Sandars'
suggestions, prompted more by Ellis' incompetent descriptions than by any independent bibliographical knowledge,
ranged from single leaves to a copy of Aquinas that finally
reached £300 (the Library did not bid on it). Of the 'odd early
bibles' recommended by Sandars, Bradshaw secured, as we
have seen, Mentelin's of 1460 and Eggestein's of 1468, for less
than £34. He also succeeded in obtaining vellum leaves of the
36- and 42-line Bibles, with Sandars' superfluous encouragement, though he chose to buy privately the leaves from the 1457
Psalter lost at the sale. The Culemann sale reveals,
more graphically than any other document, the way in which
Sandars' collecting tastes changed. His purchases, totalling
£4.8s.0d., were modest, but he would almost certainly have
chosen differently had the sale taken place a decade later. For
this sum he bought an imperfect Bible of 1491 (later discarded
and given to Trinity College),[94] a Leipzig Donatus of the mid
1490s, Schoeffer's herbal of 1484, Gregory I's commentary on
the Song of Songs, printed by Barbier in Paris in 1511, and two
liturgical works, a Lyon Breviary of 1505 – illuminated, and in
its original stamped binding, though sadly cut about – and a
sophisticated Paris *Horae*, which he also gave to his old
college.[95]

Bradshaw's present to the Library of half a dozen incunables
may perhaps have encouraged Sandars, who passed on both
the Schoeffer herbal and the Donatus. But by the time of his
death, several more of the Culemann books had passed
through Sandars' hands, nearly all of them liturgical. Thanks
to a rapid turnover in one or two collections, he was given the
second chance that collectors thirst for, when developed
interests and increased expertise could take advantage of
opportunities not at first recognized. The sale of the library of
W. H. Crawford, five years after Bradshaw's death, is beyond
the chronological limits of this book, but is essential to

---

[94] R. Sinker *A catalogue of the fifteenth-century printed books in the library of Trinity College,
Cambridge* (Cambridge 1876) no. 133 and p. 172.   [95] Sinker no. 167.

appreciating the relationship of Sandars with his mentor. What Quaritch described as 'the senseless home-rule agitations' determined Crawford to put his collections, intended for Queen's College, Cork, up for auction in 1891. Sandars was by then a respected collector, and Quaritch had recovered from his astonishment in 1881 at receiving from its author a presentation copy of Sandars' volume on vellum books in Cambridge, when he had exclaimed, 'I was not aware you were such an expert bibliographer.'[96] So, his interests now defined, Sandars bought at the W. H. Crawford sale eight leaves of an immense unrecorded *Canon missae* printed by Georg Stuchs of Nuremberg (at £4.4s.od.), an unrecorded *Horae* printed by Pigouchet, on vellum and with coloured woodcuts, and a Würzburg Missal of 1509 printed probably at Lyon. Within a few months he also picked up the entirely uncut copy of a Halberstadt Psalter of *c.* 1519, described in the Culemann catalogue as 'probably the first book printed at Halberstadt', a Bratislava Missal printed by Schoeffer in 1506, in a contemporary binding, and a manuscript. All had come originally from the Culemann collection.

Sandars became the first regular modern benefactor to the Library, but his constant interest needed sometimes to be disciplined. On one occasion he intended a copy of Thomas Raynolde's quarto *Birth of mankynde* for the Library, but on Bradshaw's pointing out that it was titivated with illustrations from a rather later folio he retrieved it and sent instead Bulwer's *Artificial changeling* – a book, in Sandars' words, 'only fitted for a public collection. I hope you will keep it under lock and key or it will soon vanish.'[97] To Sandars' request a little later that Bradshaw should keep locked away two gifts made in 1873, Peter Hausted's *Hymnus tabaci* (1651) and *Ingeni fructus, or the Cambridge jests* (*c.* 1707), because he thought the jokes of too indecent a character, Bradshaw firmly replied that he would lock them up so as to be accessible when wanted. Sandars was

---

[96] Quaritch to Sandars 27 September 1881.
[97] Sandars to Bradshaw 16 October 1879.

satisfied easily enough on this occasion, but a little more tact was needed when in 1875 he sent up to Cambridge a manuscript prayer book decorated with engravings,[98] only to be told by Bradshaw that 'as I examined the manuscript . . . I found it was so precious and so interesting that I could not resist the temptation of taking it to pieces, which I did with the utmost care and gentleness'.[99] Sandars expressed himself completely satisfied with Bradshaw's rearrangement and rebinding, but the episode is illuminating for the authority Bradshaw enjoyed over one of the Library's greatest benefactors.

Sandars first approached Bradshaw on the subject of leaving his printed books and manuscripts to the Library in 1880, when he needed advice on the wording of his will that would prevent some accident consigning his collection either to the Fitzwilliam Museum or (as Bradshaw jestingly put it) to the zoological museum.[100] In the end some sixteen hundred books came by bequest, including almost a hundred manuscripts, over a hundred incunables, and about three hundred English books printed before 1601.[101] They were the culmination of a long stream of donations of all kinds. In 1870–1, for example, the list of his gifts contained nine incunables, Defoe's *The storm* (1704) and Isaac Ware's *Designs of Inigo Jones and others*, while the early English books included two Cambridge plays: John Mason's *Excellent tragedy of Mulleases the Turk and Borgias governour of Florence* and Thomas Tomkis' *Albumazar*, originally performed by the 'gentlemen of Trinity College'. A few months later he sent in the two printed broadsides prepared in 1710 by Francis Webb, listing university officers, together with *A treatise on the tea-herb compiled by a gentleman of Cambridge*. In some years he gave only minor pieces, but the last few years of his life were outstanding: his donations in

---

[98] MS. Add. 3016.   [99] Quoted in Prothero *Bradshaw* p. 336.
[100] Bradshaw to Sandars 20 July 1880.
[101] The Library did not receive all Sandars' books, and a number were sold at Sotheby's on 3 December 1923.

1891, for example, comprised only six items but they included William Herbert's copy of Lidgate's *Life of Our Lady*, printed by Caxton, and a fragment of a Donatus grammar in the type of the 42-line Bible. The following occasion of his gifts demanded a special report to the University, recording that he had added the W. H. Crawford copy of Gerard Leeu's *Chronicles of England* (1493) as well as an admittedly imperfect copy of the St Albans Chronicles of 1485. A volume of legal texts printed at Seville doubled the Library's collection of Spanish incunables – a late development which Sandars was to increase to three by bequest with the *Constituciones* of Catalonia printed by Rosenbach of Seville in 1494. But, again, it was Bradshaw's influence (five years after his death) that formed the most important part of this gift, intended specifically to strengthen the English and Low Countries parts of the Library's collections in preparation for the catalogue of incunables that Jenkinson was considering. Despite Bradshaw's success in building up the collections in these fields, some important books had escaped him, including the Dutch *Life and passion of Jesus Christ*, the first dated book printed at Haarlem, of which what was believed to be the unique copy was sold at the Enschedé sale to Quaritch, acting for W. H. Crawford. Anxious to save it, Sandars was prepared to pay up to £80 at the Crawford sale in 1891, but he secured it at £30 – a clear sign of the depressed state of the market. Jenkinson was also able to point to the first book printed at Schiedam (also bought by Sandars from the Crawford books for £30), and the Cistercian Breviary printed at Deventer by Paffraet, as well as the 'Costerian' Aesop – an 'appropriate pendant' to the collection, as Jenkinson put it.[102]

The range of Sandars' interests, and the true measure of his importance as a collector, emerged properly only after his bequest in 1894. In many respects he was supremely conventional, but in Bradshaw he found a sympathetic friend and a

---

[102] Syndicate report 8 June 1892; *Reporter* 21 June 1892.

critical mentor whose teaching was not always wasted. From his first gifts in the late 1860s, Sandars deliberately gave books not already in the Library, and the rate at which Bradshaw was sometimes forced to refuse the lists of books submitted to him to be checked must occasionally have seemed alarming. After Sandars' decision in 1880 to bequeath his books, virtually all his important purchases were made ultimately for the Library's benefit, and following the death of his father in 1879 he was able to buy on a grander scale. His relations with the Library therefore became the more close. Occasionally, too, there were gifts of money. When in March 1881 he sent £250, Bradshaw at first planned a shopping expedition; but he could not get away to be tempted by Quaritch or Ellis, and when therefore a man turned up from Sutton Coldfield with several books and manuscripts from the Chadwick family he seized his opportunity. After beating the price down, he succeeded in buying with Sandars' money a Paris *Horae* (1521) unrecorded by Brunet (still the best authority available in 1881), what Bradshaw believed to be the first edition in English of Sir John Mandeville's travels (Wynkyn de Worde 1499), lost sight of since William Herbert had described it, and four manuscripts, all English:[103] they included an early fifteenth-century Romance of Alexander, formerly the property of Francis Blomefield the historian of Norfolk, a selection of tales from the *Gesta Romanorum* and elsewhere, with extra stories about Lincolnshire, Norfolk and Suffolk – 'one of the most interesting books of its kind I ever saw', wrote Bradshaw – and a collection of grammatical texts written in 1434–5 by John Drury, schoolmaster at Beccles, last recorded in 1748 by Thomas Tanner.[104] The East Anglian connections of these manuscripts made sense for the Library and appealed to Sandars.[105] Such gifts of money to Bradshaw and, later, to Jenkinson, bestowed freedom of inestimable value, and betokened no little trust, but Sandars was never averse to

---

[103] MSS. Add. 2827–30.
[104] Thomas Tanner *Bibliotheca Britannico-Hibernica* (1748) p. 235: the manuscript then belonged to Thomas Martin.   [105] Bradshaw to Sandars 9 May 1881.

putting forward suggestions. The Syston Park Apocalypse was virtually forced on Bradshaw, but on other, more expensive, occasions he was protected by poverty. £500 seemed to Sandars too much for a Caxton at the Syston Park sale, but he was ready to prod Bradshaw on to the next hurdle. 'I see another great sale also is coming on. Caxtons in Ld Osterleys collection: are there any there you have not got [?]', he asked.[106] Bradshaw had concentrated on the Vergauwen books instead, and for all his hopes left Sandars to watch the Osterley Park Caxton *Morte d'Arthur* (one of only two surviving copies) go at £1950 to Quaritch for Mrs Abbey Pope of Brooklyn. The Syston Park 42-line Bible went to Quaritch at £3900, with the John Carter Brown Library as underbidder.[107] Such books were well beyond the means of either the University Library or Sandars.

One of Bradshaw's most pregnant insights was to recognize the connection between a benefactor and a proper understanding of the needs of the Library. His education of Sandars was original, subtle, and ultimately to the benefit of both parties; but the University at large could not always understand the needs of benefactors for appreciation, attention and recognition. The meeting of the Library Association held under Bradshaw's presidency at Cambridge in 1882 (fig. 28) was of a body that had still to identify its over-riding interests. Bradshaw used it as an exhibition of libraries in Cambridge, and invited Sandars to it in the belief that donors (as well as potential donors) should know something of how well the Library was run, so that they would be encouraged to give more. He complained to several correspondents of the uncomprehending reaction in some circles of the University to the notion of a gathering of librarians, and both Sandars and Bradshaw were convinced that such blinkered isolationism had lost donations in the past. 'Donors generally are "kittle cattle",' wrote Sandars, 'and expect and fairly so, some little

[106] Sandars to Bradshaw 22 December 1884.
[107] Seymour de Ricci *English collectors of books & manuscripts (1530–1930) and their marks of ownership* (Cambridge 1930) p. 160.

28 Meeting of the Library Association at Cambridge, 1882, photographed outside the south door of King's College chapel. In this portion of a larger group, Henry Bradshaw, as President, sits in the centre. To his right sit George Bullen and (in an overcoat) Richard Garnett, both from the British Museum. To his left are (1) Cornelius Walford, writer on insurance, historian and the promoter of a general catalogue of English literature; (2) Henry Stevens, bookseller (see pp. 634–46, 709–11); and (3) Robert Harrison (London Library). The front row includes, left to right, (1) Samuel Sandars (benefactor); (2) Octavius Johnson (Library staff); (5) Robert Bowes (bookseller and historian of the Cambridge book trade); (8) Eiríkr Magnússon (Library staff); and (12) Henry Wheatley (see pp. 753, 756–9). H. T. Francis (Library staff) is in the top right-hand corner, and William Blades, the biographer of Caxton, is next but two to his right.

thanks for their abnegation in making presents; and a little interest on the part of the university authorities would bear fruit I am sure.'[108] Thanks to Bradshaw and, later, Jenkinson, who also saw to the establishment of the Sandars Readership as the Library's main platform on which to promote wider interest in its collections of early books, a series of major benefactors at last began to come forward. Their example was set by Bradshaw and by Sandars.

One gift, however, was uninfluenced by either. Sir David Brewster had made extensive use of parts of the mass of Sir Isaac Newton's papers at Hurstbourne Park, near Whitchurch in Hampshire, for his study of Newton in 1855. The collection was well known, but although portions had been examined thoroughly at various times since Newton's death, the archive now belonging to the Earl of Portsmouth was in some disarray. When, therefore, in 1872, the Earl of Portsmouth signified that he wished to present the scientific papers amongst it to the University, the first need was for the collection to be properly examined. The task was entrusted to a syndicate that included the expert help of George Gabriel Stokes, John Couch Adams, and G. D. Liveing, Professor of Chemistry.[109] Its report, sixteen years later in 1888, resulted in the Library's retaining all the mathematical papers, most of the correspondence apart from that connected with the Mint and family matters, and a series of printed books including proof sheets of the *Opticks* and heavily annotated copies of both the first and second editions of the *Principia*. The remainder was returned to its owners, to resurface in 1936 at Sotheby's, when many of the lots were acquired by Maynard Keynes and so passed into the library of King's College on his death.[110]

---

[108] Sandars to Bradshaw 10 August 1882.

[109] Grace of 6 November 1872. For an account of the negotiations, and the syndicate's proceedings, see D. T. Whiteside and M. A. Hoskin (eds.) *The mathematical papers of Sir Isaac Newton* I (Cambridge 1967) pp. xxx–xxxiii.

[110] Cf. *A catalogue of the Portsmouth collection of books and papers written by or belonging to Sir Isaac Newton* (Cambridge 1888) and F. Herrmann *Sotheby's; portrait of an auction house* (1980) pp. 290–2.

Bradshaw was not directly involved in negotiations for the Portsmouth papers. No part of the Library commanded his attention to the same degree as did the early printed books, and his achievement in building up the collection, never equalled in the history of the Library, has been rarely challenged elsewhere: the achievement was all the greater with a budget that was always severely limited. But he was also the director of a library of which much else was expected, both within the University and outside in the world at large. The developments of other parts of the Library will be described in the following chapter, before a final consideration of his accomplishments as an administrator and an examination of the Library's relations with the University as a whole.

18

OTHER MEN'S FLOWERS

WHILE THE YEARS of Bradshaw's librarianship are commonly – and rightly – remembered principally for the prodigious additions made to the collection of incunables and for the foundation of one of the most important collections of Irish books in existence, other acquisitions under his guidance arrived in a variety and on a scale that had never been even approached hitherto. The Library was not prepared for such an influx. In June 1875 the Syndicate found it necessary to instruct Bradshaw to take in hand the recataloguing of the fifteenth-century printed books 'as soon as possible',[1] but they were still not catalogued sixteen years later, when Francis Jenkinson turned his dilatory attention to the still larger collection.[2] For the incunables, Bradshaw was content to work from his own somewhat scattered notes, an arrangement which ensured that everyone curious about them had to apply to him. Other collections received less attention. In November 1868 the Syndics agreed to buy from Ebenezer Palmer a collection of pamphlets dating back to the seventeenth century, estimated at 40,000 items, at the rate of £2 per thousand.[3] Scarcely any headway was made in cataloguing them, the staff being preoccupied with recataloguing the existing library for the new printed catalogue, and Palmer's leviathan was added to accumulations of similar matter, to pass into staff folklore as part of the '1868 collection' – of which a portion still existed over a century later. A collection of dissertations from the University of Uppsala, surplus to the requirements of the University of Lund, languished uncatalogued after its purchase

[1] Syndicate Minutes 9 June 1875.   [2] Oates *Catalogue* Introduction p. 34.
[3] Syndicate Minutes 14 November 1868.

in 1869;[4] and over seven thousand pamphlets on Greek and Latin history and literature from the library of Friedrich Wilhelm Ritschl, bought in 1878 for £150 (the sum was charged to the Rustat Fund)[5] were attended to only in 1901. Such profusions were simply overwhelming, and too much for the staff available, so that smaller collections seemed almost a relief. A group of books of Cambridge interest was approved for purchase by the Syndics in December 1869,[6] continuing a policy established under Joseph Power. There were similar precedents for acquiring in 1877 the annotated books from the estate of Richard Shilleto, Fellow (somewhat belatedly) of Peterhouse and editor of Demosthenes and Thucydides, who had been compared variously with Porson and with Gaisford.[7] The auction of Mark Pattison's books in 1885 was of more than incidental interest to Bradshaw, who found much pause for thought in the life of Casaubon,[8] and the Library bought there a useful group of pamphlets on Oxford.

These last were, on the whole, crumbs compared with the purchases made from the library of Robert Willis. Characterized by his nephew J. W. Clark as 'almost, if not quite, the last of those great men who by their brilliant reputation in studies the most diverse – theology, mathematics, classics, science – made the first half of the present century the golden age of Cambridge',[9] Willis died on 28 February 1875. He had been Jacksonian Professor of Natural and Experimental Philosophy since 1837. After already having taken out a patent on an improvement to the harp, he entered Gonville and Caius College in 1821, and in 1826 he graduated ninth Wrangler. A fellowship came the same year, and four years later he was

---

[4] Syndicate Minutes 24 November 1869.
[5] Syndicate Minutes 8 May 1878. Ritschl's own catalogue of his collection is now MS. Add. 6285. The books came through the agency of Herman Hager, who explained that most of the rest of Ritschl's library had been bought by the university library at Dorpat, or Tartu, in Estonia (Hager to Bradshaw 29 April 1878).
[6] Syndicate Minutes 8 December 1869.
[7] A good personal account of Shilleto is in W. E. Heitland *After many years* (Cambridge 1926) pp. 129–31.   [8] Prothero *Bradshaw* pp. 417–18.
[9] Obituary in *Cambridge Chronicle* 6 March 1875.

elected an FRS. He had few rivals in the diversity of his interests, which encompassed the human larynx and its relation to the organ, as well as the more conventional applications of his chosen sphere: in 1849 he served on a commission to examine the stresses on iron railway tracks, in 1851 he served as a juror for the Great Exhibition, he spent fifteen years as lecturer at the new government school of mines in Jermyn Street, while his paper on constructing cog-wheels and his book on *Principles of mechanism* (first published in 1841) each marked major new departures in their subjects. As an architect, his work is to be seen in the west window of St Botolph's Church in Cambridge, in the vault of the Great Gate at Trinity College, and in the rather more ambitious gothic chapel for the King's Walk cemetery at Wisbech. With no subject was he more familiar than with the history of architecture, on which his reputation in the world at large was ultimately founded. His *Remarks on the architecture of the middle ages*, published by Deighton in Cambridge in 1835, was comparable with his friend Whewell's *Architectural notes on German churches*, published also in Cambridge, five years previously;[10] and besides editing – or more properly revising – the fifth edition of J. H. Parker's popular *Glossary of gothic architecture*, he was also author of a series of volumes on the architectural history of English cathedrals. Best remembered of all, the *Architectural history of the University of Cambridge*, completed after his death by his nephew J. W. Clark, who inherited his papers and part of his library, was based on techniques developed by its author years before. To his own observation and measurement, Willis added a foundation of research among documents that provided a reliable base on which to build. The first publication of a facsimile of the ninth-century plan of St Gall in 1844 provoked a long article (with a facsimile) in the *Archaeological Journal* in 1848, and he saw to the English edition of a facsimile

---

[10] On Whewell and Willis see the remarks in Walter F. Cannon 'William Whewell, F. R. S. 2: Contributions to science and learning' *Notes and Records of the Royal Society* 19 (1964) pp. 176–89.

of the notebook of the thirteenth-century architect Villard de Honnecourt now in the Bibliothèque Nationale.[11] Investigations of the Westminster Abbey archives brought further publications, and in 1869 appeared his masterly *Architectural history of the conventual buildings of the monastery of Christ Church in Canterbury* for which besides the buildings themselves and surviving archives at Canterbury he could also turn to the plans in the mid-twelfth-century Eadwine Psalter at Trinity College.

During his last years Willis was in poor health, and in 1871 he was obliged to set about selling his library. The auction at Hodgson's rooms in Chancery Lane in April 1872 presented an extraordinary array of works on architecture and art history, which took up the first four days of the sale, while the fifth and last day offered a cosmopolitan selection of principally mechanics, mathematics and music. With no exaggeration, Sir Nikolaus Pevsner described it as prodigious;[12] but for all its wealth it was by no means the whole of his collection, and the University Library was able to buy liberally by private contract. On 6 March 1872, the month before the auction, it was resolved to spend £425 from the Worts Fund[13] on a list of over six hundred works chosen from Willis' books as valued by James Bain, the bookseller in Haymarket in London. A further, smaller, selection was approved by the Syndicate when Clark offered them to the Library following Willis' death three years later: the Worts Fund again met the bill, for £127.5s.0d.[14] Unfortunately, the books were not kept together, but dispersed round the Library according to their subjects and, more importantly since they included several costly and fragile atlas folios, their value. The books encom-

---

[11] *Facsimile of the sketch-book of Wilars de Honecort, an architect of the thirteenth century* ed. M.J. Quicherat, ed. and transl. by R. Willis (1859).

[12] N. Pevsner *Robert Willis* (Northampton, Mass., 1970) p. 24. An expanded version of this paper is included in his *Some architectural writers of the nineteenth century* (Oxford 1972) pp. 52–61. On Willis' library, besides the auction catalogue and the list mentioned below, see also MS. Add. 4307, a catalogue of his books on sound.

[13] Worts Ledger 1872.   [14] Syndicate Minutes 17 March 1875.

passed the full range of Willis' interests, but were especially remarkable for those on music, the art of perspective, theatre architecture, ancient buildings, and a major series of accounts of triumphal entries and similar festive occasions. The most curious volume among the music, perhaps, was J. S. Bach's copy of Elias Ammerbach's *Orgel, oder Instrument Tabulatur* (Leipzig 1571), given to Charles Burney at Hamburg in 1772 by C. P. E. Bach; but there were also the manuals of Nicola Vicentino (1555 and 1557) and Vincentio Galilei (1581), Glareanus Δωδεκάχορδον (1547), and Zacconi's *Prattica di musica* (1596). Besides a volume containing Gafurius' *Theorica musicae* (1492) and *Practica musicae* (1496),[15] there were his *Angelicum ac diuinum opus musicae* (1508) and *De harmonia musicorum instrumentorum* (1518), all from Milan. Niclaus Burtius' *Musices opusculum* (1487) and Johannes Spadarus' scarce *Defensio musicae* (1491) came from Bologna presses, and Guilelmus de Podio's *Ars musicorum* (1495) from Valencia. Among the English music, as well as Purcell's *Orpheus Britannicus* and various later works there were Thomas Morley's *Plaine and easie introduction* (1608) and Thomas Ravenscroft's *Briefe discourse of the true use of charact'ring the degrees in measurable musicke* (1614). The eighteenth century was represented by Rousseau's dictionary in both French and English, several of Burney's works, a clutch of minor general treatises, and handbooks on the thorough bass, division viol and other instruments. Willis's music books, individually and deliberately chosen because they did not duplicate what was already in the Library, were a reminder (if any was needed) of how much and how easily the collections could be enriched in this field, but the additions to other subjects were no less satisfactory. Among several dozen books on the arts of perspective, ranging from the sixteenth to the nineteenth century, were those of Vitellio (1535), Lautensack (1564), Jean Cousin (1560), Salomon de Caus (1612), Abraham Bosse

---

[15] Oates *Catalogue* does not identify Willis' books.

(1648), Jean François Nicéron (1663), J. J. Schübler (1719) and Thomas Malton (1778–83). Of Lorenzo Sirigatti's *Pratica di prospettiva* there were both the Venice edition of 1596 and Isaac Ware's English edition of 1756; of Andrea Pozzo both John James' translation of 1707 and the Rome edition of 1758–64. As well as the first edition, of 1583, of Giacomo Barozzi da Vignola's pioneering work on theoretical perspective were two French editions of his work on the five orders of architecture, including Panséron's *Grand et nouveau Vignole*, enlarged to take account of French building and garden design. Carlo Fontana's *Anfiteatro Flavio* (1725) and Abel Blouet on the restoration of the baths of Caracalla (1838) were both of fundamental importance to the collections on Roman antiquities, while the history of architecture was given further support with Antonio dall'Abacco's *Architettura* in the 1576 edition and Fontana's more technical *Trattato dell'acque correnti*, of 1696. The selection made from Willis' books was very far from confined to the sixteenth and seventeenth centuries, but besides these notable additions to the representation of these subjects in the Library were works on chess (one of Willis' earliest exploits had been to expose a fraudulent automaton chess player),[16] on clock-making, on short-hand, part of the 1693 edition of Moxon's *Mechanick exercises* and, to descend almost to the ridiculous, the early nineteenth-century type facsimile by James Barker of Richard Head's *Life and death of Mother Shipton* (1687).[17]

The books from Willis' library, the most notable specialist collection of its kind that the Library has ever received, came thanks to J. W. Clark, who as a Syndic was in a peculiarly strong position to influence events. It is not to be supposed that Bradshaw took as close an interest in them, extraordinary though they were, as he did in the negotiations with the

[16] *An attempt to analyse the automaton chess player, of Mr. de Kempelen* (1821). Some of Willis' papers on the subject survive in his own copy (Adv. c. 98.14) and in Adv. c. 98.13.
[17] A list of the books acquired in 1872 is in the Library archives, and forms the basis of the above account. I have not been able to find quite all the books listed there.

Durham antiquary J. T. Fowler over a copy of the Coverdale Bible with a unique title-leaf. At first Fowler had it in mind to sell the book to either Francis Fry or Henry Stevens.[18] Fry's offer of £150 was not acceptable, and after describing the Bible in full in *Notes and Queries*,[19] on 12 February 1883 Fowler wrote to Bradshaw offering it to the Library at £500, a sum which Stevens was not prepared to match. Anxious to obtain the best possible price, but so far discouraged by two of the most respected authorities on the subject, Fowler played his hand cleverly and offered to accept deferred payment in instalments over ten years. For Bradshaw there were two difficulties. The price asked was, in his words, 'beyond not only our reach, but anybody's who is likely to treat the book as it ought to be treated';[20] and in the last phrase lay his fear that an ignoramus would use the copy to perfect another, less complete, one, and so destroy the bibliographical evidence for all time. In this no-one seemed above suspicion. 'Whatever happens to your copy,' he wrote to Fowler, 'it is of vital importance that the whole preliminary matter should be kept together as a *monumentum* of this state of the book. Now this is a point which (I feel absolutely certain) almost anyone – whether Mr Bullen, Mr Fry, or Mr Stevens – would entirely fail to see; and it makes me sufficiently miserable to think that the book is fated to pass into the hands of those who will certainly destroy what is really the principal feature of value in the book.' In insisting on the integrity of the volume Bradshaw was, indeed, far ahead of his time, but by either luck or judgement he struck a chord in Fowler, who replied that his father, who had owned the book, would rather have parted with a piece of his flesh than see it mutilated.[21] With the priorities and positions of each party thus established, it proved

---

[18] Stevens to Bradshaw 22 September 1882. Fry's study of *The Bible by Coverdale MDXXXV* had been published in 1867, and Stevens had made his own contribution to the subject in his catalogue of *The Bibles in the Caxton exhibition MDCCCLXXVII* (1878). [19] *Notes and Queries* 16 December 1882 pp. 481–2.
[20] Bradshaw to Fowler 13 February 1883.
[21] Fowler to Bradshaw 16 February 1883.

easy to manoeuvre, and Fowler's offer to reduce the price to £300 – less even than Stevens had offered – was accepted by the Syndicate. It was a remarkable capitulation on both sides. Fowler had received less than he had wanted, though not so very much less than a reasonable valuation, and the Library had paid a sum from the Rustat Fund that even Bradshaw described as monstrous.[22] The arguments with which he had swayed the Syndics were, moreover, novel ones, and implied for the Library a position of national importance as a research collection.

Naturally I was asked how many pages there were in your copy, which ours did not possess, and I could but answer 'Two'. Whatever was given would seem extravagant for two pages; but my point was, not that I was urging them to give a high price for a single leaf, but that I put it to them that it was worth something considerable for our Library to step in to save a particularly precious piece of evidence from being wantonly destroyed by another purchaser. This was my only standing ground, and I was content to hold to it.[23]

The paper that he promised to write on the Bible, correcting Fowler's description and setting forth his own opinion on the printing of the Coverdale Bible, was never finished. As usual, other distractions intervened, but had it been written Bradshaw would have identified the printer of the preliminary leaves as James Nycolson, the man who, nine years before the Bible was published, had contracted to glaze some of the windows in King's College Chapel.[24]

The very considerable interest of this purchase may well have taken Bradshaw's attention away from the Sunderland sales, of which there were one in November 1882 and another in March 1883, but the renewed intimacy with Stevens following the meeting of the Library Association at Cambridge in 1882 led, a few months later, to what proved to be Stevens' last major sale to the Library (the two men were to die within a few days of each other, to the despair of the

[22] Bradshaw to Fowler 1 March 1883.   [23] Bradshaw to Fowler 22 February 1883.
[24] Bradshaw to Fowler 1 March 1883; H. Wayment *The windows of King's College Chapel, Cambridge* (1972) pp. 1, 14.

bibliographical world). Despite the proximity of their interests, Bradshaw and Stevens did little business together after the 1860s, but in November 1883 Stevens produced an irresistible list of early liturgies. The Library obtained only one fifteenth-century book on this occasion, an Ingolstadt Psalter of (according to Proctor) about 1490,[25] dated by Stevens a little earlier; but the half-dozen others, of the sixteenth century, were each of particular value to the Library. At £15 a folio Bamberg Breviary, printed by Pfeyl in 1501, was the most expensive. To these Bradshaw added a folio Benedictine Breviary from Tegernsee, as well as an incomplete one of Ratisbon use published by Georg Ratdolt, a Passau Missal of 1505, an Augsburg Breviary, a Speier Agenda, and a Cantorinus.[26] Since both Bradshaw and Edward Atkinson, Master of Clare College, also bought privately from the same list, and since the best of both men's collections came to the Library, in the end the University Library did even better than these purchases suggest. The outlay was modest (it was only just over £50), but it was one of the few occasions on which Bradshaw committed the Library to expenditure in a subject where he was acknowledged by his contemporaries to be supremely competent: in the history of the liturgy, as in the history of fifteenth-century printing, his own purse bore a heavy brunt, leaving the Library to benefit after his death.

The brilliance of Bradshaw's forays into auctions in quest of suitable incunables was matched, if at all, only by the number of oriental manuscripts that arrived in the Library during the first half of his term of office, thanks to a small group of devotees of whom the principal was E. B. Cowell, Professor of Sanskrit from 1867 to 1903, friend of Edward FitzGerald, and an original member of the British Academy. The Library had never before experienced such spectacular advances in its collections of incunables and of orientalia; the latter are

---

[25] Inc. 1325.   [26] Stevens invoice, 28 November 1883.

discussed further below. Growth in other parts of the Library's purchases was somewhat more erratic. Books and manuscripts could be recommended by one of two routes, but both were supervised by the Syndicate. Following the embarrassments of Mayor's years, when the Syndicate had found itself powerless in practice to exercise control over the Librarian's expenditure, a ledger was placed prominently in the Library to receive recommendations. In the case of collections, or when bidding was contemplated at a forthcoming auction, the matter was usually referred direct to the Syndics, who also customarily allowed Bradshaw £100 against contingencies during the period of the Long Vacation, when there were no Syndicate meetings. For other items, recommendations from staff and readers alike were subject to the same procedure, and every suggestion made, whether for modern monographs, periodicals, incunables or manuscripts, was formally inspected by the Syndics or their delegated committee. The system possessed the obvious extra advantage of making it easy for readers to suggest books, but it was equally obviously cumbrous and sometimes too slow when items were recommended from catalogues of second-hand books. It attracted mixed attention, and contained fewer entries than might, perhaps, have been expected; the annual total finally topping a thousand in 1877, and fifteen hundred in 1885 – though the annual figures were unavoidably distorted on occasion by disproportionate recommendations for oriental manuscripts.

Bradshaw himself took little active part in recommending modern books for purchase, and after his first years as Librarian restricted himself to only occasional forays into the pages of the recommendations book. In 1873, besides incunables and oriental manuscripts, he also put forward Philippus de Melho's Tamil *Triumph der Waarheid* (Colombo 1753), in 1874 a volume on the American struggle for independence, in 1875 books on international law, marine mammals, a map of Cambridge and books on Belgian antiquities. Such, clearly, might have been part of the office of Librarian: to recommend what had escaped the notice of others, or on their behalf. But he did so neither consistently nor frequently. Genealogy fascinated him (his notebooks are punctuated with the family trees of acquaintances and friends), and he recommended conscientiously in the subject; but he showed little interest in building up the Library's collection of early books beyond the first years of the sixteenth century. Even new titles on palaeography or printing history were recommended more frequently by others – notably J. H. Hessels and R. L. Bensly – than by the man to whom they would mean most. His unwillingness was not shared by everyone. The names of W. H. Miller, Bensly, Cowell, F. J. A. Hort, J. E. Sandys and W. W. Skeat appeared regularly and frequently, as did those of S. S. Lewis, librarian and benefactor of Corpus Christi College, and E. G. Wood of Emmanuel College, who by the time he won the Hulsean Prize in 1866 was curate of St Clement's, and was to remain at the same church (as vicar from 1885) until 1930. W. G. Searle, historian of Queens' College, caused the Library to buy books on numismatics over a wide field, and was responsible in 1881 for recommending one of the very few Japanese books to be bought during this period. The scientific collections were encouraged by Miller, Alfred Newton (zoology), J. W. Clark (as superintendent of the Museum of Comparative Anatomy, and only later as architectural and library historian), and James Clerk Maxwell, with occasional help from others. Books on medicine were recommended only intermittently: in 1873 Charles Lestourgeon proposed half a dozen American books on dentistry, most of which the Library succeeded in obtaining, and the collection of English and foreign medical journals was gradually improved. All these men were later joined by John Venn, R. A. Neil (Lecturer in Sanskrit from 1883), and G. W. Prothero, Bradshaw's biographer. For several years the recommendations were noticeably deficient in books on modern history, until Oscar Browning began to wage, from the mid-1870s onwards, what was at first a solitary campaign. His colleague Prothero, though a later arrival, proved almost equally active, while by contrast the name of Seeley appeared only occasionally. Browning, indeed, was overwhelming. In 1879 the combined recommendations of Hort (principally patristics and early medieval history) and Browning accounted for almost half the total for the entire year. Omnivorous in his interests, Browning was as willing to suggest books on sagas, the theory of colour, or the Talmud as on history. The Library was asked to buy scarcely any music, but when it was, it tended to be at Browning's suggestion: Palestrina in 1876, Schubert in 1884, Mendelssohn in 1885. In other words, selection of modern books was erratic, irregular and uneven in coverage.

The deficiencies of such a system were obvious enough even to contemporary observers. Browning and Hort sought to do the best for their own subjects, but their enthusiasm was not matched elsewhere, and the Library staff made no consistent effort to redeem the omissions of senior members of the University. Eiríkr Magnússon, who joined the staff in 1871, recommended items from time to time, and H. T. Francis, appointed Under-Librarian in February 1877, was specifically instructed by the Syndicate to make selections from the catalogues of foreign booksellers:[27] he did much to rectify deficiencies. But while Bradshaw was capable of recommending Victor Hugo in 1877, and Francis put forward Balzac's posthumous *Les petits bourgeois* a few months later, it could not be said that foreign imaginative literature was being sought out seriously. Acquisitions from Scandinavia, despite Magnússon's presence, proceeded haphazardly, and from the rest of northern Europe hardly at all. Too great trust was placed in the catalogues of Deighton, Bell, Barthés and Lowell, Williams and Norgate, and Trübner, which formed the principal sources of recommendations whether from the Library staff or from the University at large. In place of Henry Stevens, Macmillan and Co. – later Macmillan and Bowes – became the suppliers of American books: the shop was only just across the

----

[27] Syndicate Minutes 2 May 1877.

road, and Macmillan had opened a New York branch in 1869;[28] but the extensive acquisitions made in this field by Mayor contrasted sharply with the dwindled orders of the following decades. Only occasional additions were made to the map collection. The efforts made by the Syndics to redeem so unsatisfactory a state of affairs met with little success. In February 1878 they proposed that no less than four copies of the standard German bibliography should be circulated among a dozen senior members of the University with the object of eliciting recommendations: the existing single copies of those for Italy and France seemed sufficient.[29] This procedure enabled the Syndicate to state in its submission to the University Commissioners the following June that partly as a result of purchases of foreign books having been organized into a definite system the Library's income should be substantially increased;[30] but it did not have the expected effect. Two years later the system seemed only partially satisfactory, for in neither classics nor mathematics did there seem to be sufficient recommendations, while the lack of French, Italian, and American books had become noticeable.[31] By 1881 the situation became so obvious that Henry Tedder devoted space to it in his official *Report* on the state of the Library, remarking not only the poverty of accessions from these countries but also the poor representation of foreign literature. Nor, even, was the need for ordinary older books considered. 'But little attention is paid to procuring old books and no organized system is at work to fill up the many obvious *lacunae* in the different departments of the Library as regards other than new publications.'[32]

Attempts to interest the University, and to secure the co-operation of the staff of the Library, were thus only incompletely successful. Bradshaw himself showed little concern for

[28] Charles Morgan *The House of Macmillan (1843–1943)* (1943) p. 83.
[29] Syndicate Minutes 13 February 1878.
[30] Library papers 15 June 1878 (copy in Syndicate Minutes).
[31] Syndicate Minutes 9 November 1880.
[32] H. R. Tedder *Report on the University Library, 1881.*

the question beyond what the propriety of his position made absolutely necessary, and had in any case too few staff to lend seriously to the task. At a time when the Library had a budget for books larger than ever previously it proved easier to concentrate on other acquisitions than simply newly published titles. Bradshaw was able to focus attention on incunables, and Bensly and Cowell on oriental manuscripts, while the diet was leavened with other specialist collections and, occasionally, western manuscripts. The Library's wants in these fields were easy to measure, just as it seemed easier to gauge the importance of collections when they became available: older books had a greater appeal administratively as well as within the context of the Library's collections as a whole. They added to the stature of the Library, but there were some members of the Syndicate – notably Oscar Browning – who remained uneasy at the lack of attention paid to modern books.

The acquisition of most manuscripts, however, held little interest for Bradshaw; and although the Library added more items to this part of the collection during the twenty years of his Librarianship than even John Moore had collected in a lifetime, relatively few came at his direct prompting. Todd's manuscripts had a double appeal, in having belonged to one of his closest friends and in being – for the most part – of direct Irish interest; but for no subsequent auction did Bradshaw stir himself in the same way. The name of Baumgärtner probably prompted the purchase from Boone in 1870 of a collection of 109 letters relating to the Reformation in Germany;[33] this was only eleven years after John Baumgartner of Milton Hall had given his collection of the rather different papers of Strype and Samuel Knight, and three years after the publication of a printed catalogue of them. Boone also supplied the fourteenth-century Braybrooke Missal[34] in 1867, but few other booksellers caught Bradshaw's attention. He bought even liturgical

---

[33] Add. 712.   [34] Add. 451.

manuscripts warily, a fifteenth-century Sarum Ordinal (from
J. E. Cornish)[35] and an Antiphonary, both in April 1885, being
virtually the only purchases of the kind that he made. The
latter had a curious history. It was sold to the Library by the
rector of Springfield, near Chelmsford, but Bradshaw had
known it since 1867, when he had reassembled the leaves after
it was discovered in the roof of the church. 'I have never seen a
book of the kind anything like so perfect', he had written then.
'We have but one Antiphonarium in our whole collection at
Cambridge, and that is very imperfect, so that for the sake of
comparison the Springfield Book has often been examined.'[36]
He dated it to about 1300. Generous – arguably over-generous
– with the time he gave to other people's collections and
problems (though his patience was not inexhaustible), there
were few occasions when he saw bread cast upon the waters
returned so satisfactorily.

In the auction rooms, sale after sale of manuscripts passed
without the Library's showing a flicker of interest, and even
direct approaches such as the Berlin dealer Calvary's offer of an
enticingly described group of eighty-three manuscripts from
the Braschi collection, formerly Pius VI's, for £1000 passed
without comment.[37] Some purchases were virtually inescapable, like Sir Frederic Madden's notes on manuscripts in
Cambridge libraries,[38] bought from Quaritch in 1874, or a
transcript of the printed catalogue of Sir Thomas Phillipps'
manuscripts, bought from his heir John Fenwick in 1873,[39] or

---

[35] Add. 2600. [36] Note in the front of the manuscript, Add. 2602.
[37] S. Calvary to Bradshaw 16 December 1884. Nine humanist Cicero manuscripts from
the same collection had been offered, with others, to Lord Crawford in June and July
1884: see M. R. James *A descriptive catalogue of the manuscripts of the John Rylands
University Library*, repr. with an introduction and additional notes by Frank Taylor
(Munich 1980) p. 23*, and Nicolas Barker *Bibliotheca Lindesiana* (Roxburghe Club 1977)
p. 285. Calvary still had some of the collection when his stock was sold to the University
of Chicago in 1891: see also Edgar J. Goodspeed and Martin Sprengling *A descriptive
catalogue of manuscripts in the libraries of the University of Chicago* (Chicago 1912) p. vi.
[38] Add. 1027.
[39] Add. 1028: the Library in fact already possessed most of this in its printed form (now
860.a.31). See Munby *Phillipps studies* I pp. 22–3.

– somewhat differently – a humanist Cicero bought from Thomas Ernest Jackson, an undergraduate at Trinity College, in 1879.[40] Of over a dozen Greek manuscripts, besides fragments acquired from Tischendorf, probably none was bought on Bradshaw's initiative. Of the non-liturgical and non-Biblical texts among them, one of the most inviting was a copy of Photius written out by Constantine Palaeocappa in 1554,[41] in a contemporary Parisian gilt binding, and latterly in the collections of Anthony Askew and Michael Lort: it came from Reeves and Turner, a firm with which the Library did little business, and may have been the suggestion of Ioannes Valettas, one of the leaders of the Greek community in London, from whom the Library had bought a tenth- or eleventh-century Gospels in 1870, two years previously.[42] A New Testament Lectionary, and a copy of three Gospels, both of the thirteenth century, were bought on the recommendation of Hort, and he may well have encouraged one or two other modest purchases from Quaritch. More exotically, Cambridge grasped at the experiences of the Rev. Greville Chester, who made a practice of wintering in Egypt and whose first loyalties were to Oxford (he was a member of Balliol and St Mary Hall, and compiled the catalogue of the Ashmolean Egyptian collection in 1881), when the Library acquired from him some Coptic fragments and a leaf of a sixth-century *Evangelion* in 1874.[43] Equally tantalizing were the fragments[44] bought from Tischendorf in 1876, including a piece of Genesis[45] from the incomplete copy of the Septuagint of which he had already sold (in 1855) another portion to the Bodleian:[46] further parts went to the British Museum and St Petersburg. Such accumulations, however, could not be said to constitute an active policy.

---

[40] Add. 2582.   [41] Add. 1024.   [42] Add. 720.

[43] Add. 1875–6. Cf. Craster pp. 200, 210–11 etc.

[44] Add. 1879–93.   [45] Add. 1879.7.

[46] Bodleian Library MS. Auct.T.inf.2.1; for details see the Bodleian *Summary catalogue* 28644. See also the references in P. E. Easterling 'Hand-list of the additional Greek manuscripts in the University Library Cambridge' *Scriptorium* 16 (1962) pp. 302–23.

The collections of Asian manuscripts, by contrast, made gains of fundamental importance and central interest to the University. Bradshaw took his responsibilities in the early 1860s for cataloguing and ordering the manuscripts with commendable seriousness, and in a characteristic gesture introduced help at his own expense. 'I have just set a Hungarian rabbi at work upon our Hebrew manuscripts', he wrote in June 1865, a few months after the arrival in Cambridge of Solomon Schiller-Szinessy (fig. 27b), a refugee of the Hungarian uprising of 1848 and until recently pastor of the Jewish community in Manchester: 'and with his knowledge and my method of cataloguing, I hope it may be a creditable book. But what with this, and young Palmer for the Arabic, and Miss Shields for the Vaudois manuscripts, all being paid out of my own pocket, it leaves me but little prospect of going abroad this summer.'[47] With the publication of the catalogue of western manuscripts completed in 1867, there was every reason to press on and issue similar guides to other parts of the collection. Bradshaw himself failed to complete the only catalogue of any of the printed books planned, of the incunables; but progress on the oriental manuscripts was slightly more satisfactory. The call for these catalogues imposed on the Library a need for scholars capable of expounding them; and while the arrangements made with these specialists resulted eventually in some catalogues being published, they also involved the Library in very considerable expansion and development of parts of the collections, particularly in Hebrew and manuscripts from the Indian sub-continent. The first volume of the catalogue of the Hebrew manuscripts by Solomon Schiller-Szinessy, describing seventy-two items and encompassing the scriptures and Biblical commentaries, appeared in 1876. A further portion, covering Talmudic literature, was not completed, and the

---

[47] Prothero *Bradshaw* pp. 128–9. On Schiller-Szinessy see Raphael Loewe 'Solomon Marcus Schiller-Szinessy, 1820–1890, first Reader in Talmudic and Rabbinic Literature at Cambridge' *Transactions Jewish Historical Soc. of England* 21 (1968) pp. 148–89.

sheets printed off were never formally published: the printed part of Schiller-Szinessy's work ended with the ninety-eighth item. He lavished his erudition on the project, but showed little sense of scale and lacked the determination to see the work completed, unlike the team who had produced the catalogue of western manuscripts. He finished a shelf-list of the Hebrew manuscripts by February 1868,[48] and it was agreed in 1871 to allow him £200 per annum while the catalogue went through the press, he having received only occasional gratuities of £50 previously.[49] Impatient at his tardiness, in 1878 a Syndicate sub-committee investigated Schiller-Szinessy's progress.[50] Its findings were alarming, but inconclusive. Since the publication of the first volume of his catalogue two years previously, only six more descriptions had been printed off; but on the other hand Schiller-Szinessy had been unable to engross himself in the task completely. As the only expert Hebraist in the Library he was also distracted by the need to catalogue the Hebrew printed books, by work on revision of the main catalogue, and by members of the University in need of his opinion. Bradshaw did not consider it part of his official duties to supervise the work, and had paid only casual attention to such descriptions of manuscripts as had been completed. Such want of understanding of the true needs of the Library, and failure of self-discipline in ordering his time, were traits so familiar in large libraries that they might have been predicted, and guarded against. The appointment of Schiller-Szinessy as Reader in Talmudic and Rabbinic Literature in 1879, only the second man to be appointed to a readership in any subject in the University, reflected his position in the University more accurately, but left the authorities wholly unable to insist on his continuing the catalogue of Hebrew manuscripts, which remained unpublished a century later.

The need for a proper catalogue was the more urgent as

---

[48] Syndicate Minutes 5 February 1868. See also MS. Add. 3015, a classified catalogue of Hebrew manuscripts written out by Bradshaw to Schiller-Szinessy's dictation in 1883.
[49] Syndicate Minutes 15 May 1872.   [50] Syndicate Minutes 8 and 22 May 1878.

efforts were made to buy Hebrew manuscripts for the first time. By 1878 it was estimated that there were upwards of six hundred in the Library.[51] Most of the recent purchases came from foreign sources. Hirsch Lipschütz, of Cracow, was persistent in his attention, and energetic in his search (which encompassed even Spain, Morocco, and Greece) for suitable items. Of £748 spent out of the Rustat Fund in 1868 and 1869, £338 was paid to him alone for some 140 manuscripts including a good twelfth–thirteenth-century Bible (albeit much soiled and damaged) and a fourteenth-century *Mishneh*, brought by Lipschütz from Constantinople and the only full text of its kind in the University; the second especially absorbed Schiller-Szinessy, and was extensively used by Charles Taylor for his *Sayings of the Jewish fathers* published in 1877.[52] Purchases in 1870 were equally satisfactory. With £200 from the Worts Fund the Library acquired just over fifty manuscripts from the collection of Samuel Schönblum, of Lemberg,[53] the most important among them being a copy of Rashi's commentary on the Pentateuch;[54] and the year ended triumphantly with the purchase for £100 of two Samaritan Pentateuchs, one from Beresford Hope and one, with the Arabic version as well, from George Williams,[55] and both, in Bradshaw's words, 'almost if not quite the oldest Samaritan manuscripts in Europe'. Almost as a reminder that the Hebrew printed books were not neglected either, the Worts Fund also provided the requisite sum for an edition of the Talmud in forty-two volumes. Few of the Hebrew accessions, apart from the two Samaritan manuscripts, came from English collections, and a Pentateuch with a late copy of Maimonides' commentary on the Mishneh were the result of a rare foray into the auction rooms:[56] they came from the library of W. H. Black, formerly of the Public Record Office. English booksellers had little of interest for the Library in Hebraica, a group of

[51] Syndicate Minutes 8 May 1878.   [52] Add. 465 and 470.1.
[53] Syndicate Minutes 26 January 1870.   [54] Add. 626.
[55] Add. 713 and 714. See also Palaeographical Society *Oriental Series* pl. xxviii.
[56] Add. 1019, 1020 and 1021.

seven manuscripts from Quaritch in 1876 (including an early dated copy of the *Mishneh Torah* and a copy of the *Moreh Nebhukhim* dated variously from the twelfth century onwards and once in the Sussex collection) and a further Pentateuch, from Yemen, in 1878, being virtually all that was supplied by the London trade.[57] Other groups of manuscripts continued to be approved from Fischl Hirsch. Schiller-Szinessy paid special attention to an unusual copy of Abraham ben'Ezra's commentary on the Pentateuch, appealing for an edition of the work not least because the manuscript was in appalling physical condition,[58] but Hirsch's sales also included (at £45) a Hagiographa from the southern Arabian peninsula and, after some debate by the Syndicate, a group of five manuscripts from Yemen.[59] He was responsible, too, for most of the Library's purchases from the library of G. B. Carmoly, auctioned at Frankfurt am Main in 1875, after which thirty manuscripts were added to the shelves,[60] while Nathan Coronel and Jacob Saphir supplied other, smaller, collections from Jerusalem.

While Schiller-Szinessy began to describe the Hebrew manuscripts, most of the remainder of the oriental collections – Arabic, Turkish, Persian and Hindustani – came within the province of E. H. Palmer, who had already worked on the Arabic and Persian collections at King's and Trinity before turning his attention to the University Library.[61] The Library

---

[57] MSS. Add. 1562–8: cf. B. Quaritch *Bibliotheca orientalis* (cat. 302) nos 12108 and 12112; T. J. Pettigrew *Bibliotheca Sussexiana* I i (1827) pp. xxix–xxx. The further Pentateuch from Yemen (Add. 1731) also came from Quaritch.

[58] Add. 1014.1. See also his *Catalogue* pp. 128–9.

[59] Add. 1726–30; Syndicate Minutes 30 January and 13 February 1878.

[60] Bradshaw's marked copy of the sale catalogue stands at 8880.d.40.

[61] Library Syndicate annual report 1 April 1868; Walter Besant *The life and achievements of Edward Henry Palmer* (1883) p. 41. In November 1867 Palmer was elected to a fellowship at St John's, and rather than remain in Cambridge he preferred to join an official expedition to survey Sinai, and to return to travel in the east even after the end of the expedition in the summer of 1869. In October that year he sent back to the University an account of his experiences as a Worts Travelling Bachelor (as required by the regulations for the Fund): 'It was impossible during so short a stay in Cairo to make any extensive purchases of MSS. and I therefore determined to restrict myself to making a selection of printed works which should supply the chief deficiencies which I

was by no means inactive in buying Arabic manuscripts before 1867, but thanks to a series of major gifts and purchases between then and 1878 the rate of acquisition in Arabic and Persian material accelerated rapidly. The first year of Bradshaw's Librarianship saw the arrival of two dozen Persian manuscripts, the gift of R. E. Lofft of Troston Hall, near Bury St Edmunds, whose father had spent many years in India. More arrived from the same source two years later, again of a miscellaneous kind, but while others lent their support – among them Corrie, who produced a Koran, and Cotton Mather, son of a distinguished missionary in India, who gave a group of Hindustani and Persian manuscripts in 1868 – none compared with Henry Griffin Williams, whose books formed the most important accession of its kind since the Burckhardt collection in 1819. As Sir Thomas Adams Professor of Arabic, Williams had not been especially remarkable; but he left a library containing a notable series of Arabic and Persian manuscripts. As a result of a misunderstanding with Williams' family, who wished to sell the entire collection to Cambridge, or even to give them, the manuscripts were offered by Sotheby's in February 1871 and were only withdrawn after a placatory letter from Bradshaw and a visit from Bensly. After a month of anxiety, the executors finally decided to present them.[62] Their gift brought more than a hundred items to the Library, in a collection especially strong in Persian poetry and Hindustani literature of all kinds. Williams' interests had been practical, and while there was a modest Koran there were also histories of Afghanistan and of Mysore, grammatical treatises, works on numismatics, etymology and biography, an outstanding copy of Firūzābādī's Arabic dictionary, and, among

know to exist in the University Library. Thanks to the assistance and advice of Mr. Ayrton (an English gentleman and scholar residing at Cairo and a Bey of the Turkish Empire), and with the kind co-operation of Husein Bey and other Egyptian authorities, I have procured a number of standard works selected especially for the purpose of illustrating the literature, history and theology of the East' (*Cambridge University Gazette* 27 October 1869).

[62] Bensly to Bradshaw 3 February 1871; G. B. Williams to Bradshaw 11 March 1871; Syndicate Minutes 8 February and 8 March 1871.

the poetry, three copies of the Dīwān of Sā'ib including one of unusual beauty. Bensly's part in rescuing the collection was crucial, and it was he, too, who was responsible for most (if not all) of the Library's purchases in Arabic over the next few years. While the Library did what it could to acquire lithographed texts, including a small group believed to have been among the first printed in Persia which came to Europe,[63] the Caussin de Perceval sale in Paris in November 1871, the Flügel sale in Leipzig in May 1872, and the Judas sale in Paris in May 1873 all, with Quaritch's help, provided occasions for further manuscript accessions.[64] A few other items, in both Persian and Arabic, came from private individuals, including a volume[65] containing an unusually long series of quatrains from the Rubáiyat of Omar Khayyám which its donor, the Celtic scholar Whitley Stokes, stated to have been given to him by a tailor in Madras: it could not have fallen into more appreciative hands, as Stokes had been one of the first to recognize the merits of FitzGerald's English version.[66] But with Bensly's departure from the Library in 1876 there was no-one on the staff willing to press for the purchase of Arabic books, and those which arrived subsequently came independently. The largest collection, a series of Kufic fragments of the Koran, came from an impeccable source, being bought in 1878 from E. H. Palmer and the executors of his travelling companion in the Near East C. F. Tyrwhitt Drake, whose brief and busy life was cut short by disease in 1874 at Jerusalem.[67] The collection, gathered in 1870–3 and long promised to the Library, was, however, the last such series to arrive under

---

[63] Worts Ledger 1871.
[64] Marked copies of these catalogues are bound up together in 8880.d.3.
[65] Add. 1055.
[66] Edward FitzGerald Letters ed. A. M. and A. B. Terhune (Princeton 1980) 2 p. 417; the Terhunes believed that Stokes was also responsible for the pirated version of FitzGerald's Rubáiyat published in Madras in 1862.
[67] Add. 1111–50. On Tyrwhitt Drake see W. Besant The life and achievements of Edward Henry Palmer (1883) pp. 93–109, the Quarterly Statements of the Palestine Exploration Fund, Drake's Modern Jerusalem, with a memoir (1875), and his Literary remains ed. and with a memoir by W. Besant (1877).

Bradshaw, while Palmer's estrangement from the University[68] left the subject as a whole neglected until his successor as Lord Almoner's Professor of Arabic – and Bradshaw's as Librarian – William Robertson Smith could encourage interest in his own way.

The Library could scarcely expect to be equally successful in acquiring manuscripts from the whole of the middle east, north Africa, and India, even if it had had the inclination or the money. Nonetheless, Bensly was able to make a few modest additions to Buchanan's Syriac collection. An eighteenth-century copy of the Gospels and Song of Songs from southern India was particularly appropriate in that it came from the collection of Adam Clarke,[69] but others seem to have been selected for other reasons, and with some care in that the Library bought single leaves from the La Ferté sale in May 1873[70] and the Mohl sale at Paris in 1876. At the latter it obtained a twelfth-century copy of the New Testament,[71] one of the best surviving copies of the version originally revised by Thomas of Harkel in the early seventh century and of especial importance to the Library for the light the marginalia shed on the text of the Codex Bezae: the manuscript, when it arrived, proved a pleasant surprise to Bensly, for it was discovered to contain also St Clement's Epistles to the Corinthians, a text which J. B. Lightfoot, then Lady Margaret Professor, had edited only very recently in ignorance of the significance of Mohl's copy.[72] These restrained purchases were supplemented at the Bragge sale with a Nestorian liturgical manuscript and an unusual Carshunic copy of Genesis,[73] at £1 each, but on this occasion the sale room provided much more besides. William

---

[68] Besant *Life and achievements of Edward Henry Palmer* p. 210.   [69] Add. 1167.

[70] Add. 1166 (a Psalter, lot 2218).

[71] Add. 1700. The manuscript was used shortly after Bradshaw's death by R. L. Bensly in *The Harklean version of the Epistle to the Hebrews, chapter xi.28–xiii.25, now edited for the first time* (Cambridge 1889); his posthumous edition of *The Epistles of S. Clement to the Corinthians in Syriac*, from the same manuscript, was published in 1899. See also W. H. P. Hatch *An album of dated Syriac manuscripts* (Boston 1946) no. cxxix.

[72] Cf. J. B. Lightfoot (ed.) *S. Clement of Rome. An appendix* (1877) p. 232. See also a note by Bensly in *The Athenaeum* 17 June 1876 p. 827.   [73] Add. 1866 and 1865.

Bragge, whose expertise had built railways in Brazil, installed gas lighting in Rio de Janeiro, developed armour plating in Sheffield and organized the mass production of watches in Birmingham, was yet to publish his astonishing *Bibliotheca nicotiana* in 1880, and had given his collection of works by Cervantes to Birmingham Free Library, when his manuscripts were put up for sale anonymously through Sotheby's, in a painfully inaccurate catalogue, in 1876. Their ownership was an open secret, however, and was indeed impossible to conceal since many of them were well known through exhibitions. In anticipation of the occasion Quaritch wrote to Bradshaw well before the sale to ask for his bids. But the Syndicate was cautious, allowing £100 from the Worts Fund 'provided that no manuscripts be bought which cannot be obtained at small prices.'[74] The Library refrained from bidding against the British Museum, and its caution, uninterest, and insensitivity earned their reward in the crumbs acquired subsequently.[75] While Quaritch bought nearly thirty per cent of the total for stock, and some of the finest went to Ellis for Sir Thomas Brooke, the Library made some small but unusual additions. Besides some papyrus leaves, its purchases included a small Armenian illustrated Gospels, a fine copy of the Gospels in Arabic, dating probably from the twelfth century, a thirteenth-century Porphyry, and three Ethiopic manuscripts. In 1876 there were barely more than a dozen Ethiopic manuscripts in the Library, but as, before the nineteenth century, there had been none at all that were not western copies, the collection was not unnoticeable. For Cambridge, as for other libraries in the country, the previous dearth had been banished as a result of Napier's expedition to Abyssinia in 1867–8, after which it was estimated that at least five hundred Ethiopic manuscripts had been brought back, taken mostly from the sacked fortress of Magdala, the scene of Napier's

[74] Quaritch to Bradshaw 13 April 1876; Syndicate Minutes 2 June 1876. The Library's principal marked copy of the sale catalogue is now in the National Library of Wales.
[75] Add. 1858–68.

triumph.[76] Some of the benefits were already at Cambridge, bought as occasion offered in the early 1870s, while besides those now acquired at the Bragge sale the Library also obtained in the same year a large sixteenth-century copy of the Old Testament[77] and, from Quaritch's *Bibliotheca orientalis*, a collection of homilies optimistically dated by Quaritch to the fifteenth century but more recently considered to be of the nineteenth.[78]

Such manuscripts as the Library possessed before the 1860s from the Indian sub-continent came mainly from the south. But within a few years the University was to possess one of the three or four most important collections of Sanskrit manuscripts in Great Britain. Seldom was innovation so practicable or so dramatically successful. When in 1867 E. B. Cowell delivered his inaugural lecture as the first Professor of Sanskrit he may have hoped that the Library would not be deaf to his appeal for serious study of the subject, but he could hardly have foreseen the result. His theme, from beginning to end, was the practical and political importance of Sanskrit. 'We cannot be indifferent to any study which may help us to understand that vast dependency of our empire.' 'It will be a growing danger for our empire, if we send out young Englishmen to govern millions of subject Hindus with no sympathy for the subject race, with no feeling but contempt for their customs and habits of thought . . . The love of Sanskrit *must* inspire the true student with an interest in the future welfare of the Hindus.'[79] Philological, literary and religious considerations were admitted, but only within such a context of evangelical

---

[76] W. Wright *Catalogue of the Ethiopic manuscripts in the British Museum acquired since the year 1847* (1877) pp. iii–iv; S. Streleyn *Catalogue of Ethiopian manuscripts in the British Library acquired since the year 1877* (1978) pp. ix–xi. See also S. Chojnacki 'William Simpson and his journey to Ethiopia in 1868' *Journal of Ethiopian Studies* 6 (1968) pp. 7–38, and R. Pankhurst 'The library of Emperor Tewodros II at Mäqdäla (Magdala)' *Bull. of the School of Oriental and African Studies* 36 (1973) pp. 15–42.

[77] Add. 1570, from Captain F. J. Sotham. These manuscripts are described in E. Ullendorff and S. G. Wright *Catalogue of Ethiopian manuscripts in the Cambridge University Library* (Cambridge 1961).   [78] Add. 1569.

[79] E. B. Cowell *An inaugural lecture, delivered October 23, 1867* (1867) pp. 3, 19.

conviction as to imperial responsibility, and the case was rarely put more succinctly. Although his pupils in the subject were not at first numerous,[80] the principle was clear. An Indian Languages Tripos was established in 1879, and by 1883 there were also teachers of Hindustani, Hindi and Telugu in Cambridge preparing candidates for the Indian Civil Service; and in that year the Board of Indian Civil Service Studies was established to provide more regular supervision over a still wider range of languages.[81]

Cowell's analysis of the needs of Cambridge was accurate, but the University was not unique. In 1864 B. H. Hodgson had presented a great mass of Hindi, Buddhist Sanskrit and Tibetan manuscripts collected in Nepal to the India Office,[82] and the importance attached to knowledge of India was confirmed with the passing of the (Indian) Press and Registration of Books Act in 1867 – legislation which virtually turned the India Office into a copyright deposit library for Indian publications. This was followed ten years later by a formal committee to examine the scope and purpose of the India Office Library.[83] Further manuscripts from Hodgson's collections went to the Royal Asiatic Society and to various libraries in France.[84] Bradshaw quickly took a lay interest in these developments, from which Cambridge had not, so far, benefited. He had picked up enough Sanskrit and Arabic in the early months of 1862 to be able to handle the manuscripts in his charge, and the annual report for 1867–8 recorded that he had given various printed works in Sanskrit, while his notebooks contain memoranda on the Tibetan alphabet in March 1869. These extensions to his knowledge, which he never pursued beyond an elementary level, were provident. With the arrival of two parcels in the spring of 1873 the Library began an astonishing

[80] Frederick Pollock in George Cowell *Life and letters of Edward Byles Cowell* (1904) p. 456.
[81] *Historical register* pp. 132, 942.
[82] A. J. Arberry *The library of the India Office; a historical sketch* (1938) pp. 77–8.
[83] *Ibid.*, pp. 69–71. See also J. Forbes Watson *On the measures required for the efficient working of the India Museum and Library* (1874).
[84] W. W. Hunter *Catalogue of Sanskrit manuscripts collected in Nepal, and presented to various libraries and learned societies by Brian Houghton Hodgson* (1881). For Hodgson's career see idem *Life of Brian Houghton Hodgson* (1896).

six years in which several hundred Sanskrit manuscripts
entered the building. Most came from three men: William and
Daniel Wright, and Ralph Griffith. William Wright (fig. 27c)
had resigned from his post at the British Museum, where his
brief had been to catalogue the Syriac manuscripts, on his
appointment as Sir Thomas Adams Professor in 1870; and in
his brother Daniel, surgeon at the British Residency at
Kathmandu, the University Library found an energetic,
imaginative and loyal friend. Initially he was asked only to
procure transcripts of such manuscripts as he could find,[85] but
originals were not difficult to discover and the collection grew
quickly, partly by gift and partly by purchase. Earliest in date
among what was rapidly recognized as a collection of the first
importance were a group of leaves containing various Tantric
works, dated the equivalent of A.D. 857–8 and rescued from
destruction when a temple in Kathmandu was being cleared,
and what Bendall believed was a unique *Bodhisattva-Bhūmi*.[86]
Among the manuscripts of the much more common
Mahāyāna Buddhist *Perfection of wisdom*, or *Ashṭasahasrikā
pranjñāpāramitā* were two eleventh-century copies of crucial
interest, one undated and the other dated A.D. 1015, the latter
one of only two known dated illuminated manuscripts from
Nepal: it has since been suggested that these two Cambridge
manuscripts may represent 'the earliest attempts to produce
illustrated palm-leaf manuscripts in Nepal and eastern India'.[87]

The arrival of these and about three hundred other
manuscripts, embracing virtually all surviving Sanskrit literature of northern Buddhism, was announced to the world in an
anonymous article in *The Athenaeum* on 10 June 1876, written
by either William Wright or Cowell:

All the older MSS. are on palm leaves, and many of them are dated in the
Nepalese era or Samvat, which commences A.D. 880. The three especial
treasures of the collection, in point of age, are two copies of the

---

[85] C. Bendall *Catalogue of the Buddhist Sanskrit manuscripts in the University Library,
Cambridge* (Cambridge 1883) pp. vii, 26–7.
[86] Add. 1049 and 1702. Cf. Bendall *Catalogue* pp. xxxix–li, 27–8, 191–6.
[87] Add. 1464 and 1643. Jeremiah P. Losty *The art of the book in India* (British Library 1982)
nos. 2 and 3, pp. 24–6.

Ashṭasáhasriká, which are respectively dated in the third and fifth years of the Nepalese era, corresponding to A.D. 883 and 885; and a copy of the Kárya-Káṇḍa-Kramávali, dated in the tenth year, *i.e.*, A.D. 890. Besides these, there is a copy of the Ashṭasáhasriká, dated A.D. 1008; and from this date forwards there is a continuous series of MSS., illustrating the writing of each successive century down to the present time. One great value of these MSS., therefore, consists in the fact that they are in so many instances not merely modern copies, but undoubted ancient transcripts, which have been preserved intact for ages in the secluded valleys of Nepal. They will, therefore, be of the utmost importance for future editors or translators of Northern Buddhist texts. Thus the Káraṇda vyúha has its poetical version represented by two good MSS., and its prose version by five; while Burnouf expressly says of the Paris MS. of the latter, that it was too incorrect for him to attempt to translate it, and therefore he contented himself by giving an analysis of the more modern poetical version. There are also fine old copies of the Avadán Sataka, the Mahávastu, and the 'nine dharmas,' – we may especially notice a huge copy, in five volumes, of the large edition of the Prajná-páramitá in 100,000 articles (besides a second imperfect MS.), as well as copies of the smaller editions in 25,000 and 8,000. The Tantra literature is especially well represented, and among other names we may mention the Kála-chakra and the 'Arya-Manjus' rí-mula-tantra, the historical importance of both which works Burnouf has especially dwelt upon (from Csoma di Körösi's analyses in his Tibetan Catalogue), adding, however, the words, 'mais que nous possédons malheureusement pas à Paris.' But one of the greatest treasures of the collection is a fine copy, dated A.D. 1551, of Yas'omitra's Commentary on Vasubandhu's Abhidharma-kos'a. Burnouf calls this work, 'cette inépuisable mine de renseignements précieux sur la partie spéculative du Buddhisme.' There is a MS. of it at Paris as well as at Calcutta, but both are far too incorrect to serve as the basis of an edition; the present MS. is written in a peculiar handwriting, but it appears to be transcribed with the greatest accuracy and care. The work seems to be very scarce, even in Nepal, and the pundit made a copy for himself before he would consent to part with it. The Commentary is called Sphuṭártha-abhidharma-kos'a-vyákhyá. Wilson wrote, in 1856, of the MS. treasures discovered by Mr. Hodgson, that 'the books in the Royal Asiatic Society's possession have done little more than repose in dust and oblivion upon the shelves where they were originally deposited.' It is to be hoped that Cambridge may make a better use of her new treasures, and that some young scholar with long years of happy toil before him may immortalize himself as the English Burnouf.

Daniel Wright, although not unskilled, did not profess to be an oriental scholar; but he was aware of the significance of his collection, which contained Tibetan as well as Nepalese manuscripts, and appended a list of them to his edition of Munshī Shew Shunker Singh's and Pandit Shrī Gunānand's *History of Nepal*, published in 1877. At that date, Cowell was engaged in cataloguing the manuscripts,[88] as the recognized authority, but his pioneering work was quickly overtaken and developed by his pupil, Cecil Bendall.

First as an undergraduate with Cowell and then, after taking his degree, with the encouragement of Bradshaw and Cowell together, Bendall worked towards a printed catalogue of the manuscripts. He had begun to list the Sanskrit manuscripts shortly before sitting the Indian Languages Tripos,[89] and the catalogue was published a mere three years later, in 1883.[90] Besides the catalogue proper, he introduced a long palaeographical introduction, and a historical summary on the interest of the manuscripts for Nepalese and Bengali chronology: he had already tackled this unfamiliar and complicated subject in a paper presented to the fifth international congress of orientalists in Berlin in 1881.[91] His departure in 1882 for the Oriental Department of the British Museum was a natural consequence, but did not mean that his links with Cambridge were broken. In 1884–5, and again in 1898–9, he made journeys to Nepal and northern India on behalf of the Library, on the first occasion alone returning with over five hundred Sanskrit manuscripts. They did not, however, arrive until 1886, shortly after Bradshaw's death,[92] while Bendall himself returned as Professor of Sanskrit on Cowell's death in 1903.[93]

[88] Wright *History of Nepal* (Cambridge 1877) p. 316; Syndicate Minutes 22 March 1876.
[89] Syndicate Minutes 28 January 1880.
[90] Bendall's catalogue of the Buddhist Sanskrit manuscripts was reviewed in *The Athenaeum* 15 September 1883, *Deutsche Litteraturzeitung* 22 December 1883 (by H. Oldenberg) and *Göttingische Gelehrts Anzeigen* 15 September 1884 pp. 758–60 (by Th. Zachariae).
[91] 'On European collections of Sanskrit manuscripts from Nepal: their antiquity and bearing on chronology, history and literature' *Abhandlungen des fünften Internationalen Orientalisten-Congresses gehalten zu Berlin* (Berlin 1882) pp. 189–211.
[92] Cf. C. Bendall *A journey of literary and archaeological research in Nepal and Northern India* (Cambridge 1886); Bendall's preliminary report on his discoveries and acquisitions was given to the University in May 1885 (Library papers 21 May 1885 and *Reporter*, 26 May).
[93] Bendall's career is described in H. T. Francis *In memoriam. Cecil Bendall, M.A.* (privately pr., Cambridge 1906).

While the Wrights and Bendall concentrated on Nepal, with extraordinary success, interest in Cambridge itself was by no means restricted to the far north. From Ralph Griffith, Principal of Benares Government College and translator of the *Rigveda* and other texts, the Library received a series of parcels between 1873 and 1878.[94] In 1874 T. W. Rhys Davids sent in an assortment including a significant series of Pâli books,[95] which were followed by others from Reinhold Rost, Librarian of the India Office, the following year in a parcel that also included material in Telugu and Tamil. The sums involved were considerable; and although at first it was intended that the Rustat Fund should meet the cost of Wright's Nepalese and Tibetan manuscripts, it proved inadequate, so that in February 1876 the Syndics were obliged to ask the Worts Trustees to pay Daniel Wright's bill for £356.13s.0d. The Trustees paid a further £429.11s.0d. in April for more manuscripts. These were unusual sums for the Library to find, even for collections, and were the more so as the same years also saw the Worts Fund drawn on for the Carmoly sale, a major oriental catalogue from Quaritch, the Du Bus sale at Brussels (where the Library bought principally zoological books), and the Bragge sale at Sotheby's. The same year also marked the arrival of the larger of two groups of Jain manuscripts, gathered by G. Bühler between Delhi and the Gulf of Cambay on the Arabian Sea in a systematic attempt to amass the Jain canon for Cambridge and, equally, for Berlin.[96] Overall, it is not an exaggeration to claim that at no other period in its history so far, and in no other subject of its size, had the Library made so well orchestrated an attempt, through the leading scholars in the field, to build up collections that it recognized as of crucial national, as well as university, interest, and seized the opportunity to do so before these materials became impossibly scarce and their prices prohibitive.

[94] Bradshaw's notes on these are in MS. Add. 4566.
[95] T. W. Rhys Davids 'List of Pâli manuscripts in the Cambridge University Library' *Journal of the Pâli Text Society* 1883 pp. 145–6.
[96] Bühler to Cowell 26 February 1876 (Add. 2592, no. 437); Syndicate Minutes 22 March 1876. The Worts Fund paid £77 for MSS. Add. 1755–808, and in May 1877 the Library received from Bühler Add. 1809–22.

19

BRADSHAW AT BAY

UNLIKE MAYOR, Bradshaw did not relish confrontation. After the stormy months of his predecessor's term of office, he quickly established an amicable working relationship with the Syndics that allowed him, for much of his own Librarianship, to concentrate on those parts of the collections that most appealed to him. His first interest was in the collections of manuscripts and early printed books, and even his apologists did not disguise the fact that the everyday running of the Library was not his forte: he himself was all too aware of the difficulty, with the pain of a shy man who could do little about it.

The management of most of the Library's functions therefore fell on the staff. The appointment of Bensly as an Under-Librarian in 1864 was a mixed success, as it expected too much of a man preoccupied with the scholarly demands of orientalia. When in May 1871 G. R. Crotch resigned in order to travel in pursuit of natural history,[1] there seemed to some to be another occasion when two birds might be killed with one stone: the University could employ a specialist without extra expense, and the Library a graduate who could take a responsible part in its internal affairs. Bradshaw's preference was to promote Dennis Hall, a loyal, efficient and hard-working assistant first appointed in 1855, whose salary had crept up to £104 per annum, but he did not have his way. Instead, the successful candidate was Eiríkr Magnússon, an Icelander who had come to London in 1862 to supervise the printing of an Icelandic New Testament. He had visited Cambridge in 1869, and his sociable manner had won for him a

---

[1] Library papers 2 May 1871.

wide circle of acquaintances.[2] At the election he was strongly
supported by E. B. Cowell, William Aldis Wright, and W. W.
Skeat, who may be forgiven for having less the Library's
management at heart than a shared interest in promoting
English and Germanic philology, and the establishing of a
person at Cambridge to match Guðbrandr Vigfússon at
Oxford. He was, nevertheless, at first welcomed by Bradshaw.
But the two men were far apart in temperament, and while
Magnússon pursued his philological researches, clashed violently and repeatedly with Vigfússon on all manner of subjects,
and won a popular reputation as William Morris' preceptor
and partner in a series of translations of Icelandic sagas, his
work in the Library proceeded in a manner uncomfortable to
all concerned. Much of the work of recataloguing devolved
on him, and it was he who was in large part responsible for
drawing up the cataloguing rules, based on those of Panizzi,
which were used for a century. At his suggestion the volumes
containing the catalogue were set up in a vertical position,
rather than left flat on a table, though his suggestions for a card
catalogue fell on deaf ears. His manner became irritating to
Bradshaw, who would have preferred a less aggressive
member of staff. After a stormy passage, the two men were
reconciled in a fashion, but not until the Syndicate had been
forced to intervene on several occasions. A man of stronger
action than Bradshaw (there was no doubting his will) might,
perhaps, have avoided argument by imposing his authority.
But Bradshaw was hesitant to explore the extent of his
prerogative, preferring evolution to revolution even in circumstances that demanded otherwise. While he found it easier
to concentrate on the manuscripts and early printed books, the
administration of the Library required his attention no less
urgently, and, as he was to discover, he neglected it at his peril.
The consequence was that while in some respects his librarian-

---

[2] The standard biography is S. Einarsson *Saga Eiríks Magnússonar* (Reykjavík 1933); see
also Einarsson's 'Eiríkur Magnússon – the forgotten pioneer' in B. S. Benedikz (ed.)
Studia centenalia in honorem memoriae Benedikt S. Þórarinsson (Reykjavík 1961) pp. 33–50,
and the obituary in the *Cambridge Review*, 30 January 1913, pp. 223–4.

ship saw considerable improvements, in others there was much to criticize.

Although the new Scott Building, as the latest extension to the Library came to be called after its architect, was handed over to the University in February 1867, shortly before Bradshaw's election, the rooms were not available to the Library immediately. In March the first floor room was pressed into use for examination purposes, while the ground floor, intended originally for the Librarian and general library purposes, was destined not to become part of the Library at all until after Bradshaw's death. In the room on the first floor, once it was free, Bradshaw had an ideal retreat. Bookcases were fitted in the summer of 1868, and having established his desk where he could be most easily accessible next to the Dome Room, he gathered together the Library's more notable possessions in the course of the following year. The manuscripts were moved out of the Cockerell Building, and placed here with the adversaria, books printed on vellum, the Lewis Cabinet, printed books identified since 1859 as being too valuable to remain on the open shelves, and, gradually, the incunables.

In this room was created what Bradshaw called his 'Museum typographicum', a concept which grew only slowly. At first he simply arranged the incunables in two sequences: those in the old class created by Richard Farmer of the rarest printed books, AB, and those he had gathered between 1859 and 1866 off the open shelves into the locked manuscript cases on the other side of the Library. Not until September 1883 did he grasp what he had been groping for in applying his work on incunables to the physical arrangement of the books on the shelves. The 'natural history' arrangement of catalogues, applied so successfully by Holtrop to the Royal Library in The Hague and by Bradshaw himself to the De Meyer and other collections, was now to be translated into library management.

At last I see my way about the XVth cent. books in the Library. I have always wanted to have them *arranged* not merely under countries but under towns, printers, presses. But *first*, it will always be a mistake of the first class to try and range books on the shelves in such a way that additions cannot be made, & *secondly* very few would know so exactly where to place a book.

Therefore group them *roughly* under Germany, Italy, France, &c, as I have done, & let any further subdivision be only on paper.

Call the class Inc. (Incunabula typographica) as at Munich.

Call the shelves 1, 2, 3, 4, 5, 6 as in class Sel., 1 being F3; 2, F2; 3, F, Q3; 4, Q2, O3; 5, Q, O2; 6, O, D, S.

The countries may be represented as a, b, c, d, &c. So that the shelves will be 1a, 2a, 3a, 1b, 2b, 3b, & so on; and then any one searching for types will at least find all the Italian printed books together, & so with the other countries.

All minute subdivisions must be on paper only, & should be on paper as soon as possible, but the Library-mark should in no case be more complicated than Inc. 3c. 21, showing that it was a XVth century book, in small folio, or largest quarto, printed in France, and standing 21 among its fellows.[3]

From Bradshaw's work grew Robert Proctor's fully developed system of ordering incunables and numbering presses according to a standard notation, the one still applied, with Bradshaw's size divisions (and contrary to Bradshaw's own recommendation), on the shelves of the Library.[4]

But while the benefits to incunabulists were immeasurable, the organization and housing of the books outside Bradshaw's museum and the accompanying *réserve* presented a persistent problem that required dramatic alterations to the buildings. In 1868 fifty years' accumulation of pamphlets, periodicals, school and children's books had been moved into the new room on the second floor, over the old south room. In May 1874 it was agreed that the windows on the north side of the catalogue room should be walled up as a fire precaution, but a year later it was still thought to be impossible to use this extra wall space for cases that could be made accessible via an iron gallery: a gallery was never built.[5] The position in the Library

---

[3] MS. Add. 4573 fos. 176–7. F, Q, O, D and S stand respectively for folio, quarto, octavo, duodecimo and sextodecimo. In class Sel., 1 signifies the largest books.

[4] Cf. the *Memoir* by A. W. Pollard prefixed to Robert Proctor *Bibliographical essays* (1905) pp. xix–xxi, and J. H. Hessels 'Some notes on the invention of printing' *Trans. Bibliographical Soc.* 9 (1906) pp. 11–14. See also above, p. 557.

[5] Annual Report 1 April 1868; Grace of 7 May 1874; Annual Report 5 May 1874; Library papers 26 May 1875.

as a whole was, again, becoming desperate despite the new Scott Building. Books were stored on the window-sills, and there was no space for new ones on the shelves except by removing others. Henry Wheatley, inspecting the Library formally in 1877, easily recognized that much of the muddle from rearranging and recataloguing the books was a direct result of insufficient space,[6] but he could only reiterate his remarks a year later, and point to the lack of space for new journals, the time wasted as books were shuffled round to make room for more, and the inexorable flow of new accessions under the Copyright Act.[7] The Royal Commission on the University in 1878 heard the same complaint, but could do little about the Syndics' suggestions that the Library should take over virtually the whole of the rest of the Schools including the Geological Museum and the parts of the Scott Building used for the Vice-Chancellor, Marshal and Council, as well as the Arts School and Law School. It could not support them in pressing for the completion of the west court. Nor could it advance the Syndicate's other suggestion, involving the roofing in of one or both courts to provide space for the catalogues and a general reading room:[8] the proposal, which would have transformed the building, was put forward again a few months later in a report to the University, after the Syndics had consulted Basil Champneys as to its feasibility.[9] For reasons which were not made clear, their report on the matter was not the subject of a discussion until two and a half years later,[10] after which undergraduates took up the cause, collecting over four hundred signatures to a petition from junior graduates and undergraduates in favour of a reading room.[11] The question of the courtyards was to receive a much more detailed hearing under Bradshaw's pupil and successor Francis Jenkinson, but not until the end of the century.

Only too aware of the difficulties of all kinds, Bradshaw attempted to ease matters for readers by introducing a unified

[6] Wheatley's report 15 October 1877.   [7] Wheatley's report 19 October 1878.
[8] Library papers 15 June 1878.   [9] *Reporter* 27 May 1879 pp. 632–8.
[10] *Ibid.*, 1 November 1881 pp. 81–4.
[11] *Cambridge Review* 16 November 1881, 'Summary of news'.

scheme that at least gave all of the rooms an identifying letter. But this was scarcely an answer, and his short-lived arrangements survived only in the names of the classes LA–LO, after room L, the Librarian's room on the first floor of Scott's extension, classes MA–MH (mostly natural history) in room M, the new upper floor above the south room, and, dating from a little later, class OA, in room O, on the top floor of the Scott Building.[12] Despite his early hopes,[13] he did nothing further in a practical way to extend attempts at subject classification in response to the demands of the new Moral Sciences Tripos – founded like that for natural sciences in 1848 and originally bringing together moral philosophy, political economy, modern history, general jurisprudence, and the laws of England: in the year of Bradshaw's election to the Librarianship this ambitious curriculum was amended to cover moral and political philosophy, mental philosophy, logic and political economy, and by his death this in turn had been enlarged to take more account of psychology. The Library paid little heed to these developments (so far as the arrangement of books was concerned),[14] while no full attempt to classify modern books entering the Library was made until well after Bradshaw's death.

The completion of Basil Champneys' new Divinity School

[12] '"Well, now we are at the Catalogue, what are you going to look for? Oh, you've settled your book, have you? And d'you know where to find it? That's lucky for you. Now whenever I come here and have run through the catalogue and fixed on what I'm going to read, what with the simple letters and the compound letters, and the Roman figures, and the Arabic numerals and the old English letters, and the Greek letters, and the Syro-Chaldaic symbols – oh, aren't there any? well, there might be, considering the way I get mixed up among all the different sorts of signs that they've devised, I suppose, to make the books less liable to be found and so perhaps carried off by dishonest persons – well, I never have any time to get anything done satisfactorily, but I spend it all running up and down enquiring of kind librarians if they can direct me anywhere in the slightest degree near where I want to get to, and climbing up into perilous places and getting myself all covered with dust, and then very often the book isn't there after all' (*Cambridge Review* 1 June 1881 p. 357).

[13] MS. Add. 6420 fo. 360 (datable to 1868–9).

[14] The early history of the Moral Sciences Tripos is described in Winstanley *Later Victorian Cambridge* pp. 185–90; see also the successive volumes of the Cambridge University *Calendar*.

in St John's Street in 1879 offered much needed relief, in that it released the old divinity lecture room on the ground floor of the east front, where the Syndicate agreed to block up the old central doorway and break through a new entrance at the south end.[15] Even when this had been carried out, however, the new room could still contain only about 8,600 volumes on its walls,[16] less than the number of new books added to the general catalogue alone in two years. More space was created by heightening cases in the Novel Room on the ground floor and in the west room, where the Royal Library cases were now interspersed with dwarf cases, and by shelving the catalogue room up to the roof at the risk of accident to all who ventured there.[17] A gallery to reach the upper shelves of the west room, above the eighteenth-century cases, was constructed in 1883.[18]

Nonetheless, there remained two principal rooms in the Schools that the Library had still not formally acquired, the Law School on the ground floor beneath the south room, and the Arts School below the west room. But although the Syndicate's proposal to remove the fittings from the Arts School, including the central reading desk, and to fit both with bookcases protected with wire mesh around the walls,[19] met with little opposition, the shelving of the Arts School only emphasized how much – and more – was needed. When they returned to the University less than eighteen months later, in May 1885, the Syndics took a firmer line on the Law School, and proposed in this instance to convert the whole room to library purposes, including the provision of more adequate space for staff. They also took the rather more contentious step of proposing, after a lapse of twenty years, that Scott's building should be continued round the corner to the Old Gateway and arranged to provide not only more space for ordinary books but also a properly secure room in which to store the

[15] *Reporter* 17 February 1880 pp. 294–5; their proposal was confirmed on 11 March.
[16] H. R. Tedder *Report on the University Library* (Cambridge 1881) p. 6.
[17] Wheatley's report 11 November 1882.   [18] Library papers June 1883.
[19] Library papers 31 October 1883; *Reporter* 4 December 1883 pp. 251–2 (Discussion).

manuscripts and other rare books housed at the end of Bradshaw's office.[20] No-one in the University was better qualified to comment on such drastic proposals than J. W. Clark, Syndic with only brief breaks since 1868, whose *Architectural history* of the University was in the hands of the printers and was published only the next year. He lent the first part of the proposals his unqualified support. On the question of the western court he went further, and in a speech at the University Discussion on the report treated his audience to a historical lecture spanning five hundred years, urging that the entire west range from the Scott Building to Cockerell's library should be completed.[21] Bradshaw had hesitated to put so radical a scheme forward through the Syndicate, principally because it involved the Woodwardian Museum of Geology, over which he had no jurisdiction, but there was otherwise every reason to reduce the cost and inconvenience of construction work by tackling the whole side at once. What opposition there was to the abandoning of the Law School to the Library was effectively quashed by E. C. Clark, as Professor of Civil Law and head of the Law Faculty, who showed every sympathy for Bradshaw's needs: he had himself been a Syndic since 1883, and merely expressed the hope that his displaced department would have first claim to the use of the Arts School.

Bradshaw's report was cleverly timed. It came before the University less than two months after it had been announced that Edward Grey Hancock, formerly Fellow of St John's College, had left the residue of his estate to the University, mentioning no specific purpose.[22] No other department in the University could demonstrate so obvious a need, and none was more central to its purpose, than the Library. The difficult, and sometimes disputed, calculations of cost that had accompanied every proposal to extend the Library hitherto were set aside by Hancock's bequest, and the Council of the Senate took only

[20] *Reporter* 12 May 1885 pp. 680–2; Syndicate Minutes 11 March 1885.
[21] *Reporter* 11 May 1885 pp. 717–19. [22] Clark *Endowments* pp. 460–1.

just over eight months to issue a report concluding that the fund should be applied to whatever extension to the Library was sanctioned by the Senate. A fortnight later, Bradshaw was dead, and he therefore never saw the Hancock Building, built to the designs of John Loughborough Pearson after the sketches by Scott, and handed over to the University in 1890.[23]

The schemes adopted to enlarge the Library were the most practical and the most conservative, but they were not the only ones put forward. Had a proposal circulated by Eiríkr Magnússon, the brilliant but refractory Under-Librarian, been agreed to be appropriate for Cambridge, the University might have become possessed of a library constructed like a nautilus, with a central circular reading room and the book stacks spreading out as a helix: the principal attraction of such a design, assuming that the building stood in an unrestricted open space, was that it allowed extensions to be added relatively cheaply and as they became needed.[24] But although it was bandied about as a novelty in library discussions elsewhere, it was never considered seriously at Cambridge.

Behind the simple need for extra shelving for more books there lurked two more problems of which the implications were not straightforward nor their answers obvious. The calls for a reading room – and even a specialist reading room – and the need to classify or reclassify (and so rearrange) the Library with more particular attention to subject matter, both demanded more space; but the calls came from people in whose minds the purpose, responsibilities and potential of the Library were different from those of even a generation previously. It was no longer possible for the Library to enjoy the isolation that had protected it for centuries, while the equation between

---

[23] A statue of Hancock overlooks the car park in the west court of the Old Schools.

[24] Sayle *Annals* p. 136. His proposal was described in detail on several occasions: in Cambridge in December 1885 (Library papers 4 December 1885); in the *Athenaeum* (27 February 1886 pp. 296–7); and, at greatest length and supported with specifications by Sir Alfred Waterhouse, in the *Library Journal* 11 (1886) pp. 331–9, reprinting Magnússon's paper read (by J. L. Whitney) to the American Library conference at Milwaukee in July 1886; reactions to the Milwaukee address are printed *ibid.* pp. 359–63.

the cost of the Library and the needs of other departments in both the arts and the sciences was calculated with ever increasing vigour and frequency. In itself, the Syndics' decision in March 1869 to allow undergraduates in their academical dress into the Library for an additional hour each afternoon and for the latter part of Saturday mornings was a small enough concession; but their agreement at the same meeting to place a notice board in the vestibule suitable for University notices 'for the information of Undergraduates and other members of the University'[25] hinted at more serious changes in the Library's relations with the rest of an increasingly complicated University, where the main library could no longer be regarded officially as solely a place of advanced research. Five years later, the Syndicate bowed to a petition from about two hundred undergraduates,[26] and they at last won the privilege of entering the Library whenever it was open, subject only to their tutors' recommendations.

Neither the old regulations nor the new, of course, applied to women. It was inconceivable even that they might. Girton College had admitted its first students in 1869, and Newnham in 1871, but as women did not become full members of the University until 1948 their way into the Library was neither easy nor, always, even negotiable: the consequences are to be seen in the care to establish first-class working libraries at both the colleges, which offered facilities far superior to many of the men's colleges. The regulations did, however, allow for anomalies, since there was no objection to women applying for readers' tickets on their own merits, provided they were of age. The Syndics therefore found no difficulty in granting a reader's ticket to Ella Bulley,[27] one of the original five students

---

[25] Syndicate Minutes 3 March 1869.

[26] The signatories included J. N. Keynes, later Registrary of the University, Francis Jenkinson, R. F. Scott, later Master of St. John's, J. E. C. Welldon, later dean of Durham, and J. P. Postgate, the classical scholar.

[27] Syndicate Minutes 8 November 1871. She was born in 1841 (*Newnham College register 1871–1971* I (Cambridge 1979) p. 55).

of Newnham, in 1871, since she had long since reached the age of twenty-one. But her case proved to be one of a very few, as the Syndics steadfastly refused to admit readers under the age of majority who were not members of the University. Their sentiments were tested in what might have been considered slightly different circumstances in April 1875, four months after undergraduates had been allowed into the Library at any time on presenting the necessary documentation from their tutors, but the Syndics' resolve was firm. Charlotte Martin, also of Newnham, who later had a distinguished career as an anarchist and member of the Fabian Society, was refused admission on the grounds that she was not yet of age:[28] she reached her twenty-first birthday three weeks later, and was given a ticket, with two others from the college, the following winter.[29] By the mid-1880s such applications had become a matter of course, few Syndicate meetings passing without a small group of women from Newnham or Girton being recommended, each candidate supported by two members of the Senate; but the Library remained closed to girls whose only fault was that they were not old enough.

On the only slightly less difficult subject of undergraduate admission generally, the Syndics seemingly took their decision to allow unrestricted access at all times when the Library was open with some reluctance, bowing to *force majeure*, for they continued to debate the merits of a general reading room to which undergraduates and holders of readers' tickets could be restricted: such a room, lit by gas, could also be used in the evenings without the need for keeping the rest of the Library open. In the circumstances, however, such proposals, which had the merit of at once removing some and granting other facilities, were hardly practical, and they were dropped.[30] In practice, the number of undergraduates using the Library remained small, discouraged by the lack of any special

---

[28] Syndicate Minutes 14 April 1875.
[29] Syndicate Minutes 9 February 1876.   [30] Library papers 26 May 1875.

743

provision. Within the colleges, library facilities varied alarmingly. While St John's library was open to undergraduates for three hours each day, Trinity Hall was open for only one, and at Jesus books could, seemingly, only be taken out during one hour of the week, in the first part of Friday afternoon.[31] The complaint that undergraduate hours in the University Library were still restricted, even after the Syndics' decision to allow more free access, to only a few hours – and those mostly in the afternoon, the time for recreation – was therefore the more serious. As the University Library was the only collection of any distinction accessible to many undergraduates, there were other, more theoretical, objections, as well. 'Is it not vastly more advantageous to the student that, however clumsily, and inaccurately, he should make an independent effort at classification and analysis from original sources, than that he should be wholly given up to that monstrous incubus on vital action, the general system of coaching, and text-books that are merely coaching systems in print', remarked an anonymous contributor to a debate on library provision conducted in the *Cambridge Review* in 1881.[32] 'The University Library is not very accessible to a young student, and undergraduates are almost entirely debarred from its use', pontificated Oscar Browning in pressing for a specialist history library in 1884.[33] The answer did, indeed, lie outside the walls of the University Library.

The peculiar needs of lawyers were explained to the Syndicate in December 1870 by J. T. Abdy,[34] and they were repeated more formally by his successor E. C. Clark three years later, in June 1873: for a separate reading room containing the

[31] J. Spencer Hill 'College libraries and undergraduates' *Cambridge Review* 23 March 1881 pp. 242–3. [32] *Ibid.*, 23 November 1887. Cf. also the remarks in Chapter 1.
[33] Cambridge papers FA 4528, circular of April 1884. When Browning became the first librarian of the history library in 1884, it contained about 1600 volumes, principally from the libraries of John Symonds (Regius Professor from 1771 to 1807) and his successor William Smyth, and attracted few students at first: in 1889 H. M. Gwatkin thought one or two a term a liberal estimate (Jean O. McLachlan 'The origin and early development of the Cambridge historical tripos' *Cambridge Historical Journal* 9 (1947–9) pp. 78–104, at pp. 85–6). [34] Syndicate Minutes 7 December 1870.

law books most frequently referred to and having 'somewhat ampler facilities for literary work than exist in the Library building' – words that referred as much to table space as to reference books. Clark's other reason for asking that law students should be given special privileges was to become familiar, and it is unlikely that he was the first to voice it: 'The books in question are so numerous, so expensive, and new editions of many of them are issued so frequently, that it is not to be expected that they should be purchased by individual Students, who must therefore work mainly, if not entirely, in the University Library, from which it is of course impossible that books should be removed.'[35] His plea was an urgent one, three years after the first candidates had sat for a new tripos combining law and history, and only a year before this arrangement was replaced by a Law Tripos alone.[36] Clark had his eye on the Law School as the most appropriate site for such a room, but after his plea also had fallen on stony ground at the Syndicate, he and the Board of Legal Studies next had recourse to the Council of the Senate in a tersely worded appeal proposing instead that the little-used divinity lecture room, situated on the east front between the two entrances to the Schools building, should be converted into a law reading room.[37]

It was this that led to the Syndics' report of May 1879, referred to above, on the desirability of constructing a general reading room in one of the courts; but their conclusions, based on an examination of the cramped conditions throughout the Library, served only to prove the impracticability of the Law Faculty's hopes. The Faculty finally acquired its own library as the result of the will of Miss Rebecca Flower Squire[38] in 1898,

---

[35] Library papers 3 June 1873.
[36] There were thirty successful candidates in 1873, thirty-four in 1874, thirty-six in 1875 and thirty-five in 1876 (*Historical register* pp. 861–63). The combined law and history tripos was heavily biased towards law: see the article by Jean O. McLachlan cited in n. 33 above.
[37] Considered by the Library Syndicate 27 November 1878: copy in Library papers.
[38] *Reporter* 28 March 1969 p. 1252.

but chose at least during Bradshaw's Librarianship to concentrate its hopes on special provision within the University Library, rather than on a separate institution. It was still the case that, with one or two notable exceptions, including the rather different provision for general reading at the Union Society, library facilities outside the University Library and the colleges hardly existed. The Divinity Library dated its life from the opening of the Divinity School in 1879. But while the Board of Historical and Archaeological Studies called vociferously for a separate library for candidates for the Historical Tripos when given the opportunity in a wide-ranging report prepared for the new General Board of Studies in 1883, it was the only body to do so:[39] the General Board had not even bothered to specify libraries in its enquiries, but spoke simply of 'other measures – such as the supply of additional teaching appliances' to render departmental teaching more effective.

Nevertheless, while there were few enough departmental libraries in the University, such relations as the University Library itself had with them suggested, on the whole, a new spirit of co-operation which had not been thought necessary hitherto. In 1871 the Library Syndicate agreed to deposit on loan at the New Museums Building in Downing Street such duplicate copies of natural science books that it saw fit,[40] and when in 1880 the Philosophical Society's library became too large for it to be continued either in its existing home in the New Museums or under the old arrangements for custody, it seemed obvious that one remedy would be to employ a University Library assistant, 'one properly trained in library work', as librarian. The University did not however feel able to accede to the whole of Alfred Newton's suggestion (as the President of the Philosophical Society) that a central university scientific library should be built, in which the Society's collections could be deposited. Instead, under an agreement

---

[39] A copy of the report is in the Library papers. Oscar Browning's appeal for such a library was launched separately in 1884 (Cambridge papers FA 4528: see above).
[40] Syndicate Minutes 8 February 1871.

which made the library accessible to university teaching staff (rather than Fellows of the Society only), and run by a librarian whose salary was met by the University, the collections were drawn into what was becoming a new pattern in library provision more attuned to the needs of departments than the University Library could ever expect to be.[41]

In his evidence to the Royal Commission in 1852, Power had made clear how necessary it was that the Fitzwilliam Museum and the University Library should agree on some working arrangement to avoid unnecesary expense in buying books on the history of art:[42] in the next decades, spurred on by the desperate need for space, the collections in the Library were ever more closely defined. With the erection of the Fitzwilliam Museum it no longer needed to act as the repository for all the University's works of art, and the decision in 1876 to recommend to the Senate the transfer of nineteen albums of prints and drawings to the Museum was taken with little ado. The collection had been accumulated from various sources, and included works by Hollar, Callot, Dürer, Cranach and Altdorfer as well as a major collection (said to consist of 838 items) of etchings by Rembrandt and his school. Many came from Moore's library. A few albums of inferior interest were left behind, but it was intended that the nineteen albums should join Viscount Fitzwilliam's own collections, where in many instances they would fill in gaps. G. W. Reid, of the British Museum, was then in the midst of supervising the mounting and cataloguing of the Fitzwilliam collections, and as the Syndics rightly pointed out, the Library was not equipped to look after prints or to exhibit them properly.[43] Bradshaw's own relations with the Fitzwilliam had not flourished in uninterrupted amity. He had disputed fiercely, and publicly,

---

[41] Syndicate Minutes 16 February 1881; A. Rupert Hall *The Cambridge Philosophical Society; a history, 1819–1969* (Cambridge 1969) pp. 29–30.

[42] Under Bradshaw several attempts were made to integrate the acquisitions policies for books on art history with the Museum: cf. for example Syndicate Minutes 12 March 1884 and 23 April 1884.

[43] Syndicate Minutes, letter of 24 October 1875; Library papers 15 November 1876.

with the Museum Syndicate's decision in 1872 to decline R. E. Kerrich's bequest of the whole of his collection of books and works of art and to restrict itself to a selection of what seemed then to be most valuable;[44] and as the Museum Syndics had then behaved so unsympathetically it seems odd that he did not ensure that the Library Syndicate exacted a promise to keep what was transferred in 1876. Instead, once the collection had been sorted through at the Museum, those Rembrandt etchings that were not wanted were sold off, and the Library Syndicate could only fume impotently at a meeting made perhaps the more embarrassing by the presence of Sidney Colvin, the Museum's director.[45] The episode did not, however, prevent further attempts to integrate the acquisitions policies for books in the two institutions.

Nothing, unfortunately, came of a proposal that would have joined more than these various strands together. A serious attempt at a union catalogue of all the college libraries had last been made in the seventeenth century, when it had been envisaged that all printed books of whatever date should be included. What had proved impossible in the seventeenth century was no less challenging in the nineteenth, but the publication in 1847 and 1850 of catalogues of the early printed books at Trinity College and Gonville and Caius College were reminders of the great riches in the college libraries –

---

[44] A copy of Bradshaw's flysheet of 4 June 1872 is in Cambridge Papers FA 3940, with the other relevant circulars; see also Prothero *Bradshaw* pp. 180–3. A sale of the Kerrich collection was held at Sotheby's on 18–20 July 1873.

[45] Syndicate Minutes 22 May 1878. The Fitzwilliam Museum annual report of 24 November 1877 (*Reporter* 27 November 1877 p. 137) recorded that 838 etchings by Rembrandt and his school had been removed from four of the Library's albums, and 490 from a volume in the Museum's collection. The Museum could not sell from the Founder's bequest, but on 2–3 April 1878 345 lots from the Library collection were offered at Sotheby's, and raised £1984.5s.0d. The transaction with the Library coincided with serious efforts by the Museum to improve its collection of prints from the early German and Netherlandish schools: it spent £783.2s.0d. at the Liphart sale at Frankfurt in December 1876, and in 1877 paid £200 for Martin Schongauer's *Death of the Virgin* (University Archives CUR 30.2, 5–9 December 1876). In 1878 C. H. Middleton published his *Descriptive catalogue of the etched work of Rembrandt van Rhyn*, a work dismissed by Seymour Haden (whose own hopes of such a publication were thereby dashed) as 'intrinsically unreliable' (*The etched work of Rembrandt; a monograph* (1879)).

collections with which no-one had more overall familiarity than Bradshaw himself. In 1881 John Venn, Fellow of Caius, estimated that the colleges, the Fitzwilliam Museum and the Philosophical Society between them possessed 353,000 books, only a little less than the University Library itself. Since it was axiomatic that most colleges could ill afford to keep up collections to the highest standard, and evident that if a book could not be found in the University Library there might easily be a copy in another library in Cambridge, the logical steps were first, to organize a union catalogue (which need not, Venn considered, include books published in England since 1800, which could be assumed to be in the University Library), and second, to persuade colleges each to specialize in one particular subject once a small general library was established for undergraduate needs.[46] Logic was a powerful, but not an irresistible, weapon. Prompted by Venn, the Syndicate addressed itself to the question of compiling a union catalogue of early books down to 1800 in the colleges in May 1883,[47] but came to no conclusion then and was similarly unsuccessful when it again discussed the matter in 1885: it agreed to authorize Bradshaw to buy an interleaved copy of the Bodleian catalogue for the purpose,[48] but, lacking anyone to proceed with the work, the project could only be abandoned before it had been begun. If the Syndics ever considered Venn's second proposal, which would have lessened the autonomy of the colleges and which was beyond their purview, the Minutes do not record the fact.

The Library's relations with the University had never been

---

[46] J. Venn 'College libraries' *Cambridge Review* 9 March 1881 pp. 210–11.
[47] Syndicate Minutes 2 May 1883.
[48] Syndicate Minutes 25 February 1885. A union catalogue of printed books in the Cambridge libraries had been contemplated at least three times before, in the mid-seventeenth century and in 1705/6. All that remains of the seventeenth-century attempts is recorded in Clare College O.5.26 (interleaved copies of *Appendix ad catalogum librorum in Bibliotheca Bodleiana* (Oxford 1635) and *Catalogus interpretum sacrae scripturae* (Oxford 1635)); Richard Love (Fellow of Clare, d. 1661) and another so far unidentified figure both then sought to do the same thing, but both projects were abandoned. Hearne (*Remarks and collections* 1 (1885) p. 200) noted in March 1705/6 that Joseph Wasse of Queens' was 'all for printing a Catalogue of all printed Books in ye Libraries at Cambridge': but again – and as Hearne clearly expected – the idea came to nothing.

more intricate. But while its place within the national archive and organization for research seemed to be ever more firmly established, and the University was so seriously regarded that it became the object of investigation and interference from the capital in the shape of Royal Commissions in 1852 and again in 1874, the Library was in a fragile position. Its authority in a national context was still not generally understood, and there were few occasions when it could be expounded. Discussions about the future of the archiepiscopal library at Lambeth in 1867 provided an all too rare opportunity to remind a wide and presumably interested audience in *The Times* not only that, since the books had been housed at Cambridge during the seventeenth-century interregnum, it would be appropriate for them to be returned there rather than be transferred to the British Museum, but also that the University Library expected to assume a national role – 'accessible to all real students from whatever quarter they come'.[49] Nonetheless, the Copyright Commission of 1875,[50] after listening to scarcely any evidence on the subject, recommended that the number of deposit libraries should be reduced to one only, the British Museum. It did so without really considering the implications of relying on a single deposit copy in a national context, and in the mistaken belief that the University (the assumption applied to the other libraries as well) could easily afford to buy all that it needed to an equivalent standard. Public ignorance, despite the University's exposure to the outside world, threatened proper debate. 'It is very satisfactory to find that the Commissioners join with one voice in recognition of the injustice of taxing authors and publishers for the maintenance of wealthy public libraries', remarked one partial, and influential, observer in 1879.[51] Such assumptions ignored the very foundations of the evidence facing the Royal Commissions on the University: that while

[49] Bradshaw's letter is printed in Prothero's *Memoir* pp. 158–60: the books of course stayed at Lambeth.
[50] For its Report and evidence see *Parliamentary papers* 1878.24 pp. 163–667.
[51] [Edward Marston] *Copyright, national and international, from the point of view of a publisher* (1879) p. 19.

several colleges were endowed to excess, the University itself was comparatively poor. The financial position of the Library had not improved speedily, and the Syndics' comment to the University of Cambridge Commissioners in 1878, that the current income was barely sufficient,[52] became all the more obvious as the accounts slipped into deficit: the financial situation was retrieved only after the Worts Fund had been amalgamated with the Library's General Fund, and a modest additional £500 per annum had been granted from the Common University Fund following the recommendations of the General Board in November 1883.[53]

The threat posed by the conclusions of the Copyright Commission was therefore all the more acute. For much of their time, the Commissioners concerned themselves with registration at Stationers' Hall (whether of trade labels, catalogues, or books) more than with deposit; but the deposit libraries had little support: the Secretary to the Board of Trade shared the view of William Longman and Frederic Daldy that one deposit copy was sufficient. No witness spoke specifically on behalf of the University's interest, and none of the librarians who would have been affected appeared. At Oxford, the following October, the first annual meeting of the Library Association provided a ready platform for complaint, where the voices of George Bullen and Richard Garnett, both of the British Museum, joined those of H. O. Coxe of the Bodleian, and J. T. Clark of the Faculty of Advocates' Library to express something of the widespread dissatisfaction with the Commissioners' recommendations.[54] At Cambridge the Syndics responded with circumspection. A single page in the *Reporter* suggested that the University should petition against the findings of the Royal Commission.[55] This was but a

---

[52] Library papers 15 June 1878.
[53] *Reporter* 23 November 1883 p. 205; Annual Report 4 June 1884. The Syndics had asked for £3000 per annum.
[54] H. R. Tedder and E. C. Thomas (eds.) *Transactions and proceedings of the first annual meeting of the Library Association of the United Kingdom* (1879) pp. 122, 139–40.
[55] *Reporter* 3 December 1878 p. 193.

preliminary, however, and in February 1879 a deputation headed by the High Steward of the University (the Earl of Powis), the Vice-Chancellor, and the two Members of Parliament for the University waited on Lord John Manners, the Chairman of the Commissioners, who had graduated from Trinity in 1839. Their points, summarized afterwards by William Aldis Wright, a close ally of Bradshaw's, were intended partly to correct the mistaken assumption that the Library could well afford to lose the privilege, partly to refute allegations as to the cost to publishers, partly to suggest that one copy was insufficient, and partly to make a more general point which would not have been necessary had the Library's role in the national archive been more widely understood. 'As a public institution, readily accessible to all who are engaged in the prosecution of any branch of literature or science, and placed in one of the centres of mental activity and culture, the University Library has by virtue of this right a catholicity of character which it would not possess were the choice of books governed merely by considerations of practical utility.'[56]

Their arguments, *ex post facto*, were not unavailing when joined to those of the other interested libraries,[57] for when in the following July Manners introduced a Bill 'To consolidate and amend the law relating to copyright', the clauses of the 1842 Act relating to deposit remained virtually unchanged despite the Commission's recommendation that four of the five deposit libraries should lose their privilege.[58] While there was no doubt some relief at such a turn of events, in fact the libraries were doubly saved in that the Bill was introduced too late to allow any discussion, and it was accordingly dropped. The subject was not aired again until the 1890s.

In earlier enquiries, the question of the efficacy of existing copyright legislation for deposit had taken up considerable time. But on this occasion Panizzi's reforms at the British Museum, and the related agency arrangements for the other

---

[56] Library papers 26 February 1879.
[57] Cf. also Craster pp. 63–4.   [58] Partridge *Legal deposit* pp. 93–9, 328–32.

libraries, encouraged assumptions that would hitherto have been, at the very least, matters for debate. So heavy had the work of the agency become in 1883 that the University at last agreed – after twenty years – to allow the agent, G. W. Eccles, to employ a single assistant.[59] Few suggestions could have been less controversial. But besides Eccles' advancing years and the accompanying increase in his labours, it was still clear that the Library was receiving less than its due. While noting that not one of the deposit libraries outside the British Museum received any daily newspaper through Eccles, and that the delivery of even the major London weekly journals was not uniform, in 1880 H. R. Tedder considered that the proportion of 'books worth having' not received amounted only to about five per cent.[60] His more rigorous inspection of the Library the following year proved less favourable. Of 244 works listed in the January 1881 issues of *The Bookseller* (itself by no means complete, though nonetheless the instrument used by the British Museum as the best available) he discarded twenty-one as later editions or reprints, but still discovered that ninety-one had not arrived by the following November, including twenty-six that he regarded as having some value for the Library.[61] Even on this rough calculation, the Library thus seemed to be missing some thirty-seven per cent of the whole, or eleven per cent if some selection was exercised. Henry Wheatley's report the following year repeated the warning, in less detail,[62] but it was E. W. B. Nicholson, at Oxford, who pursued publishers in the next few years with such success that in 1885 Professor H. W. Chandler believed that the Bodleian would be crushed like Tarpeia, and in 1895 a Curatorial committee actually sought to reduce the number of books received under the Act.[63]

While Bradshaw paid little attention to the remarks of

---

[59] Library papers 6 June 1883.
[60] H. R. Tedder *Report on the University Library* (Cambridge 1880) p. 4.
[61] Tedder *Report* (1881) p. 6.
[62] Library papers 11 November 1882.   [63] Craster p. 173.

Tedder and Wheatley on copyright deposit, or to their implications for a library which claimed to be one of national record, his understanding of the cognate subject of making the books available to virtually everyone, whether members of the University or not, was clear. At the centre of a web of correspondence that stretched halfway across Europe, to India and to America, as well as all over the British Isles, he was in a better position to appreciate the nature of the Library's contribution, and the world's expectations of it, than any of his predecessors. His remarks uttered in connection with the Lambeth library, about 'all real students', were no empty ones, and his services to those he deemed appropriate extended even on occasion to borrowing manuscripts on their behalf – a cumbersome procedure, since it required a Grace, but a privilege that had few parallels outside Cambridge. He understood needs of this kind, calling on the collections of manuscripts and early printed books, better than he did the daily needs of the University. 'His idea of a great library was hardly that of most modern librarians,' concluded Prothero, his biographer but also Secretary of the History Board and university lecturer in history; 'he regarded it in the light of a museum of literary and typographical records quite as much as, perhaps even more than, that of a collection of practically useful books'.[64]

When the Library Association met at Cambridge in 1882, during Bradshaw's term as President, he set down his own definition of a librarian as 'one who earns his living by attending to the wants of those for whose use the library under his charge exists; his primary duty being, in the widest possible sense of the phrase, to save the time of those who seek his services'. The definition was inadequate, and was not just to Bradshaw himself. It was also one that he sheltered behind too readily,[65] and which C. E. Grant, his obituarist in the *Library*

---

[64] Prothero *Memoir* p. 374.

[65] 'Address at the opening of the fifth annual meeting of the Library Association' (Memorandum no. 7, 1882), repr. in Bradshaw's *Collected papers* (1889) pp. 371–409; the appendix to Bradshaw's paper gives an account of the everyday work of cataloguing books.

Chronicle, was not shy of tackling: 'Mr Bradshaw's reputation as a librarian rests not upon his administrative powers, but upon his accurate knowledge of the contents of the library and upon the assistance which he gave to students in all departments of learning.' Grant was charitable, however, in attributing solely to Bradshaw's high standards the fact that, in his words, 'much valuable time was spent in the perfecting of comparatively unimportant details of departmental administration, while the general superintendence of the whole suffered'.[66]

As an administrator, Bradshaw lacked the persistent energy to maintain momentum. Accessions in some fields, notably of early printed books and, thanks to a series of enthusiastic supporters, of oriental manuscripts, were remarkable, while in others, such as modern foreign books and ordinary second-hand purchases to fill in more recent gaps, they were abysmal. It was not always for lack of money that some opportunities slipped away, or that the admittedly inadequate staff laboured with only mixed success to bring order to collections that a firmer hand might have found to be less intractable. On many matters the Syndicate bowed to his knowledge, and there was no return to the acrimony of Mayor's term of office. But he could also be called sharply to heel. In 1877 he was requested to 'use his authority for settling the differences between Mr Magnusson & O. Johnson, and to report the result to the Vice-Chancellor [Edward Atkinson] by Saturday next'.[67] The request came at the end of a meeting that had also asked him to see that donations were catalogued with as little delay as possible, criticized the cataloguing of part of the theological collections, and agreed on the unusual step of asking a complete outsider to conduct a full inspection of the Library during the Long Vacation. Hardly surprisingly, Bradshaw found these proceedings difficult to digest. His reputation outside Cambridge was higher than ever that summer (he had

[66] C. E. Grant 'In memoriam: Henry Bradshaw' *Library Chronicle* 3 (1886) pp. 25–36 at p. 29.   [67] Syndicate Minutes 13 June 1877.

refused E. B. Nicholson's invitation to become a Vice-President of the Library Association, and the Caxton quatercentenary exhibition opened on 30 June,[68] resulting in visits from Frederik Muller and M. F. A. G. Campbell), but the Library was suffering. On 18 August he told Campbell that he had been away for nearly two months,[69] but he did not tell him all his worries. 'I cannot go on at the library much longer', he wrote to another friend in July, 'and then, if I live, I ought to bring out some of the many things for which I have been collecting material all these years.'[70] By 1 September news reached Luard in Frankfurt that Bradshaw had had enough, and was thinking seriously of resigning: 'I trust it is not true – what should we do without you? I can thoroughly understand how much there must be to try and worry one in the office, and that all the years you have spent in the Library are beginning to tell on you.'[71] Luard's letter arrived within hours of another, rather less welcome. It came from Henry Wheatley, clerk to the Royal Society, and announced, 'I have just had a letter from Mr Oscar Browning with final instructions as to the Inspection and I therefore take this opportunity of letting you know that I hope to begin the work on the 19th inst. which arrangements will I hope be satisfactory to you.'[72]

The choice of Wheatley to carry out so delicate a task was an intelligent one. He had been Honorary Secretary of the Early English Text Society since 1864, and already knew Bradshaw through correspondence, though the two had never met. A few years later he was to be appreciated as the editor of the popular Book-Lover's Library, to which he contributed manuals on the choice of books, cataloguing and indexing, and to achieve fame as the editor of Pepys' diary; but in 1877 he was all but unknown outside a small circle, and his chief claims to

---

[68] The Library lent two dozen items to this exhibition. Cf. George Bullen (ed.) *Caxton celebration, 1877. Catalogue of the loan collection* (1877), and Prothero *Bradshaw* p. 232.
[69] Bradshaw *Correspondence* p. 194.   [70] Prothero *Bradshaw* p. 236.
[71] Luard to Bradshaw 1 September 1877.
[72] Wheatley to Bradshaw 1 September 1877. Browning was not, at this stage, a member of the Library Syndicate: he joined for the first time only in November 1877.

repute beyond the library world were as son of the auctioneer Benjamin Wheatley and as younger brother of Benjamin Robert Wheatley, author of the index to the catalogue of the Athenaeum library of 1845–51, friend of the bookseller Thomas Boone, librarian since 1855 of the Royal Medical and Chirurgical Society, and one of the most senior members of his profession. The younger man could offer less experience than his brother, but he proved to have an eye sufficiently acute for the Syndics' purposes. Henry Wheatley arrived as planned at Cambridge, but his efforts to interest Bradshaw in the forthcoming first international conference of librarians were to no avail. Instead, Bradshaw turned his attention away, to the fragments of Caxton's *Fifteen Oes* in the Bristol copy of the *Mirrour of the world*[73] (he soaked them off their binding on 27 September), and on 2 October he departed on a foray to libraries at Amiens, Orleans, Tours and Paris, leaving Wheatley to conduct his investigations in his absence.[74] The Syndics, through Browning, had asked Wheatley to organize his questions under eight heads, of which the first four dealt with the same problem that had plagued the Library for most of the century: like others before him, Bradshaw was unable to resist the temptation to remove books from one place on the shelves to another. He often did so with good reason, and withdrew from open access many whose value made some protection essential; but though much of this had been done in the sixties the catalogue records had still not been changed, and the only record of what now reposed safe but concealed lay in a list kept by Bradshaw himself. Other matters were more miscellaneous. In their request to Wheatley to inspect the newspapers, music, and official publications, and the means employed to preserve them, the Syndics clearly hoped for some guidance on a difficult problem. Wheatley offered little on this score, however, observing that the Newspaper Room was chiefly filled with unbound music and other books, and

73 Prothero *Bradshaw* pp. 232–4 and Bradshaw *Collected papers* pp. 341–9.
74 MS. Add. 4568(3).

that the Library's few newspapers were not catalogued. Of the manuscripts he reported that while everything had been allotted a number, none had been fully catalogued since the appearance of the printed catalogue. When he came to the new general catalogue of printed books, he found more to disagree with, some mistakes and some inconsistencies; but he concluded that on the whole the rules, for all their oddities, were 'very completely carried out'.[75] More generally, Wheatley clearly experienced difficulty in moving round a strange library, and found the numbering of the shelves after so many years full of incongruities: apart from suggesting that this should be improved he also recommended that printed directions particularly as to the use of the catalogue, the arrangement of the classes, and the whereabouts of principal subjects, should be made available. His report was dated 15 October, a day after Bradshaw had a long talk with Luard about giving the Library up.[76]

The Syndics had expected criticism, had asked for it, and were given it. Wheatley's report was considered at a series of meetings that autumn, the first of which was addressed to the critical problem of access to the select books in Bradshaw's room. By 17 November Atkinson, the Vice-Chancellor, had had enough, and at a meeting on the same day on which he had also to see through the conferring of an honorary LL.D on Charles Darwin he spoke out more clearly than he might at other times. Bradshaw recorded his own feelings in his diary. 'Rather hot meeting on Wheatley's report & very unsatisfactory. The VC felt constrained to say that, about the removals, it only wanted will & determination, & that with a man of ordinary good sense at the head the difficulties would have disappeared long ago.'[77] It was to Bradshaw's credit that

---

[75] He suggested, *inter alia*, that it should be made clear that entries such as 'George Eliot' were of pseudonyms, that anonymous novels should be entered under their titles, that the form heading 'Catalogue' should be reconsidered, that subject entries should be extended to include places as well as persons, and that titles beginning with insignificant words such as 'On', 'Our', 'De' etc. should be entered under something other than their first word.   [76] MS. Add. 4568(3) pp. 103–4.   [77] *Ibid.*, pp. 151–2.

he seems to have borne Wheatley no malice, and even contributed a paper on Godfried van der Haeghen to the first number of Wheatley's new journal *The Bibliographer* in 1881.[78]

Bradshaw remained in his office, and survived where Mayor would have resigned. The campaign for another extension to the Library was carried on as much by the Syndics, and by E. C. and J. W. Clark, as by Bradshaw, who sometimes seemed to prefer to take second place; yet his name alone appeared at the end of the crucial report of May 1885 that led to the successful completion of the west court. Besides the developments described in the last pages, there were others that became equally familiar over the years. He managed – with the help of Magnússon – to introduce improvements into the process of cataloguing, imposing order where Mayor had proceeded haphazardly.[79] By the time of his death there was a separate map room, where before there had been none.[80] The first of a long series of ever larger lists of serials received in the Library appeared in 1870, restricted initially to foreign titles; and in October 1885 the first *University Library Bulletin* was published, listing the books newly available week by week by the simple expedient of reimposing the entries for the catalogue and printing them off as small pamphlets. It was not the least of the achievements of his Librarianship not only that the stipends of Under-Librarians and of the Librarian were raised, but also that new incremental scales of pay for the assistants were introduced in 1875, replacing the old arrangement calling for a Grace to implement each annual increase of £4, and that within a few years the time taken to reach the top of the scale was reduced from twenty-three years. By no means all the

---

[78] Reprinted in his *Collected papers* pp. 354–70. Wheatley also reported on the Library in 1878, as has been mentioned above, and presented a paper on cataloguing periodicals to the meeting of the Library Association at Cambridge in 1882.

[79] Bradshaw to J. Winter Jones 18 January 1868 (*The Library* new ser. 5 (1904) pp. 431–4). The new procedures were fully described to the Library Association on the occasion of its meeting in Cambridge in 1882: see Bradshaw 'Some account of the organisation of the Cambridge University Library', repr. in his *Collected papers* pp. 385–404.

[80] Tedder *Report on the University Library* (1880) p. 2; Syndicate Minutes 17 March 1886.

improvements were inspired, or executed, by Bradshaw, who
crossed swords with Magnússon, a more energetic and
impatient man, over the manner in which the Library should
be managed. But his first appointment to the Library had been
to set the manuscripts straight, and he clung to the will to create
an orderly and well-run establishment. 'This Library has been
for some years past in a transition state, which I am doing my
best to bring to an end', he wrote to Ernest Thomas in
September 1880 in reply to a suggestion that the infant Library
Association should meet at Cambridge. 'But it is a long
business, at best. As matters stand at present, the Long Vacation
is the only opportunity I have for such a spell of uninterrupted
work as enables me to make any sensible impression upon the
mass which has to be got through.'[81] In place of the annual
meeting of the Association, the following summer found him
embroiled in appeals that he should allow himself to be put
forward as Bodley's Librarian, 'the head of my profession in
this country', as he described it,[82] in place of Coxe. Oxford
was in truth a poor temptation. In 1870, the Bodleian had
spurned his catalogue of its incunables, arranged in his
customary manner printer by printer and town by town. 'I
have never *enjoyed* the Bodleian since, as you may believe', he
confided to Falconer Madan in 1882,[83] six months after E. B.
Nicholson had been elected Bodley's Librarian unopposed by
Bradshaw. It was inconceivable that he should move, and he
had no wish to. Instead the work in the Library seemed ever
more onerous, and was not made easier by the endless
questions of all kinds that descended on him in each day's
post.[84] He had become an *éminence grise*, to the world at large,

---

[81] Bradshaw to Ernest C. Thomas 30 September 1880 (draft).
[82] Prothero *Bradshaw* p. 257.   [83] Bradshaw to Madan 8 August 1882.
[84] Hardly surprisingly, not all letters addressed to him won his immediate sympathy. He
was notorious for not replying to those even from friends, but he could also be stung
into a reply to a stranger. On 12 June 1885, for example, he wrote to John W. Warman,
'I should be very glad to give you any help in my power, but you must allow me to
suggest that if, as you say, you are writing a large work on the construction of the
Organ, it will be but of little value if you get other people to do the most important part
of the work for you, as you innocently propose, on your postcard received a day or two

to innumerable friends,[85] and to the University who demanded his time and thought as a member of both the Council
and the General Board, where his voice and influence were
crucial in shaping the new Modern Languages Tripos.

But while his memory was prodigious, and his reading – of
contemporary novels as much as of subjects suggested by the
Library's manuscripts and early printed books – enormous, it
was not in Bradshaw's character to finish many of the studies
which he set himself. He completed no catalogue of the
incunables in the end, neither did he finish his planned edition
of Chaucer, nor his investigations, which took him backwards
and forwards across France, of early Breton manuscripts.
Instead, his notes on Chaucer appeared partly as a Memorandum in 1871 and partly as notes to the work of others, and his
knowledge, probably unrivalled in his day, of Breton manuscripts emerged only in the work of his friend Whitley Stokes,
and in response to F. W. H. Wasserschleben's *Die Irische*

ago. Do not misunderstand me, or think me unkind – but, as a matter of fact, it is only
by doing this very work yourself that your book can possibly be of any use. Any single
modern book on the organ will necessarily refer to previous books, and if you can
manage to devote to this purpose even two or three days at some large library, say the
British Museum, you will find yourself gradually becoming possessed of knowledge
which is worth having, and you will then perceive that the kind of knowledge you
want is absolutely worthless unless you get it yourself . . .

Only look for a moment at the last but one of some twenty queries which you
propound. 'How much worth purchase by the Organ-builder or student of Organ-
construction?' Can you gravely suppose that I or any one else, after searching in all
manner of places for many scores of books, papers, journals, memoirs, &c. &c. &c. and
making out for your benefit a statement of the 'general nature of contents' of them all,
that we are then to read and weigh them carefully and then put down on paper our
sober judgment as to how far it may be worth your while to purchase the book in
question? I am sure you will see that if *you* were to put yourself through a course of
training and education by doing this work yourself, you would, – supposing you to be a
person of sufficient knowledge beforehand and of a sound judgment besides – find
yourself in a position to write "a large work on the construction of the Organ" with
some chance of benefiting your fellow-men by means of a work which would be worth
having.'

[85] In 1907 the Kingsman Karl Pearson, then Professor of Applied Mathematics and
Mechanics at University College, London (and on his death in 1936 the donor of a large
collection of German Reformation pamphlets to the Library), confided to Francis
Galton, 'I always feel about you, as I felt about Henry Bradshaw, that if I put a personal
difficulty, I shall get the help of a contemplative man of riper experience. I think it is a
trace of the old Quaker blood in both of you' (Karl Pearson *The life, letters and labours of
Francis Galton* (3 vols. Cambridge 1914–30) 3a p. 322).

Kanonensammlung, in 1885.[86] His work on Caxton was in some respects pre-empted by William Blades, yet he continued at it but published scarcely anything apart from a Memorandum in 1877 on the fragment of the *Fifteen Oes* in the Baptist College at Bristol. His pioneering list of Sarum service books formed some of the most absorbing pages of Procter and Wordsworth's edition of the Breviary, but the relevant volume appeared only after his death;[87] and it was left to Francis Jenkinson to see into print the first serious study ever attempted of the work of John Siberch, Cambridge's first printer.[88] No full-length monograph on any subject was ever completed, to the despair of his friends and of his successors alike, and it was not entirely the fault of his other duties. There was a bitter irony in the fact that the largest book which he saw through the press neither had his name on the title page nor needed to have been compiled by him at all: he found the task of editing the new *Statutes for the University of Cambridge and for the colleges within it*, published in 1883, a chore.

In August 1885, hopelessly overworked in the Library and in his other University duties, he collapsed, and after a brief visit to Madan at Oxford returned to Cambridge to arrange for Magnússon to act as his deputy, and to give Francis Jenkinson free run of the Library, before leaving on a holiday that took him through Caen, Le Mans, Tours, Toulouse and back to Chartres. The autumn was made the more pleasant by two stimulating series of correspondence, with Talbot Baines Reed on the history of Irish printing types, and with Mommsen on Gildas, and the less so by a row on the Council of the Senate. Almost certainly unknown to him, however, his heart was in a fatal condition, and he died in his rooms in King's on 10 February 1886 after spending the evening at a dinner

---

[86] Whitley Stokes (ed.) *The Breton glosses at Orleans* (privately pr., Calcutta 1880); Henry Bradshaw *The early collection of canons commonly known as the Hibernensis; a letter addressed to Dr. F. W. H. Wasserschleben* (Memorandum no. 8, Cambridge 1885), repr. in *Collected papers* (Cambridge 1889) pp. 410–20.

[87] H. F. Stewart *Francis Jenkinson* (Cambridge 1926) pp. 27–9.

[88] Cf. the introduction to the facsimile of Siberch's edition of *Doctissimi viri Henrici Bulloci . . . oratio* (Cambridge 1886).

party given by J. W. Clark at his house in Scroope Terrace, half a mile away. He was fifty-five years old.

Bradshaw was buried on 15 February in King's College Chapel, the building he had passed several times daily as he walked between his rooms in college and the Library. His funeral service was no ordinary occasion. The crowded proceedings, which closed with an anthem specially composed by Charles Villiers Stanford that directly quoted the Dublin Troper bought from Todd's library when Bradshaw was still fresh in his office,[89] were conducted by Brooke Foss Westcott, Regius Professor of Divinity and a Fellow of Trinity, and by E. W. Benson, Archbishop of Canterbury and an old friend for years. In their elaborate ritual the college and the University demonstrated in their own way their awareness that neither world would ever be quite the same again. The obituaries, among them those by G. W. Prothero in the *Cambridge Review*, J. W. Clark in the *Saturday Review*, and J. H. Hessels in *The Academy*, repeated the same theme. To the world of librarians and bibliographers outside Cambridge his death was one of three of national authorities within a month: Edward Edwards had died on 6 February, and Henry Stevens followed on the 28th. To everyone it was premature, and it found the University unprepared. There were many who assumed that his successor would be Francis Jenkinson, the man most obviously sympathetic to Bradshaw's interests, but Jenkinson gave his own support to William Robertson Smith, Lord Almoner's Professor of Arabic, who was elected on 24 February. Instead, Jenkinson succeeded his master at one remove, following Robertson Smith's election to the Sir Thomas Adams chair on the death of William Wright in 1889.[90]

Jenkinson's long librarianship – he died in 1923 after thirty-four years in office – makes the death of Bradshaw a necessary

[89] MS. Add. 710. Bradshaw had supplied the melody of the 'Angelus ad Virginem' to Stanford in 1882, and it was used in his opera *Savonarola*. The anthem 'Blessed are the dead which die in the Lord' was printed in the *Musical Times* for 1 August 1886 (vol. 26, no. 522). [90] Stewart *Francis Jenkinson* pp. 24, 35.

end to this volume. The erection and occupation of the Hancock Building helped to ease the difficulties facing the Library, but the question of a reading room in one of the courtyards was not resolved until it was rejected by a vote of the Senate in 1901. The tradition of gifts that Bradshaw sought to establish bore fruit under the care of Robertson Smith and Jenkinson, as major collections came from Sir Thomas Wade, John Venn, John Couch Adams, Samuel Sandars, and other, later, benefactors. Solomon Schechter's identification in 1896 of a long-lost Hebrew version of Ecclesiasticus, and his ensuing journey to Egypt which resulted in the Library's being offered most of the contents of the ancient Cairo Genizah in 1898, electrified the world of Old Testament scholarship: the subsequent arrival in Cambridge of over 100,000 fragments created a wholly new departure in the Library's collections. The gift of most of Lord Acton's books by Lord Morley in 1902 was the largest ever to have come to the Library, and brought to Cambridge a unique resource of incomparable value, besides making up for many of the failures to buy foreign historical works over the previous fifty years. Between 1914 and 1920 Jenkinson concentrated virtually all his energies on amassing a collection of books and ephemera of all kinds relating to the First World War, both civil and military, which has come to be explored only recently. The accumulation of these collections, and Jenkinson's battle preceding the Copyright Act of 1911, when the Library faced yet another, and rather more dangerous, threat to its position, must be described elsewhere. So, also, must the removal of the entire Library in 1934, after something more than five centuries on one site, to a new building on the other side of the River Cam.

APPENDIX
List of Librarians, 1686–1886

1686	John Laughton
1712	Philip Brooke
1718	Thomas Macro

	Protobibliothecarii	*Bibliothecarii*
1721	Conyers Middleton	Samuel Hadderton
1732		John Taylor
1734		Thomas Parne
1750	Francis Sawyer Parris	
1751		Stephen Whisson
1760	Edmund Law	
1769	John Barnardiston	
1778	Richard Farmer	
1783		John Davies
1797	Thomas Kerrich	
1817		Edward Daniel Clarke
1822		John Lodge
1828	John Lodge	

	Librarians
1845	Joseph Power
1864	John Eyton Bickersteth Mayor
1867	Henry Bradshaw
1886	William Robertson Smith

INDEX OF MANUSCRIPTS

GENERAL INDEX

Abdy, John Thomas, Regius Professor
of Civil Law 515, 546, 608, 744
Aberdeen, George Hamilton Gordon,
4th Earl of (1784–1860) 368
Aberdeen University Library 560
accommodation, library, in 1710 152
in 1850s 600–1
needs, in early eighteenth century
153, 155
needs, in early nineteenth century
463–5, 474
Ackermann, Rudolph 259, 467, fig. 13
Acton, Sir John Emerich Edward
Dalberg, Baron (1834–1902) 555
his library 14, 211, 764
Acts of Parliament, Salt collections of
585–6
Adam, Robert, architect (1728–92) 465n.
Adams, George, mathematical
instrument maker 307
Adams, John Couch (1819–92) 14, 608,
701
Adams, Walter 115n.
Addison, Joseph (1672–1719) 60
adversaria, cataloguing of 215, 322, 345,
548
African Association 389–90
Ainslie, Gilbert, Master of Pembroke
College 499–500
Åkerblad, J.D. 363
Albert, Prince Consort 597, 602n.
Aldines 50, 57, 100, 200, 457–8, 460, 461
Allix, Peter (1641–1715), theologian 70
almanac compensation fund (1782 etc.)
326, 411, 546
Amboise, Georges d' (d. 1516),
Archbishop of Rouen 133n.
American books 583, 596, 597, 635–7,
639–40, 642, 647, 713, 714–15
American Philosophical Society 279
American studies, readership in 646–7

Amherst, William, Lord Amherst of
Hackney (1835–1909) 692
Anderby church, Lincs. fig. 16
Anderton, William, printer 64
Anglesey, Arthur Annesley, 3rd Earl of
78, 104, 118–19
Appleyard, E.S. 611
Arabic, teaching of 238–9
Arabic manuscripts, Moore's 77, 144
Burckhardt's 388–92
accessions under Bradshaw 723–5
see also Index of manuscripts
Arabic types at University Press 238–9,
343n.
Archdall, George, Master of Emmanuel
College 500, 513
Archdeacon, John, University Printer
280
Arnold, Thomas (1795–1842) 335
Arts School, shelving of 739
taken over by Library, 1903 603–4
Ashby, George (1724–1808), antiquary
189, 190n.
Asher, A. & Co, Berlin, booksellers 662
Asher & Co., London, booksellers 649,
662
Asiatic Society 377
Askew, Anthony (1722–74), classical
scholar 677, 718
and Peter Needham 75
Taylor's adversaria owned by 190,
326–9
sale of his manuscripts (1785) 15,
326–36
his *Liber amicorum* 333
Asplen, George 597
Astle, Thomas (1735–1803),
palaeographer 338
astronomy, library for 14
Athenaeum, The, advertisement in 584
Atherton, H. 291, 308